55,95

D1416858

Springer Series on Social Work

Albert R. Roberts, Ph.D., Series Editor
Graduate School of Social Work, Rutgers,
State University of New Jersey

1997 **Research Methods for Clinical Social Workers:** Empirical Practice, *John S. Wodarski, Ph.D.*

1997 **Elder Abuse and Neglect:** Causes, Diagnosis, and Intervention Strategies, 2nd Edition, *Mary Joy Quinn, R.N., M.A., and Susan Tomita, M.S.W., Ph.D.*

1998 **The Privatization of Human Services**
Volume 1: Policy and Practice Issues
Volume 2: Cases in the Purchase of Services
Margaret Gibelman, D.S.W., and Harold W. Demone, Jr., Ph.D.

1998 **The Changing Face of Health Care Social Work:** Professional Practice in the Era of Managed Care, *Sophia F. Dziegielewski, Ph.D., L.C.S.W.*

1999 **Making TQM Work:** Quality Tools for Human Services Organizations, *John Gunther, D.S.W., and Frank Hawkins, D.S.W.*

1999 **Homeless Families with Children:** A Subjective Experience of Homelessness, *Namkee G. Choi, M.S.W., Ph.D., and Lidia J. Snyder, M.S.W.*

2000 **Evidence-based Social Work Practice with Families:** A Lifespan Approach, *Jacqueline Corcoran, Ph.D.*

Evidence-Based Social Work Practice with Families

A Lifespan Approach

Jacqueline Corcoran, PhD

 Springer Series on Social Work

Copyright © 2000 by Springer Publishing Company, Inc.

Springer Publishing Company, Inc.
536 Broadway
New York, NY 10012-3955

Acquisitions Editor: Bill Tucker
Production Editor: Helen Song
Cover design by James Scotto-Lavino

00 01 02 03 04 / 5 4 3 2 1

Library of Congress Cataloging-in-Publication Data

Corcoran, Jacqueline.
  Evidence-based social work practice with families : a lifespan approach / Jacqueline Corcoran.
    p. cm. — (Springer series on social work)
  Includes bibliographical references and index.
  ISBN 0-8261-1303-6 (hardcover)
  1. Family social work—United States. 2. Family social work.
I. Title. II. Series.
  HV699.C67 2000
362.82'0973—dc21   99-051496

Printed in the United States of America

To Rich Klein, for all his kindness and support.

Jacqueline Corcoran, Ph.D., has been assistant professor at the University of Texas at Arlington School of Social Work since 1996 and since 1997 has been codirector of the Community Service Clinic at the School of Social Work, where she supervises and trains graduate students to provide free and sliding-scale services to low-income members of the community.

Dr. Corcoran teaches in the direct practice concentration with courses such as Direct Practice Methods, Theories for Direct Practice Intervention, Family Therapy, Treatment of the Child and Adolescent, and Behavior Therapy.

Dr. Corcoran has published numerous journal articles in the areas of family therapy, solution-focused therapy, crisis intervention, and adolescent pregnancy. Her research involves the efficacy of solution-focused therapy with behavior-disordered children and their families and crisis intervention responses to domestic violence.

Prior to completing her Ph.D. from the University of Texas at Austin in 1996, Dr. Corcoran worked in the following practice arenas: treatment of juvenile offenders, home health care, university counseling, outpatient community clinic, and child abuse victim services.

CONTENTS

CONTRIBUTORS

Stephanie Basham, M.S.S.W.
Coordinator of School Based Services
Big Brothers and Sisters
Dallas, Texas

Jami Black, M.S.S.W.
District Manager
Communities in Schools
Greater Fort Worth Area, Texas

Sherry Fairchild-Kienlen, M.R.E.
Doctoral Student
University of Texas at Arlington School of Social Work
Arlington, Texas

Jane Harakal Phillips, M.S.
Doctoral Candidate
University of Texas at Arlington School of Social Work
Arlington, Texas

Cecilia Thomas, M.S.W.
Doctoral Candidate
University of Texas at Arlington School of Social Work
Arlington, Texas
and Program Specialist
Texas Department of Protective and Regulatory Services
Arlington, Texas

PREFACE

The usual approach of family therapy textbooks is to discuss the various theoretical approaches to family therapy. This knowledge is undeniably crucial, the foundation from which family practitioners operate. However, the student or beginning family therapist may then say, "Now what? How do I apply these theoretical approaches when a family with a particular problem needs my help? Do these theoretical approaches actually work?"

In order to answer these questions and to bridge the gap between theory and practice, *Evidence-based Social Work Practice with Families: A Lifespan Approach* has been written to supplement main family therapy text material on theory. It is designed from a problem-oriented perspective, examining the types of problems social workers commonly encounter in practice, such as child sexual and physical abuse and child neglect, behavior problems, substance abuse, juvenile criminal offending, domestic violence, schizophrenia, and caregiving for the elderly. Its purpose is to review and present empirically validated interventions so that practitioners will be informed on how to treat families effectively.

Social work is unique among the helping professions in its traditional commitment to vulnerable populations and social problems. In addition, social work is an applied field of study. Social workers want to know what approaches can be applied in specific problem areas. What has been shown effective? This book informs the reader of family approaches with demonstrated effectiveness. In each problem area, the research is comprehensively reviewed so that the reader will know what theoretical approaches have empirical support. Evidence-based practice is increasingly important as managed health care environments demand accountability in mental health and other health care services.

Due to increased demands for accountability, each chapter will also provide the reader with information on standardized measurements that family members encountering a particular problem can complete. Relevant self-report instruments can be used to guide assessment and clinical practice. For those interested in conducting research in a particular area, each of the instruments is provided with psychometric data that support its use.

In order to be as useful as possible to social workers who may be employed in various types of settings and who may see families with various types of problems, this book covers a range of possible problems across the lifespan. The incapacitated elderly, therefore, are included, as well as problems afflicting adults, such as schizophrenia, family violence, and substance abuse. Adolescent problem areas consist of substance abuse, juvenile offending, and eating disorders. Typical child problems include physical abuse, sexual abuse, neglect, conduct problems, and attention deficit and hyperactivity disorder.

FORMAT

The format for each chapter is as follows: First, a comprehensive review of the family treatment outcome literature in each area is offered, organized by type of theoretical orientation; a chart is then provided, briefly summarizing the studies in each area so that readers can familiarize themselves with the details of a study of particular interest; finally, information on standardized, self-report instruments that have been used to assess each problem area is presented.

DEFINITION OF FAMILIES

The social work perspective is less individually oriented than that of many other helping professions, and the impact of various systems on individual behavior is of primary importance. The family is one of the environments crucial to its influence on the individual. However, just as there has been debate about what constitutes a family, there is debate about how family therapy is defined (Shadish, Montgomery, Wilson, Wilson, Bright, & Okwumabua, 1993). Some definitions only involve the treatment of multiple family members, while other family therapy approaches are limited to work with one person. In this volume a broad definition has been applied. Essentially, approaches are considered family therapy whenever family members are involved in treatment. For example, a common method of treatment for child behavior problems involves working with parents to impact their child's behavior. Even though only the parent may be seen in practice, this type of treatment is still defined as a family intervention.

Another definitional issue involves family versus marital therapy. The purpose of this book is to examine the effectiveness of family therapy rather than marital interventions. At the same time, there are two problem areas discussed in this book—adult substance abuse and family violence—which certainly impact the entire family, and clinical approaches have discussed working with the whole family; however, the empirical literature in these areas has mainly limited itself to marital treatment. This work was included since its purpose is to be comprehensive in terms of the types of problems social workers may encounter in practice.

A final definition issue involves the nomenclature used to describe particular problem areas. In many instances throughout this book, the American Psychiatric Association (APA) *Diagnostic and Statistical Manual of Mental Disorders* (APA, 1994) criteria are used. APA diagnostic categories represent a medical model framework, a perspective that is often at odds with the systemic beliefs of both family therapy and social work. At the same time, these diagnostic labels do provide a common nomenclature so that practitioners from all helping professions will recognize the problem areas being discussed. For this reason, these labels were adopted at times throughout the book, although treatment rather than description of problems is the main thrust of *Evidence-based Social Work Practice with Families: A Lifespan Approach.*

REFERENCES

American Psychiatric Association. (1994). *Diagnostic and statistical manual of mental disorders* (4th ed.). Washington, DC: Author.

Shadish, W. R., Montgomery, L. M., Wilson, P., Wilson, M. R., Bright, I., & Okwumabua, T. (1993). Effects of family and marital psychotherapies: A meta-analysis. *Journal of Consulting and Clinical Psychology, 61,* 992–1002.

ACKNOWLEDGMENTS

I am grateful to many people in the writing of this book. First, to my parents, Myra and Patrick Corcoran, and my friends, Holly Bell, Robert Canon, Michael Owen, Paula McPartlin, and Kathy Selber, for unfailing support. They were always there when I needed them, and I am sincerely appreciative. To Mark Rosman, I give thanks for helping me take time out along the way. To Sara Olson and Cindy Moseley for putting such effort into preparation of a final draft, and to my contributors who put considerable work and time into their chapters. And finally, to Dr. Al Roberts, for supporting my efforts to create and carry out this project.

Section I

Family Treatment with Children

CHAPTER 1

Family Treatment with Child Abuse and Neglect*

FAMILY TREATMENT WITH CHILD ABUSE AND NEGLECT

Family Case:

Peggy Johnson is a White, 24-year-old, single parent with five children, Daryl (age 8), Cathy (age 6), Terry (age 4), Shawn (1 year), and a newborn. The family is supported by public assistance. The fathers of the children are not involved except for the father of the new baby, who has intermittent contact. He said that he will help pay for Pampers and groceries, but he is no longer involved romantically with Peggy.

Peggy has come to the attention of the Child Protective Services system for spanking Daryl with a belt to the point where she left marks. She says that whipping him is the only way he minds after she has yelled at him several times to do chores around the house or to take care of his brothers and sisters. She says that he is disrespectful to her and acts as if he is already grown up and can tell her what to do.

Physical abuse (acts that either cause or have the potential to cause bodily injury to children) and neglect (failure to give children basic necessities and age-appropriate care) are, in the majority of cases, perpetrated by parents (Petit & Curtis, 1997). Indeed, the National Center on Child Abuse and Neglect in 1996 estimated that 78% of child maltreatment referrals involved children's biological parents (Petit & Curtis, 1997). Reports to child protective services agencies have increased steadily; in 1991, 1.9 million reports were made according to the National Center on Child Abuse and Neglect, with approximately

---

* An adaptation of this chapter will be published in a forthcoming issue of *Children and Youth Services Review*.

40% of these validated cases (U.S. Department of Justice, 1995). As evidenced from the ratio of reports-to-validated cases, serious attention has been paid to identifying cases of abuse and neglect (Melton & Barry, 1994).

Due to the vast number of cases, intervention often consists mainly of state monitoring, supervision, and/or placement outside the home (Melton & Barry, 1994) . Out-of-home placements have increased from 1986 (280,000 cases) to 1995 (486,000 cases) by 74% (Petit & Curtis, 1997). Child welfare costs excluding Medicaid involve an annual national budget for 1996 of nearly $10 billion (Petit & Curtis, 1997). Despite these costs, methods of treating abusing and neglecting parents have not been established (Oates & Bross, 1995).

The physical consequences that may result from physical abuse in terms of bodily injury, which in some cases may be life-threatening, makes effective treatment urgent (Wolfe & Wekerle, 1993). According to National Center on Child Abuse and Neglect statistics, 977 maltreatment-related fatalities occurred in 1995 nationwide (Petit & Curtis, 1997). In addition to the observable physical consequences, recent attention has been directed toward the psychological effects of maltreatment. Most of the empirical work in this area has examined the effects of physical abuse. Short-term consequences include increased risk of aggression toward other children and reduced empathy and concern for peers (Azar, Barnes, & Twentyman, 1988; Graziano & Mills, 1992; Malinosky-Rummell & Hansen, 1993; Mueller & Silverman, 1989). Not surprisingly, abuse often impairs a child's social competence and social skills (Azar et al., 1988; Conaway & Hansen, 1989). Physically abused children's lack of self-control also manifests in frustration and poor impulse control in response to demanding tasks, such as schoolwork. Children who are unable to delay rewards and to organize and plan future behavior display academic and behavior problems in school (Graziano & Mills, 1992). Further, internalizing problems, such as depression and low self-esteem, have been demonstrated when children suffered physical abuse as compared to children from matched low socioeconomic homes (Toth, Manly, & Cicchetti, 1992).

Some cross-sectional study has also been conducted on the effects of physical abuse on adolescents and adults. In adolescence, physically abused youth demonstrate a greater likelihood of externalizing behaviors compared to their nonabused counterparts, as well as increased risk for criminal offending (Malinosky-Rummell & Hansen, 1993). For adults, both nonfamilial (violent criminal offenses) and familial (partner and child) rates of aggression are higher among those who have been physically abused (Malinosky-Rummell & Hansen, 1993). Intergenerational transmission of abuse is estimated at about a 30% rate among parents physically victimized as children (K. Kaufman & Rudy, 1991; J. Kaufman & Zigler, 1989). Although the adult research has mainly focused on violence, internalizing problems, such as self-abuse, suicidality, dissociation, somatization, depression, and anxiety, have also been reported in a variety of adult female samples (Malinosky-Rummell & Hansen, 1993).

Not as much work has been conducted exclusively with neglect samples. However, a prospective, longitudinal study indicated that out of all maltreatment groups, neglected children at ages 5 and 6 had the most problematic functioning (Erickson, Egeland, & Pianta, 1989). On cognitive tests, these children performed even more poorly than children who had been sexually abused, those whose parents were psychologically unavailable, and a matched low-socioeconomic control group. The neglected children's classroom behavior was anxious, inattentive, and lacking in initiative, and they failed to grasp academic material. By the end of their kindergarten year, 65% were either going to be retained a grade or had been referred for special education.

Because of these potentially harmful consequences, it is important to understand what constitutes effective treatment in this area. To this end, a review was conducted on treatment of families in which abuse and neglect had occurred. Reviews of this literature have been conducted in the past (Blythe, 1983; Fantuzzo & Twentyman, 1986; Oates & Bross, 1995; Schellenbach, 1998; Wolfe & Wekerle, 1993). The present review departs from the prior reviews by focusing on current research (1985 and on) and both physical abuse and neglect. Treatment after abuse and/or neglect had occurred is a focus, rather than the prevention of child maltreatment to at-risk families (i.e., Barth, 1990; Olds & Henderson, 1989; Olds, Henderson, Chamberlin, & Tatelbaum, 1986; Striefel, Robinson, & Truhn, 1998; Taylor & Beauchamp, 1988).

In addition, this review maintains an exclusive emphasis on interventions at the family level; that is, treatment involved either the entire family or, more commonly, work with maltreating parents. Studies involved specific interventions at the level of the individual parent or the family; therefore, block evaluations of demonstration projects were excluded (Cohn & Daro, 1987).

While outcome studies on child maltreatment often comprise an array of services, including some kind of unspecified family counseling, these studies were only included if they presented parent data. For instance, a residential treatment program for infants that involved training and assessing mother-child interactions (Elmer, 1986) was included in the review. However, Culp, Little, Letts, and Lawrence (1991) and Parish, Myers, Brandner, and Templin (1985) were excluded because their primary focus was on therapeutic day programs for children. Primary outcomes were child improvements on developmental skills (Culp et al., 1991; Parish et al., 1985) and peer relationships (Culp et al., 1991).

Another emphasis of this review was on non-family preservation approaches. Family preservation programs, which have been popularized over the last two decades, are marked by the provision of both therapeutic and concrete services. See chapter 2 of this volume for discussion of family preservation approaches with maltreating families.

Further, a minimum methodological standard was employed. For example, single-subject designs were excluded, as were studies with inadequate sample sizes (fewer than 10) [e.g., Dawson, de Armas, McGrath, & Kelly, 1986; Fantuzzo, Wray, Hall, Goins, & Azar, 1986].

Discussion of research in this review will begin with theoretically oriented studies (behavioral, cognitive-behavioral, family therapy, and cognitive-developmental), followed by those without a theoretical basis. A critique of studies will be offered along with recommendations for future research and service delivery.

THEORETICALLY ORIENTED OUTCOME STUDIES

Early explanations of why parents maltreat their children centered around parental psychopathology. However, research fails to find a certain profile, such as specific thought, affective, and character disorders, associated with child abuse (Graziano & Mills, 1992; Wolfe, 1987). A more recent perspective takes the view that child maltreatment involves a particular pattern of behavior, such as difficulties in managing child behavior, distorted cognitive appraisals of child behavior, lack of problem-solving skills, and the influence of the parent's own childhood history, rather than psychiatric or personality disturbances per se (Wolfe, 1987; Wolfe & McEachran, 1997). Child maltreatment is now conceptualized as an interactional sequence: Particular situational factors stimulate parental responses. In the following sections, treatments to address these situational and interactional responses include behavioral child management, cognitive-behavioral, and family therapy approaches.

BEHAVIORAL THEORY

Assuming that parents resort to physical punishment because they do not know more effective ways to manage their children, behavioral interventions teach parents the skills to more effectively reinforce prosocial behavior and to ignore or punish deviant behavior. Several advantages of behavioral parent training for working specifically with abusive parents have been noted (Azar & Wolfe, 1996; K. Kaufman & Rudy, 1991). First, resistance may be substantially reduced by the educational nature of behavioral parent training. Clients may be less resistant to an approach that emphasizes the development of skills and knowledge rather than their psychological functioning. Further, many abusive and neglectful parents function at a concrete cognitive level; therefore, insight-based approaches lack effectiveness. In contrast, behavioral techniques are problem-focused and relevant to the presenting issues. In addition, behavioral approaches have had demonstrated success with other populations displaying similar problems (K. Kaufman & Rudy, 1991). Specifically, the treatment literature on conduct disorder comprises a body of knowledge that can be utilized to inform the realm of physical maltreatment (Azar et al., 1988). Families in which conduct disorder and physical abuse occur represent considerable overlap. For example, authors have noted that children who had suffered abuse were more similar to behavior-disordered children in their disruptive behaviors than were children from nonclinic families (Gelardo & Sanford, 1987; Wolfe, Jaffe, Wilson, & Zak, 1985). In addition, the inciting incident in physical abuse cases often involves some kind of disobedience or child aggression (Gelardo & Sanford, 1987).

The connection between child abuse and conduct disorder using Patterson's behavioral coercion theory (Patterson, 1982) is discussed as a shared theoretical basis (Gelardo & Sanford, 1987; Howing, Wodarski, Kurtz, Gaudin, & Herbst, 1990). Briefly, coercion theory is based on operant conditioning behavioral principles. A key concept involves the reinforcement of behavior. Essentially, a reinforcer, either positive or negative, following a behavior increases the likelihood of that particular behavior. In coercive families, deviant behavior is reinforced on both the child's and the parent's part. The child, unable to elicit attention any other way, may use aversive behavior to gain parental attention, even if it is abusive (Azar, Fantuzzo, & Twentyman, 1984). Positive reinforcement thus occurs when a parent attends to this aversive behavior, thereby increasing the likelihood of future deviant behavior. Negative reinforcement, defined as the termination of a noxious event following a response, also occurs between parents and children. Parents are negatively reinforced for aggressive behavior when they become overly harsh or abusive and their child capitulates to their demands. Similarly, children receive negative reinforcement for deviance when parents react to their children's affective displays as intolerable and terminate their requests for child compliance. These kinds of interactive patterns are susceptible to coercive escalations. As parents habituate to child deviance, children may increase their negative behaviors to attain attention (Azar et al., 1984). Parents may also escalate their level of harshness, which may erupt into physical violence in order to induce child compliance. Also, in such households, children may observe parents engaging in coercive exchanges. Vicarious learning then takes place as this behavior is modeled for the child. As these processes continue over time, children become well versed in coercive social interactions.

The treatment of conduct problems through behavioral methods has been well established. A meta-analysis on 36 trials of parent training, for example, found that families undergoing training improved over those who did not. According to child, parent, teacher, and trained observer reports, the average child whose parent had attended training had improved 77% to 81% over those who had undergone an alternative intervention or those who had been placed in a control group (Serketich & Dumas, 1996). In addition, behavioral training methods have been found effective for parents of preschool (e.g., Webster-Stratton, Hollinsworth, & Kolpacoff, 1989; Webster-Stratton, Kolpacoff, & Hollinsworth, 1988) and school-age children (e.g., Kazdin, Hayes, Henry, Schacht, & Strupp, 1992; Sayger, Horne, Walter, & Passmore, 1988).

The body of literature on the behavioral treatment of conduct problems has been built over two decades of research. In contrast, only four studies were found for the treatment of abusive and neglectful parents using behavioral methods (*see* Table 1.1). Given this wide gap between the two research areas, it follows that the child maltreatment field can take advantage of knowledge-building that has occurred in this related area of psychotherapy-outcome research (Fantuzzo & Twentyman, 1986; Wells, 1994).

Two of the studies in the child maltreatment area were marked by methodological rigor (Brunk, Henggeler, & Whelan, 1987; Wolfe, Edwards, Manion, & Koverola, 1988). In Brunk et al. (1987), both abused and neglected school-age children were the focus of attention in which treatment was delivered over eight sessions in a group setting. Wolfe et al. (1988) concentrated on individual parents of preschool-age children with an average of 12 sessions of treatment. In both programs, parents were taught how to behaviorally specify goals for change, to track target behaviors, to positively reinforce prosocial conduct, and to punish or ignore their children's aversive behaviors. Wolfe et al. (1988) also extended their intervention beyond traditional behavioral parent training methods. The Wolfe et al. (1988) program was specifically modeled on the Forehand and McMahon (1981) approach in which therapists directly coach parents on how to apply behavioral principles with their children in the clinic setting. The program also included videotaping so parents could critique and review their own performance. Also, parents were trained in coping methods, including relaxation and diversion techniques, when they were confronted with stressful child management situations. These skills were practiced in session. In addition, promotion of children's language competencies and social interaction skills was conducted using skill-building, prompting, and rehearsals with parents.

Randomization to conditions was used in both studies. In Brunk et al. (1987), both parent training and multisystemic therapy (which will be discussed

TABLE 1.1 Behavioral and Cognitive-Behavioral Interventions with Abusive and Neglectful Parents

AUTHOR/MODEL	DESIGN/SAMPLE	MEASURES	RESULTS	LIMITATIONS
Acton & During (1992) 13-week, 90 minute session cognitive-behavioral group treatment focused on: 1) anger management training to reduce physiological arousal; 2) training in communication and problem-solving; 3) training in empathic understanding	Pretest, posttest $N = 29$ (out of 47 who started program) referred from child protective services because of physical abuse or from a child abuse program within a pediatric medical center (Canada) 69% married or common-law; 55% unemployed; 69% females	Parenting Stress Index; State-Trait Anger Scale; Index of Parenting Attitudes; Child Abuse Potential Inventory; Eyberg Child Behavior Inventory	Statistical and clinical significant positive improvements on Child Abuse Potential Inventory, Parenting Stress Index, and Index of Parenting Attitudes; State-Trait Anger Scale showed statistically but not clinically significant positive improvements; although parents reported their children's behavior as just as disruptive, they were less distressed by it	No comparison/control group; no behavioral measures of changes; no follow-up
Brunk et al. (1987) Comparison of multisystemic therapy and parent training 8 sessions	Quasi-experimental, randomized to parent training and multisystemic therapy, pretest, posttest (77% completed)	10-minute behavioral videotape self-report measures: Individual system: Symptom Checklist-90; Behavior Problem	Both family preservation and parent training were effective in reducing psychiatric symptoms in parents, parental stress, and individual,	Treatment groups were not similar on all characteristics: neglected children and their mothers in the multisystemic therapy condition were significantly older;

continued

TABLE 1.1 *(continued)*

AUTHOR/MODEL	DESIGN/SAMPLE	MEASURES	RESULTS	LIMITATIONS
	$N = 43$ parents who had been investigated for maltreatment and were mandated to receive counseling in lieu of court order; 50% chose this option 55% boys, 76% girls; 57% White, 43% African American	Checklist Family system: Family Environment Scale Social system: Family Inventory of Life Events and Changes Treatment Outcome Questionnaire	and family problems; Multisystemic therapy was more effective than parent training in improving parent-child relationships according to behavioral observations, while parent training was more helpful in ameliorating social system problems	selection bias in that only 50% took the option of counseling
Golub et al. (1987) Videotape/discussion program based on empirical descriptions of characteristics of abusive parents Ongoing weekly group Average attendance = 14.51 sessions	Pretest, posttest $N = 40$ parents (with complete pretest, posttest info.) Referred to clinic 73% female; mean income = $905/mo;	Coded parents' written responses to videotaped vignette	High dropout/compliance: of 120 who agreed to participate, 63% completed program, only 40 completed test information; Significant increases on: cooperative responses and number of reasons	Lack of theoretical framework; referral source/reason for referral unclear in sample description; child maltreatment composition of total sample given but not for those who completed pre- and posttest administration; measure

	parental education = high school; White 83%, Hispanic 17%; Marital status: single 20%, married 38%, divorced 24%, separated 18%; target child's gender = male 68%; mean age of child = 3.07 yrs		for child behavior proposed Significant decreases on: punitive responses and reasons that blame child	nonstandardized; lack of comparison/control group; no follow-up
Kolko (1996) Cognitive-behavioral treatment or family therapy 12, 1-hr weekly clinic sessions; home visits after every 1–2 clinic visits; average length of treatment = 19.1 weeks for cognitive-behavioral, 19.2 weeks for family therapy	Quasi-experimental, random assignment based on stratification in terms of child age (6–9 vs. 10–13), gender, and family constellation to cognitive-behavioral treatment (parent and child separately) or family therapy; pretest, posttest Originally 70 were screened for report of	Likert scales on severity of child/family problems, severity of anger arousal displayed by parents toward children, and use of physical discipline administered weekly to both child and parent Conflict Tactics Scales; Family Environment Scale; Child Abuse Potential Inventory;	Parents in cognitive-behavioral treatment improved over family therapy group in overall levels of anger and less use of physical discipline; parents of children diagnosed with a psychiatric disorder and longer duration of problems more likely to report heightened anger and use of physical force	Standardized measures were not administered pretest and posttest—they were just used as criterion validity measures; self-report bias; family therapy orientation not specifically named; small sample size

continued

TABLE 1.1 (*continued*)

AUTHOR/MODEL	DESIGN/SAMPLE	MEASURES	RESULTS	LIMITATIONS
	physical abuse within last 6 mos; 42 were randomized to treatment conditions, $N = 38$ completed treatment	Parenting Scale; Beck Depression Inventory (all self-report administered just at pretest to serve as criterion validity measures for above Likert scales)		
	mean age of child = 8.6 yrs, half White, half African American; 63% lived with biological mothers; 74% perpetrators' mothers; 66% of perpetrators had high school education or less; 42% unemployed; 58% received welfare			
Nicol et al. (1988) Behavioral therapy vs. play therapy 6–8 weeks of home visits 3 times/week	Quasi-experimental, randomization to treatment or comparison (individual play sessions), pretest, posttest	Family Interaction Coding System	45% dropout rate; treatment group improved statistically but not in clinically significant ways	Lack of specification on treatment methods used; lack of information on average numbers of sessions conducted; no follow-up; confound of home and clinic work; lack of no-treatment control

	$N = 38$ families in which physical abuse had occurred; 37% single parents, 29% divorced; majority unemployed and from unskilled, manual labor social class; all White		
Schinke et al. (1986) Behavioral stress management groups 10 weeks	Quasi-experimental, matched group assignment to stress management intervention or no-treatment control, pretest, posttest, follow-up (6 mos) $N = 23$ parents (57% mothers and 43% fathers) of developmentally disabled children who had been referred from child welfare Parental occupation = unskilled to semiskilled; mean age of children = 3.69	Psychometrically tested measures (but not stated what they were); blind ratings of videotaped role play demonstrations	Both at posttest and at follow-up, treatment group made significant improvements on observed child disciplining interactions and on their positive attitudes toward their children, their adaptive anger control ability, and their positive coping responses	No randomization between groups; not stated on what characteristics matching was done; no information on race of subjects; measures were allegedly completed at pretest, posttest, and follow-up but not stated what they were

continued

TABLE 1.1 *(continued)*

AUTHOR/MODEL	DESIGN/SAMPLE	MEASURES	RESULTS	LIMITATIONS
Szykula & Fleischman (1985) Reports 2 studies: Social learning theory	1) ABA repeated treatment (social learning program implemented for 9 mos) Child protective services clients; White; lower SES; 50% single parents; children 3–12	Out-of-home placements over 5-yr treatment period	83% reduction in out-of-home placements attributed to social learning program and placement rates returned to previous high levels at termination of program and later; of 85% with confirmed abuse, no further reports of maltreatment both during treatment or 1-yr follow-up, and no out-of-home placements	Doesn't specify total number of subjects; only one measure of program effects and no immediate measures of family functioning; lack of comparison group or no-treatment control; possible dilution of treatment since workers only consulted with per mo; doesn't discuss differences according to statistical significance, only percentages
	2) Experimental design, randomized to experimental and control groups after sorting into more and less difficult cases Child Protective Services clients; mainly White; low SES; 68% single parents	Out-of-home placements	Less difficult cases showed statistically significant lower out-of-home placement with SLT; for more difficult cases, differences were not statistically significant between treatment and control groups	Unknown number of subjects in study; "control" group assumed to have regular casework services; lack of other measures

| Whiteman et al. (1987)

Cognitive-behavioral

6 sessions | Experimental, random assignment to 5 groups: 1) cognitive restructuring; 2) relaxation procedures; 3) problem-solving skills; 4) treatment package of cognitive restructuring, relaxation, and problem-solving; 5) control group: regular agency services

$N = 55$ from public agency (confirmed child abusers) and private agency (at-risk child abusers)

Children's mean age = 10.5; race = 22% White, 50% Black, 24% Hispanic; about $^{1}/_{3}$ parents married, separated/divorced, or single; half received public assistance; majority female | Nonstandardized instruments created by authors: Adult Anger, Child Anger, Combined Anger, Affection Scale, Discipline Scale, Empathy Scale; Irritating Behavior Scale | Reduction in anger for subjects receiving experimental conditions with the composite treatment showing the most benefits and the relaxation technique condition the least | Too small a sample to have random assignment to 5 different groups; lack of standardized measures; no follow-up |

continued

TABLE 1.1 *(continued)*

AUTHOR/MODEL	DESIGN/SAMPLE	MEASURES	RESULTS	LIMITATIONS
Wolfe et al. (1988) Individual behavioral parent training median number of sessions—9	Experimental, random assignment to treatment (behavioral and information group sessions) or control (only information group sessions), pretest, posttest, follow-up (3 mos) $N = 30$ women who completed treatment; recruitment process: 1) under supervision with child protective service agency (Canada); 2) younger than 25 yrs; 3) child between 9 mos and 5 yrs; 4) score at-risk range on Child Abuse Potential Inventory majority single parent; receiving government assistance	Self-report measures of risk in parenting role: Child Abuse Potential Inventory; Beck Depression Inventory Observational measures of child-rearing methods: Dyadic Parent-Child Interaction Coding System; Home Observation and Measurement of the Environment Scale Measure of child behavior: Pyramid Scales Satisfaction with services: Parent's Consumer Satisfaction Questionnaire	On maternal report measures at follow-up, treatment group mothers reported fewer and less-intense child behavior problems and fewer adjustment problems; however, no differential effectiveness between groups was shown in quality of child-rearing environment (but could have been because focus was not on structured activities) or on measure of child adaptive abilities	Small sample size

further in the section on family therapy) were effective in reducing psychiatric symptoms in parents, parental stress, and individual and family problems. Each approach offered certain advantages. Multisystemic therapy was more effective than parent training in improving parent-child relationships, according to behavioral observations. Multisystemic therapy also helped physically abusive parents gain better control over their children's behavior and assisted neglectful parents in becoming more responsive to their child's needs. Parent training, on the other hand, was more helpful in ameliorating social problems. To explain this finding, the authors hypothesize that the delivery of parent training in a group setting helped reduce parental isolation and improved their support system.

Similar positive results were found for Wolfe et al. (1988). At 3-month follow-up, both treatment and comparison groups improved on the quality of child-rearing environment and on child developmental skills. Differential gains were found for the treatment group in terms of maternal reports of fewer and less intense child deviant behaviors and fewer adjustment problems. Caseworkers also reported a reduced risk of maltreatment for the treatment group as compared to the information-only controls. However, home observations of behaviors did not reflect these improvements. The authors suggest that this negative finding could have been the result of families restricting their behavior during observations. Their future recommendation is that structured activities be the focus of observation sessions in the home.

In a study conducted in England, Nicol, Smith, Kay, Hall, Barlow, and Williams (1988) compared a behavioral family approach in the home to individual child play therapy sessions in the clinic. On a family interaction behavioral assessment, statistically, though not clinically, significant improvements were made for the behavioral approach. Unfortunately, the behavioral methods used were not clearly delineated. In addition, home versus clinic treatment was confounded with theoretical model.

Another study evidenced that bachelor's degreed clinicians produced effective results with behavioral methods when out-of-home placement was the primary measure of outcome (Szykula & Fleischman, 1985). This study suggests that training child protective services caseworkers in behavioral parent training procedures could contribute to goal-oriented and therapeutic client contacts. Opportunities for in-home practice during supervision visits would increase the generalizability of learned behaviors. From home visits, practitioners could also understand and help the client problem-solve ways around the potential environmental barriers to effective implementation of techniques.

A potential problem might occur when parents do not have the opportunity to practice with their children because of out-of-home placement. However, there are often other children in the home so that new parenting techniques can be practiced. In addition, role-playing and structured visitation arrangements may be arranged (Azar & Wolfe, 1996).

Although behavioral skills training may enhance parental sense of efficacy and reduce abuse potential, one of the criticisms is that such an approach will not necessarily improve stimulation to the child. Unless stimulation is promoted, child development might still be negatively impacted. Authors have also criticized approaches that focus only on parents and not children (Azar, 1986). In order to address these concerns, parent-child interaction training has been suggested as a method of treatment (Urquiza & McNeil, 1996). Parent-child interaction training combines elements of both nondirective play therapy and operant behavioral principles. Structured play therapy sessions address individual child treatment needs. Parents are then trained in the play sessions on how to interact with their children in warm and nurturing ways. The objective of this component is to build a positive and mutually rewarding parent-child relationship. In the next component of treatment, parents are trained in operant behavioral methods: positive reinforcement (praise, attention), effective command-giving, ignoring of undesired behavior, and alternate punishments (time out, withdrawal of privileges). The assumption is that the previously established positive relationship will enhance the application of these behavioral methods (Eisenstadt, Eyberg, McNeil, Newcomb, & Funderburk, 1993). In the context of a positive relationship, children will experience their parents as a stronger source of positive reinforcement and will more willingly respond to limit-setting. In addition, mutually rewarding interaction will reduce parents' often negative perceptions of their children and the associated coercion that takes place.

Although a body of empirical work has now accumulated on the efficacy of parent-child interaction therapy with very young behaviorally disruptive children (Brestan, Eyberg, Boggs, & Algina, 1997; McNeil, Eyberg, Eisenstadt, Newcomb, & Funderburk, 1991; Schuhmann, Foote, Eyberg, Boggs, & Algina, 1998), no work has specifically been conducted with abused children and their parents. However, the approach shows promise in terms of addressing the child's maltreatment-related issues, establishing a more positive parent-child relationship, and educating the parent on more effective discipline (Urquiza & McNeil, 1996).

Other concerns about the limitations of behavioral methods involve the need to address attitudinal and cognitive factors (Azar, 1986). The next section will explore the application of cognitive-behavioral approaches to treating abusing and neglecting parents.

COGNITIVE-BEHAVIORAL

Cognitive approaches emphasize the role of an individual's beliefs, attitudes, appraisals, perceptions, and expectations as the filters through which the environment is experienced. This approach assumes that experience, in turn, influences behavior (Azar et al., 1988). Several cognitive deficits have been empirically associated with maltreatment. The first deficit involves the belief that children should demonstrate a higher level of functioning than their current developmental level would warrant (Azar et al., 1988). Since children lack the skills to communicate their motives when they inevitably fail to behave according to this standard, parents might then attribute negative intentions to their child's behavior, such as that their child is purposefully trying to antagonize or provoke them. A lack of problem-solving skills exacerbates these distorted cognitive appraisals, the third area of deficit. This combination of interpretive processes may result in chronic parental frustration, which might then lead to coercive and physically abusive responses (Hansen, Pallotta, Tishelman, Conaway, & MacMillan, 1989).

With these kinds of interactions, children not only risk physical abuse but also fail to obtain from their parents necessary feedback in order to develop appropriate age-level skills. The impact on child development therefore extends beyond the physical and emotional consequences of violence, since the development of language, cognition, and social skills requires sensitive caregiving (Azar et al., 1988). It is possible that these caregiving inadequacies account for many of the poor outcomes that have heretofore been attributed to physical violence.

In addition to their impact on parenting practices, cognitive factors have been implicated with coping in response to life stress. Further, problem-solving deficits, unrealistic beliefs and standards about interpersonal relationships, and attributions of negative intent might inhibit the maintenance of support networks. In this way, negative interpretive processes might contribute to risk factors associated with maltreating parents, such as high levels of negative stress and lack of social support (Azar et al., 1988). For example, in one study of child protective services–referred parents who attended treatment for a conduct-disordered child (Whipple & Webster-Stratton, 1991), the second best predictor of treatment outcome (after poverty) was maternal reports of high stress as well as negative appraisals of stress.

Several studies in the treatment of physically abusive parents have used cognitive-behavioral theory as their basis (*see* Table 1.1). For example, a 13-week group protocol was designed to address the following four areas of cognitive deficit: 1) physiological arousal associated with poor self-control, 2) poor communication and problem-solving skills, 3) lack of empathy, and 4) attributions of negative intentionality (Acton & During, 1992). According to self-report data, both statistical and clinical improvements were found for child abuse potential, parenting stress, and parenting attitudes from pre- to posttest. While parents related that their children were showing similar behavior problems as at the start of treatment, they were less distressed by these problems. Perhaps this is where the addition of behavioral management techniques might be helpful, so that parents can gain more effective control of their children's behavior.

In another group intervention, Schinke et al. (1986) used a behavioral stress management approach with physically abusive parents of developmentally delayed children. Children who have health or psychological handicaps are discussed in the literature as being more vulnerable to abuse (e.g., Kolko, 1993). A three-pronged approach was taken in the 13-week intervention. First, parents were trained in self-control methods through covert thoughts, relaxation, and simulated role plays. Second, parents were versed in communication skills training through discussion, modeling, and role-plays. Third, parents learned more effective discipline methods, such as how to set prosocial goals for their children and the use of positive reinforcement systems to foster these goals. Compared to a matched group that did not receive treatment, treatment parents made significant improvements on coping skills, positive attitudes toward their children, observed child discipline, and their ability to control their anger responses. These gains were retained at 6-month follow-up.

Another cognitive-behavioral approach was implemented during home visits over six sessions (Whiteman, Fanshel, & Grundy, 1987). Only a proportion of families (38%) had been referred by child protective services for physical abuse; the majority of the sample were seen as at risk for physical abuse. This study was notable in that treatment components were examined separately with random assignment to the following conditions: 1) cognitive restructuring; 2) relaxation procedures; 3) problem-solving skills; 4) a composite package of cognitive restructuring, relaxation, and problem-solving; and 5) a control group that received regular agency services. The rationale for cognitive restructuring involved maltreating parents' tendency to attribute negative intentions to child behavior. If the parent could be trained to attribute child behavior instead to developmental level, hunger, or fatigue, then anger could be controlled. The purpose of the relaxation training was to reduce the level of physiological arousal associated with anger. The objective of problem-solving training was to help parents find more effective ways to respond to their child's behavior. Problem-solving training involved educating parents on how to identify and define problems, generate alternatives, make decisions about the alternative to employ, implement the decision, and verify whether problem-solving efforts have worked.

The composite treatment employing both behavioral and cognitive techniques showed the most benefits in terms of improving child management skills and anger arousal, and the relaxation training condition was the least beneficial. Unfortunately, some limitations impact the strength of these findings and their generalizability. Sample size was small, particularly for so many different conditions. Dependent measures were assessed in nonstandardized ways, and there was no follow-up to examine whether results of the 6-week intervention were maintained over time.

Although not specifically named as cognitive-behavioral, a study by Golub, Espinosa, Damon, and Carl (1987) merits discussion here based on the focus of intervention. A pretest-posttest design of a videotape/discussion group program on parenting, which was held over an average of 14.51 sessions, found that cooperative responses and the number of reasons to explain child behavior increased, and the number of reasons blaming the child and punitive responses decreased.

Kolko (1996) compared cognitive-behavioral to family therapy with randomization to groups. Cognitive-behavioral therapy was conducted both in the clinic and in the home over an average of 19 weeks. The intervention consisted of both parent- and child-focused interventions that were parallel in nature. The first half of treatment covered sources of stress and views of and experiences with family violence. In addition, the development of coping and self-control skills was emphasized. Further, parents were educated about child development and realistic expectations for behavior. The second component of treatment involved behavioral child management techniques for the parents and training children in social skills, assertion, and how to use social support. The objective was to help the child gain control of behavior so that the risk of abusive punishment was diminished.

The cognitive-behavioral group showed improvements over the family therapy condition on a series of nonstandardized measures on aggression and the use of physical discipline. In addition, the amount of time before an abusive incident occurred was almost twice that of the family therapy condition.

Despite some of the advantages for cognitive-behavioral therapy, a narrow focus on parent-child interactions limits the value of the approach. Broader factors, such as the role of other family members and socioeconomic status, are not considered for their impact on maltreatment (Tzeng, Jackson, & Karlson, 1991). To address these limitations, a few studies have examined the role of the family beyond the maltreating parent.

FAMILY THERAPY

The main assumption of family therapy is that symptoms can only be understood in the context of the family. The family therapist seeks to change the function of the symptom by altering patterns of interactions within the family. In this view, abuse and violence are seen as problems in the boundaries of a family system, with both victim and perpetrator connected in a circular and reciprocal way (Geffner, Barrett, & Rossman, 1995). This perspective is not without controversy, however. Authors who argue against a systems approach take the position that that the family systems concept of circular causality blames the victim; instead, a linear perspective is taken, with a perpetrator clearly responsible for abusive behavior. Perhaps because of these reasons, there has been a lack of family therapy approaches to treating abuse and neglect (Wolfe & Wekerle, 1993).

In the Kolko (1996) study described above, the family therapy comparison condition was influenced by an ecological model (*see* Table 1.2). However, functionalist family therapy was also cited, along with the use of behavioral techniques, such as contracting and educating about coercive processes, and cognitive-behavioral techniques, such as problem-solving and communication skill-building, and structural family therapy techniques. Indeed, so many different approaches were combined that it is difficult to make any conclusions about the intervention, other than it was not as effective as cognitive-behavioral therapy on a series of nonstandardized measures assessing abusive behavior and attitudes. (See above section on cognitive-behavioral methods for more details on this study.)

Another study used ecological theory as the underlying framework, but with more of a theoretical rationale, with the assumption that problems must be understood within the systemic context (Brunk et al., 1987). The systemic context of maltreatment according to ecological theory (Belsky, 1980) involves parental background, family relationships, community systems, and cultural variables that support abuse and neglect. The approach evaluated is called multisystemic therapy and was developed by one of the authors (Henggeler).

TABLE 1.2 Family Therapy Interventions with Abusive and Neglectful Parents

Brunk et al. (1987) Comparison of multisystemic therapy and parent training 8 sessions	Quasi-experimental, randomized to parent training and multisystemic therapy, pretest, posttest (77% completed) N = 43 parents who had been investigated for maltreatment and were mandated to receive counseling in lieu of court order; 50% chose this option 55% boys, 76% girls; 57% White, 43% African American	10-minute behavioral videotape self-report measures: Individual system: Symptom Checklist-90; Behavior Problem Checklist Family system: Family Environment Scale Social system: Family Inventory of Life Events and Changes Treatment Outcome Questionnaire	Both family preservation and parent training were effective in reducing psychiatric symptoms in parents, parental stress, and individual, and family problems; Multisystemic therapy was more effective than parent training in improving parent-child relationships according to behavioral observations, while parent training was more helpful in ameliorating social system problems	Treatment groups were not similar on all characteristics: neglected children and their mothers in the multisystemic therapy condition were significantly older; selection bias in that only 50% took the option of counseling

continued

TABLE 1.2 *(continued)*

Kolko (1996)	Quasi-experimental, random assignment based on stratification in terms of child age (6–9 vs. 10–13), gender, and family constellation to cognitive-behavioral treatment (parent and child separately) or family therapy, pretest, posttest	Likert scales on severity of child/family problems, severity of anger arousal displayed by parents toward children, and use of physical discipline administered weekly to both child and parent	Parents in cognitive-behavioral treatment improved over family therapy group in overall levels of anger and less use of physical discipline; parents of children diagnosed with a psychiatric disorder and longer duration of problems more likely to report heightened anger and use of physical force	Standardized measures were not administered pretest and posttest—they were used only as criterion validity measures; self-report bias; family therapy orientation not specifically named; small sample size
Cognitive-behavioral treatment or family therapy		Conflict Tactics Scales; Family Environment Scale; Child Abuse Potential Inventory; Parenting Scale; Beck Depression Inventory (all self-report administered just at pretest to serve as criterion validity measures for above Likert scales)		
12, 1-hr weekly clinic sessions; home visits after every 1–2 clinic visits; average length of treatment = 19.1 weeks for cognitive-behavioral, 19.2 weeks for family therapy	Originally 70 were screened for report of physical abuse within last 6 mos; 42 were randomized to treatment conditions, $N = 38$ completed treatment			
	mean age of child = 8.6 yrs, half White, half African American; 63% lived with biological			

	mothers; 74% perpetrators' mothers; 66% of perpetrators had high school education or less; 42% unemployed; 58% received welfare			
Meezan & O'Keefe (1998) Multifamily Group Therapy (influenced by structural family therapy, group therapy, behavior modification, cognitive-behavioral therapy, parent education, and crisis intervention) 2 $\frac{1}{2}$ hrs per week for 34 weeks	Quasi-experimental, randomization to multifamily group therapy or family therapy (structural family therapy, behavior modification, and cognitive-behavioral strategies) N = 41 families referred by CPS for physical abuse or neglect child between 2–11; income level not greater than 185% of poverty line; over half White, $\frac{1}{5}$ each Hispanic, African American; $\frac{1}{3}$ not high school educated, $\frac{1}{3}$ college graduates	Family functioning (Family Assessment Form) Children's behavior (Child Behavior Checklist) Children's interpersonal behavior (Children's Action Tendency Scale; Index of Peer Relations)	Experimental group attended more sessions and for a longer period of time (6.5 mos) vs. 5.4 mos for comparison group. Experimental group more likely to have a planned case closing and showed more improvements in parent-child and caregiver interactions, and child assertiveness	Theoretical basis so eclectic difficult to ascertain what were the helpful components; experimental group also received case management services; no follow-up

Multisystemic therapy involves working with entire families in the home. In contrast with family therapy approaches, however, this model emphasizes both individual cognitive variables and broader system influences beyond the family that play a role in maintaining problems (Brunk et al., 1987).

As discussed above, multisystemic therapy was more effective than parent training in improving parent-child relationships and in helping physically abusing parents gain better control over their children's behavior. These findings are particularly commendable, given that parent training specifically focuses on parents gaining effective control over their children's behavior. In addition, the improvement of neglectful parents' responsiveness to their child's needs was notable with the multisystemic condition, since an emphasis on neglect has not often been a focus of treatment.

The third study with a family therapy focus involved multifamily group therapy, which was influenced by a variety of approaches, such as structural family therapy, group therapy, behavior modification, cognitive-behavioral therapy, parent education, and crisis intervention (Meezan & O'Keefe, 1998). A quasi-experimental study was employed with randomization to multifamily group therapy or single family therapy, both of which were informed by structural family therapy, behavior modification, and cognitive-behavioral strategies. Multifamily group families seemed more engaged in treatment: They attended more sessions and for a longer period of time (6.5 months versus 5.4 months for the comparison group), and they were less likely to prematurely drop out of treatment. According to self-report data, the multifamily group showed more improvements in terms of parent-child interactions and child assertiveness. It could be that the additional support offered in the multifamily group context and the observations of other families undergoing therapeutic interactions could have helped families learn vicariously. One of the limitations of the family therapies offered in both conditions, however, was that the array of techniques rendered the approaches almost theoretically meaninglessness. In addition, type of orientation and modality of delivery (family groups versus individual families) were confounded. A suggested improvement, therefore, would be to compare conditions along a single dimension, such as group versus individual family intervention.

In sum, little work has been done on the use of family therapy with maltreating families. Of the three studies discussed here, two were not informed by any consistent theoretical framework. Multisystemic therapy, administered in a manualized and standardized format, did show promise, especially since it impacted parenting practices in ways essential to the future prevention of maltreatment. However, multisystemic therapy goes beyond traditional family therapy in its emphasis on broader systems that may influence the occurrence of maltreatment. The following section, discusses approaches to targeting the social systems of families more directly through intervention.

SOCIAL SUPPORT/SOCIAL NETWORKS

Several studies in the literature examine interventions that target increasing social support, since social isolation has been associated with maltreatment (Milner & Chilamkurti, 1991) (*see* Table 1.3). Hornick and Clarke (1986) attempted to increase the support available to families with the use of laypersons to deliver services. Lay therapists were available for nurturance and support and to act as role models for appropriate parenting responses. Compared to regular social work services, the lay therapy group made similar improvements, with both resembling the community control group at 1 year. The lay therapy group seemed more engaged with services at this point, and perhaps for this reason, these services were more expensive.

Gaudin, Wodarksi, Arkinson, and Avery (1990–1991) used an approach called "social network interventions" to improve the supportive networks of neglectful families, since social isolation has been identified as a major factor associated with the occurrence of neglect (Crittenden & Ainsworth, 1989). The Gaudin et al. (1990–1991) approach included a comprehensive array of services:

1. personal networking in which caseworkers made direct contact with clients' family members, friends, neighbors, and work members to mediate conflicts and facilitate communication;
2. support groups, which included mutual aid and parenting skills groups (for the development of social skills, the promotion of self-esteem, and for mutual problem sharing and problem solving) and children's groups;
3. volunteer linking, which consisted of volunteers making home visits to provide support, to reinforce parenting skills, and to provide transportation to needed services;
4. neighborhood helpers, in which members of the community known to be informal helpers were identified and solicited to provide transportation, home management instruction, parenting information, child care, and modeling of appropriate child management skills; and
5. social skills training, which was delivered in the parents' group and through home visits by social workers and volunteers in which skills were rehearsed through instruction, coaching, and modeling.

TABLE 1.3   Social Network Interventions with Abusive and Neglectful Parents

Gaudin et al. (1990–1991) Social network Median length of services = 10 mos	Quasi-experimental, randomization to social network or usual casework services, pretest, 6 mo data point, follow-up (12 mos) *N* = 88 Child Protective Services neglect families 48 African American, 40 White; 78 income < $10,000/yr; 57 AFDC recipient; 69 unskilled or unemployed	Childhood Level of Living Scale; Child Neglect Severity Scale; Indicators of the Caretaking Environment for Children Scale; Childhood Level of Living Scale; Social Network Assessment Guide; Adult-Adolescent Parenting Inventory; reabuse	High dropout (31 families prior to 9 mos) *6 mos*: experimental group improved over controls on: 3 measures of parenting adequacy (Childhood Level of Living Scale, Indicators of the Caretaking Environments for Children Scale, Child Neglect Severity Scale); on Adult Adolescent Parenting Inventory, parents had more appropriate expectations of their children and were less reliant on corporal punishment; reported larger and more supportive networks *12 mos:* improvements maintained on the 3 measures of parenting adequacy; on Adult	Participation was voluntary from CPS roles; therefore, results may not be generalizable to neglectful families involved with CPS as a whole; age of children not given; because comprehensive array of services, unknown what treatment components essential to outcome

Adolescent Parenting Inventory, critical parenting attitudes improved on measures of age-appropriate expectations; although empathic understanding, corporal punishment and role reversal were higher than at pretest, scores were still below average; social networks increased by 47% while control stayed same; both groups significantly higher in perceived supportiveness of social networks; 59% of experimental group were terminated from services compared to 24% of controls

Rates of reabuse: 79% reabused once; 21% twice

continued

TABLE 1.3 *(continued)*

Hornick & Clarke (1986) Lay therapy	Longitudinal (12 mos at 6 mo intervals), experimental design with randomization to treatment (lay therapy with social worker services) or control (regular services); total sample also matched (by gender and age) with comparison group from general population (public health unit birth records) at pretest $N = 48$ mothers who had either physically abused their children or who were seen as at high-risk (Ontario, Canada)	Cattell's 16 Personality Factor Test; Coopersmith's Self-Opinion Form; Parent Interview Schedule; Parent Behavior Rating Scales (adapted from Baumrind); Client Satisfaction Questionnaire	No significant differences between groups but both lay and regular services groups improved to resemble community control mothers; however, lay group more actively involved in services at 12 mo follow-up—74% of lay group vs. 50% of standard group; lay therapy more costly	Regular services not defined; lack of demographic information on subjects

Neglectful families were randomized to either the social network intervention or the casework-as-usual condition. Despite the fact the sample was voluntary (all were involved with child protective services although they could elect to participate in this particular intervention), dropout rate was still high: 35% dropped out before the 9-month intervention was completed.

Outcome measures were taken at 6 months and 1 year. Social network families scored significantly better on scales assessing parenting functioning at both data points when compared to the casework-as-usual group. At 12 months, the social network intervention group had improved in statistically significant ways on parenting attitudes and knowledge, whereas the control group had not; however, clinically, the intervention group scores were still below normed averages. While both intervention and comparison groups reported increased perceived supportiveness of social networks at 12 months, only the intervention group reported an increase in the size of networks (by 47%). Overall, the progress made by the intervention group resulted in 59% of families being terminated from child protective services, whereas only 24% of the control group was terminated. At the same time, when maltreatment incidents were examined, 79.4% of the experimental group had committed one type of maltreatment during intervention, and 21% had been involved in two incidents. According to caseworker judgments at termination, almost 65% of these families were considered at least somewhat likely to maltreat their children in the future. In sum, although the social network intervention families improved over casework-as-usual, these families were often still not functioning adequately to prevent risk of poor parenting practices or maltreatment in the future.

ATHEORETICAL APPROACHES

Most of the treatment outcome studies without a theoretical background focus on the parents of very young children (*see* Table 1.4). Younger children are particularly vulnerable to maltreatment for a number of reasons. First, they depend on caretakers for their physical, emotional, and psychological needs. They also spend more time with their parents than do older children. In addition, they lack the ability to regulate affect, which adds to possible parental loss of control and aggression. Further, younger children are at increased risk for injury, given their size and physical vulnerability (Belsky, 1993). Child Welfare League of America statistics indicate that while children under 5 make up 35% of the U.S. population, this age group represents 85% of the fatalities from abuse and neglect (Petit & Curtis, 1997). These increased risks might explain why many of the outcome studies focus on the parents of this age group.

TABLE 1.4 Non-Theory-Based Interventions with Abusive and Neglectful Parents

Elmer (1986) Residential treatment for infants, which included parental visits; Parents could also receive individual and group counseling, advocacy, and referrals, such as job training Average 3 mo stay	Pretest, posttest, follow-up (9 mos) N = 31 infants from 0–6 mos referred by CPS or juvenile court (10 were physically abused, 21 were high-risk) mean age of child = 16.6 weeks 55% male, 45% female; 45% White, 48% African American	Bayley Scales of Infant Development and assessments of mother-baby interaction based on systematic video-tapes of feeding and teaching according to Barnard Feeding and Teaching Scales	Improvements noted in physical development of babies and in mother-baby interaction scores; maintenance was in mental functioning of children; declines were found in motor ability but reunification of parents with children did not occur "in the majority of cases"	Design described as quasi-experimental but results were reported for pre- to posttest rather than between-group differences; lack of theoretical orientation
Ferleger et al. (1988) (at least 6 sessions)	Posttest only; identifying correlates of reabuse in maltreating parents from clinic records N = 45 from child abuse treatment program in urban area with primary clientele from CPS; majority female;	Parent, child, and treatment variables from case record Outcome—reabuse known to CPS	40% reabused during treatment, 13% during follow-up	Lack of theoretical framework for treatment; unknown modalities of treatment; conservative definition of abuse (known to authorities); unknown how long reabuse records tracked; no pretest; lack of standardization of measures; lack of control or comparison group

	37% African American, 31% Hispanic, 31.1% White; Low SES		Both groups participated at comparable levels and significantly improved rate of positive child interactions, decreased criticisms and negative child interactions; however, no significant differences in attendance to children's annoying behaviors	Lack of theoretical framework, demographic information, no-treatment control, follow-up, standardized measures
Irueste-Montes & Montes (1988)	Quasi-experimental, comparing court mandated (N = 34) and voluntary (N = 22) clients progress in treatment from pre- to posttest	Behavioral observation		
Atheoretical				
Treatment package consisted of therapeutic family style day care for children, parent group meetings, and family sessions in the home	All CPS clients, physical abuse or neglect of preschool children (1–6 yrs)			
Land (1986)	Posttest only	MMPI	Positive relationship between treatment intensity and successful outcome; only when subjects received 4+ mos did they make substantial improvement; no differences found on race, MMPI or type of abuse committed on those who received less than and more than 4 mos	Although caseworkers were not assessing rehabilitation, some bias might still exist with program administrators rating improvement; "rehabilitation" outcome not standardized; no pretest; MMPI was not used to measure outcome; no follow-up; no comparison/control group
	N = 89 parents	treatment intensity (number of mos and number of hours/week of client participation		
	72% women, 28% men; 62% White, 38% African American	rehabilitation assessed by program administrator rather than caseworker rated subjects as improved (changes in		
	all children under 2 yrs; 37% high risk for abuse, 30% physical abuse, 19% neglect/failure to			

continued

TABLE 1.4 *(continued)*

	thrive, 14% both abuse and neglect	themselves as well as their relationship with child), partially improved (changes in self), or unimproved (neither changes in self nor changes in relationship with child)		
McLaren (1988) Home visits twice a week for 23 weeks	Pretest, posttest N = 13 mothers from a child welfare sample referred for neglect (Canada) low income; educational level not higher than 12 yrs; majority single-parent; majority Canadian Indian background; mean age of child = 27.5 mos	Parent and Child Together Scale; Child Behavior Test	On both self-report and behavioral observation, statistically significant improvement was shown	Selection bias in that voluntary participation; no control or comparison group; small sample size; nonstandardized measures; unknown who coded behavioral observations; program offered was one among many other services such as family aides, homemakers, support groups, education groups, day care, etc.; therefore, difficult to tell whether effects due to program or other services; no follow-up

Rivara (1985) Treatments offered: parent effectiveness training using behavior modification (6–8 weekly group sessions); individual insight-oriented therapy; stress management; marital counseling	Posttest only of case records (N = 71) for which there was complete data on physical abuse referrals Child ages: 0–6 mos 25%, 7–12 mos 35%, 13–24 mos 39%	Case records	32% of families participated in both mental health counseling and parenting training; almost 50% participated in neither; 16% complied with parenting groups only; of those who participated, an "acceptable response" was made; half physically abused index child 1+ times; at a mean of 30.8 mos after case entry; 59% of children living with at least one parent, 7 in foster care, 17% with relatives; 7% parental rights terminated; 50% of families physically abused index child more than once; $^2/_3$ of other children in families abused as well	Many different and confounded treatment options; demographic information lacking; no pretest; no follow-up; no control/comparison group; precise outcome data not given; many nonstandardized measures and outcomes (i.e., "acceptable response")

The interventions that are not theoretically based also tend to try to target many different areas of functioning. The following composite packages of services are offered (e.g., Azar, 1986): parent effectiveness training, individual insight-oriented therapy, stress management, and marital counseling (Rivara, 1985); therapeutic day care, parent group meetings, and family home treatment sessions (Irueste-Montes & Montes, 1988); residential treatment for infants, mother-child interaction training, parental individual and group counseling, advocacy, and community referrals (Elmer, 1986); and mother-child relationship-building, family aides, homemakers, support groups, education groups, and day care (McLaren, 1988). Given the combinations of services provided to families, the specific effect attributable to parental treatment is unknown. In addition, length and intensity of treatment and information on utilization of services are generally not provided. Because of these limitations, it is difficult to make conclusions about the atheoretical research in this area. Instead, brief summaries of these studies will be given.

Only one study exclusively targeted neglectful mothers (McLaren, 1988). An approach was developed to assist mother-child bonding through home visits. Although statistically significant improvements were found for nonstandardized maternal self-report data and behavioral observations from pre- to posttest, this intervention was one among many other services offered; therefore, it is difficult to know whether the effects were due to the program or other services.

Another study, this time with physical abuse families, examined the effectiveness of a residential treatment program for infants (Elmer, 1986). During parent visits, program staff discussed and then modeled appropriate interactions. Parent-child interactions were videotaped so mothers could receive feedback. Compared to a group at high risk for abuse who might have received a variety of other services, the treatment was helpful for restoring child physical development and maintaining mental functioning. While mother-infant interaction scores improved, families were not usually reunited, despite that being a goal of the program. However, the criteria involved for reunification were not discussed, nor were numbers provided on who had met this criteria.

The focus of another study was a therapeutic day care for both abused and neglected preschool children (Irueste-Montes & Montes, 1988). As part of the package of services, parent group and family home sessions were also held. When examining court-mandated status, both court-ordered and voluntary parents participated at comparable levels. It must be noted that both groups were under supervision by child protective services; however, the court-ordered group was threatened with legal consequences for nonparticipation, whereas the voluntary sample was not. Behavioral observations indicated that parents significantly improved their rate of positive child interactions and decreased their criticism. While children also reduced their negative behaviors, parents still attended to these behaviors.

The next group of studies were mainly interested in compliance, the relationship between service intensity and successful outcome, and factors associated with reabuse rather than the effects of programs per se. Typically, low rates of compliance with treatment have been found with child protective services clients. For example, Famularo, Kinscherff, Bunshaft, Spivak, and Fenton (1989) found that out of 91 clients referred for substance abuse treatment, only 21% participated. Overall, those who had both physically and sexually abused their children were less compliant than those who had been referred for neglect.

Another study looked at case records of physically abused very young children (up to 24 months old) to determine compliance (Rivara, 1985). Only 32% of parents participated in both parent training and mental health counseling; about half of those participated in neither, with only 16% complying with parenting groups. Overall, only one third complied with recommendations for treatment, despite child protective services supervision. According to case records, less than half of families who did go had an adequate response, although this was not defined. When examining reabuse rates, half of the index children were physically abused, and two thirds of other children in the home were abused as well.

In another study, Ferleger, Glenwick, Gaiues, and Green (1988) looked at variables to explain reabuse rates. A high rate of reabuse was also found in this study. Forty percent of parents physically abused their children during treatment, and 13% during follow-up. However, the reduced rate during follow-up may have been because parents were not as closely monitored. No obvious factors emerged to explain repeat physical abuse. Only interactions of variables were found; for example, if clients were married, they needed more extensive treatment (more than 6 months) in order not to resort to physical punishment. In addition, those who had severely abused their children in the past were more likely to commit reabuse if they missed appointments.

The need for treatment intensity was also evidenced by Land (1986). Improvements in both adult individual functioning and parenting occurred only when subjects had received at least 4 months of treatment. Although there was a positive relationship between hours in treatment per week and outcome, it was still also necessary that clients be seen over at least 4 consecutive months.

Although it is difficult to summarize the results of non-theoretically based treatment studies given their limitations, alarming is the high rate of noncompliance and reabuse. Overall, what is most striking from this review is the dearth of empirically and theoretically sound evaluation studies on treatment, despite the fact that child abuse and neglect are regarded as central social issues. It also should be noted that a majority of the studies have been conducted in the 1980s, with very few in recent years. In the following sections, studies in this area will be critiqued and recommendations for improving evaluative efforts and further research will be explored.

RESEARCH CRITIQUE AND RECOMMENDATIONS

Designs

The child maltreatment outcome research has been marked by an overreliance on single-subject (e.g., Dawson et al., 1986; Fantuzzo et al., 1986), posttest only (Ferleger et al., 1988; Rivara, 1985), and pretest/posttest (Acton & During, 1992; Golub et al., 1987; McLaren, 1988) designs (Kaufman & Rudy, 1991; Mash & Wolfe, 1991), although some improvements have been made with both quasi-experimental (Brunk et al., 1987; Elmer, 1986; Gaudin et al., 1990–1991; Hornick & Clarke, 1986; Irueste-Montes & Montes, 1988; Kolko, 1996; Nicol et al., 1988; Schinke et al., 1986; Szykula & Fleischman, 1985; Wolfe et al., 1988) and experimental (Whiteman et al., 1987) designs.

When comparison groups have been used, the lack of truly comparative control conditions has been noted (Mash & Wolfe, 1991; Schellenbach, 1998). For example, in Elmer (1986) the comparison group consisted of families at risk of physical abuse in contrast to the experimental group, which comprised actual physically abusing families. In addition, the comparison condition was not apt to receive any typical services (i.e., they could have received infant stimulation, foster home placement, etc.).

Another flaw found in evaluations using comparative conditions is the lack of randomization to groups (e.g., Elmer, 1986; Irueste-Montes & Montes, 1988). If randomization does not occur, it is unknown if groups are comparative. A recommendation for research in the future is the use of quasi-experimental designs with random assignment to treatment conditions (Wolfe & Wekerle, 1993). Because of ethical considerations involved in delaying treatment to maltreating families, examining the relative effectiveness of different treatments is a valid alternative to experimental designs in which a no-treatment control group is used. Though field research proves difficult, comparison groups could be provided with casework-as-usual services. In such cases, it is necessary to delineate services so that the difference between intervention and treatment-as-usual is clear. For example, Gaudin et al. (1990–1991) described regular casework services as consisting of once-monthly home visits, information, and referrals to community services.

A further flaw in evaluative research has been the lack of follow-up in studies (e.g., Acton & During, 1992; Golub et al., 1987; Irueste-Montes & Montes, 1988; McLaren, 1988; Meezan & O'Keefe, 1998; Whiteman et al., 1987). The need for an adequate follow-up period becomes crucial in evaluating child and adolescent treatment outcomes since children make remarkable developmental changes over time (Kazdin, 1993).

MEASUREMENT

There have been many problems with the measurement of outcome in treatment studies of abuse and neglect: the lack of connection to any underlying theory; the lack of operationalization of constructs; the use of measurement tools that have been created specifically for the study, with unknown or inadequate psychometric properties; and the use of subjective sources of information, such as caseworkers who provide intervention. In addition, particular concerns have been raised about the overreliance on archival records, such as case records (Mash & Wolfe, 1991). This information is unstandardized, inconsistently presented depending on the setting and geographic region, and is based on selective and biased reports (Mash & Wolfe, 1991).

Further measurement issues involve the use of measures that were originally formulated for nondeviant populations. Such measures may not capture the specific outcomes necessary for the treatment of abuse and neglect populations. Some beginning work has gone into the development of assessment instruments that reflect the domains that need to be impacted, such as the Child Abuse Potential Inventory (Milner, 1994) and the Parent Opinion Questionnaire (Azar, Robinson, Hekimian, & Twentyman, 1984; Azar & Rohrbeck, 1986). More work also needs to be done on ensuring that measurements are sensitive to different cultures and educational levels. These factors impact understanding and follow-through with measurement procedures, as well as the measurement of outcome (Mash & Wolfe, 1991; National Research Council, 1993; Wolfe & Wekerle, 1993).

Another area of concern is the reliance on only a few data sources or methods, especially ones of questionable reliability (Mash & Wolfe, 1991; Schellenbach, 1993; Wolfe & Wekerle, 1993). Since all sources and methods have certain advantages and disadvantages, a recommendation is to use a combination: standardized self-report measures, direct observations of behavior, peer ratings, and teacher ratings (Mash & Wolfe, 1991). Further, it is important that data be collected from both children and parents, as one criticism is the lack of information on child effects (Azar, 1986).

SAMPLE

Several issues relate to child maltreatment outcome samples. These include sample size, a gender bias toward mothers, the lack of definition regarding type of maltreatment, and information on dropouts.

The first issue involves the small size of samples. Adequate sample size needs to be ensured in order to obtain the necessary conditions to meet statistical power (Wolfe & Wekerle, 1993). For instance, although the Whiteman et al. (1987) study is to be commended for examining separate cognitive-behavioral treatment components, the sample size ($N = 55$) was inadequate to support five different conditions as well as seven dependent variables.

Another issue with sampling is that mothers are often the focus of interventions (Schellenbach, 1998; Wolfe, 1987) despite the fact that males are more likely to physically abuse children (Kaufman & Rudy, 1991). This focus probably stems from the fact that most of the maltreatment occurs under the care of mothers, who are usually the primary caregivers (Belsky, 1993). Future studies need to include information on which parent committed the abuse. It is possible that abuse perpetrated by mothers as opposed to fathers may have differential impact on child outcome (Azar et al., 1988). In addition, programs will need to ensure participation of fathers and examine how paternal engagement in treatment contributes to family outcome.

Other issues with samples involve the heterogeneity of the child maltreatment population in terms of type of maltreatment (abuse and/or neglect), etiology, and response to intervention (Aber, Allen, Carlson, & Cicchetti, 1989; Cicchetti & Rizley, 1981). When considering type of maltreatment, authors have discussed the need to distinguish "abuse" or "neglect" in samples, since these are two qualitatively different phenomenon (Conaway & Hansen, 1989; Lindsey, 1994): Physical abuse represents acts of commission, while neglect involves acts of ommission (Paget, Philip, & Abramczyk, 1993).

This review shows that samples often combine abuse and neglect (Ferleger et al., 1988; Irueste-Montes & Montes, 1988; Szykula & Fleischman, 1985; Wolfe et al., 1988), or they fail to specify whether samples have been referred for abuse or neglect (Golub et al., 1987; Schinke et al., 1986; Szykula & Fleischman, 1985). In addition, there was a much greater emphasis on physically abusive (Acton & During, 1992; Elmer, 1986; Hornick & Clarke, 1988;

Kolko, 1996; Rivara, 1985; Whiteman et al., 1987) than on neglectful parents (McLaren, 1988). Although neglect has tended to lack an empirical focus (Crittenden & Ainsworth, 1989), neglect remains the most common type of maltreatment. Indeed, National Child Abuse and Neglect Data statistics indicated that in 1992, 49% of investigated child maltreatment cases involved substantiated neglect, 23% involved physical abuse, and 14% were for sexual abuse (U.S. Department of Justice, 1995).

Despite the need to develop discrete categories of abuse and neglect, no specific criteria have been established for this purpose (National Research Council, 1993). Neither do criteria exist for how to specify the varying combinations, since abuse and different types of neglect often occur together (Azar et al., 1988). Further, the occurrences of abuse and neglect in families are not usually isolated incidents; maltreatment occurs as part of a family context that generally fails to enhance children's optimal development (Crittenden, 1998; Erickson, Egeland, & Pianta, 1989). Therefore, research needs to address the extent to which a child's difficulties are attributable to other problems in the home or the immediate social environment, besides maltreatment (Erickson et al., 1989; National Research Council, 1993; Schellenbach, 1998). For example, chemical dependency and partner abuse frequently co-occur along with abuse and neglect. It could well be that witnessing violence has its own unique effects outside of abuse and neglect (Mash & Wolfe, 1991). Further, the effect of poverty and its attendant stressors—inadequate housing, unsafe communities, and poor educational opportunities—may also contribute to negative outcomes, even after controlling for the presence of abuse.

Within each category of abuse and neglect, greater specification is also needed. Mash and Wolfe (1991) call for differentiation of the various dimensions of physical abuse, such as type of act, severity, chronicity, and recency. Age of onset has been a particular focus in the literature. There has been a great deal of concern with young children because of their physical and psychological vulnerability. In addition, prospective, longitudinal work suggests that the earlier abuse and neglect occurs, the more negative the consequences (Erickson et al., 1989). However, more attention needs to be paid to cases of adolescent abuse, since adolescents are also maltreated at high rates (Wolfe & Wekerle, 1993). It is not understood, for instance, what the differences are between cases that are continuations from childhood and those that involve the developmental challenges of parenting adolescents (Garbarino, 1989).

Similar issues pertain to child neglect, which constitutes a wide range of conditions, such as parental failure to provide adequate physical health care, nutrition, supervision, personal hygiene, safe housing, education, or emotional nurturing (Gaudin, 1993). However, these subcategories are not operationalized or standardized; nor is the definition of adequate care in each of these areas clear. Dilemmas in developing operational definitions involve the extent of harm to the child and the parent's intention of harm versus difficult social conditions for which parents are not responsible (Gaudin, 1993). Greater specification may be essential to determine the varying outcomes for children depending on the subtype of neglect and the impact of interventions.

Although legal and child protective services definitions have been developed, they suffer from lack of standardization and operationalism. Decisions, therefore, are often made on the basis of subjective judgments (Azar, 1986; Mash & Wolfe, 1991). Legal criteria often have an overreliance on intentionality and the consequences of the maltreatment. However, even if legal definitions were made behaviorally concrete, personnel in law enforcement, the legal profession, and social service agencies may not apply these criteria in reliable ways (Azar, 1986). Contextual factors, such as administrative, legal, and political jurisdictions, have played a larger role in defining maltreatment.

One recommendation, taken from the area of psychological disorders, is to develop diagnostic criteria for the various types of maltreatment. If theoretically neutral but precise categories of definitions were established, as well as standardized, structured interview and assessment procedures, this would contribute to clarity of communication, theory-building, and the development of research and knowledge (Cicchetti, 1989; Cicchetti & Rizley, 1981).

Another type of heterogeneity involved with child maltreatment samples involves the wide variation in treatment response (Aber et al., 1989; Cicchetti & Rizley, 1981). Because of the nonvoluntary nature of many child protective services clients, such clients may not be amenable to participation in research projects, which are, for the protection of subjects, voluntary in nature. Studies tend not to report how many families refused to participate, or the numbers and characteristics of families who drop out of research. Sampling biases would be represented in both cases, with more severe, multiproblem families showing a greater likelihood of both not participating and not following through with research protocol (Mash & Wolfe, 1991). For example, Golub et al. (1987) found that out of 120 who agreed to participate in treatment, 75 completed the program, and 40 provided complete test information.

Information on parents who fail to complete treatment is needed with delineation of the characteristics that distinguish those who drop out versus those who complete treatment. For example, Famularo et al. (1989) reported particularly low rates of compliance for child protective services clients who were referred for substance abuse treatment (21% of 91) and for those who had both physically and sexually abused their children as opposed to those who were neglectful. If certain characteristics of dropouts can be identified, treatment may be tailored to meet particular needs and family deficits. As in the conduct disorder literature, treatment may need to include adjunctive packages that address marital problems, lack of social support, and deficits in problem-solving skills (Miller & Prinz, 1990).

THEORY BASIS AND TREATMENT COMPONENTS

Already mentioned has been the tendency of child maltreatment programs to involve combinations of services (Azar, 1986). Composite services appear to be a response to the multiproblem nature of child maltreatment families. However, the essential components of interventions should be tested and applied in a more systematic way. Further, a decision-making process must be formulated so that clients with particular characteristics and circumstances undergo the appropriate type and course of treatment. A related issue involves monitoring the delivery of services to ensure they are applied in a standardized and consistent fashion (Wolfe & Wekerle, 1993). In addition, criteria for termination should be explicitly developed. As it stands, few studies describe the criteria used for making these decisions (Kaufman & Rudy, 1991). Finally, one of the more serious flaws of this research is its atheoretical nature. Interventions need to be grounded in theory that encompasses etiology and treatment so that child and family outcomes can be successfully impacted (Aber et al., 1989).

SERVICE DELIVERY AND POLICY RECOMMENDATIONS

Although insufficient study has accumulated for programs in any one theoretical orientation to make service delivery recommendations, behavioral and cognitive-behavioral approaches show promise. Beyond the few studies in this area, a strong research tradition with conduct-disorder youth and their parents, a similar population to that of child maltreatment, provides even more evidence for the effectiveness of behavioral and cognitive-behavioral methods. The conduct-disorder literature has also identified factors associated with nonresponse to treatment, such as low socioeconomic status, family violence, and substance abuse (Webster-Stratton, 1990). These same factors are both correlates of and contributors to abuse and neglect. The lack of interventions on family violence and marital distress with maltreatment populations has been attributed to males' uninvolvement in treatment (Wolfe & Wekerle, 1993). Special efforts should be made in the future so that male perpetrators, as well as nonoffending fathers and father figures, are included in the treatment process (Kaufman & Rudy, 1991).

There is also a lack of attention to substance abuse treatment (Schellenbach, 1998). According to a 1996 Child Welfare League survey, 67% of parents involved with the Child Protective Services system require substance abuse treatment (Petit & Curtis, 1997). Unfortunately, Child Protective Services agencies can provide services to only 31% of those in need (Petit & Curtis, 1997). None of the studies in this review examined treatment for chemical dependency; one study examined compliance with court-ordered treatment and found particularly low rates of compliance (20%) for substance abuse treatment (Famularo et al., 1989).

In addition, the family environments of many maltreated children are marked by low socioeconomic status. A dramatic illustration on the relationship between neglect, in particular, and poverty comes out of the National Center on Child Abuse and Neglect in 1996 (Petit & Curtis, 1997). In families with income less than $15,000 a year, 27.2 out of 1,000 children were referred for neglect. These numbers stand in stark contrast to the 11.3 children per 1,000 in the population that are referred from households of $15,000 to $29,000, and the 0.6 of children from households in which the income level was at least $30,000 per year.

While not all low-income parents mistreat their children, poverty remains a significant risk factor, not only for abuse and neglect, but also for other social problems, such as crime and delinquency, teenage pregnancy, high school dropout, and family violence. To address these social conditions, many authors have argued for policy change in the areas of health care, housing, child care, and education so that underlying, contributing factors are remedied (Belsky, 1993; Gaudin, 1993; Lindsey, 1994; Paget et al., 1993; Tarnowski & Rohrbeck, 1993). As Kendziora and O'Leary (1993) state: "Focusing psychological services indiscrimately on low-SES parents is a misuse of resources if not accompanied by changes in social policy" (p. 195).

Other authors, while acknowledging the advisability of such reforms, have also discussed that these changes are unlikely to happen, given the current political climate (Olds & Henderson, 1989). In addition, because the impact of socioeconomic changes on child abuse and neglect may be indirect, a considerable length of time may have to elapse (perhaps even generations) before changes occur. Treatment for abuse and neglect that has already occurred, however, is expensive, not only in terms of the costs of child protective services intervention, but also for the individual and social costs: reabuse, the inter-generational transmission of violence, and loss of adult productivity (Wolfe & Wekerle, 1993). Further, long-standing problems that have deteriorated to the point of abuse and neglect are much more resistant to change. Several advocate, therefore, for secondary prevention programs that target families at risk for problems (Olds & Henderson, 1989; Wolfe & Wekerle, 1993). The enhancement of the parent-child relationship through intervention would act as a protective factor against maltreatment and would foster optimal child developmental outcomes (Wolfe & Wekerle, 1993).

REFERENCES

Aber, J. L., Allen, J. P., Carlson, V., & Cicchetti, D. (1989). The effects of maltreatment on development during early childhood: Recent studies and their theoretical clinical, and policy implications. In D. Cicchetti & V. Carlson (Eds.), *Child maltreatment: Theory and research on the causes and consequences of child abuse and neglect* (pp. 580–594). Cambridge, UK: Cambridge University Press.

Acton, R. G., & During, S. M. (1992). Preliminary results of aggression management training for aggressive parents. *Journal of Interpersonal Violence, 7*, 410–417.

Azar, S. T. (1986). A framework for understanding child maltreatment: An integration of cognitive behavioral and developmental perspectives. *Canadian Journal of Behavioral Science, 18*, 340–355.

Azar, S. T., Barnes, K. T., & Twentyman, C. T. (1988). Developmental outcomes in physically abused children: Consequences of parental abuse or the effects of a more general breakdown in caregiving behaviors? *The Behavior Therapist, 11*, 27–32.

Azar, S. T., Fantuzzo, J. W., & Twentyman, C. T. (1984). An applied behavioral approach to child maltreatment: Back to basics. *Advances in Behaviour Research & Therapy, 6*, 3–11.

Azar, S. T. Robinson, D., Hekimian, E., & Twentyman, C. T. (1984). Unrealistic expectations and problem solving ability in maltreating and comparison mothers. *Journal of Consulting and Clinical Psychology, 52*, 687–691.

Azar, S. T., & Rohrbeck, C. A. (1986). Child abuse and unrealistic expectations: Further validation of the Parent Opinion Questionnaire. *Journal of Consulting and Clinical Psychology, 54*, 867–868.

Azar, S. T., & Wolfe, D. A. (1989). Child abuse and neglect. In E. J. Mash & R. A. Barkley (Eds.), *Treatment of childhood disorders* (pp. 424–492). New York: Guilford Press.

Azar, S. T., & Wolfe, D. A. (1996). Child abuse and neglect. In E. J. Mash & R. A. Barkley (Eds.), *Treatment of childhood disorders* (2nd ed., pp. 451–489). New York: Guilford Press.

Barth, R. P. (1990). An experimental evaluation of in-home child abuse prevention services. *Child Abuse & Neglect, 15,* 363–375.

Belsky, J. (1980). Child maltreatment: An ecological integration. *American Psychologist, 35,* 320–335.

Belsky, J. (1993). Etiology of child maltreatment: A developmental-ecological analysis. *Psychological Bulletin, 114,* 413–434.

Blythe, B. J. (1983). A critique of outcome evaluation in child abuse treatment. *Child Welfare, 62*(4), 325–335.

Brestan, E., Eyberg, S., Boggs, S., & Algina, J. (1997). Parent-child interaction therapy: Parents perception of untreated siblings. *Child and Family Behavior Therapy, 19*(3), 13–28.

Brunk, M., Henggeler, S. W., & Whelan, J. P. (1987). Comparison of multisystemic therapy and parent training in the brief treatment of child abuse and neglect. *Journal of Consulting and Clinical Psychology, 55,* 171–178.

Cicchetti, D. (1989). How research on child maltreatment has informed the study of child development: Perspective from developmental dsychopathology. In D. Cicchetti & V. Carlson (Eds.), *Child maltreatment: Theory and research on the causes and consequences of child abuse and neglect* (pp. 377–431). Cambridge, UK: Cambridge University Press.

Cicchetti, D., & Rizley, R. (1981). Developmental perspectives on the etiology, intergenerational transmission, and sequelae of child maltreatment. *New Directions for Child Development, 11,* 31–55.

Cohn, A. H., & Daro, D. (1987). Is treatment too late: What ten years of evaluative research tell us. *Child Abuse & Neglect, 11,* 47–64.

Conaway, L. P., & Hansen, D. J. (1989). Social behavior of physically abused and neglected children: A critical review. *Clinical Psychology Review, 9,* 627–652.

Crittenden, P. M., & Ainsworth, M. (1989). Child maltreatment and attachment theory. In D. Cicchetti & V. Carlson (Eds.), *Child maltreatment: Research and theory on the consequences of child abuse and neglect* (pp. 432–463). New York: Cambridge University Press.

Culp, R. E., Little, V., Letts, D., & Lawrence, H. (1991). Maltreated children's self-concept: Effects of a comprehensive treatment program. *American Journal of Orthopsychiatry, 61,* 114–121.

Dawson, B., de Armas, A., McGrath, M. L., & Kelly, J. A. (1986). Cognitive problem-solving training to improve the child-care judgment of child neglectful parents. *Journal of Family Violence, 1,* 209–221.

Eisenstadt, T. H., Eyberg, S., McNeil, C. B., Newcomb, K., & Funderburk, B. (1993). Parent-child interaction therapy with behavior problem children: Relative effectiveness of two stages and overall treatment outcome. *Journal of Clinical Child Psychology, 22,* 42–51.

Elmer, E. (1986). Outcome of residential treatment for abused and high-risk infants. *Child Abuse & Neglect, 10,* 351–360.

Erickson, M. F., Egeland, B., & Pianta, R. (1989). The effects of maltreatment on the development of young children. In D. Cicchetti & V. Carlson (Eds.), *Child mal-*

treatment: Theory and research on the causes and consequences of child abuse and neglect (pp. 647–684). Cambridge: Cambridge University Press.

Famularo, R., Kinscherff, R., Bunshaft, D., Spivak, G., & Fenton, T. (1989). Parental compliance to court-ordered treatment interventions in cases of child maltreatment. *Child Abuse & Neglect, 13*, 507–514.

Fantuzzo, J. W., & Twentyman, C. T. (1986). Child abuse and psychotherapy research: Merging social concerns and empirical investigation. *Professional Psychology Research & Practice, 17*, 375–380.

Fantuzzo, J. W., Wray, L., Hall, R., Goins, C., & Azar, S. (1986). Parent and social-skills training for mentally retarded mothers identified as child maltreaters. *American Journal of Mental Deficiency, 91*, 135–140.

Ferleger, N., Glenwick, D. S., Gaines, R. R. W., & Green, A. H. (1988). Identifying correlates of reabuse in maltreating parents. *Child Abuse & Neglect, 12*, 41–49.

Forehand, R., & McMahon, R. J. (1981). *Helping the noncompliant child: A clinician's guide to effective parent training.* New York: Guilford Press.

Garbarino, J. (1989). Troubled youth, troubled families: The dynamics of adolescent maltreatment. In D. Cicchetti & V. Carlson (Eds.), *Child maltreatment: Theory and research on the causes and consequences of child abuse and neglect* (pp. 685–706). Cambridge, UK: Cambridge University Press.

Gaudin, J. M., Jr., (1993). Effective intervention with neglectful families. *Criminal Justice and Behavior, 20*, 66–89.

Gaudin, J. M., Jr., Wodarski, J. S., Arkinson, M. K., & Avery, L. S. (1990–1991). Remedying child neglect: Effectiveness of social network interventions. *Journal of Applied Social Sciences, 15*, 97–123.

Geffner, R., Barrett, M. J., & Rossman, B. B. (1995). Domestic violence and sexual abuse: Multiple systems perspectives. In R. H. Mikesell, D. Lusterman, & S. H. McDaniel (Eds.), *Integrating family therapy: Handbook of family psychology and systems theory* (pp. 501–517). Washington, DC: American Psychological Association.

Gelardo, M. S., & Sanford, E. E. (1987). Child abuse and neglect: A review of the literature. *School Psychology Review, 16*, 137–155.

Golub, J. S., Espinosa, M. A., Damon, L., & Carl, J. (1987). A videotape parent education program for abusive parents. *Child Abuse & Neglect, 11*, 255–265.

Graziano, A. M., & Mills, J. R. (1992). Treatment for abused children: When is a partial solution acceptable? *Child Abuse & Neglect, 16*, 217–228.

Hansen, D. J., Pallotta, G. M., Tishelman, A. C., Conaway, L. P., & MacMillan, V. M. (1989). Parental problem-solving skills and child behavior problems: A comparison of physically abusive, neglectful, clinic, and community families. *Journal of Family Violence, 4*, 353–368.

Hornick, J., & Clarke, M. E. (1986). A cost/effectiveness evaluation of lay therapy treatment for child abusing and high risk parents. *Child Abuse and Neglect, 10*, 235–242.

Howing, P., Wodarski, J., Kurtz, P., Gaudin, J., & Herbst, E. (1990). Child abuse and delinquency: The empirical and theoretical links. *Social Work, 35*, 244–249.

Irueste-Montes, A. M., & Montes, F. (1988). Court-ordered vs. voluntary treatment of abusive and neglectful parents. *Child Abuse and Neglect, 12*, 33–39.

Kaufman, J., & Zigler, E. (1989). The intergenerational transmission of child abuse. In D. Cicchetti & V. Carlson (Eds.), *Child maltreatment: Theory and research on the causes and consequences of child abuse and neglect* (pp. 129–152). Cambridge, UK: Cambridge University Press.

Kaufman, K. L., & Rudy, L. (1991). Future directions in the treatment of physical child abuse. *Criminal Justice and Behavior, 18*, 82–97.

Kazdin, A. E. (1993). Treatment of conduct disorder: Progress and directions in psychotherapy research. *Development and Psychopathology, 5*, 277–310.

Kazdin, A. E., Hayes, S. C., Henry, W. P., Schacht, T. E., & Strupp, H. H. (1992). Case study and small sample research. In A. E. Kazdin (Ed.), *Methodological issues & strategies in clinical research* (pp. 235–242). Washington, DC: American Psychological Association.

Kendziora, K., & O'Leary, S. G. (1993). Dysfunctional parenting as a focus for prevention and treatment of child behavior problems. *Advances in Clinical Child Psychology, 15*, 175–206.

Kolko, D. (1993). Further evaluation of inpatient child behavior ratings: Consistency across settings, time, and sources. *Journal of Emotional & Behavioral Disorders, 1*, 251–259.

Kolko, D. J. (1996). Clinical monitoring of treatment course in child physical abuse: Psychometric characteristics and treatment comparisons. *Child Abuse & Neglect, 20*, 23–43.

Land, H. M. (1986). Child abuse: Differential diagnosis, differential treatment. *Child Welfare, 65*, 33–34.

Lindsey, D. (1994). *The welfare of children*. New York: Oxford University Press.

Malinosky-Rummell, R., & Hansen, D. J. (1993). Long-term consequences of childhood physical abuse. *Psychological Bulletin, 114*, 68–79.

Mash, E. J., & Wolfe, D. A. (1991). Methodological issues in research on physical child abuse. *Criminal Justice and Behavior, 18*, 8–29.

McLaren, L. (1988). Fostering mother-child relationships. *Child Welfare League of America, 67*(4), 353–365.

McNeil, C. B., Eyberg, S., Eisenstadt, T. H., Newcomb, K., & Funderburk, B. (1991). Parent-child interaction therapy with behavior problem children: Generalization of treatment effects to the school setting. *Journal of Clinical Child Psychology, 20*, 140–151.

Meezan, W., & O'Keefe, M. (1998). Multifamily group therapy: Impact on family functioning and child behavior. *Families in Society: The Journal of Contemporary Human Services, 79*, 32–44.

Melton, G. B., & Barry, F. D. (1994). Neighbors helping neighbors: The vision of the U.S. advisory board on child abuse and neglect. In G. B. Melton & F. D. Barry (Eds.), *Protecting children from abuse and neglect: Foundations for a new national strategy* (pp. 1–13). New York: Guilford Press.

Miller, G. E., & Prinz, R. J. (1990). Enhancement of social learning family interventions for childhood conduct disorder. *Psychological Bulletin, 108*, 291–307.

Milner, J. (1994). Assessing physical child abuse risk: The child abuse potential inventory. *Clinical Psychology Review, 14*, 547–583.

Milner, J. S., & Chilamkurti, C. (1991). Physical child abuse perpetrator characteristics: A review of the literature. *Journal of Interpersonal Violence, 6*, 345–366.

Mueller, E., & Silverman, N. (1989). Peer relations in maltreated children. In D. Cicchetti & V. Carlson (Eds.), *Child maltreatment: Theory and research on the causes and consequences of child abuse and neglect* (pp. 529–578). Cambridge, UK: Cambridge University Press.

National Research Council. (1993). *Understanding child abuse and neglect.* Washington, DC: National Academy Press.

Nicol, A. R., Smith, J., Kay, B., Hall, D., Barlow, J., & Williams, B. (1988). A focused casework approach to the treatment of child abuse: A controlled comparison. *Journal of Child Psychology and Psychiatry, 29*, 703–711.

Oates, R. K., & Bross, D. C. (1995). What have we learned about treating child physical abuse? A literature review of the last decade. *Child Abuse & Neglect, 4*, 463–473.

Olds, D. L., & Henderson, Jr., C. R. (1989). The prevention of maltreatment. In D. Cicchetti & V. Carlson (Eds.), *Child maltreatment: Theory and research on the causes and consequences of child abuse and neglect* (pp. 722–763). Cambridge, UK: Cambridge University Press.

Olds, D. L., Henderson, Jr., C. R., Chamberlin, R., & Tatelbaum, R. (1986). Preventing child abuse and neglect: A randomized trial of nurse home visitation. *Pediatrics, 78*, 65–78.

Paget, K. D., Philip, J. D., & Abramczyk, L. W. (1993). Recent developments in child neglect. *Advances in Clinical Child Psychology, 15*, 121–174.

Parish, R. A., Myers, P. A., Brandner, A., & Templin, K. H. (1985). Developmental milestones in abused children and their improvement with a family oriented approach to the treatment of child abuse. *Child Abuse and Neglect, 9*, 245–250.

Patterson, G. R. (1982). *Coercive family process: A social learning approach.* Eugene, OR: Castalia.

Petit, M. R., & Curtis, P. A. (1997). *Child abuse and neglect: A look at the states: 1997 CWLA stat book.* Washington, DC: CWLA Press.

Rivara, F. P. (1985). Physical abuse in children under two: A study of therapeutic outcomes. *Child Abuse & Neglect, 9*, 81–87.

Sayger, T. V., Horne, A. M., Walter, J. M., & Passmore, J. L. (1988). Social learning family therapy with aggressive children: Treatment outcome and maintenance. *Journal of Family Psychology, 1*, 261–285.

Schellenbach, C. (1998). Child maltreatment: A critical review of research on treatment for physically abusive parents. In P. Trickett & C. Schellenbach (Eds.), *Violence against children in the family and the community* (pp. 251–268). Washington, DC: American Psychological Association.

Schinke, S. P., Schilling, R. F., II, Kirkham, M. A., Gilchrist, L. D., Barth, R. P., & Blythe, B. J. (1986). Stress management skills for parents. *Journal of Child and*

Adolescent Psychotherapy, 3, 293–298.

Schuhmann, E. M., Foote, R. C., Eyberg, S. M., Boggs, S. R., & Algina, J. (1998). Efficacy of parent-child interaction therapy: Interim report of a randomized trial with short-term maintenance. *Journal of Clinical Child Psychology, 27*, 34–45.

Serketich, W. J., & Dumas, J. E. (1996). The effectiveness of behavioral parent training to modify antisocial behavior in children: A meta-analysis. *Behavior Therapy, 27*, 171–186.

Striefel, S., Robinson, M., & Truhn, P. (1998). Dealing with child abuse and neglect within a comprehensive family-support program. In J. Lutzer (Ed.), *Handbook of child abuse research and treatment* (pp. 267–289). New York: Plenum.

Szykula, S. A., & Fleischman, M. J. (1985). Reducing out-of-home placements of abused children: Two controlled field studies. *Child Abuse & Neglect, 9*, 277–283.

Tarnowski, K. J., & Rohrbeck, C. A. (1993). Disadvantaged children and families. *Advances in Clinical Child Psychology, 15*, 41–79.

Taylor, D. K., & Beauchamp, C. (1988). Hospital-based primary prevention strategy in child abuse: A multi-level needs assessment. *Child Abuse & Neglect, 12*, 343–354.

Toth, S. L., Manly, J. T., & Cicchetti, D. (1992). Child maltreatment and vulnerability to depression. *Development and Psychopathology, 4*, 97–112.

Tzeng, O. C. S., Jackson, J. W., & Karlson, H. C. (1991). *Theories of child abuse and neglect.* New York: Praeger.

Urquiza, A. N., & McNeil, C. B. (1996). Parent-child interaction therapy: An intensive dyadic intervention for physically abusive families. *Child Maltreatment, 1*, 134–144.

U.S. Department of Justice. (1995). *Bureau of Justice statistics: Sourcebook of criminal justice statistics 1995.* Washington, DC: Author.

Webster-Stratton, C. (1990). Long-term follow-up with young conduct problem children: From preschool to grade school. *Journal of Clinical Child Psychology, 19*, 144–149.

Webster-Stratton, C., Hollinsworth, T., & Kolpacoff, M. (1989). The long-term effectiveness and clinical significance of three cost-effective training programs for families with conduct-problem children. *Journal of Consulting and Clinical Psychology, 57*, 550–553.

Webster-Stratton, C., Kolpacoff, M., & Hollinsworth, T. (1988). Self-administered videotape therapy for families with conduct-problem children: Comparison with two cost-effective treatments and a control group. *Journal of Consulting and Clinical Psychology, 56*, 558–566.

Wells, K. (1994). A reorientation to knowledge development in family preservation services: A proposal. *Child Welfare League of America, 73*, 475–488.

Whipple, E. E., & Webster-Stratton, C. (1991). The role of parental stress in physically abusive families. *Child Abuse & Neglect, 15*, 279–291.

Whiteman, M., Fanshel, D., & Grundy, J. F. (1987). Cognitive-behavioral interventions aimed at anger of parents at risk of child abuse. *Social Work, 32*, 469–474.

Wolfe, D. A. (1987). *Child abuse: Implications for child development and psychopathology.* Newbury Park, CA: Sage.

Wolfe, D. A., Edwards, B., Manion, I., & Koverola, C.. (1988). Early intervention for parents at risk of child abuse and neglect. *Journal of Consulting and Clinical Psychology, 56,* 40–47.

Wolfe, D. A., Jaffe, P., Wilson, S., & Zak, L. (1985). Children of battered women: The relation of child behavior to family violence and maternal stress. *Journal of Consulting and Clinical Psychology, 53,* 657–664.

Wolfe, D. A., & McEachran, A. (1997). Child physical abuse and neglect. In E. J. Mash & L. G. Terdal (Eds.), *Assessment of childhood disorders* (3rd ed., pp. 523–568). New York: Guilford Press.

Wolfe, D. A., & Wekerle, C. (1993). Treatment strategies for child physical abuse and neglect: A critical progress report. *Clinical Psychology Review, 13,* 473–500.

MEASUREMENT OF FAMILY TREATMENT WITH CHILD ABUSE AND NEGLECT

Increasingly, practitioners are held accountable for evaluation of practice. To assist with this evaluation, this section provides information on paper-and-pencil, self-report instruments relevant to the problems of child abuse and neglect. Scores from these measurement instruments can be used to guide assessment and clinical practice. For those interested in conducting research in this area, each of the instruments provided have established psychometric data to support their use.

The following types of measures are presented: 1) child outcomes according to both child and parent report; 2) parenting practices; 3) parental adjustment; 4) family and marital functioning; and 5) client satisfaction with services.

Measures presented in this section involve the following criteria. First, instruments are self-report; that is, they are completed by family members themselves, rather than being interviewer-administered or observational measures. A second criterion for inclusion was that adequate reliability and validity information had to be available for each scale. Selected psychometric data were chosen to inform the reader on the properties of the instruments.

CHILD OUTCOMES—CHILD REPORT

CHILDREN'S DEPRESSION INVENTORY

Author: Kovacs (1980/1981)

Description:

- 27-item, self-report inventory for children from ages 8 to 13
- Measuring severity ("0" to "2") of overt symptoms of depression, such as sadness, sleep and eating disturbances, anhedonia, and suicidal ideation
- Modified from the Beck Depression Inventory for adults

Reliability:

- Internal consistency = .86
- Test-retest (1 month) reliability = .72 (Kovacs [1980/1981])
- Test-retest (3 months) reliability = .80
- Test-retest (3 weeks) reliability = .83 (Kaslow, Rehm, & Siegel, 1984)

Validity:

- Clinician's ratings of depression from a psychiatric interview correlated with Children's Depression Inventory ($r = .55$) [Kovacs, 1980/1981]
- Discriminated between psychiatric sample and nonclinic group and between child guidance and pediatric samples (Kovacs, 1980/1981)
- Children who scored high on depression for Children's Depression Inventory made more internal-stable-global attributions for failure and more external-unstable-specific attributions for success as measured by the Attributional Style Questionnaire ($r = .52$) [Kaslow et al., 1984]
- Children's Depression Inventory was negatively correlated with the Coopersmith Self-Esteem Inventory ($r = -.72$) [Kaslow et al., 1984]
- No significant relationship between Children's Depression Inventory and the Social Competence, indicating no significant relationship between child's level of depression and participation in activities, interpersonal relationships, or quality of work (Kaslow et al., 1984)
- Teachers reported depressed children as more internalizing than nondepressed children but not more externalizing (Kaslow et al., 1984)

CHILDREN'S MANIFEST ANXIETY—REVISED
(WHAT I THINK AND FEEL)

Authors: Reynolds & Richmond (1978)

Description:

- 73-item for grades 1–12
- Due to relatively high Lie score of first graders, caution should be exercised with this age child but especially grade 3 and above

Reliability:

- Alpha (for original sample) = .83; for validation sample = .85

Validity:

- High correlations with State-Trait Anxiety Inventory for Children trait scale (.85) but low correlation with State-Trait Anxiety Inventory for Children state scale (.24) [Reynolds, 1980]
- A multitrait, multimethod validation matrix indicated high correlations with trait measures of anxiety but low correlations with state anxiety measures and I.Q. (Reynolds, 1982)

STATE-TRAIT ANXIETY INVENTORY FOR CHILDREN

Author: Spielberger (1970)

Description:

- Measures anxiety in children mainly 9–12 years of age
- State scale consists of 20 statements that ask children how they feel at a particular moment in time to measure transitory anxiety (apprehension, tension, worry)
- 1–3 point scale ("very"/ "not")
- Trait scale consists of 20 statements about how children generally feel (stable feelings of anxiety proneness)
- 1–3 point scale ("hardly ever," "sometimes," and "often")

Reliability:

- Test-retest reliability (6-week) for Trait, males = .65 and females = .71
- Test-retest reliability (6-week) for State, males = .31 and females = .47
- State: alpha reliability = .82 for males, .87 for females
- Trait: alpha reliability = .78 for males, .81 for females

Validity:

- Correlations of .75 with the Children's Manifest Anxiety Scale and .63 with the General Anxiety Scale for Children
- Inverse correlations found between ability and achievement and scores

REVISED FEAR SURVEY SCHEDULE FOR CHILDREN

Author: Ollendick (1983)

Description:

- An 80-item self-report instrument assessing fears in children
- Response format involves 3-point scale ("none"/"some"/ "a lot")

Reliability:

- Internal consistency was .94 and .95 for 2 different samples
- One-week test-retest reliability was .82
- 3-month test-retest reliability was .55

Validity:

- For 2 different samples, correlations with Trait Anxiety from the State-Trait Anxiety Inventory for Children were .51 and .46, respectively, correlations with the Piers-Harris Children's Self-Concept Scale were −.23 and −.69, respectively, and correlations with the Nowicki-Strickland Locus-of-Control were −.36 and −.60, respectively
- factor analysis yielded 5 factors:
  1. Fear of Failure and Criticism
  2. Fear of the Unknown
  3. Fear of Injury and Small Animals
  4. Fear of Danger and Death
  5. Medical Fears
- Discriminates between clinic (school-phobic) and matched normal controls

LOCUS OF CONTROL SCALE FOR CHILDREN

Authors: Nowicki & Strickland (1973)

Description:

- 40-item, paper-and-pencil measure, with a yes/no response format measuring locus of control for children from 3rd to 12th grades

Reliability:

- Split-half reliabilities range from .63 for grades 2–5, .68 for grades 6–8, and .81 for grade 12

Validity:

- Internal locus of control is related to achievement
- Construct validation was confirmed when comparing the scale to other measures of locus of control

TRAUMA SYMPTOM CHECKLIST FOR CHILDREN

Author: Briere (1996)

Description:

- Child version of the adult Trauma Symptom Inventory
- 54-item instrument with 6 subscales (Anger, Anxiety, Depression, Dissociation, Posttraumatic Stress, and Sexual Concerns) for children between 8 and 15
- Unlike the Children's Impact of Traumatic Events—Revised, this scale does not orient respondents to their abuse experience and is appropriate for children who have not disclosed abuse, as well as those who have. The scale thus may be part useful with children who have experienced multiple types of abuse

Reliability:

- Alpha values for normed sample ranged from .58 to .89

Validity:

- All subscale scores correlated significantly with each other as well as with the youth and parent versions of the Child Behavior Checklist and with instruments conceptually related to the subscales, including the Child Depression Inventory, the Child Dissociative Checklist, the Children's Impact of Traumatic Events—Revised, and the Child Sexual Behavior Inventory
- Scale scores were higher among those who had experienced sexual penetration during the abuse
- Scale scores discriminated between children who had disclosed abuse and children who were evaluated for abuse but for whom abuse was not confirmed (Elliott & Briere, 1994)
- Scale scores were highest for those children who disclosed abuse (credible and partially credible), lowest for children who were believed to have been abused, but either had not disclosed or had recanted their allegations, and moderate for children who were judged not to have been abused (Elliott & Briere, 1994)

CHILD OUTCOMES—PARENT REPORT

CHILD BEHAVIOR CHECKLIST

Author: Achenbach (1991)

Description:

- Parent-report checklist assessing child functioning with response set ("0" not true/"2" very or often true) in last 6 months
- Assesses 2 primary areas:
  1. Social Competence—amount and quality of child's participation in extracurricular activities, school functioning, jobs, chores, friendships, and other activities
  2. Behavior Problems (118 items)

    8 syndromes under 2 broad groupings of syndromes:

    Internalizing
    Withdrawn, Somatic Complaints, Anxious/Depressed

    Externalizing
    Delinquent Behavior, Aggressive Behavior
    Social Problems, Thought Problems, Attention Problems, Sex Problems

Reliability:

- One-week test-retest reliability ranged from .70 to .95
- One-year test-retest reliability for competence scales was a mean correlation of .62 for competence scales and .75 for problem scales
- Two-year test-retest reliability was a mean correlation of .56 for competence scales and .71 for problem scales

Validity:

- Correlations between Child Behavior Checklist and Connors Parent Questionnaire ranged from .59 to .86, with total problem scores correlating .82
- Correlations between Child Behavior Checklist and Quay-Peterson Revised Behavior Problem Checklist ranged from .59 to .88, with total problem scores correlating .81
- Discriminates between clinic and nonclinic children

PARENTING PRACTICES—PARENT REPORT

CHILD ABUSE POTENTIAL INVENTORY

Author: Milner (1986) [A review on psychometric data conducted by Milner (1994)]

Description:

- 160-item, self-report answered in an agree/disagree format
- Third-grade readability level
- Includes a 77-item physical child abuse scale with 6 descriptive factor scales:
  1. Distress
  2. Rigidity
  3. Unhappiness
  4. Problems with child and self
  5. Problems with family
  6. Problems from others

Reliability:

- In a review of reliability (internal consistency) studies with parents characterized by different issues such as physical abuse, sexual abuse, neglecting, high risk to abuse, handicapped and developmentally delayed children; undergraduates; normal controls; and the general population, with alpha coefficients ranging from .74 to .98
- Temporal stability (ranging from 1 day to 6 months) ranged from .75 to .91

Validity:

- In adult samples, being a victim of childhood abuse, observing abuse, and severity of abuse are associated with scores
- Social isolation and perceived lack of social support are associated with scores
- Although there are some mixed results, family conflict and poor functioning are associated with scores
- Elevated scores are associated with higher levels of psychological reactiveness to both child-related and nonchild-related stimuli
- High scores are associated with low self-esteem and ego strength
- Only parent- and child-related stress are associated with abuse scores

- Respondents with high scores seem to perceive more child behavior problems and evaluated children's behaviors as more wrong, as well as to attribute more culpability to their children's behavior
- High scores were associated with aversive discipline strategies

PARENT OPINION QUESTIONNAIRE

Author: Azar & Rohrbeck (1986)

Description:

- An 80-item (agree/disagree) questionnaire indicating the degree of parental expectations for child behaviors
- Rather than solely parents' knowledge of child development, assessment of specific interpersonal sequences with children at specific developmental levels
- Total score 6 subscales (self-care, family responsibilities and care of siblings, proper behavior and feelings, help and affection to parents, leaving children alone, and punishment)

Reliability:

- Test-retest reliability at 12 weeks was .85 for 16 mothers, with subscale reliabilities ranging from .34 to .85

Validity:

- Abusive mothers had statistically higher scores than mothers whose partners were abusive
- The scale correctly predicted abusive vs. nonabusive mothers, with discriminant analyses correctly classifying 83% of mothers

THE PARENTING SCALE

Authors: Arnold, O'Leary, Wolff, & Acker (1993)

Description:

- 30 items that describe discipline practices for parents of children in response to misbehavior by preschoolers
- Written at sixth-grade level, although unknown if applicable to lower income families

- A 7-point rating scale anchored by effective and ineffective forms of parenting behavior
- Factor analyses have indicated three factors accounting for 37% of the variance: Laxness (items related to permissive discipline), Overreactivity (items reflecting behaviors such as displays of anger and irritability), and Verbosity (items reflecting verbal responses and a reliance on prolonged talking)
- A total score includes 4 additional items addressing conceptually important practices (e.g., monitoring)

Reliability:

- Internal-consistency coefficients were .83 for Laxness, .82 for Overreactivity, .63 for Verbosity, and .84 for the Total score.
- Test-retest (2-week) reliabilities were .83 for Laxness, .82 for Overreactivity, .79 for Verbosity, and .84 for the Total score.

Validity:

- Factor analyses confirmed structure
- Child Behavior Checklist correlated with Laxness (.41), Overreactivity (.54), Verbosity (.22), and the Total scale (.53)
- Locke-Wallace Marital Adjustment Test (short form) correlated with Laxness (−.50), Overreactivity (−.35), Verbosity (−.35), and the Total scale (−.53)

THE PARENT PROBLEM CHECKLIST

Authors: Dadds & Powell (1991)

Description:

- A 16-item measure of interparental parenting conflict
- Measures disagreements over rules and discipline, open conflict regarding parenting, and alienation of the child's affection

Reliability:

- A single factor has alpha = .70
- High test-retest (8-week) reliability ($r = .90$)

Validity:

- Principal component analysis indicated a single factor
- Correlates moderately with the Dyadic Adjustment Scale, with reliabilities ranging from .40 to .70, and with the Beck Depression Inventory, with reliabilities ranging from .40 to .50

PARENTING STRESS INDEX

Author: Abidin (1995)

Description:

- 120-item self-report for parents of children ages 1 month to 12 years to measure parenting stress
- Yields a total score and whether sources of stress may be related to child characteristics (child's adaptability, reinforcing qualities, demandingness, activity level, mood, and acceptability to the parent), or parental functioning (the parent's sense of competence, isolation, depression, attachment to the child, parent health, perceived restrictions of role, depression, and spousal and social system support)
- The short form (36 items) uses factor-analytically derived subscales (Total Stress, Parental Distress, Parent-Child Dysfunctional Interaction, Difficult Child) that differ from those of the PSI (Abidin, 1995)

Reliability:

- For the normative sample, alpha reliability coefficients ranged from .70 to .83 for Child Domain subscales and from .70 to .84 for Parent Domain subscales
- Abidin (1995) also reviews test-retest reliability studies: 3 weeks: .82 for Child Domain and .71 for Parent Domain; 1–3 months: .63 for Child Domain, .91 for Parent Domain, and .96 for Total Stress score; 3 months: .77 for Child Domain, .69 for Parent Domain, and .88 for Total Stress; 1 year: .55 for Child Domain, .70 for Parent Domain, and .65 for Total Stress

Validity:

- Since this was a conceptual rather than an empirically designed scale, factor analysis reveals relatively low loadings (over 50% of items in the Parent Domain and two-thirds of the items in the Child Domain have loadings less than .40)

- Evidence for construct and predictive validity found for following populations: infants with birth defects, drug-exposed infants, infant attachment, and developmentally delayed and handicapped children, mentally retarded children, and the hearing impaired, as well as children suffering from various other disabilities and long-term illnesses and behavior disorders (Abidin, 1995)
- Discriminates between clinic and matched controls and can demonstrate improvement in treatment
- Correlations with the following measures include Beck Depression Inventory, Child Abuse Potential Inventory, Eyberg Child Behavior Inventory, Family Adaptability and Cohesion Evaluation Scales II and III, Family Impact Questionnaire, Family Inventory of Resources and Management, Health Locus of Control Chance subscale, Inventory of Parent Experiences, Marital Adjustment Test, Maternal Behavior Assessment, Maternal Social Support Index, Parent Locus of Control, Child Behavior Checklist, Parenting Sense of Competence, Preschool Diabetes Behavior Checklist, Q-Set Security Scores, Family Resources Scale, and the Revised Ways of Coping
- Short form's subscales correlate with those in the full-length version in the expected pattern

PARENT ADJUSTMENT—PARENT REPORT

BECK DEPRESSION INVENTORY

Authors: Beck, Rush, Shaw, & Emery (1979); Beck, Ward, Mendelson, Mock, & Erbaugh (1961) [Review data on psychometric information by Beck, Steer, & Garbin (1988)]

Description:

- 21 items, measuring symptoms and attitudes of depression, rated from 0 to 3 in terms of intensity
- Also a short version (13 items) that correlates highly (.89 to .97) with long form although may only represent cognitively oriented symptoms rather than both cognitive and noncognitive
- Written at a fifth- to sixth-grade reading level
- Different time frames that may be ascertained
- Has been used in 1,000 research studies

Reliability:

- Mean coefficient alpha for nine psychiatric samples is .86
- Mean coefficient alpha for 15 nonpsychiatric samples is .81
- Test-retest reliability ranged from .48 to .86 for psychiatric patients and .60 to .83 for nonpsychiatric patients

Validity:

- Mean correlation coefficients between clinical ratings and the Beck Depression Inventory for psychiatric patients was .72 and for nonpsychiatric patients was .60
- Mean correlation coefficients between Hamilton Psychiatric Rating Scale for Depression and the Beck Depression Inventory for 5 psychiatric studies was .73 and for the 2 nonpsychiatric patients was .73 and .80, respectively
- Mean correlation coefficients between the Zung Self-reported Depression Scale and the Beck Depression Inventory for 8 psychiatric studies was .76 and for the 5 nonpsychiatric patients was .71
- Mean correlation coefficients between the MMPI Depression Scale and the Beck Depression Inventory for 7 psychiatric studies was .76 and for the 3 nonpsychiatric patients was .60

- Several studies have indicated that the measure discriminates between normals and psychiatric patients and psychiatric and nonpsychiatric samples
- Construct validity has been demonstrated with selected attitudes and behaviors, such as biological correlates, suicidal behaviors, alcohol problems, adjustment, medical symptoms, stress, and anxiety

SYMPTOM CHECKLIST-90—REVISED

Author: Derogatis (1977)

Description:

- A 90-item self-report inventory with ratings along a 5-point scale ("not at all"/ "extremely")
- Assesses nine dimensions of symptomatology: Somatization, Obsessive-Compulsive, Interpersonal Sensitivity, Depression, Anxiety, Hostility, Phobic Anxiety, Paranoid Ideation, and Psychoticism
- Also yields three global indices of distress: Global Severity Index (combines information numbers of symptoms and intensity of distress); Positive Symptom Total; and Positive Symptom Distress Index
- Widely used (700 published studies used this scale) [Derogatis (1993)]

Reliability:

- Alpha values for nine symptom dimensions range from .77 to .90
- Test-retest reliability ranges from .78 to .90

Validity:

- Demonstrates that the SCL-90-R is sensitive to change
- Correlates with other well-known measures of psychological functioning such as the MMPI

BRIEF SYMPTOM INVENTORY

Authors: Derogatis (1993)

Description:

- A briefer, 54-item version of the SCL-90-R
- Primary symptom dimensions:
  1. Somatization
  2. Obsessive-compulsive
  3. Interpersonal sensitivity
  4. Depression
  5. Anxiety
  6. Hostility
  7. Phobic anxiety
  8. Paranoid ideation
  9. Psychoticism

- 3 global indices:
  1. Global Severity Index
  2. Positive Symptom Total
  3. Positive Symptom Distress Index

- 0–4 ("not at all," "a little bit," "moderately," "quite a bit," and "extremely")
- Widely used (200 published studies used this scale) [Derogatis (1993)]

Reliability:

- Alpha coefficients are strong, ranging from .71 to .85
- Test-retest (2 weeks) reliabilities ranged from .68 to .91, with reliability for the Global Severity Index at .90

Validity:

- High convergence between scales of Brief Symptom Inventory and the MMPI
- High correlations (ranging from .92 to .99) between Brief Symptom Inventory and Symptom Checklist 90-Revised
- A factor analysis provided support for construct validation
- Evidence for predictive validity in that the measure has been demonstrated as an effective screening device across many varied medical settings

- Further evidence for predictive validity in that psychological distress was predicted in cancer populations, individuals with psychopathology, individuals experiencing problems with pain management, in HIV research, in student mental health, and in general clinical studies, and to predict efficacy of therapeutic interventions.

FAMILY/MARITAL FUNCTIONING

REVISED CONFLICT TACTICS SCALES

Author: Straus, Hamby, Boney-McCoy, & Sugarman (1996)

Description:

- 78-item self-report measuring psychological and physical attacks on a partner, as well as the use of negotiation, in a marital, cohabiting, or dating relationship
- Items are asked in form of questions (what the participant did and what the partner did)
- Sixth-grade reading level
- Following scales included:
  1. Physical Assault
  2. Psychological Aggression
  3. Negotiation
  4. Injury
  5. Sexual Coercion

Reliability:

- Internal consistency reliabilities for scales: physical assault (.86); psychological aggression (.79); negotiation (.86); injury (.95); sexual coercion (.87)

Validity:

- Only preliminary evidence of construct validity
- Only preliminary evidence of discriminant validity (negotiation and sexual coercion and negotiation and injury not correlated)

THE MARITAL ADJUSTMENT TEST

Authors: Locke & Wallace (1959)

Description:

- 15-item self-report measuring adjustment defined as the accommodation of partners to each other

Reliability:

- Internal consistency of .90

Validity:

- Discriminates between distressed and nondistressed couples as assessed by clinical judgments
- A correlation of .47 with Locke-Wallace Marital Prediction Test

DYADIC ADJUSTMENT SCALE

Author: Spanier (1976)

Description:

- A 32-item self-report inventory measuring marital adjustment
- Four subscales:
  1. Dyadic Consensus (agreement regarding marital issues)
  2. Dyadic Cohesion (extent to which partners are involved in joint activities)
  3. Dyadic Satisfaction (overall evaluation of relationship and level of commitment)
  4. Affectional Expression (extent of affection and sexual involvement)

Reliability:

- Adequate internal-consistency reliability for the total scale (.96) and for each of the subscales, ranging from .73 to .94

Validity:

- Discriminates between married and divorced couples
- Correlates with Locke-Wallace Marital Adjustment Scale ($r = .86$)

O'LEARY-PORTER SCALE

Authors: Porter & O'Leary (1980)

Description:

- A 20-item parent-completed questionnaire assessing the frequency of various forms of overt marital hostility (e.g., quarrels, sarcasms, and physical abuse) witnessed by the child

Reliability:

- Test-retest (2-week) reliability of 14 families: −.96

Validity:

- Correlation between this scale and Short Marital Adjustment Test: −.63

FAMILY ADAPTABILITY AND COHESION EVALUATION SCALES III

Authors: Olson, Portner, & Lavee (1985)

Description:

- A 20-item self-report measure in which members rate their families on the following dimensions, both perceived and ideal
  1. adaptability—the ability of a family system to alter structure, roles, and rules in response to situational and developmental stress
     – a continuum of scores ranges from extremely low (rigid) to moderate levels (flexible, structured) to high (chaotic)
  2. cohesion—emotional bonding
     – a continuum of scores ranges from extremely low (disengaged) to moderate (separate, connected) to extremely high (enmeshed)
- Rating scale from 1 ("almost never") to 5 ("almost always")

Reliability:

- Internal consistency was .77 for Cohesion scale, .62 for Adaptability scale, and .68 for Total scale

Validity:

- Lack of balance reported in families with different kinds of problems including schizophrenia, sex offenses, and substance abuse, but no characteristic profile in terms of adaptability and cohesion for any problem type (Olson, 1986)

FAMILY ENVIRONMENT SCALE

Authors: Moos & Moos (1981)

Description:

- A 90-item, true-false, questionnaire assessing 10 dimensions of family life:

Relationship Dimensions
1. Cohesion
2. Expressiveness
3. Conflict

Personal Growth Dimensions
4. Independence
5. Achievement Orientation
6. Intellectual—Cultural Orientation
7. Moral-Religious Emphasis
8. Active-Recreational Orientation

System Maintenance Dimensions
9. Organization
10. Control

- 3 different forms:
  1. Real form—assesses members' perceptions of their families
  2. Ideal form—measures members' preferred family environments
  3. Expectations form—assesses members' expectations about family environments

Reliability:

- Internal consistency reliabilities range from .61 to .78
- Test-retest reliabilities range from .68 to .86 for 8 weeks and from .52 to .89 for 1 year

Validity:

- Cohesion scale predicts depression
- Discriminates between normal and disturbed families

McMaster Family Assessment Device

Authors: Epstein, Baldwin, & Bishop (1983)

Description:

- A 60-item, Likert-type, self-report measure assessing overall health/ pathology in a general score as well as six areas of family functioning:
  1. Problem-solving
  2. Communication
  3. Roles
  4. Affective responsiveness
  5. Affective involvement
  6. Behavior control

Reliability:

- Internal consistency ranges from .72 to .83 for various subscales

Validity:

- Discriminates between clinic and nonclinic families
- Correlates with Locke-Wallace Marital Ajustment (.53)
- Factor analysis has shown support for validity (Kabacoff, Miller, Bishop, Epstein, & Keitner, 1990; Miller, Epstein, Bishop, & Keitner, 1985)

SATISFACTION WITH SERVICES

CLIENT SATISFACTION QUESTIONNAIRE

Authors: Attkisson & Zwick (1982); Larsen, Attkisson, Hargreaves, & Nguyen (1979); Nguyen, Attkisson, & Stegner (1983)

Description:

- 8-item, self-report inventory with 4-point anchored answer format assessing general satisfaction with services

Reliability:

- Coefficient alpha is .92

Validity:

- Factor analysis supported these 8 items as loading together from both a 31-item and an 18-item version
- Global improvement as measured by the Symptom Checklist correlated with the Client Satisfaction Questionnaire ($r = .53$)
- Therapists' ratings of their satisfaction with their work with the client correlated with the Client Satisfaction Questionnaire ($r = .42$) and how satisfied they believed their clients to be ($r = .56$)

REFERENCES FOR MEASUREMENT OF FAMILY TREATMENT WITH CHILD ABUSE AND NEGLECT

Abidin, R. R. (1995). *Parenting Stress Index* (3rd ed.), Professional manual. Odessa, FL: Psychological Assessment Resources.

Achenbach, T. M. (1991). *Manual for the Child Behavior Checklist/4–18 and 1991 Profile*. Burlington, VT: University of Vermont Department of Psychiatry.

Arnold, D. S., O'Leary, S. G., Wolff, L. S., & Acker, M. M. (1993). The parenting scale: A measure of dysfunctional parenting in discipline situations. *Psychological Assessment, 5*(2), 137–144.

Attkisson, C. C., & Zwick, R. (1982). The client satisfaction questionnaire: Psychometric properties and correlations with service utilization and psychotherapy outcome. *Evaluation and Program Planning, 5*, 233–237.

Azar, S. T., & Rohrbeck, C. A. (1986). Child abuse and unrealistic expectations: Further validation of the parent opinion questionnaire. *Journal of Consulting and Clinical Psychology, 54*(6), 867–868.

Beck, A., Rush, A., Shaw, B., & Emery, G. (1979). Cognitive therapy of depression. New York: Guilford Press.

Beck, A., Ward, C., Mendelson, M., Mock, J., & Erbaugh, J. (1961). An inventory for measuring depression. *Archives of General Psychiatry, 4*, 53–63.

Beck, A. T., Steer, R. A., & Garbin, M. G. (1988). Psychometric properties of the Beck Depression inventory: Twenty-five years of evaluation. *Clinical Psychology Review, 8*, 77–100.

Briere, J. (1996). A self-trauma model for treating adult survivors of severe child abuse. In J. Briere & L. Berliner (Eds.), *The APSAC handbook on child maltreatment* (pp. 140–157). Thousand Oaks, CA: Sage.

Dadds, M., & Powell, M. (1991). The relationship of interparental conflict and global marital adjustment to aggression, anxiety, aand immaturity in aggressive and non-clinic children. *Journal of Abnormal Child Psychology, 19*, 553–567.

Derogatis, L. (1977). *The SCL-90R: Administration and scoring procedures manual*. Baltimore: Clinical Psychometric Research.

Derogatis, L. (1993). *Brief Symptom Inventory: Administration, scoring, and procedures manual*. Minneapolis, MN: National Computer Systems.

Elliott, D., & Briere, J. (1994). Forensic sexual abuse evaluations of older children: Disclosures and symptomology. *Behavioral Sciences and the Law, 12*, 261–277.

Epstein, N., Baldwin, L., & Bishop, D. (1983). The McMaster family assessment device. *Journal of Marital and Family Therapy, 9*, 171–180.

Kaslow, N. J., Rehm, L. P., & Siegel, A. W. (1984). Social-cognitive and cognitive correlates of depression in children. *Journal of Abnormal Child Psychology, 12*, 605–620.

Kovacs, M. (1980/1981). Rating scales to assess depression in school-aged children. *Acta Paedopsychiatrica, 46*, 305–313.

Larsen, D. L., Attkisson, C. C., Hargreaves, W. A., & Nguyen, T. D. (1979). Assessment of client/patient satisfaction: Development of a general scale. *Evaluation and Program Planning, 2*, 197–207.

Locke, H., & Wallace, K. (1959). Short marital-adjustment and prediction tests: Their reliability and validity. *Marriage and Family Living, 21*, 251–255.

Milner, J. S. (1986). The Child Abuse Potential Inventory: Manual (2nd ed.). Webster, NC: Psytec.

Milner, J. S. (1994). Assessing physical child abuse risk: The child abuse potential inventory. *Clinical Psychology Review, 14*, 547–583.

Moos, R. H., & Moos, B.S. (1981). Family Environment Scale manual. Palo Alto, CA: Consulting Psychologists Press.

Nguyen, T. D., Attkisson, C. C., & Stegner, B. L. (1983). Assessment of patient satisfaction: Development and refinement of a service evaluation questionnaire. *Evaluation and Program Planning, 6*, 299–314.

Nowicki, S., & Strickland, B. (1973). A locus of control scale for children. *Journal of Consulting & Clinical Psychology, 40*, 148–154.

Ollendick, T. H. (1983). Reliability and validity of the revised fear survey schedule for children (FSSC-R). *Behaviour Research and Therapy, 21*, 685–692.

Olson, D. (1986). Circumplex model VII: Validation studies and FACES III. *Family Process, 25*, 337–351.

Olson, D., Portner, J., & Lavee, Y. (1985). FACES III: Family Adaptability and Cohesion Evaluations Scales. In D. Olson, H. McCubbin, H. Barnes, A. Larsen, M. Muxen, & M. Wilson (Eds.), *Family Inventories* (rev. ed.). St. Paul, MN: Family Social Science, University of Minnesota.

Porter, B., & O'Leary, D. (1980). Marital discord and childhood behavior problems. *Journal of Abnormal Child Psychology, 8*, 287–295.

Reynolds, C. R. (1980). Concurrent validity of What I Think and Feel: The Revised Children's Manifest Anxiety Scale. *Journal of Consulting and Clinical Psychology, 48*, 774–775.

Reynolds, C. (1982). Convergent and divergent validity of the revised children's manifest anxiety scale. *Educational and Psychological Measurement, 42*, 1205–1212.

Reynolds, C. R., & Richmond, B. O. (1978). What I think and feel: A revised measure of children's manifest anxiety. *Journal of Abnormal Child Psychology, 43*, 281–283.

Reynolds, C. R., & Richmond, B. O. (1997). What I think and feel: A revised measure of children's manifest anxiety. *Journal of Abnormal Child Psychology, 25*, 15–20.

Spanier, G. B. (1976). Measuring dyadic adjustment: New scales for assessing the quality of marriage and similar dyads. *Journal of Marriage and the Family*, 15–28.

Spielberger, C. (1970). *Current topics in clinical and community psychology: II.* New York: Academic Press.

Straus, M., Hamby, S., Boney-McCoy, S., & Sugarman, D. (1996). The Revised Conflict Tactics Scales (CTS2). *Journal of Family Issues, 17*, 283–316.

CHAPTER 2

Family Treatment with Child Maltreatment Using Family Preservation Approaches*

Family Case:

Thelma Jackson (age 32) is of African American descent and has three children, Sonya (age 7), Elijah (age 5), and Roddie (age 2). The family was investigated by Child Protective Services because Elijah had a bruise on his buttocks that was perpetrated by the father of the youngest child, Roderick. Roderick stays with Thelma a lot, she reports, but they are not married, nor are they living together. Thelma says that Roderick didn't usually discipline her children, but a couple of days ago Elijah wasn't listening to her and Roderick took over.

Thelma says she tended to have a difficult time managing her children's behavior, and that the children didn't listen to what she said until she threatened to spank them. She says that they never put away their toys or helped her around the house, and they are always fighting among themselves. They also have poor attendance at school because they don't get up in the morning and miss the bus.

The tenet behind family preservation programs, first launched in the 1970s (Wells, 1995) and variously called home-based, family-centered, in-home, and intensive family preservation services, involves the primacy of the family as a major social institution (Stroul & Goldman, 1990). Recognition of the importance of the parent-child attachment and the significant human costs inherent in child removal from the home in terms of loss, trauma, stigmatization, and

---

* A portion of this chapter will be published in a forthcoming issue of *The Crisis Intervention and Time-Limited Treatment Journal.*

identity problems have played a central role in the development of family preservation services (Nelson, Landsman, & Deutelbaum, 1990). A related role in their development involved criticisms, ongoing since the 1960s, of out-of-home placements (Wells, 1995; Whittaker & Tracy, 1990). Children were placed many times other than when strictly necessary due to lack of other options. They were often involved in unstable and overly restrictive placements. Spiraling expenses associated with these placements acted as further inducements to less costly alternatives. However, funding policies endorsed placements, rather than prevention programs or support services. As a result, children were not usually provided with services prior to placement. Although many children were never returned to their biological families, for those who were reunited, conditions had often remained unchanged, due to lack of intervention with biological parents. Further, biological families often continued to need ongoing services and support after reunification (Wells, 1995; Whittaker & Tracy, 1990).

In response to these criticisms, the Adoption Assistance and Child Welfare Act of 1980, PL 96–272, was enacted to provide comprehensive standards for the provision of child welfare services. This law requires the establishment of case plans and review mechanisms so that unnecessary placements are prevented, placements are provided in the least restrictive setting, and children are discharged in a timely manner, either to their biological parents or to adoptive families (McGowan, 1990; Wells, 1995). Other federal mandates compatible with these policies include the 1975 Education for All Handicapped Children Act, which legislates that children be treated in the least restrictive environment, and the 1974 Juvenile Justice and Delinquency Prevention Act, which states that youth status offenders be treated in their communities rather than in juvenile justice institutions (McGowan, 1990). The objectives of family preservation are compatible with these policies (Nelson et al., 1990; Wells, 1995), and government funding for these programs, as well as for their evaluation, has expanded, particularly with the enactment of the Family Preservation Act of 1993. Perhaps due to the emphasis on family primacy, a number of philanthropic foundations have also actively supported such programs (Bath & Haapala, 1994; Nelson et al., 1990).

Family preservation programs are characterized by three central characteristics (Nelson et al., 1990; Nelson & Landsman, 1992; Stroul & Goldman, 1990). The first is an emphasis on having children remain in their own homes with caretakers to whom they are attached. A second emphasis is on the whole family, rather than on just individual members. Third is the provision of and linkage with comprehensive services in the community so that families' concrete needs are met.

Beyond these commonalities, family preservation programs differ on many service delivery aspects. Programs vary in the following ways:

1. Level of intervention (whether primary, secondary, or tertiary)
2. Auspices (public or private)
3. Target group for services (abusive and neglectful families, juvenile offenders, emotionally disturbed children)
4. Primary location of service delivery (office or home)
5. Theoretical model
6. Intensity of service
7. Length of service
8. Size of worker caseload
9. Immediacy of services (time on waiting list)
10. Extent to which services are voluntary
11. Extent to which worker teams are used (Bath & Haapala, 1994)
12. Staffing patterns (paraprofessionals, entry-level professional staff, trained professional staff [e.g., MSW or other counseling degree], or specialized professional staff [e.g., family therapists]) [Nelson et al., 1990; Nelson & Landsman, 1992]

Due to these varying factors, comparisons of programs and summarization of effects are made difficult (Tracy, 1991). A recommendation has been to examine programs by shared characteristics. One such salient characteristic is theoretical orientation, as this guides the purpose and methods of programs (McGowan, 1990). Barth (1988) has discussed program models as represented by crisis intervention, social learning, family systems, and ecological theories. Social learning methods have tended to be subsumed under crisis intervention models (Barth, 1990; Nelson et al., 1990), although how these frameworks work together has not been well delineated.

This chapter, therefore, will focus on crisis intervention, family systems, and ecological theory-based programs, although it is recognized that certain family preservation programs are atheoretical in nature (e.g., Rosenthal & Glass, 1986; Smith, 1995). [The interested reader is referred to Table 2.7 for a brief summary of atheoretical studies.] The theoretically based programs will be organized in the following way. First, a brief description of each theoretical model will be delineated, followed by an examination of evaluative efforts in each area. The emphasis of this review will be on current evaluation efforts (1985 and later) and on child abuse and neglect, although it is recognized that samples are sometimes mixed in terms of child welfare, juvenile justice, and mental health referrals (e.g., Feldman, 1991; Fraser & Haapala, 1987–1988;

Nelson & Landsman, 1992). In addition, studies will be limited to those published in books or refereed journals, rather than including those presented in unpublished reports. A critique of the research and the theoretical basis will be offered as well as an exploration of key findings. A summary will conclude with recommendations for improved service delivery and research.

DESCRIPTION OF THEORY BASIS FOR FAMILY PRESERVATION PROGRAMS

CRISIS INTERVENTION

Crisis intervention theory posits that families are most amenable to change when coping mechanisms are exceeded by the demands of a crisis (e.g., Parad & Caplan, 1960). The widely used Homebuilders program, developed in Tacoma, Washington, in 1974, is based on the crisis intervention model. A little over half (53%) of states report modeling their family preservation program after Homebuilders, according to a 1996 Child Welfare League survey (Petit & Curtis, 1997).

Consistent with the assumption that there is a critical short-term period for restabilization to a former, more adaptable level of functioning, Homebuilders provides immediate services (within a day of referral) and 24-hour availability of workers (Kinney & Dittmar, 1995; Kinney, Haapala, & Booth, 1991). For this level of service intensity, workers carry a low caseload (a maximum of three families), and clients are usually seen for a brief period (between 4 and 6 weeks) by which time the crisis is assumed to be stabilized. At this time, it is also assumed that clients have attained an adequate level of functioning so that they can be assisted by more traditional means.

A main feature of Homebuilders is the provision of home-based services. In this way, services are made accessible to families and more accurate assessments of family functioning can be conducted in the natural environment. As well as offering counseling, Homebuilders either supply or link families to a variety of concrete resources that may include helping families meet basic needs for food, clothing, housing, and medical care. Financial aid, transportation, homemaker services, day care, and employment training may also be accessed (Nelson et al., 1990; Pecora, Fraser, & Haapala, 1992).

FAMILY SYSTEMS

Family systems and ecological theories are similar in that they consider the influence of factors beyond the individual. In family systems, an individual's problems are seen as a symptom of dysfunctional interactions within the family. Work is generally centered on modifying maladaptive transactions between family members so that the need for the symptom is alleviated. Family therapy interventions are borrowed from the communication, strategic, structural, and brief schools (Barth, 1988, 1990). In a recent randomized survey of family preservation programs, over a third of respondents stated that their programs employed a family systems approach (Walton & Denby, 1997).

ECOLOGICAL MULTISYSTEMIC

Ecological theory expands on environmental systems beyond the family. The crux of the orientation is that individuals and families have an interactional relationship with the environment of which they are part. Based on Bronfenbrenner's (1979) social-ecological model of development, ecological theory postulates that the following systems surrounding individuals influence behavior: the microsystems (the most direct systems that impact the child, such as the family environment), the mesosystems (the more distal influences that the child and his/her microsystems are embedded within, such as the school and the neighborhood), and the macrosystem (the larger social environment, such as cultural influences that exert their impact on individuals and families). The multisystemic model as described by Brunk, Henggeler, and Whelan (1987) extends beyond intervention with the family to the numerous systems in which the child and family are embedded that serve to maintain and impact abuse and neglect. Case management and service coordination are the methods by which both concrete and therapeutic services are delivered so that risk factors associated with out-of-home placement of children can be alleviated (Berry, 1990a, 1991, 1992; Grigsby, 1993).

CRITICAL REVIEW OF STUDIES

In this section, key findings of studies will be reported for both distal and proximal outcomes (Bath & Haapala, 1994; Fraser, 1990). Distal outcomes involve long-term goals and are the desired result of a constellation of program services and activities. Placement of children outside the home represents an indirect, distal outcome measure related to changes in family functioning. Proximal outcomes measure changes associated with specific services. Family preservation services are concerned with improving the family's level of functioning so that placement is avoided; therefore, measures of family functioning represent proximal outcomes that can be assessed to determine program effectiveness.

DISTAL OUTCOMES

The most common outcome criterion for the effectiveness of family preservation programs involves placement of children outside the home. Due to this emphasis, in the vast majority of studies, results for this outcome will be explored separately for evaluation efforts involving both pretest, posttest, and quasi-experimental designs.

Pretest, Posttest Designs

As can be seen from Table 2.1, the majority of studies of crisis intervention family preservation programs still rely on pretest, posttest–only designs. The studies in this area report favorable results with placement prevention rates ranging from an average of 77% (Scannapieco, 1994) to nearly 99% (Bath, Richey, & Haapala, 1992) at case termination and from 65% (Fraser, Pecora, & Haapala, 1991) to 83% (Bath et al., 1992; Yuan & Struckman-Johnson, 1991) at follow-up.

Several crisis intervention studies, to make up for the lack of comparison groups, divide their samples into high- and low-risk for placement cases (Scannapieco, 1994; Thieman & Dall, 1992). In these studies, the high-risk groups actually demonstrated higher placement prevention rates. Thieman and Dall (1992) suggest that these findings are the result of services being applied more intensively in high-risk cases.

Similarly, results for family systems and ecologically based family preservation studies are favorable in terms of placement prevention (*see* Tables 2.2 and 2.3). In the pretest, posttest designs, rates of prevention placement range from 55 (Bribitzer & Verdieck, 1988) to 84% (Nelson et al., 1988) for family systems–based programs. Further, ecologically based studies report remarkable success rates (96%) when using placement as an outcome criterion (Berry, 1990, 1995).

Critique of Imminent Risk Criterion   Although family preservation programs are generally targeted at families of children at "imminent risk of placement," there are many potential problems with this criterion. First, it is questionable whether "imminent risk" is the central deciding factor in admitting families to programs. To illustrate, when respondents were questioned about the criteria for acceptance to services in a recent randomized survey of family preservation programs, the following responses were given:

1. Parent gives voluntary permission
2. Child at imminent risk placement
3. Age specification
4. Residence specification (Walton & Denby, 1997)

These responses indicate that "imminent risk of placement" is only one criterion for many programs. In fact, Walton and Denby (1997) found that almost one third of the cases served by family preservation programs were not imminent-risk families.

In addition, the caseworker is only part of a larger context that might impact child placement. There are administrative factors, such as availability of placements and the extent to which alternative resources and services are present in the community (Pecora, Fraser, Nelson, McCroskey, & Meezan, 1995; Rossi, 1992b; Wells, 1994).

A third problem with the "imminent risk of placement" criterion involves the lack of definition of terms, such as "at-risk," "imminence," and "placement" (Tracy, 1991; Wells & Biegel, 1992), as well as valid and reliable measures of a child's risk for placement (Tracy, 1991). In the Walton and Denby (1997) survey, when respondents were asked "How does your agency define imminent risk?" a variety of replies were given. Most common were the following:

1. No working definition
2. Imminent risk not used as a criteria
3. Immediate placement
4. Placement occurring between 3 and 7 days
5. Potential for placement, with no specified time-frame
6. Definition decided by referral source

Given the imprecise specification of selection criteria, caseworkers may be susceptible to unstandardized decisions, often based on practice wisdom and value judgments on whom can be helped by family preservation. For example, the most common response to the question of what inhibits programs from employing imminent risk criteria was the necessity of providing prevention services (Walton & Denby, 1997). The second most popular response involved the lack of other services to troubled families. Apparently, caseworkers are influenced by an array of different and unique factors in making judgments about child placement (Feldman, 1991; Pecora et al., 1995; Wells & Tracy, 1996).

TABLE 2.1 Crisis Intervention Family Preservation Studies—Pre-Experimental Designs

AUTHOR/MODEL	DESIGN/SAMPLE	MEASURES	RESULTS	LIMITATIONS
Bath et al. (1992) Washington average hours of service = 65.8	Posttest only (1 yr after intake) $N = 1,506$ children represented 1,112 families referred from child welfare workers due to imminent risk of placement; low-income; majority White Ages 0–2 (6.9%); 3–9 (18%); 10–17 (76%)	Outcome: out-of-home placements 12 months after intake Independent variables: nonstandardized checklist of child and family characteristics	At case termination, success of avoiding placement—98.5%; at 3 mos 91.4%; 83% avoided placement	Pre-to-post not tracked; lack of control/comparison group; age groupings were not clearly laid out in demographic information; nonstandardized measures
Fraser et al. (1991) Pecora, Fraser, & Haapala (1991) Pecora et al. (1992) Pecora et al. (1995)	Pretest, posttest, follow-up (12 mos) with an overflow comparison group ($N = 27$ children) from the Utah sites $N = 581$ children from 446 families at imminent risk of placement (within 1 week)	Placement defined as outside the home for at least 2 weeks in a non-relative setting Family Risk Scales; FACES-III; Social Support Inventory (adapted from Inventory of Socially Supportive Behaviors)	93.9% of children were in home at case termination (Washington); 90.7% (Utah); children experienced placement during study (nonrelative or continous runaway behavior for at least 2 weeks): 32% (Utah), 22.5% (Washington)	Little basis for comparison group; bias for therapist ratings; social desirability for parent ratings of improvements; some measures nonstandardized; only 29% of Utah and 71% of Washington sample tracked for the full 12-mo follow-up

continued

TABLE 2.1 (continued)

AUTHOR/MODEL	DESIGN/SAMPLE	MEASURES	RESULTS	LIMITATIONS
Spaid et al. (1991) Spaid & Fraser (1991) Homebuilders 2 sites in Utah (60 days); 4 sites in Washington (30 days)	Percentages of families referred by CPS: Washington (45.5%), Utah (59%); families referred by family reconciliation, youth services, or juvenile court: Washington (54.5%), Utah (40.2%); of ethnic minority families: Washington (18.3%), Utah (13.5%); of single-parent families: Washington (42.5%), Utah (38.3%); majority income below $20,000	Nonstandardized: parent ratings of family problems; global family ratings by parents	Only 263 families served early enough to participate in 12-mo follow-up: placement prevention rate 58.8% for Utah (compared to 14.8% for comparison group), 70.2% for Washington No significant changes on FACES-III; positive significant changes in Family Risk Scales for child, parent, and family environment; significant positive changes for aversive social interactions between spouses and empathic friendships with extended kin and network members changes for parent ratings of changes	

Reference/Model	Sample/Method	Measures	Results	Comments
Fraser & Haapala (1987–1988) Homebuilders	Qualitative survey method—related "Critical incidents" during intervention and helpfulness of services related to placement (3 mos after termination of services) $N = 41$ families referred for child abuse and/or neglect, psychiatric impairment, disruptive behavior Mean age of child = 13.9 Half were single-parent families	In-home placement defined as children continuously being in the home from pretreatment to 3-mo follow-up Interview guide to discover client (independent interviews with mothers and children) and therapist versions of "Critical incidents" during sessions	Oppositional and older youth at higher risk of placement Client perceptions of global helpfulness of treatment not related to placement outcome; neither were any therapists' reports related to outcome; the provision of concrete assistance was related to positive outcome; although interruptions in home were rated by mothers as unhelpful, they were significantly related to positive outcome since they may have given therapists opportunities for teaching families	Although Homebuilders model was described generally as lasting between 2 and 5 mos duration of services, service time here not defined; no racial or SES information provided; posttest assessment delayed until 3 mos

continued

TABLE 2.1 *(continued)*

AUTHOR/MODEL	DESIGN/SAMPLE	MEASURES	RESULTS	LIMITATIONS
Scannapieco (1994)	Pretest, posttest, divided by risk (high-risk— child at risk of placement outside the home) $N = 80$ families randomly selected from 480 cases, only 45 families engaged in services 40% receiving welfare assistance Referral reasons: physical abuse (42%), sexual abuse (22%), child neglect (27%), drug abuse (53%), domestic abuse (13%), mental illness (24%)	Placement prevention; family functioning (non-standardized); completion of program; improvement of problem areas (nonstandardized)	Low-risk families made progress on identified problem area 89% of time compared to 58% of the high-risk family cases. No statistically significant differences between high- and low-risk families family functioning, program completion 59% of high-risk families completed compared to 56% of low-risk), or placement prevention (achieved in 82% of high-risk cases compared to 72% of low-risk cases)	"High risk" not defined; no specific intake criteria for program; measures nonstandardized; race not given; although 80 cases selected, only 45 engaged in services— low engagement/high dropout of concern; although services were said to be delivered intensely between 3 and 6 mos, average length of services not given

TABLE 2.2 Family Systems Family Preservation Programs—Pre-experimental Designs

AUTHOR/MODEL	DESIGN/SAMPLE	MEASURES	RESULTS	LIMITATIONS
Bribitzer & Verdieck (1988) Home-based, family-centered program Virginia Mean duration of services: 9 mos	posttest only $N = 42$ closed cases served by program for 5 yrs; 67% of families had been referred due to petition for relief from responsibility of children; rest of sample—confirmed abuse or neglect; majority White; Age of children = 0–19, mixed gender	Return of legal custody or emancipation Family and service provision characteristics	Successful outcome—55% Families with more children, with 2 adults, and no history of juvenile court involvement most likely to avoid out-of-home placement	No-pretest; no comparison or control group; small sample size; nonstandardized measurement system; lack of reliable information on SES; since a majority of the families were involved with CPS due to petition for relief from responsibility rather than abuse/neglect, not known how imminent the risk; lack of specification of interventions; unclear whether services were voluntary; lack of information about dropouts; uneven follow-up lengths

continued

TABLE 2.2 *(continued)*

AUTHOR/MODEL	DESIGN/SAMPLE	MEASURES	RESULTS	LIMITATIONS
Meezan & McCroskey (1996) Family-centered services California average 3 mos With 1–3 visits per week	Experimental, randomization to family services or regular services, pretest, posttest (3 mos), follow-up (1 yr) $N = 240$ families referred by child welfare workers 48% Latinos; 27% African American; 22% White; 33% incomes under $750; 52% incomes between $750 and $1,499 per mo; 15% had incomes over $1,500 per mo; about $^1/_2$ on government assistance Type of abuse: 43% physical abuse, 41% neglect, 18% sexual abuse, 4% emotional abuse	Parents: Brief Symptom Inventory; Child: Home Observation for Measurement of the Environment; Child Behavior Checklist Caseworkers: Family Assessment Form Teachers: Child Behavior Checklist	While families in both groups stated no problems in family functioning at pretest, at follow-up family-centered services group reported improvement in living and financial conditions; they also reported more improvements in their children's behavior; according to interviewer observation, parents of preschoolers in the family-centered service group improved their parenting skills	Criteria for referral from caseworkers not specified; lack of information on differences between groups on standardized measures

Nelson, 1991 5 programs (Iowa, Minnesota, Ohio, & Oregon) Average length of services = 5.6 mos family systems perspective	Pretest, posttest, with a comparison to populations used to develop Child Well-Being Scales $N = 248$ families; majority income below poverty line (63%); majority White (85%); majority married (60%); average age of child = 10.14; problem reported included following: child behavior (59%), parent-child conflict (56%), adult relationships (52%), and family relationships (51%); physical abuse (27%), neglect (26%), status offenses (26%), delinquency (25%), sexual abuse (19%), and substance abuse (18%)	Placement (not counted as placement if removed from a temporary placement back home before termination of services) Child Well-Being Scales	For maltreatment cases, most important predictor of placements: substance abuse, community mental health services, primary caretaker's cooperation with services	Percentage of placement rates not included; since part of criteria—that primary children of concern couldn't have been continuously out of their homes for more than 30 days preceding or following referral, seems like cases were screened out and reduced failure rate of family preservation program; measurement system relied on case records—hence, a lot of missing data (i.e., 23 of the 43 Child Well-Being Scales and only 9 were identical in content and frequency to allow comparisons); length of service time longer than most family preservation programs; lack of comparison or control group

continued

TABLE 2.2 *(continued)*

AUTHOR/MODEL	DESIGN/SAMPLE	MEASURES	RESULTS	LIMITATIONS
Nelson et al. (1988) Nelson & Landsman (1992) 11 sites (Pennsylvania, Ohio, Minnesota, Colorado, Iowa, and Oregon,) generally programs endorsed a family therapy approach average length of services = 6.5 mos	Pretest, posttest; $N =$ 533 families; Major referral source—public social services agency; reasons for referral: parent-child conflict (50.8%), child behavior problems (38.7%), delinquency (23.3%), status offenses (22.8%), adult relationship problems (20%), physical abuse (19.8%), family relationships (19.6%), child relationships (17.5%) Nearly 50% of caretakers married; predominantly White; 53.2% living below poverty level of \$10,000, 27% incomes from \$10,000 to \$20,000 for an average family size of 3.96	Questionnaire (nonstandardized); case records; placement; Child Well-Being Scales	Family factors predictive of placement: older age of child, more problems in the home, and lower functioning of caretakers and children as indicated by Child Well-Being Scales Service characteristics predictive of placement: imminence of risk at intake and psychological or psychiatric outpatient services Workers' estimated average rate of success—67.7%; Average placement rate = 16% Rate of placement for neglect cases: 24%, 10% higher than for physical or sexual abuse	Nonstandardized questionnaire; workers rated their own services on some evaluations; no control/comparison group; lack of long-term follow-up

			Rate of placement for physical abuse: 13%	
			Following termination of services, 27% of placement group and 16% of nonplacement group were transferred to another agency unit for further services	
			1992: 22% of sample re-reported for maltreatment	
Potocky & McDonald (1996) Family systems and crisis intervention	Limited time-series design, pretest, at 3 mos, and at termination (6 mos or earlier if family terminated from program prior to 6 mos)	Child Well-Being Scales; placement	When dropouts before completing 6 mos of program were compared with completers, only 1 significant difference: dropouts participated	Small sample size; African American and Hispanic race lumped together rather than delineated separately

continued

TABLE 2.2 *(continued)*

AUTHOR/MODEL	DESIGN/SAMPLE	MEASURES	RESULTS	LIMITATIONS
	$N = 27$ parents with substance abuse problems referred from local hospitals and by state child welfare agency; 75% were minority race; 70% single mothers; all unemployed and receiving welfare		less frequently in parent/child interaction group 70% stayed in home no evidence that Child Well-Being scores changed over time larger family size (average 4.8) was more predictive of placement	

TABLE 2.3 Ecological Systems Family Preservation Programs—Pre-experimental Designs

AUTHOR/MODEL	DESIGN/SAMPLE	MEASURES	RESULTS	LIMITATIONS
Berry (1990a; 1990b; 1991; 1992) Intensive family preservation services—"case management model, emphasizing time-limited, task-centered treatment that is systems-based and environmentally oriented" (p. 75)	Pretest, posttest (1 mo, 2.5 mo), and follow-up (6 mos, 1 yr) $N = 367$ families at risk of child placement; average monthly income of $572; 13% "imminent risk"	Out-of-home placements (relatives placements counted)	4% of families had placement during services; an additional 6% had placement at 6-mo follow-up; total 12% had placement at 1-yr	Lack of no-treatment control or comparison group; information on skills gains made during treatment not available on total sample; definition of "risk" changed throughout the program and broad range of criteria; worker rated all measures (biased raters)
San Francisco, Oakland California	SF sample: 35% African American, 21% White, 17% Hispanic; 7% Asian Oakland: 48% African American, 25% White; 10% Hispanic, 5% Asian		1991: No difference in placement rates for general and imminent risk families although latter ended services at lower skill levels	

continued

TABLE 2.3 *(continued)*

AUTHOR/MODEL	DESIGN/SAMPLE	MEASURES	RESULTS	LIMITATIONS
Berry (1995) Ecological focus Cases open average of 17 weeks	Pretest, posttest, follow-up (majority 3-mos) $N = 40$ families with 97 children (85% of families at imminent risk of placement) referred from CPS Children's mean age = 4; 1/3 single-parent households; 20% prior placements; 58% referred for physical abuse, 30% neglectful supervision, 25% physical neglect, 15% medical neglect; 8% sexual abuse; 5% emotional abuse, 5% abandonment; 57% White, 30% African American, 13% Hispanic; 1/3 families had parent employed; mean annual income = $8,790 (including AFDC)	Placement; maltreatment referrals to CPS and case reopenings; Family Risk Scales; family resources (food, phone, AFDC, housing, employment, ability to read and write)	96% placement prevention rate; 72% had no further reports of maltreatment; only half of all cases closed due to satisfactory progress; another 22% transferred to other services; non-placement rate of imminent risk families—88%; although a statistically significant decrease in parent-centered risk, none in child- or economic risk; subsequent reabuse not correlated with extent of risk at case termination; significantly more families received public assistance after case services	Variable follow-up times; brief follow-up period; no comparison or control group; all information provided by caseworkers (biased raters)

TABLE 2.4 Crisis Intervention Family Preservation Studies—Quasi-Experimental Designs

AUTHOR/MODEL	DESIGN/SAMPLE	MEASURES	RESULTS	LIMITATIONS
Feldman (1991) After Homebuilders (4 sites in New Jersey) 5.35 weeks	Experimental design, randomization to intensive treatment ($N = 96$) if availability of family preservation slots or community service ($N = 87$), 1-yr follow-up $N = 183$ families recruited from child welfare, county family-juvenile crisis units, crisis mental health units; mean age of child = 13; majority single-parent; 45% White; 36% African American; 20% Hispanic; 90% low SES	Placement; Family Environment Scale; Child Well-Being Scales; Life Event Scale (nonstandardized); Interpersonal Support Evaluation List; Goal Attainment Scale; Community SES	Family preservation group did significantly better avoiding out-of-home placement from case termination to 9-mo follow-up; then effect dissipated Experimental group did not do significantly better on standardized measures from pretest to follow-up	22 were "turnbacks" after randomization (didn't meet program selection criteria, caretaker refused to participate, children had to be removed)

continued

TABLE 2.4 (*continued*)

AUTHOR/MODEL	DESIGN/SAMPLE	MEASURES	RESULTS	LIMITATIONS
Walton (1996) Walton et al. (1993) modified Homebuilders Utah 90 days	Randomization to treatment (family preservation) or comparison group (once monthly visits and provision of resources so that child could return home), posttest (90 days), follow-up (6 mos) N = 110 children from computer-generated list of children in out-of-home placement; primarily White; mean age = 10.7; Neglect was the most frequent reason for the initial out-of-home placement (32.7%), followed by child disruptive behavior (18.2%), physical abuse (14.5%), and sexual abuse (14.5%); half of caretakers were	Placement; McMaster's Family Assessment Device; Index of Self-Esteem; Index of Parental Attitudes; Consumer Outcome and Satisfaction Survey; Six Mo Follow-up Survey (latter two developed by authors)	No significant differences between groups on standardized measures; significant differences were noted between groups on Six Mo Follow-up Survey, favoring family preservation; Children in family preservation group significantly more likely to be returned to the home and stayed in the home longer than control children; At 90 days, 93% of family preservation group had been returned compared to 28.3% of control children; at 6-mos 75% of family preservation families remained together compared to 49% of control group	Standardized measures not administered at 6-mo follow-up, just at 90 days; no pretest information; measures by authors not standardized

Study, Location, Duration	Design/Sample	Sample Characteristics	Measures	Results	Limitations
		divorced/separated; half of sample annual income less than $10,000		At 1 yr, 74% of children in family preservation group remained in home compared to 45% in casework-as-usual group. Costs for family preservation group were also lower	No randomization to groups; lack of information on casework-as-usual services; no posttest; selection bias found in referrals (some units were enthusiastic supporters of in-home services and many referrals, some units were not supportive and made few referrals or none)
Wood et al. (1988) Northern California 4–6 weeks	Quasi-experimental, with casework-as-usual services, provided to overflow comparison group, pretest, 1-yr follow-up $N = 50$ families referred by CPS in which child was "in danger of being removed from the home"	50% received public assistance yr prior to referral but range in income from working poor to affluent; 72% mothers White, 12% African American, 11% Hispanic, 7% Asian; 57% boys, 43% girls; children in in-home group older (mean = 8.9 yrs) than in comparison group (mean = 5.4 yrs)	Placement; Family Adaptability and Cohesion Scale-II (results to be published in another study)		

continued

TABLE 2.5 Family Systems Family Preservation Studies—Experimental/Quasi-Experimental Designs

AUTHOR/MODEL	DESIGN/SAMPLE	MEASURES	RESULTS	LIMITATIONS
Raschick (1997) family systems theory "preventative" in focus structured educational approach (curriculum)	Quasi-experimental, treatment (65 children from 33 families) and comparison (39 children from 18 families) group comprised of families who were rejected because of lack of vacancies in the program, follow-up at 180, 360, 540, 720 days Qualitative piece consisted of 10 sets of parents and 5 adolescents randomly selected from treatment group Program targets families who volunteer for services and don't have active involvement with CPS Average age of child = 9 for treatment group and 9.9 for comparison group	Restrictiveness of Living Environment Scale; General Functioning scale of Family Assessment Device; Interaction Behavior Questionnaire; Child Behavior Checklist	At end of 720 days, comparison group had 16% more placement days than treatment group; comparison group had more restrictive placements at 0–360 and 0–720 day intervals (significance at .10 level); costs were lower for treatment group—average per child placement cost of $621.40 vs. $824.67; no significant differences on any of 3 standardized measures	Recruitment into program unclear; unequal treatment and comparison groups; unknown whether comparison groups had other services

Schwartz et al. (1991) structural family therapy approach Minnesota 4-week services	Quasi-experimental design, comparison between cases in which placement had been decided and were assigned to family preservation instead if space was available (n = 58), and random selection of cases that were not assigned (58), cases tracked between 12- and 16-mo follow-up N = 116; equivalent groups of male and female children and those living in single-parent versus two-parent homes; 2/3 White; approximately half of children younger than 14, half older than 15	Out-of-home placement; goal-setting	"While comparison group had twice the placements of the home-based group and spent more days in placement, the average number of placements were about the same in each group; parental involvement in problem solving and goal achievement are strongly related to a child's likelihood of out-of-home placement" (p. 43) 56% of treatment group experienced placement (55% of these were multiple placements) by 16 mo follow-up but comparison group experienced twice as many placements	Lack of no-treatment control; lack of randomization to treatment groups; differences between groups on placements not given in terms of statistical significance

continued

TABLE 2.6 Ecological Family Preservation Programs—Experimental/Quasi-Experimental Designs

AUTHOR/MODEL	DESIGN/SAMPLE	MEASURES	RESULTS	LIMITATIONS
Brunk et al. (1987) Comparison of multisystemic therapy and parent training 8 sessions	Quasi-experimental, randomization to parent training and multisystemic therapy $N = 43$ families with parent investigated for maltreatment; parents were mandated to receive counseling in lieu of court order; 50% chose this option; 77% (33) completed posttest 55% boys, 76% girls; 57% White, 43% African American	10-minute behavioral videotape self-report measures: Individual system: Symptom Checklist-90; Behavior Problem Checklist Family system: Family Environment Scale Social system: Family Inventory of Life Events and Changes Treatment Outcome Questionnaire	Both family preservation and parent training were effective in reducing psychiatric symptoms in parents, parental stress, and individual, and family problems; Multisystemic therapy was more effective than parent training in improving parent-child relationships according to behavioral observations, while parent training was more helpful in ameliorating social system problems	Treatment groups were not similar on all characteristics: neglected children and their mothers in the multisystemic therapy condition were significantly older
Lutzker & Rice (1987) Ecobehavioral	Quasi-experimental, experimental (in-home services—352) and comparison (received	Recidivism rates for child maltreatment	Statistically significant difference between recidivism rates for in-home services and com-	No randomization to groups; characteristics of comparison group and specific services

Stress reduction, self-control training, problem-solving skill training, job-finding skill training, money management training, leisure-time counseling, social support, alcoholism referral services, parent training, child basic skills training, prenatal and postnatal training, in-home safety and home cleanliness	CPS services—358) $N = 710$ families		parison group, with a rate of 21.3% for in-home and 28.5% for comparison families; although differences were statistically significant, effects seemed to decrease over time	received unknown; unknown how long in-home services were provided; uneven follow-up (some families tracked 5 yrs, some families tracked 1)
Schuerman et al. (1994) Multisystems 7 sites in Illinois median length of service = 108 days	Experimental, randomization to treatment and control (services as usual), pretest, posttest, 1 yr follow-up $N = 6,456$ families, 10,608 children 72% African American, 3% Latino, 24% White; 51% single-parent, 24%	Structured interview guide based on Parent Outcome Interview, Social Support Interview Schedule, Life Events Inventory; placement; child maltreatment referrals	77% of family preservation families were intact at posttest and 81% intact at 1 yr; however, families in the experimental group had a statistically significant higher risk of placement than the control group; no difference between groups in length or type of placement	16% of those eligible for random assignment were exceptions and did not follow random assignment; study was conducted for 5 yrs —unclear if variable follow-up periods

continued

TABLE 2.6 *(continued)*

AUTHOR/MODEL	DESIGN/SAMPLE	MEASURES	RESULTS	LIMITATIONS
	2-parent, 21% extended families, 4% other; 52% annual incomes under $5,000; reason for referral-51% neglect, 31% abuse, 10% both, 8% unsubstantiated		estimated probability of abuse/neglect referral was .40 after 3 yrs; no significant differences between treatment and control groups Risk factors predictive of placement: cocaine and other drug problems; previous protective custody, previous referrals, parents' chronic emotional problems or mental illness, children's health, development, or learning problems No cost savings to child welfare system	

Quasi-Experimental Designs

To address the question of whether children involved with family preservation programs are truly at risk of placement, there has been some movement toward quasi-experimental designs with random assignment to family preservation and casework-as-usual services (Feldman, 1991; Walton, 1996; Walton, Fraser, Lewis, Pecora, & Walton, 1993) or the use of overflow comparison groups (Wood, Barton, & Schroeder, 1988) (*see* Table 2.4.). In crisis intervention, Feldman (1991), for example, notes that the existence of a control group was essential since only about three fifths of children screened as at "imminent risk" were placed out of the home. Walton and associates (Walton, 1996; Walton et al., 1993) also found that 28% of the casework-as-usual children had been returned to their homes after the 90-day intervention and this percentage had increased to almost 50% by 6 months. A similar percentage of placement prevention (45%) was found for the overflow comparison group in Wood, Barton, and Schroeder, (1988) at the 1-year point. In this same vein, Wells and Biegel (1992) build the argument that only children in the control group removed from their homes during the first couple of months of service represent the number of children truly at imminent risk of placement; if this proportion is employed, family preservation services prevent placement for approximately only half of children at risk.

In the quasi-experimental designs reviewed here, despite the high rates of placement prevention for the comparison groups, family preservation program families tended to have even higher prevention rates (Feldman, 1991; Walton, 1996; Wood et al., 1988), demonstrating the success of these programs. However, for the Feldman (1991) study, significant differences between groups dissipated after 9 months. This finding highlights the importance of including an adequate follow-up period for evaluation.

For the quasi-experimental designs in family systems family preservation studies, Schwartz, AuClaire, and Harris (1991) found that family preservation services had half as many placements and spent fewer days in placement than casework-as-usual services (*see* Table 2.5). Raschick (1997) reported that number of days spent in placement was statistically lower (at a .10 level of significance) for the family preservation group compared to the overflow comparison group, although it is not clear the type of services the overflow group received. However, the experimental group in the Raschick (1997) study was not necessarily at risk for placement at the start of the program due to its prevention focus.

For ecologically based family preservation programs, only a few studies used quasi-experimental designs, but only Schuerman, Rzepnicki, and Littell (1994) looked at placement (*see* Table 2.6). In this study, the family preservation group was actually more likely to experience a placement than the casework-as-usual comparison group. At the same time, however, 77% of the families were intact after family preservation services, a figure that went up to 81% at a year follow-up. These rates are only slightly lower than the highly successful outcomes that tend to be reported by other studies in this area (Berry, 1990a, 1991, 1992, 1995).

Predictors of Placement

Predictors of placement were examined in various studies, though no clear findings were indicated. Tentatively, it appears that parental involvement and cooperation and utilization of services (Nelson, 1991; Schwartz et al., 1991) and severity of problems at intake (Berry, 1991, 1992, 1995; Nelson et al., 1988) might influence placement. Presenting problems that posed difficulty in the avoidance of prevention of placement involved substance abuse of parents (Nelson, 1991), parental involvement with other mental health services (Nelson et al., 1988). In addition, neglect as a presenting problem has also been associated with a higher risk of placement (Bath et al., 1992; Berry, 1990a, 1991, 1992; Yuan & Struckman-Johnson, 1991).

Critique of Placement as Outcome

Despite successes noted when using placement as the outcome criterion, a discussion of the limitations of this outcome is warranted (e.g., Nelson & Landsman, 1992). First, an assumption of distal outcomes such as placement is that programmatic efforts account for the achievement of long-term goals (Bath & Haapala, 1994; Fraser, 1990). If this assumption is true, data indicate that the proliferation of family preservation programs has not lessened the overall time children spend in out-of-home placements, nor has it resulted in a substantial reduction in placements. Data from the Voluntary Cooperative Information System of the American Public Welfare Association indicates a 60% increase (from 273,000 to 442,000) in out-of-home care from 1985 to 1992, although the rate of increase each year has slowed since 1989 (Schuerman, Rzepnicki, & Littell, 1994). At the same time, since 1985, children tend to stay in care for longer periods of time. These figures seem to indicate that foster care placements have increased along with the availability of family preservation programs (Schwartz, 1995). The relationship between foster care and family preservation, however, is only correlational. Many other variables probably account for rates of foster care placements, such as rising rates of poverty and single parenthood, as well as policies on public assistance to families. Similarly, many other factors account for placement of children outside the home; therefore, it cannot be assumed that programmatic efforts are solely responsible for this type of distal outcome. As with the criteria for imminent risk, many contextual variables influence placement decisions (e.g., Pecora et al., 1995; Rossi, 1992a; Wells, 1994), such as the availability of placements and resources, and prevailing community attitudes. For instance, recent publicized accounts of abuse in the home may result in a movement toward out-of-home placement, while reports of abuse occurring in foster or group homes may promote the provision of family preservation services (Tracy, 1991).

Aside from contextual influences on placement, there is a lack of conceptual clarity in the definition of out-of-home placement. Some authors fail to define placement at all, while others offer varying definitions based on the duration of placement, the formality of placement in terms of licensing and payment from the state, and the involvement of relatives (Schuerman et al., 1991; Wells & Biegel, 1992).

Further, the reliability of placement data is influenced by the source of information. If information is only gleaned from case records or practitioners, the number of placements are likely to be underestimated (Pecora et al., 1992). Parental self-reports of children running away or informal neighbor or relative placements might need to supplement official records in order to obtain accurate results. In addition, agency data may not capture psychiatric hospitalizations, inpatient substance abuse treatment, and juvenile justice institutional stays. Hence, multiple indicators are needed in order to obtain precise information on placement (Fraser, 1990).

Another critique of placement outcome is the assumption that remaining in the home is always desirable for children. In some cases, substitute care or intensive treatment outside the home represents an optimal outcome (Bath & Haapala, 1994; Rossi, 1992a; Wells, 1995). Prevention of unnecessary placements while keeping children safe within their own homes embodies a more appropriate goal for family preservation programs (Tracy, 1991). A further goal is that functioning of families and living conditions are improved. In the next section, the more immediate, proximal outcomes of family preservation programs will be discussed.

PROXIMAL OUTCOMES

To assess some of the more immediate effects of family preservation, many programs relied on unstandardized checklists (i.e., Bath et al., 1992); others employed the Child Well-Being or the Family Risk Scales (Pecora et al., 1992; Thieman & Dall, 1992; Yuan & Struckman-Johnson, 1991). Although some psychometric work has been performed on these scales (Magura & Moses, 1986; Magura, Moses, & Jones, 1987), an inherent bias exists in that the practitioners involved with services also complete the instrument (Meezan & McCroskey, 1995). Given this bias, it is difficult to place much confidence in the results of these measures.

Only a small proportion of studies employed standardized self-report measures (Feldman, 1991; Fraser et al., 1991; Walton, 1996). When these were used for crisis intervention programs, no significant differences were found for family preservation families from pre- to posttest (Fraser et al., 1991) or between family preservation and comparison groups (Feldman, 1991; Walton, 1996). These trends were similar for the family systems family preservation studies. Raschick (1997) reported no significant differences between groups. Meezan and McCroskey (1995), though discussing that several standardized measures were completed by both mother and teacher of the index, seemed to limit their reporting to the Home Observation for Measurement of the Environment (HOME). On this measure, the family-centered services group showed greater improvement over the services-as-usual comparison group in the following areas: living and financial conditions, child behavior, and parenting skills of preschoolers. It is not clear whether caseworkers were responsible for HOME ratings. If they were, the limited positive findings might be susceptible to caseworker bias since caseworkers were also responsible for delivering services.

Some improvements, however, have been found for an ecologically based model called multisystemic therapy on standardized self-report data and behavioral observations (Brunk et al., 1987), although improvements were also noted for the parent training comparison condition. Both conditions produced reductions in parental psychiatric symptoms, parental stress, and both individual and family problems. Each condition also demonstrated certain advantages. Multisystemic therapy was beneficial at improving parent-child relationships according to behavioral observations. It could be that the individually designed multisystemic treatment could work with parents on their parenting practices (similar to parent training), but it also had the added benefit of being able to work with children individually as well as family members together. Parent training was more helpful for producing gains in social support. Although the multisystemic therapy was designed to target the social systems presumed to influence the family, such as the school, the neighborhood, and the peer group, it is interesting that social system functioning was more positively impacted by parent training. A possible hypothesis is that such training was conducted in the group setting and members were available to provide important support functions for each other.

Other ecological studies looked at cost savings and child maltreatment recidivism rates. Findings from these studies were mixed. Schuerman et al. (1994) failed to find cost savings or reduced child maltreatment referrals when comparing family preservation to services-as-usual. Lutzker and Rice (1987) also looked at maltreatment referrals and found recidivism rates for the in-home services group of 21.3% compared to a rate of 28.5% for the Child Protective Services group. Although these differences were statistically significant, they tended to decrease over time, suggesting the need for additional monitoring.

SUMMARY

In sum, while placement is often averted in studies, success is not as always consistently reflected in the more proximal measures of family preservation programs. Further, no child and family functioning variables were consistently associated with predicting successful outcome, although neglect as reason for referral might represent a tentative risk factor. The next section will address the contribution that the theoretical bases of programs have made to outcome followed by recommendations for research, service delivery, and policy.

CRITIQUES OF THEORETICAL BASES OF FAMILY PRESERVATION PROGRAMS

CRISIS INTERVENTION

Several criticisms have been leveled at crisis intervention as the theoretical basis for family preservation programs. One practical concern is the difficulty of referring families at the point of crisis (Tracy, 1991). Agency procedure often dictates that cases have to be processed through supervisors, committees, and/or the courts before being accepted into family preservation programs. During this time frame, events that precipitated the crisis may have been resolved, or families have adjusted and are no longer motivated for program involvement. Another practical concern involves the use of waiting lists when families are in crisis, as these are antithetical to the original conceptualization of Homebuilders (Tracy, 1991).

In addition to these logistical concerns, there is a lack of empirical support for the effectiveness of crisis intervention (Barth, 1988). For instance, in one of the studies in this review, the provision of crisis intervention services was associated with an increased risk of placement (Fraser et al., 1991). In addition, there is no empirical validity for the assumptions underlying the model (Barth, 1988). For example, one assumption of crisis intervention is that reactions are relatively brief in duration, usually about 4 to 6 weeks. However, the literature on traumatic events, such as sexual assault, does not indicate that reactions are this time-limited in nature.

Barth (1988) has also questioned the validity of crisis intervention as the underlying theory for Homebuilders. Crisis intervention was originally formulated for individuals who were functioning at an acceptable level before being confronted with untenable circumstances. These circumstances were seen as overwhelming the individual's capacity for functioning, with the goal of intervention to return the individual to prior adjustment (Parad & Caplan, 1960). Crisis intervention, therefore, is viewed as involving precipitating events rather than predisposing environmental factors, such as long-standing poverty, and personal factors, such as substance abuse, disabilities, and other impairments.

Another problem is that although Homebuilders has been associated with crisis intervention, there appears to be some conceptual confusion as to the underlying theory. Some authors, for instance, have claimed that although Homebuilders is based on crisis theory, the interventions most frequently used are from social learning theory (Barth, 1988; Nelson et al., 1990; Nelson & Landsman, 1992; Wells, 1994). Such interventions include contracting, parent-training, and self-management techniques (Lewis, 1991).

In sum, there appears little basis for utilizing crisis intervention as an underlying theoretical framework for family preservation services. Logistical concerns often preclude the provision of intervention during the crucial crisis period (Tracy, 1991). In addition, concerns have been raised about the lack of empirical evidence for the effectiveness of crisis intervention theory (Barth, 1988). The question has also been asked whether social learning theory does not better explain the methods that are being utilized with family preservation (Barth, 1988; Nelson et al., 1990; Wells, 1994). A further problem with using crisis intervention with a child welfare population is that chronic stress tends to compromise family functioning more than the acute events that are assumed to trigger a crisis response in crisis theory (Barth, 1988).

FAMILY SYSTEMS THEORY

When examining family systems family preservation programs by theoretical premise, the general conclusion is that theories undergirding programs are weak. First, when family theory is described, there is a lack of detail about the type of approach used. While family systems theory may have some general assumptions (circular causality, system-wide payoffs for symptoms), particular schools work with families in very different ways. With the exception of

Schwartz et al. (1991), who discuss a structural approach, it is unknown from what perspective family systems methods were employed.

As well as the issue of how family systems methods are being applied in family preservation programs, there are also problems with family systems theory for explaining access to concrete resources or for coping with environmental stressors (Barth, 1988, 1990). Another major limitation is that while family systems theory does account for the family system impact on the individual, it does not take into account the influence of the larger system.

ECOLOGICAL THEORY

Ecological theory takes a more expansive perspective in that wider environmental systems are implicated for their influence on individual and family functioning. However, this theoretical framework, when applied to family preservation programs, does not consider how systems can be impacted at this level. An exception involves multisystemic therapy, which was developed by Henggeler, one of the co-authors of the Brunk et al. (1987) study, and has been primarily used with juvenile offenders with demonstrated effectiveness (e.g., Henggeler, Melton, & Smith, 1992; Henggeler, Melton, Smith, Schoenwald, & Hanley, 1993). One of the major strengths of multisystemic therapy is its theoretical basis; in addition, while treatment is delivered on an individualized basis, there is adherence to a standardized and manualized treatment model. In essence, multisystemic treatment is more than simply an eclectic approach in a family preservation model (Henggeler et al., 1993).

Many of the advantages of the multisystemic treatment, however, have to do with the differences between research therapy and treatment delivered in the field (Weisz, Weiss, & Donenberg, 1992); Henggeler, Melton, Brodino, Scherer, & Hanley (1997) found that treatment adherence was the strongest predictor of good outcomes when community practitioners rather than university graduate students administered the treatment. Research therapists usually are trained in specific techniques and are guided through manualized treatment and regular supervision. In contrast, therapists in clinical practice often do not undergo intensive training; nor do they have the kind of structure and supervision present in research models. Further, due to large multiproblem caseloads and paperwork requirements, therapists in clinical practice are not able to devote themselves to select techniques (Weisz et al., 1992). These factors tend to compromise the success of many family preservation programs, but they can also work toward more effective outcomes if these factors are controlled. Other recommendations for future research will be explored below.

RESEARCH RECOMMENDATIONS

This review of crisis intervention studies demonstrates that the evaluation efforts in the area of family preservation need to be considerably strengthened. Of essential importance is that "imminent risk of placement" criterion be clarified; otherwise, claims that programs avert placement will continue to rest on a faulty assumption. One suggestion is that instead of offering family preservation when maltreatment is substantiated, services should be implemented after a court decision to place the child has been made (Rossi, 1992). In this way, family preservation services are delivered only to those children and families who truly are at imminent risk of placement. In addition, quasi-experimental designs are essential in order to discover the differential effects of family preservation. Ethical considerations preclude the use of no-treatment control groups; however, casework-as-usual services is an acceptable comparison group alternative (Rossi, 1992). At the same time, it is important that evaluators detail the casework-as-usual services, so that the differences between regular and family preservation services are clear.

The importance of an adequate follow-up period is also argued: "A treatment whose effects fade out after a few months may not be cost effective if the treated families subsequently come back into the child protective system because of additional complaints, suggesting that the main effect of treatment is to postpone recidivism" (Rossi, 1992, p. 169). Although Rossi (1992) suggests that a 2-year follow-up period be employed, only one of the programs reviewed here tracked outcomes for this time period (Raschick, 1997); most follow-ups were between 6 and 12 months.

Another recommendation is that authors articulate more clearly the theory bases for programs. As part of this effort, manualized treatment and other ways to obtain standardization need to be implemented. The importance of adherence to a standardized treatment model was highlighted in a recent study on family preservation with juvenile offenders (Henggeler et al., 1997). Treatment adherence was associated with improved outcome in terms of prevention of re-arrest and incarceration. Despite the potential importance of this issue, the family preservation literature fails to discuss efforts to ensure that therapists are following structured interventions.

A further recommendation for research in this area is that measurement of program success should not solely rely on placement outcome; standardized measurement instruments that reflect the theoretical constructs on which family preservation programs are built should also be implemented routinely (Barth, 1988; Wells & Biegel, 1992). The reliance on worker-completed evaluation instruments, such as the Child Well-Being Scales and the Family Risk Scales, must be supplemented by behavioral observation measures conducted by unbiased parties and/or by standardized self-report instruments. These recommendations will more systematically ensure that programs are not only preventing unnecessary placements, but are also keeping children safe within their own homes and improving the living conditions and functioning of families (Tracy, 1991).

CONCLUSION

Even though improvements can be made in the way family preservation is both administered and studied, Lindsey (1994) argues that neither family preservation nor any other residual program that attempts to address problems that have already occurred can be effective when inadequate residence, food, and medical care undermines parenting ability. In this nation, a substantial proportion of children live in poverty—a little over one fifth of children in 1995 (Petit & Curtis, 1997). Poverty is a serious risk factor not only for abuse and neglect but also for a host of other problems, such as academic underachievement, teenage pregnancy, marital conflict, and family violence (Lindsey, 1994). Poverty must be addressed if abuse and neglect are to be seriously impacted (Dore, 1993; Lindsey, 1994; Schuerman et al., 1994; Wells & Tracy, 1996).

REFERENCES

American Psychiatric Association. (1994). *Diagnostic and statistical manual of mental disorders* (4th ed.). Washington, DC: Author.

Barth, R. (1988). Theories guiding home-based intensive family preservation services. In J. Wittaker, J. Kinney, E. Tracey, & C. Booth (Eds.), *Improving practice technology for work with high risk families: Lessons from the "Homebuilders" social work education project* (pp. 91–113). Seattle: Center for Social Welfare Research.

Barth, R. (1990). Theories guiding home-based intensive family preservation services. In J. K. Wittaker, J. Kinney, E. M. Tracey, & C. Booth (Eds.), *Reaching high-risk families: Intensive family preservation in human services* (pp. 89–112). Hawthorne, NY: Aldine De Gruyter.

Bath, H. I., & Haapala, D. A. (1993). Intensive family preservation services with abused and neglected children: An examination of group differences. *Child Abuse and Neglect, 17*, 213–225.

Bath, H. I., & Haapala, D. A. (1994). Family preservation services: What does the outcome research really tell us? *Social Service Review, 68*, 386–399.

TABLE 2.7 Atheoretical Family Preservation Outcome Studies

AUTHOR/MODEL	DESIGN/SAMPLE	MEASURES	RESULTS	LIMITATIONS
Jones (1985) New York City Mean mos of service = 19	Experimental with randomization to experimental and control (treatment as usual); pretest, posttest, follow-up (5 yrs)	Case records (experimental group only); placement; abuse and neglect referrals; assessments of problems by workers and parents	28% of families assessed as functioning adequately, almost 75% were not	Evaluation only considered cases at risk of placement rather than foster family cases although both had family preservation services applied; criteria at each agency for case selection were different; unequal numbers in experimental and control group; nonstandardized measures
	$N = 142$ families with 243 children at risk of placement within 6 mos; majority referred from public child welfare agency; low-income; majority single-parent; approximately 50% African American, 25% Mexican-American, 20% White; 61% male, 39% female; age ranges: 0–2 25%, 3–5 21%, 6–9 23%, 10–13 27%, 14–17 4%		34% of the experimental group vs. 46% of the control group entered care (significant difference); also experimental group was significantly more delayed in their entry into care; however, experimental children did not spend significantly less time in care	
			no significant difference in maltreatment reports between groups	
			Predictive factors for placement: 1) mother's central problem was physical illness; 2)	

		placement had already been requested for child; 3) child's functioning was a factor in need for placement; 4) worker recommended that child be placed; 5) single-parent household; 6) mother not high school graduate	
Reid, Kagan, & Schlosberg (1988)	Post-hoc comparison of placed (31 families) and nonplaced (matched sample in terms of follow-up length of 55 families randomly drawn from 400 families) at average of 2 ½ yrs after case closing	Staff ratings on goal attainment for family and child	"For the placed cases, children had more problems and more serious problems; families had fewer resources, used services less, made less progress, and were less satisfied with the agency efforts" (p. 33)
New York			Lack of no-treatment control or comparison group that did not receive family preservation; unclear how long children were tracked; nonstandardized measures
minimum of 3 mos	median age of children—14, 50% boys, 50% girls; White, urban, working poor or supported by public assistance; 53% history of abuse and neglect		

continued

TABLE 2.7 *(continued)*

AUTHOR/MODEL	DESIGN/SAMPLE	MEASURES	RESULTS	LIMITATIONS
Rosenthal & Glass (1986)	Quasi-experimental, comparing a group who entered foster care services from 1977 to 1978 to those who received family preservation services from 1980 to 1981, follow-up of 36 mos $N = 240$ Mean age of child = 14; majority male	Placement by month which included foster homes, group homes, residential treatment programs, independent living programs, correctional settings, and psychiatric settings as long as child placed for > than 50% of month	Initial positive effect of family preservation seemed to dissipate, mean cost savings also decreased over 3-yr time period In both groups, a significant proportion of children experienced extended placement and poor school performance	Confound of history; because alternative intervention consisted of 4 different programs, unknown which components are responsible; no information on race; variable follow-up time; differences between groups and time periods not always given in terms of statistical significance
Rubin (1997) Although services were targeted for 90-day time periods, this was extended to 1 yr since progress wasn't made by clients	Quasi-experimental, comparing family preservation services to overflow group, who received CPS-as usual services, follow-up (12 mos). Also used a time-series design drawn from CPS cases referred from 2 yrs before family	Out-of-home placement	No differences between groups	Lack of randomization to groups; lack of comparability of groups; lack of standardized measures other than placement

	family preservation services (4 data points) to 2 yrs after following a 6-mo start-up phase (4 data points) $N = 68$ cases Criteria: substance abuse—primary presenting problem, family had to have an advocate who could take care of children if parent unavailable; 68 mothers, 35 fathers; income less than $9,000		
Smith (1995) 90 days	Pretest, posttest (90 days), follow-up (6 mos) $N = 26$ families targeted as risk of placement within 1 mo; 65% of families receiving AFDC;	Placement; Assessment sheet (money management, marital relationship, family communication, use of support systems,	Statistically significant improvements made in family relationships, supervision of children Support system, home management, did not	Caseworker bias exists in measurement system; nonstandardized measures; some pretest, posttest differences not reported in terms of statistical significance;

continued

TABLE 2.7 *(continued)*

AUTHOR/MODEL	DESIGN/SAMPLE	MEASURES	RESULTS	LIMITATIONS
	average annual income = \$915; 69.2% White, 27% African American, 4% biracial; child's average age = 3; average number of children per family = 2.3	relationship building, home management, child supervision, nurturance, and expectations)	improve statistically At program termination, 96% families still intact; at 6 mos after termination, 92% still intact 18% referred for further services after program termination	small sample size; no comparison/control group
Wald, Carlsmith, & Leiderman, Smith, & French (1988) Purpose: maintain abused and neglected children in their own homes by providing services to their families	Quasi-experimental, comparing CPS families in one county who were more likely to have services delivered in the home vs. foster care, compared to 2 other counties that were more likely to use foster care, and a low SES comparison group comprising	Health assessment and physical exam; Weschler Preschool and Primary Scale of Intelligence; Weschler Intelligence Scale for Children—Revised; academic performance; child behavior scale; social competence instrument; children's perspectives	Home placement unsuccessful in 20% of cases; little change in families with most problems for home-based Child problem outcomes: Almost half of children, in both settings, continued to evidence emotional	Ethnic minorities had to be removed from sample because confounded results (more African Americans in comparison groups since more likely to be placed in foster care); also excluded those who moved between foster care and home during study

neither abused nor neglected children Data collected at following points: caretaker (every 3 mos); child (every 6 mos); teacher and social worker (yearly) for 2 year-period $N = 32$ children excluding residential treatment placements and sexual abuse cases	about their lives; parental self-esteem; involvement with children; Moos Family Environment Scale; observational checklist on quality of physical environment	problems, and these seemed more severe among the home children; 50% of home-services mothers reported child behavior problems throughout 2 yrs; 50% of foster children perceived as problematic first yr but declined to 25% at end of 2 yrs School outcomes:Foster children missed less school and had better chances of performing	period; compared to home services baseline data which was collected close to the time of initial intervention, foster care data was collected between 6–12 weeks after intervention; some non-standardized measures; results not given re: statistical significance; at times data not presented in terms of group differences

continued

TABLE 2.7 *(continued)*

AUTHOR/MODEL	DESIGN/SAMPLE	MEASURES	RESULTS	LIMITATIONS
	White; 59% at home, 41% in foster care; 44% abused, 56% neglected; majority White single-parent and low-income children aged 5–10		adequately in school; home-services children's school social behavior declined according to teacher ratings; although many foster children also experienced social problems at school, as a group they didn't deteriorate	

Bath, H. I., Richey, C. A., & Haapala, D. A. (1992). Child age and outcome correlates in intensive family preservation services. *Children & Youth Services Review, 14*, 389–406.

Berry, M. (1990a). Preparing and supporting special needs adoptive families: A review of the literature. *Child & Adolescent Social Work Journal, 7*, 403–418.

Berry, M. (1990b). Stress and coping among older child adoptive families. *Social Work & Social Sciences Review, 1*, 71–93.

Berry, M. (1991). The assessment of imminence of risk of placement: Lessons from a family preservation program. *Children and Youth Services Review, 13*, 239–256.

Berry, M. (1992). An evaluation of family preservation services: Fitting agency services to family needs. *Social Work, 37*, 314–321.

Berry, M. (1995, Summer). An examination of treatment fidelity in an intensive family preservation program. *Family Preservation Journal*, 25–50.

Bribitzer, M. P., & Verdieck, M. J. (1988). Home-based, family-centered intervention: Evaluation of a foster care prevention program. *Child Welfare, 67*, 255–266.

Bronfenbrenner, U. (1979). *The ecology of human development.* Cambridge, MA: Harvard University Press.

Brunk, M., Henggeler, S. W., & Whelan, J. P. (1987). Comparison of multisystemic therapy and parent training in the brief treatment of child abuse and neglect. *Journal of Consulting and Clinical Psychology, 55*, 171–178.

Chamberlain, P., & Rosicky, J. (1995). The effectiveness of family therapy in the treatment of adolescents with conduct disorders and delinquency. *Journal of Marital and Family Therapy, 21*, 441–459.

Dore, M. M. (1993). Family preservation and poor families: When "Homebuilding" is not enough. *Families in Society: The Journal of Contemporary Human Services, 74*, 545–553.

Feldman, L. (1990). Target population definition. In Y. Yaun & M. Rivest (Eds.). Preserving families: Evaluation resources for practitioners and policymakers. Sage Focus editions vol. 117 (pp. 16–38). Newbury Park, CA: Sage.

Feldman, L. H. (1991). *Evaluating the impact of intensive family preservation services in New Jersey.* In K. Wells & D. Biegel (Eds.). *Family preservation services: Research and evaluation* (pp. 47–71). Newbury Park, CA: Sage.

Forehand, R., & Long, N. (1988). Outpatient treatment of the acting out child: Procedures, long term follow-up data, and clinical problems. *Advances in Behavioral Research and Therapy, 10*, 129–177.

Fraser, M. W. (1990). Program outcome measures. In Y. T. Yuan and M. Rivest (Eds.), *Preserving families: Evaluation resources for practitioners and policy makers*, (pp. 77–101). Newbury Park, CA: Sage.

Fraser, M. W., & Haapala, D. A. (1987–1988). Home-based family treatment: A quantitative-qualitative assessment. *Journal of Applied Social Sciences, 12*, 1–23.

Fraser, M. W., Pecora, P. J., & Haapala, D. A. (1991). *Families in crisis: The impact of intensive family preservation services.* Hawthorne, NY: Aldine de Gruyter.

Grigsby, R. K. (1993). Theories that guide intensive family preservation services: A second look. In E. S. Morton & R. K. Grigsby (Eds.), *Advancing family preservation practice* (pp. 16–27). Newbury Park, CA: Sage.

Henggeler, S. W., Melton, G. B., Brodino, M. J., Scherer, D. G., & Hanley, J. H. (1997). Multisystemic therapy with violent and chronic juvenile offenders and their families: The role of treatment fidelity in successful dissemination. *Journal of Consulting and Clinical Psychology, 65,* 821–833.

Henggeler, S. W., Melton, G. B., & Smith, L. A. (1992). Family preservation using multisystemic therapy: An effective alternative to incarcerating serious juvenile offenders. *Journal of Consulting and Clinical Psychology, 60,* 953–961.

Henggeler, S. W., Melton, G. B., Smith, L. A., Schoenwald, S. K., & Hanley, J. H. (1993). Family preservation using mulitsystemic treatment: Long term follow up to a clinical trail with serious juvenile offenders. *Journal of Child and Family Studies, 2,* 283–293.

Hinshaw, S., & Anderson, C. (1996). Conduct and oppositional defiant disorders. In E. Mash, & R. Barkley, et al. (Eds.) *Child psychopathology* (pp. 113–149). New York, NY: Guilford Press.

Jones, M. (1985). *A second chance for families five years later: Follow-up of a program to prevent foster care.* New York: Child Welfare League of America.

Kazdin, A. E. (1993). Treatment of conduct disorder: Progress and directions in psychotherapy research. *Development and Psychopathology, 5,* 277–310.

Kinney, J., & Dittmar, K. (1995). *Homebuilders: Helping families help themselves.* Lincoln, NE: University of Nebraska Press.

Kinney, J., Haapala, D. A., & Booth, C. (1991). *Keeping families together: The homebuilders model.* New York: Aldine De Gruyter.

Lewis, R. (1991). What elements of service relate to treatment goal achievement? In M. W. Fraser, P. J. Pecora, & D. A. Haapala (Ed.), *Families in crisis: The impact of intensive family preservation services.* Hawthorne, NY: Aldine De Gruyter.

Lindsey, D. (1994). Family preservation and child protection: Striking a balance. *Children and Youth Services Review, 16,* 279–294.

Lutzker, J. R., & Rice, J. M. (1987). Using recidivism data to evaluate project 12-ways: An ecobehavioral approach to the treatment and prevention of child abuse and neglect. *Journal of Family Violence, 2,* 283–290.

Magura, S., & Moses, B. S. (1986). *Outcome measures for child welfare services: Theory and applications* Washington, DC: Child Welfare League of America.

Magura, S., Moses, B. S., & Jones, M. A. (1987). *Assessing risk and measuring change in families: The family risk scales.* Washington, DC: Child Welfare League of America.

McGowan, B. G. (1990). Family-based services and public policy: Context and implications. In J. K. Whittaker, J. Kinney, E. M. Tracy, & C. Booth (Eds.), *Reaching high-risk families: Intensive family preservation in human services* (pp. 65–85). New York: Aldine De Gruyter.

Meezan, W., & McCroskey, J. (1995, Winter). Improving family functioning through family preservation services: Results of the Los Angeles Experiment. *Family Preservation Journal,* 9–28.

Miller, G. E., & Prinz, R. J. (1990). Enhancement of social learning family interventions for childhood conduct disorder. *Psychological Bulletin, 108,* 291–307.

Nelson, K. E. (1990). Program environment and organization. In Y. Y. Yuan & M. Rivest (Eds.), *Preserving families: Evaluation resources for practitioners and policymakers* (pp. 39–61). Newbury Park, CA: Sage.

Nelson, K. E. (1991). Populations and outcomes in five family preservation programs. In K. Wells & D. E. Biegel (Eds.), *Family preservation services: Research and evaluation* (pp. 72–91). Newbury Park, CA: Sage.

Nelson, K. E., Emlen, A., Landsman, M., Hutchinson, J., Zalenski, A., Black, R., Marcus, C., Inskeep, C., & Leung, P. (1988). *Family-based services: A national perspective on success and failure.* Iowa City, IA: The National Resource Center on Family-Based Services, The University of Iowa, School of Social Work.

Nelson, K. E., & Landsman, M. J. (1992). *Alternative models of family preservation: Family-based services in context.* Springfield, IL: Charles C. Thomas.

Nelson, K. E., Landsman, M. J., & Deutelbaum, W. (1990). Three models of family-centered placement prevention service. *Child Welfare, 69,* 3–19.

Parad, H. J., & Caplan, G. (1960). A framework for studying families in crisis. *Social Work, 5,* 3–15.

Patterson, G. R., DeBaryshe, B. D., & Ramsey, E. (1989). A developmental perspective on antisocial behavior. *American Psychologist, 44,* 329–335.

Pecora, P. J., Fraser, M. W., & Haapala, D. A. (1991). Client outcomes and issues for program design. In K. Wells and D. E. Biegel (Eds.), *Family preservation services: Research and evaluation* (pp. 3–32). Newbury Park, CA: Sage.

Pecora, P. J., Fraser, M. W., & Haapala, D. A. (1992). Intensive home-based family preservation services: An update from the FIT project. *Child Welfare, 71,* 177–188.

Pecora, P. J., Fraser, M. W., Nelson, K. E., McCroskey, J., & Meezan, W. (1995). *Evaluating family-based services.* New York: Aldine De Gruyter.

Peters, R. D. (1991). Expanding the perspective on contributing factors and service delivery approaches to childhood aggression. In D. J. Pepler & K. H. Rubin (Eds.), *The development and treatment of childhood aggression* (pp. 189–197). Hillsdale, NJ: Lawrence Erlbaum Associates.

Petit, M. R., & Curtis, P. A. (1997). *Child abuse and neglect: A look at the states: 1997 CWLA Stat Book.* Washington, DC: CWLA Press.

Potocky, M., & McDonald, T. P. (1996). Evaluating the effectiveness of family preservation services for the families of drug-exposed infants: A pilot study. *Research on Social Work Practice, 6,* 524–535.

Raschick, M. (1997). A multi-faceted, intensive family preservation program evaluation. *Family Preservation Journal, 2,* 33–52.

Reid, J. B. (1993). Prevention of conduct disorder before and after school entry: Relating interventions to developmental findings. *Development and Psychopathology, 5,* 243–262.

Reid, W., Kagan, R., & Schlosberg, S. (1988). Prevention of placement: critical Factors in program success. *Child Welfare,* 25–36.

Rosenthal, J. A., & Glass, G. V. (1986). Impacts of alternatives to out-of-home placement: A quasi-experimental study. *Children and Youth Services Review, 8,* 305–321.

Rossi, P. H. (1992a). Assessing family preservation programs. *Children and Youth Services Review, 14,* 77–98.

Rossi, P. H. (1992b). Strategies for evaluation. *Children and Youth Services Review, 14,* 167–191.

Rubin, A. (1997). The family preservation evaluation from hell: Implications for program evaluation fidelity. *Children and Youth Services Review, 19,* 77–99.

Scannapieco, M. (1994). Home-based services program: Effectiveness with at risk families. *Children and Youth Services Review, 16,* 363–377.

Schuerman, J. R., Rzepnicki, T., & Littell, J. (1991). *From Chicago to Little Egypt: Lessons from an evaluation of a family preservation program.* Newbury Park, CA: Sage.

Schuerman, J. R., Rzepnicki, T., & Littell, J. (1994). *Putting families first: An experiment in family preservation.* New York: Aldine De Gruyter.

Schwartz, I. (1995). The systemic impact of family preservation services: A case study. In I. Schwartz, P. Auclaire, et al. (Eds.), *Home-based services for troubled children. Child, youth, and family services series* (pp. 157–171). Lincoln, NE: University of Nebraska Press.

Schwartz, I. M., AuClaire, P., & Harris, L. J. (1991). Family preservation services as an alternative to the out-of-home placement of adolescents: The Hennepin County experiences. In K. Wells, & D. Biegel, et al. (Eds.), *Family preservation services: Research and evaluation.* Sage. Focus edition, vol. 129 (pp. 33–46). Newbury Park, CA: Sage.

Smith, M. K. (1995). Utilization-focusedevaluation of a family preservation program. *Family in Society, 76*(1), 11–19.

Spaid, W. M., & Fraser, M. (1991). The correlates of success/failure in brief and intensive family treatment: Implications for family preservation services. *Children and Youth Services Review, 12,* 77–99.

Spaid, W. M., Lewis, R. E., & Pecora, P. J. (1991). Factors associated with success and failure in family-based and intensive family preservation services. In M. W. Fraser, P. J. Pecora, & D. A. Haapala (Eds.), *Family in crisis: The impact of intensive family preservation services* (pp. 49–58). New York: Aldine De Gruyter.

Stroul, B. A., & Goldman, S. K. (1990). Study of community-based services for children and adolescents who are severely emotionally disturbed. *Journal of Mental Health Administration, 17,* 61–77.

Thieman, A. A., & Dall, P. W. (1992). Family preservation services: Problems of measurement and assessment of risk. *Family Relations, 41,* 186–191.

Tracy, E. M. (1991). Defining the target population for family preservation services. In K. Wells & D. E. Biegel (Eds.), *Family preservation services: Research and evaluation* (pp. 138–158). Newbury Park, CA: Sage Publications.

Wald, M., Carlsmith, J., Leiderman, P., Smith, C., & French, R. (1988). *Protecting abused and neglected children.* Stanford, CA: Stanford University Press.

Walton, E. (1996). Family functioning as a measure of success in intensive family preservation services. *Journal of Family Social Work, 1,* 67–82.

Walton, E., & Denby, R. (1997). Targeting families to receive intensive family preservation services: Assessing the use of imminent risk of placement as a service criterion. *Family Preservation Journal, 2*, 53–70.

Walton, E., Fraser, M. W., Lewis, R. E., Pecora, P. J., & Walton, W. K. (1993). In-home, family-focused reunification services: An experimental study. *Child Welfare, 72*, 473–487.

Weisz, J. R., Weiss, B., & Donenberg, G. R. (1992). The lab versus the clinic: Effects of child and adolescent psychotherapy. *American Psychologist, 47*, 1578–1585.

Wells, K. (1994). A reorientation to knowledge development in family preservation services: A proposal. *Child Welfare, 73*, 475–488.

Wells, K. (1995). Family preservation services in context: Origins, practices, & current issues. In I. M. Schwartz & P. AuClaire (Eds.) *Home-based services for troubled children* (Child, Youth, & Family Services Series, pp. 1–28). Lincoln, NE: University of Nebraska Press.

Wells, K., & Biegel, D. (1992). Intensive family preservation services research: Current status and future agenda. *Social Work Research and Abstracts, 28*, 21–27.

Wells, K., & Tracy, E. M. (1996). Reorienting intensive family preservation services in relation to public child welfare practice. *Child Welfare, 75*, 667–692.

Whittaker, J. K., & Tracy, E. M. (1990). Family preservation services and education for social work practice: Stimulus & response. In J. K. Whittaker, J. Kinney, E. M. Tracy, & C. Booth (Eds.), *Reaching high-risk families: Intensive family preservation in human services* (pp. 1–11). New York: Aldine De Gruyter.

Wood, S., Barton, K., & Schroeder, C. (1988). In-home treatment of abusive families: Cost and placement at one year. *Psychotherapy, 25*, 409–414.

Yuan, Y. Y., & Struckman-Johnson, D. L. (1991). Placement outcomes for neglected children with prior placements in family preservation programs. In K. Wells D. E. Biegel (Eds.), *Family preservation services: Research and evaluation* (pp. 92–118). Beverly Hills, CA: Sage.

MEASUREMENT OF FAMILY TREATMENT WITH CHILD MALTREATMENT USING FAMILY PRESERVATION

For measurement instruments in this area, *see* Measurement of Family Treatment with Child Abuse and Neglect, *Chapter One.*

CHAPTER 3

Family Treatment with Conduct Disorder*

Family Case:

Gwen Parson, a White female in her early 40s, brings in her child Peter, age 9, because she says that he acts "bad" all the time. He won't listen to her or to his teachers in school, and he has already been kicked out of his regular class at school only 2 months into the year. He is now attending a special school for children with conduct problems.

Gwen says that when she tries to discipline Peter, he runs away from her and calls her names. She claims he has even hit her back on a couple of occasions when she has gone to "smack him for his attitude." Gwen reports that she and her husband have been separated for the last couple of months, and Peter's behavior has been even worse since his father has been out of the home. Gwen relates that her husband can be "kind of scary when he gets mad" and that Peter will sometimes listen to his father. Gwen says she is having a difficult time supporting the children and herself with her job as a convenience store clerk, so she will probably take her husband back if he promises to get help for his drinking problem.

Behavioral problems in youth pose a serious mental health and social issue. Problems of a severe nature warrant the psychiatric diagnoses of conduct disorder and oppositional defiant disorder (American Psychiatric Association, 1994). Conduct disorder occurs between 2% and 9% of females and 6% and 16% of males. Between 6% and 16% of both males and females are diagnosed with oppositional defiant disorder. Antisocial and aggressive behaviors are also

---

* A portion of a draft of this chapter will be published in a forthcoming issue of *Research in Social Work Practice*.

the most commonly referred mental health problem in children and adolescents, accounting for between one third to one half of clinic referrals (Kazdin, 1987). Despite these prevalence rates, Peters (1991) reports a large-scale Canadian epidemiological study, indicating that only about 20% of children with conduct problems had obtained services in the last 6 months.

Effective treatment of child conduct disorders, given that early disruptive problems portend increased risk for antisocial behaviors, is crucial in adolescence and adulthood (Conduct Problems Prevention Research Group [CPPRG], 1992; Hinshaw & Anderson, 1996). Next to intelligence, aggression appears to be one of the most stable traits (Kazdin, 1987). Prospective longitudinal research shows that male childhood aggression predicts violence and criminal behavior in young adults, as well as substance abuse and unemployment (Offord & Bennett, 1994). Tremendous costs are incurred at the societal level in terms of property destruction, law enforcement, remedial education, and mental health services, particularly when antisocial behavior continues into adulthood, as it appears to do in about half of cases (Kazdin, 1997; Prinz & Miller, 1991). In addition, there are the more personal costs involved with the emotional and physical harm to victims of antisocial behavior and the distress that behavior-disordered youth and their families experience (CPPRG, 1992; Kazdin, 1997; Prinz & Miller, 1991). Because of the potential for serious consequences, the need to understand and apply effective treatment for early behavior problems has never been more urgent (Miller & Prinz, 1990).

DEVELOPMENTAL PERSPECTIVE

Viewed through a developmental perspective, conduct problems arise out of the unique developmental demands of each stage and the differing requirements from the major socializing institutions with which children interact (Forehand & Wierson, 1993; Patterson, DeBaryshe, & Ramsey, 1989). In the first section of this chapter, the possible progression of antisocial behaviors will be discussed for the preschool-age and then the school-age child, followed by the treatment outcome research in each of these areas. (For adolescent conduct disorders and juvenile offending, see Chapter Six.)

PRESCHOOL

At the preschool level, a temperamentally difficult child may stimulate coercive parenting interactions. Such a child may be unusually irritable or hyperactive as a result of neuropsychological sensitivity of the central nervous system. Research posits a variety of hypotheses to explain the development of these sensitivities, such as heredity, birth complications, or exposure to toxins (Moffitt, 1993). Caretakers find bonding more of a challenge with a temperamentally difficult child, compromising a secure attachment (Greenberg, Speltz, DeKlyen, & Endriga, 1991; Speltz, Greenberg, & DeKlyen, 1990). Although behavioral theory has been the dominant explanation for the development of early conduct problems, the importance of attachment has also been discussed (e.g., Greenberg et al., 1991).

According to attachment theory, which has been influenced by psychoanalytic, object relations, and ethological theories (Bowlby, 1973, 1980), the caretaker must recognize the child's signals and respond appropriately to the infant's physical and emotional needs in order for the child to view the self as worthy. In essence, the early infant-parent bond forms the basis for expectancies about social interaction and affects all subsequent relationships (Easterbrooks, Davidson, & Chazan, 1993). Unavailable, inconsistent, or rejecting caretakers compromise a child's ability to internalize a working model of a self capable of regulating behavior. In addition, this theory explains behavior problems as a way for the child to seek attention or gain closeness to a caretaker who fails to respond to other cues.

However, empirical work linking attachment style and preschool conduct problems has demonstrated inconsistent findings (Greenberg et al., 1993). This may be due in part to the variations in samples across studies, which have included the extent of internalizing versus externalizing problems, referral source (clinic, nonclinic), and the attachment classification system used. The conclusion at this point is that attachment might play a role in the development of some behaviors in some samples. By the same token, other factors also clearly interact with attachment to determine risk: child temperament, child gender, parental practices, and family ecology.

A behavioral conceptualization of conduct problems involves the normal development of autonomy in children between the ages of 18 months and 2 years. Children at this age struggle to balance conflicting desires between dependence on the parent and increased self-regulation, which often results in noncompliance and other problematic behaviors (Forehand & Wierson, 1993). Further, 2- to 3-year-olds have developed sufficient cognitive capacity so they are able to make basic causal connections between behaviors and their consequences. This increased cognitive capacity means children learn that their deviant and noncompliant behavior gains them attention, however negative, leading to coercive interactions between parent and child.

Coercive interactions are explained in terms of behavioral theory, specifically operant conditioning (Patterson, 1982b; Patterson et al, 1989). The central concept of operant conditioning involves *reinforcement*, defined as a consequence of an event which increases the likelihood of that response. *Positive reinforcement* occurs when parents attend to child deviant behaviors rather than prosocial behaviors, thus increasing the likelihood of future deviant behavior. *Negative reinforcement*, a response that terminates an aversive event, also plays a role. If a parent escalates into harshness and the child ceases the noxious behavior, the parent's harsh behavior is negatively reinforced. At the same time, if a child noncomplies with parental requests, and the parent terminates the request, the child's noncompliant behavior is negatively reinforced. In addition, in such a household, it is likely that the child will observe the parents engaging in coercive processes. *Vicarious learning* then takes place as this behavior is modeled for the child (Forehand & Long, 1988).

School-Age

As the conduct-disordered child grows older, the family may continue to be characterized by escalating coercive interactions (Patterson, 1982a; Patterson et al., 1989). Behavioral theorists further posit that parents of conduct-disordered children act in an indiscriminant fashion with their children (Dumas, 1990; Dumas, Serketich, & LaFreniere, 1995; Wahler & Dumas, 1989, 1987). This inconsistency, inherently noxious, stimulates children to react in coercive ways so their parents will react in a predictable, albeit negative, manner (Wahler & Dumas, 1986).

As these coercive interchanges continue, parents may avoid the negative emotions engendered by such exchanges, preferring instead that their child spend time away from the home. This rejection and avoidance of the child further erode discipline and supervision (Capaldi & Patterson, 1994). Reid (1993) reviews research on the role that coercive parenting and lack of supervision may play in the development conduct disorder. By the time the child reaches foutth grade, coercive parenting practices and poor supervision account for about 50% of the variance in conduct problems displayed in fifth grade and in both self-report and official data on seventh grade juvenile offending.

During school-age, the mastery of school and other social settings represents the child's central task. Unfortunately, the child who has been trained in coercive exchanges at home and has received little support for academic achievement enters school ill-prepared, and performance suffers (CPPRG, 1992). Poor performance may lead to frustration, particularly for a child already experiencing impulse problems and aggression. Alienation from the norms of the school system, the major socializing institution at this stage, may also result. By the time such children are about 10 to 11 years of age, they bond together in deviant peer groups (McMahon, 1994).

Environmental factors also enter into consideration. In areas marked by poverty and restricted means to opportunity, higher proportions of individuals seek deviant means to obtain identity and fulfillment (Prinz & Miller, 1991). Widespread community stressors, such as poverty, unemployment, single parenting, and lack of education, further compromise parenting practices (Forehand & Wierson, 1993).

TREATMENT

Assuming that conduct problems in young children are formed and maintained through behavioral contingencies in the family environment, parents are taught how to more effectively demonstrate their influence (Chamberlain & Rosicky, 1995; Miller & Prinz, 1990). Usually, the therapist has no direct intervention with the child (Kazdin, 1993); rather, parents are trained to implement the procedures in the home. Parents are taught the following skills:

1. to behaviorally specify goals for change
2. to track target behaviors
3. to positively reinforce prosocial conduct through the use of attention, praise, and point systems
4. to employ alternative discipline methods, such as differential attention, time out from reinforcement, response cost, and the removal of privileges

For school-age children, in addition to the above skills, parents are taught how to effectively supervise children and to implement problem-solving, negotiation, and contracting strategies (Kazdin, Esveldt-Dawson, French, & Unis, 1987).

This educational material is generally presented through a variety of formats (Miller & Prinz, 1990):

- Didactic instruction
- Interactive discussion
- Modeling
- Role play
- Feedback

Sessions further give parents the opportunity to view how techniques should be implemented, to practice employing methods, and to evaluate the progress of newly learned behaviors in the home (Kazdin, 1993).

A further treatment implication comes from Wahler and Dumas's (1986) formulation of indiscriminate maternal responsiveness. These authors recommend that treatment improve maternal sensitivity so that reactions are more responsive to the child's needs. In addition, since predictability seems important, parents are taught to terminate parent-child disputes quickly, rather than engaging in prolonged interchanges with repeated use of parental warnings that have become predictable (though noxious).

Due to developmental considerations, interventions for school-age children need to be extended beyond home reinforcement programs (McMahon, 1994). Longitudinal evidence and treatment outcome studies indicate that the school-age behavior-disordered child will require interventions in multiple settings and from a variety of agents to seriously impact problem behavior (Reid, 1993). Specifically, children at this stage require reinforcement systems at school so that behavioral and academic competencies can be built and relationship problems with peers can be addressed. Knowledge of development needs to be taken into account with such programs. For instance, because children before the third grade cannot cognitively broach the time span between behavior performed at school and reinforcement occurring later at home, separate reinforcement programs at home and at school are crucial prior to this age level (Forehand & Wierson, 1993). As the child develops and succeeds at externally controlled programs, parent training and classroom management can segue into those that are more internally based, such as problem-solving programs (McMahon, 1994).

To gain an understanding of effective family interventions in alleviating child behavior problems, the next part of this chapter will comprehensively review the treatment outcome studies in this area. Studies reviewed will be those published in academic journals from 1985 and on, as this reflects current social conditions. The emphasis is on treatment of problems that have already occurred, rather than on prevention studies targeting at-risk behaviors (e.g., Dishion, Patterson, & Kavanagh, 1992; Tremblay et al., 1992). Although some treatment outcome studies simply require that parents were seeking assistance for child noncompliance and disruptive behavior problems (e.g., Dishion et al., 1992; Holden et al., 1990; Mullin, Quigley, & Glanville, 1994; Routh, Hill, Steele, Elliott, & Dewey, 1995), most used the psychiatric diagnostic disorders of oppositional defiant disorder and conduct disorder as criteria for inclusion. Therefore, a brief description of oppositional defiant disorder and conduct disorder will follow.

Oppositional defiant disorder is represented by a pattern of angry, defiant, and disobedient behavior toward those in authority for at least the last 6 months (APA, 1994). In about one quarter of cases, youth with oppositional disorder end up developing more serious behavioral problems in the form of conduct disorder (Hinshaw & Anderson, 1996). Conduct disorder is characterized by a pattern of antisocial behavior in which violations of the rights of individuals and/or societal rules occur. The following four main types of behaviors are described:

1. aggressive conduct that causes or threatens harm to other people or animals
2. nonaggressive conduct that causes property loss or damage
3. deceitfulness or theft
4. serious violations of rules

Using this screening criteria, studies were gathered and summarized according to length and intensity of treatment, design, sample, measures used, key findings, and limitations. As can be seen from Tables 3.1 and 3.2, the majority of the family treatment studies are based on behavioral theory.

Discussion of studies will first open with results of a meta-analysis in the area of parent training (Serketich & Dumas, 1996). A meta-analysis provides a quantitative analysis of an accumulated body of knowledge, and its contributions to psychotherapy outcome research have been enumerated (Kazdin, 1994). Results of treatment outcome studies will then be discussed according to whether they are categorized as involving either preschool or school-age children. Following the reviews in each area, research and service delivery recommendations for social work will be explored.

FINDINGS OF OUTCOME STUDIES ON PARENT TRAINING

Results of a Meta-Analysis

The meta-analysis that has been conducted in this area combines outcome studies with three age groups: preschool, school-age, and adolescent youth (Serketich & Dumas, 1996). Only methodologically strong studies, those that included both an experimental and a control group, were used in the meta-analysis, and these comprised 36 trials. Dependent variables included child outcomes, parental report of child behaviors, teacher report, behavioral observation, and parental adjustment. Effect sizes by child, parent, teacher, and trained observer reports further indicated that the average child whose parent had attended training had improved from 77% to 81% over those who had undergone an alternative intervention or those who had been placed in a control group. Although parental adjustment did not show as consistently outstanding effects, participants in parent training demonstrated an improved adjustment of 67% over parents who were not involved in such training. In sum, families undergoing behavioral parent training improved over those who did not receive such training.

FAMILY TREATMENT FOR PRESCHOOL BEHAVIOR PROBLEMS

The only type of empirically validated family treatment for preschool-age behavior problems involve the training of parents in behavioral principles (*see* Table 3.1). Within the behavioral parent training model, however, different formats are applied, along with the use of various supplemental curriculums. The following sections will be organized according to these different formats: 1) programs based on modeling theory (e.g., Webster-Stratton, 1990, 1992; Webster-Stratton, Hollinsworth, & Kolpacoff, 1989); 2) programs based on live training of parents (e.g., Forehand & Long, 1988; McNeil, Eyberg, Eisenstadt, Newcomb, & Funderburk, 1991); and 3) programs with supplemental components to address lack of social support and deficts in cognitive skills.

Videotape Modeling

The parent training series with modeling theory as its basis involves a program developed by Webster-Stratton (e.g., Webster-Stratton, 1991). Behavioral techniques for the parents of children ages 3 to 8 are modeled through brief videotaped vignettes in the context of a discussion group. Discussion revolves around the correct implementation of techniques by involving parents in problem-solving, role playing, and rehearsal.

The research on the Webster-Stratton series (e.g., Webster-Stratton, 1992; Webster-Stratton, Kolpacoff, & Hollingworth, 1988) has been commended for a number of strengths (Serketich & Dumas, 1996):

1. random assignment to comparative treatment conditions (videotape behavioral parent training and group discussion series; individually administered videotape series; group discussion training) and a waiting-list control group
2. data on child behaviors are from varied sources (parents, teachers, blind observation coders)

3. data on attrition and family characteristics, such as family structure, parental behavior, stress, and personal and marital distress, included
4. follow-up information (up to 3 years) has been provided

The empirical work has supported the use of the videotape training series. At posttest, subjects in all three treatment groups, the videotape and group discussion, the individually administered videotape training, and the group discussion, demonstrated positive improvements in terms of parent ratings of child behaviors and in some of the observed behavioral interactions, but the videotape discussion group surpassed the other conditions in certain areas (Webster-Stratton et al., 1988). Compared to the waiting-list control condition, the group videotape discussion produced significantly reduced mothers' parenting stress, increased the use of praise statements by parents, and, according to fathers, decreased the intensity of child problems.

At 3-year follow-up, positive results in terms of reduced child behavior problems and increased prosocial behaviors were retained by all three treatment groups when compared to the waiting-list control group at pretest (Webster-Stratton, 1990). However, only in the combination package (videotape and group discussion) did child behaviors and parental adjustment continue to maintain improvements; the other treatment conditions demonstrated a significant increase in child behavior problems.

Therefore, it appears that over time, the videotape training series in the context of a group service delivery format offers more benefits in terms of both child and parent adjustment. It must be recognized, however, that the Webster-Stratton studies have been conducted in university settings, which, in part, has contributed to the methodological rigor of the work. Meta-analyses of psychotherapy treatment outcome studies have consistently shown that interventions conducted in university laboratories produce stronger effects than interventions conducted in conventional clinic settings (Weisz, Weiss, & Donenberg, 1992).

In response to the need to further evaluate clinic research (Weisz et al., 1992), Taylor, Schmidt, Pepler, and Hodgins (1998) compared the Webster-Stratton videotape series to eclectic treatment, including ecological, solution-focused, cognitive-behavioral, family systems, and popular-press parenting approaches. At 4-month posttest, the videotape training series showed more positive results in reducing child behavior problems than the eclectic treatment, although the latter condition still produced gains over the waiting-list control. When results were examined in terms of clinical significance, 41% of mothers in the videotape condition still demonstrated problems of a clinical nature,

TABLE 3.1 Preschool Conduct Problem Family Intervention Studies

AUTHOR/MODEL	DESIGN/SAMPLE	MEASURES	RESULTS	LIMITATIONS
Brody & Forehand (1985)	Quasi-experimental, comparing high and low marital satisfaction mothers $N = 24$ mother-child pairs referred to a university psychology clinic for child noncompliant behavior mean age of child = 62.2 mos; 14 males, 10 females; mean SES = middle class	Coded mother-child interactions; Locke Marital Adjustment Test; Parent Attitude Test	While mothers in both groups perceived their children as better adjusted after treatment, when marital distress is present, targeted behaviors improved, but changes did not generalize to nontargeted behaviors; program had positive effect on marital adjustment of mothers in distress	Lack of information on race; small sample size; lack of no-treatment control; no follow-up
Cunningham, Bremner, & Boyle (1995) Large-Group Community-Based vs. Individual Parent training 11–12 sessions	Experimental, random assignment to 1) community-based, large-group parent training, 2) individual parent training held at clinic, or 3) waiting-list control, pretest, posttest, follow-up (at 6 mos 76% completed)	Screening and outcome: Home Situations Questionnaire Outcome: Weschler Preschool and Primary Intelligence Scale; General Functioning Scale of the Family	Immigrant and English-as-a-second-language families, and parents of children with severe behavior problems were significantly more likely to enroll in community groups than clinic individual parent training	Programs differ along 2 dimensions: group vs. individual, community vs. clinic; therefore, confound of dimensions; both treatment conditions also had a child social skills program offered

continued

TABLE 3.1 *(continued)*

AUTHOR/MODEL	DESIGN/SAMPLE	MEASURES	RESULTS	LIMITATIONS
	$N = 150$ Canadian families selected from every junior kindergarten class in one city screened for home behaviors problems; children's mean age = 4.5	Assessment Device; Social Provisions Scale; Beck Depression Inventory; Achenbach Child Behavior Checklist; Parenting Sense of Competence Scale; enrollment & adherence in treatment	Parents in community groups reported greater improvements in behavior problems at home and better maintenance of these gains at 6-mo follow-up, and these groups were more cost effective	concurrently but no information provided as to how many children participated in this possible confound; limited demographic information
Dadds & McHugh (1992) Behavioral group	Quasi-experimental, pretest, posttest, follow-up (6 mos), randomization to parent-only or parent and ally group	Family Observation System; Revised Behavior Problem Checklist; Beck Depression Inventory; Perceived Social Support; Parent Daily Report	Significant statistical improvement for both groups but only 50% when clinical significance considered; improvements maintained at follow-up; no difference between groups, although social support from friends strongest predictor of improvement	Small sample size; no control group; lack of information on race
6 weeks	$N = 22$ single-parents; majority female and low SES from Australia 68% boys, 31% girls; Mean age of child: 4.5 yrs			
	Children sought treatment at clinic to meet criteria for ODD or CD. Quasi-experimental			

Study	Design/Sample	Measures	Results	Limitations
Dadds et al. (1987) Parent training (6 sessions) and Partner support training (6 sessions)	design, assigned to marital discord and no-marital-discord groups based on Locke Wallace Marital Adjustment Test, then randomized to child-parent management training (CMT) only or to parent-training and partner support training, pretest, posttest/ follow-up (6 mos) $N = 24$ middle-class families with 4- and 5-yr-olds who met criteria for ODD and CD. Recruited from newspaper solicitation (Australia)	Marital problems screened—Locke Wallace Adjustment Test Family Observation System; Child Behavior Checklist	When maritally discordant group received no marital intervention, they showed relapse at 6-mo follow-up particularly on parent ratings of child behavior and marital satisfaction rather than on observational assessment in contrast to the maritally discordant group who also received partner support training and the two maritally nondiscordant groups	Lack of no-treatment control; small sample size; lack of specification of posttest time period; no information on race and gender
Forehand & Long (1988) Parent training (average 9 sessions)	Long-term follow-up of parent training group that had met at least 4 1/2 yrs earlier (when child was between 2 and 7) and whose child was now between 11 and 14 yrs;	Parent Attitude Test; Beck Depression Inventory; Locke-Wallace Marital Adjustment Test; Parent's Consumer Satisfaction	Few significant differences between groups except that parents who received parent training reported poorer relationships with their children than did parents in com-	Attrition bias since follow-up occurred for only about 50% of sample; parents who had undergone parent training had sought additional treat-

continued

TABLE 3.1 (*continued*)

AUTHOR/MODEL	DESIGN/SAMPLE	MEASURES	RESULTS	LIMITATIONS
	21 out of 43 (49%) parents were contacted and agreed to participate compared with "normal" community sample (21 youths never referred for treatment, matched on age, gender, and SES)	Questionnaire; clinic and home-coded observations Follow-up measures: Revised Behavior Problem Checklist; Issues Checklist; Conflict Behavior Questionnaire; Children's Depression Inventory; Perceived Competence Scale for Children; Rating Scale of Child's Actual Competence; Academic grades; Parent Competency Inventory; Beck Depression Inventory; Dyadic Adjustment Scale; O'Leary-Porter Scale; Observational ratings; Consumer satisfaction measure	parison group; adolescents from parent training group also had a significantly lower grade point average than the comparison group	ment for their child in about $1/3$ of cases

Long et al. (1994)	Continued long-term follow-up of above (14 yrs after treatment) with matched community comparison group $N = 26$ youth White; middle-to-lower-middle-class SES; 65% males, 35% females; majority married	*Relationship with parents*: Conflict Behavior Questionnaire *Delinquency*: self-report measure from National Youth Survey; Michigan Alcohol Screening Test *Emotional adjustment*: Rosenberg Self-Esteem Scale; Brief Symptom Inventory *Academic achievement*	Responders to long-term follow-up were of higher SES; few differences found between experimental and control groups
Holden et al. (1990) Individual mother-child sessions (20 min 2 times/week) and weekly parent support group Uses former graduates of program to serve as instructors	Multiple baseline $N = 96$ mothers who completed treatment 114 boys, 44 girls; age = 3 yrs; enrolled in Early Intervention Project; 66% White, 18% Hispanic, 7% African American; educational level = 1 yr college; range of income (32% on AFDC, 31% earned more than $30,000/yr)	Behavioral observation of child cooperative and oppositional behaviors during mother-child play sessions	High dropout (68% completed); improvement found in child cooperation over time Since subjects were enrolled in Early Intervention Project for 3 yrs, unknown if other interventions involved; no comparison or control group; results described in terms of percentages only; no standardized measures

continued

TABLE 3.1 *(continued)*

AUTHOR/MODEL	DESIGN/SAMPLE	MEASURES	RESULTS	LIMITATIONS
McNeil et al. (1991) Parent-Child Interaction Therapy 14 sessions	Quasi-experimental, pretest, posttest, Comparison groups (treatment, normal classroom, and untreated school children with behavioral problems) $N = 30$ children referred from school; mean age = 4 yrs, 8 mos; majority male and White	Dyadic Parent-Child Interaction Coding System; Eyberg Child Behavior Inventory; Classroom Coding System; Revised Conners Teacher Rating Scale; Sutter-Eyberg Student Behavior Inventory; Walker-McConnell Test of Children's Social Skills.	Treatment children significantly improved both statistically and clinically on conduct problems but not on hyperactive/distractibility symptoms	Non-random assignment; small sample size; lack of information on SES
Funderburk et al. (1998) Parent-child interaction therapy 14 sessions	12- and 18-mo follow-up of McNeil et al. (1991) Treatment group = 12 males 1% ODD, 58% ODD & ADHD, 25% ODD, ADHD, & CD	Eyberg Child Behavior Inventory; Revised Conners Teacher Rating Scale; Sutter-Eyberg Student Inventory; Walker-McConnell Scale of Social Competence and School Adjustment: A Social	At 12 mos, parent-child interaction group maintained improvement on observed measures, teacher ratings, and social competence to the point where conduct problems and social competence were within normal ranges. At 18	Small sample size for treatment group, particularly with so many dependent variables; because of absences & problems with teacher participation, not all treatment children included in follow-up analysis);

continued

Study	Design/Sample	Measures	Results	Limitations
	Control group $N = 72$ 1) low problem group; 2) average group; and 3) behavior problem group mean age at 12-mo follow-up = 6 yrs, 2 mos mean age at 18-mo follow-up = 6 yrs, 8 mos	Skills Rating Scale for Teachers; Classroom Coding System	mos, while parent-child interaction group still showed gains in compliance, on most other measures, declines had occurred to the point of pretest levels.	
Eisenstadt et al. (1993) Parent-child Interaction Therapy 14 weeks total, 7 weeks each for parent-interaction and child-interaction	Quasi-experimental, randomized to either an initial stage of child-centered or parent-centered training, pretest, posttest (both at 7 weeks to examine differential effectiveness of components of treatment and at 14 weeks), follow-up (6 weeks) $N = 24$ families (out of 31 families who began treatment) referred to psychology clinic	Eyberg Child Behavior Inventory; Child Behavior Checklist; Werry-Weiss-Peters Activity Rating Scale; Parenting Stress Index; Therapy Attitude Inventory; Pictorial Scale of Perceived Competence and Social Acceptance for Young Children; Dyadic Parent-Child Interaction Coding System	Parent-interaction training group significantly improved over child-interaction group on child compliance and reduced disruption in both home and clinic settings; no significant differences between groups at reducing internalizing problems, improving nonverbal affection, or child self-esteem.	Lack of no-treatment control; small sample size; differential dropout for parent-interaction group (more dropout with this group), so results for follow-up not reported

TABLE 3.1 *(continued)*

AUTHOR/MODEL	DESIGN/SAMPLE	MEASURES	RESULTS	LIMITATIONS
	38% ODD & ADHD, 25% ODD, 21% ADHD & CD, 13% ADHD, 4% CD			
	Mean family income = $18,674; 33% subsisted on welfare; 46% father-absent; in each group, 25% fathers participated in treatment; 92% boys; 88% White; mean age = 4.5 yrs			
Brestan et al. (1997) Parent-child Interaction Therapy Mean number of treatment sessions = 13.8	Quasi-experimental, randomization to experimental or waiting-list control, pretest, posttest $N = 30$ siblings of children referred for disruptive behavior (Oppositional Defiant Disorder, 18 also comorbid for ADHD)	Wonderlic Personnel Test; Peabody Picture Vocabulary Test—Revised; Eyberg Child Behavior Inventory	Compared to siblings in waiting-list control group, fathers reported untreated siblings as having decreased problem behaviors; mothers rated siblings' behavior as less of a problem	Small sample size; no behavioral observation system; groups unequal on race (number of African Americans differed between groups)

	referred children: 25 boys, 5 girls; mean age = 4.53 yrs		
	siblings: 19 boys, 11 girls; mean age = 5.80 yrs		
	mean Hollingshead = 33.07; educational level—at least some college; about 50% 2-parent families; White = 70%; African American = 20%; Hispanic = 7%		High dropout; not all completed 4-mo follow-up
Schuhmann et al. (1998) Parent-child Interaction Therapy treatment time unlimited but average number of sessions = 13	Quasi-experimental, randomization to treatment or waiting list control, pretest, posttest, follow-up (4 mos) N = 64 children referred to clinic	Dyadic Parent-Child Interaction Coding System-II; Eyberg Child Behavior Inventory; Parenting Stress Index; Parental Locus of Control Scale; Peabody Picture Vocabulary Test-	high dropout (34%) _For behavior observations:_ increased description of child's behavior, praise, child compliance, and decreased criticism compared to waiting-list control

continued

TABLE 3.1 *(continued)*

AUTHOR/MODEL	DESIGN/SAMPLE	MEASURES	RESULTS	LIMITATIONS
	Criteria: 1) ODD diagnosis (33% ODD, 45% ADHD & ODD, 20% CD & ADHD, 2% CD & ODD); 2) hyperactivity medication dosage constant	Revised; Beck Depression Inventory; Dyadic Adjustment Scale; Therapy Attitude Inventory; Wonderlic Personnel Test	*Parental perceptions of child behaviors* had improved to normal range compared to waiting list group, which was still in clinical range	
	Mean age of child = 59.2 mos; 81% boys; 77% White, 14% African American, 9% Hispanic, Asian, or mixed; mean Hollingshead = 35; 62% 2-parent homes; 43 mothers, 22 fathers		*Parental adjustment:* parental locus of control increased and stress decreased For 25 families with follow-up data available: all had retained improvements	

Serketich & Dumas (1996) Behavioral Parent Training	Meta-analysis of 26 studies	Across different outcome measures, whether child behavior was evaluated by parents or observers, the average child whose parents participated in parent training was better adjusted after treatment than approximately 80% of children whose parents did not; Children whose parents participated in parent training were better adjusted at school after treatment than three quarters of their peers whose parents did not. Parents who participated in parent training were better adjusted themselves at the end of the intervention than two thirds of parents who did not	Small sample sizes in studies; Only a small percentage of studies examined comparative treatment conditions; only a few controlled studies reported follow-up

continued

TABLE 3.1 *(continued)*

AUTHOR/MODEL	DESIGN/SAMPLE	MEASURES	RESULTS	LIMITATIONS
Problem-solving training in addition to Webster-Stratton's videotape behavioral training Taylor et al. (1998)	Experimental, randomization to 1) parenting-skills groups (10 hrs) with adjunctive training in problem-solving (6 hrs); 2) parenting-skills group with facilitated discussion; or 3) waiting-list attention control (6 hrs of therapist-faciliatated discussion focusing on how parents might apply skills learned to actual child problem behaviors), pretest, posttest, follow-up (8–10 weeks) 126 parents randomly assigned to treatment conditions; N = 53 parents completed posttest; mean age of target child = 6.1 yrs; 57% boys, 43% girls	Eyberg Child Behavior Inventory; Parent Identified Problems Scale; Parenting Situation Test; Parent Behavior Inventory—Part II; Parent Attitude Test; Parenting Stress Index—Parent Domain	Dropout high: Out of 126 parents who showed interest in program, 64% participated in pretest, 42% completed posttest, 23% completed follow-up; effect of supplementary package on parental attitudes did not enhance effect of parent training at follow-up	

Taylor et al. (1998) Parent Training (groups met for 2 1/4 hrs weekly for average of 10 weeks) Eclectic individual with some groups additionally—average 8 hrs	Experimental, randomization to Webster-Stratton videotape training group, eclectic treatment, or waiting-list control, pretest, posttest (4 mos) N = 108 families contacting clinic (Canada) for conduct problems or difficulties parenting a child mean age = 5.6 yrs; 74% boys; 36% single-parent; 27% lived in subsidized housing; 30% below poverty line; median income = $30,000	Eyberg Child Behavior Inventory; Child Behavior Checklist; Parent Daily Telephone Report; Achenbach Teacher Report Form; Matson Evaluation of Social Skills with Youngsters; Beck Depression Inventory; Dyadic Adjustment Scale; Support Scale; Brief Anger-Aggression Questionnaire; Therapy Attitude Inventory	Videotape training session more effective than eclectic treatment in reducing child behavior problems according to maternal reports and was more satisfying to mothers as well as producing mental health benefits for parents although eclectic treatment also showed gains (mothers reported fewer child behavior problems than waiting-list control)	Groups co-led by Ph.D. level psychologists whereas therapists conducting eclectic treatment (not controlled for level of education of therapist); no follow-up
Webster-Stratton (1985b) Behavioral Parent training (9 weeks)	Expost facto quasi-experimental design, comparing father-involved and father-absent families, 3- to 4-	Achenbach Child Behavior Checklist; Eyberg Child Behavior Inventory; home observations coded by Dyadic	Although both groups showed improvement, involved fathers/ boyfriends at posttest and 1 yr perceived their	Father-involved families confounded with income with these families reporting a higher income; lack of a control

continued

TABLE 3.1 (*continued*)

AUTHOR/MODEL	DESIGN/SAMPLE	MEASURES	RESULTS	LIMITATIONS
	week baseline, posttest, follow-up (3 mos, 1 yr) $N = 30$ from pediatric hospital 70% boys; mean age = 60.2 mos; lower-middle class to lower-class SES	Parent-Child Interaction Coding System; Consumer Satisfaction Questionnaire	children as having significantly fewer and less intense behavior problems	group; lack of information on race
Webster-Stratton, Kolpacoff, & Hollingsworth (1988) Treatment conditions had 10–12 sessions	Experimental, randomization to 1) group discussion videotape modeling training; 2) individually administered videotape modeling training; 3) group discussion training; 4) waiting-list control, pretest, posttest (1 mo after termination) $N = 114$ families	*Parent perception of child adjustment:* Child Behavior Checklist; Eyberg Child Behavior Inventory *Mother observations:* Parent Daily Reports *Parent personal adjustment:* Parenting Stress Index *Home observations:* Dyadic Parent-Child Interaction Coding Systems	Dropouts more likely from group discussion than 2 videotape conditions; for mothers, all 3 treatment conditions resulted in improvements in maternal perception of child behaviors; for fathers, same improvements found but particularly for videotape conditions; while fathers from all 3 treatment condi-	

continued

	69% boys, 31% girls; mean age = 4 yrs, 6 mos; 69.3% were married, 30.7% single; broad range of income represented	*Teacher perceptions of child adjustment:* Behar Preschool Behavior Questionnaire *Social validity:* Consumer Satisfaction Questionnaire	tions showed behavioral improvements; differences seemed to favor combined group discussion regarding maternal stress and paternal stress and paternal reports of child behavior problem intensity, increased both parents' praise statements	
Webster-Stratton et al., (1989)	Reports 1-yr follow-up of Webster-Stratton et al. (1988) above 93.1% (94 mothers and 60 fathers) completed 1-yr follow-up assessments	Achenbach Child Behavior Checklist; Eyberg Child Behavior Inventory; Parenting Stress Index; Behar Preschool Behavior Questionnaire; Parent Daily Report; telephone assessments; home observations using the Dyadic Parent-Child Interaction Coding System; Consumer Satisfaction Questionnaire; Follow-up Satisfaction Questionnaire	All three parent-training programs led to reliable and sustained improvements at 1 yr follow-up for about ⅔ of the sample; 42% of mothers & 54.5% of fathers reported no further complaints, although group discussion & videotape training somewhat superior; most cost-effective self-administered videotape training sustained its effectiveness over time and did not reveal any deterioration, especially for fathers	No discussion of the demographics of the participants

TABLE 3.1 *(continued)*

AUTHOR/MODEL	DESIGN/SAMPLE	MEASURES	RESULTS	LIMITATIONS
Webster-Stratton (1990) Parent training 10 2-hr sessions	3-yr follow-up of Webster-Stratton et al. (1988) $N = 171$ parents who had completed at least 50% of program and posttesting (original sample) 3-yr follow-up: 82% mothers, 73% fathers completed measures (when completers of measures were compared with noncompleters, no differences between groups whether at pre- or posttest) Mean age of child at this point = 7.5		At 3-yr follow-up, while parents from all 3 treatment conditions continued to sustain decreased child behavior problems and increased positive behaviors, only discussion and videotape package combined showed stable improvements, while other 2 conditions indicated an increase in child behavior problems	

while 74% of the eclectic group mothers reported clinical problems. It is possible that a couple of different confounds were operating. For instance, the crucial variable accounting for the differences between treatment groups may have been level of experience, in that Ph.D.-level therapists administered the videotape training as compared to master's-level practitioners, who were responsible for the eclectic treatment. Alternatively, it could have been the difference between group and individual treatment, since most of the "eclectic" treatments were delivered in an individual format. Suggestive, however, is that a standardized parent training series based on modeling and group discussion may present more benefits for the treatment of behavior-disordered children than the usual approaches to such problems in regular clinic settings.

Live Training of Parents

Another type of parent training involves the supervision of parents developing their behavioral skills with their children in the session. A couple of different programs use live supervision with a one-way mirror so that the therapist can monitor progress and coach the parent. Otherwise, parents find it difficult to recognize and change their entrenched interaction patterns. In one model, during beginning sessions, parents are taught how to identify and reinforce their children's appropriate play behaviors through attention and praise (Forehand & McMahon, 1981). In the second phase, parents learn how to issue specific commands and to use time out from reinforcement when misbehavior occurs (Forehand & McMahon, 1981).

This program has been assessed over long-term follow-up: 4 years (Forehand & Long, 1988) and 14 years (Long, Forehand, Wierson, & Morgan, 1994) after treatment lasting an average of 9 weeks. Overall, the children of parents who had received training were now doing as well as a matched community samples. However, attrition for the follow-up sample was about a 50% rate (Long et al., 1994). Therefore, it could be that those who were functioning less well were also those that did not respond to follow-up contact. Further, other variables may have accounted for successful outcomes. For instance, Forehand and Long (1988) reported that one third of the parents had sought additional intervention for their children.

Another program adapted from the Hanf model is called parent-child interaction therapy (Eyberg, 1988). Again, live and immediate coaching and feedback with parents and their children are used. However, parent-child interaction therapy departs from the Hanf model in utilizing traditional play therapy techniques, and it is only when a warm, trusting, mutually rewarding relationship between parent and child has been established that operant behavioral principles are incorporated (Eyberg & Boggs, 1989).

The rationale for the order of the stages is that when parents change their negative perceptions of their children's behaviors and personalities, coercive interactions are also reduced. Further, when the relationship is improved, children find their parents a greater source of positive reinforcement (Eisenstandt, Eyberg, McNeil, Newcomb, & Funderburk, 1993). However, when the premise that the development of a positive parent-child relationship should precede parent training on operant behavioral principles was directly tested (Eisenstadt et al., 1993), results indicated that an initial parent behavioral training stage may improve child compliance and reduce disruptive behavior, both at home and in the clinic, whereas play therapy at the initial stage was not able to produce these kind of effects. Further, both initial sessions of play therapy and operant parent training techniques produced positive effects on maternal stress, child internalizing problems, and self-esteem. The authors, therefore, suggest that behavior problems, especially those that are severe, may best be treated with an initial focus on behavioral methods before the play therapy stage of treatment.

In another study, McNeil et al. (1991) found that at posttest, children who received parent-child interaction therapy significantly improved, statistically and clinically, on conduct problems, but not on hyperactivity/distractibility. Generalization of therapeutic effects to untreated siblings was found in another study according to both paternal (fathers reported sibling problem behaviors as less frequent) and maternal (mothers rated sibling behaviors as less distressing) reports (Brestan, Eyberg, Boggs, & Algina, 1997).

When results of the McNeil et al. study (1991) were tracked into follow-up, at 1-year posttest gains for both behavioral observations of classroom behaviors and teacher ratings were maintained (Funderburk, Eyberg, Newcomb, McNeil, Hembree-Kigin, & Capage, 1998). In addition, social competency was improved to within a normal range, as were conduct problems. However, subjects did not fare as well at the 18-month follow-up (Funderburk et al., 1998). Although subjects retained gains made in compliant behaviors, most of the other measures indicated a return to pretest levels of functioning.

A more recent study also indicated significant gains at 4 months in terms of increasing parent praise, reducing parent critical remarks, increasing child compliance, and improving parental adjustment (Schuhmann, Foote, Eyberg, Boggs, & Algira, 1998). While controls were still in the clinical range on parent-reported child behaviors, parents who had participated in parent-child interaction therapy rated their children within a normal range. This follow-up period is relatively brief, however. It is unknown if changes would fail to persist over time similar to the Funderburk et al. (1998) study.

Summary

In sum, both group and individual parent training approaches have been found effective. In addition to its demonstrated efficacy, a number of other advantages to parent training are apparent (Forehand & Long, 1988). First, consumer surveys indicate that clients are satisfied with the approach. Second, improvement seems to occur after a relatively brief time period (10 to 12 sessions). Third, numerous treatment manuals and training materials are available for use. Fourth, the approach can be competently administered by paraprofessionals, particularly with the younger child. For instance, a meta-analysis of child and adolescent treatment outcome studies indicates that graduate students and trained paraprofessionals (teachers and parents) were more effective with younger than older children (Weisz et al., 1995). Finally, and because of these other advantages, behavioral approaches are less expensive than other traditional forms of child psychotherapy (Serketich & Dumas, 1996).

Despite these advantages, a significant proportion of families fail to respond to parent training. According to Webster-Stratton (1990), between about 30% and 46% of parents show treatment nonresponse with the assumption that certain deficits or stressors impact individuals' abilities to parent in competent ways. To address these problems, adjunctive packages have been developed to supplement parent training (Miller & Prinz, 1990; Reid, 1993), and in the next section, studies examining adjunctive interventions will be explored. These include packages that address the negative social influences, the lack of social support, and the marital problems that afflict many parents of conduct-disordered children and the problem-solving and communication skills deficits of both parents and children. Programs for parents and children will be discussed separately.

Adjunctive Packages

Parent

Negative social environments have been related to poor parent training outcomes. Marital distress and lack of support from partner predicted nonresponse to a videotape behavioral parent training program in a follow-up study of 218 families (Webster-Stratton, 1994). High family violence rates have also been indicated, ranging from 33.8% of mothers (Webster-Stratton, 1994) to 50% of marital couples self-reporting violence in the relationship (Webster-Stratton, 1990).

In order to address these issues, Webster-Stratton designed a cognitive-behavioral supplemental curriculum consisting of 14 sessions for parents with communication, problem-solving, and self-control skills training as its basis. A 1994 study compared the addition of the supplemental package to the original 10-session intervention. Although time in treatment was left uncontrolled, improvements were shown for the supplemental package over basic parent training in the areas of child problem-solving and parent communication, problem-solving, and collaboration skills. However, there was no differential improvement for the supplemental package in terms of marital satisfaction, depression, anger, or stress. In addition, neither parental perceptions of child behavior nor coded home observations of parent-child interactions improved for the supplemental condition over the basic package. Due to the lack of follow-up for the cognitive-behavioral supplemental package, it is unknown if these findings held up over time.

In an earlier study, Spaccarelli, Cotler, and Penman (1992) had also added a six-session course of problem-solving training to the basic Webster-Stratton videotape package. The problem-solving component was found more effective at short-term only, but not at long-term. The results of these two studies (Spaccarelli et al., 1992; Webster-Stratton, 1994) seem to indicate that the extra effort involved in a cognitive-behavioral supplement adds little to a basic parent training package.

The aforementioned cognitive-behavioral packages focused on building skills that would extend to different social situations. Dadds, Schwartz, and Sanders (1987) have more directly focused on developing communication and problem-solving skills between marital partners so that sources of coercion assumed to impact parenting skills were reduced. At 6-month follow-up, mothers with marital problems who received partner support training maintained treatment gains, as did the maritally nondiscordant mothers. However, mothers with marital problems who received parent training only did not. This study suggests that in order to retain treatment improvements, the marital relationship might need special attention. Further support for this hypothesis is provided by Brody and Forehand (1985), who found that generalization of training to behaviors unspecified for intervention did not occur unless the marital relationship was targeted. At the same time, it appears that parent training can also help with the marital relationship (Brody & Forehand, 1985; Webster-Stratton, 1994).

In another approach to targeting the presumed support deficits of parents of behavior-disordered children, Dadds and McHugh (1992) had single-parent mothers invite a supportive person to participate with them in parent training. However, no differential gains were noted for this condition over the regular parent training; both groups improved. While social support from friends was the strongest predictor of improvement, the support did not necessarily need to come from the person receiving training along with the mother.

In a similar vein, Webster-Stratton (1985) examined the effectiveness of parent training when mothers' partners were involved compared to when only mothers were involved in treatment. While income was a confound in that mothers with involved partners also had higher incomes, important gains were realized at 1-year follow-up: Observed mother-child interactions maintained gains, and mothers continued to rate child behavior problems as less frequent. These results suggest the importance of involving mothers' partners in treatment since child behavior contingencies are not typically controlled by only one person in the child's environment.

Child

While the above packages focus on the parent, other programs emphasize the child, with the assumption that a child who has better social skills, problem-solving, and self-control may be easier to parent. Most studies in this area are for school-age children (e.g., Kazdin et al., 1987; Kazdin, Siegel, & Bass, 1992; Pfiffner, Jouriles, Brown, Etscheidt, & Kelly, 1990) since cognitive skills must be sufficiently advanced in order to benefit from such training. For instance, a meta-analysis on cognitive-behavioral interventions with children showed that level of cognitive development was the central mediating variable of treatment performance (Durlak, Fuhrman, & Lampman, 1991). The effect size from treatment for children ages 11 to 13, who are presumably functioning at the formal operations stage, was about twice that of children ages 5 to 11.

In order to compensate for young children's concrete operational thinking style, Webster-Stratton and Hammond (1997) designed a number of contextual supports to aid in children's learning. Their rationale for a videotape training program, for instance, is based on research demonstrating the modeling effects of television viewing, particularly for child aggression. Over 100 vignettes were developed, showing young children and fantasy characters (life-size puppets) in a variety of interpersonal situations that may challenge children with conduct problems. Modeled skills involved the use of social skills, conflict resolution skills, positive attributions, and perspective-taking. Vignettes were viewed in a group setting in which children discussed options the characters had for coping and how they could apply some of the same options to their own behaviors.

When the child cognitive-behavioral training was used in conjunction with parent training and compared to either child cognitive-behavioral or parent training alone, the combination package offered a number of advantages over either child cognitive-behavioral or parent training alone. Different areas were found to be impacted by each program component. While cognitive-behavioral training produced gains in children's problem-solving and conflict management with peers, parent training conditions led to improved parent-child interactions. Advantages were thus posed by the combination package, since these components together resulted in the best overall outcomes at follow-up (Webster-Stratton & Hammond, 1997).

Summary of Adjunctive Packages

In considering the research on adjunctive packages, more advantages seem to be present for a child rather than a cognitive-behavioral parent package, which includes both parent training and cognitive-behavioral training. A further benefit of a child focus is that training can occur while parents are in treatment for child management. This alleviates an additional treatment burden on parents.

While the parent communication, problem-solving, and self-control skills training package produced some beneficial results (Webster-Stratton, 1994), suggestive is that the marital relationship be targeted more directly (Dadds et al., 1987). Future study on adjunctive packages could include the differential effects of such approaches.

In addition, an effort should be made to involve fathers of children and mothers' partners in parent training so that mothers feel supported in their efforts and so that environmental contingencies for the child are consistent. Research could more routinely address the differences in outcome when male parental figures are involved versus when they are not.

FAMILY TREATMENT FOR SCHOOL-AGE BEHAVIOR PROBLEMS

Family treatment outcome research on school-age behavior problems is mainly comprised of behaviorally oriented studies, although a few traditional family therapy approaches have also been examined. Each of these approaches will be explored separately.

Behavioral Theory

In this section on behaviorally oriented family approaches, discussion will first center on programs that use only parent training. Then, in recognition that the school-age, conduct-disordered child might require intensive intervention beyond parent training, discussion of the research in this area also includes cognitive-behavioral treatment as an adjunct to treatment. Studies either compare the effects of parent training to cognitive-behavioral treatment, specifically problem-solving training, or examine supplemental packages in which parent training and problem-solving treatment are combined (*see* Table 3.2).

Parent-Training Only Similar to the area of preschool treatment, when parents of school-age children undergo behavioral parent training, improvements are noted. Short-term (between 10- and 16-week) parenting groups conducted in both England (Routh, Hill, Steele, Elliott, & Dewey, 1995) and Ireland (Mullin, Quigley, & Glanville, 1994) showed reductions in child behavior problem scores (Mullin et al., 1994; Routh et al., 1995) and in maternal adjustment (Mullin et al., 1994) that were sustained for 1-year (Mullin et al., 1994) and 29-month median (Routh et al., 1995) follow-up.

A couple of studies looked at behavioral improvement of children of different age spans (Dishion, Patterson, & Kavanagh, 1992; Ruma, Burke, & Thompson, 1996). The evidence indicates that school-age children can still show gains when their parents undergo, training although Ruma et al. (1996) discussed that older children tended to have more severe problems prior to treatment. In addition, Dishion, Patterson, and Kavanagh (1992) found that dropout was higher for parents of older children (6.5 to 12.5 years) compared to parents of younger children (2.5 to 6.5 years). To make more of an impact on school-age children, several programs have added cognitive-behavioral components.

Parent Training and Cognitive-Behavioral Treatments As discussed, parent training programs in this area frequently make use of cognitive-behavioral supplements. Specifically, problem-solving skills training is used with the assumption that individuals need to better cope with and manage various interpersonal challenges. Studies vary by whether parents or children are targeted for problem-solving training, and these will be examined separately.

Adult Problem-Solving Training Problem-solving training involves educating parents on a series of steps: identifying and defining problems, generating alternatives, making decisions about appropriate alternatives to apply, implementing the decision, and verifying whether problem-solving efforts have worked (Pfiffner et al., 1990). Training targets problematic situations other than child management, such as time management, work problems, and other interpersonal conflicts.

Studies examined the comparative effects of parent training and problem-solving training in both individual (Pfiffner et al., 1990) and group (Magan

& Rose, 1994) settings. Although only two studies exist in this area, it appears that combining parent training and problem-solving improves response over parent training (Pfiffner et al., 1990). When behavioral versus problem-solving skills training were compared, more benefits were found for parent training, although both conditions produced positive change in parental perception of child behavior (Magan & Rose, 1994). The behavioral training, but not the problem-solving condition, improved significantly over the control condition, and declines in parental role play performance were not as marked between posttest and follow-up (3 months) for parent training. However, it also must be noted that comparability between studies might be limited. The Pfiffner et al. (1990) sample comprised low-income, single-parent mothers and was limited to a very small sample size ($N = 11$). The sample for Magan and Rose (1994), although also mainly female, was mainly middle-socioeconomic status. Further, in this latter study, children were not screened for diagnostic disorders for inclusion in the study, whereas the Pfiffner et al. (1990) study required diagnostic criteria. One hypothesis to explain the differing results is that middle-class mothers, due to greater resources, already possess problem-solving skills. Given these differences, it is apparent that more study is needed to determine the differential effectiveness of parent training, problem-solving training, and combined packages for parents with behavior-disordered children.

Child Problem-Solving Training A small body of literature focuses on developing cognitive skills with children. Deficits in cognitive skill are presumed to influence problematic interactions with parents, teachers, and peers. Similar to training with parents, cognitive-behavioral intervention has focused specifically on problem-solving skills. Kazdin et al. (1987) describes a problem-solving model in which children are taught to generate alternative solutions to problems, to consider consequences, and to take the perspective of others. Cognitive and behavioral techniques, such as modeling, role-playing with corrective feedback, and reinforcement involving praise and tokens, are used to develop skills. Parents are also actively involved in the child problem-solving intervention. Parents observe skills training, are instructed on how to prompt and reinforce the child's use of skills, and are given written instructions on how to assist the child with homework assignments.

When this model was combined with parent training and compared against a contact control condition, improvements for the experimental group were sustained at 1-year follow-up. Gains were made not only in targeted areas, but also for child prosocial behavior in both the home and school, and for inter-

TABLE 3.2 Behavioral Family Interventions for School-Age Conduct Problems

AUTHOR/MODEL	DESIGN/SAMPLE	MEASURES	RESULTS	LIMITATIONS
Dishion, Patterson, & Kavanagh (1992) Parent training Individual average treatment time = 17 hrs	Quasi-experimental, comparison of younger children (2.5–6.5 yrs) and older children (6.5–12.5 yrs) $N = 73$ children (originally 87) referred to clinic for antisocial or disruptive behavior problems mean age = 7.5 yrs; 82% boys, 18% girls (no girls in older child sample); 47% headed by single parent	Family Interaction Coding System on 6 home observations	Overall, children improved over parent training; effectiveness of parent training doesn't vary by child's age but dropout was much higher for older children	Treatment took place between 1965 and 1978; lack of control or comparison that received another treatment; only 1 outcome measure; uneven comparison groups in terms of demographics

TABLE 3.2 *(continued)*

AUTHOR/MODEL	DESIGN/SAMPLE	MEASURES	RESULTS	LIMITATIONS
Kazdin et al. (1987) Parent training individual (13 sessions) + problem-solving skills training (20 sessions)	Experimental, randomization to treatment or contact-control, pretest, posttest, follow-ups (4, 8, and 12 mos) 1-yr follow-up: Data available from parents and teachers (82.4%) and children (79.4%) $N = 36$ children from an inpatient treatment program completed experiment; 9 girls, 31 boys; mean age = 10.1; 30% White, 25% African American; 45% from 2-parent families, 55% from single-parent families; median monthly income range = $500–$1000	Parents completed: Child Behavior Checklist Teacher ratings: School Behavior Checklist	Parent training + problem-solving skills showed greater changes at posttest and at 1-yr follow-up; changes generalized from externalizing behaviors at both home and school and to internalizing symptoms, prosocial behavior, and school adjustment; clinically, more children in the combination package were within a normal range of functioning, but at 1-yr, a majority of both the experimental and control group were in the clinical range, according to teacher and parent reports of child behaviors	Hospital milieu (individualized academic activities, structured routines and activities, discussions designed to promote socialization, etc.) might be a possible confound although both treatment and control groups received; because problem-solving and parent training delivered as a package, unknown what contributed to effectiveness

Kazdin et al. (1992) Behavioral & Cognitive-behavioral	Quasi-experimental, pretest, posttest, follow-up (1 yr), randomized to 3 experimental conditions: 1) Problem-solving skills training—25 child sessions 1 hr each week, with intense parent involvement; 2) parent management training—16 sessions for parent over 6–8 mos; 3) combination of above $N = 76$ children from psychiatric clinic completed treatment; Age = 7–13 Gender = apprx. $^3/_4$ male, 1/4 female Race = 69% Anglo, 31% African American SES = median monthly income ($1,000–$1,500)	For child: Child Behavior Checklist, Child Behavior Checklist-Teacher Report Form, Health Resources Inventory, Interview for Antisocial Behavior, Children's Action Tendency Scale, Self-Report Delinquency Checklist, Parent Daily Report For parent: Parenting Stress Index, Beck Depression Inventory	Problem-solving parent training, parent training, and problem-solving + parent training all produced significant gains in child adjustment, prosocial, and externalizing behaviors at home, school, and the community at posttest and 1-yr follow-up; at posttest and follow-up, there were few statistically significant differences between problem-solving and parent training, although problem-solving was favored in terms of school social competence and self-report of externalizing behaviors. Also, the parent training program did not sustain as many improvements at 1 yr	Approximately $^1/_4$ dropped out of treatment

continued

TABLE 3.2 *(continued)*

AUTHOR/MODEL	DESIGN/SAMPLE	MEASURES	RESULTS	LIMITATIONS
Magan & Rose (1994) Problem-solving versus Behavioral Skills Training 8-week group sessions, 2 hrs each session	Experimental design, randomization to behavioral, problem-solving, or control, pretest/posttest/follow-up (3 mos) $N = 56$ recruited from announcements to social service agencies, schools, physicians, and churches and newspaper ads 95% female caretakers; 66% married, 27% divorced, 7% single; mean income = $37,570; 94% White; mean age of child = 7.02; 30% female, 70% male	Revised Behavior Problem Checklist; Social Problem-solving Inventory; behavioral role-play test of parenting skills; observational data on client participation, client attendance, client promptness to sessions, and clients' reports of homework completion	Both groups showed significant improvements in parents' perceptions of children's behavior, with behavioral skills doing somewhat better. Only behavioral skills training showed statistically significant improvements over control. Although parents' role-play performances declined for all groups, the behavioral skills condition declines were less between posttest and follow-up. Also, the clients in the behavioral skills group had better attendance and homework completion	Voluntary population; small sample size; subjects were not screened diagnostically for entry to study

Mullin, Quigley, & Glanville (1994) Group Parent Training program (10 weeks)	Quasi-experimental, experimental and waiting-list control, pretest, posttest, & follow-up (1 yr) $N = 79$ mothers seeking treatment for child behavior problems majority married homemakers; 72% boys, 28% girls; ages 3 mos 14 yrs	Eyberg Child Behavior Inventory; General Health Questionnaire; Texas Social Behavior Inventory; Rosenberg Self-Esteem Inventory	97.2% attendance rate Experimental group improved over control on self-esteem and frequency of child problems; overall, experimental group revealed 36.5% improvement, while control group showed 9.1% improvement; changes maintained at 1 yr follow-up	Average age of child not given; lack of randomization to groups
Pfiffner, Jouriles, Brown, Etscheidt, & Kelly (1990) Intensive Parent Training (ITP) & Parent Training with Social Problem-Solving Skills Training (PTPS)	Quasi-experimental, random assignment to two comparison treatment groups, pretest, posttest & 4 mos follow-up $N = 6$ (ITP) and $N = 5$ (PTPS); Self-referred single-parent families; Children ranged in age from 4–9 (M = 6.8 yrs), 6 females and 5 males; Mothers ranged in age from 24–40 (M = 32 yrs), all had HS diploma, low-income	Achenbach Child Behavior Checklist; Observational measures; & Interobserver agreement	Parent training and parent training + problem-solving skills training families showed significant reductions on maternal perceptions of child behaviors at posttest and follow-up; parent training + problem-solving skills training families displayed on observational measures significant pre-to-post reductions on deviant child behavior	No indication of race/ethnicity. Small sample size

continued

TABLE 3.2 *(continued)*

AUTHOR/MODEL	DESIGN/SAMPLE	MEASURES	RESULTS	LIMITATIONS
Routh, Hill, Steele, Elliott & Dewey (1995) Group Parent Management Training (between 10 and 16 sessions)	Pretest & 13 to 43 mo follow-up (median = 29 mos) $N = 37$ Clinic referrals for child behavior problems Majority mothers; 50% single parents; children < 9 yrs old (average age of interviewed sample = 6.8)	Child Behavior: Eyberg Behavior Inventory Level of maternal psychopathology : General Health Questionnaire Marital harmony: Dyadic Adjustment scale Maternal attachment: Adult Attachment Interview	Dropout: 5% attended less than 25 sessions; 27% attended fewer than 50% of sessions; 43% attended at least 75% of sessions Significant decreases over time on intensity and frequency of problem behavior scores	Average number of sessions attended not given; no comparison/control group; no posttest; mothers only assessed at follow-up; variable followup time

| Ruma, Burke, & Thompson (1996) | Quasi-experimental using archival data, pretest, posttest | Achenbach Child Behavior Checklist | For the total sample, the severity of problem behaviors before treatment was the best predictor of treatment outcomes Older children tended to have more severe behavior problems before treatment, but all groups improved. Adolescents had the lowest rate of clinically significant improvements | Not a control/comparison group; no follow-up |
| Group Parent Training | $N=$ archival data from 304 mothers who attended Common Sense Parenting during 1991 & 1992 in 5 states. At the pre-post analysis, 206 mothers remained. 67% of target children were boys & 33% were girls, age range 2–16 yrs Predominantly White, African American, & Hispanic. Diverse SES & family composition | | | |

nalizing symptoms. Despite these statistically significant improvements, children were still limited in terms of clinical benefits (Kazdin et al., 1987). However, this sample involved children with sufficiently severe behavioral problems to warrant inpatient treatment. In this study, because parent training and problem-solving were combined, it is unknown the crucial components of the program that effected change. To address this limitation, Kazdin et al. (1992) investigated the differential effectiveness of parent training, problem-solving skills training for children, and parent training combined with problem-solving training. The parent training used in this study was, however, much more intensive than traditional programs. Teachers were included in monitoring and evaluating children's academic and behavioral performance and made reports to parents who reinforced progress.

While all three treatment groups made significant child behavior improvements, both at posttest and 1-year follow-up, and in multiple settings (home, school, and the community), the combined treatment produced the greatest impact in terms of both child behavior and parental adjustment. In addition, the combined package resulted in a greater number of children scoring within a normal range of functioning. Although there were few statistically significant differences between parent training and problem-solving, problem-solving showed advantages in the area of social competence at school and reduced aggression and juvenile offending, according to self-reports. In addition, the problem-solving training group was more likely to maintain some of the child behavior improvements at 1-year follow-up.

Summary Combining parent training and parent problem-solving appears to improve response. However, if a choice is offered between parent training and parent problem-solving, behavioral therapy may offer more benefits overall. Similarly, when examining child problem-solving and parent training, combined packages appear to produce the most benefits. Given a choice between parent training and child problem-solving, the problem-solving group appeared to possess certain advantages. Further study needs to compare adult and child problem-solving with the addition of parent training.

Family Therapy

A small body of literature has accumulated on the effectiveness of family therapy approaches to conduct problems in school-age children (*see* Table 3.3). One study examined systems family therapy versus parent training on child oppositional defiant disorder (Wells & Egan, 1988). Systems family therapy assumes that child behavioral symptoms can only be understood in the context of the family. The family therapist seeks to change the structure of the family through its interaction patterns; in this way, the child's symptoms are no longer necessary for the family.

Although no differences were found on parental anxiety, depression, or marital adjustment at posttest, parent training was more effective at reducing child behavior symptoms, according to coded observations (Wells & Egan, 1988). However, the authors recognize that the behaviors coded, parents' ability to attend to and reward child compliance, might have been due to this emphasis in behavioral parent training. The study might have been improved with a standardized checklist of child behaviors so that parental perception of child improvements could be assessed, not only those behaviors targeted by parent training.

There is also one model that works with the entire family over 10 weeks on behavioral techniques for discipline, as well as helping family members with their communication and self-control over thoughts, feelings, and behaviors (Sayger, Horne, & Glaser, 1993; Sayger, Horne, Walker, & Passmore, 1988). The experimental group displayed greater reductions in child behavior problems and family conflict and greater improvements on positive child behavior and family problem-solving over the waiting-list control. Marital satisfaction also improved (Sayger et al., 1993). These gains were maintained at 1 year.

Another study looked at structural family therapy, a particular model within family systems theory with an emphasis on altering the hierarchical structure of the family (Szapacznik et al., 1989). Structural family therapy was compared with individual psychotherapy in a sample of behavior-disordered Hispanic youth. Although both conditions showed improvements regarding child behavior, family functioning for the individual condition deteriorated over time. It is unknown whether this finding is specific to only Cuban-Americans and their families. Implications for research from this study and other recommendations will be explored in the following section.

CONCLUSION AND RECOMMENDATIONS

Behavioral parent training for families with conduct-disordered children has gained substantial empirical support. This emphasis on parent training reflects a general trend in the child and adolescent therapy outcome literature in that behavioral and cognitive-behavioral methods have predominated (accounting for half of all treatment outcome studies) (Kazdin, Ayers, Bass, & Rodgers, 1990). However, many other practice orientations and methods are used with conduct-disordered children in clinical practice. These include other family therapy approaches, as well as psychodynamic therapy, relationship-centered therapy, play therapy, and art therapy (Kazdin et al., 1990). In a review of over two decades' worth of literature, each of these models was the subject of empirical focus in less than 5% of studies (Kazdin et al., 1990).

A research priority, therefore, is to evaluate empirically practice methods that are commonly used in clinic settings and the way treatments are combined in eclectic ways (Kazdin, 1997). The many differences between research and clinic therapy have been delineated: Samples in research tend to be homogeneous, fitting a certain diagnostic criteria, whereas clinic cases are heterogeneous, with many different problems represented; treatment addresses one focal problem in research, whereas a range of problems is targeted for clinic therapy; research therapists usually are trained in specific techniques and are guided through manualized treatment and regular supervision, whereas therapists in clinical practice often do not undergo intensive training, nor do they have the kind of structure and supervision present in research models; finally, due to large multi-problem caseloads and paperwork requirements, therapists in clinical practice are not able to devote themselves to select techniques (Weisz et al., 1992). Given these differences, research must apply itself to identifying how treatment efficacy can be optimized in clinical practice.

A further area deserving of more attention, particularly with caregivers of infants, is attachment-informed interventions, so that parents are more able to appropriately respond to their children in nurturant and affective ways (Fantuzzo, 1990). Such interventions would be at the level of prevention, identifying high-risk samples. An example of an empirically tested program in this area involves mothers seen as at risk for anxious attachment with their children due to stressors associated with low socioeconomic status and recent immigration (Lieberman, Weston, & Pawl, 1991). Program effects included improvements in mother-child interactions and toddler behavior over an untreated control group.

A related recommendation is that approaches such as parent-child interaction therapy (Eyberg, 1988), in which both relationship and behavioral principles are integrated, need to be compared with attachment and behavioral methods. In this way, the essential elements of improving child conduct problems in preschoolers will be better understood.

Future study of these other treatment areas needs to continue the strong methodologies that have informed behavioral and cognitive-behavioral research. These trends include random assignment to comparative treatment conditions, adequate sample sizes, follow-up, and the reporting of sufficient statistical data, including information on attrition.

TABLE 3.3 School-Age Conduct Problems Family Therapy Studies

AUTHOR/MODEL	DESIGN/SAMPLE	MEASURES	RESULTS	LIMITATIONS
Sayger et al. (1988) 10 weeks Social learning + sessions on self-control, and family communication	Experimental, randomization to treatment or waiting-list control, pretest, posttest, follow-up (9 mos; 71% completed) $N = 28$ families completed (out of 37 who started) referred by school for aggression problems in children at home and school; children grades 2–6	Parent: Child Behavior Checklist; Parent Daily Report; Family Problem-Solving Behavior Coding System; Beavers-Timberlawn Family Evaluation Scale; Family Environment Scale Teachers: Daily Behavior Checklist	At posttest, families in experimental condition compared to control group, reported reductions in negative child behaviors and family conflict; increases in positive child behaviors, family cohesion, and total positive family relationships; independent observers rated families as more efficient problem-solvers and less conflictual; teachers reported fewer negative and more positive child behaviors in the classroom; changes maintained at follow-up	Small sample size; lack of demographic information on sample; modality not clear

continued

TABLE 3.3 *(continued)*

AUTHOR/MODEL	DESIGN/SAMPLE	MEASURES	RESULTS	LIMITATIONS
Sayger et al. (1993) Social learning + sessions on self-control, and family communication	Experimental, randomization to treatment or waiting-list control, pretest, posttest, follow-up (9 mo—71% of sample completed), also divided into high and low marital satisfaction groups This analysis involves 17 2-parent families of 37 families who completed treatment Children grades 2–6 referred by school; all male Child age = 11	Parents: Locke-Wallace Marital Adjustment Test; Parent Daily Report, Family Environment Scale; Beck Depression Inventory Teachers: Daily Behavior Checklist	Couples with low marital satisfaction at pretest improved (statistically significant) their satisfaction at both posttest and follow-up; both marital satisfaction groups made significant gains on Total Relationship Score on Family Environment Scale; both marital satisfaction groups improved (statistically significant) on depression scores; regardless of pretreatment levels of marital satisfaction, parents reported significant gains in child positive behaviors and both parents and teachers reported significant decreases in child negative behaviors from pretest and follow-up	71% completed follow-up; lack of demographic information on sample

Szapacznik et al. (1989) Structural Family Therapy	Experimental design randomization to SFT, individual psychodynamic therapy, and recreational control, pretest, posttest, follow-up (1 yr) $N = 69$ Hispanic males, ages 6–12 yrs; mean age = 9 yrs, 2 mos Recruited from school counselors and a media campaign 32% diagnosed as ODD, 30% CD For SES Hollinghead categories III, IV, and V accounted for 75.4% of sample	Behavioral and self report measures: Parents: Revised Child Behavior Checklist, Revised Behavior Problem Checklist Children: Children's Depression Inventory, Children's Manifest Anxiety Scale Psychodynamic child rating scale and structural family system rating	Improvements were for family functioning and individual adjustment for Structural family therapy; while individual adjustment improved, family functioning deteriorated for individual psychodynamic condition	Weren't only looking at antisocial behaviors— subjects were diagnosed with anxiety 30%, adjustment disorders 12%, and 10% other); 80% Cuban antecedent - not sure if could generalize to other Hispanic populations

continued

TABLE 3.3 (*continued*)

AUTHOR/MODEL	DESIGN/SAMPLE	MEASURES	RESULTS	LIMITATIONS
Wells & Egan (1988) Social Learning-based Parent Training & Systems Family Therapy	Quasi-experimental, random assignment to treatment conditions, pretest, posttest $N = 24$ families referred to an outpatient child psychiatry clinic; children were between 3–8 yrs of age	Direct observation using a coding system; Beck Depression Inventory; Spielberger State-Trait Anxiety Inventory; Locke Wallace Marriage Inventory	Social learning condition more effective than Systems therapy in reducing oppositional symptoms. Parent training led to significantly greater improvements in parents' abilities to pay positive attention to their children and to reward compliance than did family therapy. Few differences were noted in the effects of parent-training and family therapy on parent anxiety, depression, and marital adjustment at post-treatment	Lack of control group; small sample size; limited demographic information on sample

A further research recommendation is that attention should be paid not only to the characteristics of therapy but also to child characteristics (Kazdin et al., 1990), such as race and gender (CPPRG, 1992; McMahon & Wells, 1989; Miller & Prinz, 1990). One of the limitations of this literature is the lack of information on race. In addition, when such information is given, the interactional effects of race and intervention are not provided. However, attention to the effectiveness of interventions for families of particular racial groups is crucial, given the diversity of population in the United States (Forehand & Kotchick, 1996). The U.S. Census Bureau (1998) estimates that 17.2% of the U.S. population is composed of ethnic minorities.

In addition, people of ethnic minority, especially Hispanics, African Americans, and Native Americans, are overrepresented among those living in poverty. Indeed, 40% of Hispanic and 42% of African American children live in poverty (Children's Defense Fund, 1997). Poverty, in turn, is related to a lack of available mental health services (Forehand & Kotchick, 1996). Further, the daily stress of poverty involving unemployment, underemployment, the lack of safe child care, and inadequate housing, often in high-crime areas, may not only negatively impact effective parenting, but also inhibit utilization of any available treatment. Finally, individuals living in poverty have restricted opportunities; therefore, they may more often seek out deviant and anitisocial means to obtain identity and fulfillment (Prinz & Miller, 1991). Therefore, attention to socioeconomic conditions and improving employment opportunities, educational levels, housing, and the provision of child care is essential if families are to be meaningfully impacted (Kendziora & O'Leary, 1993; Reid, 1993).

Another child characteristic, gender, deserves special emphasis. Since the onset of puberty tends to mark an increase in the number of girls afflicted with conduct problems, school age becomes a salient period for intervention. However, gender has not been a focus for either research or service delivery. Many studies include only or mostly males. When mixed samples of both boys and girls are present, results are not analyzed separately by gender (McMahon & Wells, 1989). In addition, mental health services drastically underserve females with conduct disorder. Only 7% of adolescent conduct-disordered girls, as compared to 19% of their male counterparts, receive services (Tremblay, 1991).

A main explanation for this lack of attention is that the female presentation of the disorder tends to be less noticeable, given that nonaggressive or covert behaviors are involved (Hinshaw & Anderson, 1996). Hinshaw and Anderson (1996) cite longitudinal research indicating that behavior-disruptive girls commit offenses less often (3.2%) than boys (42%). Conduct disorder in females also co-occurs more frequently with internalizing disorders, such as depression (McMahon, 1994). These gender patterns play themselves out into adulthood. Adult females who were conduct-disordered as adolescents display internalizing disorders, such as anxiety and depression (73%), more often than adult males who were conduct-disordered as boys (26%). In contrast, males who were conduct-disordered as adolescents display externalizing problems, such as substance abuse and antisocial behaviors, more often in adulthood (73%) compared to adult females with adolescent conduct disorder (39%) (Capaldi & Patterson, 1994).

Adolescent behavior-disordered females show higher risk for becoming pregnant and bearing children as teenagers and for single parenting. Given these increased risks, a strong rationale exists for attention to this population, particularly since conduct-disordered mothers exhibit poor parenting practices, marked by coercive interchanges (Capaldi & Patterson, 1994; McMahon, 1994; Tremblay, 1991). In order to prevent perpetuation of conduct disorder between the generations, effective intervention is required. To achieve this objective, an understanding of the developmental progression of the disorder must be uncovered, given that the course and symptoms may be quite different for females than they are for males (McMahon, 1994).

In sum, a strong research tradition needs to be continued so that conduct-disordered children can be treated effectively in clinic settings. In this way, behavior problems can be prevented from extending into both adulthood and the next generation.

SERVICE DELIVERY RECOMMENDATIONS

Because the presence of early conduct problems is predictive of chronic forms of antisocial disorders (Forehand & Long, 1988), a strong case can be made for early screening and intervention. Screening can occur in health settings, such as doctors' offices and health clinics, and at child care facilities and preschools. Preschool teachers, for instance, have been able to reliably pick out children who show problems with their conduct up to 3 years later (Webster-Stratton, 1990). Screening efforts can be coordinated and conducted in a variety of mental health and community settings.

Based on positive results shown with an individually administered videotape program at 1-year follow-up in terms of improved child behavior and reduced physical punishment (Webster-Stratton et al., 1989), one recommendation is that a first line of intervention involve the availability of such an individually administered program. As well as being available in health, mental health, social service, and school settings, major videotape outlets could offer taped training packages as a community service. Free videos could be offered as incentives for parents to prove their assimilation of taped material. Following this first line of intervention, more intensive treatments could be offered for those families requiring additional assistance.

Despite the encouraging results of such behavioral interventions, it appears that about 30% to 46% of families are unable to benefit from short-term treatment (Webster-Stratton, 1990). It must be emphasized that most of the interventions presented in this review are, on average, about 12 weeks in duration. In many cases, this amount of time is insufficient to significantly impact behavior. To address the needs of the substantial proportion of families with an unfavorable treatment response and because of the potentially chronic nature of the disorder, child functioning should be assessed at regular periods, especially at developmental transitions, and further intervention should be offered at such times (Dumas, 1989; Kazdin, 1997).

REFERENCES

American Psychiatric Association. (1994). *Diapnostic and statistical manual of mental disorders* (4th ed.). Washington, D: Author.

Anastopoulos, A. D., Shelton, T. L., DuPaul, G. T., & Guevremont, D. C. (1993). Parent training for attention-deficit hyperactivity disorder: Its impact on parent functioning. *Journal of Abnormal Child Psychology, 21*, 581–596.

Atkeson, B. M., & Forehand, R. (1979). Home-based reinforcement programs designed to modify classroom behavior: A review and methodological evaluation. *Psychological Bulletin, 86*(6), 1298–1308.

Bank, L., Marlowe, J. H., Reid, J. B., Patterson, G. R., & Weinrott, M. R. (1991). A comparative evaluation of parent training interventions for families of chronic delinquents. *Journal of Abnormal Child Psychology, 19*, 15–33.

Barkley, R. A., Guevremont, D. C., Anastopoulos, A. D., & Fletcher, K. F. (1992). A comparison of three family therapy programs for treating family conflicts in adolescents in adolescents with ADHD. *Journal of Consulting and Clinical Psychology, 60*, 450–462.

Baum, C. G., & Forehand, R. (1980). Handling family violence: Situational determinants of police arrest in domestic disturbances. *Law and Society Review, 15*, 317–346.

Bierman, K. L., Miller, C. L., & Stabb, S. D. (1987). Improving the social behavior and peer acceptance of rejected boys: Effects of social skill training with instructions and prohibitions. *Journal of Consulting and Clinical Psychology, 55*, 194–200.

Blakemore, B., Shindler, S., & Conte, R. (1993). A problem-solving training program for parents of children with attention deficit hyperactivity disorder. *Canadian Journal of School Psychology, 9*, 66–85.

Bowlby, J. (1973). *Attachment and loss: Separation* (Vol. 2). New York: Basic Books.

Bowlby, J. (1980). *Attachment and loss: Loss, sadness and depression* (Vol. 3). New York: Basic Books.

Brestan, E. V., Eyberg, S. M., Boggs, S. R., & Algina, J. (1997). Parent-child interaction therapy: Parents' perceptions of untreated siblings. *Child & Family Behavior Therapy, 19*(3), 13–28.

Brody, G. H., & Forehand, R. (1985). The efficacy of parent training with maritally distressed and nondistressed mothers: A multimethod assessment. *Behavioral Research Therapy, 23*, 291–296.

Capaldi, D. M., & Patterson, G. R. (1987). An approach to the problem of recruitment and retention rates for longitudinal research. *Behavioral Assessment, 9*, 169–177.

Capaldi, D. M., & Patterson, G. R. (1991). Relation of parental transitions to boys' adjustment problems: I. A linear hypothesis. II. Mothers at risk for transitions and unskilled parenting. *Developmental Psychology, 27*, 489–504.

Capaldi, D. M., & Patterson, G. R. (1994). Interrelated influences of contextual factors on antisocial behavior in childhood and adolescence for males. In D. C. Fowles, P. Sutker, & S. H. Goodman (Eds.), *Progress in experimental personality and psychopathology research* (pp. 165–198). New York: Springer Publishing.

Chamberlain, P. (1990). Comparative evaluation of specialized foster care for seriously delinquent youths: A first step. *Community Alternatives: International Journal of Family Care, 2*, 21–36.

Chamberlain, P., & Ray, J. (1988). The therapy process code: A multidimensional system for observing therapist and client interactions in family treatment. In R. J. Prinz (Ed.), *Advances in behavioral assessment of children and families* (pp. 189–217). Greenwich: JAI Press.

Chamberlain, P., & Reid, J. B. (1991). Using a specialized foster care model for children and adolescents leaving the state mental hospital. *Journal of Community Psychology, 60*, 252–259.

Children's Defense Fund (1997). *The state of America's children: Yearbook 1997.* Washington, DC: Author.

Cicchetti, D., & Richters, J. E. (1993). Developmental considerations in the investigation of conduct disorder. *Development and Psychopathology, 5*, 331–344.

Conduct Problems Prevention Research Group. (1992). A developmental and clinical model for the prevention of conduct disorder: The FAST Track program. *Development and Psychopathology, 4*, 509–527.

Cunningham, C. E., Bremner, R., & Boyle, M. (1995). Large group community-based parenting programs for families of preschoolers at risk for disruptive behavior disorders: Utilization, cost effectiveness, and outcome. *Journal of Child Psychology and Psychiatry, 36*, 1141–1159.

Dadds, M. R., & McHugh, T. A. (1992). Social support and treatment outcome in behavioral family therapy for child conduct problems. *Journal of Consulting and Clinical Psychology, 60,* 252–259.

Dadds, M. R., Schwartz, S., & Sanders, M. (1987). Marital discord and treatment outcome in behavioral treatment of child conduct disorders. *Journal of Consulting and Clinical Psychology, 55,* 396–403.

Dishion, T. J., Patterson, G. R., & Kavanagh, K. A. (1992). An experimental test of the coercion model: Linking theory, measurement, and intervention. In J. McCord & R. E. Tremblay (Eds.), *Preventing antisocial behavior: Interventions from birth through adolescence* (pp. 153–282). New York: Guilford.

Dishion, T. J., Reid, J. B., & Patterson, G. R. (1988). Empirical guidelines for a family intervention for adolescent drug use. *Journal of Chemical Dependency Treatment, 12,* 189–224.

Dodge, K. A. (1990). Nature versus nurture in childhood conduct disorder: Is it time to ask a different question. *Developmental Psychology, 26,* 698–701.

Dubow, E. F., Huesmann, L. R., & Eron, L. D. (1987). Mitigating aggression and promoting prosocial behavior in aggressive elementary schoolboys. *Behavior Research Therapy, 25,* 527–531.

Dumas, J. E. (1986). Indirect influence of maternal social contacts on mother-child interactions: A setting event analysis. *Journal of Abnormal Child Psychology, 14,* 205–216.

Dumas, J. E. (1989). Treating antisocial behavior in children: Child and family approaches. *Clinical Psychology Review, 9,* 197–222.

Dumas, J. E. (1990). Contextual effects in mother-child interaction: Beyond an operant analysis. In E. A. Blechman (Ed.), *Emotions and the family: For better or for worse* (pp. 155–179). Hillsdale, NJ: Erlbaum.

Dumas, J. E. (1991). Commentary: From simplicity to complexity: Parent training is coming of age. In D. J. Pepler & K. H. Rubin (Eds.), *The development and treatment of childhood aggression* (pp. 331–337). Hillsdale, NJ: Erlbaum.

Dumas, J. E., Gibson, J. A., & Albin, J. B. (1989). Behavioral correlates of maternal depressive symptomatology in conduct disorder children. *Journal of Consulting and Clinical Psychology, 57,* 516–521.

Dumas, J., Serketich, W., & La Freniere, P. (1995). Balance of power: A transactional analysis of control in mother child involving socially competent, aggression, and anxious children. *Jouranl of Abnormal Psychology, 104,* 104–113.

Durlak, J. A., (Fuhrman, T., & Lampman, C. (1991). Effectiveness of cognitive-behavior therapy for maladapting children: A meta-analysis. *Psychological Bulletin, 110,* 204–214.

Easterbrooks, M. A., Davidson, C. E., & Chazan, R. (1993). Psychosocial risk, attachment, and behavior problems among school-aged children. *Development and Psychopathology, 5,* 389–402.

Eisenstadt, T. H., Eyberg, S., McNeil, C. B., Newcomb, K., & Funderburk, K. N. (1993). Parent-child interaction therapy with behavior problem children: Relative effectiveness of two stages and overall treatment outcome. *Journal of Clinical Child Psychology, 22*(1), 42–51.

Estrada, A. U., & Pinsof, W. M. (1995). The effectiveness of family therapies for selected behavioral disorders of childhood. *Journal of Marital and Family Therapy, 21*, 403–440.

Eyberg, S. (1988). Parent-child interaction therapy: Integration of traditional and behavioral concerns. *Child and Family Behavior Therapy*, 10, 22–46.

Eyberg, S., & Boggs, S. R. (1989). Parent training for oppositional-defiant preschoolers. In C. E. Schaefer & J. M. Briesmeister (Eds.), *Handbook of parent training: Parents as co-therapists for children's behavior problems* (pp. 105–132). New York: Wiley.

Fantuzzo, J. (1990). Behavioral treatment of the victims of child abuse and neglect. *Behavior Modification, 14*, 316–339.

Farrington, D. P. (1978). The family backgrounds of aggressive youths. In A. Hersov, M. Berger, & D. Shaffer (Eds.), *Aggression and antisocial behavior in childhood and adolescence* (pp. 73–93). Oxford: Pergamon Press.

Farrington, D. P. (1991). Childhood aggression and adult violence: Early precursors and later-life outcomes. In D. J. Pepler & K. H. Rubin (Eds.), *The development and treatment of childhood aggression* (pp. 5–29). Hillsdale, NJ: Erlbaum.

Feldman, J. M., & Kazdin, A. E. (1995). Parent management training for oppositional and conduct problem children. *The Clinical Psychologist, 48*, 3–4.

Fine, M. J. (1989). *The second handbook on parent education: Contemporary perspectives*. San Diego, CA: Academic Press.

Firestone, P., Crowe, D., Goodman, J. T., & McGrath, P. (1986). Vicissitudes of follow-up studies: Differential effects of parent training and stimulant medication with hyperactives. *American Journal of Orthopsychiatry, 56*, 184–194.

Fonagy, P., & Target, M. (1994). The efficacy of psychoanalysis for children with disruptive disorders. *Journal of American Academy of Child and Adolescent Psychiatry, 33*, 45–54.

Forehand, R., & Kotchick, B. A. (1996). Cultural diversity: A wake-up call for parent training. *Behavior Therapy, 27*, 187–206.

Forehand, R., & Long, N. (1988). Outpatient treatment of the acting out child: Procedures, long term follow-up data, and clinical problems. *Advances in Behavioral Research and Therapy, 10*, 129–177.

Forehand, R. L., & McMahon, R. J. (1981). *Helping the noncompliant child: A clinician's guide to parent training*. New York: Guilford.

Forehand, R., & Wierson, M. (1993). The role of developmental factors in planning behavioral interventions for children: Disruptive behavior as an example. *Behavior Therapy, 24*, 117–141.

Frick, P. J., Lahey, B. B., Loeber, R., Tannenbaum, L., Van Horn, Y., Christ, M. A. G., Hart, E. L., & Hanson, K. (1993). Oppositional defiant disorder and conduct disorder: A meta-analytic review of factor analyses and cross-validation in a clinic sample. *Clinical Psychology Review, 13*, 319–340.

Funderburk, B. W., Eyberg, S. M., Newcomb, K., McNeil, C. B., Hembree-Kigin, T., & Capage, L. (1998). Parent-child interaction therapy with behavior problem children: Maintenance of treatment effects in the school setting. *Child and Family Behavior Therapy, 20*, 17–38.

Goldberg, S., Muir, R., & Kerr, J. (Eds.). (1995). *Attachment theory: Social, developmental, and clinical perspectives.* Hillsdale, NJ: The Analytic Press.

Greenberg, M. T., Speltz, M. L., & DeKlyen, M. (1993). The role of attachment in the early development of disruptive behavior problems. *Development and Psychopathology, 5,* 191–213.

Greenberg, M. T., Speltz, M. L., DeKlyen, M., & Endriga, M. C. (1991). Attachment security in preschoolers with and without externalizing behavior problems: A replication. *Development and Psychopathology, 3,* 413–430.

Grych, J. H., & Fincham, F. D. (1990). Marital conflict and children's adjustment: A cognitive-contextual framework. *Psychological Bulletin, 108,* 267–290.

Hawkins, J. D., Catalano, R. F., Morrison, D. M., O'Donnell, J., Abbott, R. D., & Day, L. E. (1992). The Seattle Social Development Project: Effects of the first four years on protective factors and problem behaviors. In J. McCord & R. Tremblay (Eds.), *The prevention of antisocial behavior in children* (pp. 139–161). New York: Guilford Press.

Hazelrigg, M. D., Cooper, H. M., & Borduin, C. M. (1987). Evaluating the effectiveness of family therapies: An integrative review and analysis. *Psychological Bulletin, 101,* 428–442.

Henggeler, S. W., Borduin, C. M., & Mann, B. J. (1993). Advances in family therapy: Empirical foundations. *Advances in Clinical Child Psychology, 15,* 207–241.

Hinshaw, S. P., & Anderson, C. A. (1996). Conduct and oppositional defiant disorders. In E. J. Mash & R. A. Barkley (Eds.), *Treatment of childhood disorders* (pp. 113–149). New York: Guilford Press.

Holden, G., Lavigne, V. & Cameron, A. (1990). Probing the continuum of effectiveness in parent training: Characteristics of parents and preschoolers. *Journal of Clinical Child Psychology, 19,* 2–8.

Hollon, S. D., & Flick, S. N. (1988). On the meaning and methods of clinical significance. *Behavioral Assessment, 10,* 197–206.

Horn, W. F., Ialongo, N., Greenberg, G., Packard, T., & Smith-Winberry, C. (1990). Additive effects of behavioral parent training and self-control therapy with attention deficit hyperactivity disordered children. *Journal of Clinical Child Psychology, 19,* 98–110.

Ialongo, N., Horn, W. F., Pascoe, J. M., Greenberg, G., Packard, T., Lopez, M., Wagner, A., & Puttler, L. (1993). The effects of a multimodal intervention with attention-deficit hyperactivity disorder children: A 9-month follow-up. *Journal of the American Academy of Child and Adolescent Psychiatry, 32,* 182–189.

Johnson, C. (1988). A behavioral-family systems approach to assessment: Maternal characteristics associated with externalizing behavior in children. In R. J. Prinz (Ed.), *Advances in behavioral assessment of children and families* (pp. 161–187). Greenwich: JAI Press.

Kagan, S. L., Powell, D., Weissbourd, B., & Zigler, E. (1987). *America's family support programs.* New Haven: Yale University Press.

Kazdin, A. E. (1985). *In treatment of antisocial behavior in children and adolescents.* Homewood, IL: The Dorsey Press.

Kazdin, A. E. (1987). Treatment of antisocial behavior in children: Current status and future directions. *Psychological Bulletin, 102*, 187–203.

Kazdin, A. E. (1990). Premature termination from treatment among children referred for antisocial behavior. *Journal of Child Psychology and Psychiatry, 31*, 415–425.

Kazdin, A. E. (1994). Psychotherapy for children and adolescents. In A. Bergin & S. Garfield (Eds.), *Handbook of psychotherapy and behavior cChange: An empirical analysis* (pp. 543–594). New York: Wiley.

Kazdin, A. E. (1995). Child, parent and family dysfunction as predictors of outcome in cognitive-behavioral treatment of antisocial children. *Behavioral Research Therapy, 33*, 271–281.

Kazdin, A. E. (1997). Practitioner review: Psychosocial treatments for conduct disorder in children. *Journal of Child Psychology and Psychiatry, 38*, 161–178.

Kazdin, A. E., Ayers, W. A., Bass, D., & Rodgers, A. (1990). Empirical and clinical focus of child and adolescent psychotherapy research. *Journal of Consulting and Clinical Psychology, 58*, 729–740.

Kazdin, A. E., Bass, D., Siegel, T., & Thomas, C. (1989). Cognitive-behavioral therapy and relationship therapy in the treatment of children referred for antisocial behavior. *Journal of Consulting and Clinical Psychology, 57*, 522–535.

Kazdin, A. E., Siegel, T. C., & Bass, D. (1992). Cognitive problem-solving training and parent management training in the treatment of antisocial behavior in children. *Journal of Consulting and Clinical Psychology, 60*, 733–747.

Kelley, P., Kelley, V., & Williams, B. (1989, October). Treatment of adolescents: A comparison of individual and family therapy. *Social Casework: The Journal of Contemporary Social Work*, 461–468.

Kendziora, K. T., & O'Leary, S. G. (1993). Dysfunctional parenting as a focus for prevention and treatment of child behavior problems. In T. H. Ollendick & R. J. Prinz (Eds.), *Advances in clinical child psychology* (Vol. 15, pp. 175–206). New York: Plenum Press.

Larzelere, R. E., & Patterson, G. R. (1990). Parental management: Mediator of the effect of socioeconomic status on early delinquency. *Criminology, 28*, 301–323.

Laub, J. H., & Sampson, R. J. (1988). Unravelling families and delinquency: A reanalysis of the Gluecks' data. *Criminology, 26*, 355–380.

Lewis, R. A., Piercy, F., Sprenkle, D., & Trepper, T. (1990). Family-based interventions and community networking for helping drug abusing adolescents: The impact of near and far environments. *Journal of Adolescent Research, 5*, 82–95.

Liberman, A. F., Weston, D. R., & Pawl, J. H. (1991). Preventive intervention and outcome with anxiously attached dyads. *Child Development, 62*, 199–209.

Loeber, R. (1990). Development and risk factors of juvenile antisocial behavior and delinquency. *Clinical Psychology Review, 10*, 1–41.

Loeber, R., Keenan, K., Lahey, B. B., Green, S. M., & Thomas, C. (1993). Evidence for developmentally based diagnoses of oppositional defiant disorder and conduct disorder. *Journal of Abnormal Child Psychology, 21*, 377–410.

Long, P., Forehand, R., Wierson, M., & Morgan, A. (1994). Does parent training with young noncompliant children have long-term effects? *Behavior Research and Therapy, 32*(1), 101–107.

Lyons-Ruth, K., Alpern, L., & Repacholi, B. (1993). Disorganized infant attachment classification and maternal psychosocial problems as predictors of hostile-aggressive behavior in the preschool classroom. *Child Development, 64*, 572–585.

Lytton, H. (1990a). Child and parent effects in boys' conduct disorder: A reinterpretation. *Developmental Psychology, 26*, 683–697.

Lytton, H. (1990b). Child effects: Still unwelcome? Response to Dodge and Wahler. *Developmental Psychology, 26*, 705–709.

Maerov, S. L., Brummett, B., Patterson, G. R., & Reid, J. B. (1978). Coding of family interactions. In J. B. Reid (Ed.), *A social learning approach to family intervention: Observation in home settings* (pp. 21–36). Eugene, OR: Castalia.

Magan, R., & Rose, S. (1994). Parents in groups: Problem solving versus behavioral skills training. *Research on Social Work Practice, 4*, 172–191.

Mas, C. H., Alexander, J. F., & Barton, C. (1985). Modes of expression in family therapy: A process study of roles and gender. *Journal of Marital and Family Therapy, 1*, 411–415.

Mash, B. J. (1989). Treatment of child and family disturbance: A behavioral systems perspective. In E. J. Mash & R. A. Barkley (Eds.), *Treatment of childhood disorders* (pp. 3–36). New York: Guilford Press.

Mash, E. J., & Barkley, R. A. (Eds.). (1995). *Child psychopathology*. New York: Guilford Press.

McMahon, R., & Wells, K. C. (1989). Conduct disorders. In E. J. Mash & R. A. Barkley (Eds.), *Treatment of childhood disorders* (pp. 73–134). New York: Guilford Press.

McMahon, R. J. (1994). Diagnosis, assessment, and treatment of externalizing problems in children: The role of longitudinal data. *Journal of Consulting and Clinical Psychology, 62*, 901–917.

McNeil, C. B., Eyberg, S., Eisenstadt, T. H., Newcomb, K., & Funderburk, B. (1991). Parent-child interaction therapy with behavior problem children: Generalization of treatment effects to the school setting. *Journal of Clinical Child Psychology, 20*, 140–151.

Miller, G., & Prinz, R. (1990). Enhancement of social learning family interventions for childhood conduct disorder. *Psychological Bulletin, 108*, 291–307.

Moffitt, T. E. (1993). Adolescence-limited and life-course-persistent antisocial behavior: A developmental taxonomy. *Psychological Review, 100*, 674–701.

Mullin, E., Quigley, K., & Glanville, B. (1994). A controlled evaluation of the impact of a parent training programme on child behavior and mothers' general well-being. *Counseling Psychology Quarterly, 7*, 167–179.

Newlon, B. J., Borboa, R., & Arciniega, M. (1986). The effects of Adlerian parent study groups upon Mexican mothers' perception of child behavior. *Journal of Adlerian Theory, Research and Practice, 42*, 107–113.

Nicol, A. R., Smith, J., Kay, B., Hall, D., Barlow, J., & Williams, B. (1988). A focused casework approach to the treatment of child abuse: A controlled comparison. *Journal of Child Psychology and Psychiatry, 29*, 703–711.

Noble, P. S., Adams, G. R., & Openshaw, D. D. (1989). Interpersonal communication in parent-adolescent dyads: A brief report on the effects of a social skills training program. *Journal of Family Psychology, 2*, 483–494.

Offord, D. R., & Bennett, K. J. (1994). Conduct disorder: Long-term outcomes and intervention effectiveness. *Journal of the American Academy of Child Adolescent Psychiatry, 33*, 1069–1079.

Offord, D. R., Boyle, M. C., & Racine, Y. A. (1991). The epidemiology of antisocial behavior in childhood and adolescence. In D. J. Pepier & H. Rubin (Eds.), *The development and treatment of childhood aggression* (pp. 31–54). Hillsdale, NJ: Erlbaum.

Patterson, G. R. (1982a). The aggressive child: Victim and architect of a coercive system. In E. J. Mash, L. Hamerlynck, & L. Handy (Eds.), *Behavior modification and families* (pp. 267–316). New York: Brunner/Mazel.

Patterson, G. R. (1982b). *Coercive family process: A social learning approach* (3rd ed.). Eugene: OR: Castalia.

Patterson, G. R. (1986). Performance models for antisocial boys. *American Psychologist, 41*, 432–444.

Patterson, G. R., & Chamberlain, P. (1994). A functional analysis of resistance during parent training therapy. *American Psychological Association D12*, 53–70.

Patterson, G. R., Dishion, T. J., & Chamberlain, P. (1993). Outcomes and methodological issues relating to treatment of antisocial children. In T. Giles (Ed.), *Effective psychotherapy: A handbook of comparative research* (pp. 43–88). New York: Plenum.

Patterson, G. R., & Forgatch, R. S. (1985). Therapist behavior as a determinant for client noncompliance: A paradox for the behavior modifier. *Journal of Consulting and Clinical Psychology, 53*, 846–851.

Patterson, G. R., Reid, J. B., & Dishion, T. J. (1992). *Antisocial boys.* Eugene, OR: Castalia.

Patterson, G. R., Reid, J. B., & Maerov, S. L. (1978). The observation system: Methodological issues and psychometric properties. In J. B. Reid (Ed.), *A social learning approach to family intervention: Observation in home settings* (pp. 11–19). Eugene, OR: Castalia.

Pepler, D. J., & Rubin, K. H. (1991). *The development and treatment of childhood aggression.* Hillsdale, NJ: Erlbaum.

Peters, R. D. (1991). Expanding the perspective on contributing factors and service delivery approaches to childhood aggression. In D. J. Pepler & K. H. Rubin (Eds.), *The development and treatment of childhood aggression.* Hillsdale, NJ: Erlbaum.

Pfiffner, L. J., Jouriles, E. N., Brown, M. M., Etscheidt, M. A., & Kelley, J. A. (1990). Effects of problem-solving therapy on outcomes of parent training for single-parent families. *Child and Family Behavior Therapy, 12*, 1–11.

Pisterman, S., McGrath, P., Firestone, P., & Goodman, J. (1989). Outcome of parent-mediated treatment of preschoolers with attention deficit disorder with hyperactivity. *Journal of Consulting and Clinical Psychology, 57*, 636–643.

Prinz, R. J., & Miller, G. E. (1991). Issues in understanding and treating childhood conduct problems in disadvantaged populations. *Journal of Clinical Child Psychology, 20*, 379–385.

Prinz, R. J., & Miller, G. E. (1994). Family-based treatment for childhood and antisocial behavior: Experimental influences on dropout and engagement. *Journal of Consulting and Clinical Psychology, 62*, 645–650.

Reid, J. B. (1978a). Involving parents in the prevention of conduct disorder. *Community Psychologist, 24*(2), 28–30.

Reid, J. B. (1978b). *A social learning approach to family intervention: Observation in home settings*. Eugene, OR: Castalia.

Reid, J. B. (1993). Prevention of conduct disorder before and after school entry: Relating interventions to development findings. *Development and Psychopathology, 5*, 243–262.

Richters, J. E. (1993). Community violence and children's development: Toward a research agenda for the 1990's. *Psychiatry, 56*, 3–6.

Richters, J. E., & Martinez, P. E. (1993). Violent communities, family choices and children's chances: An algorithm for improving the odds. *Development and Psychopathology, 5*, 609–627.

Robin, A. L., & Foster, S. L. (1989). *Negotiating parent-adolescent conflict*. New York: Springer.

Robins, L. N. (1981). Epidemiological approaches to natural history research. *Journal of the American Academy of Child Psychiatry, 20*, 566–580.

Rogers-Wiese, M. R. (1992). A critical review of parent training research. *Psychology in the Schools, 29*, 229–236.

Routh, C., Hill, J., Steele, N., Elliott, C., & Dewey, M. (1995). Maternal attachment status, psychosocial stressors and problem behavior: Follow-up after parent training courses for conduct disorder. *Journal of Child Psychology and Psychiatry, 36*, 1179–1198.

Ruma, P. R., Burke, R. V., & Thompson, R. W. (1996). Group parent training: Is it effective for children of all ages? *Behavior Therapy, 27*, 159–169.

Satterfield, J. H., Satterfield, B., & Schell, A. M. (1987). Therapeutic interventions to prevent delinquency in hyperactive boys. *Journal of the American Academy of Child and Adolescent Psychiatry, 26*, 56–64.

Sax, L., Cross, T., & Silverman, N. (1988). Children's mental health: The gap between what we know and what we do. *American Psychologist, 49*, 800–807.

Sayger, T. V., Horne, A. M., & Glaser, B. A. (1993). Marital satisfaction and social learning family therapy for child conduct problems: Generalization of Treatment Effects. *Journal of Marital and Family Therapy, 19*, 393–402.

Sayger, T. V., Horne, A. M., Walker, J. M., & Passmore, J. L. (1988a). Multidimensionality versus inconclusiveness: The baby and the bathwater. *Journal of Family Psychology, 1*, 296–297.

Sayger, T. V., Horne, A. M., Walker, J. M., & Passmore, J. L. (1988b). Social learning family therapy with aggressive children: Treatment outcome and maintenance. *Journal of Family Psychology, 1*, 261–285.

Schuhmann, E. M., Foote, R., Eyberg, S. M., & Boggs, S. R., & Algira, J. (1998). Efficacy of parent-child therapy: Interim report of a randomized trial with short-term maintenance. *Journal of Clinical Child Psychology, 1998*(1), 34–45.

Serbin, L. A., Schwartzmann, A. E., Moskowitz, E. S., & Ledingham, J. E. (1991). Aggressive, withdrawn, and aggressive/withdrawn children in adolescence: Into the new generation. In D. J. Pepler & K. H. Rubin (Eds.), *The development and treatment of childhood aggression* (pp. 55–70). Hillsdale, NJ: Erlbaum.

Serketich, W. J., & Dumas, J. E. (1996). The effectiveness of behavioral parent training to modify antisocial behavior in children: A meta-analysis. *Behavior Therapy, 27*, 171–186.

Shadish, W. R., Montgomery, L. M., Wilson, P., Wilson, M. R., Bright, I., & Okwumabua, T. (1993). Effects of family and marital psychotherapies: A meta-analysis. *Journal of Consulting and Clinical Psychology, 61*, 992–1002.

Snyder, J. J. (1991). Discipline as a mediator of the impact of maternal stress and mood on child conduct problems. *Development and Psychopathology, 3*, 263–276.

Spaccarelli, S., Cotler, S., & Penman, D. (1992). Problem-solving skills training as a supplement to behavioral parent training. *Cognitive Theory and Research, 16*(1), 1–18.

Speltz, M. L., Greenberg, M. T., & DeKlyen, M. (1990). Attachment in preschoolers with disruptive behavior: A comparison of clinic-referred and nonproblem children. *Development and Psychopathology, 2*, 31–46.

Spitfire, A., Webster-Stratton, C., & Hollinsworth, T. (1991). Coping with conduct-problem children: Parents gaining knowledge and control. *Journal of Clinical Child Psychology, 20*, 413–427.

Strayhorn, J. M., & Weidman, C. S. (1989). Reduction of attention-deficit and internalizing symptoms in preschoolers through parent-child interaction training. *Journal of the American Academy of Child and Adolescent Psychiatry, 28*, 888–896.

Szapocznik, J., Kurtines, W. M., Foote, F. H., Perez-Vidal, A., & Hervis, O. E. (1986). Conjoint versus one-person family therapy: Further evidence for the effectiveness of conducting family therapy through one person with drug-abusing adolescents. *Journal of Consulting and Clinical Psychology, 54*, 395–397.

Szapocznik, J., Kurtines, W. M., Santisteban, D. A., & Rio, A. T. (1990). Interplay of advances between theory,research, and application in treatment interventions aimed at behavior problem children and adolescents. *Journal of Consulting and Clinical Psychology, 58*, 696–703.

Szapocznik, J., Perez-Vidal, A., Brickman, A. L., Foote, F. H., Santisteban, D., & Hervis, O. (1988). Engaging adolescent drug abusers and their families in treatment: A strategic structural systems approach. *Journal of Consulting and Clinical Psychology, 56*, 552–557.

Szapocznik, J., Rio, A., Murray, L., Cohen, R., Scopetta, M., Ribas-Vasquez, A., Nervis, O., Posada, V., & Kurtines, W. (1989). Structural Family versus psychodynamic child therapy for problematic Hispanic boys. *Journal of Consulting and Clinical Psychology, 5*, 571–578.

Szapocznik, J., Rio, A. T., Murray, E., Richardson, R., Alone, M., & Kurtines, W. (1993). Assessing change in child psychodynamic functioning in treatment outcome studies: The psychodynamic child ratings. *Revista Interamericana de Psicologia/Interamerican Journal of Psychology, 27*, 147–162.

Tayor, T., Schmidt, F., Pepler, D., & Hodgins, C. (1998). A comparison of eclectic treatment with Webster-Stratton's parents and children services in a children's mental health center: A randomized controlled trial. *Behavior Therapy, 29*, 221–240.

Todreas, R., & Bunston, T. (1993). Parent education program evaluation: A review of the literature. *Canadian Journal of Community Mental Health, 12*, 225–257.

Tremblay, R. E. (1991). Aggression, prosocial behavior, and gender: Three magic words but no magic wand. In D. Pepler & K. Rubin (Eds.), *The development and treatment of childhood aggression* (pp. 71–78). Hillsdale, NJ: Erlbaum.

U.S. Census Bureau. (1998). USA statistics in brief: Population and vital statistics. http://www.census.gor/statab

Wahler, R. G. (1990). Who is driving the interactions? A commentary on "child and parent effects in boys' conduct disorder." *Developmental Psychology, 26*, 702–704.

Wahler, R. G., Cartor, P. G., Fleischman, J., & Lambert, W. (1993). The impact of synthesis teaching and parent training with mothers of conduct-disordered children. *Journal of Abnormal Child Psychology, 21*, 425–440.

Wahler, R. G., & Dumas, J. E. (1986). Maintenance factors in coercive mother-child interactions: The compliance and predictability hypothesis. *Journal of Applied Behavior Analysis, 19*, 13–22.

Wahler, R. G., & Dumas, J. E. (1987). Stimulus class determinants of mother-child coercive interchanges in multi-distressed families: Assessment and intervention. In J. D. Burchard & S. N. Burchard (Eds.), *Prevention of delinquent behavior* (pp. 190–219). Newbury Park, CA: Sage.

Wahler, R. G., & Dumas, J. E. (1989). Attentional problems in dysfunctional mother-child interactions: An interbehavioral model. *Psychological Bulletin, 105*, 116–130.

Webster-Stratton, C., & Hammond, M. (1997). Treating children with early-onset conduct problems: A comparison of child and parent training interventions. *Journal of Consulting and Clinical Psychology, 65*, 93–109.

Webster-Stratton, C. (1985a). Predictors of treatment outcome in parent training for conduct disordered children. *Behavior Therapy, 16*, 223–243.

Webster-Stratton, C. (1985b). The effects of father involvement in parent training for conduct problem children. *Journal of Child Psychology and Psychiatry, 26*(5), 801–810.

Webster-Stratton, C. (1990). Long-term follow-up with young conduct problem children: From preschool to grade school. *Journal of Clinical Child Psychology, 19*, 144–149.

Webster-Stratton, C. (1991). Annotation: Strategies for helping families with conduct disordered children. *Journal of Clinical Child Psychology and Psychiatry, 32*, 1047–1062.

Webster-Stratton, C. (1992). Individually administered videotape parent training: "Who benefits?" *Cognitive Therapy and Research, 16*, 31–35.

Webster-Stratton, C. (1994). Advancing videotape parent training: A comparison study. *Journal of Consulting and Clinical Psychology, 62*, 583–593.

Webster-Stratton, C., & Hammond, M. (1997). Treating children with early-onset conduct problems: A comparison of child and parent training interventions. *Journal of Consulting and Clinical Psychology, 65,* 93–109.

Webster-Stratton, C., & Herbert, M. (1993). What really happens in parent training? *Behavior Modification, 17,* 407–457.

Webster-Stratton, C., Hollinsworth, T, & Kolpacoff, M. (1989). The long-term effectiveness and clinical significance of three cost effective training programs for families with conduct-problem children. *Journal of Consulting and Clinical Psychology, 57,* 550–553.

Webster-Stratton, C., Kolpacoff, M., & Hollinsworth, T. (1988). Self-administered videotape therapy for families with conduct-problem children: Comparison with two cost-effective treatments and a control group. *Journal of Consulting and Clinical Psychology, 56*(4), 558–566.

Weiss, H. B. (1989). State family support programs: Lessons from the pioneers. *American Journal of Orthopsychiatry, 59,* 32–48.

Weisz, J., Donenberg, G., Han, S., & Weiss, B. (1995). Bridging the gap between laboratory and clinic in child and adolescent psychotherapy. *Journal of Consulting and Clinical Psychology, 63,* 688–701.

Weisz, J. R., Weiss, B., & Donenberg, G. R. (1992). The lab versus the clinic: Effects of child and adolescent psychotherapy. *American Psychologist, 47,* 1578–1585.

Wells, K. C., & Egan, J. (1988). Social learning and systems family therapy for childhood oppositional disorder: Comparative treatment outcome. *Comprehensive Psychiatry, 29,* 138–146.

Whipple, E., & Webster-Stratton, C. (1991). The role of parental stress in physically abusive families. *Child Abuse and Neglect, 15,* 279–291.

Wood, B. (1985). Proximity and hierarchy: Orthogonal dimensions of family interconnectedness. *Family Process, 24,* 487–507.

MEASUREMENT OF FAMILY TREATMENT
WITH CONDUCT DISORDER

Increasingly, practitioners are held accountable for the evaluation of their practice. To assist with this evaluation, this section on measurement is to provide the reader with self-report instruments that children and their families can easily complete. Scores from these measurement instruments can be used to guide assessment and clinical practice when treating children with conduct problems. For those interested in conducting research in this area, each of the instruments provided have established psychometric data to support their usage.

The following types of measures are presented: 1) child outcomes according to parent report; 2) parenting practices; 3) parental adjustment; 4) marital functioning; 5) family functioning; and 6) client satisfaction with services.

Measures presented in this section involve the following criteria. First, instruments are self-report; that is, they are completed by family members themselves, rather than being interviewer-administered or observational measures. For example, the Self-Reported Antisocial Behavior for Young Children (Loeber, Stouthamer-Loeber, Van Kammen, & Farrington, 1989) was not included although it has been recommended by experts in this area (e.g., McMahon & Estes, 1997) because the instrument was interviewer-administered. A second criterion for inclusion in this section was that adequate reliability and validity information had to be presented in terms of correlation data rather than in some other manner, such as percentages (e.g., Loeber et al., 1989). Selected psychometric data were chosen to inform the reader on the properties of the instruments.

CHILD OUTCOME—PARENT REPORT

CHILD BEHAVIOR CHECKLIST

(See Chapter *One*, Family Treatment with Child Abuse and Neglect)

EYBERG CHILD BEHAVIOR INVENTORY

Author: Eyberg (1992)

Description:

- A parent-completed behavior rating scale specifically developed to assess disruptive behaviors in children
- 2 scales:
  1. Intensity ("Never"/1 to "Always"/7)—how often the behaviors currently occur
  2. Problem ("Yes"/"No")—identifies the specific behaviors that are currently problems

Reliability:

- Interparent agreement .86 for Intensity and .79 for Problem scales
- Internal consistency was .98 for both Intensity and Problem scales for nonreferred pediatric clinic sample and for pediatric clinic adolescents
- Test-retest reliability was .86 for Intensity and .88 for Problem Scales over 3 weeks, and .80 for Intensity and .85 for Problem Scales over 3 months

Validity:

- Problem ($r = .67$) and Intensity (.75) scores were correlated with Externalizing Scale of the Child Behavior Checklist and with Internalizing Scale (Problem = .48; Intensity = .41)
- Problem and Intensity scores correlated with Parenting Stress Index child domain scores and with parent domain scores (Problem = .62; Intensity = .59)
- When comparing preschool disruptive children and a comparison group without such problems and adolescents who were disruptive versus adolescents who were not, mean Intensity and Problem scores differentiated between groups
- Scale appears to be sensitive to treatment change in young children

PARENTING PRACTICES

CHILD ABUSE POTENTIAL INVENTORY

(*See Chapter One*, Family Treatment with Child Abuse and Neglect)

PARENT OPINION QUESTIONNAIRE

(*See Chapter One*, Family Treatment with Child Abuse and Neglect)

THE PARENTING SCALE

(*See Chapter One*, Family Treatment with Child Abuse and Neglect)

THE PARENT PROBLEM CHECKLIST

(*See Chapter One*, Family Treatment with Child Abuse and Neglect)

PARENTING STRESS INDEX

(*See Chapter One*, Family Treatment with Child Abuse and Neglect)

PARENT ADJUSTMENT

BECK DEPRESSION INVENTORY

(*See Chapter One*, Family Treatment with Child Abuse and Neglect)

SYMPTOM CHECKLIST 90–REVISED

(*See Chapter One*, Family Treatment with Child Abuse and Neglect)

BRIEF SYMPTOM INVENTORY

(*See Chapter One*, Family Treatment with Child Abuse and Neglect)

MARITAL FUNCTIONING

THE MARITAL ADJUSTMENT TEST

(*See Chapter One*, Family Treatment with Child Abuse and Neglect)

DYADIC ADJUSTMENT SCALE

(*See Chapter One*, Family Treatment with Child Abuse and Neglect)

O'LEARY-PORTER SCALE

(*See Chapter One*, Family Treatment with Child Abuse and Neglect)

REVISED CONFLICT TACTICS SCALES

(*See Chapter One*, Family Treatment with Child Abuse and Neglect)

FAMILY ADJUSTMENT

FAMILY ADAPTABILITY AND COHESION EVALUATION SCALES III

(*See Chapter One*, Family Treatment with Child Abuse and Neglect)

FAMILY ENVIRONMENT SCALE

(*See Chapter One*, Family Treatment with Child Abuse and Neglect)

MCMASTER FAMILY ASSESSMENT DEVICE

(*See Chapter One*, Family Treatment with Child Abuse and Neglect)

SATISFACTION WITH SERVICES

CLIENT SATISFACTION QUESTIONNAIRE

(*See Chapter One*, Family Treatment with Child Abuse and Neglect)

REFERENCES FOR MEASUREMENT OF FAMILY TREATMENT WITH CONDUCT DISORDER

Eyberg, S. (1992). Assessing therapy outcome with preschool children: Progress and problems. *Journal of Clinical Child Psychology, 21*, 306–311.

Loeber, R., Stouthamer-Loeber, M., Van Kammen, W. B., & Farrington, D. P. (1989). Development of a new measure of self-reported antisocial behavior for young children: Prevalence and reliability. In M. W. Klein (Ed.), *Cross-national research in self-reported crime and delinquency* (pp. 203–222). New York: Kluwer Academic Publishers.

McMahon, R., & Estes, A. (1997). Conduct Problems. In E. Mash, & L. Terdal (Eds.). *Assessment of childhood disorders* (3rd ed., pp. 130–194). New York: Guilford Press.

CHAPTER 4

Family Treatment with Attention Deficit and Hyperactivity Disorder

---

with Jami Black and Cecilia Thomas

Family Case:

An African American single mother, Shirley Watson, age 26, brings in her 6-year-old son, Tyrone, for counseling. Shirley says that her child has been referred by the school for testing of Attention Deficit-Hyperactivity Disorder, but she can't afford it. She says that Tyrone has a difficult time listening at both home and school and seems to forget directions as soon as they are issued. She says that she is constantly getting reports from the school about Tyrone's behavior: He doesn't stay in his seat, he fails to listen to directions, he doesn't complete work, and he is always talking to classmates..

Ms. Watson says that at home Tyrone also has difficulty following her directions, and she can't seem to get him to do his homework no matter how much she "gets onto him." She has tried to set the rule that he has to do his homework before he plays outside, but he usually just avoids his work and then begs and cries so he is allowed to go outside. Shirley also has a 5-month-old baby, and she is tired and worn out after being up all night with him. She finds that she likes the peace when Tyrone goes out to play with his friends. She says she loves her son, but she finds herself almost continually angry with him and yelling. She says she doesn't understand why he can't just listen and do as he's told, instead of making his own life and everyone else's so hard.

Attention deficit/hyperactivity disorder (more commonly referred to as ADHD) is marked by a characteristic pattern of inattention and/or hyperactivity-impulsivity (American Psychiatric Association, 1994). The prevalence in the United

States of ADHD has been estimated at 5% of the male and 1% of the female population (Arnold, 1996). While this may seem like a small portion of the American population, these proportions translate into over 6 million boys and/or men who have ADHD (Arnold, 1996) and into over 1 million girls and/or women. With this disorder affecting so many, it is discouraging to note that only a very small percentage of children with ADHD are receiving any treatment—perhaps only 10% to 30% (Whalen & Henker, 1991).

The lack of treatment is particularly disturbing when viewed in the context of the possible continuation of ADHD symptoms across the lifespan. The onset of ADHD occurs usually within the preschool years (Abikoff & Klein, 1992). According to a review of longitudinal studies, the early school-age years become a time when problems arise with oppositional and aggressive behavior for between 40% and 70% of children diagnosed with ADHD (Abikoff & Klein, 1992). Of children who are clinic-referred for ADHD, 35% to 60% will meet the diagnostic criteria for oppositional defiant disorder by the age of 7. Even more staggering is that between 30% and 50% of these same children will eventually meet the criteria for conduct disorder by ages 8 to 12. Indeed, for treatment-referred children diagnosed with conduct disorder, the dual diagnosis with ADHD may be as high as 90% (Abikoff & Klein, 1992). Oppositional and aggressive behaviors may combine to overwhelm children who are already at a disadvantage in terms of impulse control.

In addition to the possible coexistence of other disorders and behavior problems, ADHD children may face persistence of their symptoms over a long period of time. Although teachers and parents commonly believed at one time that childhood ADHD would subside with the onset of puberty (Faigel, Sznajderman, Tishby, Turel, & Pinus, 1995), a review of nine prospective studies ascertained that the rate of ADHD declines by only about 50% every 5 years (Hill & Schoener, 1996). Longitudinal study indicates that from about 50% to 80% of clinic-referred children will continue with the disorder into adolescence, with commensurate behavioral and academic difficulties (Barkley, Fischer, Edelbrook, & Smallish, 1990; Klein & Mannuzza, 1991). An 8-year follow-up of hyperactive children found that ADHD adolescents were still performing less well than their peers in basic reading recognition, spelling, and arithmetic skills, even after controlling for intelligence (Fischer et al., 1990). Sixty percent of these adolescents were also diagnosed with oppositional defiant disorder and/or conduct disorder (Barkley et al., 1990). High rates of other disorders have also been noted. For example, a 4-year follow-up of ADHD youth indicated not only higher rates of oppositional and conduct disorder, but also higher rates of major depression, bipolar disorder, and anxiety disorders compared to normal controls (Biederman et al., 1998).

While long-term outcome studies related to the effects of ADHD over time are few, the current research states that as many as 30% to 50% of ADHD children continue with the diagnosis into adulthood (Barkley, 1996). Further, a controlled prospective, 15-year follow-up study (Weiss, Hechtman, Milroy, & Perlman, 1985) showed trends of greater drug, alcohol, and antisocial involvement, including criminal activity, for adults who had been diagnosed with ADHD as children compared to normal controls (Weiss & Hechtman, 1993). Similar results were found for other research that tracked ADHD children through the ages of 24 to 33: ADHD children as adults continued to have elevated rates of ADHD symptomatology, substance use disorders, criminal offending, and antisocial personality disorders (Klein & Mannuzza, 1991). Indeed, 15% to 25% of ADHD clinic-referred children may later qualify for a diagnosis of antisocial personality disorder in adulthood (Barkley, 1996). Several factors appear to affect the persistence of these grave symptoms over time (Barkley, 1996):

1. the initial degree of hyperactive-impulsive behavior in childhood
2. the coexistence of conduct problems or hostile behavior
3. poor family relationships, particularly in dysfunctional parent-child interactions
4. maternal depression
5. the extent and duration of mental health interventions

Considering the substantial numbers in the American population afflicted with ADHD and the possible persistence of long-range problems, it is important to address the etiology of the disorder and its treatment. The following sections will discuss these two areas.

ETIOLOGY

While the exact causes of ADHD are not known at this time, research indicates a biological, and specifically, a genetic, causation. Development and functioning of the brain appear to be implicated, given the similarity of ADHD symptoms to the behaviors of individuals who have sustained lesions or injuries to the frontal lobes of the brain. Common symptoms involve the inability to maintain attention, control impulses, and manage emotion and urges, as well as difficulty with regulating behavior over time (Barkley, 1996).

Apparently, the development of ADHD may occur through a number of different neurological pathways, such as pregnancy and/or birth complications, acquired brain damage, toxins, infections, and heredity (Mash, 1989). Heredity is the most well-documented causal pathway, and Barkley (1996) reviews the evidence in this area. First, a high percentage of family members of ADHD children are diagnosed with ADHD. Second, adopted children show a greater similarity with their biological parents, rather than their adoptive parents on ADHD symptomatology. The heredity theory of ADHD has also been substantiated through other studies, which demonstrate a higher preponderance of ADHD among identical twins rather than fraternal twins. The assumption is that the greater amount of shared genetic material between identical twins is responsible for this phenomenon.

The most recent formulation of ADHD by Barkley (1996), an expert theoretician and researcher in this area, suggests that biological impairment of the brain may occur in the motor, output, or motivational sections of the brain, which affect behavioral self-regulation. This formulation departs from traditional thought, which considers disturbance of the sensory processing system as crucial to the development of ADHD. It may well be, however, that attentional difficulties represent an inability to sustain more complicated, goal-directed endurance with a task. Therefore, poor self-regulation, as opposed to deficits in sustained responding, may be the central mechanism. Regulation of behavior may be the end result of several other abilities:

1. prolonged activity (also referred to as working memory)
2. regulation of affect, drive, and motivation
3. the internalization of speech
4. the analysis and synthesis of information

In combination, these functions allow individuals to evaluate and manage their environment and their behavior within it. According to the recent model, an inability to control impulse (regulation of affect, drive, and motivation) may give rise to a problem with prolonged activity and working memory, exhibited as forgetfulness. The deficiency in working memory results in a diminished sense of time and therefore an impaired ability to rely on both hindsight and forethought to assist the individual in regulating behavior. ADHD, therefore, is defined by one of its earliest developmental manifestations, hyperactivity, and only minimally by its primary feature, impulsivity (Barkley, 1996).

TREATMENT

Further evidence for the salience of biological causation has been the responsiveness of ADHD symtomatology to medication. Indeed, the dominant approach to treatment has been medicating ADHD children, primarily through the use of the psychostimulant methylphenidate (otherwise known as Ritalin) (Jacobvitz, Sroufe, Stewart, & Leffert, 1990). Psychostimulants act as stimulants to the central nervous system; they affect the functioning of neurotransmitters in the brain, regulating the rate at which they fire (Jacobvitz et al., 1990). This regulation of neurotransmitters is supposed to slow down the neural processes for an overstimulated child, or to speed them up for a child who is understimulated, thereby impacting the child's behavior. The actual effect the psychostimulants have on neural processes is still being heavily debated (Jacobvitz et al., 1990), however, as these medications have been shown to produce the same effects on ADHD and non-ADHD children.

Side effects such as insomnia, loss of appetite, irritability, nausea, vomiting, mood alterations, and an increase in heart rate and/or blood pressure also make drug treatments of this type a concern for children (Ervin, Bankert, & DuPaul, 1996; Jacobvitz et al., 1990; Simeon & Wiggins, 1993). While experts explain that these side effects are usually related to dosage and can be controlled (Simeon & Wiggins, 1993), other concerns related to psychostimulant treatment need to be addressed. First, only 60% to 80% of children medicated with psychostimulants show a positive response to this treatment alone, while other children demonstrate either no effect at all or such an adverse effect that medication must be withdrawn (Ervin et al., 1996; Pelham & Murphy, 1986).

In addition, stimulant treatments typically fail to bring ADHD children to a normal level of academic (Jacobvitz et al., 1990) or social functioning (Pelham & Murphy, 1986); nor do the effects of treatment generalize to other situations and times when medication is not provided. Third, the growth-suppressant side effects of psychostimulants have resulted in physicians only prescribing them for consumption during school hours, with the effects dissipating typically 4 hours after being taken (Ervin et al., 1996). This dilemma has left parents to their own means of controlling their child's behavior during evenings, weekends, and school holidays.

Further, Simeon and Wiggins (1993) report that some ADHD-medicated children may experience a gradual decrease in their positive response to drug therapy after only a few months. Continued attempts to stop the use of these medications, or even to lower their dosage, may result in a recurrence of problematic behavior, ultimately ending in academic and behavioral difficulties

(Simeon & Wiggins, 1993). Finally, longitudinal outcome studies following children treated with psychostimulants have ultimately failed to provide any support for their long-term effect on prognosis in terms of antisocial behavior, peer relations, and academic performance (Jacobvitz et al., 1990). Therefore, the family has been targeted as a possible arena of influence for the child.

FAMILY FACTORS

While little evidence supports a purely psychosocial etiology of ADHD, environmental factors may well shape and mold the nature and severity of a genetic, hereditary disposition toward poor impulse control. In particular, the risk for certain co-morbid disorders, such as oppositional defiant disorder and conduct disorder, are largely related to family factors (Barkley, Fischer, Edelbrock, & Smallish, 1991). Psychopathology of parents, marital conflict, and any family difficulties, which contribute to inconsistent, coercive, or decreased efforts at managing the child's behavior, may serve to increase the defiant, oppositional, and aggressive behaviors in the ADHD child (Weiss & Hechtman, 1993).

As well as affecting outcomes for children with ADHD, families with an ADHD child also suffer from distress with the difficulties of managing the disorder (Barkley, 1996). Increased parenting stress, depression in mothers, abuse of substances and marital conflict, as well as an increased rate of separation and divorce, are present in families with a child diagnosed with ADHD. An 8-year follow-up tracking hyperactive children into adolescence indicated long-standing mother-child interaction problems, marked by negative and controlling behaviors on both sides (Barkley et al., 1991). Further, mothers reported more psychological distress.

The argument for this pattern is that poor parenting practices are caused by the child's coercive behavior in terms of noncompliance and poor self-control, rather than the development of ADHD in children being caused by parental practices. Evidence for this pattern is provided by studies that have looked at the effects of medication on mother-child interactions. In Barkley (1989), when children's behavior improved due to medication effects, mothers reduced the number of commands and control over child compliance.

At the same time, it is still possible that maternal perceptions and behaviors are purely in reaction to their child's action. To illustrate, Mash and Johnston (1982) compared mothers of younger (mean age 4) and older (mean age 8) hyperactive children, with both groups also compared against normal controls. While preschool hyperactive children were clearly different from controls in terms of noncompliance and inattentiveness, mothers' perceptions of older hyperactive children was more negative than behavioral observation warranted. The authors suggest that early negative experiences with a difficult child may color maternal perceptions even when child disruptive behaviors have waned. While the correlational nature of these studies precludes definitive statements on the direction of causation, Mash and Johnston (1982) suggest that coercive parent-child interactions may begin when the child is quite young. The coercion that characterizes this relationship may then limit the possibility of future positive interactions and learning experiences for the child.

Much more can be learned from prospective, longitudinal research in which children and their parents are tracked from an early age and followed over time. Sroufe and colleagues have conducted such work and reported on outcomes of children from infancy to preschool and school-age (Carlson, Jacobvitz, & Sroufe, 1995; Jacobvitz & Sroufe, 1987; Sroufe, 1989). Findings indicate, even when children have reached the age of 11, a strong relationship between early infant/caregiver attachment and the later development of ADHD (Sroufe, 1989). These results suggest that environmental, familial determinants have not been adequately explored in terms of the etiology of ADHD.

The development of ADHD in this framework concerns the acquisition of self-management and control in the child, which directly pertains to the pattern of arousal and control of behavior in the parent-child dyad (Sroufe, 1989). In this framework, the caregiver's sensitivity to infant cues during periods of arousal and interaction teaches the child invaluable lessons regarding the maintenance of behavioral organization. If the caregiver shows sensitivity to the infant's signals, then arousal remains within the limits that insure well-organized and consistent infant behavior. From these parent-child interactions, children learn that high stimulation (or arousal) does not necessarily lead to the disorganization of behavior and total loss of control (Sroufe, 1989).

On the other hand, if caregivers are unwilling or unable to follow their infants' cues regarding arousal, perhaps because of other environmental factors, such as isolation in the parenting role or a general lack of external social support (Carlson et al., 1995), interaction between parent and child is largely governed by the parents' desires, moods, and needs. Infants with this experience over time may not learn that behavior can be reorganized following stimulation (Sroufe, 1989).

During the toddler years, additional vulnerabilities for overarousal are present due to the child's movement toward independence. In their research, Sroufe and colleagues often observed parents provoking and teasing their children, initiating power struggles, and failing to set boundaries (Sroufe, 1989). Noncompliance and/or frustration on the part of the child results from these types of caregiver behaviors. The caregiver may then react with threats or punishments, which further stimulate the child, and the child fails to learn how to gain control of his or her behavior.

While the central importance of attachment for the development of ADHD symptoms has been discussed, attachment theorists suggest that multiple pathways may lead to the occurrence of this disorder. In some children, organic factors, such as motor development and medical vulnerability may explain why ADHD develops, while in others, a combination of both environmental and organic factors may provide an optimal explanation (Carlson et al., 1995).

SUMMARY OF FAMILY FACTORS

Clearly, the exact role of family factors has not been well delineated, and more longitudinal work from varying theoretical perspectives is needed. However, whether the development of ADHD is influenced by family factors, whether disruptive child behaviors negatively influence parental perceptions, thereby leading to poorer parent-child interactions, or whether child behaviors are the sole cause of negative parental perceptions and behaviors, it is obvious that work with the family is needed to help members better manage and cope as well as optimizing future outcomes for the child. Treatments focused on intervening with the family, therefore, have become a viable and important aspect of helping ADHD children, and the focus of this chapter will be to explore these family interventions.

Studies in this review were required to meet certain criteria. First, studies had to involve interventions with parents, rather than maintaining an individual focus on the child or on classroom management procedures (e.g., Pelham et al., 1993). In addition, only empirical outcome studies were included so as to examine the actual measured efficacy of the treatments being considered. A certain standard of methodological rigor was also required for inclusion. For instance, single-subject designs were excluded (e.g., Guevremont, Tishelman, & Hull, 1986), and studies had to be published in peer-reviewed academic journals. Publication dates were from 1985 and on in order to focus on the more recent developments in the ADHD treatment field.

Using these criteria for study inclusion, only behaviorally oriented family interventions were located. These interventions will be described and their effectiveness evaluated. Following, recommendations for further research and service delivery in the area of family treatment for ADHD will be explored.

REVIEW OF THE LITERATURE

The review of family intervention studies will be organized in the following manner. First, a rationale for the use of behavioral parent training programs will be offered, followed by a description of such curricula. Discussion of outcome studies will be organized according to the developmental level of the child: preschool, school-age, and teenage. Family treatment outcome studies in each of these developmental periods will be presented.

THEORETICAL BASIS AND DESCRIPTION OF PARENT TRAINING PROGRAMS

Parent training was developed from the principles of behavioral theory, specifically operant conditioning for the treatment of conduct disorder (e.g., Patterson, 1982). DuPaul and Barkley (1992) discuss that the pattern of parent-child interactions in ADHD children are prey to the same coercive cycles present in conduct disorder families, these cycles under the influence of behavioral principles.

The cycle typically begins with the parent issuing a directive to the child. The child then responds in a coercive manner through noncompliance, whining, or yelling. At that point, the parent may withdraw the command, which acts to negatively reinforce a child's disobedient behavior. Negative reinforcement is defined as the termination of an aversive event; in this case, if a parental command is withdrawn, the child's noncompliance is increased. The parent may also be negatively reinforced for coercive behavior. If, following noncompliance, the parent escalates the command (raises voice, uses physical aggression), the child may obey, which reinforces the parent's use of these aversive tactics. According to the principles of operant conditioning, positive reinforcement also plays a role in that parents attend to child deviant rather than prosocial behaviors, which increases the likelihood of future deviant behavior.

In parent training programs, behavioral principles are applied to increase child positive behaviors and decrease negative behaviors. Desirable and appropriate child behaviors are encouraged through the use of positive reinforcement techniques such as attention, praise, token economies, and privileges (Anastopoulos, Shelton, DuPaul, & Guevremont, 1993). Undesirable behaviors are decreased through ignoring and punishment, such as time-out from reinforcement (Horn, Ialongo, Popovich, & Peradotto, 1987). Parents are taught these tactics through the use of didactic presentations, modeling, role-plays, and homework assignments (Horn et al., 1987, 1991). Parent training tends to be brief in nature (9 to 12 sessions) and is administered in both group (e.g.,

Anastopoulos et al., 1993; Pisterman et al., 1989) and individual formats (e.g., Blakemore, Shindler, & Conte, 1993).

As discussed, parent training programs began with the treatment of conduct disorder. In fact, some of the curriculums for the treatment of ADHD have been directly adapted from this area (i.e., Forehand & McMahon [1981] was applied in Pisterman et al., 1989). One widely used model in this area, a program formulated by Barkley (1987), relies heavily on conduct disorder programs, but also incorporates information on ADHD. While designed for the school-age child, a variation for the Barkley (1987) program when treating adolescents with ADHD involves the substitution of withdrawal of privileges for time-out from reinforcement. A variant of parent training for preschool children is discussed below along with treatment outcome studies in this area.

Preschool

Negative patterns between parents and their children often become entrenched at the preschool stage (Mash & Johnston, 1982). For this reason, intervention with younger children may be essential. Designed for the preschool-age child exhibiting hyperactivity and disruptive symptoms, parent-child interaction training as described by Strayhorn and Weidman (1989, 1991) involves training parents in operant techniques within a context of story reading and dramatic play. The stories and games are designed to teach prosocial behavior to preschool children. Parents are taught the techniques by paraprofessionals. The parent first observes the clinician employing these techniques with the child, then the parent practices with coaching and feedback provided (Strayhorn & Weidman, 1989).

Strayhorn and Weidman (1989, 1991) have examined parent-child interaction training with a low-income, mainly African American population of hyperactive young children (*see* Table 4.1). Children and their families were randomized to treatment or information control (pamphlets and videotapes on parent-training principles) conditions. At posttest, clinically and statistically significant improvements were made after a mean number of 10 sessions of parent-child interaction therapy in terms of parent-child interactions and parent ratings of child behaviors. Teachers also rated experimental children as superior to control children with respect to improvement of attention deficit and hyperactivity symptoms. At 1-year follow-up, though, many of these positive effects had dissipated, and parent ratings and child achievement test scores between the two groups showed no difference (Strayhorn & Weidman, 1991). However, teacher ratings of decreased ADHD symptom severity were maintained. Suggestive is that a short-term treatment may not be able to sustain all improvements at 1 year after treatment (Strayhorn & Weidman, 1991). At the same time, it might be unreasonable to expect a short-term treatment to have such durable effects, given the persistence of ADHD behavior and its frequent co-occurrence with conduct problems.

School-Age

The majority of the treatment outcome studies on ADHD youngsters involve school-age children (*see* Table 4.2). This trend is not surprising, since referrals for problematic behavior multiply with increasing demands from the school system. Studies in this area typically compare parent training either to no-treatment at all or another treatment approach, such as child cognitive-behavioral therapy and medication treatments. Treatments are also sometimes combined and compared against their separate components. Given this orientation in the literature, studies will be organized in the following way: parent training versus no treatment, parent training versus cognitive-behavioral treatment, and parent training versus stimulant medication.

Parent Training versus No Treatment   Studies examining the effects of training parents versus no treatment all found positive treatment gains. Improvements in parent reports of child ADHD symptomatology (Anastopoulos et al., 1993) and behavioral observations of child compliance (Pisterman et al., 1989) enhanced parental adjustment in terms of increased self-esteem and decreased stress (Anastopoulos et al., 1993) with gains maintained at short-term follow-up.

While the Anastopoulos et al. (1993) and Pisterman et al. (1989) programs were administered through a group format, Blakemore et al. (1993) compared the effectiveness of groups versus individual applications of parent training. Stronger treatment effects were found for the individual format; perhaps attention to the individual treatment needs of particular parents may be more beneficial. However, more studies are needed comparing individual and group format programs, since the Blakemore et al. (1993) curriculum departed from standard parent training programs in a couple of crucial ways. First, there was more of an emphasis on affective issues with the parent, such as grief and loss, communication, acknowledging feelings, self-esteem, and anger management. In addition, 6 hours of consultation was offered to the child's teacher so as to increase the probability of generalization effects to the school environment.

Parent Training versus Cognitive Behavioral Self-Control Training   Along with parent training, child cognitive-behavioral training has been a dominant psychosocial treatment approach for ADHD children (Barkley, 1996; Ervin et al.,

1996). Within cognitive-behavioral approaches, problem-solving/self-control training has been a main thrust. The rationale behind self-control training is to enhance social skills and peer relationships, thereby increasing the child's ability to relate to social as well as classroom environments (Horn et al., 1990). Self-control training involves teaching the following problem-solving steps:

1. taking a "time-out" to think about whether the situation is a problem and to breathe deeply
2. defining the problem
3. thinking of as many solutions as possible
4. evaluating the effectiveness of each solution
5. choosing the best solution and trying it out
6. evaluating how the solution worked

Horn and associates have examined the differential effectiveness of parent training, child cognitive behavioral training, and combinations of these approaches (Horn et al., 1987, 1990). Interestingly, given the differing skills taught in parent training versus cognitive-behavioral training, all three treatment groups (parent training only, child cognitive-behavioral therapy only, and a combination of the two approaches) showed significant behavioral improvements in the home according to child self-report and parent checklist ratings for the initial study (Horn et al., 1987). These improvements were retained at 1-month follow-up, still with no significant differences between groups.

In the second study (Horn et. al., 1990), the program was extended from 8 to 12 sessions, but the hypothesis that combining treatments would produce even greater effects was only minimally supported: A higher proportion of children made clinically significant improvements on externalizing behavior and self-concept. Suggestive is that a slightly longer treatment period (an increase of four sessions) may represent some advantages for a combined intervention. At the same time, the combined treatment group failed to generalize significant treatment effects from the home to the classroom, although it is not mentioned whether the other conditions also failed to produce generalization effects (Horn et al., 1990).

Treatment Combined with Medication for the Child As discussed, the primary treatment method for ADHD involves the use of psychostimulant medication. In order to understand differential effectiveness of alternative approaches for the school-age child, drug treatment has been compared against behavioral approaches in the following studies.

In a Canadian study, Firestone, Crowe, Goodman, and McGrath (1986) randomized children to either parent training combined with medication, parent training with a placebo medication, or medication only. The medication conditions only produced short-term improvements on attentional, behavioral, and hyperactivity problems. The 2-year follow-up showed little difference between any of the treatment conditions, but this result appeared mainly because many of the subjects from the placebo and parent training group had to switch to medication treatments because effective treatment was necessitated due to their symptoms.

Other research examined the effectiveness of group parent training and child self-control training as compared to medication alone (Horn et al., 1991; Ialongo et al., 1993) and found no advantages even when parent and child training were combined (Horn et al., 1991). Limited support was found for combining a low dose of psychostimulant medication with behavioral therapy to achieve the same results as a high-medication dose (Horn et al., 1991) as both the benefits and the undesirable effects of the medication seem to increase with the dose (Horn et al., 1991)

In the 9-month follow-up, the benefit of medication rapidly dissipated when the medication was withdrawn (Ialongo et al., 1993). In addition, there was no evidence to support the hypothesis that behavioral interventions combined with medication would better maintain treatment effects than medication alone. However, when parent training was combined with self-control training of the child, parent ratings of ADHD symptoms and externalizing behaviors were significantly reduced when compared to medication alone (Ialongo et al., 1993).

The final study on family intervention versus medication involved two samples of school-age males: The first cohort received stimulant medication as the primary treatment; the second cohort received "intensive psychotherapy" (including group, family, and individual sessions) together with medication (Satterfield, Satterfield, & Sahell, 1987). Intensive psychotherapy consisted of a variety of techniques and methods. ADHD symptoms were targeted by behavior management techniques; emotional and behavioral symptoms of the child were treated with a combination of behavioral, cognitive, and interpretive techniques; and parents were treated using cognitive, interpretive, or directive techniques depending on the parents' intelligence, motivation, and insight capacity (Satterfield et al., 1987). A limitation of this study is that "intensive psychotherapy" is not clearly explained, nor is mean length and intensity of varying approaches and modalities described. Further, no posttest was conducted so as to assure a minimum equal length of treatment for both treatment groups (Satterfield et al., 1987). Instead, only a 9-year follow-up was employed.

At this point, the group receiving intensive psychotherapy and medication had lower rates of delinquency and institutionalization when compared to the drug-treatment-only group, although participants had to have remained in treatment for between 2 and 3 years for this treatment impact to occur (Satterfield et al. 1987). This study therefore suggests that a child with ADHD and his or her family may have to participate in multi-modal therapy for at least a few year's duration in order to prevent some of the possible negative consequences of ADHD, and to demonstrate the possibility of greater efficacy with a longer duration of treatment.

Adolescence

Only one study in this review concentrated on treatment for teenagers (Barkley, Guevremont, Anastopoulos, & Fletcher, 1992) (see Table 4.3). However, intervention for this age child is crucial, given the high likelihood of continuation into adolescence of ADHD symptoms (e.g., Barkley et al., 1990; Klein & Mannuzza, 1991).

Barkley et al. (1992) compared three different family conditions for teenagers referred for ADHD treatment and their mothers: behavior management training, problem-solving and communication training, and structural family therapy, each of which lasted for 8 to 10 weeks. The behavior management curriculum was similar to the school-age program described earlier by Barkley (1987), except that grounding was substituted for time-out as punishment because of the age of the child. The problem-solving and communication training approach developed by Robin and Foster (1989) involved three major methods for reducing parent-adolescent conflict:

1. problem-solving training
2. communication skills training
3. identifying and restructuring irrational beliefs that either teens or parents hold about the other party's behavior

The structural family therapy condition, originally formulated by Minuchin (1974), focused on the development of a strong parental hierarchy so that parents can gain control of their adolescent's behavior. However, the child's ADHD symptomatology in this model is seen as a symptom of a weak parental hierarchy and other related maladaptive transaction processes, such as disengaged or enmeshed boundaries between family subsystems, transgenerational coalitions, scapegoating, and triangulations. The therapist stimulates interaction in the session to help families alter these maladaptive processes.

TABLE 4.1 Treatment Outcome Studies with Preschoolers

AUTHOR/MODEL	DESIGN/SAMPLE	MEASURES	RESULTS	LIMITATIONS
Strayhorn & Weidman (1989) Parent-Child Interaction Training average 7 sessions Treatment consisted of group sessions for the didactic portion, individual sessions with parent and child for interactive sessions	Experimental, randomization to experimental or control (videotapes on time out and positive reinforcement, pamphlet on parenting practices), pretest, posttest $N = 89$ through Head Start meetings, ads, pediatric and mental health referrals Age = 2–5 SES = low, 74% on public assistance Race = 64% African American, 30% White, and 6% other Gender = 44% male & 56% female	Parent Practices Scale, Commands Self-Report, Parent Behavior in Play with Child Scale, Beck Depression Inventory, Shipley Scale, Consumer Satisfaction Question, Child Behavior in Play with Parent Scale, Behar Preschool Behavior Questionnaire, Depression Factor Items from Child Behavior Checklist, Parents ratings on DSM-III-R items, Frequency of Behavior for Preschoolers, Verbal Ability Measures	Experimental group showed significant improvement over control on: Commands Self-Report; Parent Behavior in Play with Child Scale; Child Behavior in Play with Parent Scale; Behar Anxious and Hyperactivity subscales; Frequency of Behavior for Preschoolers; parent responses to DSM-III-R attention deficit items	Posttest not immediately after last session (average 33 days after)

Strayhorn & Weidman (1991)	1-yr follow-up of above data on 84 children from 77 caretakers	Parents: Behar Preschool Behavior Questionnaire; DSM-III checklist for opposi-tional and attention deficit disorders; Depression Factor Items from Child Behavior Checklist; Parent Practices Scale Teachers: Behar Preschool Behavior Questionnaire; Depression Factor Items from Child Behavior Checklist; reading por-tion of California Achievement Test	Although parent ratings and child achievement test scores indicated no difference between experimental and con-trol groups, teachers reported treatment chil-dren as improved over controls for ADHD symptoms and in ratings of child behavior

TABLE 4.2 Treatment Outcome Studies for School-Age Children

AUTHOR/MODEL	DESIGN/SAMPLE	MEASURES	RESULTS	LIMITATIONS
Anastopoulos et al. (1993) Parent training 9 sessions	Experimental, random-ization to parent training or waiting-list control, pretest, posttest, follow-up (2 mos) $N = 34$ referred to a university medical center clinic; 74% boys and 26% girls; mean age = 97.7 mos; majority 2-parent	Parenting Stress Index; Parenting Sense of Competence Scale; Global Severity Index of Symptom Checklist 90—Revised; Locke-Wallace Marital Adjustment Scale; Test of ADHD Knowledge	Parent training condi-tion produced improve-ments on child ADHD symptoms, parent func-tioning (reduced stress and increased self-esteem) over waiting-list control	Small sample size
Blakemore et al. (1993) 12 weekly parent training sessions with parent prob-lem-solving training with 2 follow-up sessions at 3 and 6 mos 6 hrs of school consulta-tion with teacher was also available	Experimental, random-ization to group, individ-ual or waiting-list control, with stratified sampling procedure so that groups were similar regarding age of child, Oppositional Defiant Disorder, and children on Ritalin, pretest, posttest, follow-up (3 mos)	Nonstandardized: parental decision-mak-ing; measure of family functioning; nonstandardized coding of observations of par-ent-child interactions; Parenting Stress Index, Child Behavior Checklist, Eyberg Child Behavior Inventory, IOWA Conners; WRAT-	Stronger results with individual treatment and for mothers than fathers (mother effects persisted at follow-up); for hypo-thetical problem-solving situations, both individ-ual and group condi-tions showed improvement in strate-gies when child was vic-tim and in	Although children with conduct disorders were screened from the study because of the different etiological factors involved, oppositional defiant disorder was not screened out; states that waiting-list control group was made aware of other services available that they may access prior to their

	$N = 24$ both parents required to attend treatment referred from client list of the agency, community physicians, and ads in newspapers and other media	Peabody Picture Vocabulary Test	parent-created troublesome situation, but only for group was there significant effects when child was aggressor	starting date," so unknown whether this group received other services; some measures nonstandardized; tiny sample size; some findings not discussed in terms of statistical significance; demographic information (e.g., gender of subjects, SES, ethnicity) not mentioned
Horn et al. (1991) Additive effects of psychostimulants, parent training, and self-control therapy with ADHD children 12 90-minute weekly sessions	Experimental, randomization to 1) low-dose stimulant medication alone; 2) high-dose stimulant therapy alone; 3) medication placebo plus behavioral group parent training and child self-control instruction; 4) medication placebo alone $N = 77$ completed pre to posttest (out of original 96)	Child outcomes: Child Behavior Checklist; SNAP Checklist; Conners Teacher Rating Scale; Teacher Checklists of Children's Peer Relations and Social Skills; Continuous Performance Test; clinic-based; clinic-based observational paradigm, modeled after Structured Observation of Academic and Play	Analysis of those who completed at least 9 of 12-week sessions showed no evidence of the combined treatment producing better effects than medication alone, although some support was indicated for combining a low dose of psychostimulant medication with parent training to produce the same effects as a high dose of medication	Small sample size; since behavioral parent training and child self-control training delivered as package, unknown what components are essential

continued

TABLE 4.2 *(continued)*

AUTHOR/MODEL	DESIGN/SAMPLE	MEASURES	RESULTS	LIMITATIONS
	referred to a university-based psychological clinic; mean age = 8.27; 77.4% male, 22.6% female; majority White; mean yearly income = $25,019; majority intact families	Settings; Wide Range Achievement Test-Revised 2; Piers-Harris Self-Concept scale; Nowicki-Strickland Locus of Control scale; Peabody Picture Vocabulary Test—Revised Family functioning: Family Relations subscale from Personality Inventory for Children-Revised Format Consumer Satisfaction Questionnaire		
Satterfield et al. (1987) Multimodal therapy (medication + intensive psychotherapy)	Two samples of White males between 6 and 12 referred to outpatient treatment in consecutive 2-yr periods and then followed for 9 yrs: one	Arrest histories	Comparing the multimodal group with 2–3 yrs of treatment: mean number of arrests and institutionalizations for felony offenses was	Lack of randomization to groups, subjects were assigned to conditions based on their treatment cohort in time; selection bias operating on who

group received psychostimulant medication only ($N = 81$ out of original 116) [mean follow-up time = 9.3 yrs when 17.4 yrs old]; $N = 50$ out of original 70 males, receiving multimodal therapy (mean follow-up time = 8.7 yrs when 17.6 yrs old)

greater in drug-only group compared to multimodal group that received more treatment; the group with less treatment did better than the drug-only groups but differences weren't significant; only significant differences between more and less treatment in multimodal was that the more treatment group had fewer institutionalizations

was available for follow-up; individualized treatment program for multimodal, therefore, not a standardized package; various components comprising intensive psychotherapy not given in terms of average numbers of sessions attended

At posttest, all three treatment conditions reported significant improvements in a number of areas: family communication and conflict, child internalizing and externalizing behaviors, and maternal depression. There were few differences between groups, and all changes were maintained at follow-up.

SUMMARY AND SERVICE DELIVERY RECOMMENDATIONS

Early family intervention for ADHD children seems to be important, given that negative maternal perceptions may develop when the child is young and may persist over time (Mash & Johnston, 1982). Entrenched negative perceptions may preclude the formation of an optimal parent-child bond and the interaction may instead be characterized by coerciveness. Parent-child interaction training, sensitive to the developmental requirements of the preschool child by involving play and stories, shows promising results at posttest (on average of 10 sessions). It also offers the advantage of being administered by trained paraprofessionals from the community rather than degreed professionals. Parent-child interaction therapy indicates some promise in terms of gains at posttest (Strayhorn & Weidman, 1989). One year later, improvements persisted according to teacher ratings of inattention and hyperactivity symptom, although compared to controls, the benefit perceived by parents had dissipated, as well as child achievement scores (Strayhorn & Weidman, 1991). Suggestive is that brief treatment may not be able to sustain all improvements over this period of time. However, given the persistence of ADHD behavior and its frequent co-occurrence with conduct problems, it might be unreasonable to expect a short-term treatment to have such durable effects in all settings. Impressive is that the effects of the parent-child interaction training generalized to the school setting when the lack of generalization of treatment effects have been noted for youngsters diagnosed with ADHD (Barkley, 1996). If these findings were to be replicated, a rationale might develop for early screening and intervention. Screening could occur in health settings, such as doctors' offices and health clinics, at the school, and at child care facilities. At the earliest stages, intervention could be targeted at infants with medical or temperamental vulnerabilities and with mothers who are isolated in the caregiving role or who lack social support. Services could be targeted at promoting secure mother-child attachment, since findings from longitudinal study indicate that an insecure attachment may contribute to the development of ADHD (e.g., Carlson et al., 1995).

When examining school-age children, studies comparing the differential impact of alternative approaches provide the most information about effective treatments. For instance, when parent training was compared against cognitive behavioral child treatment, no differences were found, despite the very different emphases of these treatments. It could well be, then, that parent training offers no special advantages over cognitive-behavioral treatment. Child treatment tends to be more amenable to parents who in parent training have to bear the effort for attendance in treatment and applying the new principles they have learned (Pelham & Murphy, 1986).

The additional effort required to treat both the parents with behavioral therapy and the child with cognitive-behavioral therapy may not produce gains beyond either treatment alone (Horn et al., 1987, 1990). When treatment was extended from 8 (Horn et al., 1987) to 12 sessions (Horn et al., 1990), however, the combined intervention did show some limited advantages in terms of greater proportions of children making clinical improvements on their externalizing behavior and their self-concept.

When looking at behavior therapy versus medication and combined treatments, there appears little advantage to either behavior therapy alone or combining treatments over medication. While parent training appears to improve child noncompliance and aggression, it seems unable to change core symptoms of ADHD consistently over the effects of medication (Estrada & Pinsof, 1995). However, the long-term outcome of behavioral parent training alone or in combination with other treatments has never been studied (Pelham et al., 1993). Such a study may not retain the purity of treatment conditions over time, though, if Firestone et al. (1986) is any indication of what occurs over time. In this study, treatment groups no longer maintained their integrity because of the necessity for subjects in the combined parent training placebo medication group to receive more effective treatment. The evidence, taken together, is that only when psychosocial treatment is combined with medication and applied in an intense fashion and targeting several child and parent domains (e.g., Satterfield et al., 1987) might long-term benefits be gained at least in terms of criminal offending and institutionalization. Therefore, the Satterfield et al. (1987) study provides support for the clinical recommendation that treatment of ADHD be multimodal in nature (Faigel et al., 1995; Hechtman, 1993; Horn et al., 1987; Ialongo et al., 1993; Whalen & Henker, 1991). Interventions may have to include psychopharmacological therapy, child cognitive-behavioral training, parent training, classroom behavioral management systems, and special education (Mash, 1989). These interventions may also have to be applied over a long period of time.

TABLE 4.3 Treatment Outcome Studies with Adolescents

AUTHOR/MODEL	DESIGN/SAMPLE	MEASURES	RESULTS	LIMITATIONS
Barkley et al. (1992) Behavioral Management, Structural, & Problem-Solving/Communication Training 8–10 individual sessions	Quasi-Experimental, randomization to 1) behavioral management; 2) structural; & 3) problem-solving/ communication training, pretest, posttest, follow-up (3 mos) $N = 61$ Age = 12–18 Race = White Clinic referrred ADHD diagnosed	Child Behavior Checklist, Conflict Behavior Questionnaire, Issues Checklist, Locke-Wallace Marital Adjustment Test, Beck Depression Inventory, Parent Adolescent Interaction Coding System, Therapist rating of family cooperation, Consumer Satisfaction Survey	All groups showed statistically but not clinically significant change at both posttest and follow-up for child behavior problems; family members from all groups also displayed higher adjustment and less distress	Small sample size, especially for number of dependent measures; groups were evaluated individually rather than being compared statistically; gender not given

CRITIQUE OF THE RESEARCH AND RESEARCH RECOMMENDATIONS

Although the research on family interventions with ADHD children possesses a number of strengths, such as the use of experimental and quasi-experimental designs with follow-up and the administration of standardized measures, there are also several limitations. One rather common limitation of studies is small sample size. At the same time, studies are usually characterized by a large number of dependent measures. The size of the sample often does not contribute to sufficient statistical power; nor does it support this type of multivariate statistical analysis. Future studies need to ensure adequate sample sizes.

Another limitation of the research involves the lack of demographic information, particularly socioeconomic status and ethnicity. When this information is provided, it is apparent that research on treatment outcome has focused on ADHD children who are White and of at least middle class. Although children of color and those from low socioeconomic backgrounds are no more likely to have a diagnosis of ADHD (Barkley, 1996), the effectiveness of treatments with children from these groups needs to be established.

Other limitations of the research involve gender. The first germane issue in this area is gender of the parents included in parent training outcome studies. Out of 17 research studies, only about a third included any information on which parent attended. Regarding the studies that did not mention gender of participating parents, it could be that we are to assume both parents attended. This is a rather large assumption to make, however, when out of those five studies, four of them required mothers to attend, or families were not allowed to continue in the study (Anastopoulos et al., 1993; Barkley et al., 1992; Horn et al., 1987; McNeil et al., 1991). With the exception of Blakemore et al.'s study (1993), which required both parents to participate, fathers were generally only "encouraged" to attend if they lived in the home. This trend in the research appears to perpetuate the myth that somehow mothers are responsible for the problems their children possess (Phares, 1992). This assumption is present not only in behavioral therapy but also in attachment theory. The longitudinal work presented by Sroufe and colleagues, for example, followed mothers and their children over time, rather than examining the impact of the fathers of these children. The operating belief appears to be that parenting is the domain only of mothers, despite the fact that a significant proportion of women now work outside the home (Phares, 1992). For example, recent statistics demonstrate that approximately 62% of women with children under 6 are part of the labor force (Children's Defense Fund, 1996).

For families with ADHD children, fathers and other male figures often play a significant role in the negative interactions that take place in the home. Further, ADHD children are at risk for developing conduct problems when parental psychopathology, such as parental antisocial behavior and substance abuse, is present. Therefore, failing to require fathers' attendance in therapy seems self-defeating. In both service delivery and research, involvement of fathers deserves a greater emphasis in order to achieve improved outcomes and to remove some of the burden of responsibility from mothers.

Another issue of gender is that out of 17 studies, a little over half (9) mentioned the gender of the participating child. Of these, only a couple included a significant proportion of females (22.6% in Ialongo et al. [1993]; 56% in Strayhorn & Weidman [1989]). It is interesting that the later age of onset commonly documented for females (Arnold, 1996) is not reflected in the treatment outcome studies reported here. Strayhorn and Weidman (1989) has both the highest percentage of females (more than half) and the youngest age group.

The debate in the literature on the later age of onset for females concerns whether this just reflects insensitivity to early precursors in girls, or whether it represents an actual difference in the way ADHD presents in females. In addition, fewer girls tend to be diagnosed, even controlling for referral bias, because females as a group have a lower base level of inattentiveness and hyperactivity than their male counterparts. Therefore, they have to deviate much further from girls without symptoms in order to be diagnosed (Arnold, 1996). As a result, discussion has been generated on appropriate diagnostic criteria for females. Another area of concern involves the children of mothers with ADHD. Not only are females with ADHD possibly more likely to have adolescent pregnancies, they are also more likely to abuse substances than are their non-ADHD counterparts. In addition, the quality of their child care may be marked by inattention, inconsistency, or impulsivity. Therefore, their children are not only more genetically vulnerable, but they are also more physiologically and psychologically vulnerable (Arnold, 1996). With the prevalence rate of ADHD among girls and/or women in the United States (as mentioned earlier, approximately 1 million females), it is a matter of concern that they are not being given fair representation in the research. The needs of these girls and women, as well as the children they bear, require attention in research. The research population must match the population needing treatment if interventions are to be evaluated effectively.

Aside from limitations of the studies themselves, a general problem in the research literature is the lack of study on family treatments other than behavioral theory. The emphasis on behavioral therapy is not, however, restricted to ADHD. Behavioral and cognitive-behavioral methods predominate in child and adolescent treatment outcome research. However, many other practice orientations and methods are used with ADHD-diagnosed children in clinical settings, and these deserve further research attention (Kazdin, Ayers, Bass, & Rodgers, 1990). One option is to use alternative treatment conditions against the behavioral therapy condition. For example, Barkley et al. (1990) compared behavioral therapy, structural family therapy, and parent and adolescent communication and problem-solving skills training, with all groups showing equal effects.

Another issue deserving of further study involves the similarity of symptoms between ADHD and conduct problems and the high rate of co-morbidity. Apparently, the two disorders are separate with a high degree of overlap; however, little is still known about the developmental unfolding of these disorders, the ways in which they are intertwined, and how they influence each other at different periods of development (McMahon, 1994). Further, it is not understood whether and how ADHD by itself is different from when it occurs alongside a conduct disorder, and how treatment needs may differ based on these factors (Abikoff & Klein, 1992). For example, one hypothesis is that combining treatments (parent training and medication) might be more beneficial for children with dual diagnoses (Estrada & Pinsof, 1995). To understand more about the presentation of these two disorders and treatment requirements, a recommendation is to examine, within studies, subjects who demonstrate a pure form of each disorder, as well as those who are co-morbid for both disorders. While treatment outcome studies need to be studied in this manner, much can be learned particularly from longitudinal research, in which over time, the patterns of the disorders can be revealed (McMahon, 1994).

More longitudinal work could also uncover the role of attachment (and not just maternal-infant relationships) and the development of ADHD. Carlson et al. (1995) suggest that there may be several different pathways to ADHD: intrusive and overstimulating caregiving in the context of lack of parental support; organic factors, such as motor development or medical vulnerability; or an interaction of these factors. The delineation of certain pathways to ADHD and the factors that maintain or deflect the child from these pathways may be essential to an understanding of how ADHD differs from other disorders, such as conduct problems and school failure. Given the serious, chronic, and pervasive nature of this disorder, as well as its potential for long-term negative outcomes, a clearer understanding of the disorder and its responsiveness to treatment is urgently required.

REFERENCES

Abikoff, H., & Klein, R. G. (1992). Attention-deficit hyperactivity and conduct disorder: Comorbidity and implications for treatment. *Journal of Consulting and Clinical Psychology, 60,* 881–892.

American Psychiatric Association. (1994). *Diagnostic and statistical manual of mental disorders* (4th ed.). Washington, DC: Author.

Anastopoulos, A. D., Shelton, T. L., DuPaul, G., & Guevremont, D. C. (1993). Parent training for attention-deficit hyperactivity disorder: Its impact on parent functioning. *Journal of Abnormal Child Psychology, 21,* 581–596.

Arnold, L. E. (1996). Sex differences in ADHD. *Journal of Abnormal Child Psychology, 24*(5), 555–569.

Barkley, R. A. (1987). *Defiant children: A clinician's manual for parent training.* New York: Guilford Press.

Barkley, R. A. (1989). Hyperactive girls and boys: Stimulant drug effects on mother-child interactions. *Journal of Child Psychology and Psychiatry, 30,* 379–390.

Barkley, R. A. (1996). Attention-deficit/hyperactivity diorder. In E. J. Mash & R. A. Barkley (Eds.), *Child psychopathology* (pp. 63–112). New York: Guilford Press.

Barkley, R. A., Fischer, M., Edelbrook, C., & Smallish, L. (1990). The adolescent outcome of hyperactive children diagnosed by research criteria: I. An 8-year prospective follow-up study. *Journal of the American Academy of Child and Adolescent Psychiatry, 29,* 546–557.

Barkley, R. A., Fischer, M., Edelbrock, C., & Smallish, L. (1991). The adolescent outcome of hyperactive children diagnosed by research criteria—III. Mother-child interactions, family conflicts and maternal psychopathology. *Journal of Child Psychology and Psychiatry, 32,* 233–255.

Barkley, R. A., Guevremont, D. C., Anastopoulos, A. D., & Fletcher, K. E. (1992). A comparison of three family therapy programs for treating family conflicts in adolescents with attention-deficit hyperactivity disorder. *Journal of Consulting and Clinical Psychology, 60,* 450–462.

Biederman, J., Faraone, S. V., Taylor, A., Sienna, M., Williamson, S., & Fine, C. (1998). Diagnostic continuity between child and adolescent ADHD: Findings from a longitudinal clinical sample. *Journal of the American Academy of Child and Adolescent Psychiatry, 37,* 305–313.

Blakemore, B., Shindler, S., & Conte, R. (1993). A problem solving training program for parents of children with attention deficit hyperactivity disorder. *Canadian Journal of School Psychology, 9,* 66–85.

Carlson, E. A., Jacobvitz, D., & Sroufe, L. A. (1995). A developmental investigation of inattentiveness and hyperactivity. *Child Development, 66,* 37–54.

Children's Defense Fund. (1996). *The state of America's children: Yearbook 1996.* Washington, DC: Author.

DuPaul, G. J., & Barkley, R. A. (1992). Social interactions of children with attention deficit hyperactivity disorder: Effects of methylphenidate. In J. McCord & R. E. Tremblay (Eds.), *Preventing antisocial behavior: Interventions from birth through adolescence* (pp. 89–116). New York: Guilford Press.

Ervin, R. A., Bankert, C. L., & DuPaul, G. J. (1996). Treatment of attention-deficit/hyperactivity disorder. In M. Reinecke, F. Dattlio, & A. Freeman (Eds.), *Cognitive therapy with children and adolescents: A casebook for clinical practice* (pp. 38–61). New York: Guilford Press.

Estrada, A. U., & Pinsof, W. M. (1995). The effectiveness of family therapies for selected behavioral disorders of childhood. *Journal of Marital and Family Therapy, 21*, 403–440.

Eugene, A. L. (1996). Sex differences in ADHD. *Journal of Abnormal Child Psychology, 24*, 555–569.

Faigel, H. C., Sznajderman, S., Tishby, O., Turel, M., & Pinus, U. (1995). Attention deficit disorder during adolescence: A review. *Journal of Adolescent Health, 16*, 174–184.

Fischer, M., Barkley, R. A., Edelbrock, C. S., & Smallish, L. (1990). The adolescent outcome of hyperactive children diagnosed by research criteria: II. Academic, attentional, and neuropsychological status. *Journal of Consulting and Clinical Psychology, 58*, 580–588.

Firestone, P., Crowe, D., Goodman, J. T., & McGrath, P. (1986). Vicissitudes of follow-up studies: Differential effects of parent training and stimulant medication with hyperactives. *American Journal of Orthopsychiatry, 56*, 184–194.

Forehand, R. L., & McMahon, R. J. (1981). *Helping the noncompliant child: A clinician's guide to parent training*. New York: Guilford Press.

Guevremont, D. C., Tishelman, A. C., & Hull, D. B. (1986). Teaching generalized self-control to attention-deficient boys with mothers as adjunct therapists. *Child and Family Behavior Therapy, 7*, 23–37.

Hechtman, L. (1993). Aims and methodological problems in multimodal treatment studies. *Canadian Journal of Psychiatry, 38*, 458–464.

Hill, J. C., & Schoener, E. P. (1996). Age-dependent decline of attention deficit hyperactivity disorder. *American Journal of Psychiatry, 153*, 1143–1146.

Horn, W., Ialongo, N., Greenberg, G., Packard, T., & Smith-Winberry, C. (1990). Addictive effects of behavioral parent training and self-control therapy with attention deficit hyperactivity disordered children. *Journal of Clinical Child Psychology, 19*, 98–110.

Horn, W. F., Ialongo, N. S., Pascoe, J. M., Greenberg, G., Packard, H., Lopez, M., Wagner, G., & Putler, L. (1991). Additive effects of psychostimulants, parent training, and self-control therapy with ADHD children. *Journal of the American Academy of Child and Adolescent Psychiatry, 30*, 233–240.

Horn, W. F., Ialongo, N., Popovich, S., & Peradotto, D. (1987). Behavioral parent training and cognitive-behavioral self-control therapy with ADD-H children: Comparative and combined effects. *Journal of Clinical Child Psychology, 16*, 57–68.

Ialongo, N. S., Horn, W. F., Pascoe, J. M., Greenberg, G., Packard, T., Lopez, M., Wagner, A., & Puttler, L. (1993). The effects of a multimodal intervention with attention-deficit hyperactivity disorder children: A 9-month follow-up. *Journal of the American Academy of Child and Adolescent Psychiatry, 32*, 182–189.

Jacobvitz, D., & Sroufe, A. (1987). The early caregiver-child relationship and attention-deficit disorder with hyperactivity in kindergarten: A prospective study. *Child Development, 58*, 1496–1504.

Jacobvitz, D., Sroufe, L. A., Stewart, M., & Leffert, N. (1990). Treatment of attentional and hyperactivity problems in children with sympathomimetic drugs: A comprehensive review. *Journal of the American Academy of Child and Adolescent Psychiatry, 29*, 492–518.

Kazdin, A. E., Ayers, W. A., Bass, D., & Rodgers, A. (1990). Empirical and clinical focus of child and adolescent psychotherapy research. *Journal of Consulting and Clinical Psychology, 58*, 729–740.

Klein, R. G., & Mannuzza, S. (1991). Long-term outcome of hyperactive children: A review. *Journal of the American Academy of Child and Adolescent Psychiatry, 30*, 383–387.

Mash, E. (1989). Treatment of child and family disturbance: A behavioral-systems perspective. In E. Mash & R. Barkley et al. (Eds.), *Treatment of childhood disorders* (pp. 3–36). New York: Guilford Press.

Mash, E. J., & Johnston, C. (1982). A comparison of the mother-child interactions of younger and older hyperactive and normal children. *Child Development, 53*, 1371–1381.

Minuchin, S. (1974). *Families and family therapy*. Cambridge, MA: Harvard University Press.

Patterson, G. R. (1982). *Coercive family process: A social learning approach* (3rd ed.). Eugene, OR: Castalia.

Pelham, W. E., & Murphy, H. A. (1986). Behavioral and pharamacological treatment of attention deficit and conduct disorders. In M. Hersen (Ed.), *Pharmacological and behavioral treatment: An integrative approach* (pp. 108–148). New York: Wiley.

Pelham, Jr., W. E., Carlson, C., Sams, S. E., Vallano, G., Dixon, M. J., & Hoza, B. (1993). Separate and combined effects of methylphenidate and behavior modification on boys with attention deficit-hyperactivity disorder in the classroom. *Journal of Consulting and Clinical Psychology, 61*, 506–515.

Phares, V. (1992). Where's Poppa? The relative lack of attention to the role of fathers in child and adolescent psychopathology. *American Psychologist, 47*, 656–664.

Pisterman, S., McGrath, P., Firestone, P., Goodman, J. T., Webster, I., & Mallory, R. (1989). Outcome of parent-mediated treatment of preschoolers with attention deficit disorder with hyperactivity. *Journal of Consulting and Clinical Psychology, 57*, 628–635.

Robin, A. L., & Foster, S. (1989). *Negotiating parent-adolescent conflict*. New York: Guilford Press.

Satterfield, J. H., Satterfield, B. T., & Schell, A. M. (1987). Therapeutic interventions to prevent delinquency in hyperactive boys. *Journal of the Academy of Child and Adolescent Psychiatry, 26*, 56–64.

Simeon, J. G., & Wiggins, D. M. (1993). Pharmacotherapy of attention-deficit hyperactivity disorder. *Canadian Journal of Psychiatry, 38*, 443–448.

Sroufe, L. A. (1989). Pathways to adaptation and maladaption: Psychopathology as developmental deviation. In D. Cicchetti (Ed.), *Rochester Symposium on Developmental Psychopathology* (pp. 13–41). Hillsdale, NJ: Lawrence Erlbaum and Associates.

Strayhorn, J., & Weidman, C. S. (1989). Reduction of attention deficit and internalizing symptoms in preschoolers through parent-child interaction training. *Journal of the American Academy of Child and Adolescent Psychiatry, 28,* 888–896.

Strayhorn, J., & Weidman, C. S. (1991). Follow-up one year after parent-child interaction training: Effects on behavior of preschool children. *Journal of the American Academy of Child and Adolescent Psychiatry, 30,* 138–143.

Weiss, G., & Hechtman, L. (1993). *Hyperactive children grown up: ADHD in children, adolescents, and adults.* New York: Guilford Press.

Weiss, G., Hechtman, L., Milroy, T., & Perlman, T. (1985). Psychiatric status of hyperactives as adults: A controlled prospectus 15-year follow-up of 63 hyperactive children. *Journal of the American Academy of Child Psychiatry, 24,* 211–220.

Whalen, C. K., & Henker, B. (1991). Therapies for hyperactive children: Comparisons, combinations, and compromises. *Journal of Consulting and Clinical Psychology, 59,* 126–137.

MEASUREMENT OF FAMILY TREATMENT WITH ATTENTION DEFICIT AND HYPERACTIVITY DISORDER

Increasingly, practitioners are held accountable for the evaluation of their practice. To assist with this evaluation, this section on measurement provides the reader with self-report instruments that children and their families can easily complete. Scores from these measurement instruments can be used to guide assessment and clinical practice when treating children with ADHD. For those interested in conducting research in this area, each of the instruments provided has established psychometric data to support its usage.

The following types of measures are presented: 1) child outcomes according to parent report, 2) parenting practices, 3) parental adjustment, 4) family and marital functioning, and 5) client satisfaction with services.

Measures presented in this section involve the following criteria. First, instruments are self-report; that is, they are completed by family members themselves, rather than being interviewer-administered or observational measures. A second criterion for inclusion was that adequate reliability and validity information had to be available for each scale. Selected psychometric data were chosen to inform the reader on the properties of the instruments.

CHILD OUTCOMES—PARENT REPORT

CONNERS PARENT QUESTIONNAIRE

Author: Conners (1990)

Description:

- Screens for childhood disorders and rates the degree problems may be present for children ages 3 to 17 years old
- Originally developed for documenting behavior change during pharmacotherapy among hyperactive children
- Parent report short and long forms: 93, 48, 39, 28, with 4 responses ("not at all," "just a little," "pretty much," "very much")
- 93-item scale includes, 1) Conduct Disorder, 2) Anxious-Shy, 3) Restless-Disorganized, 4) Learning, 5) Psychosomatic, 6) Obsessive-Compulsive, 7) Antisocial, and 8) Hyperactive-immature
- 48-item scale includes 1) Conduct Problem, 2) Learning Problem, 3) Psychosomatic, 4) Impulsive-Hyperactive, and 5) Anxiety.
- All versions also include the 10-item Hyperactivity Index

Reliability:

93-item scale:
- Test-retest reliabilities range from .40 (Psychosomatic) factor to .70 (Immature-Inattentive and Hyperactive-Impulsive)
- Maternal and paternal correlations on factors average .85

48-item scale:
- Inter-rater reliabilities range from .46 (Psychosomatic) to .57 (Conduct Problem) with mean correlation of .51
- Item-total correlations range from .13 to .65

39-item scale:
- Average internal consistency of .94 for various factors

Hyperactivity Index:
- Maternal and paternal ratings correlate .55
- Alpha internal-consistency reliability coefficient of .92

Validity:

39-item scale:
- Scores correlate with observed motor activity and disruptive behavior and peer ratings
- Predictive validity: a 3-year follow up of children with minor neuro-developmental disorders and generalized hyperkinesis at 7 years highly predictive of hyperactivity at 10
- Discriminative validity: discriminates between hyperactive boys and controls and juvenile offenders and controls
- Strong correlation between factors and externalizing scales of the Child Behavior Checklist
- In normal control and clinic samples, subscales had moderate-to-strong correlations with the Quay-Peterson subscales

93-item scale:
- Discriminates between boys with attention deficit disorder, learning disabilities, and matched controls
- In normal control and clinic samples, subscales had moderate-to-strong correlations with the Quay-Peterson subscales

Hyperactivity Index:
- Discriminates between behavior-disordered children and both normal controls and the learning-disabled
- Strong correlations between teacher ratings and 2 other hyperactivity rating scales, the Behavior and Temperament Survey (.89) and the School Behavior Survey (.76)

HOME SITUATIONS QUESTIONNAIRE

Authors: Barkley & Edelbrock (1987)

Description:

- Lists 16 different situations for which parents observe and handle their child's behavior
- Parents indicate ("yes"/ "no") whether problem behaviors occur in these situations; if so, parents rate severity of the problem (1/ "mild" to 9/ "severe")
- Yields 2 summary scores

1. Number of Problem Situations: An index of the situational variance of problem behaviors
2. Mean Severity Score: An index of problem behavior severity across situations

Reliability:

- Test-retest reliabilities estimated by correlating initial scores with scores from the placebo condition of drug trial (1–3 weeks apart) were .66 for Number of Problem Situations and .62 for Mean Severity Score

Validity:

- Number of Problem Situations correlated with the following scales of the Child Behavior Profile: Aggressive (.83); Hyperactive (.73); Delinquent (.48); Depressed (.62); Social Withdrawal (.62)
- Mean Severity Score correlated with the following scales of the Child Behavior Profile: Aggressive (.69); Hyperactive (.66); Delinquent (.60); Depressed (.46); Social Withdrawal (.61)
- Number of Problem Situations correlated with the following Child Domain scales of the Parenting Stress Index: Adaptability (.78); Distractibility/Hyperactivity (.76); Mood (.73); Demanding (.70)
- Mean Severity Score correlated with the following Child Domain scales of the Parenting Stress Index: Adaptability (.63); Distractibility/ Hyperactivity (.75); Mood (.61); Demanding (.59)
- Summary scales correlated with the Adjustment, Depression, Hyperactivity, Social Skills, and Psychosis scales of the Personality Inventory for Children, ranging from .72 to .81
- Discriminates between normal children and children with ADHD and ADHD children and their normal siblings

EYBERG CHILD BEHAVIOR INVENTORY

(*See Chapter Three,* Family Treatment with Conduct Disorder)

CHILD BEHAVIOR CHECKLIST

(*See Chapter One*, Family Treatment with Child Abuse and Neglect)

PARENTING PRACTICES

THE PARENT PROBLEM CHECKLIST

(*See Chapter One,* Family Treatment with Child Abuse and Neglect)

THE PARENTING SCALE

(*See Chapter One*, Family Treatment with Child Abuse and Neglect)

PARENTING STRESS INDEX

(*See Chapter One*, Family Treatment with Child Abuse and Neglect)

PARENT ADJUSTMENT

BECK DEPRESSION INVENTORY

(*See Chapter One*, Family Treatment with Child Abuse and Neglect)

SYMPTOM CHECKLIST 90-REVISED

(*See Chapter One*, Family Treatment with Child Abuse and Neglect)

BRIEF SYMPTOM INVENTORY

(*See Chapter One*, Family Treatment with Child Abuse and Neglect)

MARITAL OUTCOMES

THE MARITAL ADJUSTMENT TEST

(*See Chapter One*, Family Treatment with Child Abuse and Neglect)

DYADIC ADJUSTMENT SCALE

(*See Chapter One*, Family Treatment with Child Abuse and Neglect)

O'LEARY-PORTER SCALE

(*See Chapter One*, Family Treatment with Child Abuse and Neglect)

REVISED CONFLICT TACTICS SCALES

(*See Chapter One*, Family Treatment with Child Abuse and Neglect)

FAMILY OUTCOMES

FAMILY ADAPTABILITY AND COHESION EVALUATION SCALES III

(*See Chapter One*, Family Treatment with Child Abuse and Neglect)

FAMILY ENVIRONMENT SCALE

(*See Chapter One*, Family Treatment with Child Abuse and Neglect)

MCMASTER FAMILY ASSESSMENT DEVICE

(*See Chapter One*, Family Treatment with Child Abuse and Neglect)

SATISFACTION WITH SERVICES

CLIENT SATISFACTION QUESTIONNAIRE

(*See Chapter One*, Family Treatment with Child Abuse and Neglect)

REFERENCES FOR MEASUREMENT OF FAMILY TREATMENT WITH ATTENTION DEFICIT AND HYPERACTIVITY DISORDER

Barkley, R. A., & Edelbrock, C. (1987). Assessing situational variation in children's problem behaviors: The home and school situations questionnaires. *Advances in Behavioral Assessment of Children and Families, 3*, 157–176.

Conners, C. K. (1990). *Manual for Conners' rating scales.* North Tonawanda, NY: Multi-Health Systems.

CHAPTER 5

Family Treatment with Sexual Abuse

Family Case:

Tricia Reilly, a White female, age 11, made allegations that she was sexually abused by her stepfather of 2 years. The sexual abuse consisted of her stepfather, Bill Coons, fondling Tricia's vagina on three occasions while Tricia's mother, Betty Coons, was at work. Tricia first told a school counselor after a sexual abuse prevention program held at school.

When Child Protective Services became involved, Tricia's mother initially expressed skepticism at Tricia's account, stating her suspicion that the prevention program had maybe planted an idea in Tricia's head on how to get rid of her stepfather. Betty Coons said that Tricia had not wanted her mother to get married to her stepfather because she had enjoyed all the attention she used to get from her mother when they lived alone together. Tricia also claimed that her stepfather was "mean" and "yelled too much."

When the Child Protective Services investigator stated that Tricia might have to stay with someone else if Tricia's mother did not ask the stepfather to leave the home, Betty Coons said that of course she would have him leave if it meant losing her daughter.

However, a Child Protective Services case was opened because Tricia reported that after he had moved out, her stepfather had been allowed to visit the home. Tricia denied that he had made any sexually abusive gestures toward her; in fact, she said he had ignored her completely. As part of the case, Tricia and her mother have been mandated into treatment.

High rates of sexual abuse have been reported in the general population. Probability samples of adults indicate that between 13% (Elliott & Briere, 1995) and 16% (Finkelhor, Hotaling, Lewis, & Smith, 1990) of males experience sexual abuse as children. For females, survey estimates vary: 27% (Finkhelhor et al., 1990), 32% (Elliott & Briere, 1995), 38% (Russell, 1984), and 45% (Wyatt, 1985). These high rates are of concern, particularly when the potentially deleterious effects of child sexual abuse are considered.

The effects of sexual abuse have been well documented. The empirical literature reports a range of behavioral and emotional problems, which include internalizing symptoms (Kendall-Tackett, Williams, & Finkelhor, 1993), such as depression (Brooks, 1985; Koverola, Pound, Heger, & Lytle, 1993; Mennen & Meadow, 1994), anxiety (Mennen & Meadow, 1994), somatic concerns (Miller, McCluskey-Fawcett, & Irving, 1993), and externalizing behaviors (Kendall-Tackett et al., 1993), such as sexual acting-out (Friedrich, 1993), aggression, conduct disorders, and delinquency (Friedrich, 1988). Additionally, post-traumatic stress disorder (Kendall-Tackett et al., 1993; Wolfe, Sas, & Wekerle, 1994), lowered self-esteem (Kendall-Tackett et al., 1993; Mennen & Meadow, 1994), and impaired self-concept (Orr & Downes, 1985) are implicated with sexual abuse.

Meta-analyses have also been conducted on the effects of sexual abuse on long-term adjustment (Jumper, 1995; Neumann, Houskamp, Pollock, & Briere, 1996) and found the following symptom constellations: depression, low self-esteem, somatization, anger, anxiety, obsessions and compulsions, sexual dysfunctions, self-mutilation, suicidality, dissociation, substance abuse problems, revictimization, relationship problems, and post-traumatic stress symptomatology. The cumulative results of these studies indicate that children who have been sexually abused are at substantial risk for impaired adult mental health and adjustment.

A recent movement in the sexual abuse literature has been the growing awareness of the distress and possible negative sequelae to nonoffending caretakers upon disclosure of sexual abuse of their children (Corcoran, 1998). This trend is in contrast to the earlier clinical literature, which tended to implicate mothers in their children's abuse and negatively focus on maternal inadequacy (e.g., Forward, 1978; James & Nasjleti, 1983; Justice & Justice, 1979; Mayer, 1983; Sgroi & Dana, 1982).

Empirical work with mothers of intrafamilial sexual abuse victims indicates that these mothers are similar to mothers of extrafamilial abuse survivors (Deblinger, Hathaway, Lippmann, & Steer, 1993; Peterson et al., 1993) and clinic mothers (Wagner, 1991), and that symptom distress appears to be related to the demands of disclosure, rather than to pre-existing pathology (DeJong, 1988; Newberger, Gremy, Waternaux, & Newberger, 1993). Further, Deblinger et al. (1993) specifically compared mothers whose partners had sexually abused their children to mothers whose children were abused by other relatives and found no differences.

Attention to maternal adjustment and response to disclosure is crucial, as it may mediate children's recovery. A meta-analysis on the short-term effects of sexual abuse indicate the importance of maternal support (Kendall-Tackett et al., 1993), which comprises both belief and protective action. Belief involves validation of the child's account, placing the responsibility on the adult rather than the child, and conveying an attitude of concern. Protective action involves behaviors that protect the child from further abuse and aid in recovery, such as cooperating with the child protective services and criminal justice agencies, removing the child from perpetrator access, and seeking counseling (Corcoran, 1998). Clinician assessments (Adams-Tucker, 1982; Conte & Schuerman, 1987; Division of Child Psychiatry, 1984; Everson, Hunter, Runyon, Edelsohn, & Coulter, 1989) and retrospective reports from adult survivors (Edwards & Alexander, 1992; Gold, 1986; Nash, Hulsey, Sexton, Harralson, & Lambert, 1993; Peters, 1988; Wind & Silvern, 1994; Wyatt & Mickey, 1988) also demonstrate the importance of maternal support for both short- and long-term adjustment.

Despite the potential deleterious consequences of sexual abuse to both the child and nonoffending caretakers, outcome research on treatment for either the child or parent has been sorely lacking (Finkelhor & Berliner, 1995). To illustrate, a review of the group therapy literature found that out of 25 intervention reports, only three employed empirical methods (Stauffer & Deblinger, 1996). The lack of evaluation is further reflected in the practice arena. A national questionnaire of 2,258 child sexual abuse programs found that only 38% of program respondents reported employing both pre- and posttesting, and only 27% conducted follow-ups (Keller, Cicchinelli, & Gardner, 1989).

In order to effectively intervene with sexually abused children and their families, it is important that clinicians be informed by empirically based knowledge. To this end, a review of interventions that included both the child and the nonoffending caretaker was conducted. Although studies had to demonstrate a minimum methodological standard in order to be included, studies still possessed flaws, such as lack of theoretical frameworks, the use of nonstandardized measures (e.g., Downing, Jenkins, & Fisher, 1988), and uncontrolled confounding factors, such as the provision of individual, group, and family therapy to various family members for varying lengths of time (e.g., Friedrich, Luecke, Beilke, & Place, 1992) (*see* table 5.1). Therefore, discussion of this review will concentrate on the three different streams of research that are both theoretically based and methodologically strong.

DEBLINGER AND ASSOCIATES

Deblinger and associates were the first to evaluate cognitive-behavioral intervention with a specific focus on post-traumatic stress due to its relative frequency as an effect of abuse (Kendall-Tackett et al., 1993). Deblinger, McLeer, and Henry (1990) discuss a behavioral conceptualization of post-traumatic stress disorder (PTSD) involving both classical and operant conditioning. In classical conditioning, an initially neutral stimulus becomes paired with an unconditioned stimulus. In cases of sexual abuse, certain places, people, and sensory experiences, such as smells or hearing certain words or phrases, for example, may become associated with the trauma. The neutral stimulus then becomes a conditioned stimulus, capable of evoking anxiety. Operant conditioning comes into play as the child avoids such anxiety-provoking stimulus. The relief associated with the avoidance of anxiety is negatively reinforced and increases the frequency of avoidance behavior in the future.

Treatment for the child emphasizes gradual exposure to abuse-related memories in order to disconnect the respondently conditioned stimuli. Coping skills, such as relaxation training, emotional expression, and cognitive restructuring, are taught. In this way, victims can manage the anxiety produced by gradual exposure and thereby both cognitively and affectively process the abusive experience. A final module of treatment comprises education on sexuality and sexual abuse. In addition, both behavioral rehearsal and role-plays are used so that children are prepared to protect themselves in the event of further inappropriate advances.

The parental component of the cognitive-behavioral treatment initially focuses on sexual abuse education, with the assumption that an understanding of dynamics will mediate emotional distress. For example, maternal feelings of guilt may be allayed by knowledge of the prevalence of sexual abuse among the general population. Understanding aspects of perpetration, such as grooming and its secretive nature, may help explain why mothers might not have learned of the abuse earlier.

After parents' emotional reactions have been processed, they are trained through the use of modeling and role-plays to communicate about the sexual abuse to their children. Further, they are trained in gradual exposure techniques to assist in reducing their children's anxiety toward abuse-related stimuli. Parents also learn behavior management skills in order to reinforce appropriate age-level behavior and extinguish any inappropriate behaviors their children have learned through experiencing victimization.

Based on this model, Deblinger and associates have conducted an increasingly sophisticated series of studies, beginning with a pretest, posttest design with a control baseline period (Deblinger et al., 1990), and 3-month follow-up (Stauffer & Deblinger, 1996), to an experimental design with randomization to experimental conditions (parent-only, child-only, parent and child, community control) with a planned 6-, 12-, and 24-month follow-up (Deblinger, Lippmann, & Steer, 1996). The positive impact of cognitive-behavioral interventions was found for school-age children and their caretakers delivered in an individual format (Deblinger et al., 1990, 1996) and for preschool children and their nonoffending caretakers in groups (Stauffer & Deblinger, 1996).

The Deblinger et al. (1996) study was designed to address some of the earlier limitations, such as the lack of randomization to treatment and control conditions and the difficulty of ascertaining the essential elements of treatment when both children and parents received the intervention. In this study, children were screened for post-traumatic symptoms and had to meet a minimum criterion of at least three symptoms. Unfortunately, the authors neglect to mention how many children were excluded for this reason.

Results of Deblinger et al. (1996) specify intervention components necessary for targeting certain symptoms. First, parents' engagement in treatment was associated statistically and clinically with reductions in child externalizing problems. A substantial body of literature has accumulated on the effectiveness of parent training programs on child externalizing symptoms (e.g., Kazdin, 1987, 1997). Therefore, it is curious that the Stauffer and Deblinger (1996) study did not also find such improvements. One hypothesis to explain the contrasting results might have to do with the screening criteria. Deblinger et al. (1996) specifically screened for the inclusion of post-traumatic stress symptomatology, whereas inclusion in the Stauffer and Deblinger (1996) study was based on parental interest. It could be that the similarity of symptom behaviors in the former sample furthered positive intervention effects.

In Deblinger et al. (1996), parents' engagement in treatment was also associated with statistically significant reductions in depression, according to child reports. While these improvements suggest that parents' recovery through treatment helps mediate child distress, clinical significance was not positively impacted, nor were parents' perceptions of child internalizing symptoms. Since these results were also found for Deblinger et al. (1990), it appears that child-focused interventions to target depression might be a beneficial addition to the cognitive-behavioral protocol. Cognitive-behavioral interventions addressing social skills and coping strategies have had demonstrated success with children and adolescents (Peterson et al., 1993) and would be theoretically consistent with the Deblinger program. A further rationale for such a focus is a meta-analysis on the effects of sexual victimization. Kendall-Tackett et al. (1993) reported that sexual abuse predicted internalizing symptoms, such as depression and withdrawal, contributing 35% to 38% of the variance.

The necessity for child-focused interventions are also seen with recovery from post-traumatic stress symptomatology (Deblinger et al., 1996). Although parents were trained in gradual exposure techniques to enable their children to process abuse-related thoughts, memories, and other stimuli, it appeared that their efforts were much less effective than when clinicians directly worked with their children.

COHEN AND MANNARINO

Another cognitive-behavioral curriculum was developed and tested by Cohen and Mannarino (1993), who argue that a specialized treatment protocol for the preschool-age group and their caretakers is of necessity, citing statistics that one third of sexual abuse victims are below the age of 6 years. The parent curriculum addresses the following concerns: belief and support; ambivalence toward the abuser; attributions of fault and responsibility; history of abuse in the parent's background, if applicable; legal issues; and management of children's anxieties and inappropriate sexual behaviors. The child curriculum includes prevention of further abuse, assertiveness training, attributions of blame, ambivalence toward the abuser, regressive and sexual acting-out behaviors, and coping with fear and anxiety. To target these symptoms, cognitive-behavioral interventions involve reframing, positive imagery, thought-stopping, problem-solving, and parent management training.

With the rationale that symptom reduction was the central objective of treatment, children were screened for a minimum symptom level (Cohen & Mannarino, 1997). Children and parents were then randomized to either the 12-week cognitive-behavioral treatment or "nonspecific" treatment (Cohen & Mannarino, 1996a). The nonspecific condition involved elements presumed common to many therapeutic approaches: reflective listening, conveying empathy, and making clarifying and supportive statements. Neither interpretations nor directive advice was provided, nor was there an emphasis on sexual abuse issues. For the child condition, these nonspecific elements were essentially described as nondirective play therapy.

Results supported the efficacy of cognitive-behavioral treatment over the nonspecific treatment on all measures except for child social competence. The lack of empirical support for play therapy for maltreated preschoolers has also been found in an earlier study (Reams & Friedrich, 1994). When examining predictors that contribute to outcome, Cohen and Mannarino (1996b) discuss that children with more advanced cognitive capacity were able to utilize cognitive-behavioral interventions more effectively. Further, maternal distress was associated with poorer child outcomes (Cohen & Mannarino, 1996b). The authors postulated that modeling may be the mechanism, in that children may master fewer adaptive coping strategies from parents who are struggling with their own emotional reactions (Cohen & Mannarino, 1996b).

At 6- and 12-month follow-ups, parental distress decreased in its impact on child adjustment; at this point, social support available to parents was a more potent mediator for outcomes. Overall, cognitive-behavioral treatment was the strongest predictor of superior outcomes (Cohen & Mannarino, 1998), with gains made at posttest maintained over time (Cohen & Mannarino, 1997). Further study could address, similar to Deblinger et al. (1996), crucial components of the intervention. For example, is it the parent or the child treatment that is associated with certain positive outcomes?

CELANO, HAZZARD, AND ASSOCIATES

Celano, Hazzard, Webb, and McCall (1996) departed from the emphasis on cognitive-behavioral treatment by using Finkelhor and Browne's (1985) four-factor traumagenic model, which addresses domains of functioning presumably impacted by sexual abuse. The model assumes that sexual abuse negatively impacts four areas crucial to the child's development: 1) self-esteem, 2) feelings of trust in others, 3) healthy sexuality, and 4) sense of efficacy. The model hypothesizes how children's affective and cognitive capacities are distorted within each of these areas with the four traumagenic factors (Finkelhor, 1990). The first is self-blame/stigmatization, the negative reactions of shame and guilt that are communicated to the child and then internalized into the child's self-image. The second involves betrayal, the discovery that a trusted person on whom children depend has harmed them. The third is traumatic sexualization, the process by which the child's sexuality is inappropriately conditioned and develops in a dysfunctional manner with faulty beliefs and assumptions about sexual behavior. The fourth factor is powerlessness, which arises from the child's inability to escape or stop the boundary violations associated with sexual abuse. Little study has been conducted to test the traumagenic model due to its complexity, the amount of mechanisms that have been put forth to explain the effects, and the challenge of definition and measurement (Kendall-Tackett et al., 1993). Therefore, the Celano et al. (1996) treatment model is notable.

The protocol devotes two sessions each to the four factors for a total of eight sessions. Cognitive-behavioral and "metaphoric" techniques target affect, behavior, and beliefs of sexually abused children and their caretakers regarding each domain. Children and caretakers are seen individually for the most part with some conjoint work as well. The model and protocol are outlined in Table 5.2.

Compared to "treatment-as-usual," the four-factor treatment model was not significantly different in its effects for children: Both groups of children showed improvements in post-traumatic stress symptoms and beliefs reflecting self-blame and powerlessness. Unfortunately, betrayal and traumatic sexualization were not significantly impacted. For caretakers, both groups showed increased supportiveness according to clinician ratings, with the experimental group showing more support toward their children. The same trend was found for maternal self-blame. Caretakers were less blaming of themselves, with experimental group mothers showing the most reductions in self-blame. Another difference was that mothers in the experimental group became more optimistic about their children's future in regard to the possible negative effects of sexual abuse, whereas the comparison group became more pessimistic.

Although a differential treatment effect was not found for children in the experimental curriculum (Celano et al., 1996), an advantage named by the authors was its structuring of clinical material for beginning therapists. In contrast, an advantage of treatment-as-usual was its flexibility in addressing the particular concerns of individual victims and their parents. It is encouraging, however, that so much change occurred for both groups in such a short time frame (8 weeks, 1-hour sessions). The authors suggest that a combination treatment, both structured and sensitive to individual concerns, might be most beneficial to victims and their families, although they also recognize that such a program would be difficult to empirically validate.

SUMMARY AND RECOMMENDATIONS

Empirically validated treatment models have begun to be tested on sexual abuse victims and their caretakers, and initial outcome studies have demonstrated positive results within brief time periods (8 to 12 sessions). Results of studies point to certain tentative conclusions. Suggestive, for instance, is that sexual abuse issues need to be targeted directly in therapy, rather than relying on a nondirective process (Celano et al., 1996; Mannarino & Cohen, 1996). In addition, cognitive-behavioral treatments appear to be effective for addressing children's sexual acting-out behavior (Mannarino & Cohen, 1996; Stauffer &

Deblinger, 1996). Authors have discussed the intractable nature of victimized children's tendency to exhibit sexualized behaviors, such as excessive and overt masturbation, sexual overtures toward children and adults, and compulsive talk and play about sexual topics (Kendall-Tackett et al., 1993). Indeed, both cross-sectional and longitudinal research indicate that sexual victimization explains 43% of the variance for inappropriate sexual behavior (Kendall-Tackett et al., 1993).

This research review also highlights methodological and treatment issues that deserve attention in future studies. These issues include the confounding of treatments, the symptoms that interventions target, the type of control conditions used, and the applicability to voluntary and nonvoluntary populations.

The first issue involves the confounding of treatments in which both parent and child are seen concurrently, a limitation of all studies, with the exception of Deblinger et al. (1996). Unfortunately, when parents and children both attend counseling, it is difficult to ascertain whether intervention is effective and the essential components of treatment needed to target particular symptoms. This issue is especially crucial for sexual abuse, since there is no dominant symptom constellation that victims universally experience. According to a meta-analysis on sexual abuse effects, any particular constellation is demonstrated in only about 20% to 30% of victimized children (Kendall-Tackett et al., 1993). The Deblinger et al. (1996) study shows that child externalizing problems are best addressed by parent treatment, whereas PTSD symptoms in children require child-focused interventions. Further study is needed to find out whether these results are generalizable to other samples.

A related issue is whether treatments should be targeted at specific symptoms, such as the Deblinger treatment protocol for PTSD. PTSD seems most prevalent in samples of children who suffer severe ritualistic abuse. When ritualistic abuse studies were removed from the meta-analysis, the mean percentage of children diagnosed with PTSD were similar to those of other common symptom constellations, such as impaired self-esteem (35%) and behavior problems (37%) (Kendall-Tackett et al., 1993). In addition, sexually abused children may suffer commonly from such symptoms as guilt, fear, autonomic arousal, nightmares, and somatic problems; it is unknown whether these are symptomatic of PTSD or other problems. Finally, although PTSD is more prevalent in sexual abuse samples compared to other clinic populations, this diagnosis is not unique to sexual victimization (Kendall-Tackett et al., 1993).

Both Deblinger et al. (1996) and Cohen and Mannarino (1997) screened for symptoms before children and caretakers were included in their studies.

However, questions about apparently asymptomatic sexually abused children have been raised, given that one third of children do not display ill effects (Kendall-Tackett et al., 1993). Several possible hypotheses may explain these findings. The first is that appropriate measures may not have been used to capture the effects of sexual abuse, as only a limited range of symptoms was assessed (Kendall-Tackett et al., 1993). The second is that available measures might not possess sufficient sensitivity to capture symptoms. A third explanation is that such children have as yet to show symptoms. Perhaps children are suppressing their symptoms, or they have not yet processed the abuse.

Another hypothesis for apparently asymptomatic children involves the role of development. Perhaps children experience greater distress when the sexual abuse experience attains more significance, for example, in adolescence, when sexuality becomes more salient.

A final hypothesis to explain lack of symptoms in children is that some children may not be as affected. Certain factors, for instance, have been associated with increased impact: lack of maternal support, maternal use of avoidant coping mechanisms, intrafamilial child abuse, and being part of a sexual abuse case that results in acquittal (Wolfe & Birt, 1997). In addition, children without symptoms may be those with the most resources (psychological, social, and/or treatment). Given the various hypotheses that have been put forth, it is clear that the issue of apparently asymptomatic children, and whether such children can benefit from treatment, deserves more attention. Related is the issue of whether studies should screen for and target particular symptoms.

Another issue in this literature is the construction of adequate control/comparison conditions, since it is unethical to deny treatment to sexual abuse victims. Each of the researchers came up with a different way to structure these conditions. In Deblinger et al. (1996), the control was represented by a "community" condition, whereby parents were encouraged to seek treatment for their families from community agencies and services. As a result, a great deal of variability existed in the control condition: Some families received no treatment; others attended a varying amount of sessions in a variety of different modalities over varying lengths of time. It could be argued that such a condition fails to possess an adequate level of homogeneity to serve as a basis for comparison.

In the Celano et al. (1996) study, the solution was for subjects in the alternative condition to receive "treatment as usual" for the same length of time as the experimental condition. Some issues with treatment-as-usual involve "bleed-over" effects from the treatment to comparison groups as training, supervision, and discussion between colleagues takes place. In addition, treat-

TABLE 5.1 Treatment Outcome Studies for Family Interventions

AUTHOR/MODEL	DESIGN/SAMPLE	MEASURES	RESULTS	LIMITATIONS
Celano et al. (1996) Finkelhor and Browne's (1985) traumagenic factor model Eight 1-hr sessions divided between caregiver and child; 2–3 conjoint sessions	Quasi-experimental, comparing Recovering from Abuse program and treatment as usual (supportive and unstructured) $N = 32$ families (sexually abused girls and nonoffending caregiver) Girls' ages = 8–13 Race = 75% African American, 22% White, & 3% Hispanic Low SES 72% mothers, 13% aunts, 13% grandmothers, & 3% stepmothers Recruited from pediatric emergency room, CPS, & Victim Assistance programs	Child: Child Behavior Checklist, Children's Impact of Traumatic Events Scales-Revised, Children's Global Assessment Scale For caregiver: Parent Reaction to Incest Disclosure Scale; Parental Attribution Scale (nonstandardized)	No significant difference between groups for children: both groups showed reduced PTSD symptoms, & beliefs reflecting self-blame & powerlessness; traumatic sexualization and betrayal were not impacted. For mothers, both groups showed improved supportiveness of their children and reduced self-blame, with an emphasized positive effect for the experimental group. Experimental groups also became more positive regarding the potential negative effects of the sexual abuse on their children whereas comparison group mothers became more pessimistic	Small sample size due to high dropout (17); lack of no-treatment control group

continued

TABLE 5.1 (*continued*)

AUTHOR/MODEL	DESIGN/SAMPLE	MEASURES	RESULTS	LIMITATIONS
Cohen & Mannarino (1996a, 1996b) Cognitive-behavioral 12 sessions, individual with both parent and child	Quasi-experimental, randomization to cognitive behavioral or individual supportive therapy, pretest, posttest, follow-up $N = 67$ completed treatment (out of 86) Sexual abuse had been confirmed and a minimum level of symptomatology was present Mean age = 4.68; about half male, half female; about half White and half African American; Mean Hollingshead = IV	Child: Preschool Symptom Self-Report Parent: Child Behavior Checklist; Child Sexual Behavior Inventory; Weekly Behavior Report Study on predictors of outcome: Child: Battelle Developmental Inventory; Peabody Picture Vocabulary Test-R; Parent completed: Child Behavior Checklist; Child Sexual Behavior Inventory; Weekly Behavior Report; Beck Depression Inventory; Family Adaptability and Cohesion Scale-III; Parent Emotional Reaction Questionnaire; Parental Support Questionnaire; Maternal Social Support Index	Experimental condition produced greater improvements on almost all outcomes over non-specific control group to non-clinical ranges; social competence one area that showed equivalent modest improvement for both groups even though neither group had initial scores within clinical range Predictors of treatment outcome: problems with parental depression and parents' negative emotional reaction to abuse associated with behavioral and emotional child problems	Because both parents and children attended sessions, unknown as to the crucial intervention strategy

Cohen & Mannarino (1997)	12-mo follow-up of above $N = 43$	Cognitive-behavioral treatment maintained significant improvements over non-specific therapy on total scores on Child Behavior Checklist as well as Internalizing and Externalizing scores and Weekly Behavior Report
Cohen & Mannarino (1998)	Reports on predictors of outcome at 6- and 12-mo follow-up	Parental distress became less important at 6- and 12-mo follow-ups; instead, amount of support parents had became stronger predictors of child outcome; treatment was the most important predictor with experimental group showing positive changes over nondirective supportive therapy

continued

TABLE 5.1 *(continued)*

AUTHOR/MODEL	DESIGN/SAMPLE	MEASURES	RESULTS	LIMITATIONS
Deblinger et al. (1990) Cognitive-behavioral individual treatment for child and nonoffending parent 12 sessions	Baseline 2 to 3 weeks prior to beginning treatment, pretest, posttest $N = 19$ girls who were sexually abused, mainly by relatives; met criteria for PTSD; mean age = 7.8 yrs	Child Behavior Checklist; Child Depression Inventory; Spielberger State-Trait Anxiety Inventory	PTSD symptoms child behaviors, anxiety, and depression improved after intervention	No information on social class or race; no comparison or control group; small sample size; study cannot tease out whether parent or child interventions were crucial to the results

Deblinger et al. (1996) Cognitive-behavioral 12 sessions	Experimental, pretest, posstest/follow-up (6, 12, & 24 mos), randomization to 3 experimental conditions: parent-only, child-only, parent & child, & community control $N = 90$ children Age = 7–13 Gender = males 17%, females 83% Race = 72% White, 20% African American, 6% Hispanic Caregivers = 76% biological or adoptive mothers, 4% long-term foster mothers, & 20% other female relatives Recruited from hospital in which forensic medical exam had taken place, CPS, & prosecutor's office	Schedule for Affective Disorders & Schizophrenia for school-age children State/Trait Anxiety Inventory for Children, Child Depression Inventory, Child Behavior Checklist For parent: Parenting Practices Questionnaire (adapted for parents of sexual abuse victims)	When parents were involved in treatment, they reported significant improvements in parenting skills & in child's externalizing behaviors; children also reported reductions in depression When children involved in treatment, depression levels decreased When more stringent critieria used (clinical cutoff scores), externalizing symptoms only remained significant	Follow-up data in process; small numbers in each group

continued

TABLE 5.1 (continued)

AUTHOR/MODEL	DESIGN/SAMPLE	MEASURES	RESULTS	LIMITATIONS
Stauffer & Deblinger (1996) Cognitive-behavioral groups for both parents and children 11 2-hr sessions	Pretest, posttest, and follow-up (3 mos), $N = 19$ nonoffending caregivers and their sexually abused children who completed treatment; Ages = 2–6 Gender = 26% male, 74% female Race = Mostly White; Parents' educational levels: 42% completed high school, 37% had some college, 11% Bachelor's degrees; 5% master's degree Recruited from: medical facility for assessment of sexual abuse	For child (completed by parent): Child Behavior Checklist, Child Sexual Behavior Inventory For parent: Symptom Checklist-90—Revised Global Severity Index, Impact of Events Scale, Parent Practices Questionnaire	From pretest to posttest, significant changes on following: Child Sexual Behavior Inventory, Symptom Checklist-90—Revised Global Severity Index, Avoidance Subscale of Impact of Events Scale, Parent Practices Questionnaire; although no significant change to follow-up, treatment effects were maintained	High number of dropouts (44%) from initial treatment sample; no randomization to groups; small sample size; because both parents and children attended group, impossible to tease out essential elements of treatment; no comparison group

Downing et al. (1988) Comparison between psychodynamic and reinforcement theory	Quasi-experimental pretest, posttest only (1 yr) $N = 22$ children ranging in age from 6–12 from 5 elementary schools and seeking help from 4 private practitioners, middle to lower-middle class, 90% sexually abused by a nonbiological relative living in home	Home observations by parents: child's acting-out behavior, sleep disturbances, enuresis, sexual self-stimulation, and sexual play school observations from teachers on general in-school behavior and parent-school personnel relations summarized by school counselors	Both groups reported improvements except with sexual self-stimulation and to a lesser extent, enuresis	Although reinforcement theory sounds behavioral, no mention of that orientation; lack of randomization to treatment; lack of standardized measures; differences between pre- and posttests and differences between groups not reported in terms of statistical significance
Friedrich et al., (1992) Multimodal treatment consisting of individual, group, and family therapy Average of 20 sessions of group, 4 family sessions, 4 parent sessions, and 5 individual sessions over 8-mo period	Pretest, posttest $N = 33$ boys who had been sexually abused and completed treatment (9 noncompleters); referred from within agency, CPS, other agencies, and professionals in community; majority had received prior treatment; primarily White, age range =	Parent: Beck Depression Inventory; Faces II; Sibling Behavior Problem Checklist and Social Support Measure (both derived from Health and Daily Living Manual of the Stanford Ecology Laboratory); Achenbach Child Behavior Checklist; Child Sexual Behavior Inventory; Rated satis-	Boys did not improve on self-esteem or depression; on Child Behavior Checklist, all scales showed improvement except for hyperactivity; mothers reported reduced depression, number of sibling behavior problems; mothers reported improved social support and adaptability and cohesion	No theoretical model specified; confounded effects of treatment; no comparison or control group; lack of follow-up

continued

TABLE 5.1 *(continued)*

AUTHOR/MODEL	DESIGN/SAMPLE	MEASURES	RESULTS	LIMITATIONS
	4–16; majority from single-parent households; predominantly lower middle class	faction with treatment (unstandardized) Child: Child Depression Inventory; Piers Harris Self-Esteem Inventory; Martinek-Zaichkowsky Self-Concept Scale; 2 cards from Roberts Apperception Test for Children; kinetic-family drawings		
Winton (1990) Open-ended group support for parents of sexual abuse victims 13 weeks for 2 hrs weekly "Eclectic" incorporating parent effectiveness training and parent training	Pretest, posttest $N = 27$ caretakers 70% mothers; mean age of child = 4.63; 85% White, 15% African American	Therapist rating forms (nonstandardized) Louisville Behavior Checklist; Parenting Stress Index; Subjective Evaluation Form	While parenting stress did not decrease, child behavior problems improved	No comparison/control group; no follow-up; lack of theoretical framework

TABLE 5.2   Celano et al. (1996) Individual Child and Parent Protocol Based on Finkelhor and Browne's (1985) Four Traumagenic Factor Model

GOALS FOR FACTOR	CHILD	PARENT
Self-blame/stigmatization	1. Reduce self-blame 2. Increase self-esteem	1. Decrease attributions of blame toward child 2. Increase attribution of blame toward perpetrator 3. Attribute specific blame to self, if appropriate 4. Reduce global self-blame ("I am a bad mother")
Betrayal	1. Address sense of betrayal by perpetrator 2. Assess perceptions of people's reactions to disclosure and how trust was effected 3. Help child find balance between excessive distrust and overdependence on others	1. Address betrayal by perpetrator and possibly victim 2. Improve communication between child and mother so that trust can be rebuilt 3. Identify support system
Traumatic sexualization	1. Reduce abuse-reactive sexual behaviors 2. Reduce confusion and/or anxiety about sexual activities and functioning	1. Parent learns origins of child's inappropriate sexual behaviors 2. Learn strategies for handling inappropriate sexual behaviors 3. Increase mother-child communication about developmentally appropriate sexual matters
Powerlessness	1. Reduce abuse-related helplessness and anxiety 2. Improve assertiveness skills	1. Address perceptions of powerlessness 2. Improve mother's skills to reduce risk of further abuse

ment-as-usual may lack sufficient homogeneity within a certain setting. On the other hand, it could also be that a certain setting may possess a particular orientation; therefore, treatment-as-usual may vary considerably depending on the setting, which would undermine comparisons across studies.

In their study, Cohen and Mannarino (1996a) utilized "nonspecific therapy" to control for common aspects of therapy, such as support and validation provided by a concerned professional over a period of time. The Cohen and Mannarino (1996a) solution appears to hold a number of advantages. Ethical considerations are accounted for, with families receiving some basic therapeutic support; at the same time, sufficient homogeneity is maintained. Despite these advantages, future studies should strive to utilize a control condition that takes into account the feasibility of the design and the limitations associated with field research.

A final issue involves treatment efficacy with voluntary versus nonvoluntary populations. Parents in the reviewed studies seem largely voluntary, rather than the mandated samples associated with child protective services. It is recognized that the population of mothers of sexual abuse victims is heterogeneous (Corcoran, 1998), and a variety of factors, such as personality variables, relationship to the perpetrator, circumstances of disclosure, characteristics of the child and the abuse, and mothers' experience of physical victimization are associated with a mother's ability to support her child (De Jong, 1988; Division of Child Psychiatry, 1984; Everson et al., 1989; Lyon & Kouloumpos-Lenares, 1987; Myer, 1985; Sirles & Franke, 1989). The next stage of research needs to examine effectiveness of treatment programs with nonvoluntary mothers, those whose lack of support necessitates child protective services involvement.

Despite the presumed voluntary nature of caretakers in this review, a high rate of noncompliance was still demonstrated. For example, Stauffer and Deblinger (1996) reported that 44% of mothers invited to participate either failed to initially engage or stopped attending after one session. High drop-out rates were also indicated for Celano et al. (1996) (35%) and Cohen and Mannarino (1996a) (22%).

A couple of studies examined characteristics of dropouts. Longer duration of abuse (an average of almost 2 years compared to 9.8 months for completers) was found to distinguish dropouts (Friedrich et al., 1992). Longer duration of abuse suggests not only the likelihood of more severe child problems, but also that parents are less able to protect and support (Friedrich et al., 1992). Lower socioeconomic status might also be associated with high dropout, since families overwhelmed with meeting basic necessities may not find counseling a priority (Cohen & Mannarino, 1996a). The high rate of dropout in the Celano et al. (1996) study (35%) may have involved the predominance of African Americans (75%) in the sample. High rates of dropout are indicated for African Americans in treatment (Sue, Zane, & Young, 1994), although Celano et al. (1996) discussed their efforts to make treatment culturally sensitive.

In order to address these questions and issues raised, a greater expansion of the outcome research is essential in order to intervene effectively with families. Given the negative consequences of sexual abuse to both child victims and nonoffending mothers, empirical study of treatment efficacy urgently requires more attention.

REFERENCES

Adams-Tucker, C. (1982). Proximate effects of sexual abuse in childhood: A report on 28 children. *American Journal of Psychiatry, 139,* 1252–1256.

Briere, J., & Runtz, M. (1993). Childhood sexual abuse: Long-term sequelae and implications for psychological assessment. *Journal of Interpersonal Violence, 8,* 312–330.

Brooks, B. (1985). Sexually abused children and adolescent identity development. *American Journal of Psychotherapy, 39,* 401–410.

Browne, A., & Finkelhor, D. (1986). Impact of child sexual abuse: A review of the research. *Psychological Bulletin, 99,* 66–77.

Celano, M., Hazzard, A., Webb, C., & McCall, C. (1996). Treatment of traumagenic beliefs among sexually abused girls and their mothers: An evaluation study. *Journal of Abnormal Child Psychology, 24,* 1–17.

Cohen, J. A., & Mannarino, A. P. (1993). A treatment model for sexually abused preschoolers. *Journal of Interpersonal Violence, 8,* 115–131.

Cohen, J. A., & Mannarino, A. P. (1996a). A treatment outcome study for sexually abused preschool children: Initial findings. *Journal of the American Academy of Child and Adolescent Psychiatry, 35,* 42–50.

Cohen, J. A., & Mannarino, A. P. (1996b). Factors that mediate treatment outcome of sexually abused preschool children. *Journal of the American Academy of Child and Adolescent Psychiatry, 34,* 1402–1410.

Cohen, J. A., & Mannarino, A. P. (1997). A treatment study for sexually abused preschool children: Outcome during a one-year follow-up. *Journal of the American Academy of Child and Adolescent Psychiatry, 36,* 1228–1235.

Cohen, J. A., & Mannarino, A. P. (1998). Factors that mediate treatment outcome of sexually abused preschool children: Six- and 12-month follow-up. *Journal of the American Academy of Child and Adolescent Psychiatry, 37,* 44–51.

Conte, J., & Schuerman, J. (1987). Factors associated with an increased impact of child sexual abuse. *Child Abuse and Neglect, 11,* 201–211.

Corcoran, J. (1998). In defense of mothers of sexual abuse victims. *Families in Society, 79,* 358–369.

Deblinger, E., Hathaway, C. R., Lippmann, J., & Steer, R. (1993). Psychosocial characteristics and correlates of symptom distress in nonoffending mothers of sexually abused children. *Journal of Interpersonal Violence, 8*, 155–168.

Deblinger, E., Lippmann, J., & Steer, R. (1996). Sexually abused children suffering posttraumatic stress symptoms: Initial treatment outcome findings. *Child Maltreatment, 1*, 310–321.

Deblinger, E., McLeer, S., & Henry, D. (1990). Cognitive-behavioral treatment for sexually abused children suffering post-traumatic stress: Preliminary findings. *Journal of the American Academy of Child and Adolescent Psychiatry, 29*, 747–752.

De Jong, A. (1988). Maternal responses to the sexual abuse of their children. *Pediatrics, 81*, 14–21.

Division of Child Psychiatry, Tufts New England Medical Center. (1984). *Sexually exploited children: Service and research project* (Final report for the Office of Juvenile Justice and Delinquency Prevention, U.S. Department of Justice). Unpublished Manuscript, Tufts New England Medical Center, Boston.

Downing, J., Jenkins, S. J., & Fisher, G. L. (1988). A comparison of psychodynamic and reinforcement treatment with sexually abused children. *Elementary School Guidance and Counseling, 22*, 291–298.

Edwards, J. J., & Alexander, P. C. (1992). The contribution of family background to the long-term adjustment of women sexually abused as children. *Journal of Interpersonal Violence, 7*, 306–320.

Elliott, D. M., & Briere, J. (1995). Posttraumatic stress associated with delayed recall of sexual abuse: A general population study. *Journal of Traumatic Stress Studies, 8*, 629–648.

Everson, M. D., Hunter, W. H., Runyon, D. K., Edelsohn, G. A., & Coulter, M. A. (1989). Maternal support following disclosure of incest. *American Journal of Orthopsychiatry, 59*, 197–207.

Finkelhor, D. (1990). Early and long-term effects of child sexual abuse: An update. *Professional Psychology—Research and Practice, 21*, 325–330.

Finkelhor, D., & Berliner, L. (1995). Research on the treatment of sexually abused children: A review and recommendations. *Journal of the American Academy of Child and Adolescent Psychiatry, 34*, 1408–1423.

Finkelhor, D., & Browne, A. (1985). The traumatic impact of child sexual abuse: A conceptualization. *American Journal of Orthopsychiatry, 55*, 530–541.

Finkelhor, D., Hotaling, G., Lewis, I. A., & Smith, C. (1990). Sexual abuse in a national study of adult men and women: Prevalence, characteristics, and risk factors. *Child Abuse and Neglect, 14*, 123–133.

Forward, S. (1978). *Betrayal of innocence: Incest and its devastation.* New York: St. Martin's Press.

Friedrich, W. (1988). Behavior problems in sexually abused children: An adaptational perspective. In G. E. Wyatt & G. J. Powell (Eds.), *Lasting effects of child sexual abuse* (pp. 171–192). Newbury Park, CA: Sage.

Friedrich, W. (1993). Sexual victimization and sexual behavior in children: A review of recent literature. *Child Abuse and Neglect, 17*, 59–66.

Friedrich, W. N. (1990). *Psychotherapy of sexually abused children and their families.* New York: Norton.

Friedrich, W. N., Luecke, W., Beilke, R., & Place, V. (1992). Psychotherapy outcome of sexually abused boys. *Journal of Interpersonal Violence, 7,* 396–409.

Gold, E. R. (1986). Long-term effects of sexual victimization in childhood: An attributional approach. *Journal of Consulting and Clinical Psychology, 54,* 471–475.

Gomes-Schwartz, B., Horowitz, J. M., & Sauzier, M. (1985). Severity of emotional distress among sexually abused preschool, school-age, and adolescent children. *Hospital and Community Psychiatry, 36,* 503–508.

Haskett, M., Nowlan, N., Hutcheson, J., & Whitworth, J. (1991). Factors associated with successful entry into therapy in child sexual abuse cases. *Child Abuse and Neglect, 15,* 467–475.

James, B., & Nasjleti, M. (1983). *Treating sexually abused children and their families.* Palo Alto, CA: Consulting Psychologists Press.

Johnson, B. J., & Kenkel, M. B. (1991). Stress, coping, and adjustment in female adolescent incest victims. *Child Abuse and Neglect, 15,* 293–305.

Jumper, S. A. (1995). A meta-analysis of the relationship of child sexual abuse to adult psychological adjustment. *Child Abuse and Neglect, 19,* 715–728.

Justice, B., & Justice, R. (1979). *The broken taboo: Sex in the family.* New York: Human Sciences Press.

Kazdin, A. E. (1987). Treatment of antisocial behavior in children: Current status and future directions. *Psychological Bulletin, 102,* 187–203.

Kazdin, A. E. (1997). Practitioner review: Psychosocial treatments for conduct disorder in children. *Journal of Child Psychology and Psychiatry, 38,* 161–178.

Keller, R. A., Cicchinelli, L. F., & Gardner, D. M. (1989). Characteristics of child sexual abuse treatment programs. *Child Abuse and Neglect, 13,* 361–368.

Kendall-Tackett, K. A., Williams, L. M., & Finkelhor, D. (1993). Impact of sexual abuse on children: A review and synthesis of recent empirical studies. *Psychological Bulletin, 113,* 164–180.

Koverola, C., Pound, J., Heger, A., & Lytle, C. (1993). Relationship of child sexual abuse to depression. *Child Abuse and Neglect, 17,* 393–400.

Lyon, E., & Kouloumpos-Lenares, K. (1987). Clinician and state children's services worker collaboration in treating sexual abuse. *Child Welfare, 66,* 517–527.

Mannarino, A. P., & Cohen, J. A. (1996). Abuse related attributions and perceptions, general attributions and locus of control in sexually abused girls. *Journal of Interpersonal Violence, 11,* 162–180.

Mayer, A. (1983). *Incest: A treatment manual for therapy with victims, spouses, and offenders.* Holmes Beach, FL: Learning Publications.

Mennen, F. E., & Meadow, D. (1994). Depression, anxiety, and self-esteem in sexually abused children. *Families in Society, 75,* 74–81.

Miller, D. A., McCluskey-Fawcett, K., & Irving, L. M. (1993). The relationship between childhood sexual abuse and subsequent onset of bulimia nervosa. *Child Abuse and Neglect, 17,* 305–314.

Myer, M. (1985). A new look at mothers of incest victims. *Journal of Social Work and Human Sexuality, 3,* 47–58.

Nash, M. R., Hulsey, T. L., Sexton, M. C., Harralson, T. L., & Lambert, W. (1993). Long-term sequelae of childhood sexual abuse: Perceived family environment, psychopathology, and dissociation. *Journal of Consulting and Clinical Psychology, 61*, 276–283.

Neumann, D. A., Houskamp, B. M., Pollock, V. E., & Briere, J. (1996). The long-term sequelae of childhood sexual abuse in women: A meta-analytic review. *Child Maltreatment, 1*, 6–16.

Newberger, C. M., Gremy, I., Waternaux, C. M., & Newberger, E. H. (1993). Mothers of sexually abused children: Trauma and repair in longitudinal perspective. *American Journal of Orthopsychiatry, 63*, 92–102.

Orr, D. P., & Downes, M. C. (1985). Self-concept of adolescent sexual abuse victims. *Journal of Youth and Adolescence, 14*, 401–410.

Peters, S. D. (1988). Child sexual abuse and later psychological problems. In G. E. Wyatt & G. J. Powell (Eds.), *Lasting effects of child sexual abuse* (pp. 101–117). Newbury Park, CA: Sage.

Peterson, A., Compas, B., Brooks-Gunn, J., Stemmler, M., Ey, S., & Grant, K. (1993). Depression in adolescence. *American Psychologist, 48*, 155–168.

Reams, R., & Friedrich, W. (1994). The efficacy of time-limited play therapy with maltreated preschoolers. *Journal of Clinical Psychology, 50*, 889–899.

Russell, D. E. H. (1984). *Sexual exploitation: Rape, child sexual abuse, and workplace harassment.* Beverly Hills, CA: Sage.

Russell, D. E. H. (1986). *The secret trauma: Incest in the lives of girls and women.* New York: Basic Books.

Scott, R., & Stone, D. (1986). MMPI profile constellations in incest families. *Journal of Consulting and Clinical Psychology, 54*, 364–368.

Sgroi, S. M., & Dana, N. T. (1982). Individual and group treatment of mothers of incest victims. In S. M. Sgroi (Ed.), *Handbook of clinical intervention in child sexual abuse* (pp. 191–214). Lexington, MA: Lexington Books.

Sirles, E. A., & Franke, P. J. (1989). Factors influencing mothers' reactions to intrafamily sexual abuse. *Child Abuse and Neglect, 13*, 131–139.

Stauffer, L. B., & Deblinger, E. (1996). Cognitive behavioral groups for nonoffending mothers and their young sexually abused children: A preliminary treatment outcome study. *Child Maltreatment, 1*, 65–76.

Strayhorn, J. M. (1987). Control groups for psychosocial intervention outcome studies. *American Journal of Psychiatry, 144*, 275–282.

Sue, S., Zane, N., & Young, K. (1994). Research on psychotherapy with culturally diverse populations. In A. E. Bergin & S. L. Garfield (Eds.), *Handbook of psychotherapy and behavior change* (4th ed., pp. 783–817).

Wagner, W. G. (1991). Depression in mothers of sexually abused vs. mothers of nonabused children. *Child Abuse and Neglect, 15*, 99–104.

Wind, T. W., & Silvern, L. (1994). Parenting and family stress as mediators of the long-term effects of child abuse. *Child Abuse and Neglect, 18*, 439–453.

Winton, M. (1990). An evaluation of a support group for parents who have a sexually abused child. *Child Abuse and Neglect, 14*, 397–405.

Wolfe, D. A., Sas, L., & Wekerle, C. (1994). Factors associated with the development of posttraumatic stress disorder among child victims of sexual abuse. *Child Abuse and Neglect, 18*, 37–50.

Wolfe, V. V., & Birt, J. A. (1997). Child sexual abuse. In E. J. Mash & L. G. Terdal (Eds.), *Assessment of childhood disorders* (pp. 569–623). New York: Guilford Press.

Wyatt, G. E. (1985). The sexual abuse of Afro-American and White American women in childhood. *Child Abuse and Neglect, 9*, 507–519.

Wyatt, G. E., & Mickey, M. R. (1988). The support by parents and others as it mediates the effects of child sexual abuse: An exploratory study. In G. E. Wyatt & G. J. Powell (Eds.), *Lasting effects of child sexual abuse* (pp. 211–226). Newbury Park, CA: Sage.

MEASUREMENT OF FAMILY TREATMENT
WITH SEXUAL ABUSE

Increasingly, practitioners are held accountable for the evaluation of their practice. To assist with evaluation, this section provides the reader with self-report instruments that children and their families can easily complete. Scores from these measurement instruments can be used to guide assessment and clinical practice when treating children who have been sexually abused. For those interested in conducting research in this area, each of the instruments provided has established psychometric data to support usage.

The following types of measures are presented: 1) child outcomes according to the child's own report and then the parent's report, 2) parenting practices, 3) parental adjustment, 4) family functioning, and 5) client satisfaction with services.

Measures presented in this section involve the following criteria. First, instruments are self-report; that is, they are completed by family members themselves, rather than being interviewer-administered or observational measures. A second criterion for inclusion was that adequate reliability and validity information had to be available for each scale. Selected psychometric data were chosen to inform the reader of the properties of the instruments.

CHILD OUTCOME—CHILD REPORT

CHILDREN'S DEPRESSION INVENTORY

(See Chapter One, Family Treatment with Child Abuse and Neglect)

CHILDREN'S MANIFEST ANXIETY—REVISED
(WHAT I THINK AND FEEL)

(See Chapter One, Family Treatment with Child Abuse and Neglect)

STATE-TRAIT ANXIETY INVENTORY FOR CHILDREN

(See Chapter One, Family Treatment with Child Abuse and Neglect)

CHILDREN'S IMPACT OF TRAUMATIC EVENTS SCALE—REVISED

Authors: Wolfe & Gentile (1991); Wolfe, Gentile, Michienzi, Sas, & Wolfe (1991)

Description:

- Original 54-item child report (very true/somewhat true/not true) assessing perceptions and attributions concerning sexual abuse of children ages 8 to 16
- Although could be used as a self-report, suggested that measure be administered with an interviewer reading the questions and indicating the child's responses (due to sensitive nature of the questions)
- Revised scale: 78 items based upon a factor analysis and a multimethod-multitrait analysis of the original 54-item scale plus DSM-III-R diagnostic criteria
- 11 scale scores, which fall into 4 areas: 1) PTSD (Intrusive thoughts, Avoidance, Hyperarousal, and Sexual Anxiety); 2) Attributional Issues (Self-Blame/Guilt, Empowerment, Personal Vulnerability, and Dangerous World); 3) Social Reactions (Negative Reactions from Others, Social Support); 4) Eroticization.

Reliability:

- For the revised scale: alpha values for the total scale (.89) and the subscales (.57 to .88) (Wolfe et al., 1991)

Validity:

- Convergent validity evidenced by significant correlations between the following subscales and measures:
    1. Intrusive Thoughts, Avoidance, and Sexual Anxiety subscales and the PTSD subscale of the Child Behavior Checklist List and the Sexual Abuse Fear Evaluation
    2. Negative reactions from others and Social Support and Child's Attitude Toward Mother, the Child's Attitude toward Father, and Index of Parental Attitudes (all Hudson, 1982, scales)
    3. Self-blame and Guilt, Empowerment, Vulnerability, and Dangerous World and the Attributional Style Questionnaire for Children
    4. Eroticism and the Child Behavior Checklist Sex Problems Scale and the Child Sexual Behavior Inventory (Wolfe et al., 1991)

- Discriminant validity evidenced by low correlations between the subscales and the alternate method scales assessing different variables (Wolfe et al., 1991)

TRAUMA SYMPTOM CHECKLIST FOR CHILDREN

(*See Chapter One,* Family Treatment with Child Abuse and Neglect)

CHILD OUTCOMES—PARENT REPORT

CHILD BEHAVIOR CHECKLIST

(*See Chapter One,* Family Treatment with Child Abuse and Neglect)
Child Behavior Checklist—Sexual Problems Subscale

Description:

- Consists of six items, which are scored for children ages 4 to 11
- Although it contributes to the overall count for the Total Behavior Problems scale, the subscale is not considered as part of either the Internalizing or Externalizing scores
- Since the six items were endorsed relatively infrequently in the normative sample, Achenbach (1991) cautions that scores should be interpreted in general terms (i.e., low, moderate, or high range)

Reliability:

- One-week test-retest reliability is .83
- Interparent agreement on the scale is poor (.50 for girls and .54 for boys)
- Alpha values for the Sexual Problems scale are also poor (.56 for boys and .54 for girls), probably because of low endorsement of these items

CHILD SEXUAL BEHAVIOR INVENTORY

Authors: Friedrich et. al. (1992)

Description:

- A 35-item parent report measuring sexual behaviors such as self-stimulation, sexual aggression, gender role discrepancies, and personal boundary violations on a 4-point scale for the previous 6-month period
- Designed to assess children ages 2 to12 years (although does not appear to be as sensitive for girls ages 7 to 12 years)

Reliability:

- Alpha values for the normative sample was .82 and for the clinical sample .93
- Four-week test-retest reliability for the normative sample was .85
- Three-month test-retest reliability for the clinic sample was .47

Validity:

- 26 of the 35 items discriminated between sexually abused and nonsexually abused children
- Correlates with teacher report of child sexual behavior
- Correlates with characteristics of the sexual abuse including force, severity, and number of perpetrators

PARENT OUTCOMES—PARENT REPORT

BECK DEPRESSION INVENTORY

(*See Chapter One,* Family Treatment with Child Abuse and Neglect)

SYMPTOM CHECKLIST-90—REVISED

(*See Chapter One,* Family Treatment with Child Abuse and Neglect)

BRIEF SYMPTOM INVENTORY

(*See Chapter One,* Family Treatment with Child Abuse and Neglect)

FAMILY ADJUSTMENT

FAMILY ADAPTABILITY AND COHESION EVALUATION SCALES III

(*See Chapter One,* Family Treatment with Child Abuse and Neglect)

FAMILY ENVIRONMENT SCALE

(*See Chapter One,* Family Treatment with Child Abuse and Neglect)

McMASTER FAMILY ASSESSMENT DEVICE

(*See Chapter One,* Family Treatment with Child Abuse and Neglect)

SATISFACTION WITH SERVICES

CLIENT SATISFACTION QUESTIONNAIRE

(*See Chapter One,* Family Treatment with Child Abuse and Neglect)

REFERENCES FOR MEASUREMENT OF FAMILY
TREATMENT WITH SEXUAL ABUSE

Achenbach, T. M. (1991). *Manual for the Child Behavior Checklist/4–18 and 1991 profile*. Burlington, VT: University of Vermont Department of Psychiatry.

Friedrich, W., Grambsch, P., Damon, L., Hewitt, S., Koverola, C., Lang, R., Wolfe, V., & Broughton, D. (1992). Child sexual abuse inventory: Normative and clinical comparisons. *Psychological Assessment, 4*, 303–311.

Wolfe, V. V., & Gentile, C. (1991). *The Children's Impact of Traumatic Events Scale— Revised*. Unpublished manuscript, London Health Sciences Centre, London, Ontario, Canada.

Wolfe, V. V., Gentile, C., Michienzi, T., Sas, L., & Wolfe, D. A. (1991). The children's impact of traumatic events scale: A measure of post-sexual-abuse PTSD systems. In (Ed.), *Behavioral assessment* (pp. 359–383). Elmsford, NY: Pergamon Press.

Section II

Family Treatment with Adolescents

CHAPTER 6

Family Treatment with Eating Disorders

Family Case:

Jordan Adams, age 16, is brought to treatment by her mother, Monica Adams. Monica explains that her husband couldn't make it because he is working late. Monica states that her daughter has always been a "perfect" child—she gets good grades and has always helped her around the house. The only area where there has ever been any trouble is the arguments Jordan and her 15-year-old sister, Ashley, get into, which can get "pretty vicious."

Monica reports that recently, however, after Jordan's boyfriend of 4 months broke up with her, Jordan lost 15 pounds. Monica discovered that Jordan has been using laxatives and throwing up her food. Monica has also found Jordan up in the middle of the night eating her way through whole packets of cookies.

Jordan is embarrassed by her mother's revelations and she says she only threw up "that one time" when her mother "made her" eat Thanksgiving with all their relatives. She said that she has only used laxatives a couple of times, and it is her sister that has just "blown the whole thing out of proportion," and her mother always believes Ashley over her.

Although diagnosable eating disorders afflict 2% of the population (APA, 1994), eating disorders severe enough to fulfill diagnostic criteria may be the extreme end of a continuum, with relatively normative concerns about weight and body dissatisfaction at the other (Hsu, 1990). For example, a review of surveys reported that almost 19% of female undergraduates reveal symptoms of bulimia (Hoek, 1995). In addition, at least a third of those entering clinic treatment for eating disorders fail to meet diagnostic criteria for either anorexia or bulimia nervosa (Beumont, 1995).

Alarmingly, the rate of eating disorders has increased in recent decades among industrialized nations (Hsu, 1990). Feminist scholars have explained these normative concerns among women (90% of victims are female in both clinic and population samples; Anderson, 1995; APA, 1994) as involving the discrepancy between an increasingly thin female cultural ideal and the biological realities of female bodies, resulting in widespread body image dissatisfaction (Streigel-Moore, 1995). It is also acknowledged that besides sociocultural influences, individual and family risk factors interact and contribute to the development of eating disorders. This chapter will focus specifically on the families of eating-disordered individuals and the interventions in this area. Prior to this discussion, definitions of eating disorders will be provided, along with associated health risks.

Anorexia nervosa and bulimia nervosa are disorders marked by disturbances in eating behavior and distorted perception of body weight and shape (APA, 1994). Pathological fears of becoming overweight lead to behaviors intended to cause or maintain weight loss (Garfinkel, 1995). Anorexia nervosa is distinguished by refusal to sustain a minimal body weight (85% of what is normal for body height and age; APA, 1994), achieved through either restricting or binge-eating and purging, and these represent subtypes of the disorder. Restricting anorexics maintain underweight through dieting or excessive exercise. Binge-eating/purging types engage in binge eating, purging behaviors, or both. Another criterion for the diagnosis of anorexia nervosa is the manifestation of an endocrine problem, namely amenorrhea in females.

In bulimia nervosa, pathological fears of overweight lead to purging behaviors, such as self-induced vomiting, and/or misuse of laxatives, diuretics, or other medications. Nonpurging types rely on fasting or excessive exercise in order to influence weight (APA, 1994). Binge eating and compensatory behaviors occur about twice a week for at least 3 months.

Serious health complications can result from eating disorders. Specific risks to anorexia nervosa include starvation and malnutrition, which impacts many of the systems of the body (Fairburn, 1995; Hsu, 1990). Endocrine problems may include amenorrhea and metabolic abnormalities. Cardiovascular disturbances include electrolyte imbalances, hypotension, arrhythmia, and heart failure. Other problems impact the hematologic system (anemia) and the musculocutaneous system (hair covering body, sensitivity to cold) (Hsu, 1990). Ten percent of the anorexic group may eventually die from the disorder, either through starvation, heart failure, or suicide (APA, 1994).

For bulimia nervosa, purging behaviors may lead to enlarged salivary glands and the erosion of dental enamel (Hsu, 1990; Mitchell, 1995). More seriously, electrolyte imbalance and chronic dehydration increase the likelihood of both cardiac arrhythmia and renal failure. These potentially serious outcomes necessitate the discovery of effective treatments. The situation is made even more urgent by the finding that only about a quarter of community-based samples seem to be receiving treatment (Fairburn, 1995).

The role of the family has been implicated in the development and maintenance of eating disorders and, therefore, has been a target of intervention. Risk factors in the family will first be explored, followed by systemic family therapy formulations and a discussion of findings of family-based treatments in the empirical literature.

THE ROLE OF THE FAMILY

Certain risk factors may be present in the families of individuals with eating disorders. Correlational studies indicate that family members of eating-disordered individuals seem to experience an increased risk for both eating disorders and affective disorders themselves, at a rate of three times higher than for the families of normal controls (Cooper, 1995). For individuals with bulimia specifically, relatives have an increased risk of substance abuse (Cooper, 1995) and obesity (APA, 1994; Hsu, 1990). Different causal processes within the family environment may be implicated in the development of eating disorders. However, whether they are due to genetic mechanisms, childhood experiences, family concerns about weight, family psychopathology, or family transactional processes is unknown at this time (Cooper, 1995; Wilson, Heffernan, & Black, 1996).

To explain the role of the family transactional processes, systemic family therapy postulates that individual symptoms (eating disorders) serve a function for the family system in terms of their stabilizing role. In structural family therapy, a specific school of family systems theory formulated by Minuchin and colleagues, symptoms are seen as arising from a lack of functional structure in the family (Minuchin, 1974). Structuralists contend that well-functioning families should be hierarchically organized, with parents exercising more power than children. In a family in which eating disorders develop, it is assumed that the child is aligned with one parent or the other, rather than parents being united as a team. Further, Minuchin and colleagues formulated a model of "psychosomatic" families, which was originally applied to families with a child with diabetes unexplained by organic causes (Minuchin et al., 1975). This model was extended to families in which there was an anorexic member (Minuchin, Rosman, & Baker, 1978). Four patterns were described in these families: enmeshment, overprotectiveness, rigidity, and lack of conflict resolution (especially between the parents so that the marriage need not be threatened). Enmeshment is defined as a blurring of boundaries, a pattern of overinvolvement and hyperresponsivity, in which family members attempt to control and regulate the intake of others. Overprotection involves excessive concern of family members for each other, which tends to restrict autonomy. Rigidity concerns the maintenance of fixed patterns that are no longer functional. Lack of conflict resolution means that psychosomatic families possess low tolerance for conflict, especially between parents (Minuchin et al., 1978).

In a series of studies, Kog and associates constructed behavioral and self-report measures in order to empirically test Minuchin's model of psychosomatic families. In the initial study involving 10 families with an anorexic child, no specific family profile was found (Kog, Vertommen, & Vandereycken, 1987). In later studies using both observational and self-report measures, many of Minuchin's concepts appeared to overlap, rather than representing distinct theoretical dimensions (Kog & Vandereycken, 1989; Kog, Vertommen, & Vandereycken, 1987). However, observational support was found for the following concepts: interpersonal boundaries, the family's adaptability, and the family pattern of managing conflict. Because behavioral, rather than self-report, evidence was indicated for three of the concepts, this may provide support for the systemic nature of family interactions.

The work of Kog and colleagues is from Belgium; the results of family treatment in the following discussion are from studies conducted from other parts of the world: Argentina (Herscovici & Bay, 1996), Canada (Woodside et al., 1995), Germany (Shugar & Krueger, 1995), Great Britain (Crisp et al., 1991; Dare, Eisler, Russell, & Szmukler, 1990, Gowers et al., 1989, 1994; Le Grange, Eisler, Dare, & Russell, 1992; Russell, Smukler, Dare, & Eisler, 1987; Szmukler & Dare, 1991; Szmukler, Eisler, Russell, & Dare, 1985), Israel (Danziger, Carel, Tyano, & Mimouni, 1989), the Netherlands (van Furth et al., 1996), and the United States (Robin, Siegel, Koepke, Moye, & Tice, 1994; Robin, Siegel, & Moye, 1995). In the following discussion on study findings, a question remains whether results of studies from a particular country will generalize to another, given cultural differences. The organizational system to follow will involve discussion of studies according to design. The more sophisticated designs, experimental and quasi-experimental, will be explored first, followed by pretest, posttest, and posttest-only designs.

EXPERIMENTAL AND QUASI-EXPERIMENTAL DESIGNS

A great deal of the work in this area has been generated from Great Britain. Two different streams of research are represented (Gowers, Crisp, and colleagues; Russell, Dare, Szmukler, Le Grange, and colleagues), and discussion in this section will begin with their research (*see* Table 6.1). In the first study of their series, Gowers et al. (1989) describe an experimental design with random allocation to four groups conducted with anorexic adolescents seeking treatment. The first condition comprised inpatient treatment, which consisted of individual, conjoint family therapy, group therapy, dietary counseling, and occupational therapy. The second condition was outpatient treatment involving psychodynamic individual therapy, family conjoint sessions, and four sessions of nutritional counseling. The family component focused on the establishment of boundaries and reducing enmeshment and conflict avoidance. The second outpatient condition comprised concurrent group sessions for the individual client and her parents, as well as nutritional counseling. The client group addressed conflict avoidance, family relationships, feeling identification and management, communication, and relationship skills. In the parents' group, a key intervention involved getting the parents to come together as a team to handle the eating disorder. Also addressed were parental discord and difficulties with children's autonomy. The fourth condition was a control group, which consisted of assessment only. However, this group could have sought treatment from the community.

Crisp et al. (1991) reported 1-year follow-up. Weight gain was significant across all groups over time, but only the outpatient treatment groups improved significantly when compared to the control group. The global score for the Morgan-Russell scale also improved for all groups. When examining subscales, the following changes were noted: the cessation of amenorrhea (all groups), sexual adjustment (inpatient and control), and socioeconomic status (outpatient individual and conjoint family therapy). Despite the gains made in these many areas, there were no significant improvements in "mental state" for any of the conditions.

Findings suggest that there may be no more advantages to inpatient over outpatient treatment. There also may be few advantages to outpatient treatment over the community control group, the members of which improved on weight gain, cessation of amenornhea, and sexual adjustment. However, it must be noted that the control group might have received treatment, although this was not tracked or controlled. In addition, Gowers et al. (1994) reported that the outpatient samples received only an average of 12 sessions over a 10-month

TABLE 6.1 Family Treatment Outcome Studies with Eating Disorders

AUTHOR/MODEL	DESIGN/SAMPLE	MEASURES	RESULTS	LIMITATIONS
Danziger et al. (1989) No theory identified	Post-hoc comparison between 2 groups: 1) only received refeeding inpatient for 2 mos; 2) received refeeding inpatient program and community individual or family therapy for those 2 mos $N = 45$ anorexics from pediatric day care unit (Israel) mostly female mean age $= 14.7$	Weight gain	Weight gain program without psychotherapy achieved better weight gain	No randomization into groups; theoretical orientation, number of sessions, and intensity for individual and family treatment not given; no other measures of functioning other than weight gain; possible confound—all patients exposed to "therapeutic milieu" (multidisciplinary team along with cooperation of parents)
Gowers et al. (1989) Crisp et al. (1991) [Reports 1-yr follow-up of Gowers et al. (1989)] 12 sessions of 1–1 ½ hrs over 10 mos	Experimental, random allocation to 4 groups: 1) inpatient (psychodynamic individual, family conjoint, and nutritional counseling); 2) outpatient (individual, family	Morgan & Russell scales	Crisp et al. (1991): Weight change was significant across all groups over time but only the outpatient treatment groups improved significantly when compared to	Lack of compliance with design, particularly inpatient (only 60% complied with this condition); small sample size; confounded treatments in conditions

conjoint, and nutritional); 3) outpatient (separate group therapy for client and parents, nutritional); 4) control (assessment only) $N = 90$ anorexics seeking treatment (England)			the control group. The global score for the Morgan-Russell scale also improved for all groups. When examining subscales, the following changes were noted: the cessation of amenorrhea (all groups); sexual adjustment (inpatient and control); socioeconomic status (outpatient individual and conjoint family therapy). Despite the gains made in these many areas, there were no significant improvements in "mental state" for any of the conditions.	Crisp et al. (1991): 1-yr follow-up for all conditions rather than when treatment was completed (no posttest)
Gowers et al. (1994)	Reports 2-yr follow-up of Gowers et al. (1989), the outpatient part of sample receiving individual and conjoint family ($N = 20$) compared to controls ($N = 20$)	Morgan & Russell scales	High dropout (only 50% of original 20 completed 12 sessions); no significant differences between treatment and control except for SES (treatment group higher); sig-	Small sample size; control group subjects may have received treatment elsewhere; mix of family and individual therapy makes it difficult to draw conclusions; question-

continued

TABLE 6.1 *(continued)*

AUTHOR/MODEL	DESIGN/SAMPLE	MEASURES	RESULTS	LIMITATIONS
			nificant improvement for both groups in all areas except mental state	able why one outpatient group was included in follow-up and not other two treatment conditions
Herscovici & Bay (1996) Family Systems Model	Posttest only $N = 30$ follow-up (2–6 mos) of 46 adolescent anorexics in original sample from hospital (Argentina) 88% female; majority middle- and upper-class	Morgan & Russell scales	Global Outcome Measure: "good" for 60%; "intermediate" for 30%; "poor" for 10%"	Length and intensity of treatment not discussed; no control/comparison group; no pretest; theoretical model not well-described; confounded treatments—patients also received nutritional therapy program, some received individual treatment and some were hospitalized; follow-up time was variable
Le Grange et al. (1992) Family therapy (conjoint family sessions) and family counseling (separate sup-	Quasi-experimental, random assignment to 2 groups of family treatment, pretest, posttest	Individual: Eating Attitude Test; Rosenberg Self-Esteem Score; Morgan-Russell Assessment Schedule;	Improvements in weight gain and individual psychological variables similar for both groups; in video observation,	Small sample size; lacks no-treatment control

portive sessions for patient and parent) for average of 9 sessions for 6 mos Structural	$N = 18$ mostly female anorexics, ages 12–17, from hospital referrals (England); no other major psychiatric diagnosis	weight; menstrual status Family: video recordings were used for Expressed Emotion ratings; Family Adaptability and Cohesions Scales-III	critical comments were higher for conjoint group compared to family counseling group although similar improvements for FACES	
Robin et al. (1994) Behavioral family systems 16 mos, treatment weekly for first 8 mos and biweekly thereafter	Quasi-experimental, random assignment to behavioral family therapy or ego-oriented individual + bimonthly separate sessions for parents, pretest, posttest $N = 22$ middle-class, White female anorexics (onset within 1 yr) ages 12–19 referred from school personnel, psychologists and social workers (U.S.A.)	Quetelet's Body Mass Index; Eating Attitudes Test (parent completed modified version of their daughter's eating attitudes); Body Shape Questionnaire; Eating Disorder Inventory subscales, Dissatisfaction Scale, Ineffectiveness, Interpersonal Distrust, and Interoceptive Awareness; Beck Depression Inventory; Child Behavior Checklist Internalizing Behavior Problems Score; Parent-Adolescent Relationship Questionnaire	No significant differences between groups but both groups improved significantly on body mass index, eating attitudes, interoceptive awareness, depression, internalizing behavior problems, and eating-related family conflict from both adolescent and parent self-report	Small sample size, particularly given number of measures; possible confound in that participants also underwent a medical and dietary regimen and some were hospitalized due to low body weight or health problems

continued

TABLE 6.1 (continued)

AUTHOR/MODEL	DESIGN/SAMPLE	MEASURES	RESULTS	LIMITATIONS
Robin et al. (1995)	Reports 1-yr results of Robin et al. (1994)		Improvements maintained at follow-up; both treatments associated with improvements in body mass index, menstruation, and family interactions; although family group improved statistically, differences not clinically; family group showed a decrease in negative and increase in positive communication in behavioral observations	
Russell et al. (1987) Dare et al. (1990) Szmukler & Dare (1991) Outpatient offered for a year	Quasi-experimental, clients were stratified into subgroups: 1) onset of anorexia before age 18 and duration of less than 3 yrs; 2) onset of anorexia	Morgan & Russell Scales; Crown-Crisp Experiential Index Szmukler & Dare (1991): Expressed Emotion	Family was more effective than individual therapy only for clients whose eating disorder was not chronic (not longer than 3 yrs) and had started before the age of 19 and this group	One-yr follow-up rather than posttest; small sample size; some clients were on anti-depressants and some were rehospitalized; no psychometric information about the CCEI

before age 18 and onset
over 3 yrs;
3) onset of anorexia at
age 19 or above;
4) bulimics and then
randomly assigned to
family or individual
therapy after an inpa-
tient therapeutic nutri-
tional program

Measures were taken
preadmission, after
nutritional program, and
at 1 yr

$N = 80$ clients present-
ing to eating disorders
hospital unit in England
(73 completed treat-
ment)

Mainly female:
71% anorexic; 29%
bulimic

had low expressed emo-
tion; no significant dif-
ferences between
conditions in other sub-
groups (anorexics for
whom disorder had
become chronic despite
younger age of onset
and bulimics)

continued

TABLE 6.1 (*continued*)

AUTHOR/MODEL	DESIGN/SAMPLE	MEASURES	RESULTS	LIMITATIONS
Shugar & Krueger (1995) Systemic family therapy 12–14 weeks with weekly sessions	Pretest, posttest $N = 15$ families of anorexic females admitted to inpatient treatment (Germany) ages 13–16; middle or upper SES	Family Aggression Scale; Eating Attitudes Test; Body Mass Index	Statistically significant improvement on Eating Attitudes Test; the more direct rather than covert or indirect expression of anger was associated with more weight gain	Small sample size; no comparison/control group; no follow-up; treatment also included mandatory regular meals, daily weighing and individual cognitive-behavioral treatment so unknown effect of family treatment
Van Furth et al. (1996) "All patients treated received some form of family therapy/family counseling, combined in 50% of the cases with individual therapy on an eclectic basis" (p. 22) Outpatients received on average of 14.9 individual	Pretest, posttest, follow-up (1 yr) $N = 49$ adolescents referred to eating disorders program of psychiatric unit of university hospital (the Netherlands) 37% anorexic, 39% bulimic, 14% both anorexic and bulimic,	Morgan-Russell Outcome Assessment Schedule (adjusted to accommodate bulimics) Camberwell Family Interview (adapted for use with eating-disordered population)	13 families dropped out of testing administration from pretest to posttest and an additional 3 dropped out before follow-up	Theoretical orientation not discussed; no comparison/control group; type of therapy, modality of therapy, duration of therapy, combinations of therapy all uncontrolled

	and 5.9 family therapy sessions for a mean duration of 12.6 mos	10% for eating disorder not otherwise specified	Parental Expressed Emotion at pretest low but still lower at posttest; maternal critical comments best predictor of average outcome score of Morgan-Russell scale; Emotional Overinvolvement only subscale to significantly decrease over time; at termination of treatment, although 1/3 had same diagnosis as they had in beginning, 45% did not meet criteria for eating disorder	
	30% received inpatient treatment for a mean of 20.2 mos	10.2% male; mean age = 17.3 yrs; mean duration of illness = 23 mos		
Woodside et al. (1995)	Pretest, posttest		Family Assessment Measure	
Brief, psychoeducation and symptom-focused family therapy	N = 91 bulimics who completed treatment at hospital (Canada) and for whom there is complete data (out of 118 originally)		At pretest, only patient showed distressed family functioning which significantly improved at posttest	Possible confounds—nutritional rehabilitation and group therapy theoretical model not well-clarified
	mean age = 24.8 yrs			

period; therefore, treatment intensity was limited. Moreover, dropout was high, with only 50% completing 12 sessions. It could be that treatment applied in a more intensive fashion would produce better results.

Gowers et al. (1994) reported the 2-year follow-up for only the outpatient condition receiving individual and family conjoint treatment, although it is unknown why only this subsample was reported. When compared against the control group, both groups improved over time, except in the area of "mental state adjustment," consistent with the 1-year follow-up findings. Again, there seemed to be no more advantages to the outpatient treatment structured with both individual and family conjoint treatment over the community control condition.

Another group of British researchers compared individual to family therapy (Dare et al., 1990; Russell et al., 1987; Szmukler & Dare, 1991). Eighty individuals who had first received inpatient treatment with a focus on weight gain were then subdivided into four groups: 1) onset of anorexia before age 18 and duration of less than 3 years, 2) onset of anorexia before age 18 and duration over 3 years, 3) onset of anorexia at age 19 or older, and 4) individuals with bulimia nervosa. Groups were then randomly assigned to family therapy or individual therapy.

Family treatment consisted of both structural and nonstructural techniques. At the beginning of treatment, the "family meal" intervention from Minuchin (Minuchin et al., 1978), in which the family was seen for a lunchtime session, was used so that the therapist could assess and intervene with the way the family organized itself around the eating behavior of the eating-disordered member.

In initial sessions, Dare et al. (1990) departed from Minuchin with an emphasis on weight gain and diet. The therapists attempted to arouse anxiety about the dangers of starvation so that they would unite the parents in taking control of their daughter's symptoms. Reframing was used to reduce blame. The family was reframed as close, loving, and highly committed to each other. When weight gain was achieved, more attention was given to increasing the adolescent's autonomy and structuring the parents' marital relationship. Another departure was to explore and foster an understanding of the eating disorder as it relates to intergenerational patterns in the family in the style of Milan systemic (Selvini-Palazzoli, Boscolo, Cecchin, & Prata, 1978) or psychodynamic intergenerational therapy (Boszormenyi-Nagy & Spark, 1973) to reduce blame and resistance in the immediate family.

In this study, family therapy was more effective than individual therapy only for clients whose eating disorder was not chronic (not longer than 3 years) and had started before the age of 19. This group of adolescents also had parents low on "expressed emotion" at pretest (Szmukler et al., 1985). Expressed emotion is a measure of family affective communication assessed through the Camberwell Family Interview. This measure includes five subscales: 1) critical comments, 2) hostility, 3) emotional overinvolvement, 4) warmth; and 5) positive remarks. The critical comments of relatives has, especially, been a strong predictor of treatment response for mental illness (Hogarty, 1986; Vaughn, Snyder, Jones, Freeman, & Falloon, 1984).

In this study, "critical comments" by parents were associated with dropout from psychotherapy (Szmukler & Dare, 1991). In addition, when family, but not individual, therapy was involved, high levels of expressed emotion were correlated with poor outcome. These findings suggest that if a parent is critical, then family therapy may be contraindicated until this is under control.

In a later study, Le Grange et al. (1992) examined "critical comments" with 18 adolescents seeking treatment, the majority of whom were diagnosed with anorexia nervosa. A quasi-experimental design was used with random assignment to two groups of family treatment: conjoint family sessions (family was seen together) and family counseling (separate supportive sessions for patient and parent). The family treatment was similar to the one described above for Dare et al. (1990) for both the conjoint and separate counseling sessions. When working with the parents separately, although the therapist could not intervene directly with the interactions, suggestions could be made for how family members could modify their behavior around the adolescents' symptoms. With the individual adolescent, the therapist provided support and education about attitudes toward eating, body shape, and weight until sufficient weight gain was made. Adolescents and their parents were seen for an average of nine sessions for 6 months.

Both the conjoint and separate conditions showed improvements in weight gain, individual psychological variables, and on the standardized self-report inventory of family functioning. However, a video observational assessment revealed a higher level of critical comments for the conjoint group, compared to the separate family counseling group. Apparently, separate parental sessions reduce criticism toward the identified patient. The importance of critical comments were also reported in another study (van Furth et al., 1996). Maternal critical comments were the strongest predictor of the average outcome score on the Morgan-Russell scale, explaining 28% to 34% of the variance.

Robin et al. (1994) used a behavioral family systems approach. These researchers compared behavioral family systems therapy to ego-oriented individual therapy for the eating-disordered individual with separate bimonthly sessions for parents. Treatment was conducted over a 16-month time span; sessions were weekly for the first 8 months and biweekly thereafter. No significant differences were found between groups, with both groups making significant positive changes on body mass index, eating attitudes, interoceptive awareness, depression, internalizing behavior problems, and eating-related family conflict, according to adolescent and parent self-report. At the 1-year follow-up, both family and separate individual and parent treatments were associated with improvements in body mass index, menstruation, eating-related family conflict, and other family interactions.

On behavioral observations, the mothers in the family group showed a decrease in negative and an increase in positive communication (Robin, Siegel, & Moye, 1995), whereas mothers who received separate treatment did not. Due to the comparable treatment gains, Robin et al. (1995) argue that changes on family interactions can be produced without conjoint family therapy.

Unfortunately, potentially confounding variables limited the results: Subjects also received nutritional counseling, and some were hospitalized due to low body weight or health problems. These are common confounds in the research on family treatment of eating disorders. One study explicitly addressed this issue, comparing anorexics' weight gain when they underwent only an inpatient hospital weight-gain program and when they also attended individual and/or family therapy (Danziger et al., 1989). Although the type of psychotherapy received (modality, length, intensity, theoretical orientation) was not controlled, psychotherapy with a weight-gain program was less optimal than an initial emphasis on weight gain only. The authors hypothesized that psychotherapy might generate conflict, which would interfere with the anorexic's gaining weight.

PRETEST, POSTTEST, AND POSTTEST-ONLY DESIGNS

Herscovici and Bay (1996), Shugar and Krueger (1995), and Woodside et al. (1995) all used pre-experimental designs. Although the first two identify themselves with family systems (and Shugar and Krueger identify themselves with structural and more specifically with Milan systemic), and Woodside et al. (1995) describe their approach as "brief, psychoeducation and symptom-focused family therapy," there is insufficient description in each of these cases to clearly understand the nature of the interventions. Therefore, findings of studies will be summarized briefly and limitations of studies will be further detailed under the following section, which is a critique of the research in this area.

Shugar and Krueger (1995) report statistically significant improvements on eating-disordered attitudes after adolescents diagnosed with anorexia nervosa underwent treatment. The more direct rather than covert or indirect expression of anger was associated with more weight gain, which lends support for Minuchin et al.'s (1978) conceptualization of the psychosomatic family and that conflict avoidance can be targeted for change.

Herscovici and Bay (1996) also looked specifically at anorexia nervosa and found at posttest (without measuring pretest) that improvement was made for 60% of the sample, 30% were somewhat improved, and 10% had not improved (according to Global Outcome of the Morgan-Russell Scale).

The only study to specifically examine individuals with bulimia nervosa was with a slightly older sample (mean age of 25). Woodside et al. (1995) found that individuals reported lower levels of family functioning at pretest than did their parents, who scored in a comparatively normal range. However, improvements were made over time for the patient.

SUGGESTIONS FOR SERVICE DELIVERY

This section will explore some of the tentative findings gleaned from studies. However, given the methodological limitations of studies (which will be discussed in the critique section following), these findings must be subjected to further empirical investigation before any definitive statements can be made about family treatment in this area.

First, studies suggest that patient weight be stabilized before initiating psychotherapy at least in an inpatient setting (Danziger et al., 1989). The hypothesis is that psychotherapy might generate conflict and inhibit the positive impact of a weight-gain program. It is unknown if this finding would still hold true with psychotherapeutic approaches that focus on initial weight gain before moving on to other issues, such as the Dare et al. (1990) and Le Grange et al. (1992) interventions. In any case, the Le Grange et al. (1992) conclusion was that the conjoint structural family therapy condition was too confrontational for reducing criticism and dissatisfaction. Other researchers also found conjoint family therapy to be no more effective than separate sessions for the individual eating-disordered client and for parents (Crisp et al., 1991; Robin et al., 1995). Critical comments from parents in family sessions were associated with dropout (Szmukler & Dare, 1991) and poor outcome (Szmukler & Dare, 1991; van Furth et al., 1996). Apparently, critical comments from parents need to be under control before conjoint family therapy is indicated. A final finding from studies is that when inpatient and outpatient treatments are compared, similar gains are found (Crisp et al., 1991; Dare et al., 1990). Dare et al. (1990), in particular, suggest that outpatient family therapy might be the treatment of choice for adolescents under age 18 with anorexia nervosa of early onset.

CRITIQUE AND RESEARCH RECOMMENDATIONS

Overall, despite the magnitude and severity of the problem, few studies have examined treatment, particularly family treatment, of eating disorders. In a review of 223 child and adolescent psychotherapy outcome studies from 1970 to mid-1989, less than 1% of studies included the treatment of eating disorders (Kazdin, Bass, Ayers, & Rodgers, 1990). In addition, the research on family treatment of eating disorders is methodologically so weak as to call into question any reported findings. First, studies often fail to report any theory underlying the treatment offered; instead, "family therapy" and "individual therapy" are discussed in generic terms. Second, information on the length and intensity of treatment is often not provided. Third, programs often combine many different treatments with nutritional counseling, individual and group therapy, antidepressant medication, and rehospitalization as common confounds. When so many different combinations of treatments with varying lengths and intensity are offered, it is difficult to attribute changes made to the family component of treatment alone.

In essence, the state of the empirical literature has remained almost unchanged since 1987, when Vandereycken wrote:

> There is a strong tendency toward a multimodal eclectic approach that, to a varying degree and usually in a flexible way, combines individual and family therapy, often intertwining behavioral, psychodynamic, structural, strategic, and other interventions. Treatment is then aimed at different levels of functioning, but such a multidimensional approach requires an integrative way of thinking on the part of the therapist or the therapeutic team. This is necessary in order to avoid the unproductive "supermarket" treatment in which an accidental accumulation of techniques is used as a machine-gun to ensure that at least some targets are hit. (p. 459)

This literature suffers also from a weakness of designs, with an overreliance on pretest/posttest and posttest-only designs (e.g., Herscovici & Bay, 1996;

Shugar & Krueger, 1995; van Furth et al., 1996; Woodside et al., 1995). Due to the potentially life-threatening nature of eating disorders, ethical considerations preclude the use of no-treatment control groups. An acceptable alternative is the use of comparative treatment conditions. However, it is important that the necessary components of treatment be delineated systematically.

Length of follow-up needs consideration as well. A recent 20-year follow-up study by Ratnasuriya, Eisler, Szmukler, and Russell (1991) revealed that the pattern of outcome is determined at 5 years (Steinhausen, 1995). Therefore, 5-year follow-up is optimal for treatment outcome studies.

Another way in which studies have been compromised is by small sample size. Future study needs to attend to adequate sample size in order to obtain conditions necessary for statistical power. Samples in studies were also plagued by high dropout. For example, 18 subjects in the Gowers et al. (1989) inpatient sample alone did not participate, and in the outpatient sample only 50% completed 12 sessions (Gowers et al., 1994); Woodside et al. (1995) reported 27 dropouts. Although some studies discuss how dropouts differ from those who complete treatment (e.g., Szmukler & Dare, 1991), dropout data need to be reported on a routine basis.

Samples in studies consist usually of individuals with anorexia nervosa (e.g., Gowers et al., 1989; Le Grange et al., 1992; Robin et al., 1994, 1995; Shugar & Krueger, 1995). Although bulimia nervosa has a later age of onset than anorexia nervosa, this does not rule out a family approach (Friedrich, 1995). In addition, individual interpersonal therapy has shown positive results for treatment of bulimia nervosa (e.g., Fairburn et al., 1991; Fairburn et al., 1995; Wilfley et al., 1993). Interpersonal therapy, a short-term psychodynamic approach, focuses on relationship factors that trigger and maintain disorders, such as eating disorders and depression. The effectiveness of this approach indicates the salience of relationship factors for the development of bulimia nervosa, and one important domain of relationships involves the family environment. While the family treatment literature on anorexia nervosa has been slightly more developed, no specific approaches or modalities have consistently demonstrated effectiveness with anorexia nervosa. This state of the research is in contrast to bulimia nervosa, for which both individually-oriented interpersonal therapy and cognitive behavioral therapy have shown positive results (e.g., Blouin et al., 1995; Cooper & Steere, 1995; Treasure, Schmidt, Troop, & Todd, 1996).

Although inpatient treatment has been a traditional approach (Fichter, 1995), particularly for anorexia nervosa, a recommendation is that more research should be conducted in outpatient settings, before the disorder deteriorates to the point where hospitalization is required. As insurance companies are no longer reimbursing so extensively for hospitalization, outpatient care of eating disorders will gain increasing importance. In addition, more work needs to be targeted toward earlier detection and treatment of cases. Based on a review by Hoek (1995), it appears that approximately 43% of diagnosable anorexia nervosa patients are screened by general practitioners, and about three quarters are referred for treatment. Even fewer cases of bulimia nervosa are screened: General practitioners detect only 11% of cases, with half of these being referred for treatment (Hoek, 1995). Medical and social service screening efforts need improvement, along with the provision of appropriate referrals for treatment. Clearly, more empirical attention needs to be directed toward prevention and treatment of eating disorders.

REFERENCES

Andersen, A. E. (1995). Eating disorders in males. In K. D. Brownell & C. G. Fairburn (Eds.), *Eating disorders and obesity: A comprehensive handbook* (pp. 177–182). New York: Guilford Press.

American Psychiatric Association. (1994). Diagnostic statistical manual of mental disorders (4th ed.). Washington, DC: Author.

Beumont, P. (1995). The clinical presentation of anorexia and bulimia nervosa. In K. D. Brownell & C. G. Fairburn (Eds.), *Eating disorders and obesity: A comprehensive handbook* (pp. 151–158). New York: Guilford Press.

Blouin, J., Schnarre, K., Carter, J., Blouin, A., Tener, Zuro, C., & Barlow (1995). Factors affecting dropout rate from cognitive-behavioral group treatment for bulimia vervosa. *International Journal of Eating Disorders, 17,* 323–329.

Boszormenyi-Nagy, I., & Spark, G. M. (1973). *Invisible loyalties: Reciprocity in intergenerational family therapy.* New York: Harper & Row.

Cooper, P., & Steere, J. (1995). A comparison of two psychological treatment for bulimia nervosa: Implications for models of maintenance. *Behaviour Research Therapy, 33,* 875–885.

Cooper, Z. (1995). The development and maintenance of eating disorders. In K. D. Brownell & C. G. Fairburn (Eds.), *Eating disorders and obesity: A comprehensive handbook* (pp. 199–206). New York: Guilford Press.

Crisp, A. H., Norton, K., Gowers, S., Halek, C., Bowyer, C., Yeldham, D., Levett, G., & Bhat, A. (1991). A controlled study of the effect of therapies aimed at adolescent and family psychopathology in anorexia nervosa. *British Journal of Psychiatry, 159,* 325–333.

Danziger, Y., Carel, C. A., Tyano, S., & Mimouni, M. (1989). Is psychotherapy mandatory during the acute refeeding period in the treatment of anorexia nervosa? *Journal of Adolescent Health Care, 10,* 328–331.

Dare, C., Eisler, I., Russell, G., & Szmukler, G. (1990). The clinical and theoretical impact of a controlled trial of family therapy in anorexia nervosa. *Journal of Marital and Family Therapy, 16*, 39–57.

Fairburn, C., Jones, R., Peveler, R., & Carr, S. (1991). Three psychological treatments for bulimia nervosa: A comparative trial. *Archives of General Psychiatry, 48*, 463–469.

Fairburn, C., Norman, P., Welch, S., & O'Conner, S. (1995). A prospectus study of outcome in bulimia nervosa and the long-term effects of three psychological treatments. *Archives of General Psychiatry, 52*, 304–312.

Fairburn, C. G. (1995). The prevention of eating disorders. In K. D. Brownell & C. G. Fairburn (Eds.), *Eating disorders and obesity: A comprehensive handbook* (pp. 289–293). New York: Guilford Press.

Fichter, M. M. (1995). Impatient treatment of anorexia nervosa. In K. D. Brownell & C. G. Fairburn (Eds.), *Eating disorders and obesity: A comprehensive handbook* (pp. 336–343). New York: Guilford Press.

Garfinkel, P. E. (1995). Classification and diagnosis of eating disorders. In K. D. Brownell & C. G. Fairburn (Eds.), *Eating disorders and obesity: A comprehensive handbook* (pp. 125–134). New York: Guilford Press.

Gowers, S., Norton, K., Halek, C., & Crisp, A. (1993). Outcome of outpatient psychotherapy in a random allocation treatment study of anorexia nervosa. *International Journal of Eating Disorders, 15*, 165–177.

Gowers, S., Norton, K., Yeldham, D., Bowyer, C., Levett, A., Heavey, A., Bhat, A. V., & Crisp, A. (1989). The St. George's prospective treatment study of anorexia nervosa: A discussion of methodological problems. *International Journal of Eating Disorders, 8*, 445–454.

Hoek, H. W. (1995). The distribution of eating disorders. In K. D. Brownell & C. G. Fairburn (Eds.), *Eating disorders and obesity: A comprehensive handbook* (pp. 207–211). New York: Guilford Press.

Hogarty, G. (1986). Family psychoeducation, social skills training, and maintenance chemotherapy in the after care of schizophrenia: One-year effects of a controlled study on relapse and expressed emotion. *Archives of General Psychiatry, 43*, 633–642.

Hsu, L. K. G. (1990). *Eating disorders.* New York: Guilford Press.

Kazdin, A., Bass, D., Ayers, W., & Rodgers, A. (1990). Empirical and clinical focus of child and adolescent psychotherapy research. *Journal of Consulting and Clinical Psychology, 58*, 729–740.

Kog, E., & Vandereycken, W. (1989). Family interaction in eating disorder patients and normal controls. *International Journal of Eating Disorders, 8*, 11–23.

Kog, E., Vertommen, H., & Vandereycken, W. (1987). Minuchin's psychosomatic family model revised: A concept-validation study using a multitrait-multimethod approach. *Family Process, 26*, 235–253.

Le Grange, D., Eisler, I., Dare, C., & Russell, G. (1992). Evaluation of family treatments in adolescent anorexia nervosa: A pilot study. *International Journal of Eating Disorders, 12*(4), 347–357.

Minuchin, S. (1974). *Families and family therapy.* Cambridge, MA: Harvard University Press.

Minuchin, S., Rosman, B. L., & Baker, L. (1978). *Psychosomatic families: Anorexia nervosa in context.* Cambridge, MA: Harvard University Press.

Mitchell, J. E. (1995). Medical complications of bulimia nervosa. In K. D. Brownell & C. G. Fairburn (Eds.), *Eating disorders and obesity: A comprehensive handbook* (pp. 271–277). New York: Guilford Press.

Ratnasuriya, R., Eisler, I., Szmukler, G., & Russell, G. (1991). Anorexia nervosa: Outcome and prognostic factors after 20 years. *British Journal of Psychiatry, 158,* 495–502.

Robin, A. L., Siegel, P. T., Koepke, T., Moye, A. W., & Tice, S. (1994). Family therapy versus individual therapy for adolescent females with anorexia nervosa. *Developmental and Behavior Pediatrics, 15,* 111–116.

Robin, A. L., Siegel, P. T., & Moye, A. (1995). Family versus individual therapy for anorexia: Impact on family conflict. *International Journal of Eating Disorders, 17*(4), 313–322.

Russell, G., Szmukler, G., Dare, C., & Eisler, I. (1987). An evaluation of family therapy in anorexia nervosa and bulimia nervosa. *Archives of General Psychiatry, 4,* 1047–1056.

Selvini-Palazzoli, M., Boscolo, L., Cecchin, G. F., & Prata, G. (1978). *Paradox and counterparadox: A new model in the therapy of the family in schizophrenic transaction.* New York: Aronson.

Shugar, G., & Krueger, S. (1995). Aggressive family communication, weight gain, and improved eating attitudes during systemic family therapy for anorexia nervosa. *International Journal of Eating Disorders, 17,* 23–31.

Steinhausen, H. (1995). The course and outcome of anorexia nervosa. In K. D. Brownell & C. G. Fairburn (Eds.), *Eating disorders and obesity: A comprehensive handbook* (pp. 234–237). New York: Guilford Press.

Striegel-Moore, R. H. (1995). A feminist perspective on the etiology of eating disorders. In K. D. Brownell & C. G. Fairburn (Eds.), *Eating disorders and obesity: A comprehensive handbook* (pp. 224–229). New York: Guilford Press.

Szmukler, G., Eisler, I., Russell, G., & Dare, C. (1985). Anorexia nervosa, parental "expressed emotion" and dropping out of treatment. *British Journal of Psychiatry, 147,* 265–271.

Treasure, J., Schmidt, U., Troop, N., & Todd, G. (1996). Sequential treatment for bulimia nervosa incorporating a self-care manual. *Britich Journal of Psychiatry, 168,* 94–98.

Vandereycken, W. (1987). The constructive family approach to eating disorders: Critical remarks on the use of family therapy in anorexia nervosa and bulimia. *International Journal of Eating Disorders, 6,* 455–467.

van Furth, E. F., van Strien, D. C., Martina, L. M. L., van Son, M. J. M., Hendrickx, J. J. P., & van Engeland, H. (1996). Expressed emotion and the prediction of outcome in adolescent eating disorders. *International Journal of Eating Disorders, 20,* 19–31.

Vaughn, C. E., Snyder, K. S., Jones, S., Freeman, W. B., & Falloon, I. R. (1984). Family factors in schizophrenic relapse: Replication in California of British research on expressed emotion. *Archives of General Psychiatry, 41,* 1169–1177.

Wilfley, D., Agras, W., Stewart, T., Christy, F., & Rossiter, E. (1993). Group cognitive-behavioral therapy and group interpersonal psychotherapy for the nonpurging bulimic individual: A controlled comparison. *Journal of Consulting and Clinical Psychology, 61*, 296–305.

Wilson, G., Heffernan, K., & Black, C. (1996). Eating disorders. In E. Mash & R. Barkley (Eds.), *Child psychopathology* (pp. 541–571). New York: Guilford Press.

MEASUREMENT OF FAMILY TREATMENT
WITH EATING DISORDERS

Increasingly, practitioners are held accountable for the evaluation of their practice. To assist with evaluation, the following section provides the reader with self-report instruments for individuals with eating disorders and their family members. Scores from these measurement instruments can be used to guide assessment and clinical practice. For those interested in conducting research in this area, each of the instruments provided has established psychometric data to support its usage.

The following types of measures are presented: 1) eating disorder outcomes, 2) adjustment outcomes for the individual with the eating disorder, 3) parent adjustment, 4) parental marital adjustment, 5) family functioning, and 6) client satisfaction with services.

Measures presented in this section involve the following criteria. First, instruments are self-report; that is, they are completed by family members themselves, rather than being interviewer-administered or observational measures. A second criterion for inclusion was that adequate reliability and validity information had to be available for each scale. Selected psychometric data were chosen to inform the reader of the properties of the instruments.

EATING DISORDER OUTCOMES—CLIENT REPORT

THE BINGE SCALE

Author: Hawkins & Clement (1980)

Description:

- A 9-item self-report screening inventory assessing behavioral and attitudinal aspects of bingeing, such as intensity or severity

Reliability:

- Alpha coefficient = .68
- Test-retest reliability (1-month) = .88

Validity:

- Discriminates between women in treatment for binge eating and a college student sample
- Factor analysis indicated a main factor (71% of variance) representing guilt/concern about binge eating, and a secondary factor (16% of variance) involved duration and satiety feelings associated with binges

THE EATING ATTITUDES TEST

Author: Garner & Garfinkel (1979)

Description:

- Assesses the symptoms of anorexia nervosa
- A self-report instrument with 40 items rated on a 6-point ("always–never") scale
- 7 factors: food preoccupation, body image for thinness; vomiting and laxative abuse; dieting; slow eating; clandestine eating; perceived social pressure to gain weight
- Reduced to 26 items after factor analysis and scores on 2 scales were significantly correlated (Garner, Olmsted, Bohr, & Garfinkel, 1982)
- 3 factors (Garner et al., 1982):
  1. Dieting (an avoidance of high-caloric food and a preoccupation with thinness)

2. Bulimia and food preoccupation (bulimic thoughts and thoughts about food)
3. Oral control (self-control of eating and perceived pressure from others to gain weight)
4. May be used as a screening device for nonclinical settings or to measure clinical outcomes

Reliability:

- Overall alpha coefficient = .94
- Alpha coefficients range from .83 to .92 for both the 26-item and 40-item versions (Garner et al., 1982)

Validity:

- Although not significantly related to measures of dieting, weight fluctuation, or neuroticism, indicating discriminant validity, scores discriminated between female patients with anorexia nervosa and normal university students
- Normal-weight females and obese females scored lower than did anorexic patients
- 26-item version correlates with 40-item version ($r = .98$) (Garner et al., 1982).

EATING QUESTIONNAIRE—REVISED

Authors: Williamson, Davis, Goreczny, McKenzie, & Watkins (1989)

Description:

- 15-item self-report assessing symptoms of bulimia

Reliability:

- Internal consistency of .87
- Test-retest reliability (2-week) is .90

Validity:

- Correlates with Eating Attitudes Test and Bulimia Test—Revised
- Distinguishes between individuals with bulimia, individuals with obesity, and normal controls

BODY IMAGE AVOIDANCE QUESTIONNAIRE

Authors: Rosen, Srebnik, Saltzberg, & Wendt (1991)

Description:

- 19-item self-report (6-point format) assessing behaviors, particularly avoidance of situations, associated with body image disturbance

Reliability:

- Internal consistency is .89
- Test-retest reliability is .87

Validity:

- Correlates at .78 with Body Shape Questionnaire
- Distinguishes between individuals with bulimia nervosa and nonclinical groups

BULIMIA TEST—REVISED

Authors: Thelan & Smith (1991)

Description:

- 28-item self-report assessing DSM-III criteria for bulimia nervosa

Reliability:

- Internal consistency was reported as .97
- Test-retest reliability (2 months) was .95

Validity:

- Discriminates between individuals with bulimia nervosa and normal controls
- Correlates with original scale at .99
- Correlates with Binge Scale at .85

PERSONAL ADJUSTMENT

YOUTH SELF-REPORT

Author: Achenbach (1991)

Description:

- Assesses 11- to 18-year-olds' self-reports of their own problems and competencies for the last 6 months
- Items are parallel to Child Behavior Checklist
- 3-response format (0/ "not true," 1/ "somewhat" or "sometimes true," 2/ "very true" or "often true")
- 17 competence items include:
  1. Activities
  2. Social
  3. Academic performance
- 103 problem items
  1. Thought problems
  2. Attention problems
  3. Self-destructive/identity problems (only for boys)
- Internalizing
  4. Withdrawn
  5. Somatic complaints
  6. Anxious/depressed
- Externalizing
  7. Delinquent behavior
  8. Aggressive behavior

Reliability:

- One-week test-retest reliabilities: mean .76 for competence scores and mean .72 for problem scores
- Six-month test-retest reliabilities: mean of .69 for problem scores
- Seven-month test-retest reliabilities: mean of .50 for competence scales and .49 for problem scales

Validity:

- Discriminates between referred and nonreferred youth

BECK DEPRESSION INVENTORY

Authors: Beck, Rush, Shaw, & Emery (1979); Beck, Ward, Mendelson, Mock, & Erbaugh (1961)
[Review data on psychometric information by Beck, Steer, & Garbin (1988)]

Description:

- 21 items, measuring symptoms and attitudes of depression, rated from 0–3 in terms of intensity
- Also a short version (13 items) that correlates highly (.89 to .97) with long form, although may only represent cognitively oriented symptoms rather than both cognitive and noncognitive
- Written at a fifth- to sixth-grade reading level
- Different time frames may be ascertained
- Has been used in 1,000 research studies

Reliability:

- Mean coefficient alpha for nine psychiatric samples is .86
- Mean coefficient alpha for 15 nonpsychiatric samples is .81
- Test-retest reliability ranged from .48 to .86 for psychiatric patients and .60 to .83 for nonpsychiatric patients

Validity:

- Mean correlation coefficients between clinical ratings and the Beck Depression Inventory for psychiatric patients was .72 and for nonpsychiatric patients was .60
- Mean correlation coefficients between Hamilton Psychiatric Rating Scale for Depression and the Beck Depression Inventory for 5 psychiatric studies was .73 and for the 2 nonpsychiatric patients was .73 and .80, respectively
- Mean correlation coefficients between the Zung Self-Reported Depression Scale and the Beck Depression Inventory for 8 psychiatric studies was .76 and for the 5 nonpsychiatric samples was .71
- Mean correlation coefficients between the MMPI Depression Scale and the Beck Depression Inventory for 7 psychiatric studies was .76 and for the 3 nonpsychiatric patients was .60
- Several studies have indicated that the measure discriminates between normals and psychiatric patients and psychiatric and nonpsychiatric samples

- Construct validity has been demonstrated with selected attitudes and behaviors, such as biological correlates, suicidal behaviors, alcohol problems, adjustment, medical symptoms, stress, and anxiety

BRIEF SYMPTOM INVENTORY

Authors: Derogatis (1993)

Description:

- A briefer, 54-item version of the SCL-90-R
- Primary symptom dimensions:
  1. Somatization
  2. Obsessive-compulsive
  3. Interpersonal sensitivity
  4. Depression
  5. Anxiety
  6. Hostility
  7. Phobic anxiety
  8. Paranoid ideation
  9. Psychoticism
- 3 global indices:
  1. Global Severity Index
  2. Positive Symptom Total
  3. Positive Symptom Distress Index
- 0–4 ("not at all," "a little bit," "moderately," "quite a bit," and "extremely")
- Widely used (200 published studies used this scale) (Derogatis, 1993).

Reliability:

- Alpha coefficients are strong, ranging from .71 to .85
- Test-retest (2 weeks) reliabilities ranged from .68 to .91, with reliability for the Global Severity Index at .90

Validity:

- High convergence between scales of Brief Symptom Inventory and the MMPI
- High correlations (ranging from .92 to .99) between Brief Symptom Inventory and Symptom Checklist 90—Revised
- A factor analysis provided support for construct validation

- Evidence for predictive validity in that the measure has been demonstrated as an effective screening device across many varied medical settings
- Further evidence for predictive validity in that psychological distress was predicted in cancer populations, individuals with psychopathology, and individuals experiencing problems with pain management in HIV research, in student mental health, and in general clinical studies, and to predict efficacy of therapeutic interventions

PARENT ADJUSTMENT

BECK DEPRESSION INVENTORY

(*See Chapter One*, Family Treatment with Child Abuse and Neglect)

SYMPTOM CHECKLIST 90—REVISED

(*See Chapter One*, Family Treatment with Child Abuse and Neglect)

BRIEF SYMPTOM INVENTORY

(*See Chapter One*, Family Treatment with Child Abuse and Neglect)

MARITAL ADJUSTMENT

THE MARITAL ADJUSTMENT TEST

(*See Chapter One*, Family Treatment with Child Abuse and Neglect)

DYADIC ADJUSTMENT SCALE

(*See Chapter One*, Family Treatment with Child Abuse and Neglect)

O'LEARY-PORTER SCALE

(*See Chapter One*, Family Treatment with Child Abuse and Neglect)

FAMILY OUTCOME—MEMBERS' REPORTS

FAMILY ADAPTABILITY AND COHESION EVALUATION SCALES III

(*See Chapter One*, Family Treatment with Child Abuse and Neglect)

FAMILY ENVIRONMENT SCALE

(*See Chapter One*, Family Treatment with Child Abuse and Neglect)

MCMASTER FAMILY ASSESSMENT DEVICE

(*See Chapter One*, Family Treatment with Child Abuse and Neglect)

SATISFACTION WITH SERVICES

CLIENT SATISFACTION QUESTIONNAIRE

(*See Chapter One*, Family Treatment with Child Abuse and Neglect)

REFERENCES FOR MEASUREMENT OF FAMILY TREATMENT WITH EATING DISORDERS

Achenbach, T. M. (1991). *Manual for the youth self-report and 1991 profile.* Burlington, VT: University of Vermont Department of Psychiatry.

Beck, A., Rush, A., Shaw, B., & Emery, G. (1979). *Cognitive therapy of depression.* New York: Guilford Press.

Beck, A., Ward, C., Mendelson, M., Mock, J., & Erbaugh, J. (1961). An inventory for measuring depression. *Archives of General Psychiatry, 4,* 53–63.

Beck, A. T., Steer, R. A., Garbin, M. G. (1988). Psychometric properties of the Beck Depression Inventory: Twenty-five years of evaluation. *Clinical Psychology Review, 8,* 77–100.

Cooper, P. J., Taylor, M. J., Cooper, Z., & Fairburn, C. G. (1987). The development and validation of the Body Shape questionnaire. *International Journal of Eating Disorders, 6*(4), 485–494.

Derogatis, L. (1993). *Brief Symptom Inventory: Administration, scoring, and procedures manual.* Minneapolis, MN: National Computer Systems.

Garner, D. M., & Garfinkel, P. E. (1979). *The eating attitude test: An index of the symptoms of anorexia nervosa* (9th ed.). Cambridge, MA: Cambridge University Press.

Garner, D. M., Olmsted, M. P., Bohr, Y., & Garfinkel, P. E. (1982). The eating attitudes test: Psychometric features and clinical correlates. *Psychological Medicine, 12,* 871–878.

Hawkins II, R. C., & Clement, P. F. (1980). Development and construct validation of a self-report measure of binge eating tendencies. *Addictive Behaviors, 5,* 219–226.

Rosen, J., Srebnik, D., Saltzberg, E., & Wendt, S. (1991). Development of a body image avoidance questionnaire. *Psychological Assessment, 3,* 32–37.

Thelan, M., & Smith, M. (1991). A revision of the bulimia test: The BULIT-R. *Psychological Assessment, 3,* 119–124.

Williamson, D., Davis, C., Goreczny, A., McKenzie, S., & Watkins, P. (1989). The Eating Questionnaire—Revised: A symptom checklist for bulimia. In P. A. Keller & S. R. Heyman (Eds.), *Innovations in clinical practice, 8,* 321–326.

CHAPTER 7

Family Treatment
with Juvenile Offending

with Stephanie Basham

Family Case:

Vincent Lopez, an Hispanic male, age 15, and his single parent, Constance Lopez, were mandated into treatment by the juvenile court. Vincent has recently been placed on probation because he had been caught for auto theft. Ms. Lopez said that Vincent was "a good boy" until he started hanging around "with a bad crowd" and sneaking out of the house at night and stealing cars. She said that although she yells at Vincent and has tried grounding him, he just sneaks out of the house.

She explained that since she can't control him anymore, she wanted his father to take him for awhile. However, Vincent's father claims he can't take Vincent because he has two new children from another marriage, as well as his current wife's three children from a previous relationship, to support. Vincent now sees his father about once a month. Ms. Lopez says he only pays a quarter of his child support.

Perpetration of crimes by adolescents, juvenile offending, has become a serious problem in our society. According to self-reports of victims and offenders, Federal Bureau of Investigation (FBI) statistics, and police arrest data, large proportions of crimes are perpetrated by juvenile offenders (U.S. Department of Justice, 1996a). Arrests by juveniles for violent crimes have continued to increase in the last decade (67.3% from 1986 to 1995), whereas the increase for property crimes was only by 8% over the same time period. Clearly juvenile crime, especially violent crime, is a costly and dangerous problem in our nation today.

RATIONALE FOR A FOCUS ON THE FAMILY

Many researchers have noted the strong association of certain family characteristics on the development and maintenance of antisocial behavior and delinquent behavior (Capaldi & Patterson, 1994; Kazdin, 1997; Loeber & Stouthamer-Loeber, 1986; Robins, 1991). For example, Loeber and Stouthamer-Loeber (1986) found that the strongest predictors of delinquency were poor monitoring; harsh, inconsistent, or poor discipline; lack of parent involvement/attachment; and parental rejection. While demographics of the family, particularly education and occupation, and stresses impinging upon the family are also associated with the development of delinquency, family processes appear to be key. For instance, Laub and Sampson (1988) reported that maternal supervision, discipline style, and attachment were much more predictive of delinquency than factors external to the family, such as parental involvement with the law, alcohol use, poverty, and single-parent status. In addition, Larzelere and Patterson (1990) indicated that parent management practices were more important than socioeconomic status in predicting later delinquency. That is not to say that these factors were unimportant (evidence has suggested that these factors actually complicate intervention, [e.g., Miller & Prinz, 1990; Webster-Stratton, 1990)]), but their effect seems to be mediated by the presence or absence of family process variables.

Given the importance of family factors, much attention has been given to family interventions. Although authors have noted no single intervention or treatment to date that has been found entirely effective with antisocial behavior (Kazdin, 1995, 1997; Miller & Prinz, 1990; Reid, 1993; Webster-Stratton, 1991), Kazdin (1995b, 1997) has identified four approaches that provide the best research evidence for effectiveness with treating conduct disorders. These were cognitive problem-solving skills training, and then three types of family interventions: parent-management training, functional family therapy, and multisystemic therapy. Similarly, Chamberlain and Rosicky (1995) in their review of family therapy, considered social learning family therapy (also known as parent training), structural family therapy, and multi-ecological targeted treatment (including family preservation and multisystemic treatment) to be effective with antisocial youth and their families.

Cognitive problem-solving skills therapy focuses on treating the individual by teaching social problem-solving skills (Kazdin, 1997). Antisocial children are characterized by a style of cognitive processing that impedes their ability to effectively problem-solve in social situations (Dodge, Price, Bachorowski, & Newman, 1990). For example, they are more likely to make hostile attributions regarding neutral events (Bienert & Schneider, 1995), which contributes to aggressive behavior. Individual treatment targeted at their problem-solving skills has produced reductions in antisocial behavior, but generally has not shown a good deal of generalization to various settings (Kazdin, 1997). Even so, it is often used as a component of therapy in some family interventions (i.e., family preservation, multisystem treatment) which will be explained in more detail elsewhere. For reviews of individual cognitive-behavioral interventions with antisocial behavior, the reader is directed to Durlak, Fuhrman, and Lampman (1991) and Kazdin (1995, 1997).

The other interventions tested with offending youth have focused on the family as the system for intervention. Parent training targets the parent-child relationship; functional family therapy focuses on the entire family system; and family preservation and multisystemic therapy involve working closely and intensely with the family to impact several of the systems with which the offending adolescent is involved. The effectiveness of these interventions is of great concern, noting the stability and poor prognosis of antisocial behavior.

In this review, studies examining family interventions published since 1985 were examined. Studies were from refereed journals and provided empirical outcome data. Single subject design and case studies were not included. Studies with adolescent offenders exclusively were examined, in which subjects' mean age was at least 12 years of age. Subjects were offenders and conduct-disordered youth with a record of offending, rather than simply those at risk of offending. Therefore, studies focused on treatment (interventions which took place after indications of offending behavior, such as probation, arrest, or incarceration) rather than prevention efforts, which take place prior to offending behavior (e.g., Dishion, Patterson, & Kavanagh, 1992; Forehand & Long, 1991; Fraser, Hawkins & Howard, 1988; Tremblay et al., 1992).

This review first gives an overview of the development of offending behavior and then examines the research on family interventions. The organizational framework for this chapter involves a range of less to more intense and comprehensive interventions. Parent training in which the focus is the parent-child interaction is examined first, followed by functional family therapy in which the entire family's interactions are involved. Next, discussion will revolve around family preservation approaches which address family resource needs as well as interactions, and finally multisystemic treatment, where the interactions within the family, as well as between the family and other systems, are of concern.

DEVELOPMENT OF CONDUCT PROBLEMS

The development of juvenile offending, has been conceptualized as either limited to the developmental period of adolescence or as being persistent across the life span (Moffitt, 1993). Life-course persistent antisocial behavior may be influenced by early development, especially neurological traits, which may be determined by either genetics or the environment. Moffitt (1993) hypothesizes that a neurologically vulnerable and difficult child develops antisocial behavior in the context of parental interactions. The child's individual traits evoke distinctive, negative reactions from parents, and these responses in turn heighten the child's tendency toward difficult behavior. Reciprocal interactions between individual traits, and interactions and reactions in the environment serve to develop and sustain antisocial behavior.

Patterson and associates (Patterson, 1982, 1986; Patterson, DeBaryshe, & Ramsey, 1989) have formulated a model to explain how this occurs. The cycle begins with the application of an aversive stimulus. A typical aversive stimulus involves the parent issuing a command to the child. This command is then followed by a coercive response by the child, such as noncompliance, whining, yelling, or crying. Two main response types are then displayed by the parent: the parent may remove the aversive stimulus (withdraw the command); alternatively, the parent may reapply the aversive stimulus (raising voice to repeat command, physical aggression to encourage compliance). The child may also respond in certain ways: he/she may comply, which reinforces the parent's aversive behavior; or he/she may escalate, reinforcing the parent's withdrawal of commands. As both family members train each other to become increasingly averse in their interactions, coerciveness is generated and maintained. This negative reinforcement for antisocial behavior, along with the modeling of the coercive responses by the parent, serves to teach the child a behavior pattern that is increasingly expanded to other social environments, such as the school setting and the peer group (Conduct Problems Prevention Research Group [CPPRG], 1992; Forehand & Long, 1988; Moffitt, 1993). At the same time, parents, in an attempt to avoid the negative emotions engendered by such exchanges, prefer instead that their child spend time away from the home. This rejection and avoidance of the child further erode discipline and supervision (Capaldi & Patterson, 1994; Reid, 1993).

As a result, instead of learning and enhancing prosocial skills at each level of development, life-course persistent antisocial children actually learn to be more evocative of others and are increasingly rejected by parents, teachers and peers. For example, difficulty with teachers may contribute to poor school performance. Alienation from the norms of the school system may result, and by the time such children are about 10 to 11 years of age, they bond together in deviant peer groups (McMahon, 1994).

Adolescent-limited antisocial behavior, on the other hand, is actually influenced by these deviant peers (Moffitt, 1993). A normal desire for adolescents is to want the privileges of adulthood, such as independence and a diminished need for adult accountability. Antisocial behavior considered adolescent-limited is motivated by these desires. Adolescents may engage in antisocial behavior, such as skipping school or stealing a car, in order to achieve what to them is adult status. As more acceptable adult roles are obtained and environmental contingencies alter for adolescents progressing to young adulthood, antisocial behavior is discontinued.

The family environment and the adolescent's own developmental course, therefore, impact the initiation of offending behavior. However, treatment models have not yet been formulated that reflect onset of behavior problems. As previously discussed, though, the home environment has been given a considerable amount of attention in explaining the development of offending. The next section will examine the family intervention that targets the simplest family system: the parent-child dyad.

FAMILY INTERVENTIONS

PARENT TRAINING

Parent training, which focuses on changing the interaction style of the parent, has shown much promise as an intervention for younger antisocial children, by changing parent's behavior, parent's perception of child's behavior, and children's behavior (Kazdin, 1997; Miller & Prinz, 1990; Webster-Stratton, 1990, 1991; Webster-Stratton & Hammond, 1997). Parent training has been recommended for juvenile offenders, but with little empirical evidence to support it (e.g., Fraser et al., 1988). Very few studies have examined the effectiveness of parent training with adolescents specifically (Kazdin, 1995, 1997). In fact, only one study could be found that met the criteria for this review. In order to understand the intervention of parent training, its theoretical basis must first be understood.

Theoretical Basis of Parent Training

Based on a social learning theory of behavior (Horne & Sayger, 1990; Miller & Prinz, 1990), conduct disorder is assumed to develop and sustain itself from social learning processes in the family. Parent training intervenes in these interactional processes (Kazdin, 1993, 1995, 1997; Offord & Bennett, 1994). The goal of parent management training is to change this interactional pattern so that prosocial behavior is reinforced and antisocial behavior diminished (Kazdin, 1995, 1997). The poor parenting interaction may result from lack of knowledge about how to implement effective skills, or from some additional outside interference (Forehand & Long, 1988). For example, interference such as parental adjustment, marital discord, and parental depression has been related to poor parenting skills (Forehand & Long, 1988; Webster-Stratton, 1990). Parents are taught to change the interpersonal consequences and antecedents that are maintaining and triggering the antisocial behavior (Kazdin, 1995, 1997; Webster-Stratton, 1991). Although it is recognized that the parent is not solely responsible for this interactional process, altering this pattern is targeted via the parent (Kazdin, 1995, 1997; Patterson, 1986).

Definition of Parent Training

Parent training focuses on the improvement of parenting skills or addressing other factors that may be interfering with parenting (Forehand & Long, 1988). Patterson and his colleagues developed a program at the Oregon Social Learning Center that has been quite influential in the field of parent training (Patterson, 1982). Originally formulated for preadolescents, the program involves five family management practices: accurate observation of problem behaviors, reinforcement techniques, discipline procedures, monitoring, and problem solving. This model was adapted for parents of adolescents by Bank, Marlowe, Reid, Patterson, and Weinrott (1991), who examined parent training with juvenile offenders. The intervention included training parents to identify prosocial and antisocial behavior, as well as behavior that may place the child at risk for offending. Parents tracked the occurrence of specific behaviors, such as class attendance, violating curfew, usage of drugs, association with deviant peers, and completion of homework. In addition to close monitoring of activities, parents were instructed to talk with their adolescent about any activities the parent was not able to directly observe. Parents were also trained to have close and frequent contact with the school to monitor homework and attendance. Teachers supplied information on classroom behavior that was used in a behavioral contract agreed upon by the parent and adolescent, which included rewards and punishments for prosocial and antisocial behavior. As opposed to the use of time-out, which is typically taught to the parents of younger children, alternative punishments—such as loss of points, restriction of free time, and work details—were used with adolescents. The program also addressed stressors that affected the family, such as marital discord and parental depression, by providing additional services, such as individual therapy, to the parents.

Outcomes from the program (Bank et al., 1991) included arrest rates at 1-, 2-, and 3-year follow-up for juvenile offenders whose families received parent training compared to those who received family therapy (*see* Table 7.1). Overall, no significant differences were found between groups at 3-year follow-up; both had decreased arrest rates over time. However, the parent training group experienced more rapid improvement than the family therapy group, and the juveniles spent slightly less time incarcerated.

Limitations of Parent Training with Adolescent Offenders

It is noteworthy that Bank et al. (1991) provided a level of parent training beyond basic parenting skills, since the level of family dysfunction and stress plays a role in parent training effectiveness. Generally, greater dysfunction has been associated with less effectiveness of parent training programs alone (Dadds & McHugh, 1992; Dumas & Wahler, 1983; Reid, 1993). More intensive work with parents themselves may need to be done in these cases, especially since families of offenders are characterized by multiple stressors. Parents of adolescents in particular are believed not only to drop out of treatment more often, but also may be less likely to change their parenting style (Kazdin, 1995).

However, as discussed, there is a shortage of recent studies that have actually examined parent training with adolescents. A couple of studies looked at behavioral improvement of children of differing age spans (preschool vs. school-age; Dishion & Patterson, 1992; Ruma, Burke, & Thompson, 1996). The evidence indicates that school-age children can still show gains when their parents undergo training, although Ruma et al. (1996) discussed that older children tend to have more severe problems prior to treatment. In addition, Dishion and Patterson (1996) found that dropout was higher for parents of older children (6.5 to 12.5 years) compared to parents of younger children (2.5 to 6.5 years). These studies suggest that at adolescence, while behavior problems may be more entrenched and dropout from treatment may be higher, families may still benefit.

Clearly, more work needs to be conducted on the effectiveness of parent training with conduct-disordered adolescents and juvenile offending youth. Perhaps treatment with adolescents could be enhanced to include the important role that peers and other outside influences play in behavior. For example,

TABLE 7.1 Parent-Training Programs with Juvenile Offenders

AUTHOR/MODEL	DESIGN/SAMPLE	MEASURES	RESULTS	LIMITATIONS
Bank et al., (1991) Social-interactional mean session hours: 21.5 hrs, phone contact 23.3 hrs	Quasi-experimental, random assignment to treatment (parent training) or comparison (services as usual—family therapy [combination behavioral and systems generally] & group [social skills and drug counseling if needed]), pretest, posttest, 3-yr follow-up $N = 55$ repeat offender youths all males; average age 14; 38.5% father-absent; parents high school educated and either semi-skilled workers or skilled manual workers	Offense records; Family Interaction Coding System; Parent Daily Report (latter 2 measures only experimental group)	Both groups demonstrated reduced rates of offending during follow-up years. Experimental group boys spent significantly less time in institutional settings than boys in comparison group. Significant positive change according to Parent Daily Report but not on home observational data; staff in experimental group experienced "burnout"	Information on race/ethnicity excluded; comparison group did not have standardized measures

parents could be trained to monitor activities with peers more closely (e.g., Bank et al., 1991) or teach skills for social competency (e.g., Kazdin, Siegel, & Bass, 1992). In addition, since the relationship is viewed as interactional, adolescents may have to take a more active part in the intervention, possibly learning to alter their communication and rewards/punishments toward parents. Given the success of parent training with younger children with antisocial problems, it seems premature to write it off completely for adolescents without further investigation.

FUNCTIONAL FAMILY THERAPY

The next family intervention, functional family therapy, focuses not only on the interaction between parent and child, but also on other interactions in the family system, such as within the parental dyad. Although other family therapy approaches have been used with juvenile offenders, either these approaches are weak methodologically (Green, Vosler, & Bader, 1989) or the family intervention is only one component in a package of services (Minor & Elrod, 1994). (*See* Table 7.2.) The theoretical basis and description of functional family therapy, along with an empirical investigation of its effectiveness, will be provided in the following sections.

Theoretical Basis of Functional Family Therapy

Alexander and Parsons, (1982) developed functional family therapy in which systems, cognitive, and behavioral theories are integrated. Juvenile offending and other clinical problems are conceptualized from the standpoint of the functions they serve the family system, as well as the function for individual family members (Alexander & Parsons, 1982; Kazdin, 1995, 1997). Behavior is viewed in the context of family relationships in which the individual may be attempting to achieve greater closeness, greater separation, or some balance between the two in the relationship. For example, behavior problems may unite parents around their child's difficult behavior; alternatively, conduct problems may be the child's attempt to signal that the family is too restrictive. Since maladaptive processes within the family develop in lieu of more direct means of fulfilling these functions, the goal of functional family therapy is to alter interaction and communication patterns so that more adaptive functioning is experienced. As well as communication patterns of the family, coercive interactions between parent and child are also targets for functional family intervention (Alexander & Parsons, 1982). Functional family therapy combines knowledge about parent-child interactions and social learning (the basis of parent train-

TABLE 7.2 Juvenile Offender Family Therapy Studies

AUTHOR/MODEL	DESIGN/SAMPLE	MEASURES	RESULTS	LIMITATIONS
Barton et al., (1985) Functional Family Therapy (by undergraduates trained in the model) average number of sessions: 10.3 Time frame of services not given	I. posttest only at 13 mos $N = 27$ families referred by the court II. Post-hoc comparison between families seen with Functional Family ($N = 109$) therapy and casework-as-usual ($N = 216$) services) Parent-initiated referrals for cases in which there might be a protective issue III. $N = 74$ seriously delinquent adolescents having family therapy after being incarcerated in a state training school	I. Recidivism; Defensive & Supportive Communication coding scheme for direct observation II. Proportion of cases placed in foster care shelter for at least 72 hrs III. Offenses	I. Undergraduates achieved comparable results (26% recidivism) to graduate therapists in other studies; compared to annual recidivism rate for juvenile court district, this was significant II. Before functional family therapy, rate of foster care was 48% and 11% following functional family therapy but no change in foster care rate for comparison group III. At end of 15-mo follow-up, 60% of experimental group were charged with	I. No comparison/ control group; small sample size; lack of demographic information on participants; pretest, posttest differences not reported in terms of statistical significance; coding schema lacking evidence of reliability II. Lack of demographic information; potentially biased ratings by caseworkers who administered treatment and coded comparison cases; statistically significant tests were not computed for group comparison; confound of highly motivated workers who carried

	compared to a matched group incarcerated for similarity of offenses		offense compared to 93% of comparison group; for those who committed subsequent offenses in experimental group, they were fewer in number than in the comparison group (but not less severe)	out the treatment group; no measures other than foster care; families might also have received remedial education, job training and placement, and school placement; therefore, changes could be attributed to these other services
Gordon et al. (1988) Functional Family Therapy Mean # of sessions = 16	Quasi-experimental, assigned to family condition only if criteria met: family conflict; family wanted out-of-home placement for child; child at risk of recidivism Treatment condition also involved probation, compared against probation only, pretest, follow-up (mean of 27.8 mos for treatment group after pretest; for comparison group, mean of 31.5 mos)	Recidivism rates	Annualized recidivism rates: Treatment group averaged 1.3 offenses for a year, comparison group averaged 10.3 Average rates of recidivism: 5% for treatment group, 25% for comparison group	No random assignment; no other measures than recidivism; no posttest

continued

TABLE 7.2 *(continued)*

AUTHOR/MODEL	DESIGN/SAMPLE	MEASURES	RESULTS	LIMITATIONS
	$N = 28$ family therapy, 27 in probation only 69% males, 29% females; all White; 80% from lower and lower middle-income and 20% from middle income			
Gordon et al. (1995) Functional family therapy	3-yr follow-up for Gordon et al. (1988) 82% from treatment, 81% from comparison		Recidivism rates 8.7% treatment vs. 40.9% for comparison group	
Green, Vosler, & Bader (1989) Bowenian Family Therapy, Satir's communications approach, & Haley's Strategic Family Therapy	Quasi-experimental, to one of three treatment groups; pretest, posttest $N = 80$ families who were referred because they had an adolescent probationer, 39% intact	Family Awareness Scale, Dyadic Adjustment Scale, Parent Adolescent Communication Inventory, Locus of Control Scale for Children, Piers-Harris Children's Self-Concept	No differences between groups; mothers, fathers, and adolescents all improved on reports of family functioning; for dyadic functioning, maternal, paternal, and child scores on parent-	No control group; no random assignment; confounded effect of treatment length and intensity—treatment lasted between 6 and 9 mos for Bowenian and strategic groups and 3

	families, 24% blended, 38% single-parent. 69% boys & 31% girls. 83% White, 15% African American, mean age = 15.2 yrs, low to middle income	Scale, State-Trait Anxiety Inventory, Emotional Maturity Scale	child communication improved, while maternal marital quality scores did not show a significant improvement, and fathers' perception of marital quality decreased at a significant level; on individual psychosocial measures: mothers did even more poorly on trait anxiety; men, women and children improved on locus of control, and adolescents also improved on self-esteem	mos with "multiple and varying modalities"
Kelley, Kelley, & Williams (1989) Individual & Family Therapy Models	Posttest only (archival data) $N = 253$ closed case records from a 6-yr period regarding adolescents who received outpatient treatment. 185 received family therapy and 68 received individual therapy	Therapist judgment	Overall, family therapy was more effective than was individual therapy in treating teens with acting-out behavioral problems. The girls improved at a higher rate than did boys regardless of type of treatment	No pretest; no comparison or control group; lack of standardized measures; biased measure of outcome; lack of demographic information Confound family therapy

continued

TABLE 7.2 *(continued)*

AUTHOR/MODEL	DESIGN/SAMPLE	MEASURES	RESULTS	LIMITATIONS
Minor & Elrod (1994) Alternative probation (4 job-preparation workshops, 3-day outdoor adventure, and 7 family skill-building workshops) implemented over a 3-mo period Family component—7 2-hr workshops held over 7 weeks	Randomization by 2 groups (intensive and moderate probationers) to treatment or control (probation services as usual), pretest, posttest (3 mos after termination) $N = 45$; 82.2% male; 60% White, 35.6% African American, 4.4% Hispanic; average age = 15.07 yrs; SES—low- to middle status	Client and family participation (unstandardized); Self-Concept Scale; Locus of Control Scale; Perceptions of Juvenile Justice	Few differences on outcomes between treatment and services as usual	with other treatment components; many of the measures adopted from other measures and therefore, unstandardized; posttest sometimes not conducted until 3 mos after treatment

ing) along with knowledge about individual cognitive styles that influence juvenile offending. With the combination of theoretical concepts, the model has also been referred to as behavioral-systems family therapy (Gordon, Arbuthnot, Gustafson, & McGreen, 1988).

Treatment is divided into three phases: assessment, therapy, and education (Alexander & Parsons, 1982). In the assessment phase, behavior patterns and the contingencies that reinforce behaviors are examined. Information is also obtained from collateral agencies, such as the school and the justice system. In the therapy phase, practitioners use many techniques to change the relationships between family members, as well as the meaning the problem holds for the family (Alexander & Parsons, 1982). Techniques include changing beliefs, cognitions, expectations, and reactions between family members. Interactions between family members are the focus of intervention, instead of the behavior of the adolescent. The education phase involves the family members learning new skills, including parenting, communication, and problem-solving skills.

Empirical Evidence Concerning Functional Family Therapy

For the most part, the few studies on functional family were mainly conducted in the 1970s (Gordon et al., 1988; Kazdin, 1997) and no studies have been published in the last few years. Findings show much promise, however, for functional family therapy, which was beneficial in modifying communication within offending families and reducing recidivism of offending behavior at both two and 5-year follow-up when compared against probation only (Gordon et al., 1988). Further, Barton, Alexander, Waldron, Turner, and Warburton (1985) reported on three replications of functional family therapy in three different settings: probation, state family services, and juvenile detention. Functional family therapy produced the following notable changes:

1. reduced recidivism
2. improved communication
3. reduced out-of-home placement, as well as commensurate costs
4. decreased number and frequency of offenses among juvenile offenders

Of note in Barton et al. (1985), it was found that undergraduates trained in functional family therapy achieved comparable results to the graduate therapists. This finding suggests that bachelor's-level practitioners in the court setting may, with appropriate training and supervision, facilitate positive family change and reduce juvenile offending with the functional family model.

In a more controlled study, Gordon et al. (1988) tested functional family therapy as an in-home rather than a clinic-based intervention for court-ordered offenders. Recidivism rates for youths who received functional family therapy were 11% at 2-year follow-up. This rate was in marked contrast to comparison youths who received regular probation services, with a recidivism rate of 67%. At 5-year follow up, the recidivism rate for the experimental group was 8.7%, as compared to 40.9% for the probation group (Gordon, Graves, & Arbuthnot, 1995). Gordon et al. (1995) argue the importance of this finding, since subsequent violations increase dramatically the likelihood that offending will continue.

Limitations of Functional Family Therapy

Although results are promising, functional family therapy has not undergone extensive investigation. Because the model comprises techniques from different theoretical models, comparing it to either parent training or systems therapy would assist in an understanding of the crucial components of the intervention. Studies would also benefit from more diverse outcome measures besides recidivism, such as the adolescent's relationship with peers, or other measures of antisocial behavior, such as parent or teacher report, school performance, and parent's functioning (level of stress, depression). A final criticism of this research has been the homogeneity of the subjects tested, who have been largely middle-class (Gordon et al., 1995).

FAMILY PRESERVATION

Definition of Family Preservation

Going a step beyond functional family therapy and growing out of family system interventions is family preservation, which involves intervention with other systems besides the family alone. Family preservation is considered a model of service delivery characterized by home-based, intensively delivered, time-limited, and goal-oriented interventions (Haapala & Kinney, 1988). Family preservation has evolved from both home-based services, which seek to bring services to a family in its natural environment, and family-based services, which aim to intervene with the whole family as opposed to the individual (Rodenhiser, Chandy & Ahmed, 1995). Prevention of out-of-home placement and the maintenance of youth in their natural environment have been the main concerns of the model (Haapala & Kinney, 1988). The original family preservation model, Homebuilders, has been used with adolescent offenders and includes a variety of therapeutic interventions such as behavior modification, crisis intervention, assertiveness training, and client-centered therapy (Haapala & Kinney, 1998). Since families at risk of having a member placed out of the home tend to be characterized by multiple stressors, family preservation offers a variety of services to families above and beyond therapy, such as the provision of resources, transportation, and advocacy with agencies that affect the family.

Empirical Evidence Concerning Family Preservation

While a vast body of literature exists in family preservation with child abuse and neglect (*see* Chapter Two, this volume), few studies concentrate solely on outcome with adolescent offenders. In the studies that were located (e.g., Haapala & Kinney, 1988; Rodenhiser et al., 1995), disposition of the adolescent (i.e., whether or not they were placed out of the home) is the common outcome measure. Haapala and Kinney (1988) examined 1-year disposition of offenders and found the majority to have avoided placement. These results were maintained at 4-year follow-up. In addition to avoidance of placement, children's well-being and parent's ability to handle the child's behavior have been shown to improve after family preservation (Rodenhiser et al., 1995).

Limitations of Family Preservation

It is difficult to correctly interpret the findings of family preservation studies, since the many interventions that are provided confound effects. Generally, family preservation research lacks methodological rigor, as evidenced by the lack of both standardized measures and control/comparison groups (Chamberlain & Rosicky, 1995). While placement is an important outcome variable, reduction of offending, improvements in family functioning, and school performance are also relevant outcomes that have not been examined. The most difficult hurdle for this treatment approach to overcome is its lack of specificity, which makes replication difficult. Indeed, family preservation is viewed by many as a service-delivery model rather than a treatment (Henggeler, Borduin, & Mann, 1993). Most discouraging is that some researchers have concluded that the effects of family preservation quickly diminish after the intervention is terminated (Wells & Biegel, 1992).

MULTISYSTEMIC TREATMENT FOR JUVENILE OFFENDING

Theoretical Basis of Multisystemic Treatment

Henggeler and colleagues (e.g., Henggeler, 1989; Henggeler & Borduin, 1990) have created a model emphasizing the multiple systems that impact the development of delinquency. Using Bronfenbrenner's (1979) theory of the social-ecological model of development, this theory postulates that the systems surrounding the individual influence his/her behavior in both direct and indirect ways. The microsystems (the most direct systems that impact the child, such as immediate and extended family) and mesosystems (more distal influences that the child and his/her microsystems are embedded within, such as the school or neighborhood) impact the child and are impacted by the child in a systemic fashion. Systems that affect and are affected by delinquent behavior include the child's own intrapersonal system (i.e., cognitive ability, social skills), parent-child system, the family system, the school system (interactions with teachers), and child-peer system (Henggeler, 1991; Henggeler, Cunningham, Pickrel, Schoenwald, & Brondino, 1986).

Mulitsystemic therapy is considered a form of family therapy in that the family is viewed as a system and behavior as an interactional response within that system (Henggeler & Borduin, 1990; Henggeler et al., 1993, 1996). Multisystemic therapy extends beyond family therapy, however, in that it targets not only the family system but also the numerous systems in which the adolescent is embedded that serve to maintain and impact delinquent behavior (Henggeler, 1989; Henggeler et al., 1996). For example, the impact of other systems besides the family, such as the peer group or school setting, on antisocial behavior is acknowledged.

Multisystemic therapy is also considered a family preservation model in that a central objective involves keeping the adolescent in the home rather than being institutionalized due to criminal behavior. Maintaining youths in their natural environment, as well as enhancing generalization, is an important goal of the therapy. As a result, treatment is often conducted in the home or a community setting. Also, similar to family preservation models, multisystemic therapy represents a combination of treatment modalities and venues of service provision. In common to both models, treatment is individualized; however, multisystemic therapy appears to have a more consistent theoretical basis and its procedures are more systematic (for instance, treatment is manualized).

Several characteristics serve to define multisystemic therapy (Henggeler et al., 1996). Social learning and behavior principles are the basis for change within this treatment, which also includes cognitive and behavioral techniques (Henggeler & Borduin, 1990; Henggeler et al., 1996). Therapy is highly individualized, so that each family's unique interactions and systems, along with each member's individual strengths and limitations, are taken into account. Treatment is also goal-focused, providing accountability for practitioners. The therapist works with the family to determine specific behavioral goals such as following curfew, completing chores, and separating from antisocial peers. Multisystemic treatment is further considered time-limited and present-focused, targeting change that is possible to make within the family. Therapists seek to collaborate with the family rather than instruct or direct the family.

Empirical Evidence to Support Multisystemic Treatment

Multisystemic therapy has been extensively studied (*see* Table 7.3). Outcomes examined are relevant to those systems the treatment aims to impact, such as the individual, the parent dyad, the parent-child relationship, the child's relationships with peers, and the family's relationship with the school (Henggeler & Borduin, 1990). In the following section, interventions within each system will be provided, along with their outcomes.

The individual Individual functioning may include cognitions, behavior, social capabilities, and psychological adjustment. As stated earlier, antisocial youth tend to make more errors in their cognitive processing than their peers, which may contribute to aggressiveness (Dodge et al., 1990). Delinquent youth also display deficits in specific social skills (Bierman, Miller, & Stabb, 1987). Lower IQ further has been associated with delinquent behavior (Henggeler, 1991; Moffitt, 1993). Any of these areas may be targeted for intervention with the child and the parent (Henggeler & Borduin, 1990). Interventions for the child may include social skills training, problem-solving training, or even academic tutoring (Heneggeler & Borduin, 1990).

Effects on individual adjustment Reported behavior problems, as well as psychiatric symptomatology of both youth and parents, have been examined to determine the effectiveness of the intervention within the intrapersonal system. Families receiving multisystemic treatment have reported decreases in youth's behavior problems (Borduin et al., 1995; Henggeler et al., 1986; Henggeler, Melton, Brondino, Scherer, & Hanley, 1997; Scherer, Brondino, Henggeler, Melton, & Hanley, 1994). These findings are noteworthy because comparison groups have not fared as well in these areas.

Adolescents who received multisystemic therapy also showed a significant decrease in psychiatric symptomatology (such as withdrawal, anxiety, and aggression) from referral to termination (Borduin et al., 1995; Henggeler et al., 1986). Adolescents in comparison groups have either showed slight improvement (Scherer et al., 1994), no change (Henggeler et al., 1996), or reported increases in such problems (Borduin et al., 1995; Henggeler et al., 1997). Youth who received probation services actually reported an increase in

TABLE 7.3 Juvenile Offender Family Preservation and Multisystemic Studies

AUTHOR/MODEL	DESIGN/SAMPLE	MEASURES	RESULTS	LIMITATIONS
Borduin et al. (1995) Multisystemic therapy Mean hrs of treatment: 23.9 for multisystemic; 28.6 for individual therapy	Experimental, random-ization to treatment or comparison (individual therapy), pretest, posttest, follow-up (for criminal activity 3.95 yrs) N = 126 youth referred from juvenile justice system with at least 2 arrests Mean age = 14.8; 67.5% male; 70% White, 30% African American; 53.3% lived in 2-parent families	Adolescent: (Symptom Checklist 90; Revised); Revised Behavior; Missouri Peer Relations Inventory; criminal activity Problem Checklist) Family relations: (Family Adaptability and Cohesion Scales—II); observed family interactions (Unrevealed Differences Ques-tionnaire —Revised)	21.5% dropout rate *At posttest:* Multisystemic condition produced improvements over comparison group on:1) perceived family relations (increased cohesion and adaptabil-ity); 2) observed family interactions (increased supportiveness and decreased conflict-hos-tility across family dyads); 3) parent adjust-ment; 4) youth behav-iors (based on parental reports) *At 4-yr follow-up,* reduced rates of: 1) arrests; and 2) serious offenses	

Haapala & Kinney (1988) Family Preservation sites offered in 4 of most populous Washington counties	Posttest only (1yr) 678 status offenders referred to a family preservation service in Washington state. Description of subsample of 64 youths: 64% male; mean age = 13; 81% White, 6% African American, 5% Hispanic, 5% Other; 68% had never been in out-of-home placement; 36% from single female parent homes, 20% from intact families	Computer records of placement	12 mos after intake, 87% of youths had avoided removal from their homes; follow-up over 4 yrs maintained placement avoidance rates of 84.7% to 91%	No descriptive information is given of whole sample; unknown whether subsample is representative of population of families served; follow-up of 4 yrs only conducted on some cases that were seen at the beginning of service; no comparison/control group; no standardized measures; additional counseling services received after family preservation services may have confounded the effects

continued

TABLE 7.3 (continued)

AUTHOR/MODEL	DESIGN/SAMPLE	MEASURES	RESULTS	LIMITATIONS
Henggeler et al. (1997) Multisystemic Average length of treatment = 120 days	Quasi-experimental, randomization to multisystemic therapy and usual juvenile justice services, pretest, posttest, follow-up (1.7 yrs) N = 155 violent or chronic offenders and were at imminent risk of being placed outside of home because of criminal involvement (140 completed study); mean age = 15.22; 81.9% male; 80.6% African American; 19.4% White; caregivers 92.2% female; most mothers (55.6%) and many fathers (38.1%) had not completed high school; median family income between $5,000–$10,000	Global Severity Index of Brief Symptom Inventory; Revised Problem Behavior Checklist; Self-Report Delinquency Scale; arrest and incarceration histories; Family Adaptability and Cohesion Evaluation Scales; Monitoring Index; Missouri Peer Relations Inventory; MST Adherence Measure	Multisystemic therapy produced a 26% reduction in rearrest (not statistically significant), a 47% reduction in days incarcerated, and a significant improvement in adolescent psychiatric symptomatology; Therapist adherence to multisystemic treatment predicted low rates of rearrest, self-reported offenses, and incarceration	

Study	Design and Sample	Measures	Findings
Henggeler et al., (1992) Multisystemic therapy	Quasi-experimental, random assignment to treatment and comparison (services as usual), pretest, posttest, & 59 weeks post-referral follow-up $N = 84$ serious juvenile offenders (but only 77% of treatment condition and 56% of usual services completed pre- and posttest data); mean age of 15.2 yrs; 56% African American, 42% White, 2% Hispanic; 26% did not live with biological parent; semi-skilled social status	Criminal behavior and incarceration: Archival records; Self-Report Delinquency scale Family relations: Family Adaptability and Cohesion Evaluation Scales Peer relations: Missouri Peer Relations Inventory Symptomatology : Revised Behavior Problem Checklist (adolescent); Symptom Checklist-90-Revised (adult) Adolescent social competence: Social Competence scale of the Child Behavior Checklist	High attrition rates: 23% for Multisystemic & 44% for usual services; the multisystemic condition vs. comparison group resulted in: 1) fewer arrests; 2) self-reported offenses; 3) fewer weeks incarceration (average 10 weeks less); 4) decreased aggression with peers; and 5) for families, increased cohesion

continued

TABLE 7.3 *(continued)*

AUTHOR/MODEL	DESIGN/SAMPLE	MEASURES	RESULTS	LIMITATIONS
Henggeler et al., (1993) Multisystemic Therapy	Follow-up of Henggeler et al., (1992) average 2.4 yrs post-referral	Rearrest rates	Mean time for re-arrest in multisystemic condition was 56.2 weeks compared to 31.7 weeks for youths receiving traditional services; at 120 week follow-up, 39% of Multisystemic group had not been rearrested, as compared with 20% of group receiving usual services	
Henggeler et al., (1986) Multisystemic Family Therapy Mean hrs of treatment = 20	Quasi-experimental, assignment to multisystemic treatment, alternative treatment and normal control group, pretest, posttest *N* = 57 families of delinquent adolescents with complete pre- and posttest information	Individual measures: Behavior Problem Checklist; Eysenck Personality Inventory Self-reported family relations: Family Relationship Questionnaire	Adolescents who received multisystemic treatment evidenced significant decreases in conduct problems, anxious-withdrawn behaviors, immaturity, and association with delinquent peers. The mother-adolescent interaction and marital rela-	Lack of randomization; no follow-up; subjective criteria for termination: "Families were terminated from treatment when the identified problems were well-ameliorated or when further therapeutic change was unlikely" (p. 135)

	Sample	Measures	Results	Limitations
	Mean age = 14.8 yrs; 84% male; 65% African American; 75% lower-income; 62% father absent	Observational measures of family relations: Unrevealed Differences Questionnaire	tions in these families were significantly warmer, and the adolescent was significantly more involved in family interaction. The families who received the alternative treatment evidenced no positive change and showed deterioration in affective relations	
Nugent, Carpenter, & Parks (1993) Family Preservation	Archival data comparing families who were intact when entering services and those whose teens were not living at home N = 10,191 families of status offenders who had complete data information; Majority females; White; average age = 15 yrs	Placement	Predictors of out of home placement: *3 demographic variables:* for every year older, odds less likely that child stay in home; not attending school; abuse as presenting problem. *2 client history variables:* involvement with CPS or juvenile justice system. *3 service vari-*	No standardized measures; post-hoc; placement not defined clearly; only cases studied which had complete information (selection bias); a lot of variability in way therapy was conducted in 23 different agencies; atheoretical

continued

TABLE 7.3 *(continued)*

AUTHOR/MODEL	DESIGN/SAMPLE	MEASURES	RESULTS	LIMITATIONS
			ables: if residential care used at any time; if family therapy was not provided and if family had not completed all planned services:	
Rodenhiser et al. (1995) Family preservation (Homebuilders) 5 sites in North Dakota Length of services = appx. 1 mo	Pretest, posttest N = 87 families referred by court system and public social service agencies primarily for adolescent conflict and status offenses, representing 255 children seen as at "imminent risk" for placement; 78% White, 17% Native American; average educational level of parents = 12 yrs; 47% were married and 36% were	Placement data; Family Risk Scale; Child Well-Being Scale	At posttest, significant improvements for parents: mental health, knowledge of child care, motivation to solve problems, supervision of teenage children, constructive verbal discipline, affection; at posttest, significant improvements for children: mental health, school adjustment, and home-related behavior. The use of physical punishment, sexual abuse,	Children's gender not delineated; no comparison or control group; caseworker bias in reporting; don't know how placement was defined and if limited to worker knowledge rather than being supplemented by additional sources

	single-parent; Age: 0–6 (16.1%); 6–12 (40.4%); 13–19 (43.5%)		and delinquency signifi-cantly decreased. Families remained together 74% of time	No control group or ran-dom assignment. No dis-cussion of treatment effects; some measurs non-standardized
Watson, Henggeler, & Borduin (1985) Family-Ecological Systems Therapy	pretest, posttest $N = 52$ families Adolescents between 10–17 who had been arrested. 62% African American; 87% boys, 71% lower-class, 58% father-absent	Behavior Problem Checklist, Unrevealed Differences Questionnaire, thera-pist's assessment report, progress notes, & termi-nation summary, recidivism	Therapist reports of improved marital rela-tions were related to therapist reports of: (1) improved father-adoles-cent & mother-adoles-cent relations, (2) improved school perfor-mance. Therapist reports of improved mother-adolescent relations cor-related with therapist reports of: (1) improved father-adolescent rela-tions, (2) improved school performance, (3) improved adolescent-peer relations	

psychiatric symptomatology after treatment (Henggeler et al., 1997) or no change at all (Scherer et al., 1994).

Parents have reported decreased psychiatric symtomatology after multisystemic treatment as well (Borduin et al., 1995; Scherer et al., 1994), while parents in comparison groups have showed either an increase in psychiatric symptoms (Borduin et al., 1995) or no change at all (Scherer et al., 1994).

The family system   The parental dyad and the single-parent support system are also targets of intervention. Parental systems of antisocial youth are often characterized by high levels of marital conflict and low levels of acceptance and affection (Henggeler, 1989). Interventions may include marital therapy, building support networks for single parents, or even training in how to deal with stress or anger (Heneggeler et al., 1986, 1996; Scherer et al., 1994).

The parent-child relationship is often a focus of intervention, due to several factors empirically shown to characterize families of offenders. These factors include poor parental monitoring, inconsistent discipline, and a lack of clear rules in the household (Loeber & Stouthamer-Loeber, 1985; Patterson, 1986), along with impaired communication between parents and adolescents (Henggeler, 1989). Interventions in this system may include parent training, communication training, and/or behavioral contracting.

Effects on child-parent interactions and family functioning   Positive effects on family conflict and supportiveness have been associated with this treatment (Borduin et al., 1995; Henggeler et al., 1986). Mother-adolescent relations became more warm and affectionate, and fewer aggressive verbalizations were displayed following multisystemic treatment (Henggeler et al., 1986). Adolescent communication with fathers improved as well. Further, increased support, as well as decreased hostility and conflict, between family members was evident after multisystemic treatment, compared to the decline in relations that occurred in families whose adolescent received individual treatment (Borduin et al., 1995).

Two important dimensions of family functioning are cohesion and adaptability (Olsen, Sprenkle, & Russell, 1979). Cohesion involves the sense of closeness or distance (i.e., boundaries) between family members; adaptability involves the amount of flexibility a family employs in responding to change or new influences. Borduin et al. (1995) found increased cohesion and adaptability in families who received multisystemic treatment, compared to individual-treatment families, who reported decreased cohesion and adaptability. Similarly, a probation comparison group reported decreased cohesion, while multisystemic treatment families demonstrated improved cohesiveness (Henggeler, Melton, & Smith, 1992).

The family-school relationship Multisystemic treatment departs from more typical family interventions in that systems beyond the family are targeted. One major ecological system involves the school, as delinquency has been strongly associated with poor school performance as well as dropout (Loeber, 1990; Patterson et al., 1989). These factors will subsequently affect employment level and income status (Moffitt, 1993). Improving the adolescent's relationship with the school is therefore crucial. Again, since programs are individualized, practitioners may work with teachers in designing and implementing behavioral modification systems for the classroom, work with the school administration in readmitting students, or even involve youth in extracurricular activities (Henggeler et al., 1996). Despite the emphasis on interaction with the school, none of the studies on multisystemic treatment have specifically included outcomes in this area, such as teacher observations, grade reports, or attendance records.

The peer group Early peer rejection has been associated with the development of antisocial behavior (Bierman et al., 1987). It is postulated that once rejected by "normal" peers, deviant youth form their own peer group and serve to enhance each other's antisocial behavior (e.g., McMahon, 1994). Increasing an adolescent's ability to make and maintain positive peer relationships is, therefore, a concern. Social skills training may be offered so that the adolescent is taught to respond appropriately to internal and external cues in order to enhance the likelihood of gaining and maintaining positive peer relationships (Henggeler & Borduin, 1990).

Effects on peer relations Results have been inconsistent regarding the offending youth's relationship with peers. When emotional bonding, aggression, and maturity were examined, youth who received multisystemic treatment showed either no effects (Borduin et al., 1995), inconsistent effects (Henggeler et al., 1997), or decreased peer aggression (Henggeler et al., 1992). Decreased socialized aggression was observed by parents in some cases (Henggeler et al., 1986; Scherer et al., 1994).

The criminal justice system Criminal justice system involvement in terms of arrest and incarceration has been referred to as an "ultimate outcome" of the treatment (Borduin et al., 1995, p. 573). Number of arrests is an important outcome, since arrests and subsequent legal proceedings are costly to taxpayers. In addition, Gordon et al. (1995) cite evidence that the risk of chronicity of arrest is cumulative. That is, after a certain number of arrests (three), the probability of another arrest increases at about a 75% rate; hence, the importance of interventions that seek to maintain a low arrest rate.

Multisystemic programs have shown some impact in this area. Henggeler and colleagues found that a little over a year after referral, youths who received multisystemic treatment had not only fewer self-reported offenses but also fewer arrests (Henggeler et al., 1992, 1993). In 1993, Henggeler et al. examined survival rates and discovered that time of rearrest for serious offenders was quite significantly prolonged for youth who received multisystemic treatment. In fact, mean rearrest time for multisystemic treatment youths was 56.2 weeks in comparison to the probation group, which was 31.7 weeks. In addition, 120 weeks after referral, nearly 40% of the multisystemic treatment group had not been rearrested, whereas only 20% of the probation group had not been arrested.

At long-term follow-up (4 years), Borduin et al. (1995) found that youth who completed multisystemic treatment were significantly less likely than those who completed individual treatment to be rearrested. If rearrested, offenses were less likely to be of a serious nature. Only 26.1% of multisystemic youths had been arrested at follow-up, compared with 71.4% of youths receiving individual therapy. Even when previous arrests were controlled, type of treatment the youth received emerged as the more significant predictor of arrests for violent crimes.

Interestingly, when those who completed treatment were compared to dropouts and those who refused treatment altogether, multisystemic treatment dropouts were at significantly lower risk of arrest than those who dropped out of individual treatment or those who refused any treatment. To account for these findings, Borduin et al. (1995) have suggested that multisystemic treatment is concerned with empowering families and intervening quickly in systems relevant to the family.

One consistent and promising finding has involved the ability of multisystemic treatment to achieve results with diverse clients and those who have traditionally been more resistant to treatment. For example, Borduin et al. (1995) found that treatment efficacy was not affected by various demographic variables, such as gender, age, race, social class, or the number of pretreatment arrests. Henggeler et al. (1992) also found that multisystemic treatment was effective in reducing arrests and incarceration, regardless of the youth's gender or ethnic background or the family's level of cohesion.

Therapist's adherence to the treatment, however, has been related to effectiveness (Henggeler et al., 1997), with decreased levels of adherence to the model associated with lower levels of effectiveness. In 1997, Henggeler et al. again tested the model, with youths at risk of out-of-home placement, comparing multisystemic treatment to probation services. Treatment was administered by professionals in the community already working for the local department of juvenile justice, as opposed to the master's- or doctoral-level university students employed in previous studies. Although multisystemic treatment youths experienced a 26% reduction in rearrests after treatment, these results were nonsignificant when compared to the probation condition (Henggeler et al., 1997). Multisystemic treatment youths, however, did show significant differences in days incarcerated, with 47% fewer days than probationers.

Multisystemic treatment has helped to reduce time incarcerated for serious offenders (Henggeler et al., 1992, 1993). Recidivism rates for offending youth who received multisystemic treatment in a family preservation model compared to those who received probation were 42% and 62%, respectively, at 59 weeks after referral (Henggeler et al., 1992). Probation and multisystemic treatment youth differed significantly on number of days incarcerated as well, with multisystemic treatment youth incarcerated for an average of 73 fewer days than their probation counterparts. The total number of youth incarcerated after referral differed as well, with 68% of probationers being incarcerated compared to only 20% of multisystemic treatment youth.

These dramatic differences in time spent institutionalized translate into tangible cost savings for multisystemic treatment. For example, Henggeler et al. (1992) reported that the cost per client of multisystemic treatment was $2,800, as compared to the average cost of local institutional placement at $16,300. Henggeler et al. (1997) reported that the cost per client for multisystemic treatment was $4,000. This investment resulted in an estimated savings of $7,440 for each youth who received multisystemic treatment, based on a projected reduction of incarceration over a 2-year period.

Limitations of multisystemic treatment Overall, multsystemic treatment has strong empirical validation in impacting the intrapersonal system, the parental dyad, the parent-child relationship, and especially the adolescent's interactions with the criminal justice system. Additionally, the results have been backed by methodologically sound studies including comparison/control groups, standardized measures, long-term follow-up, and standardized pre- and post-treatment measures.

At the same time, some improvements can be made in how treatment is examined by researchers. Although multisystemic treatment is considered by its developers to be primarily family therapy, many other treatments are used as necessary to facilitate change in the clients' systems. The usefulness of combined treatments is logically apparent, given the resistant nature of antisocial behavior to treatment (e.g., Kazdin, 1997; Kazdin, Esveldt-Dawson, French, & Unis, 1987). In addition, the constituent elements of multisystemic treatment are those that have evidence on their behalf (e.g., problem-solving skills training, parent training), so that the combination of treatments is not haphazard (Kazdin, 1997). Practitioners should be cautioned, however, that it is not yet known if multisystemic treatment is more effective than any one of the interventions that comprises it (Kazdin, 1997), although one study comparing multisystemic therapy with parent training was conducted with parents at risk of physically abusing and neglecting their children (Brunk, Henggeler, & Whelan, 1987). Similar types of studies would be helpful in the area of juvenile offending, so that the component parts of multisystemic treatment could be more thoroughly examined within the context of the treatment itself.

In addition, future research needs to uncover the essential elements that contribute toward change for families with particular characteristics. Given that treatment is so highly individualized, comparing families who received a similar array of services is recommended, so that the possible effects of certain types of treatments or combinations can be ascertained. For example, it would be helpful to know within a treatment group which families received primarily systemic family therapy versus parent training, and the effect these differing interventions may have had on outcome.

The most glaring limitation of this treatment is that for many practitioners, the delivery of multisystemic treatment is, unfortunately, unfeasible. Without the sanction and support of the agency involved, the intense nature of this treatment cannot be provided, and without adherence to the treatment through adequate supervision, monitoring, and training, outcome is compromised. Multisystemic treatment is more than simply an eclectic approach in a family preservation model (Henggeler et al., 1993) and seems to require some level of skill and knowledge beyond that available in training sessions alone.

The results of Henggeler et al. (1997) as compared to previous studies point to the fact that treatments tend not to produce the same results in the field as they do in the university setting (Weisz, Weiss, & Donenberg, 1992). Research therapists usually are trained in specific techniques and are guided through manualized treatment and regular supervision. In contrast, therapists in clinical practice often do not undergo intensive training, nor do they have the kind of structure and supervision present in research models. Further, due to large multiproblem caseloads and paperwork requirements, therapists in clinical practice are not able to devote themselves to select techniques (Weisz et al., 1992).

CONCLUSION

The sophisticated development of multisystemic treatment has been a breakthrough for the treatment of offending, but simpler forms of treatment (such as parent training) have not been thoroughly examined and tested. While it is clear that family therapy in general has been effective with adolescent offenders (Chamberlain & Rosicky, 1995; Henggeler et al., 1993; Kazdin, 1997; Liddle, 1996; Tolan, Cromwell, & Brasswell, 1986) and certainly may be more beneficial than individual therapy alone (Kelley et al., 1989), it is understating the case to recommend that more investigation and knowledge-building needs to be done. The area deserves more attention, given the increased rates of juvenile offending over the past decade, and the commensurate costs that are incurred at the societal level in terms of property destruction, law enforcement, incarceration, remedial education, and mental health services (Kazdin, 1997; Prinz & Miller, 1991). In addition, there are the more personal costs involved with the emotional and physical harm to victims of antisocial behavior and the distress that juvenile-offending youth and their families experience (CPPRG, 1992; Kazdin, 1997; Prinz & Miller, 1991). Because of the potential for negative consequences, the need to understand and apply effective treatment for adolescent antisocial behavior is clearly warranted (Miller & Prinz, 1990).

REFERENCES

Alexander, J., & Parsons, B. V. (1982). *Functional family therapy*. Monterey, CA: Brooks/Cole.

Bank, L., Marlowe, J. H., Reid, J. B., Patterson, G. R., & Weinrott, M. R. (1991). A comparative evaluation of parent-training interventions for families of chronic delinquents. *Journal of Abnormal Child Psychology, 19*, 15–33.

Barton, C., Alexander, J. F., Waldron, H., Turner, C. W., & Warburton, J. (1985). Generalizing treatment effects of functional family therapy: Three replications. *American Journal of Family Therapy, 13*, 16–26.

Bienert, H., & Schneider, B. H. (1995). Deficit-specific social skills training with peer-nominated aggressive-disruptive and sensitive-isolated preadolescents. *Journal of Clinical Child Psychology, 24*, 287–299.

Bierman, K. L., Miller, C. L., & Stabb, S. D. (1987). Improving the social behavior and peer acceptance of rejected boys: Effects of social skill training with instructions and prohibitions. *Journal of Consulting and Clinical Psychology, 55*, 194–200.

Borduin, C. M., Mann, B. J., Cone, L. T., Henggeler, S. W., Fucci, B. R., Blaske, D. M., & Williams, R. A. (1995). Multisystemic treatment of serious juvenile offenders: Long-term prevention of criminality and violence. *Journal of Consulting and Clinical Psychology, 63*, 569–578.

Bronfenbrenner, U. (1979). *The ecology of human development: Experiments by nature and design*. Cambridge, MA: Harvard University Press.

Capaldi, D. M., & Patterson, G. R. (1994). Interrelated influences of contextual factors on antisocial behavior in childhood and adolescence for males. In D. C. Fowles, P. Sutker, & S. N. Goodman (Eds.), *Progress in experimental personality and psychopathology research* (pp. 165–198). New York: Springer Publishing.

Chamberlain, P., & Rosicky, J. G. (1995). The effectiveness of family therapy in the treatment of adolescents with conduct disorders and delinquency. *Journal of Marital and Family Therapy, 21*, 441–459.

Conduct Problems Prevention Research Group. (1992). A developmental and clinical model for the prevention of conduct disorders: The FAST track program. *Development and Psychopathology, 4*, 509–527.

Dadds, M. R., & McHugh, T. A. (1992). Social support and treatment outcome in behavioral family therapy for child conduct problems. *Journal of Consulting and Clinical Psychology, 60*, 252–259.

Dishion, T. J., Patterson, G. R., & Kavanagh, K. A. (1992). An experimental test of the coercion model: Linking theory, measurement, and intervention. In J. McCord & R. E. Tremblay (Eds.), *Preventing antisocial behavior* (pp. 253–282). New York: Guilford Press.

Dodge, K. A., Price, J. M., Bachorowski, J., & Newman, J. P. (1990). Hostile attributional biases in severely aggressive adolescents. *Journal of Abnormal Psychology, 99*, 385–392.

Dumas, J. E., & Wahler, R. G. (1983). Predictors of treatment outcome in parent: Mother insularity and socioeconomic disadvantage. *Behavioral Assessment, 5*, 301–313.

Durlak, J. A., Fuhrman, T., & Lampman, C. (1991). Effectiveness of cognitive-behavioral therapy for maladapting children: A meta-analysis. *Psychological Bulletin, 110*, 204–214.

Forehand, R., & Long, N. (1988). Outpatient treatment of the acting out child: Procedures, long-term follow-up data, and clinical problems. *Advances in Behaviour Research and Therapy, 10*, 129–177.

Fraser, M. W., Hawkins, J. D., & Howard, M. O. (1988). Parent training for delinquency prevention. *Child and Youth Services, 1*, 93–125.

Gordon, D. A., Arbuthnot, J., Gustafson, K. E., & McGreen, P. (1988). Home-based behavioral-systems family therapy with disadvantaged juvenile delinquents. *American Journal of Family Therapy, 16*, 243–255.

Gordon, D. A., Graves, K., & Arbuthnot, J. (1995). The effect of functional family therapy for delinquents on adult criminal behavior. *Criminal Justice and Behavior, 22*, 60–73.

Green, R., Vosler, N., & Bader, W. (1989). Reverberative change: Family therapy with adolescent probationers. *Family Therapy, 16*, 145–160.

Haapala, D. A., & Kinney, J. M. (1988). Avoiding out-of-home placement of high-risk status offenders through the use of intensive home-based family preservation services. *Criminal Justice and Behavior, 15*, 334–348.

Henggeler, S. W. (1989). *Delinquency in adolescence*. Newbury Park, CA: Sage.

Henggeler, S. W. (1991). Multidimensional causal models of delinquent behavior and their implications for treatment. In R. Cohen & A. W. Siegel (Eds.), *Context and development* (pp. 211–231). Hillside, NJ: Erlbaum.

Henggeler, S. W., & Borduin, C. M. (1990). *Family therapy and beyond: A multisystemic approach to treating the behavioral problems of children and adolescents.* Pacific Grove, CA: Brooks/Cole.

Henggeler, S. W., Borduin, C. M., & Mann, B. J. (1993). Advances in family therapy. *Advances in Clinical Child Psychology, 15*, 207–241.

Henggeler, S. W., Cunningham, P. B., Pickrel, S. G., Schoenwald, S. K., & Brondino, M. J. (1996). Multisystemic therapy: An effective violence prevention approach for serious juvenile offenders. *Journal of Adolescence, 19*, 47–61.

Henggeler, S. W., Melton, G. B., Brondino, M. J., Scherer, D. G., & Hanley, J. H. (1997). Multisystemic therapy with violent and chronic juvenile offenders and their families: The role of treatment fidelity in successful dissemination. *Journal of Consulting and Clinical Psychology, 65*, 821–833.

Henggeler, S. W., Melton, G. B., & Smith, L. A. (1992). Family preservation using multisystemic therapy: An effective alternative to incarcerating serious juvenile offenders. *Journal of Consulting and Clinical Psychology, 60*, 953–961.

Henggeler, S. W., Melton, G. B., Smith, L. A., Schoenwald, S. K., & Hanley, J. H. (1993). Family preservation using multisystemic treatment: Long term follow up to a clinical trial with serious juvenile offenders. *Journal of Child and Family Studies, 2*, 283–293.

Henggeler, S. W., Rodick, J. D., Borduin, C. M., Hanson, C. L., Watson, S. M., & Urey, J. R. (1986). Multisystemic treatment of juvenile offenders: Effects on adolescent behavior and family interaction. *Developmental Psychology, 22*, 132–141.

Horne, A. M., & Sayger, T. V. (1990). *Treating conduct and oppositional defiant disorders in children*. Elmsford, NY: Pergamon.

Kazdin, A. E. (1993). Treatment of conduct disorder: Progress and directions in psychotherapy research. *Development and Psychopathology, 5*, 277–310.

Kazdin, A. E. (1995). *Conduct disorders in childhood and adolescence* (2nd ed.). Thousand Oaks, CA: Sage.

Kazdin, A. E. (1997). Practitioner review: Psychosocial treatments for conduct disorder in children. *Journal of Child Psychology and Psychiatry, 38*, 161–178.

Kazdin, A. E., Esveldt-Dawson, K., French, N. H., & Unis, A. S. (1987). Effects of parent management training and problem-solving skills training combined in the treatment of antisocial child behavior. *Journal of the American Academy of Child and Adolescent Psychiatry, 26*, 416–424.

Kazdin, A. E., Siegel, T. C., & Bass, D. (1992). Cognitive problem-solving skills training and parent management training in the treatment of antisocial behavior in children. *Journal of Consulting and Clinical Psychology, 60*, 733–747.

Kelley, P., Kelley, V., & Williams, B. (1989). Treatment of adolescents: A comparison of individual and family therapy. *Social Casework: The Journal of Contemporary Social Work*, 461–468.

Larzelere, R. E., & Patterson, G. R. (1990). Parental management: Mediator of the effect of socioeconomic status on early delinquency. *Criminology, 28*, 301–324.

Laub, J. H., & Sampson, R. J. (1988). Unraveling families and delinquency: A reanalysis of Glueck's data. *Criminology, 26*, 355–379.

Liddle, H. A. (1996). Family-based treatment for adolescent problem behaviors: Overview of contemporary developments and introduction to the special section. *Journal of Family Psychology, 10*, 3–11.

Loeber, R. (1990). Development and risk factors of juvenile antisocial behavior and delinquency. *Clinical Psychology Review, 10*, 1–41.

Loeber, R., & Stouthamer-Loeber, M. (1986). Family correlates and predictors of juvenile conduct problems and delinquency. In M. Tonry & N. Morris (Eds.), *Crime and justice: An annual review of research* (Vol. 7). Chicago: University of Chicago Press.

McMahon, R. (1994). Diagnosis, assessment, and treatment of internalizing problems in children: The role of longitudinal data. *Journal of Consulting and Clinical Psychology, 62*, 901–917.

Miller, G. E., & Prinz, R. J. (1990). Enhancement of social learning family interventions for childhood conduct disorder. *Psychological Bulletin, 108*, 291–307.

Minor, K., & Elrod, P. (1994). The effects of a probation intervention on juvenile offenders' self-concepts, loci of control, and perceptions of juvenile justice. *Youth and Society, 25*, 490–511.

Moffitt, T. E. (1993). Adolescence-limited and life-course-persistent antisocial behavior: A developmental taxonomy. *Psychological Review, 100*, 674–701.

Nugent, W. R., Carpenter, D., & Parks, J. (1993). A statewide evaluation of family preservation and family reunification services. *Research on Social Work Practice, 3*, 40–65.

Offord, D. R., & Bennett, K. J. (1994). Conduct disorder: Long-term outcomes and intervention effectiveness. *Journal of the American Academy of Child and Adolescent Psychiatry, 33*, 1069–1078.

Olsen, D. H., Sprenkle, D. H., & Russell, C. S. (1979). Circumplex model of marital and family systems: I. Cohesion and adaptability dimensions, family types, and clinical applications. *Family Process, 18*, 3–28.

Patterson, G. R. (1982). *Coercive family process*. Eugene, OR: Castalia.

Patterson, G. R. (1986). Performance models for antisocial boys. *American Psychologist, 1*, 432–444.

Patterson, G. R., DeBaryshe, B. D., & Ramsey, E. (1989). A developmental perspective on antisocial behavior. *American Psychologist, 44*, 329–335.

Prinz, R. J., & Miller, G. E. (1991). Issues in understanding and treating childhood conduct problems in disadvantaged populations. *Journal of Clinical Child Psychology, 20*, 379–385.

Reid, J. B. (1993). Prevention of conduct disorder before and after school entry: Relating interventions to developmental findings. *Development and Psychopathology, 5*, 243–262.

Robins, L. N. (1991). Conduct disorder. *Journal of Child Psychology and Psychiatry, 37*, 193–212.

Rodenhiser, R. W., Chandy, J., & Ahmed, K. (1995). Intensive family preservation services: Do they have any impact on family functioning? *Family Preservation Journal*, 69–85.

Ruma, P. R., Burke, R. U., & Thompson, R. W. (1996). Group parent training: Is it effective for children of all ages? *Behavior Therapy, 27*, 159–169.

Scherer, D. G., Brondino, M. J., Henggeler, S. W., Melton, G. B., & Hanley, J. H. (1994). Multisystemic family preservation therapy: Preliminary findings from a study of rural and minority serious adolescent offenders. *Journal of Emotional and Behavioral Disorders, 2*, 198–206.

Tolan, P. H., Cromwell, R. E., & Brasswell, M. (1986). Family therapy with delinquents: A critical review of the literature. *Family Processes, 25*, 619–649.

Tremblay, R. E., Vitaro, F., Bertrand, L., LeBlanc, M., Beauchesne, H., Boileau, H., & David, L. (1992). Parent and child training to prevent early onset of delinquency: The Montreal longitudinal-experimental study. In J. McCord & R. E. Tremblay (Eds.), *Preventing antisocial behavior*. New York: Guilford Press.

U.S. Department of Justice. (1996a). *Bureau of Justice statistics sourcebook of criminal justice statistics, 1995*. Washington, DC: Author.

U.S. Department of Justice. (1996b). *Crime in the United States, 1995: Uniform crime reports*. Washington, DC: Author.

Watson, S., Henggeler, S., & Borduin, C. (1985). Interrelations among multidimensional family therapy outcome measures. *Family Therapy, 12*, 185–196.

Webster-Stratton, C. (1990). Long-term follow up of families with young conduct problem children: From preschool to grade school. *Journal of Clinical Child Psychology, 19*, 144–149.

Webster-Stratton, C. (1991). Annotation: Strategies for helping families with conduct disordered children. *Journal of Child Psychology and Psychiatry, 32*, 1047–1062.

Webster-Stratton, C., & Hammond, M. (1997). Treating children with early-onset conduct problems: A comparison of child and parent training interventions. *Journal of Consulting and Clinical Psychology, 65*, 93–109.

Weisz, J. R., Weiss, B., & Donenberg, G. R. (1992). The lab versus the clinic: Effects of child and adolescent psychotherapy. *American Psychologist, 47,* 1578–1585.

Wells, K., & Biegel, D. E. (1992). Intensive family preservation services research: Current status and future agenda. *Social Work Research and Abstracts, 28, 21–27.*

MEASUREMENT OF FAMILY TREATMENT WITH JUVENILE OFFENDING

Increasingly, practitioners are held accountable for the evaluation of their practice. To assist with evaluation, the reader is provided with self-report instruments for juvenile offenders and their family members. Scores from these measurement instruments can be used to guide assessment and clinical practice. For those interested in conducting research in this area, each of the instruments provided has established psychometric data to support its usage.

The following types of measures are presented: 1) adolescent behavior problems and adjustment according to both the child and the parent, 2) parent adjustment, 3) family functioning, and 4) client satisfaction with services.

Measures presented in this section involve the following criteria. First, instruments are self-report; that is, they are completed by family members themselves, rather than being interviewer-administered or observational measures. A second criterion for inclusion was that adequate reliability and validity information had to be available for each scale. Selected psychometric data were chosen to inform the reader of the properties of the instruments.

ADOLESCENT BEHAVIOR PROBLEMS AND ADJUSTMENT— ADOLESCENT REPORT

SELF-REPORT DELINQUENCY SCALE

Authors: Elliott, Huizinga, & Ageton (1985)

Description:

- 47-item version for 11- to 19-year-olds derived from offenses in Uniform Crime Reports
- Also assesses for substance use
- Report of frequency of each behavior in past year
- 40-item version used in National Youth Survey includes a General Delinquency scale giving a summary measure of criminal offenses and an Index Offense scale that includes only relatively serious offenses

Reliability:

- Test-retest reliabilities range from .80 to .99 (Elliott, Ageton, Huizinga, Knowles, & Canter, 1983)

Validity:

- Good discriminant and predictive validity with chronic (Dunford & Elliott, 1984) and serious offenders (Elliott et al., 1985)

YOUTH SELF-REPORT

(*See Chapter Six*, Family Treatment with Eating Disorders)

ADOLESCENT BEHAVIOR PROBLEMS AND ADJUSTMENT— PARENT REPORT

CHILD BEHAVIOR CHECKLIST

(*See Chapter One*, Family Treatment with Child Abuse and Neglect)

PARENT ADJUSTMENT

BECK DEPRESSION INVENTORY

(*See Chapter One*, Family Treatment with Child Abuse and Neglect)

SYMPTOM CHECKLIST 90—REVISED

(*See Chapter One*, Family Treatment with Child Abuse and Neglect)

BRIEF SYMPTOM INVENTORY

(*See Chapter One*, Family Treatment with Child Abuse and Neglect)

FAMILY FUNCTIONING

FAMILY ADAPTABILITY AND COHESION EVALUATION SCALES III

(*See Chapter One*, Family Treatment with Child Abuse and Neglect)

FAMILY ENVIRONMENT SCALE

(*See Chapter One*, Family Treatment with Child Abuse and Neglect)

MCMASTER FAMILY ASSESSMENT DEVICE

(*See Chapter One*, Family Treatment with Child Abuse and Neglect)

SATISFACTION WITH SERVICES

CLIENT SATISFACTION QUESTIONNAIRE

(*See Chapter One*, Family Treatment with Child Abuse and Neglect)

References for Measurement of Family Treatment
with Juvenile Offending

Dunford, F., & Elliott, D. (1984). Identifying career offenders using self-reported data. *Journal of Research in Crime and Delinquency, 21*, 57–86.

Elliott, D., Huizinga, D., & Ageton, S. (1985). *Explaining delinquency and drug use.* Beverly Hills, CA: Sage Publishing.

CHAPTER 8

Family Treatment with Adolescent Substance Abuse

with Stephanie Basham

Family Case:

Arturio Gomez (age 15) is on probation for possession of marijuana. He is brought to treatment by his parents, Hector and Felicia Gomez. Hector is originally from Mexico; Felicia is American-born, although her parents were from Mexico.

Mr. and Mrs. Gomez report that Arturio has been smoking marijuana for about the last 3 years. Hector Gomez scolds Arturio in the session, stating, "What do you want to do? End up like your brother, throwing your life away?" It turns out Arturio's older brother is in prison for dealing drugs. Arturio says he doesn't want to be like his parents either, working all the time (Hector works construction, Felicia cleans houses) with nothing to show for it. Hector gets mad at Arturio for being disrespectful. Felicia says that Arturio is really a good boy and helps her out in the house when he is there, but he is often with his friends "smoking weed," coming back with "his eyes all red." She said that she tells him the only way he's going to make it is to get his education, but he is behind a grade at school. Hector says that she is not strict enough with Arturio and what Arturio needs is to go to the construction site with his father every day so he will know how easy he has it.

According to the 1996 National Household Survey on Drug Abuse, the rate of marijuana use in the month prior to being surveyed has doubled since 1992 (from 3.4% to 7.1%) (Substance Abuse and Mental Health Services Administration, 1998). For high school students specifically, the use of marijuana in the last month was at a rate of 25.3% and for inhalants was 20.3% (Substance Abuse and Mental Health Services Administration, 1998).

Moreover, heavy episodic drinking in the past 30 days was reported by 32.6% of high schoolers surveyed. Given such high rates of alcohol and drug use, service providers working with adolescents need to familiarize themselves with the effective treatments available.

There are many different views on how substance abuse in adolescents develops and how it should be treated. Several of these frameworks discuss the necessity of family work. The rationale for including the family in treatment involves the fact that adolescents usually still live with their families and parents can, at least potentially, exert an enormous influence on the adolescent's behavior. Also, because parents are still involved in the care of their adolescents, they are responsible for ensuring that their children attend treatment. If parents are not involved in the treatment process, the adolescent's participation is often compromised (Joanning, Quinn, Thomas, & Mullen, 1992).

Beyond these fairly practical reasons for involving families, different theoretical perspectives pose certain rationale for the necessity of family work. This chapter will present only theoretical viewpoints that have been reflected in treatment outcome studies. For a more complete discussion of etiological theories on adolescent substance use, the interested reader is referred to a review in Petraitis, Flay, and Miller (1995).

Treatment outcome studies were included in this review only if they presented empirical data on the effects of programs treating alcohol- or drug-abusing adolescents and their families. A family component of the treatment also had to be delineated. Only studies published in academic referred journals were selected. In order to further ensure a certain standard of methodological rigor, single-subject designs and studies comprised of fewer than 10 subjects per treatment group (i.e., Bry & Krinsley, 1992) were excluded. This review focuses on research published since 1985 so that the more recent developments in the adolescent substance abuse treatment field are reflected.

Employing these criteria, only studies evaluating drug treatment were located; none involved alcohol. In addition, three main categories of outcome studies were located: behavioral family therapy, systemic family therapy, and multisystemic treatment. The following review will therefore be organized according to these theoretical perspectives. After discussion of findings in each of these areas, recommendations for service delivery and future research will be made.

BEHAVIORAL FAMILY THERAPY

The basic theoretical premise of behavior theory involves the importance of environmental contingencies for shaping behavior. For children, parents are the main environmental influence. Therefore, the context for understanding adolescent substance abuse involves the salience of parenting practices for the development of child deviant and antisocial behaviors of all kinds, including conduct problems, juvenile offending, and substance abuse (Dishion, Reid, & Patterson, 1988). As the predominant environmental influence, parents train their children in behavior that may be coercive as well as antisocial in nature (Loeber, 1990, 1991; Patterson, 1982; Patterson & Stouthamer-Loeber, 1984). Such parents reinforce deviant behavior through their attention to it, fail to reinforce prosocial behavior, and negatively reinforce child noncompliance by giving in to it. Further, they may model for their children interactions that are either coercive or antisocial (Patterson, 1986; Patterson, De Barshye, & Ramsey, 1989). Specifically, parents may have substance abuse problems themselves. According to the 1996 National Household Survey on Drug Abuse, approximately 3 million children resided with at least one parent who was drug-dependent; 6 million lived with an alcohol-dependent parent (Substance Abuse and Mental Health Office of Applied Studies, 1998).

Besides exhibiting an inability to apply effective discipline, such parents fail to appropriately monitor their children's activities, friends, and interests. Structural equations modeling has established the veracity of this model. Dishion et al. (1988) found that poor family management practices, including ineffective disciplining and modeling, were related to the increased likelihood of child drug use. In addition, the child's lack of appropriate social and problem-solving skills results in rejection by prosocial peers, causing the child at about the age of 10 or 11 to seek out other deviant peers (McMahon, 1994). Therefore, in this model, the peer's role in substance use is seen as secondary to the parent's poor family management skills. This model assumes that these parental deficits facilitate early association with deviant peers (Dishion et al., 1988). Indeed, other etiological models of adolescent substance abuse (e.g., Oetting & Beauvais, 1987) have posited that the role of peers involves selection rather than negative influence. In other words, teens choose friends who are like themselves in terms of willingness to experiment with and use substances.

While the role of family management factors in the development of substance use behavior has been established through empirical testing (Dishion et al., 1988), only one study has actually used behavior therapy with parents of adolescent drug users (Azrin, Donahue, Besalel, Kogan, & Acierno, 1994). (See Table 8.1.) Further, in this study, the parent component was only one aspect of treatment that mainly involved behavioral self-control and stimulus training with the adolescent. Behavioral interventions with the parents included contracting to supervise the child's therapeutic homework and providing rewards for child activities incompatible with drug use, including cooperation with monitoring. In this study, the behavioral condition was compared to an adolescent process group revolving around drug issues. Behavioral therapy was found to improve school and work attendance and family relationships, as well as reduce depression and use, over the alternative condition.

Future study in this area needs to address the necessary components of behavioral treatment for adolescents with subatance abuse problems. For example, adolescent behavior control and stimulus training could be compared against a condition involving this training and a family component to understand how parental involvement affects outcome.

Given that the role of parenting practices in adolescent substance abuse behavior has been established through empirical testing, more interventions designed to alter parenting practices are indicated. In addition, a body of knowledge has already developed on the treatment of child conduct problems through behavioral parent training. While behavioral family treatment of adolescent antisocial behavior has not been given much empirical attention, the approach with adolescent substance abuse shows promise.

FAMILY SYSTEMS THEORY

Family systems theory is another main approach in the treatment of adolescent substance abuse with models often combining approaches with a common systemic framework. For example, Szapocnik et al. (1988) employ a strategic-structural approach adapted from the work of Stanton, Todd, and associates (1982). Joanning, Quinn, Thomas, and Mullen (1992) used a combination of structural, strategic, and Milan systemic methods. Lewis, Piercy, Sprenkle, and Trepper (1990) employed a structural, strategic, behavioral, and functional approach, while Friedman, Tomko, and Utada (1991) used a functional approach. In turn, functional family therapy is viewed as a conglomeration of systems and cognitive and behavioral theories (Alexander & Parsons, 1982). Given that these approaches share some common family systems features, the central concepts from family systems therapy—circular causality, homeostasis, the functional nature of problems, and the importance of structure—will be presented and illustrated with examples from the treatment studies.

Circular Causality

Many models of psychopathology, such as the medical, psychodynamic, and behavior theory models, are linear in nature. That is, prior events are seen as the cause of a current problem, disorder, or conflict. In contrast, family systems theory espouses circular causality, which involves the nature of systems to be comprised of repeated patterns of interpersonal interactions (Weakland, Fisch, Watzlawick, & Bodin, 1974). Therefore, treatment focuses on the interaction between family members rather than on the individual characteristics of its members. Applying this concept to adolescent substance abuse, drug use behaviors, rather than being caused by individual characteristics (a genetic predisposition, personality problems), stem from the current interactions with other family members.

The concept of circular causality also means that change in one part of the system may produce changes in other parts of the system. Empirical support for this concept has been provided by a study involving one-person family therapy with drug-abusing Hispanic youth (Szcapocznik, Kurtines, Foote, Perez-Vidal, & Hervis, 1986). One-person family therapy not only produced comparable gains in terms of family functioning as the conjoint condition but also showed greater reductions in drug use. These findings suggest that change in one member's interaction creates change in the way symptom patterns manifest, as well as the way other family members relate.

Homeostasis

Another feature of systems is their tendency toward homeostasis, that is, the nature of systems to remain in a steady state or a status quo position (Jackson, 1965). Symptoms, such as drug abuse, and the family's resistance to change are viewed as mechanisms for self-regulation. To examine more closely how families organize themselves in circular interaction patterns around a problem, certain family therapy models, specifically Milan systemic therapy, emphasize the tracking of interaction sequences (Palazzoli-Selvini, Boscolo, Cecchin, & Prata, 1980). For instance, in the Lewis, Piercy, Sprenkle, and Trepper (1991) model, practitioners inquire about how family members react before, during, and after times that drug abuse has occurred to learn the predictable interaction patterns family members display.

In order to work with the natural family tendency of ambivalence toward change, strategic family therapy uses several interventions designed to side with family resistance (Haley, 1976; Watzlawick, Weakland, & Fisch, 1974). For instance, the family is urged to resist changing too quickly, as there is prob-

TABLE 8.1 Behavior Interventions

AUTHOR/MODEL	DESIGN/SAMPLE	MEASURES	RESULTS	LIMITATIONS
Azrin et al. (1994) Behavioral therapy sessions 6 mos, twice a week initially, then sessions diminished in intensity as progress was seen	Quasi-experimental, randomization to behavioral or supportive treatment $N = 26$ adolescents who had used a drug other than alcohol within last month Ages 13–18; 77% male, 22% female; 19% minority (either Hispanic or African American); 19% school dropouts	*Each session:* urinalysis; parent and child reports at each session on type and frequency of drug use, school attendance, employment, institutionalization, and arrests *Monthly:* Parent Satisfaction Scale; Youth Satisfation Scale; Beck Depression Inventory; Quay Problem Behavior Checklist	In behavioral condition, drug use had decreased from 73% at 1 mo to 26% by 6 mo and from 7 days/mo to 2 days/mo. In supportive condition, drug use increased from 7 to 9 days/mo; alcohol use decreased 50% in behavioral condition while increasing 50% in supportive condition; behavioral participants also showed significantly reduced depression, significantly increased attendance at school/work and improved family relationships when compared with the suppportive treatment condition	Average session attendance not provided; small sample; no follow-up; results were not always reported in terms of statistical significance

ably a functional reason for symptoms. Rather than focusing on the necessity for change, the family is asked to explore all the negative consequences that change would bring. Lewis et al. (1991) give some examples of negative consequences if an adolescent was no longer involved in drug behavior: There might be more conflict in the family if a child is not medicated; the family might have to deal with other issues members had been avoiding; parents may not spend as much time with their children. Relabeling or reframing is also used so that family members can see the positive intent behind negative behaviors. For instance, the adolescent is congratulated for sacrificing himself or herself through a drug problem in the service of getting parents to interact with each other again (Lewis et al., 1991). The shift in perception and meaning that presumably occurs with a reframe results in the possibility of a different response from family members.

FUNCTIONS OF SYMPTOMS

Another systemic concept involves the functions that symptoms serve for the system. One particular family therapy model has developed out of this concept: functional family therapy (Alexander & Parsons, 1982). The basic idea in this model is that substance abuse, as well as other clinical problems, serve a function for the family system, as well as for individual family members (Alexander & Parsons, 1982). Examples of the functions that adolescent substance abuse may serve for the system include either a distancing or an intimacy function. The abuse may serve a distancing functioning if disengagement from parents results, such as through long absences away from the home (Lewis et al., 1991). In contrast, an intimacy function might be involved in the substance abuse behavior if greater involvement with parents results (being grounded at home, visits to a therapist as a family). After the purpose of the symptom has been identified, the family practitioner helps the family find more acceptable ways to meet this same purpose. For example, if more closeness is desired, then the family can establish a contingency management program in the home. If, however, greater distance is needed, other ways of increasing adolescent independence are explored, such as allowing a later curfew, for example, once the adolescent establishes that he/she can be trusted with some basic rules (Lewis et al., 1991).

THE IMPORTANCE OF STRUCTURE

In addition to an emphasis on circular interaction patterns, certain family therapy models (structural, strategic) emphasize structure, the repetitive patterns of interactions by which families are organized. Optimally, families should be hierarchically organized, with parents exercising more power than children and with older children having more responsibilities and privileges than younger children (e.g., Minuchin, 1974). Subsystems are comprised of family members who join together to perform various functions. Boundaries, the invisible barriers surrounding individuals and subsystems, govern the amount of contact members have with each other and define both proximity and hierarchy. When boundaries are too open, relationships are enmeshed or fused; when boundaries are too closed, disengagement occurs (Minuchin, 1974).

In a review of family structural issues, Mackensen and Cottone (1992) found that families with chemical dependence often show signs of boundary disturbance, although one single pattern is not characteristic. Malkus (1994), for instance, reported lower levels of family cohesion and more rigidity among substance abuse families compared to "normal" families. However, Friedman, Utada, and Morrissey (1987) found that families with substance abuse problems were about equally characterized as either enmeshed or disengaged.

The important point is that normal families modify their structure to accommodate to changed circumstances; pathological families increase the rigidity of structures that are no longer functional. Changes in structure are required when the family or one of its members faces external stress and when transitional points of growth are reached. Structural and structurally informed strategic interventions particularly focus on the challenges associated with families experiencing developmental change. Substance abuse is associated with the developmental stage of adolescence and may involve struggles around allowing the adolescent to experience autonomy. In order for the family to accommodate to this stage, presumably the rules governing the system must change through restructuring the way the family is organized.

To reduce family resistance to change, the practitioner must first join the family so that members accept the therapist and will receive direction. Szapocznik et al. (1988) combine both joining and restructuring to increase engagement in treatment as dropout for treatment of substance abuse is high (Liddle & Dakof, 1995). Structural aspects preventing the family from coming into treatment, such as a disengaged father or an adolescent who has a lot of power in the family, are targeted. In this study, the structural intervention was compared to an "engagement-as-usual" condition in which the practitioner was empathic and supportive of the family member who called in for treatment. The structural engagement process proved very effective. For the engagement-as-usual condition, 58% of families did not end up coming to treatment, whereas only 7% of families in the structural intervention were lost.

A quarter of the engagement-as-usual cases were terminated successfully, while over three quarters were successfully terminated in the treatment condition (Szapocznik et al., 1988). Findings from this study suggest that a structured intervention to induce engagement into treatment is beneficial not only for getting families into treatment but also for successful completion of treatment. Additional findings from other family systems treatment outcome studies will be discussed below.

Findings

Overall, the family systems treatments were beneficial when compared to alternative treatment conditions (*see* Table 8.2). A couple of studies indicated that the family systems approach produced greater reductions in drug use over family drug education (Joanning et al., 1992; Lewis et al., 1990). These findings lend support to the family systems idea that change occurring at the level of information is merely first-order change. For change to occur at a meaningful level, however, it must be enacted at the level of second-order change. Second-order change involves an alteration of the rules governing system interactions (Watzlawick et al., 1974).

Given the improvements in drug abuse patterns with the family systems condition, it is surprising that such changes were not reflected in measures of family functioning. Indeed, Joanning et al. (1992) found that none of the three conditions (family systems, family drug education, and the adolescent group) improved appreciably on family functioning, other than adolescent's perception of the quality of communication with parents.

Friedman et al. (1991) was the only study to compare a family systems approach to another condition in which parents participated in therapy. In this case, the alternative condition consisted of a parent group (parent communication skills training). Both conditions showed reductions in adolescent drug use, improved psychological functioning, and gains in parent-adolescent communication according to maternal and paternal reports. It appears that more gains are made in treatment when parents are involved in some kind of therapeutic process besides education alone, although treatment does not necessarily have to consist of a conjoint approach. There are advantages and disadvantages offered by group treatment with parents. Groups, while more cost-effective, are more difficult to get started due to problems with recruitment. They are also marked by higher rates of dropout: The family therapy condition had a 93% attendance rate, while the parent group rate was 67%. Rates of high dropout were also noted in the group treatment condition with adolescents (Joanning et al., 1992).

TABLE 8.2 Family Systems

AUTHOR/MODEL	DESIGN/SAMPLE	MEASURES	RESULTS	LIMITATIONS
Friedman (1989) Friedman et al. (1991) Functional family therapy 24 weekly sessions	Quasi-experimental design, randomization to family therapy or parent group, 15-mo follow-up Majority White, male; mean age = 17.9; mean number of years of education = 9.3 yrs; mainly marijuana use	Adolescent: Parent-Adolescent Communication Form; Drug Severity Index; Brief Symptom Inventory; Rosenberg Self-Esteem Scale; Family Role Task Behavior Scale; Family Environment Scale Parents: Family Role Task Behavior Scale; Parent-Child Relationship Problems Scale; Emotional/Psychological Problems Inventory	93% of families engaged in treatment when assigned to family therapy compared to 67% in group conditions but no differences between groups on outcomes; improvement reported by both clients and their mothers at follow-up in terms of reduction in drug use and improvements in Parent-Adolescent Communication Inventory and Family Role Task Behavior Scale	In addition to family treatment, some adolescents also received individual or peer group counseling; no posttest; lack of no-treatment control; some measures lacked standardization; unknown gender composition of parents who attended treatment

Joanning et al. (1992) Family systems (combination of structural and strategic approaches informed by Stanton, Todd, & associates [1982])	Quasi-experimental, random assignment with replacement to family systems therapy (7–15 sessions), adolescent group therapy (weekly for 12 sessions), and family drug education, pretest (biweekly for 6 sessions), posttest, follow-up (6 mos) N = 82 families completed posttest out of 134 families of adolescents referred with drug abuse problems. Both parents tested 75% of time; 25% single-parent families; low-to-moderate income; high school education; maternal race: White 68%, Mexican-American 29%, African American	Dyadic Adjustment Scale; Parent-Adolescent Communication Questionnaire; Family Coping Strategies; Self-Report Family Inventory; drug use by urinalysis, drug involvement survey, videotaped family assessment interviews, therapist evaluations, school records, and legal involvement	High dropout especially in adolescent group therapy; family systems therapy had improved outcomes on drug use (rate of family therapy youth drug-free at posttest was 2 times greater than family drug education and 3 times greater than adolescent group therapy); no differences in changed family functioning for any condition, but all perceived improved communication	Amount of time spent in treatment was not equal for all groups; selection bias for follow-up: (only 41% out of those who completed posttest)

continued

TABLE 8.2 (*continued*)

AUTHOR/MODEL	DESIGN/SAMPLE	MEASURES	RESULTS	LIMITATIONS
	2%; paternal race: White 74%, Mexican-American 23%, African American 3%			
	Mean age of adolescent = 15.4 yrs;			
Lewis, Piercy, Sprenkle, & Trepper, (1990) Structural, strategic, behavioral, functional approach (12 sessions) vs. family-oriented drug education	Quasi-experimental, randomization to conditions, pretest, posttest $N = 84$ adolescents from 2-yr longitudinal study; referred from court, probation or police (51.2%), school and agency (33.8%); 19% females and 81% males; mean age = 16 yrs; 35.5% living with single parents	Family Adaptability and Cohesion Evaluation Scales; Parent-Adolescent Communication Inventory; Family Problem Assessment Scale; Family Sculpture Test; Dyadic Formation Inventory; Poly-drug Use History Questionnaire; Index of Drug Severity; random urinalysis tests	55% of family systems approach made clinically significant positive changes in drug use compared to 38% of drug education group	Results not reported in terms of statistical significance; no follow-up Non-standardized mea-

| Szapocznik et al. (1988)

Strategic-structural | Quasi-experimental, randomization to strategic-structural engagement and engagement-as-usual (the therapist empathizes with and is supportive of the caller but doesn't attempt to restructure family's resistance)

N = 108 families of adolescents who were suspected of or were observed partaking in drugs; range in age = 12–21 yrs; 77% males; All Hispanic; 82% Cuban origin; 60% families 2-parent; mean head-of-household catio$N$ = 10th grade | Self-report of drug use; Drug Abuse Syndrome List; rate of engagement and maintenance of therapy; symptom reduction of identified patient (Psychiatric Status Schedule, Client-Oriented Data Acquisition Process) | In 62% of cases, adolescent was unwilling to come to treatment; in 10% of cases, both adolescent and father resisted; in 6%, father resisted; fathers and adolescents combined accounted for resistance 78% of the time; experimental conditions resulted in much higher level of engagement (93% came for intake) than service-as-usual (42% came); successful termination: 77% for experimental condition and 25% for comparison group; from pretest to posttest, significant reduction in drug use | surements; no comparisons made between groups on drug use at posttest |

continued

TABLE 8.2 *(continued)*

AUTHOR/MODEL	DESIGN/SAMPLE	MEASURES	RESULTS	LIMITATIONS
Szapocznik et al. (1986) Compares conjoint family therapy and 1-person family therapy (both brief strategic) Maximum sessions allowed 12–15	Quasi-experimental, randomization to conditions, pretest, posttest, follow-up $N = 35$ Hispanic-American families of adolescents (mean age = 17); 77% Cuban-American; middle- to lower-class	Psychiatric Status Schedule; Behavior Problems Checklist, and Structural Family Task Ratings	One-person family therapy was as effective as conjoint family therapy for both individual and family functioning and more effective than conjoint at sustaining improved family functioning at follow-up	Unknown if generalizes to other Hispanic families; unclear reason as to how the subsample for this analysis was chosen; lack of specification as to when follow-up occurred; treatment duration not clear

MULTISYSTEMIC TREATMENT

THEORETICAL BASIS

Multisystemic therapy is a form of family therapy in that the family is viewed as a system and behavior as an interactional response within that system (Henggeler, Pickrel, Brondino, & Crouch, 1996). Therapy is highly individualized with the family and is based on structural and strategic family therapy, as well as social learning and behavior principles (Henggeler & Borduin, 1990; Henggeler et al., 1996). Maintaining youths in their natural environment and enhancing generalization are important goals of the therapy. As a result, treatment is often conducted in the home or a community setting (Henggeler, Melton, & Smith, 1992).

However, multisystemic therapy extends beyond family therapy in targeting not only the adolescent's family system but also the numerous systems in which he/she is embedded that serve to maintain and impact substance abuse behavior (Henggeler, 1989; Henggeler & Borduin, 1990; Henggeler, Borduin, & Mann, 1993). Multisystemic treatment takes into account the research on the multidimensional nature of adolescent substance abuse (*see* Henggeler et al., 1991, and Pickrel & Henggeler, 1996, for reviews). For example, given the role of social skills and other interpersonal skills in substance abuse, treatment may actually target the individual system for change (Henggeler et al., 1991). Since research has indicated involvement with deviant peers is strongly associated with substance use (e.g., Loeber & Schmaling, 1985; Simons & Robertson, 1989), decreasing the adolescent's association with negative peers may be a goal of treatment (Henggeler et al., 1991). Promoting school performance may also be a focus for intervention, since the developers of the model cite research linking poor school performance and substance use. Therefore, multisystemic therapy represents a combination of treatment modalities and venues of service provision (Henggeler & Borduin, 1990).

EFFECTIVENESS OF MULTISYSTEMIC TREATMENT

While less research on multisystemic treatment with substance-abusing adolescents has been conducted than on juvenile offending youth (*see* Chapter Seven), successful effects have been noted (*see* Table 8.3). Multisystemic treatment has shown effectiveness in reducing arrests and incarceration for juvenile offenses in general (Borduin et al. 1995; Henggeler, Melton, Brondino, Scherer, & Hanley, 1997; Henggeler et al., 1992; Henggeler, Melton, Smith, Schoenwald, & Hanley, 1993) and with reducing arrests for substance-related offenses (Borduin et al., 1995; Henggeler et al., 1991). Although the juvenile offenders in Henggeler et al. (1991) were not necessarily in multisystemic treatment for substance abuse, at 4-year follow-up, those who received even some dosage of multisystemic treatment had significantly lower substance-related arrest rates than those who had received individual therapy. Self-reported drug use was also found to be significantly lower for offenders who received multisystemic treatment than for those who received probation only (Henggeler et al., 1991, 1997).

One significant finding has involved the surprisingly low attrition rates for multisystemic treatment with substance abusers (Henggeler et al., 1996). This is particularly important given the difficulties of recruitment, engagement, and retention of families with adolescent substance abuse problems (Liddle & Dakof, 1995). Although costs for multisystemic treatment are initially high (e.g., staffing), one study showed that overall costs to the community are reduced, since cost-shifting is less likely with the intensive treatment (Schoenwald, Ward, Henggeler, Pickrel, & Patel, 1996). The researchers found that youth being treated for substance abuse using multisystemic treatment were less likely to utilize out-of-home placements, including incarceration, when compared to youth on probation.

LIMITATIONS

Although multisystemic therapy has been successful in reducing substance-related offenses, lack of arrests may not reflect the absence of substance use, but rather increased adeptness at hiding such use. In addition, limiting outcomes to arrests has not demonstrated how the various systems, such as the family, the individual, the peer system, and the school, are impacted by treatment. Measurement outcomes should reflect these other areas targeted for change. In addition, research on multisystemic treatment has been limited to youth who have been involved with the criminal justice system for juvenile offending. More studies need to be conducted with youth whose chief complaint is substance abuse, rather than substance-related offending behavior.

RECOMMENDATIONS

Although family interventions with adolescent substance abuse show considerable promise, the research in this area could be substantially strengthened. First, more treatment outcome data must be compiled to establish the efficacy of approaches. As a review by Liddle and Dakof (1995) noted, more studies have been published in recent years, but still most of the discussion revolves around theories and techniques.

Future study in this area should continue the tradition of quasi-experimental designs with randomization to groups, but other methodological features, a standard posttest for all subjects, follow-up, and the reporting of results in terms of statistical significance, should also be routinely implemented. In addition, samples of studies have tended to be limited to White, male subjects, with sample size inadequate to analyze separate effects for different gender and racial groups. Therefore, gender and culturally sensitive models of intervention have not yet been developed, with the notable exception of Szapocznik et al. (1988), who successfully applied a strategic structural approach to working with Cuban-American youth (Liddle & Dakof, 1995). More attention to effective family treatment with females, as well as males, and diverse ethnic groups is required.

Future outcome studies should also establish with greater specificity the essential components of treatment. Many treatment studies in this review tend to take a conglomeration of approaches. For example, models have often combined various schools of family therapy; multisystemic therapy involves interventions targeted at various systems impacting adolescent substance abuse; the behavioral intervention involves individual treatment for the child as well as a parental component. Although the multivariate nature of adolescent substance abuse has been recognized (e.g., Petraitis et al., 1995), it is important to establish the components of treatment contributing to positive outcome.

Appropriate substance abuse outcomes for adolescents is another area worthy of attention. Adolescent substance abuse may differ in significant ways from adult substance abuse. Unfortunately, there is no precise definition of abuse for adolescents; instead, definitions of adult substance abuse are just applied to adolescents without sufficient empirical exploration (Jenson, Howard, & Yaffe, 1995). Another controversial area involves the definition of success for adolescents who have substance abuse problems. The predominant philosophy of treatment in the substance abuse field is based on the Alcoholics Anonymous model. In this view, success is defined as total abstinence. However, some authors have questioned the expectation that adolescents refrain from the use of substances their whole lives, and have suggested that reduced and controlled use might represent a more realistic outcome (e.g., Selekman & Todd, 1991). Certainly, the issue of how adolescent and adult substance abuse differ and how success of treatment is defined should be addressed in future inquiry.

TABLE 8.3 Multisystemic

AUTHOR/MODEL	DESIGN/SAMPLE	MEASURES	RESULTS	LIMITATIONS
Henggeler & Pickrel (1996) Multisystemic 130 days	Quasi-experimental, randomization to multisystemic or usual community service (referred by probation officer to receive outpatient substance abuse services, which typically entailed weekly attendance at adolescent group meetings after completing a 12-step program), pretest, posttest, follow-up (6 mos and 1 yr) $N = 118$ substance abusing or dependent juvenile offenders and their families; average age = 15.7 yrs; 79% male; 50% African American, 47% White; median family income = $15,000–$20,000; 72% had comorbid disorder	Service utilization was documented by contact logs and montly telephone interview	98% of multisystemic families completed treatment compared to usual services youths and families, 78% of whom received neither substance abuse nor mental health services; 7% received mental health treatment only, 10% received substance abuse treatment only, 5% received both mental health and substance abuse services	Differences between groups not given in terms of statistical significance

Henggeler et al. (1991) I. Multisystemic (average 24 hrs) Individual counseling (average 28 hrs)	I. Quasi-experimental, randomization to multisystemic therapy or individual counseling, tracked for 4 yrs $N = 200$ referred by juvenile court after a recent arrest (12% of families refused treatment) mean age = 14.4 yrs; 67% male; 70% White; 30% African American; 88% lived with single-parent, 54% had 2 parent homes	I. Arrest for a substance-related offense	I. Only a small percentage of multisystemic youth had a substance-related arrest during 4-yr follow-up compared with comparison group. Even when dropouts were counted into both conditions, multisystemic (15 terminated prematurely) had significantly lower rates of substance-related arrests (3% vs. 15%) than did individual therapy subjects (21 terminated prematurely)	Underestimates of drug use given outcome measure

continued

TABLE 8.3 *(continued)*

AUTHOR/MODEL	DESIGN/SAMPLE	MEASURES	RESULTS	LIMITATIONS
II. Multisystemic (Average 36 hrs over 4 mos)	II. Quasi-experimental, randomization to multisystemic or usual services (provided by Department of Youth Services), pretest, posttest $N = 47$ at imminent risk of out-of-home placement for having recently commited a serious offense Mean age = 15.1 yrs; 72% male; 74% African American, 26% White; 80% lived with biological mother and 47% lived with biological father; low SES	II. Self-Report Delinquency scale (soft drug use and hard drug use subscales) in the National Youth Survey	II. Self-reported soft drug use was significantly lower at posttest for multisystemic youth than for usual services	89% of MST-referred families agreed to participate, but no such figures were given for usual services group; time of posttest not given; lack of follow-up

Schoenwald et al. (1996) Multisystemic Average of 130 days, including average of 40 direct service hrs	Quasi-experimental with random assignment to treatment or services as usual (probation and 12-step program), pretest, posttest, follow-up (6 mo) $N = 118$ offenders who met diagnostic criteria for substance abuse or dependence Mean age = 15.7 yrs 79% male; 50% African American, 47% Caucasian; average income = $15–20,000	Days of incarceration, days in other out-of-home placements, services utilized in the last month (by type), including frequency and duration Medicaid rates were used to examine costs	Total days incarcerated was significantly less for multisystemic condition Authors concluded that although multisystemic therapy was more costly to provide than usual services, this was offset by the reduction in days in out-of-home placement	No specific cost data

A further recommendation involves examining how family structure inter-acts with family functioning to affect treatment outcomes. For example, fam-ily variables such as single-parent status, larger family size, and younger birth order contribute to a higher risk of adolescent substance use (Malkus, 1994). Because such structural factors exert a considerable influence, the interactions of structure and functioning can be examined in future research to develop more specificity on the appropriate interventions to employ with certain subgroups.

Another area worthy of concern involves the screening, treating, and study-ing of disorders in adolescents that are co-morbid to substance abuse (Liddle & Dakof, 1995). Although it is recognized that adolescent substance abuse does not occur in isolation, and that it is usually associated with other prob-lems and deviant behaviors (e.g., Dishion et al., 1988; Jessor, Donovan, & Costa, 1991), the family treatment outcome studies in this area have not addressed other possible problems and disorders. However, high rates of depression and anxiety, as well as conduct disorder, have been found among adolescent substance abusers (e.g., Neighbors, Kempton, & Forehand, 1992). Clearly, other factors either contributing to, exacerbating, or stemming from the substance abuse need to be addressed so that teens and their families are free of distress and are functioning optimally.

REFERENCES

Alexander, J., & Parsons, B. V. (1982). *Functional family therapy*. Monterey, CA: Brooks/Cole.

Azrin, N. H., Donohue, B., Besalel, V. A., Kogan, E. S., & Acierno, R. (1994). Youth drug abuse treatment: A controlled outcome study. *Journal of Child and Adol-escent Substance Abuse, 3*, 1–16.

Borduin, C. M., Mann, B. J., Cone, L. T., Henggeler, S. W., Fucci, B. R., Blaske, D. M., & Williams, R. A. (1995). Multisystemic treatment of serious juvenile offenders: Long term prevention of criminality and violence. *Journal of Consulting and Clinical Psychology, 63*, 569–578.

Bry, B. H., & Krinsley, K. E. (1992). Booster sessions and long-term effects on behav-ioral family therapy on adolescent substance use and school performance. *Journal of Behavior Therapy and Experimental Psychiatry, 23*, 183–189.

Dishion, T. J., Reid, J. B., & Patterson, G. R. (1988). Empirical guidelines for a family intervention for adolescent drug use. In Coombs (Ed.), *The family context of ado-lescent drug use* (pp. 189–224). New York: Haworth.

Friedman, A., Tomko, L., & Utada, A. (1991). Client and family characteristics that predict better family therapy outcome for adolescent drug abuses. *Family Dynamics of Addiction Quarterlym, 1*, 77–93.

Friedman, A. S., Utada, A., & Morrissey, M. R. (1987). Families of adolescent drug abusers are "rigid": Are these families either "disengaged" or "enmeshed" or both? *Family Process, 26*, 131–148.

Haley, J. (1976). *Problem-solving therapy.* San Francisco: Jossey-Bass.

Henggeler, S. (1989). *Delinquency in adolescence.* Newbury Park, CA: Sage Press.

Henggeler, S. W., & Borduin, C. M. (1990). *Family therapy and beyond: A multisystemic approach to treating the behavioral problems of children and adolescents.* Pacific Grove, CA: Brooks/Cole.

Henggeler, S., Borduin, C., & Mann, B. (1993). Advances in family therapy: Empirical foundations. *Advances in Clinical Child Psychology, 15*, 207–241.

Henggeler, S. W., Borduin, C. M., Melton, G. B., Mann, B. J., Smith, L. A., Hall, J. A., Cone, L., & Fucci, B. R. (1991). Effects of multisystemic therapy on drug use and abuse in serious juvenile offenders: A progress report from two outcome studies. *Family Dynamics of Addiction Quarterly, 1*, 40–51.

Henggeler, S. W., Cunningham, P. B., Pickrel, S. G., Schoenwald, S. K., & Brondino, M. J. (1996). Multisystemic therapy: An effective violence prevention approach for serious juvenile offenders. *Journal of Adolescence, 19*, 47–61.

Henggeler, S. W., Melton, G. B., Brondino, M. J., Scherer, D. G., & Hanley, J. H. (1997). Multisystemic therapy with violent and chronic juvenile offenders and their families: The role of treatment fidelity in successful dissemination. *Journal of Consulting and Clinical Psychology, 65*, 821–833.

Henggeler, S. W., Melton, G. B., & Smith, L. A. (1992). Family preservation using multisystemic therapy: An effective alternative to incarcerating serious juvenile offenders. *Journal of Consulting and Clinical Psychology, 60*, 953–961.

Henggeler, S. W., Melton, G. B., Smith, L. A., Schoenwald, S. K., & Hanley, J. H. (1993). Family preservation using multisystemic treatment: Long-term follow-up to a clinical trial with serious juvenile offenders. *Journal of Child and Family Studies, 2*, 283–293.

Henggeler, S. W., Pickrel, S. G., Brondino, M. J., & Crouch, J. L. (1996). Eliminating (almost) treatment dropout of substance abusing and dependent delinquents through home-based multisystemic therapy. *American Journal of Psychiatry, 153*, 427–428.

Jackson, D. D. (1965). The study of the family. *Family Process, 4*, 1–20.

Jenson, J. M., Howard, M. O., & Yaffe, J. (1995). Treatment of adolescent substance abusers: Issues for practice and research. *Social Work in Health Care, 21*, 1–15.

Jessor, R., Donovan, J. E., & Costa, F. M. (1991). *Beyond adolescent: Problem behavior and young adult development.* Cambridge, England: Cambridge University Press.

Joanning, H., Quinn, W., Thomas, F., & Mullen, R. (1992). Treating adolescent drug abuse: A comparison of family systems therapy, group therapy, and family drug eduction. *Journal of Marital and Family Therapy, 18*, 345–356.

Lewis, R. A., Piercy, F. P., Sprenkle, D. H., & Trepper, T. S. (1990). Family-based interventions for helping drug-abusing adolescents. *Journal of Adolescent Research, 5*, 82–95.

Lewis, R. A., Piercy, F. P., Sprenkle, D. H., & Trepper, T. S. (1991). The Purdue brief family therapy model for adolescent substance abusers. In T. C. Todd & M. D. Selekman (Eds.), *Family therapy approaches with adolescent substance abusers* (pp. 29–48). Boston: Allyn and Bacon.

Liddle, H. A., & Dakof, G. A. (1995). Efficacy of family therapy for drug abuse: Promising, but not definitive. *Journal of Marital and Family Therapy, 21,* 511–543.

Loeber, R. (1990). Development and risk factors of juvenile antisocial behavior and delinquency. *Clinical Psychology Review, 10,* 1–41.

Loeber, R. (1991). Antisocial behavior: More enduring than changeable? *Journal of the American Academy of Child and Adolescent Psychiatry, 30,* 393–397.

Loeber, R., & Schmaling, K. B. (1985). Empirical evidence for overt and covert patterns of antisocial conduct problems: A meta-analysis. *Journal of Abnormal Child Psychology, 13,* 337–352.

Mackensen, G., & Cottone, R. R. (1992). Family structural issues and chemical dependency: A review of the literature from 1985 to 1991. *American Journal of Family Therapy, 20,* 227–241.

Malkus, B. M. (1994). Family dynamic and structural correlates of adolescent substance abuse: A comparison of families of non-substance abusers and substance abusers. *Journal of Child and Adolescent Substance Abuse, 3,* 39–52.

McMahon, R. (1994). Diagnosis, assessment, and treatment of externalizing problems in children: The role of longitudinal data. *Journal of Consulting and Clinical Psychology, 62,* 901–917.

Minuchin, S. (1974). *Families and family therapy.* Cambridge, MA: Harvard University Press.

Neighbors, B., Kempton, T., & Forehand, R. (1992). Co-occurrence of substance abuse with conduct, anxiety, and depression disorders in juvenile delinquents. *Addictive Behaviors, 17,* 379–386.

Oetting, E. R., & Beauvais, F. (1987). Peer cluster theory, socialization characteristics, and adolescent drug use: A path analysis. *Journal of Counseling Psychology, 34,* 205–213.

Palazzoli-Selvini, M., Boscolo, L., Cecchin, G., & Prata, G. (1980). Hypothesizing—circularity—neutrality: Three guidelines for the conductor of the session. *Family Process, 19,* 5–12.

Patterson, G. R. (1982). *Coercive family Process: A social learning approach* (3rd ed.). Eugene, OR: Castalia.

Patterson, G. R. (1986). Performance models for antisocial boys. *American Psychologist, 41,* 432–444.

Patterson, G., De Baryshe, B., & Ramsey, E. (1989). A developmental perspective on antisocial behavior. *American Psychologist, 44,* 329–335.

Pickrel, S. G., & Henggeler, S. W. (1996). Multisystemic treatment for adolescent substance abuse and dependence. *Child and Adolescent Psychiatric Clinics of North America, 4,* 201–211.

Schoenwald, S. K., Ward, D. M., Henggeler, S. W., Pickrel, S. G., & Patel, H. (1996). Multisystemic therapy treatment of substance abusing or dependent adolescent offenders: Costs of reducing incarceration, inpatient, and residential placement. *Journal of Child and Family Studies, 5*, 431–444.

Selekman, M. D., & Todd, T. C. (1991). Crucial issues in the treatment of adolescent substance abusers and their families. In T. C. Todd & M. D. Selekman (Eds.), *Family therapy approaches with adolescent substance abusers* (pp. 3–28). Boston: Allyn and Bacon.

Simons, R. L., & Robertson, J. F. (1989). The impact of parenting factors, deviant peers, and coping style upon adolescent drug use. *Family Relations, 38*, 273–281.

Stanton, M. D., Todd, T., & associates (1982). *The family therapy of drug abuse and addiction.* New York: Guilford Press.

Szapocznik, J., Kurtines, W. M., Foote, F., Perez-Vidal, A., & Hervis, O. (1986). Conjoint versus one-person family therapy: Further evidence for the effectiveness of conducting family therapy through one person with drug-abusing adolescents. *Journal of Consulting and Clinical Psychology, 54*, 395–397.

Szapocznik, J., Perez-Vidal, A., Brickman, A. L., Foote, F. H., Santisteban, D., & Hervis, O. (1988). Engaging adolescent drug abusers and their families in treatment: A strategic structural systems approach. *Journal of Consulting and Clinical Psychology, 56*, 552–557.

Watzlawick, P., Weakland, J., & Fisch, R. (1974). *Change: Principles of problem formation and problem resolution.* New York: Norton.

MEASUREMENT OF FAMILY TREATMENT WITH ADOLESCENT SUBSTANCE ABUSE

Increasingly, practitioners are held accountable for the evaluation of their practice. To assist with evaluation, the reader is provided with self-report instruments that family members can easily complete. Scores from these measurement instruments can be used to guide assessment and clinical practice when treating adolescents with substance abuse problems and their families. For those interested in conducting research in this area, each of the instruments provided has established psychometric data to support its usage.

The following types of measures are presented: 1) substance abuse screening instruments, 2) adolescent outcomes, 3) parent adjustment, 4) family functioning, and 5) client satisfaction with services.

Measures presented in this section involve the following criteria. First, instruments are self-report; that is, they are completed by family members themselves, rather than being interviewer-administered or observational measures. A second criterion for inclusion was that adequate reliability and validity information had to be available for each scale. Selected psychometric data were chosen to inform the reader of the properties of the instruments.

SUBSTANCE USE OUTCOMES

PERSONAL EXPERIENCE SCREENING QUESTIONNAIRE

Author: Winters (1992)

Description:

- 18-item self-report with 4-point response option (never/once or twice/sometimes/often)
- screens for adolescent alcohol and drug problems

Reliability:

- High internal consistency (.90–.91)

Validity:

- High correlations (.55–.94) with the Personal Experience Inventory Basic Problem Severity Scales
- Differentiates between drug clinic (highest scores), juvenile offender (next highest scores), and normal school groups
- A discriminant function analysis correctly classified 87% of the school clinic group

ADOLESCENT DRUG INVOLVEMENT SCALE

Authors: Moberg & Hahn (1991)

Description:

- Measures level of drug involvement (defined in terms of consequences, motivations, and sense of control) in adolescents (but has not been tested on minority or inner-city youth)

Reliability:

- Internal consistency is alpha coefficient of .85

Validity:

- High correlations with self-reported levels of drug use (.72), teens' perceptions of drug use severity (.79), and clinical assessments (.75)

ADOLESCENT OUTCOMES—ADOLESCENT REPORT

SELF-REPORT DELINQUENCY SCALE

(*See Chapter Seven*, Family Treatment with Juvenile Offending)

YOUTH SELF-REPORT

(*See Chapter Six*, Family Treatment with Eating Disorders)

BRIEF SYMPTOM INVENTORY

(*See Chapter Six*, Family Treatment with Eating Disorders)

ADOLESCENT OUTCOME—PARENT REPORT

CHILD BEHAVIOR CHECKLIST

(*See Chapter One*, Family Treatment with Child Abuse and Neglect)

PARENT ADJUSTMENT

BECK DEPRESSION INVENTORY

(*See Chapter One*, Family Treatment with Child Abuse and Neglect)

SYMPTOM CHECKLIST 90-REVISED

(*See Chapter One*, Family Treatment with Child Abuse and Neglect)

BRIEF SYMPTOM INVENTORY

(*See Chapter One*, Family Treatment with Child Abuse and Neglect)

FAMILY FUNCTIONING

FAMILY ADAPTABILITY AND COHESION EVALUATION SCALES III
(*See Chapter One*, Family Treatment with Child Abuse and Neglect)

FAMILY ENVIRONMENT SCALE
(*See Chapter One*, Family Treatment with Child Abuse and Neglect)

MCMASTER FAMILY ASSESSMENT DEVICE
(*See Chapter One*, Family Treatment with Child Abuse and Neglect)

SATISFACTION WITH SERVICES

CLIENT SATISFACTION QUESTIONNAIRE
(*See Chapter One*, Family Treatment with Child Abuse and Neglect)

REFERENCES FOR MEASUREMENT OF FAMILY TREATMENT WITH ADOLESCENT SUBSTANCE ABUSE

Moberg, D. P., & Hahn, L. (1991). The adolescent drug involvement scale. *Journal of Adolescent Chemical Dependency, 2*, 75–88.

Winters, K. C. (1992). Development of an adolescent alcohol and other drug abuse screening scale: Personal experience screening questionnaire. *Addictive Behaviors, 17*, 479–490.

Section III

Family Treatment with Adults

CHAPTER 9

Family Treatment with Adult Substance Abuse

with Cecilia Thomas

Family Case:

Myrna Stebbins, age 45, comes to treatment, upset over her 22-year marriage to her husband, Jack, age 49. She says that Jack has had a drinking problem ever since she met him, although she didn't realize it at first. She figured from her own family background that all men got drunk after they finished a day's work.

However, when children started coming along (they are now 13, 10, and 8 years of age, all boys), Jack's drinking began to concern Myrna more. Rather than spending time with his children, Jack would prefer to drink with his construction work cronies, often not coming home until 10 at night. She says he was never abusive like some men she knew who drank, but he would just turn on the TV and pass out, uninterested in anything to do with her and the kids. If Myrna ever tried to have a conversation with him about his drinking, he would say that he worked hard to provide for his family, and he deserved a little fun and relaxation after all that.

Myrna says that she went with a friend to an Al-Anon meeting and heard that the alcoholics have to hit bottom before getting help. Myrna says she thought Jack would never hit bottom since he had been going along like this for years. He didn't miss work, and his health didn't seem to be suffering, although he has also not gone for a check-up in years. He was charged, however, with a DWI 2 years ago, and she wonders if her sons' problems are due to their father's alcoholism. She says her 13-year-old son has been in trouble at school for smoking marijuana, and the youngest boy has been diagnosed with attention deficit/hyperactivity disorder. Myrna says that she has thought about leaving her husband, but she doesn't know how she would financially provide for her children since she hasn't worked since high school. Myrna says what she would like most of all is a way to get her husband to seek help.

Alcohol and drug abuse involve severe negative social consequences in terms of health and medical problems, accidents, and criminal behavior, with commensurate cost estimated at $276.3 billion in the United States (Substance Abuse and Mental Health Services Administration, 1998). The prevalence of substance abuse is indicated by the numbers of people seeking intervention and national expenditures for such treatment. When considering detoxication programs, inpatient hospitals, and outpatient settings, over 1.5 million individuals in this nation seek treatment, and costs for treatment have reached $12.6 billion (Substance Abuse and Mental Health Services Administration, 1998).

Considering the prevalence of the problem, the negative social impact of substance abuse includes its toll on family functioning in terms of family violence, financial distress, and divorce. A 1996 National Household Survey on Drug Abuse indicates that about 6 million children in this nation live with a parent who is dependent on alcohol, and 3 million are with a drug-dependent parent (Substance Abuse and Mental Health Services Administration, 1998). The debilitating effects for these children include increased risks for disturbed affect, low educational performance, conduct problems, juvenile offending, and substance abuse (Substance Abuse and Mental Health Services Administration, 1998).

In recognition of the negative impact on families, a traditional approach in the treatment field is to encourage family members to attend Al-Anon groups. A self-help approach, Al-Anon is an outgrowth of the Alcoholics Anonymous model. Many treatment models rely heavily on an Alcoholics Anonymous framework, with Al-Anon typically representing aftercare support (Edwards & Steinglass, 1995). The philosophy of Al-Anon centers on the necessity for family members to focus on improving their quality of life, independent of the addict's behavior. Al-Anon members are discouraged from attempts to change or control the addict; instead, the family member is given support for allowing the addict to suffer the consequences of his or her own actions. In so doing, an attitude of detachment for the partner of the alcoholic is created (Barber & Gilbertson, 1996).

Although the focus of Al-Anon is not necessarily to impact on the addict, accumulating empirical evidence indicates that family involvement and support can aid in the addict's recovery. In one study on predictors of relapse for alcoholics attending an inpatient program, qualities of the family, such as warmth, limited criticism, and overinvolvement, resulted in increased abstinence (Fichter, Glynn, Weyerer, Liberman, & Frick, 1997). Further, McKay et al. (1993) found that alcoholics exhibiting low autonomy responded positively to improved functioning of their families during treatment, resulting in reduced drinking at follow-up. Other studies have examined more directly the impact on recovery of treating family members. A review of this literature will explore specific models of family treatment interventions with chemically addicted individuals, followed by recommendations for future research and service delivery.

REVIEW OF FAMILY TREATMENT

The search for appropriate studies included various databases—*Psychinfo, Social Work Abstracts, Socioabs, Criminal Justice Abstracts, Nursing and Allied Health Database,* and *Medline*—reviews of applicable journals, and references cited from other sources. The following criteria were used to locate studies for this review:

- Treatment specified a family focus
- Treatment involved adult samples (for family treatment of adolescent substance, *see* Chapter Eight)
- Outcome data were specified
- Publication in peer-reviewed journal articles since 1985
- A minimum methodological standard (at least 10 subjects per treatment group, comparative treatment designs)

When employing these criteria, a pool of 11 studies, two of which involved meta-analysis, were located. The meta-analyses will be discussed first to provide an overall statistical summary of this literature.

The Edwards and Steinglass (1995) meta-analysis specifically focused on the family treatment of alcoholism. Their criterion for study inclusion was the use of either experimental or quasi-experimental designs, though it was not necessary for randomization to groups to have occurred. Further, some type of objective measure of alcohol use or drinking-related problems was required. Outcomes were organized along three phases of the treatment process: engagement in treatment, treatment/rehabilitation, and aftercare. Irregardless of the treatment phase, a higher rate of improvement was found when families or couples were involved compared to when they were not.

Stanton and Shadish (1997) concentrated on the treatment of drug abuse and included studies that randomized subjects to at least two comparison/control conditions. The 15 studies compiled, involving both adolescent and adult substance abusers, evidenced the effectiveness of family treatment. Family or couples interventions were superior to alternative conditions (individual treatment, treatment-as-usual, group treatment, or placebo control) in terms of longer length in treatment and reduced drug use. This positive effect might have been greater, but since family treatment approaches tend to have fewer dropouts, family approaches were penalized compared to other treatments in which dropouts were not included in the analysis (Stanton & Shadish, 1997).

Overall, the meta-analyses demonstrate the considerable benefits of involving the family members of substance abusers. A more detailed analysis of the recent, published literature indicates two broad approaches for family treatment: interventions involving only the family member/spouse of the addict (without the addict's presence) and therapy with the family and addict together. These two different approaches will be detailed below.

FAMILY MEMBER TREATED ALONE

Interventions that have focused on seeing the partner/family member alone, variously called unilateral therapy (Barber & Gilbertson, 1996; Thomas, Santa, Bronson, & Oyserman, 1987) or reinforcement training (Sisson & Azrin, 1986), have typically been used in the treatment of alcoholism (as opposed to drug treatment). The focus is to treat the family member to exert an influence on the addict, which eventually may motivate the addict to change.

While the unilateral approach has the more express goal of inducing the problem drinker to seek help (eventually the addict is directly requested to enter treatment), there are many similarities between reinforcement training and unilateral therapy. Both approaches emphasize that the family member is in no way responsible for the alcoholic's behavior; rather, the family member removes any conditions in the environment supportive of drinking, reinforces appropriate behavior of the addict (Sisson & Azrin, 1986; Thomas et al., 1987), gives feedback of any inappropriate behavior while drinking (Sisson & Azrin, 1986), and provides consequences if behavior exceeds agreed-upon limits (Barber & Gilbertson, 1996). Length of treatment ranges from brief models in which family members are seen for 5 (Barber & Gilbertson, 1996) to 7 weeks (Sisson & Azrin, 1986), or members may attend sessions for as long as 6 months (Thomas et al., 1987).

FAMILY/COUPLE TOGETHER

The other main approach to family treatment of chemical addiction involves approaches in which the addict and the family member are seen together. Since the work in this area predominantly focuses on couples therapy, this review will concentrate on this area (*see* Table 9.3 for other approaches).

The main objective of couples therapy is to alter interactional patterns that maintain chemical abuse and to instead build a relationship that more effectively supports sobriety (O'Farrell & Cutter, 1984). Cognitive-behavioral in nature, treatment entails communication skill-building, planning family activities, initiating caring behaviors, and expressing feelings (O'Farrell, 1993). Techniques to learn these skills include homework, role-playing, and covert rehearsal. Treatment is generally brief, consisting of 10 (e.g., O'Farrell, Choquette, Cutter, Brown, & McCourt, 1993), 12 (Fals-Stewart, Birchler, & O'Farrell, 1996), or 15 weekly sessions (e.g., McCrady et al., 1986). Treatment is delivered in the context of either individual (e.g., McCrady et al., 1986) or group couples sessions (e.g., O'Farrell et al., 1993).

The work in this area, represented by two main streams of research, McCrady and colleagues (McCrady et al., 1986; McCrady, Stout, Noel, Abrams, & Nelson, 1991) and O'Farrell and colleagues (Fals-Stewart et al., 1996; O'Farrell et al., 1993, 1996; O'Farrell, Cutter, Choquette, Floyd, & Bayog, 1992; O'Farrell, Cutter, & Floyd, 1985), tend to be methodologically strong, involving randomization to at least three different treatment conditions, some of which also include other types of family interventions. These varying comparative treatment conditions are summarized and displayed in Table 9.1.

OUTCOMES

Studies on both the family member alone (*see* Table 9.2) and when the family member is seen in the context of couples therapy (*see* Table 9.3) involve some common outcome measures. These include engagement in treatment, substance use behavior, marital adjustment, and, less frequently, the personal adjustment of the family member, and these will be discussed in the sections below.

ENGAGEMENT IN TREATMENT

A critical consideration in the substance abuse treatment field is the high rate of dropout. At its converse, the length of time spent in treatment correlates with

TABLE 9.1 Comparative Treatment Conditions for Marital Behavior Therapy Studies

TREATMENT CONDITION	DESCRIPTION
McCrady et al., 1986; 1991 *Minimum spouse involvement treatment*	Directed toward the alcoholic in presence of spouse, emphasis on coping skills training and behavioral self-control methods
McCrady et al., 1986; 1991 *Alcohol-focused spouse involvement treatment.*	Includes skills from the minimum spouse involvement approach, as well as training spouses in abstinence support and coping skills
McCrady et al., 1986; 1991 *Alcohol behavioral marital therapy*	Consists of the skills mentioned for the above two conditions, as well as a combination of strategies for couples in treatment including instruction on reinforcing abstinence, expressing feeling, using relaxation skills, and problem-solving
O'Farrell et al., 1985; 1992 *Interactional couples group therapy*	Designed to promote the ventilation and sharing of feelings to assist couples in gaining verbal insight into their relationships
O'Farrell et al., 1993 *Relapse Prevention*	An additional 15 sessions to help the couples identify high-risk situations and early warnings for possible relapse, and to effectively cope with any drinking behaviors. Unresolved marital issues are addressed, and couples practice the skills previously learned
Fals-Stewart et al., 1996 *Individually based treatment*	Comprised of twice-weekly individual therapy sessions and one group session per week. Influenced by cognitive-behavioral coping skills training and may include cognitive-behavioral restructuring, relaxation training, and anger management

better outcomes for the substance abuser (Stark, 1992). A treatment program's mandate for family involvement may succeed in increasing treatment participation for addicts (Sorensen, Gibson, Bernal & Deitch, 1985), but even when the family member is seen without the addict, approaches have been successful in this regard (Barber & Gilbertson, 1996; Sisson & Azrin, 1986; Thomas et al., 1987). For example, two studies compared unilateral or reinforcement training to an Al-Anon condition (Barber & Gilbertson, 1996; Sisson & Azrin, 1986). Al-Anon has a similar focus in espousing that addicts should experience the consequences of their behavior; however, the Al-Anon philosophy is that partners should remain detached from the behaviors of the addict without trying to control or change them. The belief is that if the addict is allowed to suffer the consequences of his or her own behavior, he or she might eventually "hit bottom" and be motivated to seek help. Given this philosophy, it is not surprising that in the Al-Anon conditions, no addicts entered treatment (Barber & Gilbertson, 1996; Sisson & Azrin, 1986).

Apart from the underlying philosophical differences between treatment approaches, it could also be that the effectiveness of reinforcement training may be due to its greater treatment length. Subjects in this condition averaged seven sessions, whereas those in the alternative treatment condition averaged only 3.5 sessions of Al-Anon and weekly supportive counseling and education meetings (Sisson & Azrin, 1986).

One of the expressed goals, when treating family members without the addict present, is to induce them to get their relatives into treatment. Given this goal, treatment engagement has been a common outcome measure. In comparison, few studies involving conjoint treatment approaches examine treatment engagement. Nonetheless, the results are similar to those found for the unilateral interventions: Reduced rates of dropout are associated with conditions involving a marital component (McCrady et al., 1986).

SUBSTANCE USE

Drinking outcomes are typically the defining measure of treatment effectiveness and have been assessed in various ways:

1. number of days drinking
2. number of days intoxicated
3. use of Antabuse
4. amount of ethanol consumed
5. reductions in drinking

TABLE 9.2 Non-Addict Treatment Only

AUTHOR/MODEL	DESIGN/SAMPLE	MEASURES	RESULTS	LIMITATIONS
Barber & Gilbertson (1996) 5 weeks	Quasi-experimental, randomization to: individual unilateral intervention; unilateral group intervention; waiting list control; referral to Al-Anon $N = 48$ partners of alcohol abusers resistant to change; higher than threshold score for dependence on Short Michigan Alcoholism Screening Test; recruited from newspaper (Australia) 94% females, 6% males	Partner competed: Life Satisfaction Scale; Marital Consensus Scale; checklist on problems experienced because of abuser's drinking (nonstandardized) Criteria for change in alcohol abusers: 1) seek treatment; 2) cease drinking for at least 2 weeks; 3) reduce consumption to a level acceptable for partners (partner kept drinking diary of alcohol abuser's behavior to measure)	Both unilateral treatments produced change in problem drinker over comparison conditions; individual unilateral and Al-Anon conditions improved nondrinking spouses' adjustment; only individual unilateral condition showed gains on marital adjustment	6–12 weeks elapsed after pretest but before intervention; small sample size; lack of follow-up; lack of information on SES, race

Study	Design/Sample	Measures	Results	Limitations
Sisson & Azrin (1986) Behavioral Treatment Reinforcement Training = 7.2 Sessions Traditional program = 3.5 Sessions	Quasi-experimental, random assignment to reinforcement (7.2 sessions) or traditional program (3.5 sessions), tracked for 5 mos $N = 12$ adult women who had contacted a community alcoholism treatment program due to a male relative (primarily husband) having a drinking problem	Attendance in counseling; number of days drinking and sobriety; frequency of Antabuse administration	Reinforcement training for relative reduced drinking 50% before alcoholic client entered treatment; alcoholic client entered treatment in almost all cases, whereas none of traditional group did	Tiny sample size
Thomas et al. (1987) Unilateral approach (6 mos) Atheoretical	Experimental, randomization to unilateral family therapy and delayed treatment control, pretest, posttest $N = 25$ spouses recruited from newspaper ad; 85% had some college; majority White; majority female; median household income = $25,000–$29,0000	20 assessment instruments included: spouse coping (Life Distress Scale), family functioning (Dyadic Adjustment Scale), and abuser drinking behavior (Quantity-Frequency Schedule)	53% reduction in drinking when spouses underwent treatment, while drinking increased slightly for the problem drinkers of spouses who did not have treatment	Instruments were not all listed; in addition, the small sample size preclude statistical analysis for this number of measurements

TABLE 9.3 Addict and Family in Treatment Together

AUTHOR/MODEL	DESIGN/SAMPLE	MEASURES	RESULTS	LIMITATIONS
Boylin, Doucette, & Jean (1997) Total program: psychoeducational (Alcoholics Anonymous); multifamily therapy Weekly Average length of stay = 65 days	Post-hoc comparison between groups that only received standard rehabilitation based on psychoeducation model (AA) and those that received standard rehab + multifamily therapy $N = 219$ inpatients in substance abuse treatment 50% sent by legal system; 30% dual diagnosis; majority sample male (77% male, 23% female)	Length of stay in treatment	While males had a significantly longer stay in treatment in general, women who attended multifamily therapy had a longer stay in treatment than women who did not attend	Although total program described as psychoeducational in nature (AA), family treatment component not described as particular theory other than "multifamily"; lack of assignment to groups; possible selection bias, with those attending family therapy also having more family and other resources; lack of information on type of substance abuse problem, SES, race, age; unclear the other interventions clients received during treatment; no follow-up

Study/Treatment	Design/Sample	Measures	Results	Limitations
Fals-Stewart et al., (1996) Behavioral couples therapy once weekly for 12 weeks	Quasi-experimental, randomization to behavioral couples therapy or individually based treatment, pretest, posttest and follow-up (3, 6, 9, 12 mos) $N = 80$ husbands and their partners seeking treatment for non-alcohol substance abuse problems at community-based outpatient clinics; majority referred by criminal justice system	Random urine and blood alcohol breath samples (weekly); Marital Happiness Scale (weekly); Locke-Wallace Marital Adjustment Test; Areas of Change Questionnaire; Responses to Conflict Questionnaire; Addiction severity Index; time-line follow-back procedure; Client Satisfaction Questionnaire	Behavioral marital therapy resulted in significant improvement in marital adjustment, area of change, conflict, and days separated compared to individually based treatment in which there were no improvements	Lack of demographic information on sample. Possible confounds: 1) higher educated clinicians administered behavioral marital therapy 2) some subjects received antidepressant medication
McCrady et al. (1986) Behavioral 15 sessions	Quasi-experimental design, randomization to minimal spouse involvement; alcohol-focused spouse involvement; alcohol behavioral marital therapy, pretest, posttest, follow-up (82% at 6 mos)	Timeline follow-back interviewing procedure; Marital Adjustment Test; coded videotaped interaction; PFI	High dropout: 30 subjects either did not begin treatment or dropped out before 5th session; all 3 groups improved, with less drinking, increased life satisfaction, marital satisfaction, sexual activity, and job stability. Compared	Small sample size

continued

TABLE 9.3 *(continued)*

AUTHOR/MODEL	DESIGN/SAMPLE	MEASURES	RESULTS	LIMITATIONS
	$N = 45$ married couples with a spouse abusing alcohol; had to have completed at least 5 sessions; recruited through community agencies, advertising, and admissions office and inpatient units of psychiatric hospital; 73% male abusers; 51% had high school education or less		to alcohol-focused treatment, behavioral marital condition had more rapid reductions in drinking, more maintenance of gains, more stable and higher marital satisfaction	
McCrady et al. (1991)	Quasi-experimental, randomization to minimal spouse involvement, alcohol-focused spouse involvement; and alcohol behavioral marital therapy, pretest, posttest, follow-up (6, 12, and 18 mos) $N = 45$ addicts with problems at least 2 yrs and their spouses	Locke-Wallace Marital Adjustment Test; Areas of Change Questionnaire; Psychosocial Functioning Inventory; Occupational Functioning	All groups exhibited improvement; behavioral marital therapy produced greatest benefits with gradual improvements over follow-up	Demographic information not reported; small sample size

O'Farrell et al. (1985) Behavioral marital therapy Couples group 10 weekly sessions	Quasi-experimental design, randomization to behavioral marital treatment control group; interactional couples group; or no-marital treatment control group, pretest, posttest $N = 34$ couples recruited from VA sample who had completed inpatient treatment, or who had presented for outpatient treatment; high school educated	Locke-Wallace Marital Adjustment Test; Areas of Change Questionnaire; Marital Status Inventory; Marital Interaction Coding System; Drinking adjustment (Timeline Drinking Behavior Interview)	All 3 groups improved in short-term drinking; behavioral marital therapy and interactional therapy improved on marital stability and observational measures of communication	Small sample size; results might not be generalizable to other than VA population; lack of information on race
O'Farrell et al. (1992)	Two-yr follow-up of O'Farrell et al. (1985)		At 2 yrs, behavioral marital therapy and individual counseling showed improved marital adjustment for wives only who had higher scores on Marital Adjustment compared to no-marital counseling condition; initial gains of behavioral marital therapy diminished by 2-yr follow-up	

continued

TABLE 9.3 (continued)

AUTHOR/MODEL	DESIGN/SAMPLE	MEASURES	RESULTS	LIMITATIONS
O'Farrell et al. (1993) Behavioral marital therapy Over 4-to-5 mo period, including 6–8 weekly sessions and 10 weekly behavioral couples group sessions	Quasi-experimental, randomization to behavioral marital therapy or behavioral marital therapy plus relapse prevention, pretest, posttest, follow-up (3, 6, and 12 mo) $N = 59$ couples from VA sample; completed inpatient treatment, presented for outpatient treatment or in response to media announcements; male alcoholics Criteria for alcohol abuse or dependence; in past 6 mos no other psychoactive substance use disorder, schizophrenia, delusional disorder, bipolar disorder, or other psychotic disorders average of almost 6 prior hospitalizations for treatment	Drinking outcome measure (Timeline Drinking Behavior Interview) with spouse corroboration Marital outcome measure (Marital Adjustment Test) Treatment targeted behavior: Couples Behaviors Questionnaire Measures predictive of outcome: Michigan Alcoholism Screening Test; Alcohol Dependence Scale Marital Adjustment Test; Marital Status Inventory; Conflict Tactics Scale	Significant improvements through 12-mo follow-up in drinking and marital adjustment regardless of extent of aftercare. Relapse prevention group improved even more in terms of days abstinent and targeted drinking behaviors. To a lesser extent, marital adjustment also showed more improvements with addition of relapse prevention	Small sample size; results might not be generalizable to other than a VA population; lack of information on SES and race

6. consumption of alcohol
7. percent of days not alcohol-involved
8. urges to drink
9. alcohol-related consequences
10. alcohol physical and psychological dependence
11. days abstinent
12. abstinence

All of the studies for treatment of family members by themselves demonstrated decreased drinking for the alcoholic (Barber & Gilbertson, 1996; Sisson & Azrin, 1986; Thomas et al., 1987), at a rate of about a 50% reduction (Sisson & Azrin, 1986; Thomas et al., 1987). In comparison, a slight increase in alcohol consumption occurred for alcoholics in the delayed treatment condition (Thomas et al., 1987), and drinking patterns were not significantly changed for addicts whose families participated in Al-Anon (Barber & Gilbertson, 1996; Sisson & Azrin, 1986). As discussed, this latter finding may not be surprising, given the orientation of Al-Anon.

In the conjoint family treatment studies, decreased substance use was noted for all types of treatment conditions, whether marital or individual, behavioral or non-behavioral marital (*see* Table 9.3). This reduction was evident for up to 2 years after treatment had ended, although drinking tended to increase as time elapsed. When the relapse prevention component was added to behavioral marital treatment and compared against behavioral marital only, changes were even more marked: increased days of abstinence and fewer days drinking at both 6- and 12-month follow-up (O'Farrell et al., 1993). A cost-benefit and cost-effectiveness analysis was later conducted to determine the differential effects of these two types of treatments (O'Farrell et al., 1996). Although both conditions reduced health care and legal system expenses, the lower cost of the basic behavioral marital therapy package produced a more optimal benefit-to-cost ratio. It was also more cost-effective for this reason.

Only one of the conjoint studies concentrated on drug rather than alcohol abuse treatment, and indicated that while drug use decreased, alcohol use had not (Fals-Stewart et al., 1996). This finding highlights the controversy involving controlled substance use versus abstinence as an outcome. Controlled drinking remains controversial and contrary to the philosophy of Alcoholics Anonymous models (Edwards & Steinglass, 1995; Holder, Longabaugh, Miller, & Rubonis, 1991). Edwards and Steinglass (1995) recognized abstinence as the preferred treatment goal and therefore adapted it for the evaluation of studies in their meta-analysis. However, some investigators suggest the potential usefulness of controlled drinking as a process (Edwards & Steinglass,

1995) or outcome goal (Barber & Gilbertson, 1996; Thomas et al., 1987) at levels comfortable to the partner and if the drinker is not adversely affected (Barber & Gilbertson, 1996).

MARITAL ADJUSTMENT

Perhaps due to the emphasis on impacting the addict's behavior and improving the coping of the family member, it is not unexpected that when the relative of an addict is seen alone, marital outcomes are not consistently impacted. It appears that only when spouses of alcoholics were seen in an individual modality (Thomas et al., 1987) versus group (Barber & Gilbertson, 1996) were positive changes found in affectional expression, sexual satisfaction (Thomas et al., 1987), and marital adjustment (Barber & Gilbertson, 1996). Although more study needs to be conducted, suggestive is that improved outcomes with individual treatment may allow for a more personal focus on specific relationship issues.

When examining the research on conjoint therapy, couples therapy had a significant positive impact on marital functioning, no matter how it was defined (marital satisfaction, marital stability, frequency of sexual activity), compared to individual treatment at most follow-up periods (up to 2 years) and in particular for wives (O'Farrell et al., 1992). However, couples therapy did not necessarily have to be cognitive-behavioral in nature, and other marital components produced comparable gains. But when a relapse training adjunct was added to cognitive-behavioral marital therapy, even greater improvements were made over the basic cognitive-behavioral package (O'Farrell et al., 1993). When the impact on marital adjustment was examined in terms of cost-effectiveness, though, these two treatment conditions were equivalent (O'Farrell et al., 1996).

This suggests that marital therapy (and not necessarily a cognitive-behavioral approach) contributes to improved marital functioning. In addition, even when family members are seen alone, a positive impact is made on the marital system. On the other hand, change for the individual addict fails to subsequently impact the marital system (e.g., O'Farrell et al., 1985; O'Farrell et al., 1992). These results suggest the necessity for family members being seen, either alone or as part of a couple, so that the couple relationship can improve its functioning.

FAMILY MEMBER WELL-BEING

Well-being of the family member of the addict as a result of treatment has not been consistently studied. When adjustment has been examined, different outcome measures have been used, such as reduction in personal problems or increased coping (Barber et al., 1996; Thomas et al., 1987). Perhaps because of the differences in the way adjustment is measured, improvements in personal functioning are not always supported.

While Thomas et al. (1987) had reported improved marital functioning (see above), level of spouse adjustment did not show gains as a result of treatment. It could also be that specific treatment conditions need to be in place for positive change to occur. For example, Barber and Gilbertson (1996) found reductions in personal problems only when partners of addicts attended an individual version of unilateral treatment or when they attended Al-Anon groups. The Al-Anon focus on cultivating family member well-being, rather than trying to change the addict, may have improved the effectiveness of the group in reducing personal problems. The extent to which family treatment effects personal change in the nonaddict deserves further attention and needs to be consistently assessed. If a partner is sufficiently motivated to attend treatment, then their suffering and distress should also be reduced as a result. Other limitations of the research and recommendations for future work in this area will be offered below.

RESEARCH CRITIQUE AND RECOMMENDATIONS

The methodology of this research is characterized by a number of strengths. Studies are represented by either experimental or quasi-experimental designs, and they utilize standardized measurement instruments. Further, many studies had the added benefit of follow-up reporting for substance abuse outcomes, a major area of concern in determining the efficacy of interventions (Liddle & Dakoff, 1995). However, there are also some limitations in the studies that future research endeavors may address.

One limitation is the difficulty of synthesizing results when substance abuse is measured in various ways (e.g., consumption of alcohol; percent of days not alcohol-involved; days abstinent; urges to drink; alcohol-related consequences; alcohol physical and psychological dependence). It is essential that a standard measure of effect be adopted, so knowledge-building can better inform service delivery (Breslin, Sobell, Sobell, & Sobell, 1997; Edwards & Steinglass, 1995; Holder et al., 1991). Number of days abstinent has been suggested, as this measure will take into account abstinence as a treatment goal without making it a dichotomous outcome. Adoption of this measure would also allow for continued assessment of the relative merits and long-term outcomes involved with abstinence versus controlled use.

Another area deserving of attention in future endeavors involves the samples of studies. These issues include small sample size, inadequate information on samples and dropouts, and limited generalizability of samples.

The first issue, small sample sizes of studies, compromises available statistical power. This issue is of even greater concern when there are a number of treatment conditions in a single study along with several dependent variables (Sisson & Azrin, 1986; Thomas et al., 1987). In these instances, assumptions of various statistical procedures are violated, which subsequently hinders any conclusions that can be made.

Inadequate descriptions of the study population are also an area of concern. Even general demographic information is often omitted, such as socioeconomic status, race/ethnicity, and age. Inclusion of information about dropouts is also critical and must be reported in order to accurately assess the effectiveness of treatment; otherwise, conclusions are made on a biased population of subjects who choose to remain in treatment for a set number of sessions (Liddle & Dakof, 1995; Stanton & Shadish, 1997).

A final issue involves the lack of generalizability due to the samples that have been selected for study. For example, many of the marital behavior treatment studies used Veteran Administration clientele who were mostly White and male (e.g., O'Farrell et al., 1985, 1992, 1993). The only conclusion that can be drawn from these studies is that for a small cross section of the entire substance-abusing population, interventions including the spouse can produce improved outcomes.

Future research should choose a broader selection of subjects from varying backgrounds for study. In particular, targeted populations should include women, people from minority groups, and lower socioeconomic backgrounds, as well as those who present with other affective disorders. Understanding how family approaches work with these different populations will help develop a knowledge base of effective substance abuse treatments (Liddle & Dakof, 1995).

In addition, other family members of addicts, particularly their children, may suffer a tremendous negative impact, and need to be included in interventions that are examined empirically. The necessity for establishing effective treatments in this area is particularly salient as substance abuse may be an intergenerational phenomenon (Substance Abuse and Mental Health Services Administration, 1998).

RECOMMENDATIONS FOR SERVICE DELIVERY

The dominant treatment approach for substance abuse still remains an Alcoholics Anonymous model, with Al-Anon offered to family members. Until recently, inpatient treatment has also been the treatment-of-choice, despite its very high costs ($213 to $585 per day) and without evidence of improved outcomes (Holder et al., 1991). However, practitioners must recognize that other treatment models not only have demonstrated effectiveness but are also lower in costs. For example, interventions involving the family, specifically behavioral marital therapy and community reinforcement, are in a category of service represented by "medium-low" costs ($200 to $599 for total treatment costs), as well as having empirically validated positive results (Holder et al., 1991). Clear benefits have been demonstrated in terms of reduced substance abuse and greater marital satisfaction when families are involved in treatment. Therefore, the cost-effectiveness of family treatment must continue to be given consideration in view of typically high costs for substance abuse treatment

REFERENCES

Barber, J. G., & Gilbertson, R. (1996). An experimental study of brief unilateral intervention for the partners of heavy drinkers. *Research on Social Work Practice, 6*, 325–336.

Boylin, W. M., Doucette, J., & Jean, M. F. (1997). Multifamily therapy in substance abuse treatment with women. *American Journal of Family Therapy, 25*, 39–46.

Breslin, F. C., Sobell, S. L., Sobell, L. C., & Sobell, M. B. (1997). Alcohol treatment outcome methodology: State of the art 1989–1993. *Addictive Behaviors, 22*, 145–155.

Edwards, M. E., & Steinglass, P. (1995). Family therapy treatment outcomes for alcoholism. *Journal of Marital and Family Therapy, 21*, 475–509.

Fals-Stewart, W., Birchler, G. R., & O'Farrell, T. J. (1996). Behavioral couples therapy for male substance-abusing patients: Effects on relationship adjustment and drug-using behavior. *Journal of Consulting and Clinical Psychology, 64*, 959–972.

Fichter, M. M., Glynn, S. M., Weyerer, S., Liberman, R. P., & Frick, U. (1997). Family climate and expressed emotion in the course of alcoholism. *Family Process, 36*, 203–219.

Holder, H., Longabaugh, R., Miller, W. M., & Rubonis, A. V. (1991). The cost effectiveness of treatment for alcoholism: A first approximation. *Journal of Studies on Alcohol, 52*, 517–540.

Kang, S., Kleinman, P. H., Woody, G. W., Millman, R. B., Todd, T. C., Kemp, J., & Lipton, D. S. (1991). Outcomes for cocaine abusers after once-a-week psychosocial therapy. *American Journal of Psychiatry, 148*, 630–635.

Liddle, H. A., & Dakok, G. A. (1995). Efficacy of family therapy for drug abuse: Promising but not definitive. *Journal of Marital and Family Therapy, 21*, 511–543.

McCrady, B. S., Noel, N. E., Abrams, D. B., Stout, R. L., Nelson, H. F., & Hay, W. M. (1986). Comparative effectiveness of three types of spouse involvement in outpatient behavioral alcoholism treatment. *Journal of Studies on Alcohol, 47*, 459–467.

McCrady, B. S., Stout, R., Noel, N., Abrams, D., & Nelson, H. (1991). Effectiveness of three types of spouse-involved behavioral alcoholism treatment. *British Journal of Addiction, 86*, 1415–1424.

McKay, J. R., Longabuach, R., Beattie, M., Maisto, S., & Noel, N. (1993). Changes in family functioning during treatment and during outcomes for high and low autonomy alcoholics. *Addictive Behaviors, 86*, 1415–1424.

O'Farrell, T. J. (1993). *Treating alcohol problems: Marital and family interventions.* New York: Guilford Press.

O'Farrell, T. J., Choquette, K. A., Cutter, H. S., Brown, E., Bayog, R., McCourt, W., Lowe, J., Chan, A. & Deneault, P. (1996). Cost-benefit and cost-effectiveness analyses of behavioral marital therapy with and without relapse prevention sessions for alcoholics and their spouses. *Behavior Therapy, 27*, 7–24.

O'Farrell, T. J., Choquette, K. A., Cutter, H. S., Brown, E. D., & McCourt, W. F. (1993). Behavioral marital therapy with and without additional couples relapse prevention sessions for alcoholics and their wives. *Journal of Studies on Alcohol, 54*, 652–666.

O'Farrell, T. J., & Cutter, H. S. (1984). Behavioral marital therapy for male alcoholics: Clinicdures from a treatment outcome study in progress. *American Journal of Family Therapy, 12*, 33–46.

O'Farrell, T. J., Cutter, H. S., Choquette, K. A., Floyd, F. J., & Bayog, R. D. (1992). Behavioral marital therapy for male alcoholics: Marital and drinking adjustment during the two years after treatment. *Behavior Therapy, 23*, 529–549.

O'Farrell, T. J., Cutter, H. S., & Floyd, F. J. (1985). Evaluating behavioral marital therapy for male alcoholics: Effects on marital adjustment and communication from before and after treatment. *Behavior Therapy, 16*, 147–167.

Sisson, R. W., & Azrin, N. H. (1986). Family-member involvement to initiate and promote treatment of problem drinkers. *Journal of Behavioral Therapy and Experiential Psychiatry, 17*, 15–21.

Sorensen, J. L., Gibson, D., Bernal, Q., & Deitch, D. (1985). Methadone applicant dropouts: Impact of requiring involvement of friends or family in treatment. *International Journal of the Addictions, 20*, 1273–1280.

Stanton, M. D., & Shadish, W. R. (1997). Outcome, attrition, and family-couples treatment for drug abuse: A meta-analysis and review of the controlled, comparative studies. *Psychological Bulletin, 122*, 170–191.

Stark, M. J. (1992). Dropping out of substance abuse treatment: A clinically oriented review. *Clinical Psychology Review, 12*, 93–116.

Substance Abuse and Mental Health Services Administration. (1998). *Substance abuse and mental health statistics source book.* Washington, DC: Department of Health and Human Services.

Thomas, E. J., Santa, C., Bronson, D., & Oyserman, D. (1987). Unilateral family therapy with the spouses of alcoholics. *Journal of Social Service Research, 10*, 145–162.

MEASUREMENT OF FAMILY TREATMENT
WITH ADULT SUBSTANCE ABUSE

Increasingly, practitioners are held accountable for the evaluation of their practice. To assist with evaluation, this section provides the reader with self-report instruments that family members can easily complete. Scores from these measurement instruments can be used to guide assessment and clinical practice when treating families with substance abuse problems. For those interested in conducting research in this area, each of the instruments provided has established psychometric data to support its usage.

The following types of measures are presented: 1) substance abuse screening instruments, 2) personal adjustment, 3) marital adjustment, 4) family functioning, and 5) client satisfaction with services. Because the empirical work in this area has focused on couples rather than children, readers interested in assessing the effects of substance abuse on children should consult Chapter One, Family Treatment with Child Abuse and Neglect.

Measures presented in this section involve the following criteria. First, instruments are self-report; that is, they are completed by family members themselves, rather than being interviewer-administered or observational measures. A second criterion for inclusion was that adequate reliability and validity information had to be available for each scale. Selected psychometric data were chosen to inform the reader of the properties of the instruments.

SUBSTANCE USE OUTCOMES

MICHIGAN ALCOHOLISM SCREENING TEST

Author: Selzer, Vinokur, & van Rooijen (1975)

Description:

- A 24-item index of severity of alcohol misuse, response format 0–1

Reliability:

- Coefficient alpha = .93 (Skinner, 1979)

Validity:

- Factor analysis yielded 5 factors along with a strong unidimensional component (Skinner, 1979):
  1. Recognition of alcohol problem by self and others
  2. Legal, work, and social problems
  3. Help-seeking
  4. Marital-family difficulties
  5. Liver pathology
- Correlations with following Personality Research Form constructs: Impulsivity (.24), Affiliation (–.24), Hypochondriasis (.25), Depression (.29), Anxiety (.24), Thinking Disorder (.20), Social Introversion (.24), Self-Depreciation (.32), and Deviation (.26) [Skinner, 1979]
- Scores correlated with lifetime daily average consumption (.58) [Skinner, 1979]

DRUG ABUSE SCREENING TEST

Author: Skinner (1982)

Description:

- 28 items ("yes"/"no") tapping various consequences of drug use
- Parallels items on Michigan Alcoholism Screening Test

Reliability:

- Internal consistency = .92

Validity:

- Factor analysis indicates a single dimension
- High scores correlated with stable accommodation, work record, and family contact
- High scores correlated with more frequent use of cannabis, barbiturates, and opiates other than heroin
- High scores correlated with Impulse Expression and Social Deviation of Basic Personality Inventory

PERSONAL ADJUSTMENT

BECK DEPRESSION INVENTORY

(*See Chapter One*, Family Treatment with Child Abuse and Neglect)

SYMPTOM CHECKLIST 90-REVISED

(*See Chapter One*, Family Treatment with Child Abuse and Neglect)

BRIEF SYMPTOM INVENTORY

(*See Chapter One*, Family Treatment with Child Abuse and Neglect)

MARITAL OUTCOMES

THE MARITAL ADJUSTMENT TEST

(*See Chapter One*, Family Treatment with Child Abuse and Neglect)

DYADIC ADJUSTMENT SCALE

(*See Chapter One*, Family Treatment with Child Abuse and Neglect)

O'LEARY-PORTER SCALE

(*See Chapter One*, Family Treatment with Child Abuse and Neglect)

REVISED CONFLICT TACTICS SCALES

(*See Chapter One*, Family Treatment with Child Abuse and Neglect)

FAMILY FUNCTIONING

FAMILY ADAPTABILITY AND COHESION EVALUATION SCALES III

(*See Chapter One*, Family Treatment with Child Abuse and Neglect)

FAMILY ENVIRONMENT SCALE

(*See Chapter One*, Family Treatment with Child Abuse and Neglect)

MCMASTER FAMILY ASSESSMENT DEVICE

(*See Chapter One*, Family Treatment with Child Abuse and Neglect)

SATISFACTION WITH SERVICES

CLIENT SATISFACTION QUESTIONNAIRE

(*See Chapter One*, Family Treatment with Child Abuse and Neglect)

REFERENCES FOR MEASUREMENT OF FAMILY
TREATMENT WITH ADULT SUBSTANCE ABUSE

Selzer, M. L., Vinokur, A., & van Rooijen, L. (1975). A self-administered short Michigan alcoholism screening test (SMAST). *Journal of Studies on Alcohol, 36,* 117–126.

Skinner, H. (1979). A multivariate evaluation of the MAST. *Journal of Studies on Alcohol, 40,* 831–843.

Skinner, H. (1982). The drug abuse screening test. *Addictive Behavior, 7,* 363–371.

CHAPTER 10

Family Treatment with Family Violence

Family Case:

Jane and Paul Vanders, a White couple in their early 30s, present for marital counseling. Jane is an administrative assistant at a building company, and Paul is a vending machine stocker. The couple has two children, a daughter, age 4, and a son, age 7.

The Vanders reveal that on a couple of recent occasions, Paul has physically restrained and shoved Jane when she threatened to leave in the middle of an argument. Jane says, "When he gets like that, there is no use talking to him, so I just want to leave so he can cool off." He says, "I want her to stay and talk it out with me because by the time she finally comes back, I'm so mad there's no cooling down anytime soon."

When asked about any other kind of violence, Paul denies further episodes, but after a moment's hesitation, Jane reveals that Paul has also hit her across her face early in their relationship. She threatened to leave him if he ever did that again, and there has not been a repeat of that behavior. Paul says the only reason that incident happened was because he had drunk a lot of Jack Daniels that day. Now he just sticks to beer.

Both Jane and Paul admit to a lot of verbal abuse between them. They swear at each other and bring up incidents from the past. Jane says that now her 7-year-old son shows the same kind of disrespect toward her that his father does. Paul says if she was just stricter with their son, this wouldn't happen. He further says if Jane wouldn't nag so much and tell him what he was doing wrong, he wouldn't have to call her names and shout at her in front of their son.

Violence against women by intimate partners continues to be a serious social issue. The injuries women receive at the hands of their partners are more severe than those received from strangers (U.S. Department of Justice, 1995). In addition, 28% of female victims of homicide (1,414 women) were killed by their partners or ex-partners, in comparison to about 3% of male victims of homicide (637 men) who were killed by their partners or ex-partners (U.S. Department of Justice, 1995). The serious consequences are not only limited to women victims in terms of physical injury, psychological pain, and distress. There are also negative effects on children who witness violence in their homes, including emotional, behavioral, social, and cognitive adjustment problems (Kolbo, Blakely, & Engleman, 1996). The necessity for effective treatment to end violence in the home, therefore, needs to be understood by practitioners and applied so that suffering may be alleviated.

The dominant approach involves an advocacy stance, which focuses on the man's responsibility for changing violent behavior (Geffner, Barrett, & Rossman, 1995). The advocacy approach is informed by feminist theory, which assumes that men have been socialized into a position of dominance over women. Violence in intimate relationships is one of the ways men demonstrate their entitlement to power and control (Avis, 1992; Bograd, 1992). In this approach, law enforcement policies encourage arrest and legal consequences. The batterer is treated separately from his partner (Hansen, 1993; Willbach, 1989). Women obtain support and empowerment to leave their abusive situations through individual and group treatment. Men's treatment groups emphasize the use of cognitive-behavioral techniques in order to build skills to successfully communicate and resolve conflict without resorting to violence. Profeminist content is, therefore, usually incorporated into group treatment so that men are educated about sex-role socialization and their beliefs about entitlement to power and control in relationships (Tolman & Edleson, 1995).

In contrast to an advocacy approach, in which women are encouraged to leave their abusive relationships, others have argued for couples treatment of violence. Several rationales for this approach have been offered. First, women often desire to stay in their relationships (Cook & Frantz-Cook, 1984; Sirles, Lipchick, & Kowalski, 1993), and even when they leave, they often return (Hansen & Goldenberg, 1993). Further, men in such relationships are frequently reluctant to seek treatment for themselves and are more motivated to attend when the violence is framed within the context of a relationship problem (Hansen & Goldenberg, 1993). A final pragmatic rationale for couples treatment is the mutuality of violence that many times is present (Gelles & Maynard, 1987). Straus (1995) reports results of a survey that both men and women commit minor assaults at a similar rate (at over 90 per 1,000 couples), although it is recognized that a woman's smaller size and physical strength would render her more vulnerable to injury (Flynn, 1995).

The philosophical rationale for couples treatment involves a family systems view. Advocates of a systems view of family violence believe that any system, including a couple relationship, is comprised of repeated patterns of interpersonal interactions (Sexton, 1994). Rather than linear causality, in which one member is blamed for the violence perpetrated on the "victim," circular causality is assumed, in which communication and relationship transactions contribute to the violence that occurs (Gelles & Maynard, 1987; Neidig & Friedman, 1984; Sexton, 1994; Weitzman & Dreen, 1982). The relationship context, therefore, is the focus of treatment.

The use of conjoint therapy for family violence, however, has generated a lot of controversy (Geffner et al., 1995). Foremost have been concerns for victim safety, in that a woman may have violence perpetrated on her for revealing the abusive nature of the relationship (Aldarondo & Straus, 1994; Hansen, 1993). Further, failing to encourage a woman to leave an abusive situation might place her at further risk for abuse.

Another criticism is leveled against the concept of reciprocal sequences and circular interaction patterns. This concept is viewed as diffusing male responsibility and implying that victims have some responsibility for their abuse (Willbach, 1989). Seeing members of couples together may implicitly reinforce male dominance over the relationship and convey that women are, at least in some part, to blame (Geffner et al., 1995). While the systemic nature of relationships is emphasized, larger systemic influences are ignored for their impact on interpersonal relationships, such as sex-role socialization and cultural and social sanctions for domestic violence (Hansen, 1993; Tolman & Edleson, 1995).

Another argument against couples counseling involves the reduced likelihood that the couple will reveal the full extent and severity of the abuse (Aldarondo & Straus, 1994; Hansen, 1993). There are many reasons why couples may not make full disclosure: A woman may fear retribution; the couple may view the violence as unrelated to the presenting problem or merely asymptomatic of their underlying problems; and/or the couple may, in the interest of self-enhancement, want to present themselves in a positive light and avoid exposing themselves and other family members to possible shame and public condemnation (Aldarondo & Straus, 1994).

Abusive partners also have a tendency to minimize their aggressive behaviors, and their partners frequently collude with their accounts (Hansen, 1993). Many violent men fail to see they have a problem and may be more willing, as mentioned earlier, to attend treatment if the problem is couched in relationship terms. In such situations, the woman may be more motivated for help-seeking, which may result in an emphasis on her part in relationship problems, rather than a focus on the perpetrator's violent behavior. The therapist is also more likely to direct attention on where the system is most amenable to change, which may further reinforce the female partner's contribution and take responsibility away from the abuser.

Some of these concerns may be incorporated into couples approaches. For example, Geffner et al. (1995) describe an approach in which abuse is seen as stemming from both personal (linear) and couple (circular) dynamics, but with the perpetrator, not the victim, taking responsibility for the abuse. It is also suggested that the concept of reciprocal and circular interactions can be more helpful for an understanding of why the victim stays in the abusive relationship, rather than her being responsible for the abuse that has occurred.

Couples approaches that integrate an advocacy stance need to be sensitive to double messages about sustaining the relationship (Tolman & Edleson, 1995). The balance should always fall toward safety of the victim, which should remain foremost over the needs of the relationship, and various preconditions should be met to ensure safety (Geffner et al., 1995). Contraindications for the use of couples treatment include the following situations: 1) when a woman's safety is jeopardized; 2) when frequent and severe abuse occurs; 3) when the victim does not want couples counseling; 4) when substance abuse problems are present; and 5) when mental illness exists (e.g., Jennings & Jennings, 1991; Taylor, 1984).

Some of the contraindications lend themselves to the preconditions that need to be in place before a couple embarks on conjoint therapy. These include the following: 1) the victim and perpetrator desire conjoint treatment; 2) the victim has a safety plan in case of potential danger; 3) a lethality evaluation suggests a low probability of danger; 4) the perpetrator does not display obsessional thoughts or behaviors toward the victim; 5) no psychotic behavior is present on either part of the couple; 6) neither are abusing substances (if so, then specialized treatment is required); and 7) therapists are trained in both family therapy and domestic violence (Eiskovits & Edleson, 1989; Geffner et al., 1995; Gelles, 1998).

If a conjoint approach is decided upon, certain safeguards need to be addressed for the victim. For instance, Cook and Frantz-Cook (1984) discuss that partners first need to be seen separately and then continue to have separate treatment throughout the couples' sessions. In this way, disclosure of any abusive behaviors can take place in a safe context.

HOW EFFECTIVE ARE COUPLES' APPROACHES?

A search of the empirical literature was conducted on family approaches to the treatment of domestic violence. Recent efforts were emphasized (1985 to the present), and two main approaches were found: group couples counseling and conjoint couples treatment. The review will be organized according to these two categories. Within each of these categories, interventions used in studies will be described, followed by results (*see* Table 10.1). After a discussion of findings, a critique of the research will be provided along with future recommendations.

COUPLES GROUP COUNSELING

Although many interventions have the theoretical orientation of systems theory, techniques are generally not systemic in nature (Eisikovits & Edleson, 1989). Instead, cognitive and behavioral techniques are used to build skills so that abusive conflict can be avoided. Cognitive-behavioral training is described in two main group protocols, the Deschner and Neidig models (Deschner, 1984; Deschner, McNeil, & Moore, 1986). Through instruction, behavioral rehearsal (during class exercises and as assignments for homework), and feedback, several interventions are used. First, couples are taught that violence does not erupt suddenly or happen at random or in isolation. Instead, violence is the end result of a coercive process that builds in a sequence of small steps. Couples are taught to become aware of this process and recognize cues, such as bodily symptoms, cognitions, and feelings that signal the need for a time-out. Time-out involves separating at signs of rising conflict for a brief designated time period, which allows anger to subside and cognitive evaluation to occur before the couple comes together again. Couples are also trained in stress-management techniques, such as relaxation and visual imagery, and to apply these techniques to identified anger cues and stressors that may trigger conflict and abuse.

Another major intervention is cognitive restructuring with an emphasis on self-talk. Both the Deschner and Neidig models draw heavily on Albert Ellis's Rational Emotive Therapy with the identification of automatic thoughts and irrational assumptions that may underlie anger. Couples are further trained in techniques to manage interpersonal conflict. Assertiveness and communication skills training emphasize reflective listening, validation of feelings, and the use of "I" messages to express emotions and convey requests.

Both the Deschner and Neidig models have been subjected to empirical study, although a number of methodological problems limit the favorable out-

TABLE 10.1 Family Intervention Treatment Outcome Studies for Domestic Violence

AUTHOR/MODEL	DESIGN/SAMPLE	MEASURES	RESULTS	LIMITATIONS
Brannen & Rubin (1996) Cognitive-behavioral (based on model developed by Neidig & Friedman [1984]) 12 sessions 1–$\frac{1}{2}$ hrs long	Quasi-experimental, pretest, posttest, follow-up (6 mos), randomization to couples or gender-specific groups $N = 42$ Court-referred Average educational level = 12.06 yrs; 75% employed; 8% African American, 23% White, 67% Hispanic; average income = $19,772	Modified Conflict Tactics Scale McMaster Family Assessment Device Marital Satisfaction Inventory Long-term Evaluation Form (telephone interview at 6 mos to measure recidivism and confirmed by police and probation records)	Only for those with alcohol histories (were currently in court-monitored Antabuse programs) were couples groups more effective, both at posttest and at follow-up (62% were represented at follow-up)	Lack of no-treatment control group; small sample size; did not state how many men were screened with alcohol problems and how many were attending court-monitored Antabuse program; unknown if any other treatment (other than Antabuse) was used for alcohol treatment
Deschner & McNeil (1986) Cognitive-behavioral group 10 weeks of 3-hr sessions	Pretest, posttest, follow-up (4 mos to 1-yr) $N = 82$ that attended 4 + times, but usable pretest, posttest data were collected from 69 referrals from child wel-	Anger diaries (weekly) Degree of satisfaction with marriage and children (weekly)	At posttest, 22 participants in 1st 2 groups rated themselves as less angry, depressed, and less prone to violence; for 47 participants in later groups, although	Mixed group of child abuse and domestic violence; not stated how many partners attended; possible bias in that usable data not collected from 12% of sample;

Study/Intervention	Sample	Measures	Results	Comments/Limitations
	fare, media announcements; 1/3 middle-class; 2/3 working-class; average age early 30s; majority White		the decrease in number of arguments and reductions in anger ratings were statistically significant, the decrease in violence was not	variable follow-up time (from 4 mos to 1 yr); only 64% able to be contacted at follow-up; lack of no-treatment control or comparison group; lack of standardized measures; was not mentioned that physical violence would be measured and in what way, but then given in results; results for total sample not given
Deschner et al. (1986) Cognitive-behavioral group (mostly couples) 10 weeks 2 1/2-hr sessions	Reported data on 47 individuals from later groups (see Deschner & McNeil, 1986)	Arguments per week Anger during argument (1–10 scale) Perception of partner's anger Violent incidents per week Marital happiness (0–10)	Arguments per week, anger during arguments, and marital happiness all improved at the .01 significance level at posttest	Lack of demographic information; nonstandardized measurement system; lack of comparison/control group; follow-up information at 8 mos involved only 15 subjects and results not discussed in terms of statistical significance; referral source not explicit

continued

TABLE 10.1 *(continued)*

AUTHOR/MODEL	DESIGN/SAMPLE	MEASURES	RESULTS	LIMITATIONS
Harris (1986) Conjoint couples counseling using Walker's model Mean number of sessions attended = 5 Cognitive-behavioral (although Walker did not name as such)	Follow-up only (2 mos to 3 yrs) $N = 30$ couples (from original 40 randomly selected cases from agency rolls) Annual income = $18,300; police intervention 46%; alcohol and drug abuse 50% of time	Stopping violence assumed to be outcome measure but not defined	73% success, 27% failed; statistically significant factors associated with success: 1) increased age of perpetrator; 2) higher income; 3) later onset of violence in relationship; 4) greater number of couple sessions attended	Individual counseling for both partners used initially and interspersed with conjoint sessions so difficult to tease out effects of conjoint; participants may also have been attending separate group sessions; the requirement of a male and female therapist may present logistical concerns as well as labor-intensive use of therapists' time; variable follow-up time (2 mos to 3 yrs); outcome measure not defined; unknown whether follow-up reports were from victim or perpetrator

| Johannson & Tutty (1998)

Following a 24-week separate-gender group, treatment consisted of a 12-week couples group 2 times weekly

Social learning, feminist, cognitive, communication, and stress theories | Pretest/posttest

$N = 13$ couples (Canada)

Had to have completed 24-week, separate-gender group program

Average income level for couples = \$38,652 | Modified Conflict Tactics Scale (pretest, posttest data available only on 10)

Family Assessment Measure-Dyadic Relationship Scale (pretest, posttest data available only on 9) | Women reported that they themselves and their partners had significantly reduced the frequency of their psychological abuse and its severity. Women also reported that they had significantly reduced the frequency of their physical abuse. The men, too, reported significant changes in the frequency of their own psychological abuse. On the family functioning measure, both males and females significantly improved their scores on the overall score and all the subscales except for men's Values and Norms. 1-yr followup with 11 of couples —7 still in relationships, with 4 reporting no other violence | No comparison/control group; small sample; may not have generalizability because violence levels were carefully monitored and high levels of motivation of couples who attended both single-gender groups for 24 weeks and a 12-week couples group; lack of information on race, legal involvement |
| --- | --- | --- | --- | --- |

continued

TABLE 10.1 *(continued)*

AUTHOR/MODEL	DESIGN/SAMPLE	MEASURES	RESULTS	LIMITATIONS
Neidig (1986) Neidig & Friedman (1984)—described Social learning and cognitive restructuring 10 weekly 2-hr sessions	Pretest, posttest, follow-up (6 mos) $N = 40$ military personnel who had self-reported violence and their wives	Locus of Control Scale; Dyadic Adjustment Scale; military police reports and self-reports of violence by subjects and wives (at 6 mos)	Significant improvements on Dyadic Adjustment Subscales (except for Affectional Experience) and Locus of Control for both men and women; according to majority of self-reports from men and wives at 6 mos, no additional violence	Unknown how many contacted for follow-up; unknown how many wives participated in program; no comparison or control group; self-reports of males suspect
Rynerson & Fishel (1993) Cognitive-behavioral couples group (Neidig & Friedman [1984]) 8 2-hr weekly sessions	Pretest, posttest $N = 149$ Referred from court 56% males, 43% females; 50–50 Anglo- and African American; 87% of sample high school educated or less; 96% of men skilled manual labor or less; 86% employed with median income of $10,400	Locus of Control Scale Dyadic Adjustment Scale	Both males and females scored significantly lower on the external Locus of Control Scale, although participants were still in the external range; after treatment, females significantly more satisfied with their relationships	Lack of control/comparison group; posttest information missing for a lot of sample (62% of men, 45% of women); attrition not tracked precisely; employment of women not assessed; lack of follow-up; although discussed that self-reports of violence during treatment were tracked, these results not reported

Sirles et al. (1993) Solution-focused couples (93%) or individual therapy Average 4 sessions	Posttest only $N = 42$ individuals either who had been arrested for family violence (all male) or whose partner had been arrested (90% female); 15 couples were represented, 7 male batterers, 5 female victims; 58% African American, 28% White, 14% mixed racial origin	Phone interview using "structured interview" including violence experienced	For men: 54% found therapy to be positive, stating they had acquired skills in controlling their drinking, arguing, and avoiding violence; 23% mixed in response; 23% negative toward counseling Women tended to be more satisfied: 84% positive; 6% mixed; 11% dissatisfied 86% still in couple relationship and planned to stay	No pretest; no comparison/control group; lack of standardized measures

comes presented. The Deschner results include data on 82 individuals who attended their cognitive-behavioral group program (Deschner & McNeil, 1986; Deschner et al., 1986). While a majority of group members were reported to be couples, it is unknown how many. It is also unexplained why data are reported separately for an earlier group of 22 participants who attended the first two groups and for the 47 participants in later groups. The earlier group rated themselves as less angry, depressed, and less prone to violence as measured by nonstandardized anger logs, but the changes were not discussed in terms of statistical significance. In addition, it is not known how violence was defined and from what source it was collected (perpetrator or victim). For the 47 individuals who attended the later groups, arguments per week, anger during arguments, and marital happiness had all improved at statistically significant levels from pretest to posttest, although the reduction in violence was not significant (Deschner & McNeil, 1986; Deschner et al., 1986).

The Neidig program was used by Neidig himself and by two other researchers. Neidig (1986) reported results on 40 military personnel and their wives who had attended the 10-week, 2-hour group sessions. Significant improvements were made on standardized self-report measures at posttest. At 6-month follow-up, the majority of men and wives reported no additional violence. It is unknown how many were contacted for follow-up, however, and how many of the reports were from wives. This latter issue is crucial, as violent men tend to minimize and thus underreport their behavior (Tolman & Edleson, 1995).

Rynerson and Fishel (1993) report results of a cognitive-behavioral couples group that was modeled after Neidig and Friedman (1984), although it was slightly shorter in length (eight 2-hour weekly sessions). Of the 149 individuals attending, both males and females scored significantly lower on external locus of control, but participants still demonstrated scores in the external range. Following treatment, the women only were significantly more satisfied with their relationship. Unfortunately, a substantial amount of posttest information was missing (62% of men, 45% of women); it is unknown if these respondents would have reported even worse outcomes. Another flaw of the study was that though self-reports of violence during treatment were allegedly tracked, these results were not reported.

Brannen and Rubin (1996) also modeled their program after Neidig and Friedman (1984). This study was the only one to employ a quasi-experimental design with randomization to either couples or separate gender-specific groups. The separate gender group curriculums were adapted from the Domestic Abuse Project in Minneapolis, Minnesota. Cognitive-behavioral in nature, they differ from the Neidig and Friedman (1984) program in an emphasis on profeminist content.

Safety concerns were of particular importance in this study, since over a third of the abusive incidents for which spouses were court-referred were severe, involving kicking, punching, choking, and/or the use of a weapon. In addition, many of the men were assessed with alcohol problems and were attending a court-monitored Antabuse program. These types of concerns have been addressed in clinical discussions as contraindications for the use of couples treatment (e.g., Jennings & Jennings, 1991; Taylor, 1984).

Sensitivity to victim safety was addressed through several ways (Brannen & Rubin, 1996). First, victims attended a separate orientation in which they were encouraged, if they felt threatened in their relationship, to call their group facilitators, the primary investigator of the research (who also provided a 24-hour emergency number), and/or law enforcement officials. They were also provided the number for the battered women's shelter and were instructed on how to access the shelter in an emergency. A second way that safety was insured involved weekly administration of a version of the Modified Conflict Tactics Scale. These measures were reviewed by both the group facilitators and the primary investigator. If necessary, contact was made with the victim to ensure safety and to provide information on accessing emergency services.

Individuals in both the couples and the separate gender groups improved according to standardized, self-report measures. Couples counseling did produce statistically significant gains over the separate gender groups on reducing victims' reports of physical abuse and severe physical abuse only for those perpetrators who were also receiving treatment for alcohol problems. The authors hypothesize that both alcohol abuse and domestic violence involve denial and minimization. In a group context, possible confrontation by the other partner, group members, or the facilitator might reduce the extent of such minimization. It may also be that cultural factors contribute to the effectiveness of couples treatment since a majority of the sample (67%) were Mexican-American. The importance of family factors for Mexican-Americans has been discussed in the clinical literature (Falicov, 1996; Ho, 1987). Future research with different racial groups is necessary in order to understand if race was a key factor in these findings.

The most recent couples group treatment in the literature involves a Canadian study with a theoretical basis described as social learning, feminist, cognitive, communication, and stress theories (Johannson & Tutty, 1998). The study reported findings of a 12-week couples group that met two times weekly. A requirement of participation was that partners first had to complete a 24-

week separate gender group. The emphasis of the couples group was on reinforcing the skills training learned in the gender-separate groups, involving communication, problem-solving, and conflict resolution skills. It was not mentioned whether these were court-referred participants, although a substantial amount of motivation must have been involved for this level of treatment intensity. Given this level of intensity, it is not surprising that sample size was so small (13 couples).

The following safety considerations were taken: 1) severe violence was screened out with the Modified Conflict Tactics Scale; 2) telephone contact was made with each female partner to inquire about any ongoing physical abuse; 3) at entry to group, all couples signed a "no violence" contract; 4) partners were asked during each group check-in about any abusive incidents; 5) at 4-week intervals, each participant was questioned privately to find out if violence had occurred; 6) group facilitators were available for contact if a crisis developed; and 7) couples who presented with safety concerns were offered additional counseling sessions and were monitored by telephone contact (one third of couples were monitored at some point throughout the group process).

Findings were reported separately for males and females. Women reported significantly reduced frequency and severity of psychological abuse for themselves and their partners. Women also reported that they had significantly reduced the frequency of their own physical abuse. The men, too, reported significant changes in the frequency of their psychological abuse.

On the family functioning measure, both males and females significantly improved their overall score on all subscale scores, except for the Values and Norms subscale for men. At 1 year, 11 of the 13 couples were contacted. Seven were still in relationship with each other, and four others reported no further violence. It must be recognized that findings may not have generalizability to other couples because violence levels were so carefully monitored and couples seemed to be highly motivated in their attendance.

COUPLES CONJOINT

Less research has been conducted on couples conjoint treatment, with only two studies reported. In 1986, Harris discussed the use of a cognitive-behavioral model originally developed by Walker (1979) for conjoint counseling. In this model, partners build awareness of how their own behavior contributes to violence. They learn anger control, problem-solving, and communication skills. Cognitive strategies are also taught, primarily through the use of rational emotive therapy, so that assumptions each partner makes about the other's actions and any maladaptive thoughts are clarified. Harris (1986) emphasizes how this model departs from more traditional types of couples counseling.

In traditional counseling, the main goal is to improve the relationship, with individual needs sometimes compromised to achieve this goal. With domestic violence, however, the needs of the relationship are secondary to the safety of the victim. The priority of safety is also ensured through several mechanisms, including individual counseling for both members of the couple preceding conjoint therapy and interspersed between couples sessions. Participants may have also attended separate group counseling concurrently. Another difference between traditional counseling and conjoint treatment for domestic violence involves the limited exchange, particularly of anger, between partners in the latter approach. This is achieved through the presence of both a male and female co-therapist. Communication is mainly limited to the client and therapist of the same gender while the other pair observes, evaluates, and discusses their responses between themselves. The purpose of this strategy is for clients to express feelings without incurring blame and anger and for each partner to be able to hear more clearly what is being stated. In this way, resentments are reduced and violence is avoided.

Results of this study include follow-up contact with 30 of the 40 couples who could be reached. Those who attended more sessions were more available at follow-up, which took place anywhere between 2 months and 3 years after completing treatment. Success was assumed to mean reduced violence, but this was never defined; nor was the source of information clarified. With these limitations, 73% of cases were defined as successes and 27% as failed. Factors associated with success were the following: 1) increased age of perpetrator, 2) higher income, 3) later onset of violence in relationship, and 4) greater number of couple sessions attended.

Other types of counseling in the form of individual and/or group make it difficult to tease out the effects of conjoint therapy. Further, the additional counseling to ensure victim safety and the presence of both a male and female therapist at each session seem to preclude the cost-effectiveness of this approach.

In contrast to this rather intensive approach, more recently Sirles et al. (1993) report the use of brief, solution-focused therapy (an average of four sessions) with couples in which the male partner was arrested for family violence. The solution-focused approach is the most recent development out of systemic family therapy, which emphasizes the interactional context of behavior. An advantage to solution-focused therapy is that methods have been developed for use with nonvoluntary clients; individuals who batter are often court-mandated to attend treatment. Solution-focused therapy examines exceptions to the problem and enlarges upon the resources individuals use during these nonproblem times. For batterers and their partners, this comprises times when the violence is avoided and conflict is resolved. The model focuses on the strengths of the relationship and the individuals involved.

Evaluation of solution-focused therapy involved follow-up with a nonstandardized measure of satisfaction and effectiveness. Women overall were more satisfied: 84% were positive about their experience in counseling, 6% reported mixed feelings, and 11% were dissatisfied. For men, 54% found therapy to be positive, stating they had acquired skills in controlling their drinking, arguing, and avoiding violence; 23% were mixed in their response; and 23% were negative toward counseling. Despite positive findings reported, methodological problems, such as the lack of pretest, posttest, reports from the victim on their partner's violent behavior, and standardized measures call into question these results.

SUMMARY OF COUPLES TREATMENT

Studies of couples treatment for domestic violence began in the 1980s. Studies in that decade were flawed by a number of methodological problems and make positive findings reported somewhat suspect. For a period of years, the approach seemed to fall out of favor, at least in the empirical literature, due to a feminist orientation that took over the field, with an emphasis on legal consequences for batterers, separate gender treatment, and encouraging battered women to leave their spouses.

The 1990s have seen a beginning re-emergence of the couples approach with an increased sensitivity to victim safety. Although a lot of controversy still exists against the use of couples therapy for family violence (Geffner et al., 1995), one study at least has indicated that couples therapy works as well as separate-gender treatment, and for alcohol-abusing batterers in a program to monitor use, the couples approach may be even more effective (Brannen & Rubin, 1996) .

When considering the body of research in this area as a whole, however, it appears the literature has not progressed much beyond the conclusion by Eisikovits and Edleson in their 1989 review: "In summary, the research on intervention with couples is, at present, inadequate. Given the shortcomings in the existing research, additional studies will be needed before couple intervention will have proven itself a viable intervention with men who batter and their victims" (p. 392).

CRITIQUE AND RECOMMENDATIONS

As discussed, studies on couples treatment of family violence reveal serious methodological flaws. With the exception of one quasi-experimental design, all were pretest, posttest, or follow-up-only designs. Given the ethical considerations involved in withholding treatment from violent men and their victims, future studies should strive to use quasi-experimental designs with comparison treatment conditions, a viable alternative.

Attention to adequate sample size is also needed so that statistical power is ensured. Information on the sample, such as how many individuals and couples attended, the percentage of wives with violence problems, and demographic information, such as race and socioeconomic status, should be routinely provided.

Another problem with designs is either a lack of follow-up or the variable time period involved with follow-up. Follow-up contact is required to determine if gains made at posttest are maintained over time. Contact should be made with victims, as victim reports tend to be more accurate than those made by batterers, who often deny or minimize their violence (Tolman & Edleson, 1995). The earlier studies in this review often fail to reveal the source that provided information about long-term violence. If these studies relied on statements by batterers, the positive effects of intervention reported may have been compromised.

One of the recent studies supplemented follow-up data with police and probation records (Brannen & Rubin, 1996). These official indicators are probably still less likely to be accurate than are victim reports (Tolman & Edleson, 1995). Abusive incidents may have taken place without law enforcement ever being called to the scene.

In addition to reports on violence, future studies should also ensure that standardized measures are used. Suggested measures include those that assess psychological adjustment of victims and the improvement of couple functioning (Tolman & Edleson, 1995). In addition, it is important to understand how outcome is related to theoretical orientations. For example, gains in rational thinking, the use of cognitive self-management techniques, and locus of control could be assessed for cognitive-behavioral interventions. Attitudes about domestic violence and sex roles could be assessed for programs with a feminist orientation.

One particular theoretical critique of the couples treatment literature is the lack of consistency between systems theory and cognitive-behavioral interventions (Eisikovits & Edleson, 1989). No unifying schema has been developed that logically explains the connection between theory and technique.

However, some similarities are noted between these two theories. In family systems theory, change or problems in one part of the system are assumed to impact other parts of the system. In a similar manner, behavioral theory views violence as reinforced by the behavior of others in interaction (e.g., Deschner, 1984). Magill and Werk (1985) attempt to reconcile these views in that violent behavior may have been learned (behavioral theory), but then violence becomes a habitual pattern of interaction (systems theory).

Another way to reconcile these two theories involves the controversial assumption of circular causality in family systems theory. Rather than viewing the victim as responsible for the violence, the concept of reciprocal interactions can be used to understand her remaining in the relationship. If members of couples are taught tools of clear communication through cognitive-behavioral techniques, communication based on threat, emotional abuse, and manipulation is reduced, and clarity may be gained for how the victim has been caught up in the relationship.

One question arises with the systemic assumption that change in one part of the system impacts other parts of the system. If this assumption is in operation, why is there a need for couples treatment? If men are treated separately in groups designed to build their skill levels, then change in this part of the system can be assumed to change the relationship system, calling into question the systemic assumption that members of the couple should be seen together.

The only purely systemic model in this empirical review involved a solution-focused approach to treating batterers and their partners (Sirles et al., 1993). Solution-focused therapy has not typically been discussed in the literature as applied to batterers, although there have been some beginning clinical discussions about its use with victims of domestic violence (Corcoran, 1999; Greene, Lee, Trask, & Rheinscheld, 1996).

In the Sirles et al. (1993) study, although men and, particularly, women were satisfied with the approach, repeat violence was not specifically measured for outcome. Therefore, it is unknown if solution-focused therapy is effective in reducing violence for batterers. In addition, a study conducted in Israel (Eisikovits, Edleson, Guttmann, & Sela-Amit, 1995) calls into question the solution-focused assumption that people have the resources to solve their own problems. The objective of the Eisikovits et al. (1995) study was to examine whether cognitive deficits or attitudes about violence toward women underlie battering behavior. When comparing violent to nonviolent men on cognitive deficits and attitudes about violence toward women, attitudes were the strongest predictor of violence toward partners. To a lesser extent, rational thinking also predicted abusive behavior. Because of the different cultural context that may be operating, it is suggested that the Israeli study be replicated with United States samples to test the theoretical assumptions behind interventions. However, the results of this study suggest that attitudes about domestic violence might need to be targeted for interventions involving education and awareness. The deficits found in rational thinking also imply the need for training in this area, rather than assuming that people have the resources to prevent future violence. At the same time, solution-focused therapy might hold some advantages for work with violent men, who are so often mandated to attend treatment. Solution-focused therapy is unique in having methods to intervene with nonvoluntary clients, whereas most models, including cognitive-behavioral, assume some voluntary motivation on the part of the client. These issues demonstrate the need for more theoretical and empirical work at unifying underlying frameworks and techniques.

Additionally, in the past the approach was to consider all violent men and their partners as a homogeneous population with similar treatment needs. Work is now under way, however, to consider the possible types of battering populations. For example, Stuart and Holtzworth-Munroe (1995) have created a classification of maritally violent men based upon severity and frequency of the abuse, psychopathology, and the extent of assaultive and criminal behavior occurring outside the family. From these dimensions, the following three subtypes of batterers have been formulated: family-only, dysphoric/borderline, and generally violent/antisocial, with increasing levels of psychopathology, severity/frequency of partner violence, and generality of violence outside the family.

Implications for intervention have been developed from these typologies. The family-only type of batterer, comprising about half of community samples of violent men, is characterized by intermittent and less severe abuse with family members. The family-only type may benefit from the traditional type of intervention currently mandated for all batterers: cognitive-behavioral treatment to include communication skills, problem-solving, anger management, and assertiveness training. Couples counseling may also be beneficial for the family-only type of batterer. Legal interventions are likely to be effective; since these men tend to hold jobs, the threat of arrest is a deterrent for further violence.

The second classification, the dysphoric/borderline type, characterizes about 25% of community populations of maritally violent men. These men inflict moderate to severe abuse mainly on partners, although violence and criminal behavior outside the family may also be evident. These men are typified by depression, psychological distress, and emotionally instability, and may also demonstrate substance abuse problems. Cognitive-behavioral interventions for this type of violent man would have to be more intensive and of longer duration, and rigid sex-role beliefs and attitudes would require additional targeting. Substance abuse treatment might also be indicated. Further, a psychodynamic approach may be employed to address interpersonal problems. Although legal interventions may not act as a deterrent for violence, sanctions may motivate treatment attendance.

The third type of maritally violent man is the generally violent/antisocial batterers, representing the remaining 25%. These men engage in moderate to severe marital violence, as well as extrafamilial aggression, and have a history of criminal behavior and legal involvement. They are also likely to have substance abuse problems and to present with antisocial personality disorder. For the antisocial subtype, intervention might best be restricted to severe legal sanctions. The authors suggest that psychological intervention could possibly expose the partner to further risk, since it may raise her hopes about the possibility of rehabilitation.

While this conceptual schema needs to be subjected to empirical testing, similar multidimensional classificatory schema for battered women and couples with clear treatment implications would be an invaluable asset to the field. Rather than an either-or approach being taken to couples or separate-gender treatment, a continuum of battering relationships in all likelihood exists, with some that might benefit from couples counseling and others that do not.

Another way in which populations may not be homogeneous involves whether the batterers' violence has come to the attention of law enforcement. Cases in which violent men have been mandated to attend counseling might represent a more extreme end of abusive behavior in terms of severity, frequency, or both. The difference might also be in the characteristics of a victim who is more willing to call police when violence does occur or when she feels threatened. Men whose violence has not come to the attention of the authorities are more likely to present in couples conjoint counseling than in men's anger control groups. Anger control groups are more likely to contain court-ordered samples, or in rarer cases, men whose partners have either left or have threatened to leave unless they attend. Before this level of severity is reached, couples counseling is probably more often attempted at earlier stages. Couples therapists therefore serve an important screening function. As Aldarondo and Straus (1994) point out, there are many reasons why couples may fail to reveal the occurrence of violence: A woman may fear retribution or punishment; the couple may view the violence as unrelated to the presenting problem or merely asymptomatic of their underlying problems; and/or the couple may, in the interest of self-enhancement, want to present themselves in a positive light and avoid exposing themselves and other family members to possible shame and public condemnation. Therefore, those who work with couples need to be sensitized and be able to assess for the presence of family violence (Aldarondo & Straus, 1994). In cases where violence is present, the couples therapist may need to assist the female partner in formulating a safety plan, which would include calling upon law enforcement in crisis situations, and make appropriate referrals. No empirical work has yet been performed on couples who voluntarily seek conjoint work for family violence before it has reached the attention of the courts. It is unknown how the treatment needs of this population differ from that of court-mandated samples.

Another area worthy of future inquiry is a close examination of relationships in which violence has been overcome (Hansen, 1993). When reviewing family violence treatment outcomes, Tolman and Edleson (1995) report that long-term recidivism of men who attend treatment is approximately equal to that of men in the community who do not receive treatment. The characteristics of these couples and the individuals who comprise them are important to understand so this knowledge can be applied to other relationships in need of assistance.

A final area needing more attention in the empirical literature is not only couples treatment, but interventions for the whole family in which violence has occurred. In a review of the effects on children who witness domestic violence, Kolbo et al. (1996) cite that between 3 million and 10 million children see violence perpetrated against their mothers by intimate partners. Such children often suffer from behavioral problems, such as aggression and antisocial disorders, and emotional problems, such as depression and anxiety, and may also be impacted in social and cognitive domains (Kolbo et al., 1996; Margolin, 1998). Given these serious consequences on children, authors have proposed interventions for child witnesses (Jaffe, Wolfe, & Wilson, 1990). Many of these involve group treatment, and there have been some empirical efforts in this area (e.g., Wager & Rodway, 1995). However, no family interventions have been empirically tested. A treatment outcome literature has begun to develop in the sexual abuse field that may inform interventions for battered women and their children. Although sexual abuse involves perpetration by a parental figure on a child rather than between intimate partners, there are some similarities in terms of boundary violations and harm between family members (Geffner et al., 1995). Cognitive-behavioral treatment has proved effective in individual, group, and conjoint settings for sexual abuse victims and their nonoffending caretakers (e.g., Cohen & Mannarino, 1996; Deblinger, Lippmann, & Steer, 1996). Interventions may be adapted for use with women victims and child witnesses of domestic violence. The clinical literature speaks to the motivation battered women may have to leave a relationship, not for themselves, but for the impact they see it has on their children. Interventions that include both mothers and their children may bolster women's motivation to protect both themselves and their families.

This review and critique indicates that if couples interventions are to become a viable option in the treatment of family violence, the empirical and theoretical evidence needs to be strengthened. While more recent interventions are to be commended for attending to the safety needs of the victim (e.g., Brannen & Rubin, 1996; Johannson & Tutty, 1998), the cost-effectiveness of these efforts must be taken into account when considering the appropriateness of couples treatment. Comparison studies with different populations of batterers and their partners undergoing different types of treatment would continue to enhance knowledge-building in this area.

REFERENCES

Aldarondo, E., & Straus, M. A. (1994). Screening for physical violence in couple therapy: Methodological, practical, and ethical consideration. *Family Process, 33*, 425–436.

Avis, J. M. (1992). Where are all the family therapists? Abuse and violence within families and family therapy's response. *Journal of Marital and Family Therapy, 18*, 225–232.

Bograd, M. (1992). Values in conflict: Challenges to family therapists' thinking. *Journal of Marital and Family Therapy, 18*, 245–256.

Brannen, S. J., & Rubin, A. (1996). Comparing the effectiveness of gender-specific and couples groups in a court-mandated spouse abuse treatment program. *Research on Social Work Practice, 6*, 405–424.

Cohen, J. A., & Mannarino, A. P. (1996). A treatment outcome study for sexually abused preschool children: Initial findings. *Journal of the American Academy of Child and Adolescent Psychiatry, 35*, 835.

Cook, D. R., & Frantz-Cook, A. (1984). A systemic treatment approach to wife battering. *Journal of Marital and Family Therapy, 10*, 83–93.

Corcoran, J. (1999). A continuum of the duration and chronicity of woman battering: A solution-focused application. *Crisis Intervention and Time-Limited Treatment.*

Deblinger, E., Lippmann, J., & Steer, R. (1996). Sexually abused children suffering posttraumatic stress symptoms: Initial treatment outcome findings. *Child Maltreatment, 1*, 310–321.

Deschner, J. P. (1984). *The hitting habit: Anger control for battering couples.* New York: Free Press.

Deschner, J. P., & McNeil, J. S. (1986). Results of anger control training for battering couples. *Journal of Family Violence, 1*, 111–120.

Deschner, J. P., McNeil, J. S., & Moore, M. G. (1986). News and views: A treatment model for batterers. *Social Casework: The Journal of Contemporary Social Work*, 55–60.

Eisikovits, Z., & Edleson, J. (1989, September). Intervening with men who batter: A critical review of the literature. *Social Service Review*, 384–413.

Eisikovits, Z. C., Edleson, J. L., Guttmann, E., & Sela-Amit, M. (1995). Cognitive styles and socialized attitudes of men who batter: Where should we intervene? In S. M Smith & M. S. Straus (Eds.), *Understanding partner violence* (pp. 69–76). Minneapolis: National Council on Family Relations.

Falicov, C. J. (1996). Mexican families. In M. McGoldrick, J. Giordano, & J. K. Pearce (Eds.), *Ethnicity and family therapy* (pp. 169–182). New York: Guilford Press.

Flynn, C. P. (1995). Understanding partner violence: Prevalence, causes, consequences, and solutions. In S. M. Stith & M. A. Straus (Eds.), *Understanding partner violence: Prevalence, causes, consequences, and solutions* (pp. 51–57). Minneapolis: National Council on Family Relations.

Geffner, R., Barrett, M. J., & Rossman, B. B. (1995). Domestic violence and sexual abuse: Multiple systems perspectives. In R. H. Mikesell, D. Lusterman, & S. H. McDaniel (Eds.), *Integrating family therapy: Handbook of family psychology and systems theory* (pp. 501–517). Washington, DC: American Psychological Association.

Geller, J. A. (1998). Conjoint therapy for the treatment of partner abuse: Indications and contraindications. In A. R. Roberts (Ed.), *Battered women and their families: Intervention strategies and treatment programs* (pp. 76–96). New York: Springer.

Gelles, R. J., & Maynard, P. E. (1987). A structural family systems approach to intervention in cases of family violence. *Family Relations, 36*, 270–275.

Greene, G. J., Lee, M., Trask, R., & Rheinscheld, J. (1996). Client strengths and crisis intervention: A solution-focused approach. *Crisis Intervention, 3*, 43–63.

Grusznski, R. J., Brink, J. C., & Edleson, J. L. (1988). Support and education groups for children of battered women. *Child Welfare, 67*, 431–443.

Hansen, M. (1993). Feminism and family therapy: A review of feminist critiques of approaches to family violence. In M. Hansen & M. Harway (Eds.), *Battering and family therapy* (pp. 69–81). Newbury Park, CA: Sage.

Hansen, M., & Goldenberg, I. (1993). Conjoint therapy with violent couples: Some valid considerations. In M. Hansen & M. Harway (Eds.), *Battering and family therapy: A feminist perspective* (pp. 82–92). Newbury Park, CA: Sage.

Harris, J. (1986). Counseling violent couples using Walker's model. *Psychotherapy, 23*, 613–621.

Ho, K. (1987). *Family therapy with ethnic minorities.* Newbury Park, CA: Sage.

Jaffe, P. G., Wolfe, D. A., & Wilson, S. K. (1990). Children of battered women. *Developmental Clinical Psychology and Psychiatry, 21*, 85–127.

Jennings, J. P., & Jennings, J. L. (1991). Multiple approaches to the treatment of violent couples. *American Journal of Family Therapy, 19*, 351–361.

Johannson, M. A., & Tutty, L. M. (1998). An evaluation of after-treatment couples' groups for wife abuse. *Family Relations, 47*, 27–36.

Kolbo, J. R., Blakely, E. H., & Engleman, D. (1996). Children who witness comestic violence: A review of empirical literature. *Journal of Interpersonal Violence, 11*, 281–293.

Magill, J., & Werk, A. (1985). A treatment model for marital violence. *The Social Worker, 53*(2), 61–63.

Margolin, G. (1998). Effects of domestic violence on children. In P. Trickett & C. Schellenbach (Eds.), *Violence against children in the family and the community* (pp. 57–101). Washington, DC: American Psychological Association.

Neidig, P. H. (1986). The development and evaluation of a spouse abuse treatment program in a military setting. *Evaluation and Program Planning, 9*, 275–280.

Neidig, P. H., & Friedman, D. H. (1984). *Spouse abuse: A treatment program for couples*. Champaign, IL: Research Press.

Rynerson, B. C., & Fishel, A. H. (1993). Domestic violence prevention training: Participant characteristics and treatment outcomes. *Journal of Family Violence, 8*, 253–276.

Sexton, T. L. (1994). Systemic thinking in a linear world: Issues in the application of interactional counseling. *Journal of Counseling and Development, 72*, 249–258.

Sirles, E. A., Lipchik, E., & Kowalski, K. (1993). A consumer's perspective on domestic violence interventions. *Journal of Family Violence, 8*, 267–276.

Straus, M. A. (1995). Trends in cultural norms and rates of partner violence: An update to 1992. In S. M. Stith & M. A. Straus (Eds.), *Understanding partner violence: Prevalence, causes, consequences, and solutions* (pp. 30–33). Minneapolis: National Council on Family Relations.

Stuart, G., & Holtzworth-Munroe, A. (1995). Identifying subtypes of maritally violent men: Descriptive dimensions, correlates and causes of violence, and treatment implications. In S. Stith, & M. Strauss (Eds.). *Understanding Partner Violence: Prevalence, Cause, Consequences, & Solutions* (pp. 162–172). Minneapolis, MN: National Council on Family Relations.

Taylor, J. W. (1984). Structured conjoint therapy for spouse abuse cases. *Social Casework, 65*, 11–18.

Tolman, R. M., & Edleson, J. L. (1995). Interventions for men who batter: A review of research. In S. M. Stith & M. A. Straus (Eds.), *Understanding partner violence: Prevalence, causes, consequences, and solutions* (pp. 262–274). Minneapolis: National Council on Family Relations.

U.S. Department of Justice (1995). Women usually victimized by offenders they know. Bureau of Justice Statistics. http://www.ojp.usdoj.gov

Wager, J. M., & Rodway, M. R. (1995). An evaluation of a group treatment for children who have witnessed wife abuse. *Journal of Family Violence, 10*(3), 295–306.

Walker, L. E. A. (1979). *The battered woman*. New York: Harper & Row.

Weitzman, J., & Dreen, K. (1982). Wife beating: A view of the marital dyad. *Social Casework: The Journal of Contemporary Social Work, 63*, 259–265.

Willbach, D. (1989). Ethics and family therapy: The case management of family violence. *Journal of Marital and Family Therapy, 15*, 43–52.

MEASUREMENT OF FAMILY TREATMENT
WITH FAMILY VIOLENCE

Increasingly, practitioners are held accountable for the evaluation of their practice. To assist with evaluation, this section provides the reader with self-report instruments that children and their families can easily complete. Scores from these measurement instruments can be used to guide assessment, clinical practice, and research with families who have experienced violence between partners. Instruments to assess the level of violence abuse are presented, as well as those assessing marital adjustment. Although the empirical work in the family treatment of family violence is primarily focused on couples, children may also be assessed for the impact of witnessing such violence. The interested reader may refer to Chapter One Family Treatment with Child Abuse and Neglect for the use of relevant instruments for children.

Measures presented in this section involve the following criteria. First, instruments are self-report; that is, they are completed by family members themselves, rather than being interviewer-administered or observational measures. A second criterion for inclusion was that adequate reliability and validity information had to be available for each scale. Selected psychometric data were chosen to inform the reader of the properties of the instruments.

ASSESSMENT OF VIOLENCE

REVISED CONFLICT TACTICS SCALES

Author: Straus, Hamby, Boney-McCoy, & Sugarman (1996)

Description:

- 78-item self-report measuring psychological and physical attacks on a partner, as well as the use of negotiation, in a marital, cohabiting, or dating relationship
- Items are asked in form of questions (what the participant did and what the partner did)
- Sixth-grade reading level
- Following scales included:
  1. physical assault
  2. psychological aggression
  3. negotiation
  4. injury
  5. sexual coercion

Reliability:

- Internal consistency reliabilities for scales: physical assault (.86); psychological aggression (.79); negotiation (.86); injury (.95); sexual coercion (.87)

Validity:

- Only preliminary evidence of construct validity (correlates of sexual coercion, relation of assault to injury, psychological aggression and physical assault, relationships with social integration)
- Only preliminary evidence of discriminant validity (negotiation and sexual coercion and negotiation and injury not correlated)

MARITAL ADJUSTMENT

THE MARITAL ADJUSTMENT TEST

Authors: Locke & Wallace (1959)

Description:

- 15-item self-report measuring adjustment defined as the accommodation of partners to each other

Reliability:

- Internal consistency of .90

Validity:

- Discriminates between distressed and nondistressed couples as assessed by clinical judgments
- A correlation of .47 with Locke-Wallace Marital Prediction Test

DYADIC ADJUSTMENT SCALE

Author: Spanier (1976)

Description:

- A 32-item self-report inventory measuring marital adjustment
- Four subscales:
  1. Dyadic Consensus (agreement regarding marital issues)
  2. Dyadic Cohesion (extent to which partners are involved in joint activities)
  3. Dyadic Satisfaction (overall evaluation of relationship and level of commitment)
  4. Affectional Expression (extent of affection and sexual involvement)

Reliability:

- Adequate internal-consistency reliability for the total scale (.96) and for each of the subscales, ranging from .73 to .94

Validity:

- Discriminates between married and divorced couples
- Correlates with Locke-Wallace Marital Adjustment Scale ($r = .86$)

O'LEARY-PORTER SCALE

Authors: Porter & O'Leary (1980)

Description:

- A 20-item parent-completed questionnaire assessing the frequency of various forms of overt marital hostility (e.g., quarrels, sarcasms, and physical abuse) witnessed by the child

Reliability:

- Test-retest (2-week) reliability of 14 families—.96

Validity:

- Correlation between this scale and Short Marital Adjustment Test—.63

PERSONAL ADJUSTMENT

SYMPTOM CHECKLIST 90—REVISED

Author: Derogatis (1977)

Description:

- A 90-item self-report inventory with ratings along a 5-point scale ("not at all"/ "extremely")
- Assesses nine dimensions of symptomatology: Somatization, Obsessive-Compulsive, Interpersonal Sensitivity, Depression, Anxiety, Hostility, Phobic Anxiety, Paranoid Ideation, and Psychoticism
- Also yields three global indices of distress: Global Severity Index (combines information numbers of symptoms and intensity of distress), Positive Symptom Total, and Positive Symptom Distress Index
- Widely used (700 published studies used this scale) [Derogatis (1993)]

Reliability:

- Alpha values for nine symptom dimensions range from .77 to .90
- Test-retest reliability ranges from .78 to .90

Validity:

- Demonstrates that the SCL-90-R is sensitive to change
- Correlates with other well-known measures of psychological functioning such as the MMPI

BRIEF SYMPTOM INVENTORY

Authors: Derogatis (1993)

Description:

- A briefer, 54-item version of the SCL-90-R
- Primary symptom dimensions:
  1. Somatization
  2. Obsessive-compulsive
  3. Interpersonal sensitivity

  4. Depression
  5. Anxiety
  6. Hostility
  7. Phobic anxiety
  8. Paranoid ideation
  9. Psychoticism
- 3 global indices:
  1. Global Severity Index
  2. Positive Symptom Total
  3. Positive Symptom Distress Index
- 0–4 ("not at all," "a little bit," "moderately," "quite a bit," and "extremely")
- Widely used (200 published studies used this scale) [Derogatis (1993)]

Reliability:

- Alpha coefficients are strong, ranging from .71 to .85
- Test-retest (2 weeks) reliabilities ranged from .68 to .91, with reliability for the Global Severity Index at .90

Validity:

- High convergence between scales of Brief Symptom Inventory and the MMPI
- High correlations (ranging from .92 to .99) between Brief Symptom Inventory and Symptom Checklist 90—Revised
- A factor analysis provided support for construct validation
- Evidence for predictive validity in that the measure has been demonstrated as an effective screening devise across many varied medical settings
- Further evidence for predictive validity in that psychological distress was predicted in cancer populations, individuals with psychopathology, individuals experiencing problems with pain management, in HIV research, in student mental health, and in general clinical studies, and to predict efficacy of therapeutic interventions

BECK DEPRESSION INVENTORY

Authors: Beck, Rush, Shaw, & Emery (1979); Beck, Ward, Mendelson, Mock, & Erbaugh (1961) [Review data on psychometric information by Beck, Steer, & Garbin (1988)]

Description:

- 21 items, measuring symptoms and attitudes of depression, rated from 0–3 in terms of intensity
- Also a short version (13 items), which correlates highly (.89 to .97) with long form although may only represent cognitively oriented symptoms rather than both cognitive and noncognitive
- Written at a fifth- to sixth-grade reading level
- Different time frames that may be ascertained
- Has been used in 1,000 research studies

Reliability:

- Mean coefficient alpha for nine psychiatric samples is .86
- Mean coefficient alpha for 15 nonpsychiatric samples is .81
- Test-retest reliability ranged from .48 to .86 for psychiatric patients and .60 to .83 for nonpsychiatric patients

Validity:

- Mean correlation coefficients between clinical ratings and the Beck Depression Inventory for psychiatric patients was .72 and for nonpsychiatric patients was .60
- Mean correlation coefficients between Hamilton Psychiatric Rating Scale for Depression and the Beck Depression Inventory for 5 psychiatric studies was .73 and for the 2 nonpsychiatric patients was .73 and .80, respectively
- Mean correlation coefficients between the Zung Self-Reported Depression Scale and the Beck Depression Inventory for 8 psychiatric studies was .76 and for the 5 nonpsychiatric patients was .71
- Mean correlation coefficients between the MMPI Depression Scale and the Beck Depression Inventory for 7 psychiatric studies was .76 and for the 3 nonpsychiatric patients was .60
- Several studies have indicated that the measure discriminates between normals and psychiatric patients and psychiatric and nonpsychiatric samples
- Construct validity has been demonstrated with selected attitudes and behaviors, such as biological correlates, suicidal behaviors, alcohol problems, adjustment, medical symptoms, stress, and anxiety

REFERENCES FOR MEASUREMENT OF FAMILY TREATMENT WITH FAMILY VIOLENCE

Beck, A., Rush, A., Shaw, B., & Emery, G. (1979). *Cognitive therapy of depression.* New York: Guilford Press.

Beck, A., Ward, C., Mendelson, M., Mock, J., & Erbaugh, J. (1961). An inventory for measuring depression. *Archives of General Psychiatry, 4,* 53–63.

Beck, A. T., Steer, R. A., & Garbin, M. G. (1988). Psychometric properties of the Beck Depression Inventory: Twenty-five years of evaluation. *Clinical Psychology Review, 8,* 77–100.

Derogatis, L. (1977). *The SCL-90R: Administration and scoring procedures manual.* Baltimore: Clinical Psychometric Research.

Derogatis, L. (1993). *Brief Symptom Inventory: Administration, scoring, and procedures manual.* Minneapolis: National Computer Systems.

Locke, H. J., & Wallace, K. M. (1959). Short marital-adjustment and prediction tests: Their reliability and validity. *Journal of Marriage and Family Living, 21,* 251–255.

Porter, B., & O'Leary, D. (1980). Marital discord and childhood behavior problems. *Journal of Abnormal Child Psychology, 8,* 287–295.

Spanier, G. B. (1976). Measuring dyadic adjustment: New scales for assessing the quality of marriage and similar dyads. *Journal of Marriage and the Family, 15–28.*

Straus, M., Hamby, S., Boney-McCoy, S., & Sugarman, D. (1996). The Revised Conflict Tactics Scales (CTS2). *Journal of Family Issues, 17,* 283–316.

CHAPTER 11

Family Treatment with Schizophrenia

---

with Jane Harakal Phillips

Family Case:

Mitch is a 23-year-old male. He and his family have experienced multiple approaches to treating his illness over the past few years. He is the second oldest of three children. His father works the night shift at the local automobile manufacturing plant, and his mother is a homemaker. An older sister is married and lives in another state. His younger brother lives with Mitch and his parents. His parents describe his early childhood as uneventful with no significant trauma.

Mitch's first signs of schizophrenia occurred when he was 19, but he had been deteriorating for about 2 years prior to that time. Throughout his childhood and early adolescence, Mitch and his father would talk about Mitch's future and the likelihood that he would be the first in the family to attend college. However, by 11th grade, Mitch began to have trouble in school and in relationships with his peers.

During this time, Mitch's parents first brought him for mental health treatment, although he was against it. They were told that Mitch was simply going through a period of adolescent rebellion and everything would be okay. Nevertheless, after 5 months of treatment, there was still no change and he declined further intervention. There were several more treatment efforts, including a series of group sessions after Mitch had attempted suicide. When no improvement was evident, he again discontinued treatment. Eighteen months later, Mitch experienced his first psychotic episode, characterized by hallucinations and extreme withdrawal. He was hospitalized and diagnosed with paranoid schizophrenia. Several antipsychotic drugs in various dosages were tried, and he was involved in group therapy as well as individual therapy. He was released after a brief hospital stay.

Mitch made two more suicide attempts, and his parents reported despairing that they would be able to keep him alive. They were overwhelmed by their attempts to care for Mitch and thought he should be trying harder to improve. At the end of this time, Mitch moved out of his parents' home and was gone for about 14 months, during which time he had no contact with his family. The family was worried about what was happening to him, yet at the same time they were relieved that there was some peace and order in the home. Mitch's family then received a call from the local police department saying that Mitch had been living in a shelter for the homeless and was in need of psychiatric care. His parents picked him up at the police station and had him committed to a public psychiatric hospital against his wishes. It was at this time that the family became involved in an intervention that included Mitch as well as his parents.

According to the DSM-IV (American Psychiatric Association, 1994), schizophrenia is a disorder characterized by "delusions, hallucinations, disordered speech, grossly disorganized or catatonic behavior, and/or negative symptoms" (p. 285). Positive symptoms tend to represent distortions or excesses of normal demeanor, including delusions and hallucinations (APA, 1994; Farmer, Walsh, & Bentley, 1998; Leff, 1996), whereas negative symptoms tend to appear as a reduction in normal functioning, such as "apathy, inertia, social withdrawal, paucity of speech and lack of emotion" (Leff, 1996, p. 264). Although onset might occur as young as 5 or 6 years of age, or as late as the mid-40s, the usual age of onset is between 15 and 29 years (APA, 1994). Onset in males occurs slightly earlier (late teens) than in females, who are likely to experience their first episode in their early 20s.

Due to the chronic nature of the disorder, prevalence rates are typically based on the number of new cases or cases under treatment, during a given time period (Norquist, Regier, & Rupp, 1996). It is estimated that the United States has an annual prevalence rate of approximately 0.5% to 1%, with similar prevalence rates occurring in most other parts of the world (APA, 1994). In numerical terms, it is estimated that 2.74 million adults and 770,000 children age 17 and under exhibit active schizophrenic symptoms or have been in treatment for the disorder during the past year (Norquist et al., 1996). Although complete remission of schizophrenia rarely occurs, the course does not necessarily worsen over one's lifetime; it is generally considered variable, with periods of exacerbation and remission (Farmer et al., 1998).

As the trend toward deinstitutionalization of psychiatric patients continues, schizophrenia increasingly becomes a disorder that affects the family as well as the individual; it is not uncommon for a schizophrenia patient to rely on family members for housing and caretaking (Leff, 1996). Due to the nature of the illness, with its attendant characteristics of confusion and distortion of reality, the family may experience a variety of consequences in the home: Interactions between nonschizophrenic family members and an identified patient may be emotionally charged (Leff, 1996; Leff et al., 1989, 1990; Nugter, Dingemans, Van der Does, Linszen, & Gersons, 1997), there may be denial of the illness or unrealistic expectations for the patient (Randolph et al., 1994), or family members may experience anxiety and a sense of vulnerability from living with a schizophrenic relative (Anderson, Reiss, & Hogarty, 1986). The negative symptoms of schizophrenia often cause the most distress in relationships between patients and family members; patients exhibiting negative symptoms are often mistakenly considered unmotivated or lazy (Anderson et al., 1986).

Zubin and Spring (1977) proposed a vulnerability-stress model as an explanation for the onset of a psychotic episode in patients with schizophrenia. According to this model, individuals who have a biological predisposition toward schizophrenia, when exposed to environmental stressors, exceed their coping capacities and experience psychotic breaks. The integration of biological and environmental influences are presumed to be inextricably related.

The concept of expressed emotion (EE) as a predictor of relapse grew out of the vulnerability-stress model. Expressed emotion is defined as the level of emotional involvement family members have with one another, including the amount of hostility and dominance displayed (Brown, Monck, Carstairs, & Wing, 1962). In a study of patients hospitalized for long periods of time, Brown et al. (1962) discovered that those patients who were discharged into the care of parents or spouses had much higher rates of relapse or rehospitalization than those who were discharged to live alone, with siblings, or with a nonrelative roommate or landlord. It was also found that patients with less family contact actually had more rapid recoveries than those patients who had more family contact (Hooley, 1986). Upon examination of these findings, and with further study, it was determined that patients who had extensive contact with other family members and whose family households exhibited high levels of criticism and hostility, overinvolvement, and lack of warmth (characteristics of high expressed emotion) also experienced higher rates of relapse than patients in families without these characteristics, or in which they were minimized (Hooley, 1986; Leff, 1996).

With the role of the family in predicting the potential for psychotic episodes, one may be tempted to hold family members responsible for an individual's illness. In fact, first attempts to provide psychotherapeutic care for schizophrenic patients and their families seemed to implicate the patient's parents or family of origin as the primary cause of the illness, and, therefore, the focus of treatment. Bateson, Jackson, Haley, and Weakland (1956), building on communications theory, suggested that people with schizophrenia often find themselves in double-bind situations. The double bind represents a series of events beginning with a parent issuing a negative injunction, which, if not honored, results in the child's punishment. The child is then given another injunction in conflict with the first, and, therefore, is forced to violate either of the parent's demands in order to carry out the other. For example, the parent might instruct the child to do something the child finds very unpleasant, such as visiting a grandparent who is dying (first injunction). The parent might then tell the child s/he must not feel sad about the visit or about losing the grandparent to death (second injunction). Presumably, the child subsequently develops a defensive stance vis-à-vis the parent and begins to respond to double-bind situations indirectly or metaphorically, as a way of preserving safety; if no direct answer is given in response to a question or request, the child might reason, negative consequences can be avoided. For instance, in the case of the dying grandparent, if the parent asks the child if s/he is sad about the situation, the child might respond by talking about someone stepping on bugs, rather than specifically talking about the death of a grandparent.

Bateson et al.'s (1956) theory placed considerable emphasis on the mother-child relationship as the cause of schizophrenia in the child. Treatment consisted of establishing therapeutic *double binds*. Bateson and his colleagues provide, as an example of this form of therapy, a description of an encounter with a schizophrenia patient who has constructed an elaborate religion for herself, which includes several gods. At the beginning of therapy, the patient tells the psychiatrist that she must consult with one of the gods about proceeding with the session and the psychiatrist informs the patient that he does not believe in the gods, so therapy must continue without their assistance; he then instructs the patient to tell the gods that they have not helped her for the 9 years that she has been ill and that the doctor would like a chance to help. The double bind occurs in that the patient must engage with the psychiatrist by admitting doubt in her gods and her willingness to accept therapy. However, if she continues to insist that her gods are real, she must inform the gods that the psychiatrist is more powerful than they are, which demonstrates her engagement in therapy.

Research has since shown, however, that the antecedents of schizophrenia are much more complex. Liberman (1986), in reviewing the research, points to a multitude of nonspecific stressors, such as household tension or employment difficulties, in interaction with specific psychobiological responses, such as exacerbation of psychotic symptoms or depression, as the etiological framework for understanding schizophrenia. Certainly, the family may be a source of stress, as well as support, and it is in this context that family intervention may be seen as beneficial to the patient as well as to family members. Whereas researchers previously viewed family communication patterns as the cause of schizophrenia, and changing these patterns as the cure (e.g. Bateson et al., 1956), now the focus of intervention is on developing coping strategies for family members, decreasing emotional tension in the home, increasing the patient's medication compliance in an effort to control symptoms, and preventing relapse, without the expectation of a cure.

EMPIRICAL RESEARCH ON FAMILY INTERVENTIONS IN THE TREATMENT OF SCHIZOPHRENIA

Family interventions with schizophrenia take one of two general approaches. The intervention may include several families in a psychoeducation or support group, or it may take the form of single family therapy. Research with these two approaches has focused on both individual characteristics of the person suffering from schizophrenia, as well as outcomes for the family as a whole. There has been a proliferation of research in the field since the 1980s, and the body of literature has grown to be quite expansive; several outstanding reviews of previous research exist (e.g. Dixon & Lehman, 1995; Gingerich & Bellack, 1995; Lam, 1991). The present review, therefore, focuses on more recent studies addressing only those published 1985 or later. Further, only treatment studies reporting empirical data and those published in referred journals are included. Similar to the previous reviews, interventions will concentrate on those that involve parents or other family members, rather than treatment solely focused on the person with schizophrenia.

The present chapter will address the two broad categories of interventions, multifamily groups and those that address single families. Then, within each of these categories, outcomes relating to the individual with schizophrenia and those relating to the family as a whole will be discussed. The chapter will conclude by discussion of limitations of the current research and recommendations for future studies.

MULTIFAMILY GROUP INTERVENTIONS

Multifamily group interventions may take one of two theoretical approaches to working with participants, and are generally considered either psychoeducational (Abramowitz & Coursey, 1989; Anderson et al., 1986; Cañive et al., 1993, 1996; Hugen, 1993; Kane, DiMartino, & Jiminez, 1990; McFarlane, Link, Dushay, Marchal, & Crilly, 1995; McFarlane et al., 1995; Posner, Wilson, Kral, Lander, & Mcllwraith, 1992; Reilly, Rohrbaugh, & Lackner, 1988; Smith & Birchwood, 1987; Solomon, Draine, Mannion, & Meisel, 1996, 1997) or supportive (Kane et al., 1990) in their focus. Some groups may encompass both aspects of intervention.

The goal of family psychoeducation for patients with schizophrenia is to convey information about the illness to the family in an effort to provide them with realistic expectations (Anderson et al., 1986). Posner et al. (1992) emphasize the need to teach families about theories of schizophrenia, potential side effects of medication, stress as a possible antecedent to the exacerbation of symptoms, and the availability of community resources. It is important that they be prepared to deal with concerns and situations as they may arise. As well as information about the expected course of the illness, Anderson et al. (1986) have developed a framework for psychoeducation that incorporates an understanding of the family's emotional responses to schizophrenia, including guilt, embarrassment, anger, and a myriad of other emotions; and a consideration of family strengths.

For example, one particular family strength might be the existence of a large and compassionate social network which is able to provide respite care for their ill relative when the tasks of providing care become temporarily overwhelming. Whether psychoeducation is used with groups of families, or with individual families, with the identified patient present, or in the patient's absence, many of the components remain the same (Anderson et al., 1986; McFarlane, Link et al., 1995; McFarlane, Lukens, et al., 1995).

Another important feature of multifamily group therapy involves the benefits of group processes and dynamics in relieving burden and stress, in improving coping mechanisms for those families with a schizophrenic member, and in providing information about available resources for the patient and family. These support functions may be integral to the sustenance of families coping with the chronicity of schizophrenia, particularly in terms of reducing stigma, allowing for cross-parenting within a group (sharing parenting skills and ideas), and normalizing communication (McFarlane et al., 1995).

Several research efforts have focused on the effectiveness of particular multifamily group interventions in improving individual and family functioning in families where at least one member of the household has been diagnosed with schizophrenia. Individual outcome measures have included relapse and rehospitalization rates, work-related activities, and medication compliance. Measures of family outcomes have focused on an increased knowledge of schizophrenia, coping behaviors, subjective distress or burden, self-efficacy, social support, depression, grief, family conflict as exhibited through expressed emotion (EE) constructs, and self-blame for a relative's illness (*see* Table 11.1).

INDIVIDUAL PATIENT OUTCOMES WITH MULTIFAMILY GROUP THERAPY

Relapse Rates

Several measures of relapse have been used to discern the effectiveness of various family group interventions. Hugen (1993) defined relapse as hospitalization, or changes in symptomatology and social functioning as reported by significant others. McFarlane, Link, et al. (1995) identified relapse as "the re-emergence of major psychotic, schizophrenic symptoms that had persisted continuously for a minimum of 7 days . . ." (p. 135). Posner et al. (1992), Reilly et al. (1988), and Schooler et al. (1997) used rehospitalization as a measure of relapse.

In a 4-year longitudinal study, McFarlane, Lukens, and colleagues (1995) attempted to isolate the components of intervention that produce the greatest benefits for patients and families. When controlling for other factors, they found that the multifamily group format appeared to result in the fewest number of relapses. These findings were attributed to the extension of social networks provided by the multiple-family group format, especially as they were able to absorb the distress that occurred during psychotic episodes.

Hugen (1993) found similar results in a study of the effect of a 1-day educational workshop provided for family members of schizophrenia patients. Three months after the workshop, a significant number of family members reported reduced conflict in the home, as well as a lower rate of hospitalization for the patient during the 3 months following the intervention than during the 3 months prior to the intervention.

Caution must be exercised when interpreting hospitalization as a measure of relapse rates and, therefore, a measure of the success of an intervention. As Hugen (1993) notes, "hospitalization is to some degree a function of family coping abilities and is used frequently as a supportive respite for family members themselves" (p. 149). Another possibly confounding variable in the identification of hospitalization as a measure of relapse involves the financial burden of inpatient hospitalization. In situations where neither public health care nor private insurance is available, the likelihood of hospitalization (despite exacerbation of symptoms) may be significantly reduced because of financial constraints. Therefore, an interaction effect between household affluence and hospitalization rates is likely to occur. Even with this caveat, it is apparent that relapse is reduced or delayed when psychoeducation is part of the patient's therapeutic plan.

Work-related Activities

According to Anderson et al. (1986), people with schizophrenia may encounter many difficulties as they seek or attempt to maintain employment. It is likely that by the time a diagnosis of schizophrenia has been made, the individual has already experienced problems with employment and may fear continuing problems. Due to the disorganized thought processes that may occur with the illness, the patient could experience difficulty in communication or in carrying out the requirements of a job. In terms of vocational rehabilitation, the goal of therapy, then, is to help the individual navigate successfully in the job market. The importance of working in an environment that is stimulating, while not overwhelming, is often emphasized to families and employers as they attempt to help the schizophrenia patient cope with various aspects of employment. Families are in a unique position to empower their family members to learn such things as conflict resolution skills and the importance of personal hygiene, which may go a long way toward improving employment situations (Anderson et al., 1986).

Understanding that work-related activities may be a measure of the effectiveness of family interventions, McFarlane, Lukens, et al (1995), in their 2-year study of multifamily group and single family group interventions, found that patients whose families participated in group psychoeducation fared much better in terms of work-related activities than those patients whose families were involved in individual family psychoeducation. An important factor in the McFarlane, Lukens, et al. (1995) interventions was the absence of the identified patient in family intervention sessions; thus a patient's improvement was seen to be a result of improvement in family functioning.

Medication Compliance

One of the most significant factors in reducing schizophrenic symptomatology is the establishment and maintenance of a therapeutically effective level of medication. It may take time to identify the optimal dose and schedule that will work best for each individual, but once this has been done, compliance

TABLE 11.1 Multifamily Interventions with Schizophrenia

AUTHOR/MODEL	DESIGN/SAMPLE	MEASURES	RESULTS	LIMITATIONS
Abramowitz & Coursey (1989) Educational support group Family members only, no patients Multifamily group	Quasi-experimental, pretest, posttest, follow-up. Nonrandom assignment to experimental and control (medication only) conditions $N = 48$ families Family members: Majority female; majority White Patients: Non-hospitalized sample; 31% African American, majority male	State/Trait Anxiety Inventory: trait form; Relatives' Stress Scale; 9-item scale developed to measure use of community resources; Generalized Self-Efficacy Scale	Experimental group experienced significantly less trait anxiety than the control group	Families were assigned to experimental conditions based on availability of times scheduled: nonrandom; lack of psychometric data on some scales; small sample size
Cañive et al. (1993) Psychoeducation 1 $^{1}/_{2}$ hr classes once a week for 6 weeks Multifamily groups	Pretest, posttest Patient Sample: $N = 45$: 67% male, 33% female; average age of 26; almost all were sin-	McGill assessment instrument designed to measure respondents' knowledge about schizophrenia (translated to Spanish); Symptom	Knowledge about schizophrenia was significantly more after intervention for both mothers and fathers	No comparison or control group; lack of psychometric data on some scales; effect of treatment on patients was not discussed

gle; 67% high school graduates, 36% had at least 1 yr of college; average previous hospitalizations = 3	Checklist-90; scale assessing parents' sense of isolation, guilt, leisure time, and financial hardship as measures of the social impact of the patient's illness; Scale measuring parents' annoyance, modified from Smith and Birchwood's (1987) scale	Subjective distress, perceptions of social impact, annoyance with the patient, and expectations about recovery were not significantly reduced after intervention
Parent Sample: $N = 68$ 40% fathers, 60% mothers; majority married		
Cañive et al. (1996) Follow-up (9-mo) of above authors		24% of patients completing the study relapsed during the follow-up period. Knowledge scores declined somewhat at the follow-up but were still significantly different than the initial scores
Follow-up data were available for 67% of fathers and 59% of mothers		On all measures of subjective distress, mother's scores were significantly higher than fathers' before and after

continued

TABLE 11.1 *(continued)*

AUTHOR/MODEL	DESIGN/SAMPLE	MEASURES	RESULTS	LIMITATIONS
			intervention. The psychoeducational group did not significantly affect subjective distress in mothers or fathers, nor did it affect parents' perceptions of social impact or parents' annoyance with patients' behavior, or parents' expectations for recovery	
Hugen (1993)

Family psychoeducation

One-day workshop for family members only (no patients)

Multifamily group | Pretest, posttest, follow-up (3 mos)

$N = 22$ family members; 64% participants were parents, others were spouses, siblings or children of the patients; 77% female

Mean age of patient = 40; predominantly White; 77% female; 55% of ill relatives were male | Knowledge About Schizophrenia Inventory; Semantic differential scale measuring changes in family attitudes; family members' perception of responsibility for the etiology of schizophrenia; Family Conflict Inventory; relapse rates | Participants gained new information and retained it over a 3-mo period; attitudes toward ill family members did not change significantly; family conflict was lessened; hospitalization rates decreased following intervention; those for whom blame was an issue appeared to accept less blame following intervention | Inadequate psychometric data on instruments; no comparison group; limited information about patients |

Kane et al. (1990) Short Term Psychoeducation Group: four sessions of 2 hrs each; relatives only (no patients) Short Term Multifamily Support Groups: four sessions of 2 hrs each; relatives only (no patients)	Quasi-experimental, pretest, posttest, nonequivalent comparison groups 37 families totaling 49 participants: predominantly White; 55% mothers, 29% fathers, 16% other relatives; Mean age of participants = 49; Mean age of patients = 26; Mean number of prior hospitalizations = 4	Knowledge acquisition measured by the Mental Illness Questionnaire; Perceived Social Support Questionnaire; distress and coping measured by the Family Questionnaire; depression subscale of the Symptom Distress Checklist; Budner's (1962) Intolerance of ambiguity measure; CSQ-8 measure of satisfaction with the group experience	Psychoeducation group reported less depression and greater satisfaction with intervention than the support group Knowledge about schizophrenia improved in both groups	Lack of randomization to conditions; no follow-up; limited information about patients and family members
McFarlane, Lukens et al. (1995) Multifamily group psychoeducation: with no patients present, there were 3 weekly single-family sessions, then an educational Survival Skills workshop was presented to six fami-	Quasi-experimental: pretest, posttest, follow-up with random assignment to groups 172 patients and their families from six sites in northeast U.S.; patient characteristics: 73.3% males, 52.9%	Brief Psychiatric Rating Scale (BPRS) Schedule for the Assessment of Negative Symptoms Dichotomous employment question developed for the present study	When controlling for medication compliance, there were no statistically significant differences in relapse rates for Multifamily group and single-family; the difference in relapse rates increased over time: the Multifamily condition	Insufficient data on family members; insufficient psychometric data on instruments used; lack of information about family members; sample consisted only of patients who were being discharged from a hospital; small sample size

continued

TABLE 11.1 (*continued*)

AUTHOR/MODEL	DESIGN/SAMPLE	MEASURES	RESULTS	LIMITATIONS
lies who then began to meet bi-weekly for a period of 2 yrs	Caucasian, 40.7% African American, 6.4% other; 87.2% never married, 33% high school graduates; 33.7% at least some college; 77.9% unemployed; 82.6% residing with family; mean age at symptom onset = 19.5	Symptomatic, Clinically Significant, and Total Relapse Rates	resulted in significantly fewer relapse episodes during the 2-yr period; there was no difference in hospitalization rates between treatment modalities; overall, the multifamily intervention resulted in extended remission and enhanced functioning when compared to the single-family intervention	
Single-family psychoeducation (SFT): with no patient present		Hollingshead Index		
Minimum of 5 face-to-face contacts by at least one family member		Research Diagnostic Criteria (RDC) used in diagnosing schizophrenia		
Two-yr treatment period				
McFarlane, Link et al. (1995)	Four-yr follow-up of above		Psychoeducational, multifamily groups had the lowest relapse rates; by the end of 4 yrs, 78% of single family group patients had relapsed at least once	

Posner et al. (1992) Family psychoeducational support groups, without patients attending 90-min sessions once a week for 8 weeks	Quasi-experimental pretest, posttest, 6-mo follow-up with random assignment to the treatment condition or the waiting-list control condition Patient sample, $N = 59$: 39 men, 16 women; mean age = 29.1, average of 4.4 previous hospitalizations, average education = 12.1 yrs 21.8% employed Relative sample, $N = 59$: 50.9% mothers, 58.2% lived with the patient	Schizophrenia Knowledge Test; Consumer Satisfaction Questionnaire; Negative Feelings for Patient Questionnaire; Ways of Coping; General Health Questionnaire; psychiatric hospitalizations; Family Satisfaction Scale	Participants in the experimental condition increased their knowledge about schizophrenia; they judged health care services more positively than those in the control group The experimental group did not differ significantly from the control group in terms of changes in coping behavior, family satisfaction, or psychological welfare. Further, relapse rates did not differ between groups	Patients participated in a variety of therapeutic interventions, which were not controlled for in the study; medication types and dosages varied; 29.1% attrition rate

continued

TABLE 11.1 *(continued)*

AUTHOR/MODEL	DESIGN/SAMPLE	MEASURES	RESULTS	LIMITATIONS
Reilly et al. (1988) Multifamily group 2-hr Family Psychoeducation Workshop with patients present 2-hr Family Psychoeducation Workshop with patients absent	Quasi-experimental: pretest, posttest, follow-up (3 to 4 mos). Random invitation to one of four conditions: (1) workshop with patient present, (2) workshop with patient absent, (3) hospital tour only, (4) no contact control group $N = 15$ relatives, 8 patients in condition 1, 12 relatives and 7 patients in condition 2, 6 relatives and 4 patients in condition 3, 19 cases were in the control group Patient sample: mean age = 31, $2/3$ were female, $2/3$ African American, $2/3$ diagnosed with schizophrenia	Patient Rejection Scale designed to measure the criticism element of expressed emotion; items measuring attributions of illness and responsibility, attitudes about mental health care professionals, and workshop satisfaction	There were no differences between groups on measures of outcome: rehospitalization, number of psychiatric crises, continuation of outpatient family therapy; little change from pretest to posttest on measures of attribution; group processes differed when patients were present; participation rates of relatives were lower when patients were present; patients were often disruptive in the workshop; relatives in the patient-present group, in contrast to the patient-absent group rated mental health professionals as significantly more helpful	Inadequate description of samples; no psychometric data provided about measures used; small sample size

	Relative sample: mean age = 50, over 80% were the patient's parent; there were slightly more females	Only patients with frequent family contact were included, possibly excluding older or married patients, so generalizability is limited
Schooler et al. (1997) Compared Applied Family Management (single-family intervention, in-home sessions with and without patient present, 13 sessions) with Supportive Family Management group or the Supportive Family Management group, and within each group, participants were divided into standard dose medication, low dose, or targeted dose 2 yrs	Quasi-experimental: Repeated measures. Stratified random assignment to groups: Patients were randomly assigned to the Applied Family Management (multifamily group meetings 1 1/2 hrs monthly every month during stabilization and maintenance) Assessments of clinical symptoms were made monthly with detailed assessments at 6, 12, 18 and 24 mos while in the maintenance phase, and 20 weeks after the use	*Patients*: Hillside anchored version of the Brief Psychiatric Rating Scale; Modified version of the Scale for Assessment of Negative Symptoms; severity and improvement items from the Clinical Global Impressions; Neurological Rating Scale; Early Signs questionnaire to measure prodromal signs Behavioral Family Therapy Competency Scale assessed clinician's adherence to applied family management components and skills	Mean time to psychotic relapse was 431 days in the Target Dose group and 609 days with the Standard dose group; no significant differences between family intervention groups; rehospitalization occurred in the target dose group in an average of 456 days, and occurred in the low-dose group in an average of 579 days; home visits, communication training, problem solving skills appeared not to have an effect on rehospitalization rates; relatively low doses appeared to be benefi-	Only patients who were clinically stable were included

continued

TABLE·11.1 *(continued)*

AUTHOR/MODEL	DESIGN/SAMPLE	MEASURES	RESULTS	LIMITATIONS
	of rescue medication if it was used		cial to 50% of patients for 2 yrs	
	$N = 313$ patients: 66% male, 40% White, 18% never married, mean age = 29.6			
Smith & Birchwood (1987) Brief family psychoeducation 4 weekly sessions Multifamily group	Quasi-experimental: pretest, posttest, follow-up with random assignment to treatment conditions: educational sessions with a therapist or information booklets with homework assignments, sent to the family's home at weekly intervals $N = 40$ family members of 23 schizophrenic patients. 78% patients were males, with a mean age = 36.4 and mean	Questionnaire designed to measure knowledge acquisition, beliefs about schizophrenia and the treatment of schizophrenia, and worry and fear Symptom-related Behavioural Disturbance Scale Symptom Rating Test	The relatives assigned to the psychoeducation group were more optimistic about the family's role in treatment than those relatives who received educational materials in the mail At the end of treatment, fear about safety was greatly reduced in both groups with no significant differences between groups. At 6 mos, though, the relatives who had received infor-	Length of individual treatment sessions is unknown; lack of psychometric data on some measures; worry, for the cohort that received intervention by mail, was higher at baseline than that of the support group cohort; limited information about family members

	duration of illness = 7.9 yrs, 65% were unmarried	Family Distress Scale	mation in the mail were significantly less fearful than the group relatives; stress in both groups was greatly reduced by the end of treatment but had returned to baseline levels at 7 mos; behavioral disturbances remained constant for both groups; the effect of knowledge acquisition remained at 6 mos	
Solomon et al. (1996) Brief Individualized consultation: 6–15 hrs available for 3 mos Group psychoeducation: 2-hr sessions once a week for 10 weeks	Quasi-experimental: pretest, posttest; random assignment to treatment conditions: individual and family consultation, group family psychoeducation, or 9-mo waiting list (control) *Patients:* 63.5% were diagnosed with schizo-	Pai and Kapur (1981) measure of burden; Norbeck Social Support Questionnaire; adaptation of Scherer et al.'s (1982) self-efficacy scale; Greene et al.'s (1982) measure of stress; Texas Inventory of Grief; Hatfield's self-efficacy scale for coping skills	Significantly greater attrition from the group psychoeducation condition; no differences were found between those who dropped out and those who remained; specific self-efficacy was the only improvement significantly affected by either experimental interventions;	Study included not only patients diagnosed with schizophrenia, but also those diagnosed with a major affective disorder; limited psychometric data on some measures; no follow-up data were reported

continued

TABLE 11.1 *(continued)*

AUTHOR/MODEL	DESIGN/SAMPLE	MEASURES	RESULTS	LIMITATIONS
	phrenia; 33.9% had more than 5 hospitalizations; 36% had been arrested at some time; 11.8% had alcohol problems; 9.5% had drug problems *Family members*: 88% female; 84% White; majority parents; majority middle class		individual consultation compared to group psychoeducation was more effective immediately, though individual consultation requires greater resource expenditures	
Solomon et al. (1997)	Follow-up (6 mos) of above		Both experimental conditions had statistically significant improvement in self-efficacy scores at the end of the intervention and at follow-up. At 6-mo follow-up, there was no statistically significant difference between the intervention groups and the control group	Informal conversations after group meetings were stifled in order to maintain research integrity; coping strategies may have been hindered by reducing opportunities to engage in coping behaviors

with the medication regime is considered to be essential for improvement in the symptoms of schizophrenia (Anderson et al., 1986; Falloon et al., 1985; Glick, Clarkin, Haas, Spencer, & Chen, 1991; Haas et al., 1988; Hogarty et al., 1991; Leff et al., 1989; McFarlane, Link, et al., 1995; McFarlane, Lukens, et al., 1995; Randolph et al., 1994; Schooler et al., 1997).

Although medication compliance should not be the sole measure of the effectiveness of an intervention, it is a critical component in relapse prevention and remission. McFarlane (1994) suggests that psychoeducational family groups may serve to reinforce the importance of proper medication usage, which, in turn, may translate to better compliance and more successful outcomes.

FAMILY OUTCOMES WITH MULTIFAMILY GROUP INTERVENTIONS

Research on the role of family interventions in the treatment of schizophrenia often focuses on outcomes for family members, as well as the identified patient (Abramowitz & Coursey, 1989; Cañive et al., 1993, 1996; Hugen, 1993; Kane et al., 1990; Posner et al., 1992; Smith & Birchwood, 1987; Solomon et al., 1996, 1997). Anderson et al. (1986), when addressing the role of family psychoeducation in the treatment of schizophrenia, aptly point out the catastrophic impact the disease has for family members as well as for the identified patient. Therefore, goals in therapy may go beyond improvement in patient functioning, to include improvement in family functioning.

Knowledge Acquisition

A primary consideration in the family treatment of schizophrenia is the dissemination of information about the illness to the patient and to the family. According to Anderson et al. (1986), psychoeducational interventions should be designed in such a way that family members will gain an understanding of several key themes: The relative's illness has a biological basis; the patient is not responsible for the occurrence of the illness; the situation is not hopeless since new theories about schizophrenia and its treatment are developed regularly; the patient is not in control of the illness and, therefore, is not being lazy or purposefully disagreeable when psychotic; though it is not necessary for relatives to plan their lives around an ill family member, they may alleviate some distress for the patient by decreasing expectations of participation in the life of the family; and the struggles they are facing are not unique to their family alone. Therefore, a key variable in the study of the effectiveness of interventions is the extent to which patients and family members are able to assimilate and retain this information about the illness.

It is relatively common for participants in family psychoeducational groups to have immediate, though perhaps temporary, increases in their knowledge of schizophrenia (Cañive et al., 1993, 1996; Hugen, 1993; Smith & Birchwood, 1987). Interestingly, when comparing psychoeducational groups with support-only groups, Kane et al. (1990) indicated knowledge increased following support-only interventions. Kane et al. (1990) and Posner et al. (1992) found that family members usually had spent many years adapting to life with a schizophrenic relative, and the authors suggested that part of the coping process was the result of being educated by others who had found ways to cope in similar situations.

Expressed Emotion and Family Conflict

As discussed earlier, the vulnerability-stress model of schizophrenia places considerable emphasis on the role of the family in creating or alleviating stress in a patient's life (Zubin & Spring, 1977). Of particular concern is the reduction of expressed emotion; it has been hypothesized that reducing expressed emotion in a household will permit the patient to recover more rapidly and completely (Falloon et al., 1985; Hogarty et al., 1986, 1991; Hugen, 1993; Leff, 1996; Leff et al., 1989; Nugter et al., 1997; Posner et al., 1992; Randolph et al., 1994; Reilly et al., 1988; Smith & Birchwood, 1987; Tarrier et al., 1988; Vaughan et al., 1992; Zastowny, Lehman, Cole, & Kane, 1992).

As previously noted, the concept of expressed emotion was first proposed by Brown et al. (1962) when they studied the relapse rates of recently released schizophrenia patients. The hypothesis that there was a direct positive relationship between emotional involvement with the family and relapse was not disproved in their research. The concept of expressed emotion emerged as a description of the home environment, with low expressed emotion households reflecting low levels of emotional involvement between family members as demonstrated by an absence of hostility and overcontrolling behaviors. High expressed emotion households were those in which family members or the identified patient displayed hostility toward others, or attempted to dominate other family members (Brown et al., 1962).

Though most studies of expressed emotion have involved single-family interventions, Hugen (1993) and Smith and Birchwood (1987) conducted research on multiple-family group interventions to determine their effectiveness in reducing family conflict or expressed emotion. Both studies found that psychoeducation appeared to play a role in reducing expressed emotion in families.

Coping Behaviors and Subjective Distress or Burden

Often, family members fail to realize the importance of developing coping skills as a means of helping themselves and the patient; the provision of management tools for family members to use in adapting to life with a chronically ill relative is a goal shared by psychoeducation and support group models of intervention. In group settings employing a psychoeducational model, relatives are reassured that taking care of their own emotional and social needs is, in fact, beneficial to the patient; if the caregiving relative is overwhelmed, with no external support, the relative has fewer resources at hand to use in coping with and caring for the patient (Anderson et al., 1986).

Some families must adjust to living with a relative who has disorganized thinking and communication patterns, or bizarre behavior, but who does not pose a physical threat to self or others. However, the very real difficulty exists for some families that members reside with a patient who engages in dangerous behaviors. These behaviors may include but are not limited to violence against others, threats of suicide, wandering away from home, or a general inability to use sound judgment. It is important that strategies are in place to handle such situations in the event that they occur; planning for patient and family safety may be aided by input from other patients' family members participating in group sessions (Anderson et al. 1986).

With an understanding that coping skills may improve during and after family intervention, and that an improvement in these skills may lead to better outcomes for patients and their relatives, several studies included measures of coping behaviors in their research on family interventions (Abramowitz & Coursey, 1989; Cañive et al., 1993, 1996; Kane et al., 1990; Posner et al., 1992; Smith & Birchwood, 1987; Solomon et al, 1996, 1997). Not surprisingly, it was found that the greater a relative's distress about the illness, the less that person was able to employ coping strategies, and correspondingly, the less able a relative was to employ coping strategies, the greater the distress (Kane et al., 1990).

Findings about the effectiveness of psychoeducation in reducing burden are mixed. Cañive et al. (1993, 1996), Posner et al. (1992), and Solomon et al. (1996, 1997) found no changes in perceived burden or distress following participation in psychoeducational groups, while other studies have reported reduced trait anxiety (Abramowitz & Coursey, 1989), fear of safety, and general stress (Smith & Birchwood, 1987). The disparity in these findings does not appear to be due to the length of treatment or to the presence of the patient during group session. Further study will be necessary to determine whether multifamily psychoeducation groups contribute significantly to a reduction in stress and burden, or if perhaps other interventions may prove more effective.

Depression and Grief

Two variables related to burden and distress are depression and grief. Kane et al. (1990) and Anderson et al. (1986) suggest that depression may be a relatively common condition in relatives of schizophrenia patients. Understandably, the failure of a loved one to achieve expectations may result in a sense of sadness and grief; dreams for the future are dashed and hope is lost, especially as family members realize that the patient is unlikely to be the same as before succumbing to illness. The grief may be particularly acute for parents, especially if the patient is their only child. A sense of grief and loss is also common for spouses who, after schizophrenia is diagnosed, may mourn the loss of a healthy companion and hopes for a future that had been planned together (Anderson et al., 1986).

It is uncertain whether depression is reduced as a result of psychoeducational intervention. The couple of studies using depression as an outcome measure show mixed results when comparing psychoeducation versus support groups. Kane et al. (1990) found decreased depression in the psychoeducation group, while Solomon et al. (1996) reported no differences. These differences may have occurred as a result of differences in administering psychoeducational interventions—didactic versus interactive—or due to the length of treatment. The interactive program employed by Kane et al. (1990) might have provided relatives the opportunity to practice skills, which may have made it easier for them to implement the skills in other settings with the patient. With short-term treatment (one 2-hour session per week for 4 weeks in the Kane et al. [1990] study, vs. one 2-hour session per week for 10 weeks with the Solomon et al [1996, 1997] study), there may have been a temporary relief of symptoms that returned as time passed. However, in neither study was an account of symptoms over time provided, since data were collected at the end of treatment with no follow-up studies reported. Nonetheless, given the impact grief and depression make on an individual's ability to function, further research in this area would be beneficial.

Self-Efficacy

The term "self-efficacy" in the area of caretaking for a schizophrenic family member refers to one's ability to understand how mental illness affects a relative and to cope with its effects (Solomon et al., 1996, 1997). It would include refusing to accept blame for a relative's illness, gaining others' acceptance of the ill relative, allowing the patient to help herself/himself as much as possible, responding appropriately to psychotic symptoms, and availing the family of necessary resources (Solomon et al., 1996). Multifamily group psychoeducation deals very specifically with the elements of self-efficacy; research examining self-efficacy as a measure of treatment outcome consistently found improved self-efficacy following family psychoeducation (Hugen, 1993; Smith & Birchwood, 1987; Solomon et al., 1996, 1997).

SINGLE-FAMILY INTERVENTIONS

We now turn our attention to single family interventions. Comparable to multifamily interventions, those used with single families study individual patient outcomes and outcomes for the family as a whole. Interventions used with individual families may contain psychoeducational components (Glick et al., 1991; Haas et al., 1988; Hogarty et al., 1986, 1991; Nugter et al., 1997; Randolph et al., 1994; Spencer et al., 1988; Spiegel & Wissler, 1987; Tarrier et al., 1988, 1989; Xiang, Ran, & Li, 1994; Zastowny et al., 1992). Alternatively, standard family therapy models may be utilized with single families, such as behavioral family therapy (Hogarty et al., 1986, 1991; Tarrier et al., 1988, 1989), systemic therapy with paradoxical components (DeGiacomo et al. 1997), interactional family therapy (Chandra, Varghese, Anantharam, & Channabasavanna, 1994), or solution-focused therapy (Eakes, Walsh, Markowski, Cain, & Swanson, 1997). A brief review of these will follow.

Behavioral family therapy has evolved from social learning theory and exchange theory in its premise that consequences for behaviors serve to reinforce and maintain behaviors; presumably, by altering consequences, behaviors can be modified. According to behavioral therapists, successful relationships are maintained when individuals perceive interpersonal rewards as greater than costs associated with the relationship (Serketich & Dumas, 1996). Tarrier et al. (1988, 1989) tested the differences between two levels of behavioral management: one level was symbolic, wherein families were taught through lecture and discussion, but without concrete demonstrations, and the other level was enactive, wherein families were given an opportunity to actively participate in skill-building by engaging in role-plays, practices, record-keeping, and the like. Relatives were taught stress-reduction methods and ways to monitor stress reactions while learning effective coping skills. They were also taught to set goals based on specific issues in need of change.

In a variation of the behavioral model of family therapy, Hogarty et al. (1986, 1991) employed social skills training with their clients. The focus was on the patient's behaviors at the microsocial level and on strategies for dispute avoidance; the intent was to change patterns of conflict into those of negotiation, both within the family and externally in other social contexts. The overall goal of family intervention was to empower the patient to resume expected roles within the community.

The systemic model, with paradoxical elements, employed by DeGiacomo et al. (1997) explicitly avoided any type of psychoeducation, as well as social skills training. Instead, their model utilized a team approach to family therapy that involved assigning paradoxical interactions to patients and their families, rather than engaging in interactions that would be straightforward and direct. For example, in the case of a patient who was receiving nearly constant attention from his family, the therapist instructed the family "to watch the patient intently but in such a way that he would not notice, and for the patient to watch very carefully whether he was being observed, but to pretend he was quite unaware of being watched" (DeGiacomo et al., p. 185). The purpose of such an assignment was to create an ordeal for the family that was worse to carry out than it was to maintain the symptoms of the illness, thus taking the emphasis off the illness and breaking ineffectual patterns of family interaction (Haley, 1984), with the goal of reducing symptomatology in the patient.

Chandra et al. (1994) worked with patients who had forms of schizophrenia that were resistant to treatment. They hypothesized a relationship between family dysfunction and severity of the illness, suggesting, as did Bateson et al. (1956) years before, that family communication patterns may be the root of schizophrenia in unremitting cases. The model they employed involved delineating sources of stress for families with a schizophrenic member, with a specific focus on the family's interaction and structure. Once the interactive style was identified, they sought to explain the impact of the family communication patterns vis-à-vis the patient, then worked with the family to change the patterns that appeared to impact the course of the illness.

The brief solution focused model utilized by Eakes and her colleagues (1997) grew out of the systemic school and relied on a team approach to treating schizophrenia. The therapy was designed to build on the strengths of families coming into treatment; particular emphasis was given to identifying both individual and family competencies, with magnifying past successes as a way of solving present difficulties.

Many of the outcome measures identified in studies of multiple family group interventions are also utilized in single family interventions. Individual patient measures include relapse rates, suicide, medication compliance, and social functioning or social adjustment. Family outcome measures identified in the research include self-efficacy, subjective distress and burden, social support, depression, expressed emotion, and family interactions.

Single-family interventions encompass five general models, including psychoeducation, behavioral therapy, systemic therapy, interactional therapy, and solution-focused therapy. When examining the effects of single family interventions on individual schizophrenia patients, research addresses relapse rates, medication compliance, and social functioning and adjustment; outcomes for family members include self-efficacy, subjective distress or burden, depression, expressed emotion, and family interaction variables (*see* Table 11.2).

Relapse Rates

As with the various definitions of relapse identified in the multifamily group studies, there are several definitions used in research on single family interventions. However, two broad types of relapse were identified in the literature. The first type was considered as a change from nonpsychotic behavior to psychotic behavior, and the second type was the exacerbation of unremitting symptoms.

Several studies of single family psychoeducational intervention reported significantly different relapse rates for treatment group participants when compared with control (usually medication-only) group participants. Treatment group participants had lower relapse rates (regardless of the definition used for relapse) immediately following intervention, though the differences tended to disappear over time after treatment ended (Falloon et al., 1985; Hogarty et al., 1991; Randolph et al., 1994). According to Tarrier et al. (1988, 1989), it is likely that psychoeducation serves to postpone relapse, rather than prevent it. Further, upon finding no changes in relapse rates between their psychoeducation participants and comparison group participants, they suggest that short interventions do little to reduce the potential for relapse, emphasizing the need for long-term intervention to maintain remission. It is possible that treatment needs to be ongoing throughout the lifespan of schizophrenia patients, or that families may periodically need psychotherapeutic support to prevent relapse.

McFarlane, Lukens, et al. (1995) and McFarlane, Link, et al. (1995) explored the effectiveness of single-family psychoeducation when compared with multifamily psychoeducation and found that relapse rates for the two groups were not significantly different at the end of treatment, but that, over time, the single-family group experienced higher rates of relapse. These results indicate that there may be additional factors operating in the group setting, which provide protection against relapse, that are not present when treating individual families. Tarrier et al. (1988, 1989) and Hogarty et al. (1986, 1991)

TABLE 11.2 Single-family Interventions with Schizophrenia

AUTHOR/MODEL	DESIGN/SAMPLE	MEASURES	RESULTS	LIMITATIONS
Chandra et al. (1994) Interactional family intervention	Posttest only $N = 30$ families of consecutive referrals of schizophrenia patients to a family psychiatry center in Bangalore, India. 30% male, 83% ill for more than 2 yrs, all urban, nuclear families, 93% of families were in "launching out" stage of development	Family Assessment Form; evaluation of individual psychological problems, family interaction problems, communication, affective patterns	Depression was the most common problem for relatives; 20% of relatives had adjustment disorders; 10% of relatives were substance abusers; 10% of relatives had a diagnosis of schizophrenia; 75% of the discord in families with interaction problems were in the marital dyad	Descriptive study only; no pretest; no comparison group; no psychometric data provided about measures; small sample size
DeGiacomo et al. (1997) Paradoxical family therapy Patient included: 1 session a week for 10 weeks	Quasi-experimental: pretest, posttest with random assignment to treatment conditions (parodoxical or medication only) $N = 38$ patients	*Patients*: Brief Psychiatric Rating Scale; Strauss-Carpenter Outcome Scale for social improvement *Parents*: Five Minutes Speech Sample evaluating emotional expres-	None of the patients in either group required hospitalization; statistically significant advantages for experimental group: social improvement; lower psychiatric scores; patients demonstrated greater ability to	Although comparison group patients received lithium and depot, experimental group patients did not; no standardization of drug therapy; lack of psychometric data; extremely limited information about family

	sion, Clinical Global Impression	interact appropriately with others	member or patient demographics
	All family members except patient: Adjective Check List evaluating behavior and feelings		
	All family members: Synthesis and Scission-1 Test evaluating the interactive style of the participants		
Eakes et al. (1997) Solution-focused Total of 5 sessions held every other week	Quasi-experimental pretest, posttest. First five families under care assigned to experimental condition (solution-focused + 20-min medical checks), next 5 cases medical check only 10 community mental health clinic patients	Family Environment Scale	Following intervention, significant improvements for solution-focused over control: expressiveness; active-recreational orientation; decrease in scores on incongruence scale Comparison group only improved on moral religious emphasis scores	Very small sample size; lack of randomization to treatment conditions; lack of follow-up; lack of information on family members

continued

TABLE 11.2 *(continued)*

AUTHOR/MODEL	DESIGN/SAMPLE	MEASURES	RESULTS	LIMITATIONS
	diagnosed with schizophrenia, and family members; all male; 60% African American, 40% White Experimental group: mean age = 31.4, mean number of hospitalizations = 7.4 Comparison group: mean age = 40, mean number of hospitalizations = 4.6			
Falloon et al. (1985) Long term family management based on behavioral family therapy: In-home weekly sessions for 3 mos, bi-weekly	Quasi-experimental: pretest, posttest, follow-up; consecutive hospital admissions meeting, randomly assigned to treatment conditions: family management or	Camberwell Family Interview; questions about family stressors; Expressed Emotion index; plasma levels of neuroleptics; Brief Psychiatric Rating Scale	Patients in the Family Management group had significantly less severe exacerbation of symptoms than those in the individual therapy condition	Wide variety of neuroleptic drugs was used, as were drugs to minimize side effects, or other conditions. The varying effects of medication may have con-

sessions for 6 additional mos, monthly session thereafter for a total of 2 yrs' intervention	individual therapy $N = 36$, mean age = 25.8, 67% male, 42% White, 36% African American, 17% Hispanic, 61% from 1-parent family	Target Ratings of Schizophrenia; Hopkins' Symptom Checklist	Significantly fewer patients in the family management group than in the individual therapy group were admitted to hospitals during the initial 9 mos of the study Throughout the 24 mos, 83% of family management patients, compared with 17% of the individual treatment patients, did not have a reoccurrence of a schizophrenic episode	founded treatment effects Small sample size; psychometric data on measures were not reported; more highly critical families in the family management group than individual therapy group; limited information about family members
Glick et al. (1985) Inpatient family intervention with a psychoeducation component; mean number of sessions = 8.6	Quasi-experimental, pretest, posttest, follow-up, random assignment to treatment conditions: hospitalization with inpatient family intervention, or hospitalization only comparison group	*Patient Measures:* Overall functioning measured with the Global Assessment Scale; Ratings of symptoms and clusters of symptoms measured by the Psychiatric	Patients with good prehospitalization functioning who received inpatient family intervention had better outcomes at discharge than those with good prehospitalization func-	Lack of demographic information about participants; despite random assignment to groups, there were proportionately more females in the inpatient family intervention group and those

continued

TABLE 11.2 (continued)

AUTHOR/MODEL	DESIGN/SAMPLE	MEASURES	RESULTS	LIMITATIONS
	$N = 144$ 44% patients diagnosed with major affective disorder, 56% diagnosed with schizophrenia, hospital stay of at least 21 days	Evaluation Form; Role Performance and Treatment Scale; Patient's Self-Evaluation of Current Status *Family Members' Measures*: Family Member's Evaluation of Current Status; Treatment and Medication Compliance Data Sheet; Family Attitude Inventory developed for this study; Goal Attainment Scale; Family Goal Scale	tioning who received standard treatment; differences disappeared at 6-mo follow-up; those who had poor pre-hospitalization functioning showed no difference between treatment conditions	receiving inpatient family intervention had higher socioeconomic status; comparison group received more individual psychotherapy to compensate for time experimental group spent in family therapy; limited psychometric data available about measures; differential treatment following discharge from hospital; no evaluation of clinician-adherence to protocol in the treatment manual; difficult to establish strict experimental controls in a hospital setting due to severity of illness

| Haas et al. (1988) | Follow-up on 169 patients and their families in the above study following discharge | Although more patients in inpatient family group than in comparison group failed to complete treatment, of patients with good prehospital functioning, female patients in the inpatient family group had significant positive outcomes, though there was no effect for males. No treatment effects were noted for patients in the poor prehospital functioning group

Of those in the poor prehospitalization functioning group, families of male patients had better outcomes in the hospitalization-only comparison group, while families of female patients had better outcomes in the inpatient family group. Of those | Multimodal nature of hospital treatment may have confounded results; inpatient family group spent more time with a therapist; may be time, not actual therapy that resulted in improvements for that group |

continued

TABLE 11.2 *(continued)*

AUTHOR/MODEL	DESIGN/SAMPLE	MEASURES	RESULTS	LIMITATIONS
			in the good prehospitalization functioning group, families of both male and female patients had better outcomes with inpatient family than those in the comparison group	
Spencer et al. (1988)	Follow-up data (6 and 18 mos) on 158 patients and their families in the above study		At 6 mos, females in the comparison group had better outcomes At 18 mos, females in the treatment group showed better outcomes, but there was little effect on males Attitude toward treatment and "openness to social support" improved for treatment group males and females at 6 mos, but	Limited description of patient and family samples; marital status was different for treatment and comparison groups and may have played a role in outcomes; posthospital treatment was not controlled—could have been responsible for differential outcomes; medications and dosages varied

			the effects had disappeared by 18 mos		52% of comparison group families refused a repeated CFI schedule at 1 yr or at the time of relapse
			Those patients and families that achieved the goals set during family intervention had positive outcomes at discharge, 6 mos and 18 mos		
Hogarty et al. (1986)	Quasi-experimental, pretest, follow-up; blind random assignment to treatment conditions	Relapse rates	No relapses occurred in households which changed from high EE to low EE, regardless of treatment condition		Lack of information about family members
Family treatment (psychoeducation and management) biweekly for 24 mos; individual social skills training weekly for 21 mos, biweekly sessions for 3 mos; family treatment and social skills training	$N = 103$ consecutively admitted patients diagnosed with schizophrenia or schizoaffective disorder from families with high expressed emotion; randomly assigned to the treatment or medication-only comparison condition. Within the treatment condition, further random assignment was made to either a family	Expressed emotion (EE) measured with the Camberwell Family Interview Schedule (CFI)	Even in households where EE remained high, there were no relapses in families that had been in the family treatment with social skills training group		Too much time between discharge and follow-up with measures being administered only at admission and follow-up; intervening variables, or the passage of time, may have accounted for differences between groups
			A combination of hostility and criticism in the relatives is most frequently associated with relapse		

continued

TABLE 11.2 *(continued)*

AUTHOR/MODEL	DESIGN/SAMPLE	MEASURES	RESULTS	LIMITATIONS
	treatment only group or a family treatment with social skills training group			Minimum requirements for inclusion in study are reported, but averages are not
	mean age = 27.7, 66% male; 81% White; 76% never married; 69% living with parents; 88% high school graduates			
Hogarty et al. (1991) Minimum of 5 face-to-face contacts by at least one family member; 2-yr treatment period	Follow-up (1 and 2 yrs of above)		Family treatment significantly delayed relapse within a 2-yr period; the effect of social skills training observed at 1 yr posthospitalization was no longer evident; no longer an additive effect of combining social skills training as in 1-yr post-hospitalization; patients relapsing late (more than 1 yr after	Intervening treatments were not controlled

continued

			hospitalization) had significantly more severe relapses than those who relapsed prior to 1 yr; medication compliance was greatest in 3 experimental conditions; effect of family treatment was independent of medication compliance; relapses for ¾ of cases occurred in conjunction with vocational or family stress	Experimental group had a significantly longer history of unemployment before admission than did the comparison group; limited information provided about relatives; therapy was not standardized; small sample size; 4 comparison group relatives received other treatment; no psy-
Leff et al. (1986) Family intervention with three elements: education, relatives' group, family sessions in the home including the patient	Quasi-experimental, pretest, posttest, follow-up. Based on high or low EE, stratified random assignment to experimental (single family intervention) condition ($N = 12$) or comparison (relatives' support group) condition ($N = 12$);	Time budget of a typical week; Camberwell Family Interview; knowledge interview designed for this study; relapse rates (schizophrenic symptoms recurring and detected by the Present State Examination after patients had been discharged free of symp-	Improvements in experimental group over comparison group: 1) mean overinvolvement score for the experimental group dropped; 2) reduction in the mean number of critical comments; 3) patients in experimental group whose families experienced reduced face-to-	

TABLE 11.2 *(continued)*

AUTHOR/MODEL	DESIGN/SAMPLE	MEASURES	RESULTS	LIMITATIONS
	50% male; 50% living with parents, 50% living with spouse or sibling	toms, or exacerbation of symptoms in those patients who were still actively schizophrenic at discharge); history of medication compliance	face contact and reduced Expressed Emotion had no relapses, which was significantly different from the comparison group; 4) relapse rate for experimental group was 8% at 9 mos, compared to 50% for the comparison group No difference between groups on reduction of face-to-face contact or on drug compliance (compliance was excellent for both)	chometric data provided about measures
Leff et al. (1989) Family therapy support group (using combined models of therapy) versus a	Quasi-experimental, pretest, posttest, follow-up. Random assignment to 1) family therapy group: $N = 12$, 8 males,	Camberwell Family Interview; Knowledge Interview	Lack of participation by almost half the support group and high attrition; delusions of persecution more common in family	Lack of clarity of demographic data; small sample size; no nontreatment comparison group; lack of psychometric data on

relatives' support group with a psychoeducation component

Relatives in the family therapy group had a median of 17 1-hr sessions in 9 mos. Patients were included

Relatives in the support group had a median attendance of 4.5 times at the 1 $^1/_2$ hr meetings. Patients were not included

mean age = 26; 2) relatives' support group (no therapy): $N = 11$, 5 males, mean age = 27

therapy group; significant decrease in the number of critical comments in both groups during the follow-up period, and there was no difference between groups

Initially there were 26 high-EE relatives; at follow-up, 10 were low-EE

Expressions of warmth increased in both groups

In three relapses, there was noncompliance with social interventions

The highest rate of relapse was in the support group condition with families whose relatives did not attend the group meetings

measures; medication types and levels varied; since more than one relative from a family could participate, the results are vague in terms of treatment effects for relatives

continued

TABLE 11.2 *(continued)*

AUTHOR/MODEL	DESIGN/SAMPLE	MEASURES	RESULTS	LIMITATIONS
			In analyzing two separate trials, it was found that attendance at support groups was associated with a reduction in EE and family therapy was associated with a reduction in contact between the patient and family member	
McFarlane, Lukens, et al. (1995) Multifamily group Psychoeducation: With no patients present, there were 3 weekly single-family sessions, then an educational Survival Skills workshop was presented to 6 families	Quasi-experimental: pretest, posttest, follow-up with random assignment to groups 172 patients and their families from six sites in northeast U.S.; patient characteristics: 73.3% males, 52.9% White,	Brief Psychiatric Rating Scale; Symptomatic, Clinically Significant, and Total Relapse Rates	When controlling for medication compliance, there were no statistically significant differences in relapse rates between multifamily and single-family participants; MFG intervention resulted in extended remission and enhanced functioning	Insufficient data on family members Insufficient psychometric data on instruments used Lack of information about family members

Design/criteria	Sample	Results	Limitations
who then began to meet bi-weekly for a period of 2 yrs Single-family psychoeducation: with no patient present Minimum of 5 face-to-face contacts by at least one family member Two-yr treatment period	40.7% African American; 82.6% residing with family	when compared to the SFT intervention; the MFG cohort had greater reduction in positive symptoms, greater medication compliance with lower dosages required, and higher rates of employment. Negative symptoms had improved more for patients in the MFG cohort at discharge, but the differences between cohorts disappeared by the 2-yr follow-up; the difference in relapse rates increased over time; the multi-family condition resulted in significantly fewer relapse episodes during the 2-yr period; no difference in hospitalization rates between treatment modalities	Sample consisted only of patients who were being discharged from a hospital Small sample size

continued

TABLE 11.2 *(continued)*

AUTHOR/MODEL	DESIGN/SAMPLE	MEASURES	RESULTS	LIMITATIONS
McFarlane, Link et al. (1995)	Follow-up (4 yrs) of above study		Psychoeducational, multifamily groups had the lowest relapse rates; by the end of 4 yrs, 78% of single family group patients had relapsed at least once	
Nugter et al. (1997) Behavioral family treatment Inpatient phase: 3 mos including 2 sessions of psychoeducation for groups of families Family treatment began after discharge and occurred as 18 sessions during a 12-mo period	Quasi-experimental, pretest, posttest. Sample was stratified and randomly assigned to groups: Families were classified as high or low EE and then, within these classifications, randomly assigned to treatment conditions: individual treatment or individual treatment plus family treatment $N = 48$ patients with schizophrenia, schizo-	Camberwell Family Interview; Five Minute Speech Sample; Brief Psychiatric Rating Scale; Relapse rates	No significant differences between treatment groups; in both treatment groups, relapse rates were unrelated to changes in EE	Initial assessment for EE to determine inclusion in the sample was accomplished with the Camberwell Family Interview, whereas post-treatment assessment for EE was accomplished with the Five Minute Speech Sample; EE raters were not blind to treatment conditions; limited information about family members; no nontreatment comparison group

Mean number of sessions attended by each family = 17	phreniform disorders, schizoaffective disorders and other psychotic disorders, mean age = 20 yrs, 69% male, 79% lived with parents, mean duration of illness before hospitalization = 8 mos, 73% were low socioeconomic level	
	$N = 86$ family members participated in the study	
Randolph et al. (1994)	Quasi-experimental: repeated measures. Consecutive admissions to a Veteran's Administration hospital: random assignment to experimental or comparison (medication only) conditions	Brief Psychiatric Rating Scale; Camberwell Family Interview
Behavioral family management		Both groups of patients were generally compliant with medication and were well monitored during the course of the study; this resulted in relatively low levels of symptoms
25 BFM sessions during a 12-mo period, with contact decreasing over time		
Patient included	Relatives' Sample: $N = 41.$ 68% were parents, 20% were spouses	Posttest was at 1 yr, no follow-up; home visits were made to some participants in the experimental group, but not to all; limited information about family members; very general demographic information about patient sample

continued

TABLE 11.2 *(continued)*

AUTHOR/MODEL	DESIGN/SAMPLE	MEASURES	RESULTS	LIMITATIONS
	Patients: $N = 41$, all males; mostly high school graduates, mostly African American, relatively low SES, most never married, most from households with high expressed emotion			
Schooler et al. (1997) Compared Applied Family Management (single-family intervention, in-home sessions with and without patient present, 13 sessions); with Supportive Family Management (multifamily group meetings 1 ½ hrs monthly every month during stabilization and maintenance)	Quasi-experimental; Repeated measures. Stratified random assignment to groups: Patients were randomly assigned to the Applied Family Management group or the Supportive Family Management group, and within each group, participants were divided into standard dose medication, low dose, or targeted dose.	*Patients:* Hillside anchored version of the Brief Psychiatric Rating Scale; Modified version of the Scale for Assessment of Negative Symptoms; Severity and improvement items from the Clinical Global Impressions; Neurological Rating Scale, modified from the Simpson-Angus Scale for	Mean time to psychotic relapse was 431 days in the Target Dose group and 609 days with the Standard dose group; no significant differences between family intervention groups; home visits, communication training, and problem solving skills did not appear to have an effect on rehospitalization rates	Only patients with frequent family contact were included, possibly excluding older or married patients, so generalizability is limited Only patients who were clinically stable were included

2 yrs	Assessments of clinical symptoms were made monthly with detailed assessments at 6, 12, 18 and 24 mos while in the maintenance phase, and 20 weeks after the use of rescue medication if it was used	Extrapyramidal Side Effects; Early Signs questionnaire to measure prodromal signs	
	$N = 313$: 66% male, 40% White, 18% never married, mean age = 29.6		
Solomon et al. (1996) Brief	Quasi-experimental, pretest, posttest; random assignment to treatment conditions: Individual and Family consultation, Group Family Psychoeducation, or 9-mo waiting list (comparison)	Pai and Kapur (1981) measure of burden; Norbeck Social Support Questionnaire; adaptation of Scherer et al.'s (1982) self-efficacy scale; Greene et al (1982) measure of stress; Texas Inventory of Grief; Hatfield's self-efficacy scale for coping skills; instrument developed to measure satisfaction with intervention	There was significantly greater attrition from the group psychoeducation condition; no differences were found between those who dropped out and those who remained
Individualized consultation: 6–15 hrs. Service was available for 3 mos			
Group psychoeducation: 2-hr sessions once a week for 10 weeks	*Patients:* 64% were diagnosed with schizophrenia; 34% had more than 5 hospitalizations;		Self-efficacy was the only improvement significantly affected by either experimental intervention
			Study included not only patients diagnosed with schizophrenia, but also those diagnosed with a major affective disorder; limited psychometric data reported on measure of burden, measure of grief and instrument measuring satisfaction with intervention; although prior participation in a support group was included in the

continued

TABLE 11.2 *(continued)*

AUTHOR/MODEL	DESIGN/SAMPLE	MEASURES	RESULTS	LIMITATIONS
	average time since original diagnosis = 12.7 yrs; 36% had been arrested at some time; 12% had alcohol problems; 10% had drug problems *Family Members:* 88% female; 84% White; 77 % were parents of an adult child who was mentally ill; 11% were siblings, 4% were spouses, 6% were adult children of mentally ill parents; mostly middle class		Individual consultation compared to group psychoeducation was more effective immediately, though individual consultation requires greater resource expenditures	analyses, no standardization of support group involvement is noted; no follow-up data were reported
Solomon et al. (1997)	Follow-up (6 mos) of above study		Both experimental conditions had statistically significant improvement in self-efficacy scores at the end of the intervention; scores remained	Informal conversations after group meetings were stifled in order to maintain research integrity; coping strategies may have been hin-

			statistically significant improved at follow-up. At 6-mo follow-up, there was no statistically significant difference between the intervention groups and the comparison group	dered by reducing opportunities to engage in coping behaviors
Spiegel & Wissler (1987) Consultation with psycho-education and crisis intervention Periodic visits made with families for a maximum of 8 mos following hospital release Mean number of visits = 4.6	Quasi-experimental, pretest, posttest, follow-up Sample was stratified on the basis of residence: with family of origin or family of procreation, then randomly assigned to comparison (medication only) or treatment group $N = 36$ Mean age of patients = 36.7; patients had previously been hospitalized a mean of 6.8 times	Vets Adjustment Scale; Personal Adjustment and Role Skills Scale; Number of days spent rehospitalized; Family Environment Scale	At 3-mo follow-up, the treatment group had spent significantly fewer days in the hospital than had the comparison group, though at 1 yr, there was no statistically significant difference between groups No significant differences in scores on the Vets Adjustment Scale or PARS existed at 3 mos. After 1 yr, participants in the treatment group rated themselves significantly better	Variable length and duration of treatment for individual families; inconsistent application of models of therapy; small sample size; unequal sample sizes in groups (comparison group = 22, treatment group = 14); lack of psychometric data provided about measures; lack of information about family members

continued

TABLE 11.2 *(continued)*

AUTHOR/MODEL	DESIGN/SAMPLE	MEASURES	RESULTS	LIMITATIONS
			adjusted than did those in the comparison group, though scores on the PARS showed no differences	
Tarrier et al. (1988) Behavioral family intervention 9 mos	Quasi-experimental, stratified random assignment to: 1) Routine treatment; 2) Education only; 3) Enactive behavioral intervention; 4) Symbolic behavioral intervention $N = 73$ patients, mean age = 35.3, 65% female; 54% single, 35% married or cohabiting, 11% separated or divorced; mean number of admissions = 2.8	Camberwell Family Interview; medication compliance rates calculated in neuroleptic equivalents to haloperidol; frequency and compliance with appointments for outpatient psychiatric care; relapse rates; General Health Questionnaire; Symptom Rating Scale; Family questionnaire measuring the relative's perception of the problem behavior of the patient	Between admission and 4.5 mos, the high-EE Symbolic group changed significantly from high to low EE; between 4.5 and 9 mos, there were no significant differences between groups; by 9 months, the high-EE Symbolic and high-EE Enactive groups changed significantly from high to low EE; no significant differences in medication compliance existed between any groups;	Participants who dropped out were included in analysis even though they did not receive the full intervention; very small cell sizes for statistical analyses; analyses did not include relatives of patients who had relapsed during the follow-up period; lack of psychometric data on measures

Relatives: 53% female; 42% mothers, 24% fathers, 18% husbands, 6% wives; low educational attainment		high-EE Education and Routine Treatment group, when returning to a high-EE household, had higher relapse rates than those returning to a low-EE household; both behavioral family intervention groups (Enactive and Symbolic) had significantly reduced relapse rates for high-EE families; in high-EE families, education alone had no significant effect on relapse
Tarrier et al. (1989) Follow-up (2 yrs) of above study Original 6 groups were collapsed into 3 groups: (1) Enactive and Symbolic groups were combined into one behavioral intervention group. (2) The high EE	Examination of hospital admission records to determine readmission rates as a measure of relapse	Between 9 and 24 mos, the comparison group had better outcomes than the experimental conditions; family intervention may have delayed relapse without actually preventing it	Readmission rates may be a weak measure of relapse; EE could not be reassessed at follow-up due to interviewer errors; 5 admissions from the intervention group were for one patient

continued

TABLE 11.2 *(continued)*

AUTHOR/MODEL	DESIGN/SAMPLE	MEASURES	RESULTS	LIMITATIONS
	education only group and the routine treatment groups were combined into one high EE comparison group. (3) One low-EE group was made from the 2 low EE groups			
Vaughan et al. (1992) Parents received 1-hr sessions once a week for 10 weeks. Mean number of sessions attended = 8.6 Patient not included	Quasi-experimental: random assignment to treatment conditions, pretest, posttest, 9 mo follow-up $N = 36$ patients in high EE homes; $1/2$ randomly assigned to comparison group (medication/support only), $1/2$ assigned to treatment group	Phillips premorbid personality ratings; Camberwell Family Interview; Relapse rates; therapist's rating of counseling outcomes	No significant differences in relapse rates between the comparison group and treatment group; no significant differences in terms of rehospitalization between the comparison and treatment groups; 4 suicides in comparison group, none in treatment group According to therapists' assessments, 78% of parents in the treatment	Very limited information provided about relatives; measures were not well-defined; no psychometric data reported for measures used; therapy was not standardized from family to family; components of behavioral therapy were applied but were not exclusive

			group were better able to understand schizophrenia, 72% had lowered levels of expectation, and burden and guilt were reduced in 67% of parents in the treatment group	
Xiang et al. (1994)

Family Psychoeducation

4 mos | Quasi-experimental, pretest, posttest with random assignment to groups: family psycho-education or comparison (medication only)

$N = 77$ patients; mean age = 41; duration of illness = 15 yrs | Medical records; Social Disability Screening Schedule | After treatment, the rate of full compliance and the total rate of improvement in the experimental group was significantly higher than for the comparison group; percentage of families giving insufficient care in the experimental group declined significantly after treatment; there was no change in the comparison group; experimental group experienced significantly higher total rates of improvement | Sample included those with affective disorders (12%); no data provided about family members; insufficient demographic data provided about patients; unclear whether or not patients participated in groups |

continued

TABLE 11.2 *(continued)*

AUTHOR/MODEL	DESIGN/SAMPLE	MEASURES	RESULTS	LIMITATIONS
			than the comparison group; after treatment, the experimental group families were more likely to take an active role in caring for the patient were better able to recognize the disorder and seek professional help at an early stage so there would be no delay in treatment	
Zastowny et al. (1992) Behavioral and Supportive family treatment Two sessions (2 hrs each) of psychoeducation for all participants All families: 1.5 hrs once a week for 16 weeks	Quasi-experimental with repeated measures, random assignment to treatment conditions: behavioral family management or supportive family management. Assessments at 4 times $N = 30$ patients; 70% White; 81% middle-	*Patient functioning:* scale assessing negative symptoms; Global Assessment Scale; Social Behavior Assessment Schedule; Quality of Life Interview; Brief Psychiatric Rating Scale *Family functioning:*	The behavioral family management group experienced higher rates of explicit problem-solving behaviors and communications teaching; patients' prior level of functions and medication routine were predictors of current functioning; both	In addition to family treatment, all patients had individualized family care plans, which may have confounded the findings; lack of psychometric data on some measures; the use of many measures with a small sample may provide inaccurate statistical

class; mean age = 24; 80% male; average 3.7 previous hospital admissions	Communication and Interpersonal Problem Solving Assessment; Mental Illness Questionnaire measuring knowledge about schizophrenia; Community Resources Scale; measure of family conflict; family burden as measured by the "Adverse Effect on Others" section of the Social Behavior Assessment Schedule; expressed emotion index identifying feelings of family members and rating emotional overinvolvement with the patient; rating scale developed to examine family therapy sessions	groups showed improvement in scores on Global Assessment Scale; both groups improved over time; Supportive Family Management group had fewer rehospitalization	results; no non-treatment comparison group; limited information about family members

suggest that a combination of psychoeducation and behavioral interventions may show the most promise in promoting long-term remission.

Hogarty et al. (1986) examined relapse rates in terms of expressed emotion and found that no relapses occurred in households that demonstrated a change from high to low expressed emotion, and that even in households where expressed emotion remained high, those who had participated in family treatment experienced no relapses at 1 year. It was suggested that this was due, in some way, to interpersonal coping strategies that were nurtured through family intervention and ultimately facilitated relapse prevention. In their follow-up study, Hogarty et al. (1991) found that patients relapsing after 1 year had significantly more severe relapses than those who relapsed early. Therefore, the benefits of postponing relapse are unclear. On the one hand, postponement may be beneficial if the patient is able to avoid stress and become healthier, thus postponing relapse indefinitely. On the other hand, it is not always possible to avoid stress, and a patient may experience a severe relapse in the face of family or vocational stress. Given the apparent effect of late relapse, it is likely that reducing stressors may significantly improve one's chances of remaining in remission.

Although not considered a relapse, suicide is a very real possibility in unremitting cases of schizophrenia (Leff et al., 1990; Vaughan et al., 1992). The only group of researchers to examine suicide as an outcome variable, however, were Vaughan and his colleagues (1992). In their study of 36 patients from high expressed emotion homes, they found that behavioral therapy may have been a deterrent to suicide, though further research specifically addressing suicide as an outcome variable would lend insight into these findings.

Medication Compliance

As with interventions involving multifamily groups, treatment of individual families also involves the patient's adequate maintenance of a medication regime in order to provide the greatest likelihood of recovery (Glick et al., 1991; Haas et al., 1988; Hogarty et al., 1991; McFarlane, Lukens et al., 1995). Compliance may be measured in different ways, including evaluation of blood samples to determine drug concentration levels (Falloon et al., 1985), medication records kept by patients and family members (Glick et al., 1991; Hogarty, 1986; McFarlane, Lukens et al., 1995), and clinic records of visits for injections and/or prescriptions (Haas et al., 1988; Randolph et al., 1994). Regardless of the measure of compliance used, results of research on single family interventions are similar to those of multiple-family interventions in that medication compliance tends to reduce relapse rates.

Social Functioning and Adjustment

Of particular concern when dealing with schizophrenia patients is the ability of the patient to function at a level that will allow participation in family, vocational, and social experiences (Anderson et al., 1986). Measures of social functioning may include scores on rating instruments (DeGiacomo et al, 1997; Glick et al., 1985; Haas et al., 1988; Spencer et al., 1988; Spiegel & Wissler, 1987), an ability to maintain employment (Xiang et al., 1994), or patients' and family members' reports on adjustment (Zastowny et al., 1992).

A consideration of prediagnosis or prehospital functioning is important when evaluating outcomes in this area. Patients' prehospital functioning appears directly related to their ability to function in community roles following discharge; those functioning well prior to hospitalization, and who had participated in family intervention, were more likely to continue to function at a higher level upon discharge than those who had either poor prehospital functioning or those who had not received family intervention (Glick et al., 1985; DeGiacomo et al., 1997; Xiang et al., 1994; Zastowny et al., 1992).

FAMILY OUTCOMES WITH SINGLE-FAMILY INTERVENTIONS

As previously discussed, treatment outcomes are relevant not only to the identified patient, but also to the patient's family, especially when the intervention takes place while the patient is living with family members, or when the patient will return to live with the family following hospitalization (Chandra et al., 1994; Eakes et al., 1997; Leff et al., 1989, 1990; McFarlane, Link, et al., 1995; McFarlane, Ludens, et al., 1995; Solomon et al., 1996, 1997; Spencer et al., 1988; Tarrier et al., 1988; Vaughan et al., 1992; Xiang et al., 1994; Zastowny et al., 1992). Empirical studies of the effects of single family interventions on the family have examined self-efficacy (Eakes et al., 1997; Solomon et al., 1996, 1997; Vaughan et al., 1992; Xiang et al.,1994), subjective distress and burden (Chandra et al., 1994; Solomon et al., 1996, 1997; Vaughan et al., 1992), social support (McFarlane, Link et al., 1995; Solomon et al., 1996, 1997; Spencer et al., 1988), depression (Chandra et al., 1994; Solomon et al., 1996, 1997), and expressed emotion or family interaction (Chandra et al., 1994; Leff et al., 1989, 1990; Tarrier et al., 1988; Zastowny et al., 1992).

Self-Efficacy

Self-efficacy is concerned with understanding how mental illness affects a family member and is an integral part of the coping process (Solomon et al.,

1996). It may be thought of as the specific application of knowledge about schizophrenia to one's own relative. Studies of family intervention that applied a psychoeducation model reported gains in self-efficacy immediately following treatment (Solomon et al., 1996, 1997; Xiang et al., 1994). However, it is possible that psychoeducation may simply serve to expedite the process of self-efficacy, which may actually be an artifact of maturation, rather than a direct result of intervention. Xiang et al. (1994) noted, though, that those family members who had participated in psychoeducation were more likely to take an active role in caring for their schizophrenic family member, as well as being more likely to recognize the disorder and seek professional assistance at an early stage so that there would be no delay in treatment. This understanding of the course of the disease in a relative was thought to assist in the family's coping process.

The solution-focused model employed by Eakes and her colleagues (1997) also yielded improvements in self-efficacy, with treatment-condition participants reporting greater understanding between patients and family members than those in the medication-only control group. It was suggested that these findings are due, in part, to the way patients and family members were encouraged to externalize the illness as they sought solutions to any problems the illness was seen to cause in the family. Meanwhile, they also sought to identify existing strengths in the family that could be drawn on to improve family functioning. Vaughan et al. (1992) report similar results following behavioral family treatment.

Subjective Distress or Burden

As discussed in the section on multiple-family interventions, perceived stress reduces one's ability to cope with severe and chronic mental illness. Therefore, a not uncommon goal of intervention is to reduce the relative's burden, which is assumed to be a result of caring for an ill relative (Chandra et al., 1994; Solomon, 1996, 1997; Vaughan, 1992). Vaughan et al. (1992) reported positive results following behavioral therapy with families, which were attributed to training the parents received in identifying problems, devising solutions, and assessing consequences using a strategy agreed upon by the family as a whole. Solomon et al. (1996, 1997), however, reported no change in perceived distress or burden following a brief psychoeducational intervention. The lack of change may have been due to the brevity of the intervention rather than to the model used.

Social Support

Individual family interventions are concerned with the role of social support in a relative's ability to cope with the severe mental illness of a family member. Whereas multiple-family groups construct somewhat artificial social networks in an attempt to provide support to group members, the emphasis with individual family intervention is on extant social networks, and empowering family members to call on them for support. Additionally, family members are encouraged to establish new social support networks or to join other groups whose members have a relative with a schizophrenia diagnosis (Spencer et al., 1988). McFarlane, Link et al. (1995), in their comparative study of multifamily group psychoeducation and single family psychoeducation, suggest that long-term positive outcomes may be due more to the nature of multifamily groups than to the psychoeducation component, indicating that social support is the operative factor in improvement in family functioning.

Depression

Chandra et al. (1994) reported depression as the most common problem for relatives of schizophrenia patients and suggested the need to alleviate it through interactional therapy, rather than through standard psychoeducation alone. They emphasize the importance of evaluating family stressors, including difficult interaction patterns, as predictors of depression, then addressing dysfunctional interactions between family members. They stress the benefits of using circular hypotheses and a systems approach to treatment, though they have not yet tested their model.

Family Interactions

Although the family is not responsible for causing schizophrenia in one of its members, it has been consistently shown that stress and difficult interpersonal interactions may precipitate the onset of psychotic symptoms (e.g., Anderson et al., 1986; Chandra et al., 1994; Leff et al., 1989, 1990; Tarrier et al., 1988; Zastowny et al., 1992). Therefore, one of the goals of family intervention has been to improve the quality of interactions among family members. Anderson et al. (1986) suggest that it is not uncommon for marital partners to blame each other for difficulties experienced with an ill child or family member. Therefore, treatment that attends to marital discord may prove to be helpful to the patient, as well. Zastowny et al. (1992) emphasized the importance of developing problem-solving behaviors and good communication skills as techniques to reduce problems in family interactions. They found that a behavioral intervention did, indeed, have a positive effect on family interactions.

Expressed Emotion

Expressed emotion is a common outcome measure of the effectiveness of family intervention (Leff et al., 1989, 1990; Tarrier et al. 1988). Low-level expressed emotion households are considered the optimal environments for improving patient functioning and reducing stress. One way to reduce levels of expressed emotion is by reducing face-to-face contact, thereby maximizing the social distance between the patient and family members, and hence reducing conflict (Leff et al., 1989, 1990).

Summary

The single family interventions explored in the research demonstrate a reduction in relapse rates, lower suicide rates, greater medication compliance, better social functioning, increased self-efficacy, reduced caregiver burden, improved social support, improved family interactions, and lower levels of expressed emotion following treatment. Results, however, may depend on the type of intervention utilized and the contingent factors in the family's environment.

LIMITATIONS AND RECOMMENDATIONS FOR RESEARCH

Perhaps the most obvious strengths of the current literature are reflected in the attention paid to experimental design. In an effort to ensure methodological rigor, studying the effects of intervention on families of schizophrenia patients only, most researchers (with the exception of Solomon and his colleagues [1996, 1997]) excluded patients with dual-diagnoses organic brain disorders, or other physiological disorders that may have produced confounding results. All of the studies identified engaged in the ethical practice of research by avoiding the use of true control groups, in which no treatment would have been delivered to schizophrenia patients. Given the biological components of schizophrenia, the researchers tended to use as comparison groups those patients receiving medication only, with no other type of intervention.

And yet, the research on family interventions in schizophrenia has been fraught with difficulties common to all studies in the social sciences: the use of comparison groups rather than control groups, lack of random assignment to treatment conditions, in adequate sample sizes, difficulty implementing techniques for random selection of participants, use of nonstandarized instruments, lack of controlled administration of treatments, and attrition at follow-up. Of particular note in the present review, with only a few exceptions (Eakes et al., 1997; Haas et al., 1988; Hogarty et al., 1986; McFarlane, Link, et al., 1995; Nugter et al., 1997; Randolph et al., 1994; Schooler et al., 1997; Solomon et al., 1997; Spencer et al., 1988; Xiang et al., 1994), is the large number of studies providing insufficient information about the psychometric properties of their measures, or using measures with low reliability and/or validity. In one study (Nugter et al., 1997), measures at pretest and posttest were not consistent. Patients were chosen for inclusion in the study based on expressed emotion as determined by responses to the Camberwell Family Interview, while posttest expressed emotion was measured using the Five Minute Speech Sample (Magana et al., 1986, as cited in Nugter et al., 1997). Though these instruments may be parallel scales, no evidence of this was demonstrated through reliability and validity tests. In order to accurately reflect changes that have occurred due to the intervention, the same concepts must be measured in the same way; it is possible that with different measurement tools, different constructs were measured at baseline than those measured after treatment. If differences exist after treatment, we cannot know if they are artifacts of the measurement tools that were used, or actual differences due to the intervention being tested.

In addition, multiple instruments have been used to measure the various outcomes discussed in the literature, making it difficult to compare the outcomes even when the same model for intervention has been used. There are some exceptions to this, such as the use of the Brief Psychiatric Rating Scale (DeGiacomo et al., 1997; Falloon et al., 1985; McFarlane, Link et al., 1995; McFarlane, Lukens et al., Nugter et al., 1997; Randolph et al, 1994; Schooler et al., 1997; Zastowny et al., 1992) and the Research Diagnostic Criteria (Hogarty et al., 1986, 1991; McFarlane, Link et al., 1995; McFarlane, Lukens et al., 1995; Spiegler & Wissler, 1987). However, many measures were developed to evaluate the specific intervention being tested. Some of these were self-report measures and some were administered by interviewers.

The problem with self-report measures is that the participants' understanding of the instruments and their ability to accurately convey their understandings, as well as the possibility of variation in interpretations between different participants, may affect responses. Yet with interviewer-administered measures, there is the risk that responses to questions may be subject to the interpretation of the person administering the instrument.

The use of standardized instruments would facilitate an understanding of the most effective interventions for use with schizophrenia patients and their families. Although scales may be normed on populations other than those with which they are used, the replication of findings among different populations would build a strong case for the validity and reliability of the measures. The use of measures that have been shown to be valid and reliable with a variety of populations allows for a broader application of findings and generalizability to several settings, therefore creating a sound foundation on which to base inferences about the interventions being tested.

Additionally, demographic information about family members is frequently missing, and often is not reported for patients either. The difficulty with these omissions is that differences in treatment outcomes may apply to particular subgroups of participants and not to others. By knowing if specific groups are more likely to benefit from one type of intervention or another, the therapist may plan the most appropriate treatment for any given family.

Perhaps most interesting is the importance placed on treatment for positive and negative symptoms, yet no outcome measures are used that identify the types of symptoms being alleviated or maintained. Positive symptoms are those that represent excesses of usual behavior, such as hallucinations, whereas negative symptoms are those that appear as reduced functioning, such as withdrawal and diminished social interactions. This is important in that specific treatment models may be more effective with one or the other type of symptom.

Another difficulty is that patients are not always included in the interventions, even within the same model. Only Reilly et al. (1988) studied the impact of the patient's presence on the effectiveness of an intervention. They found that the presence of patients in a psychoeducation group session negatively affected the dynamics within the group. The patients tended to dominate the session, and family members were less likely to actively participate because of this. Vaughan et al. (1992) suggest including patients in treatment only when they are asymptotic. Further studies to compare the effectiveness of interventions while controlling for the presence or absence of the identified patient are necessary to determine if the patient's presence is beneficial or detrimental to treatment.

Another issue of concern is the amount of treatment families and patients actually receive. Although a given intervention may be designed to take place over a period of several weeks, unless participants actually attend all sessions or a very high percentage of the sessions, it is difficult to determine the efficacy of the intervention. Hogarty et al. (1986, 1991) adhered to a protocol that delineated participants' minimum treatment requirements for inclusion in the study, an example that should be emulated in future research. A similar dilemma is the possibility that interventions may not have been implemented in a controlled manner when several practitioners were responsible for providing services. In some studies (Hogarty et al., 1991; Posner et al., 1992; Randolph et al., 1994; Spencer et al., 1988; Spiegel & Wissler, 1987; Vaughan et al., 1992; Zastowny et al., 1992), although interventions were designed to follow a particular model, their implementation was not rigorously controlled, or in some cases, the patient and family members availed themselves of treatment opportunities outside of the constraints of the interventions being studied. In these instances, differences in outcome may have been due to differences in the way practitioners provided services or the use of extraneous services rather than actual differences due to the intervention.

Finally, sample sizes are consistently small, making generalizability suspect. If we know that there are over 3 million people who have a schizophrenia diagnosis (APA, 1994), sample sizes of a few dozen people are unlikely to provide the statistical power necessary to make inferences about the outcomes of the interventions being tested. Studies on a much larger scale, or those that accurately replicate previous research designs are necessary to provide reliable evidence that given interventions are effective.

RECOMMENDATIONS FOR SERVICE DELIVERY

In light of the volume of research pertaining to family interventions in schizophrenia, several observations are relevant. First, given the biological origins of the disorder, family intervention in the absence of psychotropic drug treatment is not likely to be successful. A team approach to patient management, including medical intervention, is crucial to the realization of long-term positive outcomes.

Second, however, is that family intervention, rather than intervention with only the identified patient, appears to provide the most positive outcomes for patients. As Falloon et al. (1985) have noted, family therapy appears to have several advantages over individual therapy, including the enhancement of the patient's stability over time and a decrease in the need for hospitalization.

Third, it is apparent that multiple-family group interventions provide a level of support not found in single family interventions, regardless of the therapeutic modality employed, and that the support is a valuable resource for patients and family members. There may be additional factors operating in the group setting that provide protection against relapse, but that are not present when treating individual families.

Fourth, multiple-family groups have the advantage of providing a cost-effective form of intervention for families dealing with schizophrenia. Due to the usually long-term nature of the illness, it behooves the mental health care provider and family to identify methods of therapy that will be financially accessible and feasible; reducing financial burden may be necessary for some families. Smith and Birchwood (1987) found a unique method of minimizing the financial costs of treatment. They mailed materials to participants in their comparison group and found that there were no differences in outcomes for the comparison group participants versus those in the experimental group that received psychoeducational group intervention. Both groups reported reduced stress, improved self-efficacy, and increased knowledge about schizophrenia. These findings have important cost-containment implications if they are replicated in other studies.

Finally, continued research is necessary to determine optimum treatment approaches for subgroups of schizophrenia patients and their families; rigorous studies using psychometrically sound measures and widely accepted design standards will facilitate the development of the most effective protocols. For instance, most of the family interventions have included the mother as the primary caretaker of the schizophrenia patient, though caregiving is a shared role in many homes (Cañive, et al., 1993, 1996). At the same time, the current body of literature is disproportionately weighted toward the study of male patients, though the illness has been shown to affect females with equal frequency (APA, 1994). Additionally, though the disparity is not as great for ethnicity as it is for gender, many studies have employed samples that include a larger percentage of White than ethnic minorities. This is not an accurate reflection of the distribution of schizophrenia in the population. Further, cultural variations in family intervention with schizophrenia have received scant attention in the literature. Ideally, future empirical studies will address the varying needs of different groups of patients, including, but not limited to females, ethnic minorities, those who are married, those with dual diagnoses, those with substance-abuse problems, the very young or very aged, and those who are resistant to treatment.

It is encouraging to note that positive outcomes can result from family interventions for patients and families coping with schizophrenia. With adherence to a medication regimen and appropriate long-term family interventions, many schizophrenia patients may hope to enjoy long periods of remission, with decreased severity of relapse and improved day-to-day functioning.

REFERENCES

Abramowitz, I. A., & Coursey, R. D. (1989). Impact of an educational support group on family participants who take care of their schizophrenic relatives. *Journal of Consulting and Clinical Psychology, 57*, 232–236.

American Psychiatric Association (1994). *Diagnostic and statistical manual of mental disorders* (4th ed.). Washington, DC: Author.

Anderson, C. M., Reiss, D. J., & Hogarty, G. E. (1986). *Schizophrenia and the family: A practitioner's guide to psychoeducation and management.* New York: Guilford.

Bateson, G., Jackson, D., Haley, J., & Weakland, J. (1956). Towards a theory of schizophrenia. *Behavioral Science, 1*, 252–256.

Bently, K. J., & Harrison, D. F. (1989). Behavioral, psychoeducational, and skills training approaches to family management of schizophrenia. In B. Thyer (Ed.), *Behavioral family therapy* (pp. 147–168). Springfield: Charles C. Thomas.

Brown, G. W., Monck, E. M., Carstairs, G. M., & Wing, J. K. (1962). Influence of family life on the course of schizophrenic illness. *British Journal of Preventive Social Medicine, 16*, 55–68.

Budner, S. (1962). Intolerance of ambiguity as a personality variable. *Journal of Personality, 30*(3), 29–50.

Cañive, J. M., Sanz-Fuentenebro, J., Tuason, V. B., Vasquez, C., Schrader, R. M., Alberdi, J., & Fuentenebro, F. (1993). Psychoeducation in Spain. *Hospital and Community Psychiatry, 44*, 679–681.

Cañive, J. M., Sanz-Fuentenebro, J., Vasquez, C., Qualls, C., Fuentenebro, F., Perez, I. G., & Tuason, V. B. (1996). Family psychoeducational support groups in Spain: Parents' distress and burden at nine-month follow-up. *Annals of Clinical Psychiatry, 8*, 71–79.

Chandra, P. S., Varghese, M., Anantharam, Z., & Channabasavanna, S. M. (1994). Family therapy in poor outcome schizophrenia: The need to look beyond psychoeducation. *Family Therapy, 21*, 47–54.

DeGiacomo, P., Pierri, G., Rugiu, A. S., Buonsante, M., Vadruccia, F., Zavoianni, L. (1997). Schizophrenia: A study comparing a family therapy group following a paradoxical model plus psychodrugs and a group treated by the conventional clinical approach. *Acta Psychiatrica Scandinavica, 95*, 183–188.

Dixon, L. B., & Lehman, A. F. (1995). Family interventions for schizophrenia. *Schizophrenia Bulletin, 21*, 631–643.

Eakes, G., Walsh, S., Markowski, M., Cain, H., & Swanson, M. (1997). Family centred brief solution-focused therapy with chronic schizophrenia: A pilot study. *Journal of Family Therapy, 19*, 145–158.

Falloon, I. R. H., Boyd, J. L., McGill, C. W., Williamson, M., Razani, J., Moss, H. B., Gilderman, A. M., & Simpson, G. M. (1985). Family management in the prevention of morbidity of schizophrenia: Clinical outcome of a two-year longitudinal study. *Archives of General Psychiatry, 42*, 887–896.

Farmer, R. L., Walsh, J., & Bentley, K. J. (1998). Schizophrenia. In B. A. Thyer & J. S.

Wodarski (Eds.), *Handbook of empirical and social work practice* (Vol. I, pp. 245–270). New York: Wiley

Gingerich, S. L., & Bellack, A. S. (1996). Research-based family interventions for the treatment of schizophrenia. *Research on Social Work Practice, 6*, 122–126.

Glick, I. D., Clarkin, J. F., Haas, G. L., Spencer, J. H., & Chen, C. L. (1991). A randomized clinical trial of inpatient family intervention: 6. Mediating variables and outcome. *Family Process, 30*, 85–99.

Glick, I. D., Clarkin, J. F., Spencer, J. H., Haas, G. L., Lewis, A. B., Peyser, J., DeMane, N., Good-Ellis, M., Harris, E., & Lestelle, V. (1985). A controlled evaluation of inpatient family intervention: 1. Preliminary results of the six-month follow-up. *Archives of General Psychiatry, 42*, 882–886.

Haas, G. L., Glick, I. D., Clarkin, J. F., Spencer, J. H., Lewis, A. B., Peyser, J., DeMane, N., Good-Ellis, M., Harris, E., & Lestelle, V. (1988). Inpatient family intervention: A randomized clinical trial: 2. Results at hospital discharge. *Archives of General Psychiatry, 45*, 217–224.

Haley, J. (1984). *Ordeal therapy*. San Francisco: Jossey-Bass.

Hogarty, G. E., Anderson, C. M., Reiss, D. J., Kornblith, S. J., Greenwald, D. P., Javna, D., & Madonia, J. J. (1986). Family psychoeducation, social skills training, and maintenance chemotherapy in the aftercare treatment of schizophrenia: 1. One-year effects of a controlled study of relapse and expressed emotion. *Archives of General Psychiatry, 43*, 633–642.

Hogarty, G. E., Anderson, C. M., Reiss, D. J., Kornblith, S. J., Greenwald, D. P., Ulrich, R. F., & Carter, M. (1991). Family psychoeducation, social skills training, and maintenance chemotherapy in the aftercare treatment of schizophrenia: 2. Two-year effects of a controlled study on relapse and adjustment. *Archives of General Psychiatry, 48*, 340–347.

Hooley, J. M. (1986). An introduction to EE measurement and research. In M. J. Goldstein, I. Hand, & K. Hahlweg (Eds.), *Treatment of schizophrenia* (pp. 25–34). Heidelberg, Germany: Springer-Verlag.

Hugen, B. (1993). The effectiveness of a psychoeducational support service to families of persons with a chronic mental illness. *Research on Social Work Practice, 3*, 137–154.

Kane, C. F., DiMartino, E., & Jimenez, M. (1990). A comparison of short-term psychoeducational and support groups for relatives coping with chronic schizophrenia. *Archives of Psychiatric Nursing, 4*, 343–353.

Kriesman, D., Simmons, S., & Joy, V. (1979). *Deinstitutionalization and the family's well-being*. New York: Guilford Press.

Lam, D. H. (1991). Psychosocial family intervention in schizophrenia: A review of empirical studies. *Psychological Medicine, 21*, 423–441.

Leff, J. (1996). Working with families of schizophrenic patients: Effects on clinical and social outcomes. In M. Moscarelli, A. Rupp, & N. Sartorius (Eds.), *Handbook of mental health economics and health policy. Volume I. Schizophrenia* (pp. 261–270). Chichester, England: John Wiley & Sons.

Leff, J., Berkowitz, R., Shavit, N., Strachan, A., Glass, I., & Vaughn, C. (1989). A trial of family therapy v. a relatives group for schizophrenia. *British Journal of Psychiatry, 154,* 58–66.

Leff, J., Berkowitz, R., Shavit, N., Strachan, A., Glass, I., & Vaughn, C. (1990). A trial of family therapy versus a relatives' group for schizophrenia: Two-year follow-up. *British Journal of Psychiatry, 157,* 571–577.

Leff, J., Kuipers, L., Berkowitz, R., Eberlein-Vries, R., Sturgeon, D. (1986). Controlled trial of social intervention in the families of schizophrenic patients. In M. J. Goldstein, I. Hand, & K. Hahlweg, (Eds.), *Treatment of schizophrenia: Family assessment and intervention* (pp. 153–165). New York: Springer-Verlag.

Liberman, R. P. (1986). Coping and competence as protective factors in the vulnerability-stress model of schizophrenia. In M. J. Goldstein, I. Hand, & K. Hahlweg, (Eds.), *Treatment of schizophrenia: Family assessment and intervention* (pp. 201–215). New York: Springer-Verlag.

Magaña, A. B., Goldstein, M. J., Karno, M., Miklowitz, P. J., Jenkins, J., Falloon, I. R. H., (1980). A brief method for assessing expressed emotion in relatives of psychiatric patients. *Psychiatry Research, 17,* 203–212.

McFarlane, W. R. (1994). Multiple-family groups and psychoeducation in the treatment of schizophrenia. *New Directions for Mental Health Services, 62,* 13–23.

McFarlane, W. R., Link, B., Dushay, R., Marchal, J., & Crilly, J. (1995). Psychoeducational multiple family groups: Four-year relapse outcome in schizophrenia. *Family Process, 34,* 127–144.

McFarlane, W. R., Lukens, E., Link, B., Dushay, R., Deakins, S., Newmark, M., Dunne, E. J., Horen, B., & Toran, J. (1995). Multiple-family groups and psychoeducation in the treatment of schizophrenia. *Archives of General Psychiatry, 52,* 679–687.

Nichols, M., & Schwartz, R. (1995). *Family therapy: Concepts and methods.* Needham Heights, MA: Allyn and Bacon.

Norquist, G. S., Regier, D. A., & Rupp, A. (1996). Estimates of the cost of treating people with schizophrenia: Contributions of data from epidemiologic surveys. In M. Moscarelli, A. Rupp, & N. Sartorius (Eds.), *Handbook of mental health economics and health policy, Schizophrenia* (pp. 95–101). Chichester, England: John Wiley & Sons.

Nugter, A., Dingemans, P., Van der Does, J. W., Linszen, D., & Gersons, B. (1997). Family treatment, expressed emotion and relapse in recent onset schizophrenia. *Psychiatry Research, 72,* 23–31.

Posner, C. M., Wilson, K. G., Kral, M. J., Lander, S., & McIlwraith, R. D. (1992). Family psychoeducational support groups in schizophrenia. *American Journal of Orthopsychiatary, 62,* 206–218.

Randolph, E. T., Eth, S., Glynn, S. M., Paz, G. G., Leong, G. B., Shaner, A. L., Strachan, A., VanVort, W., Escobar, J. I., & Liberman, R. P. (1994). Behavioural family management in schizophrenia: Outcome of a clinic-based intervention. *British Journal of Psychiatry, 164,* 501–506.

Reilly, J. W., Rohrbaugh, M., & Lackner, J. M. (1988). A controlled evaluation of psychoeducation workshops for relatives of state hospital patients. *Journal of Marital and Family Therapy, 14,* 429–432.

Schooler, N. R., Keith, S. J., Severe, J. B., Matthews, S. M., Bellack, A. S., Glick, I. D., Hargreaves, W. A., Kane, J. M., Ninan, P. T., Allen, F., Jacobs, M., Lieberman, J. A., Mance, R., Simpson, G. M., & Woerner, M. G. (1997). Relapse and rehospitalization during maintenance treatment of schizophrenia. *Archives of General Psychiatry, 54,* 453–463.

Serketich, W. J., & Dumas, J. E. (1996). The effectiveness of behavioral parent training to modify antisocial behavior in children: A meta-analysis. *Behavior Therapy, 27,* 171–186.

Smith, J. V., & Birchwood, M. J. (1987). Specific and non-specific effects of educational intervention with families living with a schizophrenic relative. *British Journal of Psychiatry, 150,* 645–652.

Solomon, P., Draine, J., Mannion, E., & Meisel, M. (1996). Impact of brief family psychoeducation on self-efficacy. *Schizophrenia Bulletin, 22,* 41–50.

Solomon, P., Draine, J., Mannion, E., & Meisel, M. (1997). Effectiveness of two models of brief family education: Retention of gains by family members of adults with serious mental illness. *American Journal of Orthopsychiatry, 67,* 177–186.

Spencer, J. H., Glick, I. D., Haas, G. L., Clarkin, J. F., Lewis, A. B., Peyser, J., DeMane, N., Good-Ellils, M., Harris, E., & Lestelle, V. (1988). A randomized clinical trial of inpatient family intervention: 3. Effects at 6-month and 18-month follow-ups. *American Journal of Psychiatry, 145,* 1115–1121.

Spiegel, D., & Wissler, T. (1987). Using family consultation as psychiatric aftercare for schizophrenic patients. *Hospital and Community Psychiatry, 38,* 1096–1098.

Tarrier, N., Barrowclough, C., Vaughn, C., Bamrah, J. S., Porceddu, K., Watts, S., & Freeman, H. (1988). The community management of schizophrenia: A controlled trial of a behavioural intervention with families to reduce relapse. *British Journal of Psychiatry, 153,* 532–542.

Tarrier, N., Barrowclough, C., Vaughn, C., Bamrah, J. S., Porceddu, K., Watts, S., & Freeman, H. (1989). Community management of schizophrenia: A two-year follow-up of a behavioural intervention with families. *British Journal of Psychiatry, 154,* 625–628.

Vaughan, K., Doyle, M., McConaghy, N., Blaszczynski, A., Fox, A., & Tarrier, N. (1992). The Sydney intervention trial: A controlled trial of relatives' counselling to reduce schizophrenic relapse. *Social Psychiatry and Psychiatric Epidemiology, 27,* 16–21.

Walsh, J. (1988). Social workers as family educators about schizophrenia. *Social Work, 23,* 138–141.

Xiang, M., Ran, M., & Li, S. (1994). A controlled evaluation of psychoeducational family intervention in a rural Chinese community. *British Journal of Psychiatry, 165,* 544–548.

Zastowny, T. R., Lehman, A. F., Cole, R. E., & Kane, C. (1992). Family management of schizophrenia: A comparison of behavioral and supportive family treatment. *Psychiatric Quarterly, 63*, 159–186.

Zubin, J., & Spring, B. (1977). Vulnerability: A new view of schizophrenia. *Journal of Abnormal Psychology, 86*, 103–126.

MEASUREMENT OF FAMILY TREATMENT WITH SCHIZOPHRENIA

Increasingly, practitioners are held accountable for the evaluation of their practice. To assist with evaluation, this section provides the reader with self-report instruments for family members of individuals with schizophrenia. Scores from these measurement instruments can be used to guide assessment, clinical practice, and research in this area.

Measures presented in this section involve the following criteria. First, instruments are self-report; that is, they are completed by family members themselves, rather than being interviewer-administered or observational measures. (Because the individual with schizophrenia may not be capable of completing a measure reliably, there is no discussion on self-report instruments for these individuals.)

A second criterion for inclusion was that adequate reliability and validity information had to be available for each scale. This area of research tends to be marked by the use of nonstandardized measures.

Measures presented include a scale on attitudes toward the schizophrenia individual by the family. Measures on the family members' adjustment is also included, along with an instrument to assess client satisfaction with services. Selected psychometric data from the measurement instruments are outlined.

ATTITUDES TOWARD INDIVIDUAL WITH SCHIZOPHRENIA

PATIENT REJECTION SCALE

Authors: Kreisman, Simmens, & Joy (1979)

Description:

- 11-item, self-report scale assessing the extent of anger or critical feelings directed toward family members with mental illness who have returned to live with their families ("often," "sometimes," "never")
- Conceptually overlaps with hostility and critical comments components of the index of expressed emotion

Reliability:

- Coefficient alpha is .78 at 4 months postdischarge and .79 at 8 months
- Test-retest reliability (4-month) is .72

Validity:

- Significant correlation with rehospitalization (.20)
- Compares favorably to Vaughn and Leff (1976) findings between expressed emotion and relapse and critical comments and relapse

CAREGIVER ADJUSTMENT

BECK DEPRESSION INVENTORY

Authors: Beck, Rush, Shaw, & Emery (1979); Beck, Ward, Mendelson, Mock, & Erbaugh (1961) [Review data on psychometric information by Beck, Steer, & Garbin (1988)]

Description:

- 21 items, measuring symptoms and attitudes of depression, rated from 0–3 in terms of intensity
- Also a short version (13 items) that correlates highly (.89 to .97) with long form although may represent only cognitively oriented symptoms rather than both cognitive and noncognitive
- Written at a fifth- to sixth-grade reading level
- Different time frames that may be ascertained
- Has been used in 1,000 research studies

Reliability:

- Mean coefficient alpha for nine psychiatric samples is .86
- Mean coefficient alpha for 15 nonpsychiatric samples is .81
- Test-retest reliability ranged from .48 to .86 for psychiatric patients and .60 to .83 for nonpsychiatric patients

Validity:

- Mean correlation coefficients between clinical ratings and the Beck Depression Inventory for psychiatric patients was .72 and for nonpsychiatric patients was .60
- Mean correlation coefficients between Hamilton Psychiatric Rating Scale for Depression and the Beck Depression Inventory for 5 psychiatric studies was .73 and for the 2 nonpsychiatric patients was .73 and .80, respectively
- Mean correlation coefficients between the Zung Self-Reported Depression Scale and the Beck Depression Inventory for 8 psychiatric studies was .76 and for the 5 nonpsychiatric patients was .71
- Mean correlation coefficients between the MMPI Depression Scale and the Beck Depression Inventory for 7 psychiatric studies was .76 and for the 3 nonpsychiatric patients was .60

- Several studies have indicated that the measure discriminates between normals and psychiatric patients and psychiatric and nonpsychiatric samples
- Construct validity has been demonstrated with selected attitudes and behaviors, such as biological correlates, suicidal behaviors, alcohol problems, adjustment, medical symptoms, stress, and anxiety

SYMPTOM CHECKLIST 90—REVISED

Author: Derogatis (1977)

Description:

- A 90-item self-report inventory with ratings along a 5-point scale ("not at all"/ "extremely")
- Assesses nine dimensions of symptomatology: Somatization, Obsessive-Compulsive, Interpersonal Sensitivity, Depression, Anxiety, Hostility, Phobic Anxiety, Paranoid Ideation, and Psychoticism
- Also yields three global indices of distress: Global Severity Index (combines information numbers of symptoms and intensity of distress), Positive Symptom Total, and Positive Symptom Distress Index)
- Widely used (700 published studies used this scale) (Derogatis 1993)

Reliability:

- Alpha values for nine symptom dimensions range from .77 to .90
- Test-retest reliability ranges from .78 to .90

Validity:

- Demonstrates that the SCL-90-R is sensitive to change
- Correlates with other well-known measures of psychological functioning such as the MMPI

BRIEF SYMPTOM INVENTORY

Author: Derogatis (1982)

Description:

- A briefer, 54-item version of the SCL-90-R
- Primary symptom dimensions:
  1. Somatization
  2. Obsessive-compulsive
  3. Interpersonal sensitivity
  4. Depression
  5. Anxiety
  6. Hostility
  7. Phobic anxiety
  8. Paranoid ideation
  9. Psychoticism
- 3 global indices:
  1. Global Severity Index
  2. Positive Symptom Total
  3. Positive Symptom Distress Index
- 0–4 ("not at all," "a little bit," "moderately," "quite a bit," and "extremely")
- Widely used (200 published studies used this scale) (Derogatis 1993)

Reliability:

- Alpha coefficients are strong, ranging from .71 to .85
- Test-retest (2 weeks) reliabilities ranged from .68 to .91 with reliability for the Global Severity Index at .90

Validity:

- High convergence between scales of Brief Symptom Inventory and the MMPI
- High correlations (ranging from .92 to .99) between Brief Symptom Inventory and Symptom Checklist 90—Revised
- A factor analysis provided support for construct validation
- Evidence for predictive validity in that the measure has been demonstrated as an effective screening device across many varied medical settings
- Further evidence for predictive validity in that psychological distress was predicted in cancer populations, individuals with psychopathology, individuals experiencing problems with pain management, in HIV research,

in student mental health, and in general clinical studies, and to predict efficacy of therapeutic interventions.

SOCIAL SUPPORT BEHAVIORS SCALE

Authors: Vaux, Riedel, & Stewart (1987)

Description:

- 45-item, Likert-type, self-report inventory designed to assess the following 5 different types of supportive behavior:
  1. Emotional
  2. Socializing
  3. Practical
  4. Financial
  5. Advice/guidance
- Each of the types of behaviors is assessed separately for family and friends

Reliability:

- Internal consistency for the subscales above .82

Validity:

- Factor analysis indicated support for loadings on the five types of behaviors tested

SATISFACTION WITH SERVICES

CLIENT SATISFACTION QUESTIONNAIRE

Authors: Attkisson & Zwick (1982); Larsen, Attkisson, Hargreaves, & Nguyen (1979); Nguyen, Attkisson, & Stegner (1983)

Description:

- 8-item, self-report inventory with 4-point anchored answer format assessing general satisfaction with services

Reliability:

- Coefficient alpha is .92

Validity:

- Factor analysis supported these 8 items as loading together from a 31-item and an 18-item version
- Global improvement as measured by the Symptom Checklist correlated with the Client Satisfaction Questionnaire ($r = .53$)
- Therapists' ratings of their satisfaction with their work with the client correlated with the Client Satisfaction Questionnaire ($r = .42$) and how satisfied they believed their clients to be ($r = .56$)

REFERENCES FOR MEASUREMENT OF FAMILY TREATMENT WITH SCHIZOPHRENIA

Attkisson, C. C., & Zwick, R. (1982). The client satisfaction questionnaire: Psychometric properties and correlations with service utilization and psychotherapy outcome. *Evaluation and Program Planning, 5*, 233–237.

Beck, A., Rush, A., Shaw, B., & Emery, G. (1979). *Cognitive therapy of depression.* New York: Guilford Press.

Beck, A., Ward, C., Mendelson, M., Mock, J., & Erbaugh, J. (1961). An inventory for measuring depression. *Archives of General Psychiatry, 4*, 53–63.

Beck, A. T., Steer, R. A., Garbin, M. G. (1988). Psychometric properties of the Beck Depression Inventory: Twenty-five years of evaluation. *Clinical Psychology Review, 8*, 77–100.

Derogatis, L. (1977). *The SCL-90R: Administration and scoring procedures manual.* Baltimore: Clinical Psychometric Research.

Derogatis, L. (1993). *Brief Symptom Inventory: Administration, scoring, and procedures manual.* Minneapolis: National Computer Systems.

Kreisman, D. E., Simmens, S. J. & Joy, V. D. (1979). Rejecting the patient: Preliminary validation of a self-report scale. *The Schizophrenia Bulletin, 5*, 220–222.

Larsen, D. L., Attkisson, C. C., Hargreaves, W. A., & Nguyen, T. D. (1979). Assessment of client/patient satisfaction: Development of a general scale. *Evaluation and Program Planning, 2*, 197–207.

Nguyen, T. D., Attkisson, C. C., & Stegner, B. L. (1983). Assessment of patient satisfaction: Development and refinement of a service evaluation questionnaire. *Evaluation and Psychological Medicine, 12*, 871–878.

Vaux, A., Riedel, S., & Stewart, D. (1987). Modes of social support: The Social Support Behaviors (SS-B) Scale. *American Journal of Community Psychology, 15*, 209–237.

Section IV

Family Treatment with the Elderly

CHAPTER 12

Family Treatment with Caregivers of the Elderly

with Sherry Fairchild-Kienlen and Jane Harakal Phillips

Family Case:

Jason Freeman, a White male in his early 50s, is confronted with life decisions for his 80-year-old mother, who has been diagnosed with Alzheimer's disease. With repeated situations in which his mother has become disoriented and lost her way while driving, Jason must face the reality that his mother is no longer capable of driving her car to purchase her weekly groceries or living alone in her home. Jason remembers he promised his mother he would always take care of her. Nursing home placement in an Alzheimer's unit seems like a cold and indifferent response to his needy mother.

With the daily caregiving contact required of him, his wife complains about the amount of time he spends away from home. Jason's wife refuses to allow his mother to live in their home. She feels that his mother never really accepted her into the family and made her life difficult by interfering in her parenting of their three daughters, now 20, 16, and 8 years of age.

For the first time in human history, old age has become a common phenomenon in the developed world. The statistics paint a picture of dramatic changes: In the United States of 1900, life expectancy at birth was 47 years, and by 1989, that figure had soared to 75.3 years (Zarit & Edwards, 1996). An overall decline in birth rates has led to a greater relative increase in the elderly, and the populous generation born between 1946 and the early 1960s will begin to reach age 65 in 2011 (U.S. Senate Special Committee on Aging, 1991).

These demographic changes have made it necessary for millions of individuals to add another identity to the roles of worker, homemaker, spouse, and child: that of caregiver. Caregiving is defined as one family member helping another member on a regular basis (e.g., daily) with tasks necessary for living independently, such as with transportation, shopping, bathing, and ongoing supervision. Caregiving is distinct from usual family exchanges, such as an older married couple helping each other by sharing household tasks, for example (Zarit & Edwards, 1996).

According to a national survey by the National Alliance for Caregiving and the American Association of Retired Persons (1997), almost a quarter of U.S. households have at least one caregiver. Of these, about three quarters are currently caring for a relative or friend who is at least 50 years old, and the average age of the care recipient is 77 years. The typical caregiver is a married woman in her late 40s. In fact, more than 7 in 10 caregivers are females working full time. Typical caregivers provide care for 18 hours a week, but about one in five provides "constant care," or at least 40 hours of care a week.

There are two primary caregiving approaches: formal and informal. Formal caregiving encompasses paid caregivers, respite care services, and nursing home placements, while informal caregiving includes family members, friends, and associates of the elderly. Within the informal category, family members account for 85% of all caregiving time. The decision whether to place an impaired relative in a formal institution is a critical event faced by family caregivers and a pivotal transition (Townsend, 1990; Zarit & Edwards, 1996).

Although many individuals in their 60s and 70s are healthy, a large number of them are living with disabilities due to chronic illnesses and need assistance. To a greater extent than ever before, families are taking care of their older relatives, even though higher percentages of women are working and families are becoming smaller. Increasingly, adult children are migrating away from their elderly parents. Such "distance caring" presents challenges, like deciding when an intervention is necessary. And with the proportion of one-child families reaching a high of 40% in the United States in the 1980s, many children are the only source of support for their elderly parents (Zarit & Edwards, 1996).

Though caregiving can be a rewarding experience, providing caregivers with a strong sense of fulfillment, it can also be one of the most stressful events in the caregiver's life (McCallion, Toseland, & Diehl, 1994; Skaff & Pearlin, 1992; Zarit & Edwards, 1996). Primary stressors are defined as those actions related to the elderly person's disability and the provision of direct assistance. For example, having to respond to agitated behavior by an elder suffering from dementia can physically and emotionally deplete the caregiver, make the caregiver feel trapped, and cause anxiety that he or she is losing the relationship with the elder.

The act of caregiving can also create negative ramifications, or "secondary stressors," in the caregiver's life, such as introducing turmoil into a marital relationship, awakening long-standing familial conflicts, disrupting work (especially for blue-collar workers, who do no have the same time flexibility as professionals), and curtailing social activities (McCallion et al., 1994; Zarit & Edwards, 1996).

One signal of the distress caregivers experience is the high rate of depression associated with the caregiver role (Bourgeois, Schulz, & Burgio, 1996; McCallion et al., 1994; Zarit & Edwards, 1996). For example, Gallagher, Rose, Rivera, Lovett, and Thompson (1989) found that almost half of a sample of caregivers of Alzheimer's patients met diagnostic criteria for a depressive disorder.

Given the distress caregivers experience and the projected future increase in size of the disabled elderly population, it is important to know the interventions that are effective with caregivers of the elderly. To this purpose, this chapter will review the treatment outcome studies that have been conducted with caregivers. Although there are a variety of caregiver types, such as those that are professionally paid, only family caregiver interventions are included. In addition, interventions are defined as therapeutic in nature; therefore, respite care interventions, in which family members obtain relief from caregiving by having services provided to the care recipient, are excluded. Further, an intervention with the caregiver had to be described along with data on attendance of the intervention. For example, if a study indicated that referrals were made to an intervention but then did not describe the intervention, the numbers who attended, and for how long, then this study was not included (e.g., Ferris, Steinberg, Shulman, Kahn, & Reisber, 1987). Only empirical outcome studies and those published in peer-referred academic journals will be examined. Another criterion for the review was that a minimum standard of methodological rigor was attained. For example, some measurement of program effects had to be provided, rather than just correlations associated with positive outcome (e.g., Quayhagen & Quayhagen, 1988) or global assessments of approval (e.g., Pinkston, Linsk, & Young, 1988). In addition, intervention groups with fewer than 10 subjects completing each treatment condition were excluded (e.g., Quayhagen & Quayhagen, 1989; Robinson, 1988; Schmidt et al., 1988) as were single-subject designs (e.g., Kaplan & Gallagher-Thompson, 1995; Teri & Uomoto, 1991). Because the literature on caregiving has vastly expanded in the last decade (Gallagher-Thompson, 1995), this review will discuss the more recent work from 1985 on.

FAMILY CAREGIVER INTERVENTIONS

Using these criteria, the majority of studies located focused on dementia and Alzheimer's disease, with a few involving other chronic illnesses such as Parkinson's disease, strokes, and depression in the frail elderly. In addition, four major types of family caregiver interventions were identified and synthesized following an adapted organizational schema from Bourgeois et al. (1996): mutual support groups, psychoeducational/skills groups, individual/family counseling, and multicomponent interventions. The discussion below will revolve around each of these four types of interventions and their outcome measures.

GROUP INTERVENTIONS

Practitioners are often faced with the decision about when to recommend individual or group treatment for clients, since caregivers are a heterogeneous group with a broad range of needs. Family caregiver literature indicates that the primary need for the caregiver of the elderly relative is often for emotional support, along with some type of skills training in handling their new family circumstance (Pratt, Schmall, Wright, & Cleland, 1985; Zarit, Todd, & Zarit, 1986). Reflecting these needs, group interventions usually take one of two theoretical approaches to working with family caregivers, and are generally considered either mutual support groups or psychoeducational/skills training groups. Overall, the purpose of mutual support groups is for group members to gain support and share experiences with other caregivers, while psychoeducational/skills groups are more structured, with the goal of learning skills and other methods to cope with the caregiving experience. Each of these two types of group interventions will be explained in more detail, followed by outcome findings of the studies in each area.

Mutual Support Groups

The accumulation of stressors over time may debilitate family members' abilities to care for their elderly relatives, which may, in turn, jeopardize the elderly person's ability to reside within the community. In order to provide relief from some of the stressors associated with caregiving, mutual support groups have developed (Toseland & Rossiter, 1989). Such groups are designed to reduce isolation and to provide a forum for caregivers to share their caregiver experiences with others in similar circumstances. Even the facilitators of such groups tend to have shared similar caregiving experiences. Indeed, layperson facilitation is a distinctive feature of mutual support groups (McCallion & Toseland, 1995), although professionally led groups are also in existence (e.g., Farran & Keane-Hagerty, 1994).

In mutual support groups, psychological closeness is provided to group members through the exchange of concerns and the receipt of understanding and validation. Mutual support group members further offer information about the effects of certain disabilities, coping strategies, and community resources (Toseland & Rossiter, 1989). Mutual aid is provided and a group identity based on a common life situation is formed.

Mutual support groups usually meet from 8 weeks (Farran & Keane-Hagerty, 1994; Glosser & Wexler, 1985; Goodman, 1991; Kaye & Applegate, 1993; Toseland, Rossiter, & Labrecque, 1989) to 24 weeks (Winogrond, Fisk, Kirsling, & Keyes, 1987). The length of the group needed may be related to the stage of caregiving. For example, a time-limited, relatively structured group may be advantageous for caregivers of a relative who is in the earlier stages of dementia (Farran & Keane-Hagerty, 1994), whereas in coping with the later stages of the illness, an ongoing support group may be most beneficial. It also may be that length of group treatment may depend on the level of burden and the amount of informal support available to the caregiver. If a caregiver reports a high level of burden along with a lack of adequate informal support, an ongoing group might be preferable.

As is evident from this discussion, support groups vary on a number of variables: group membership size, frequency of sessions, length of program, type of leadership, and nature of the common problem (the particular condition of the elderly person) (Gallagher-Thompson, 1995). As a result, there is some challenge in synthesizing the results of studies. A further issue is that one of the main outcomes studied in mutual support groups has been satisfaction with services (e.g., Glosser & Wexler, 1985; Kaye & Applegate, 1993). It has been noted in the literature that caregivers generally report satisfaction whether or not they have improved on other objective measures (e.g., Toseland & Rossiter, 1989). Therefore, satisfaction will not be discussed in this review, just as it was not included as an outcome measure for a meta-analysis on caregiver interventions (Knight, Lutzky, & Macofsky-Urban, 1993). However, the interested reader is referred to Table 12.1 for an overview of study findings, which include service satisfaction outcomes. It will also be noted from Table 12.1 that a great deal of inconsistency exists in the outcomes reported among studies. Indeed, the only consistent outcome is caregiver burden, which will be the focus of the discussion in the next section.

Mutual Support Group Outcomes   A main outcome consistently presented across the research on mutual support groups, as well as the family caregiver intervention literature as a whole, involves the impact of caregiver burden (Goodman, 1991; Knight et al., 1993; Toseland et al., 1989; Winogrond et al., 1987; Zarit et al., 1986). A broad definition of caregiver burden involves the amount of decline that caregivers perceive in their emotional or physical health, social life, and financial status as a result of the caregiving experience (Zarit et al., 1986). However, caregiver burden might be better conceptualized as a multidimensional concept. Specifically, caregiver burden may contain two central aspects: objective and subjective burden (Biegel, 1995; Montgomery, Gonyea, & Hooyman, 1985). Objective burden is defined as actual time and effort spent caring for another person's needs, which includes time involved, tasks and services provided, and the financial resources expended. Subjective burden, on the other hand, refers to perceptions, feelings, and attitudes about caregiving tasks (Biegel, 1995).

For the two studies on mutual support groups examining caregiver burden, burden was not significantly impacted (Toseland et al., 1989; Winogrond et al., 1987). In fact, a portion of caregivers (those whose Alzheimer's-afflicted relatives had shown the highest cognitive functioning at pretest) reported increased burden after a 6-month intervention. It could be that when patients display a drastic decline in functioning, the experience of burden is increased, despite any programmatic effects. It could also be, however, that caregiver burden has not been adequately measured. Indeed, instruments assessing burden do not have the necessary psychometric data establishing their validity and reliability. The lack of standardized measurement instruments to assess caregiver burden casts doubt on any findings on mutual support groups or any other caregiver interventions. Clearly more work needs to be done in this area.

Specific to the area of mutual support, the lack of consistent outcomes other than client satisfaction and caregiver burden is disappointing. Studies should routinely measure stress levels, coping, and social support, all aspects of functioning mutual support groups purport to effect.

Psychoeducational/Skills Training Groups

Although mutual support groups often provide education about the disease process and the caregiving role within that process, information is provided on an informal basis, rather than through the formalized presentation of material and curricula as in psychoeducational groups. Material presented is to help caregivers learn specific skills, the central goal of psychoeducational groups (Bourgeois et al., 1996). Psychoeducational groups provide members with education on disabilities, techniques for problem solving, strategies for improving problematic family relationships, and/or skills training in specific areas of psychological functioning, such as stress, anger, behavior, or depression management (Goldstein, 1990; McCallion, Toseland, & Diehl, 1994; McCallion & Toseland, 1995).

Psychoeducational groups vary as to whether they include a theoretical framework guiding the interventions. Theoretical frameworks include a cognitive-behavioral model for helping female caregivers of the elderly to cope with and express more constructively their feelings of anger and frustration toward the care recipient. Cognitive-behavioral strategies included relaxation training, techniques for identifying and challenging dysfunctional thoughts, and assertiveness and communication skills (Gallagher-Thompson & DeVries, 1994).

Two different theoretical models for the treatment of depression were examined in another study: Lewinsohn's social learning theory of depression and D'Zurilla's problem-solving model (Lovett & Gallagher, 1988). In Lewinsohn's model, the often unpleasant demands of caretaking preclude more pleasant activities. This negative balance of activities, in turn, contributes to the experience of depression. In the problem-solving condition, the assumption is that if caregivers are taught problem-solving skills, they will be better able to manage the potentially stressful situations that caregiving brings, thereby minimizing their emotional distress.

Psychoeducational/skills training groups may meet for varying lengths of times: as infrequently as a 1-day workshop format (Sherrill, Frank, Geary, Stack, & Reynolds, 1997); 6 to 8 weeks (Barusch & Spaid, 1991; Greene & Monahan, 1987; Robinson, 1988; Toseland, Rossiter, Peak, & Smith, 1990; Toseland & Smith, 1990; Zarit, Anthony, & Boutselis, 1987); or as often as 10 or more weeks (Gallagher-Thompson & De Vries, 1994; Lovett & Gallagher, 1988).

Outcomes Outcome variables of interest for psychoeducational/skills training groups include a slightly broader range of measures than in the mutual support group research, but are primarily concerned with positively impacting

TABLE 12.1 Mutual Support Group

AUTHOR/MODEL	DESIGN/SAMPLE	MEASURES	RESULTS	LIMITATIONS
Farran & Keane-Hagerty (1994) Dementia Caregivers Educational & Chapter Support Groups, 8 weeks for support	Quasi-experimental, pretest, posttest, self-selected nonrandom assignment to 2 types of support groups or control group. $N = 139$, Subjects recruited from Alzheimer's disease diagnostic center, local chapter, and community settings. 82% White; 13% African American; 3% Hispanic; wives = 29%; SES = between middle- & upper-middle class	Dementia Behavior Scale; Caregiver Concerns; Activity of daily living	Findings suggest that during earlier stages of dementia and moderate levels of concerns for the future, caregivers more likely to select and benefit from time-limited educational group	Self selections to groups, nonequivalent groups; no follow-up
Glosser & Wexler (1985) Educational Support Groups, 8 weeks 2 hr sessions	Posttest only. $N = 84$ completed the program but $N = 54$ completed the evaluation questionnaire. Full range of socioeconomic levels	Nonstandard 5-point Likert scale for 17 aspects of the group experience	Evaluations were generally very positive. The supportive aspects of the group and the information provided about medical and behavioral management of the	Lack of demographic information; no standardized measurers used; no follow-up

Relatives of patients with diagnosis of progressive dementia			patient were most highly rated. Resolution of intrafamilial conflict and information pertaining to specific legal/social problems were evaluated as somewhat less helpful	
Goodman (1991) Support Groups for caregivers of dementia relatives	Post-hoc comparison between caregiver who continued in group and those who attended briefly (less than 6 sessions), $N = 69$; 12% minority; 85% White income ranged 10,000 to 30,000. 58% spouse, 42% adult child	Memory and Behavior Checklist, Perceived Social Support Scale, Supportive Behaviors of the Group Leader and Members Scale, Burden Interview, Group Therapy Survey, Cohesiveness subscale, Intragroup similarity	Attendees had increased burden, and were more likely to be primary caregivers	No pretest; no follow-up; some non-standardized measures used

continued

TABLE 12.1 (*continued*)

AUTHOR/MODEL	DESIGN/SAMPLE	MEASURES	RESULTS	LIMITATIONS
Kaye & Applegate (1993) Male Caregivers' Participation in Support Groups, varying groups met at different time intervals: 62% met monthly, 20% met twice a month, 1–2 hrs meetings; 60% had been meeting 3+ yrs, 90% of the groups were ongoing	Posttest only, $N = 148$. Majority of members were White; caregiver for a spouse	Task performance index (frequency, competence & satisfaction); Barriers to Caregiving Index; Perceived levels of affection by recipients; Sex Role Index, ADL Index, Life Satisfaction Index; Zarit Caregiver Burden Index	Generally members felt comfortable sharing in the support groups and were satisfied with the group process. Males tended to be frequent attenders and those satisfied with the group process reported reduced stress	No pretest; no follow-up; no comparison groups. lack of demographic information; no standard group length time
Toseland et al. (1989) Peer-Led & Professionally-Led Caregivers Support Groups for adult daughter & daughter-in-law caregivers of family members with chronic disabilities, 8 2-hr weekly sessions	Experimental, pretest, posttest, randomization to 2 treatment groups or 1 control group. $N = 56$ subjects recruited by extensive media campaign; White; majority of caregivers married	Extent of Caregiving Scale; Zarit Burden Inventory; Problems with Caregiving Scale; Bradburn Affect Balance Scale; Brief Symptom Inventory; Community Resource Scale; Pressing Problem Index; Drug and Alcohol Use Scale; Personal change Scale	Both groups indicated significant improvements in psychological functioning, increases in informal support networks and positive personal changes. Professionally-led group resulted in greater gains in psychological functioning & peer-led group resulted in increases in informal support networks	No SES information. No follow-up. Not all Alzheimer's disease patient caregivers. Some nonstandardized measures used

| Winogrond et al. (1987) Family Caregivers' Support Group, weekly meetings, 6 months | Pretest, posttest after participation for 6 mos $N = 18$, voluntary patients from day hospital program, mean age + 71.5 (11 female, 7 male) Family caregivers were 9 spouses, 5 children, 3 siblings and 1 friend | Caregiver measures: Tolerance of behavior, Burden of care, Morale (Life Satisfaction Index-2); Patient measures: Cognitive function, Behavior function | Patient cognitive functioning decreased. Burden of care and morale were not significantly reduced. Caregiver improved in coping | No control group; small sample; no follow-up; some changes not discussed in terms of statistical significance; some nonstandardized measures used |

psychological functioning and reducing caregiver burden. One patient outcome, nursing home placement, is also included here (*see* Table 12.2).

Caregiver Well-Being Psychological functioning and caregiver burden will be presented together under the category of "caregiver well-being" as these two outcomes are assumed to be related (i.e., caregivers will be better adjusted when their burden is diminished). Another rationale provided by some authors is that the different aspects of burden should be examined on specific domains of the caregiver's experience (Neundorfer, 1991). One of these domains is in the area of emotional and psychological adjustment. A final rationale for including adjustment and burden together is due to the lack of standardized instrumentation for burden, which limits the accurate assessment of this construct and precludes its strength as an independent outcome.

Several different areas of psychological functioning are addressed in psychoeducational groups, including depression, stress, and anger. The use of cognitive-behavioral techniques seems to predominate. For example, relaxation techniques, assertive communication skills, and cognitive training were used in a program specifically designed to help female relatives more effectively cope with anger toward the recipient. The program appeared effective, with a significant decrease on anger/hostility that persisted through 18-month follow-up (Gallagher-Thompson & DeVries, 1994).

In another study employing cognitive-behavioral methods, a problem-solving model for the management of troublesome behaviors in the elderly person was used. Gains made in psychological functioning and reductions in caregiver burden were maintained at 1-year follow-up (Zarit et al., 1987). However, at posttest (7 sessions), the improvements made by both the psychoeducational group and the individual/family conditions were no different than those made by the waiting-list control group.

Another study, as well, showed few differences between a psychoeducational group (cognitive-behavioral skills building for the management of difficult caregiver emotions), a support group, and a waiting-list control condition (Haley, Brown, & Levine, 1987). In addition, measures of depression, life satisfaction, and the quality of the caregiver-care recipient relationship showed little improvement over time. In a follow-up study 29 months after treatment was begun, some decrease in stress was noted for treatment groups, with over half pursuing nursing home placement (Haley, 1989).

Another study used a cognitive-behavioral perspective, comparing a social learning and a problem-solving model. Both conditions were beneficial in increasing morale and reducing depression over the waiting-list control condition, but stress levels were not significantly impacted (Lovett & Gallagher, 1988).

More consistent positive gains were found for studies examining coping effectiveness (Barusch & Spaid, 1991; Chiverton & Caine, 1989). For Barusch and Spaid (1991), coping effectiveness improved more in the group in which patients were not present; however, objective burden was perceived as less of a problem when patients were present in groups. Subjective burden improved significantly for all conditions (group with family member, group without family member, and in-home work with only the caregiver), with no differences between groups. These findings seem to lend support to the concept of burden as a multidimensional concept, although again, burden in this study was not assessed through standardized measures. It appears in studies that even when other positive changes are noted in studies, levels of burden experienced are often not affected.

Nursing Home Placement Nursing home placement usually occurs at a point when the caregiver is unable to continue the level of care to maintain the elderly person in the home. As such, it represents a measure of an individual's inability to cope with the demands of caregiving. A few studies examined nursing home placement, or the likelihood of that placement (Barusch & Spaid, 1991), in order to determine the success of the intervention. However, none of the studies found differing rates of placement as a result of treatment (Barusch & Spaid, 1991; Greene & Monahan, 1987; Whitlatch, Zarit, & Von Eye, 1991; Zarit et al., 1987).

Summary Overall, psychoeducational group interventions seem to offer benefits in terms of improved psychological adjustment in some areas, although positive effects are not always consistent. Caregiver burden seems to be less positively impacted. When comparing group to individual interventions, the meta-analysis on interventions with caregivers indicated lower average effect sizes for group interventions on both psychological adjustment and caregiver burden (Knight et al., 1993). The next section will explore in more depth the work that has been conducted with individual caretakers. Interventions in which individual counseling is only one of the services received (e.g., Mittlelman et al., 1991; Oktay & Volland, 1990) will be discussed in a forthcoming section on multicomponent interventions.

TABLE 12.2 Psychoeducational/Social Skills Groups

AUTHOR/MODEL	DESIGN/SAMPLE	MEASURES	RESULTS	LIMITATIONS
Barusch & Spaid (1991) Spousal Caregiver Short-term Support Training. 6 2-hr sessions weekly, family participation treatment group, individual condition, and in-home condition	Quasi-experimental, Pretest, posttest, 6-mo follow-up, randomization to family participation treatment group or nonrandom in home condition group $N = 131$ (95 completed). Inclusion criteria of at least 20 hrs of care per week for 3 mos; 95% White; 70% women; income ranged from $10,001 to $15,000	Coping Inventory; Standardized measures used: Zarit Caregiver Burden, Montgomery, Gonyea, and Hooyman Objective Burden, Perceived Placement Scale, Zarit Patient Functional Status	28% improvement in coping effectiveness with a decline in failure to cope dropping 47%; small, significant reduction in caregiver burden. There was more significant improvement in the group-format condition and limited improvement for the in-home condition. Positive response to psychoeducational interventions was associated with lower institutionalization of patients	Lack of random assignment to in-home condition group; no control group; some nonstandardized measures
Chiverton & Caine (1989) Psychoeducational Program, Brief Education	Quasi-experimental, pretest, posttest, alternately assigned to treatment or control group	Health Specific Family Coping Index for Non-Institutional Care, for assessment of overall family coping with both	For treatment group educational program was beneficial in improvement of care-	Lack of information on SES; no follow-up

Program, 3 sessions lasting 2 hrs. Home visit by a registered nurse, total of 4 contact sessions Alzheimer's disease	$N = 40$ Subjects recruited from local hospital, Alzheimer's chapters. Inclusion criteria: eligible family members were restricted to spouses, had to be caring for the AD patient at home at the time of the study	potential and actual health problems in psychosocial & physical domains: physical independence, knowledge of condition, application of principle of personal hygiene, attitude toward health care, emotional competence, family living patterns, physical environment, & use of community resources. Severity of illness measured by the Clinical Dementia Rating Scale	givers' emotional competence and knowledge. No relationship between gender of the spouse & coping ability
Gallagher-Thompson & DeVries (1994) Psychoeducational/Skills Training Anger Management for female caregivers of relative with Alzheimer's desease or related dementia disorder, 8 2-hr sessions plus 2 booster sessions at 1 & 2 mo follow-up	Experimental, pretest, posttest, follow-up, randomization to 1 of 2 treatment conditions or control groups $N = 179$ sujects recruited from media, community agencies	Hostility indicators from Multiple Affect Adjective Checklist, caregiver satisfaction reports, follow-up survey	Overall 20% attrition rate. Significant decrease in hostility scores. At follow-up caregivers reported using techniques at home, particularly relaxation and CBT techniques for controlling negative feelings	Description given of only one treatment condition; use of nonstandardized measures

continued

TABLE 12.2 *(continued)*

AUTHOR/MODEL	DESIGN/SAMPLE	MEASURES	RESULTS	LIMITATIONS
	85% White; 15% minority; SES-middle to upper levels			
Greene & Monahan (1987) Professionally-Led Support-Education Caregiver Groups 8 weeks, 2-hr sessions	Quasi-experimental, nonrandom assignment, self-select to treatment or control group, pretest, posttest, follow-up (6 mos); $N = 289$ subjects recruited from community social agencies Mean age = 58 yrs, 86% female, 47% spouse, 25% Hispanics, mean yrs caregiving = 5.25	For caregivers: symptom checklist-90; modified Zarit Burden Scale For patients: ADL; IADL; cognitive dysfunction; psychological and behavioral problems; institutionalization	Significant decrease in anxiety and depression, with little effect on burden and hostility for treatment group	Non random assignment; self-selection
Haley et al. (1987) Psychoeducational/Skills Program for Alzheimer's disease caregivers 10 90-min weekly	Experimental, random assignment to 1 of 2 types of support groups or control wait list, pretest, posttest, follow-up (4 mos)	Beck Depression Inventory, Life Satisfaction Index; Elderly Caregiver Family Relationship, Health and Daily Living	Results indicated that although caregivers rated the treatment groups as quite helpful, group participation did not lead to improve-	Some nonstandardized measures

Group 1: educational support group meetings, Group 2: support group plus	$N = 54$ spouses & daughters recruited from agencies majority White; female; average income = $24,000	Form; Social Network; Program Satisfaction Questionnaire	ments on objective measure of depression, life satisfaction, social support, or coping variables
Relaxation & stress management skills training			
Haley (1989)	$N = 48$ caregivers who completed all follow-up measures at 29 mos after pretreatment assessment		Findings suggest that treatment group participants decreased level of stress and facilitated some caregivers' successful pursuit of nursing home placement (50% whose patients were still living). Marked stability indicated on measures of caregiver depression, life satisfaction, social activity, social network, and health
Follow-up to Haley et al. (1987)			

continued

TABLE 12.2 *(continued)*

AUTHOR/MODEL	DESIGN/SAMPLE	MEASURES	RESULTS	LIMITATIONS
Lovett & Gallagher (1988) Psychoeducational Classes, 10 weekly, 2-hr sessions Group 1: Increasing life satisfaction Group 2: Problem-solving skills Alzheimer's, Parkinson's, stroke, or other dementing illness Lewinsohn's model of increasing pleasant activities to enhance mood and D'Zurilla's model of problem-solving	Experimental, pretest, posttest, randomly assigned to 2 different groups or wait-list control condition; $N = 107$ subjects recruited from agencies; predominately females (83%); 55% spouse, 41% adult child; caregiver time spent = 30 mos	Perceived Stress Scale; Philadelphia Geriatric Center Morale Scale; Beck Depression Inventory; Schedule for Affective Disorders & Schizophrenia; Memory & Behavior Problem Checklist		No information on SES; no follow-up

Sherrill et al. (1997)	Posttest only	Cumulative illness Rating Scale for Geriatrics; Pittsburgh Sleep Quality Index; General Life Functioning Scale; Older American Resources Scale; Interpersonal Support Evaluation List; Hamilton Rating Scale for Depression; Global Assessment Scale; Brief Symptom Inventory; non-standardized self-report measures on satisfaction with content and quality of workshops	Attendees reported a higher average number of years of formal education. Low self-esteem scores were associated with higher rates of refusal to attend workshops. 85% of respondents indicated the workshop as moderately or extremely helpful	No pretest or comparison/control group; lack of follow-up
Psychoeducational Workshops for elderly with late-life depression, & their families, 3-hr workshops	$N = 108$ attendees of workshop, also compared with 24 who elected not to attend; Subjects (132 patients and 182 family members or significant others). SES on workshop attendees: 93% Whites; 29% males; 71% females; 44% married or cohabiting			

INDIVIDUAL AND FAMILY COUNSELING

Caregivers bring to individual counseling a variety of concerns. In their analysis of caregiver concerns, Smith, Smith, and Toseland (1991) found that the largest category of identified problems, discussed by one third of the caregivers, who were daughters or daughters-in-law of the elderly person, was in the area of coping skills. This category included time management and coping with stress. Another area of concern for caregivers involved family issues. Caregivers often lamented the lack of time, for instance, they had to spend with their husbands. They also wanted their husbands, as well as their siblings, more involved with the care of their elderly relative. Resentment was often expressed because siblings did not offer more assistance. Less salient family issues involved the impact of caregiving on the caregiver's children and the grief and loss associated with the approaching death of a family member.

Another category representing 16% of caregivers' concerns involved responding to the elderly person's emotional and behavioral needs. Most of these involved emotional needs, such as helping care recipients make meaning of their lives, helping them maintain their friendships and interests, and in other ways enriching the elderly person's existence. The physical and safety needs of the care recipient were much less of an issue, and financial and legal concerns were even lower on caregivers' list of priorities. Other concerns, shared about equally among a small proportion of caregivers, involved the quality of the relationship with the elder, eliciting formal and informal support, guilt and feelings of inadequacy, and long-term planning.

To address these concerns, individual interventions tend to be structured and relatively short-term, and some are theoretically driven. Toseland and Smith (1990), for example, used an "ecological practice perspective" in which counselors used "problem identification, problem solving, stress reduction, time management, and behavioral and cognitive coping strategies" (Smith, Tobin, & Toseland, 1992, p. 346).

In another intervention, cognitive-behavioral therapy and brief psychodynamic therapy were compared for their effect on depression in caregivers (Gallagher-Thompson & Steffen, 1994). Cognitive-behavioral therapy was used to help caregivers challenge their dysfunctional thoughts and develop more adaptive ways to perceive distressing events. In addition, behavioral strategies were taught, such as increasing daily pleasant events, to enhance mood and to gain mastery over circumstances. The psychodynamic condition involved the assumption that conflicts over dependence and independence were reactivated by the caregiving experience and that an understanding of past losses and conflicts through reenactment in the therapeutic relationship is necessary.

Other interventions that are included under individual work with caregivers involve those with a technological basis. One example is a computer network, ComputerLink, to enable caregivers to obtain information and support regarding caregiving decisions (Brennan, Moore, & Smyth, 1995). A nurse moderator served as facilitator and clinical expert. There were three major options for communication involving Alzheimer's caregivers: a public bulletin board; private mail; and an anonymous question and answer segment. Caregivers were allowed free access, 24 hours daily. Another technological intervention involved a 12-week telephone support program, utilizing both peer telephone support and telephone-accessed taped lectures for family caregivers of elderly Alzheimer's patients (Goodman & Pynoos, 1990).

Advantages of these types of technological support services involve privacy, access, convenience, and lower cost (Haas, Benedict, & Kobos, 1996). Family caregivers often do not seek professional counseling due to the perceived stigma of needing to go for "therapy," or they delay counseling until the care recipient's health is declining rapidly. Telephone counseling interventions and computer telecommunications offer anonymity and the ability to ask professionals about caregiving problems as they arise (Gallienne, Moore, & Brennan, 1993; Wright, Bennet, & Gramling, 1998), as well as ensuring that caregivers do not have to make travel arrangements or additional care arrangements for the elderly person (Skipwith, 1994). These types of support programs can also help caregivers combat the time constraints of attending traditional counseling and respite care services, particularly so that caregivers do not have further loss of time from work responsibilities. In addition, services can be offered on a 24-hour basis and access is provided to isolated or rural caregivers (Skipwith, 1994; Wright et al., 1998).

Outcomes

Outcomes for individual counseling involve first, caregiver well-being, defined as both psychological adjustment and caregiver burden. Less of a focus of studies has been on relationship functioning, social support, and the elderly patient's behavior. These outcomes will be explored below (*see* Table 12.3).

Caregiver Well-Being Despite the high rates of depression of caregivers reported in the literature (e.g., Bourgeois, Schulz, & Burgio, 1996; Gallagher et al., 1989; McCallion et al., 1994; Zarit & Edwards, 1996), only 10% of caregiver-identified concerns in the Smith et al. (1991) analysis involved client

Table 12.3 Interventions with Individual Caregivers

AUTHOR/MODEL	DESIGN/SAMPLE	MEASURES	RESULTS	LIMITATIONS
Brennan, Moore, & Smyth (1995) *AD Caregivers Computer Link Telecommunication Counseling*, 1 yr, caregivers averaged 2 encounters per week, average of 13 minutes each. Each subject in experimental group received a Wyse 30 terminal system, 3 major functions to caregivers: information, decision support, & communication. Caregivers could access Computer Link 24 hrs a day at no charge. Comparison groups subjects received a placebo training experience identifying local services & resources	Quasi-experimental, posttest only, random assignment to either the ComputerLink group or comparison group. N = 102, mean age = 64. Subjects recruited from 3 sources: AD research center, AD area chapter support groups, & self-referral. Criteria required that family caregiver live w/ AD person. Demographic data indicate that 67% were females, 72% were White, 86% were educated at or beyond high school	Standardized & non-standardized self-report measures *Decision-making confidence* by modified decision confidence scale by Saunders & Courtney; *Decision-making Skill* assessed by an investigator developed self-report instrument; Instrumental & Expressive Social Support Scale; *Burden* measured by impact of Caregiving Scale; *Depression* Measured by Epidemiological Studies Depression scale; *Patient functional status* By Clinical Dementia Rating	Subjects with access to ComputerLink experienced greater improvement in confidence in decision-making than subjects in the comparison group. Decision-making skill was unaffected. ComputerLink access did not lead to changes in social isolation. The decision-support function was used least often	Some measures nonstandardized. No pretest

Gallagher-Thompson, & Steffen (1994) *Cognitive-Behavioral and Brief Psychodynamic Psychotherapies* For depressed family caregivers, 20 sessions	Quasi-experimental, Pretest, posttest, & follow-up at 3 & 12 mos; random assignment to either cognitive-behavior or brief psychodynamic psychotherapy; N = 66 subjects recruited through referrals from other health care professionals, self-referred, or newspaper articles. Mean age = 62 yrs; average education = 14 yrs; reported being caregivers for average of 49 mos; 73% living with the elderly relative; 92% were female; 68% of caregivers had a diagnosis	Hamilton Rating Scale for Depression; Geriatric Depression Scale; Beck Depression Inventory; Schedule for Affective Disorders & Schizophrenia interview	21% (14 caregivers) dropped out before completing the course of therapy. Caregivers who dropped out of the 2 conditions had been caregiving longer than those who completed treatment. Subjects who had been caregivers for a shorter period showed improvement in the psychodynamic condition versus those who had been caregivers for at least 44 mos improved with CB therapy. By conclusion of therapy, 71% of all caregivers no longer had an RDC diagnosis of depression, 8% moving from major to minor depressive disorder. At 3 mo posttest, the 2 conditions did not differ	No control treatment used

continued

TABLE 12.3 (continued)

AUTHOR/MODEL	DESIGN/SAMPLE	MEASURES	RESULTS	LIMITATIONS
Goodman & Pynoos (1990) *Telephone Support Program*, 2 types of support over the telephone. Group 1 = peer telephone networks for 12 wk; Group 2 = 12 telephone-accessed taped lectures. *Alzheimer's, Nonspecific Abdominal Pain*	Experimental, random assignment to 2 treatment groups, pretest, posttest Subjects recruited through agency contacts & media announcements. N = 66, subjects paired according to relationship to patient, age, and gender	Zarit Burden Interview, Memory & Behavior Problem Checklist, Caregiver-Elder Relationship Scale, Mental health Scale, Social Network, Perceived Social Support for caregiving, Knowledge of AD Test	Both groups indicated gains in information, perceived social support satisfaction with social supports. Group 2 indicated greater information gain & more frequent emotional support from family & friends. No changes in relief from burden, improved caregiver-elder relationship, distress with relative's problem, or mental health	Some nonstandardized measures. No no-treatment control group
Schmidt, Bonjean, Widem, Scheftt, & Steele (1988) *Individual Counseling*, four-1 hr sessions, Group 1: Problem-solving, Group 2: Emotional expression plus problem-solving focus for dealing the dementia relative	Quasi-experimental, pretest, posttest, random assignment to one of 2 treatment conditions. N = 20	Standardized measures used: Zarit Burden of Care Scale, Wood Life Satisfaction Scale, Brief Symptom Inventory, Structural Analysis of social Behavior; nonstandardized measure used: Expectation of Therapy Form	Group 2—Emotional expression plus problem solving tx. Reduced psychiatric symptoms and improved caregiver-relative relationship. No other significant difference on other outcome measures	No control group. No SES or race indicated; recruitment procedures not specified

Toseland, Rossiter, Peak, & Smith (1990) *Individual versus Group Interventions*, 8 weekly 1-hr sessions for individual counseling, and 8 weekly 2-hr sessions for group counseling	Quasi-experimental, pretest, posttest, random assignment to respite only control group, and 2 treatments. Groups. N = 154. Subjects recruited by extensive publicity campaign of social service, religious, & civic organizations. Limited to adult daughters & daughters-in-law. Demographic data indicate that subjects in the 3 groups did not differ significantly in age, sex employment status, race,	Effectiveness was measured by self-perceived change in 4 areas: 1) *emotional response to caregiving* measured by Bradburn Affect Balance Scale & Zarit Burden Interview; 2) *psychiatric symptoms* Measured with Brief Symptoms Inventory; 3) *informal social support* assessed by different 3 & 4 point scales & Community Resource Scale; 4) *changes in the caregiver-care receiver*	Individual intervention produced more positive effects on caregiver's psychological functioning and well-being than did the group intervention, whereas group intervention produced greater improvements in caregiver's social supports. Participants in both interventions experienced significant improvements in coping with caregiving stress. Psychological issues respond best to individ-	Mix of measures included some that were nonstandardized and only given at posttest. Study only used females that were daughters or daughter-in-laws. No follow-up

continued

TABLE 12.3 *(continued)*

AUTHOR/MODEL	DESIGN/SAMPLE	MEASURES	RESULTS	LIMITATIONS
	or health. (White, African American, Other)	*relationship* with measures developed for this study, given at posttest only. Personal Change Scale, scale for perceived change in interpersonal competence as a caregiver, improvement in their relationship due to treatment. To examine similarities & differences in therapeutic process that occurred in group versus individual intervention conditions, audio tapes were rated using the Vanderbilt Psychotherapy Process Scales	ual intervention, & social support issues respond best to group intervention	
Toseland & Smith (1990) *Individual Counseling by Professional & Peer Helpers* for daughters &	Quasi-experimental, pretest, posttest; Randomly assigned to 3 conditions: either	Standardized measures: *emotional response to caregiving* by Bradburn Affect Balance Scale, &	Both types of counseling demonstrated no sign effect on caregivers' formal & infor-	Investigators cautioned about lack of generalizability to other primary caregivers such as

daughters-in-law, 8 weekly sessions *Frail elderly*	individual counseling by professional, peer, or no treatment control group. N = 87 subjects recruited from extensive media campaign (TV & radio)	Zarit burden Interview; *psychiatric symptomatology* by Brief Symptom Inventory; Non-standardized measures: *social supports by self-reports & new Community Resource Scale; change in caregiver-care-receiver relationship* by Self-appraisal of Change Scale, Community Resource Scale	mal social support networks. No significant differences found between professional or peer counseling on the outcome measures, however those receiving professional counseling indicated significantly better outcome than the no-treatment control group in subjective well-being, level of psychiatric symptomatology, and perceived changes in caregiving relationship. Subjects receiving peer counseling did not improve significantly. More than did control group in subjective well-being	spouses, men, & members of specific ethnic groups
Smith, Tobin, & Toseland, 1992 *Follow-up Study to previous Toseland & Smith (1990)*			Investigator examined the therapeutic processes occurring during peer and profes-	

continued

TABLE 12.3 (continued)

AUTHOR/MODEL	DESIGN/SAMPLE	MEASURES	RESULTS	LIMITATIONS
			sional individual sessions. Findings indicate that professionals were significantly warmer and friendlier, engaged in great exploration, & gave more & different types of advice than peer counselors	
Zarit, Anthony, & Boustsellis (1987) *Support Group and Individual & Family Counseling*, 8 sessions *Stress Management Psychoeducational Dementia*	Experimental, pretest, posttest, & 1 yr follow up, randomly assigned to 2 different treatment groups & 2 control groups. N = 184, but only N = 119 completed the program. Recruited from community agencies. Subjects were family members or friends	Standardized & non standardized measures used. Assessed in 4 ways: changes in caregivers' reports of stress by Burden Interview & Brief Symptom Inventory; improvement in management of pt's problem behaviors by Memory & Behavior Problems Checklist; increased use of social support & caregivers'	Although subjects in treatment groups made significant gains over time, they did not differ from wait-list subjects who showed similar improvements. One yr follow-up interviews indicated that gains made during the treatment period were maintained	Mix of measures included some that were nonstandardized. High attrition rate. Intervention differed in important ways from typical support groups & these differences could have accounted for the modest results

	perception of treatment benefits by nonstandardized measures	
Whitlatch, Zarit, & von Eye, 1991. *Follow-Up Study to Zarit, Anthony, & Boutselis, 1987*		Compared with subjects on a waiting list or support group members, caregivers in individual and family counseling were more likely to have successful outcome on all dependent measures: Brief Symptom Inventory, personal strain and role strain

affect, and these usually presented as either guilt or feelings of inadequacy. However, emotional well-being and psychological adjustment have been a major focus of outcomes in research, and one study has specifically targeted the treatment of depression. In this study, two different conditions were used: cognitive-behavioral therapy and brief psychodynamic therapy (Gallagher-Thompson & Steffen, 1994). At the end of treatment (between 16 and 20 sessions), 71% of the subjects no longer had a diagnosis of depression, and an additional 8% moved from a major to a minor depressive disorder. At follow-up, 63% were still no longer fitting diagnostic criteria for depression. No differences were indicated between cognitive-behavioral therapy or brief psychodynamic therapy. However, there were some differential results based on the length of time that individuals had been involved in caregiving: shorter-term caregivers had improved more in the psychodynamic condition, while longer-term caregivers seemed to find cognitive-behavioral treatment more beneficial. The authors hypothesize that with caregivers who became depressed earlier, psychodynamic therapy is more responsive to the grief they may be experiencing about the impending loss of the elderly person and the decline in functioning. However, for longer-term caregivers emphasizing the loss did not seem as beneficial as the acquisition of specific skills for managing negative emotions and difficult patient behaviors.

Two studies have examined the outcomes of psychological adjustment and caregiver burden when comparing the differential effectiveness of group versus individual treatment. In Zarit et al. (1987), a problem-solving model for management of care recipient behaviors was used, comparing a psychoeducational group and an individual condition. Although psychological functioning improved and caregiver burden was decreased by the end of the intervention for both treatment conditions, these findings were not significantly greater than the waiting-list condition. At the same time, treatment groups did maintain their improvements at 1-year follow-up.

In Toseland et al. (1990), the individual condition produced greater overall improvement on caregiver well-being and psychological functioning for adult children (daughters and daughters-in-law) and reduced caregiver burden than the group condition. Despite these gains, neither condition improved significantly over the waiting-list control group. In this latter study, the group intervention was more support-oriented than psychoeducational in nature. From these two studies, it appears that psychoeducational groups (over support groups)might produce gains comparable to individual caregiver counseling. The differences between these two studies, however, could also be because the samples were slightly different: The Toseland et al. (1990) sample was comprised of female, adult child caregivers, while Zarit et al. (1987) was divided between adult children and spouses of the elderly. It could be that spouse caregivers' greater social isolation (McCallion et al. (1994) may mean they receive more benefits from participation in a group.

A process analysis of the individual and group sessions revealed that interaction in the individual treatment intervention focused more on problem-solving and the exploration of feelings, whereas groups were more social and emphasized the sharing of caregiving experiences. Toseland and colleagues (1990) suggest that the types of problems experienced by a particular caregiver might be the basis for determining the most effective treatment modality for that individual.

Comparisons have also been made between professional- and peer-led individual interventions with caregivers. Toseland and Smith (1990) found that the professional-led condition produced more improvements overall on well-being and adjustment. Again, however, these improvements failed to translate into reductions in caregiver burden.

In an analysis of the therapeutic processes occurring within sessions, Smith et al. (1992) discovered some differences between the professional- and the peer-led sessions. Professionally led sessions involved a greater variety of interventions. When facing client impasses, professional counselors were able to more deeply explore caregiver issues, while peer-led counselors were more likely to use confrontation. Perhaps partly due to this factor, professional counselors were better able to maintain warmth and friendliness throughout the duration of the eight-session treatment. Another factor possibly impacting peer counselors' attitudes toward clients was their discomfort with terminating clients after eight sessions; many of these counselors expressed that ongoing work was needed. Finally, peer counselors were more apt to share their personal caregiving experiences in session than were professional counselors. These in-session differences may have accounted for the greater improvements in psychological adjustment for caregivers in the professional-led condition.

Given that peer counseling involves a less costly way of delivering services, additional training may be warranted so that peer counselors are able to maintain an attitude of consistent warmth toward the client and so that they can better negotiate client impasses. Future studies could then be conducted to determine the differential effects of professional versus peer counseling with both adult child and spousal caregivers.

Caregiver-Care Receiver Relationship Change Concerns about the quality of the relationship between the caregiver and the recipient did not tend to rank high in the problems identified by those seeking individual counseling according to Smith et al. (1991). The authors hypothesize that caregivers may attribute difficulties in the relationship to long-standing problems that occurred in the past rather than to the current caregiving situation. However, when studies examined this outcome, the effect was positive. This positive effect occurred regardless of theoretical model (e.g., Gallagher-Thompson & Steffen, 1994) or whether the intervention was led by professionals or peers (Toseland & Smith, 1990).

Care Recipient Behavior   A limitation of the caregiver literature is a lack of study on the effects of intervention on the elderly individual (Bourgeois et al., 1996). One study in the area of individual interventions with the caregiver focused on the impact of training caregivers to behaviorally reinforce the elderly person for appropriate behaviors (Pinkston & Linsk, 1988). A series of single-subject designs ($N = 21$) indicated that improvements were made in several areas: self-care tasks, social activities, and negative verbalizations. Although positive changes were maintained in these areas at 8-month median follow-up, negative caregiver recipient behaviors, such as fighting and smoking cigarettes, failed to show improvement. However, scores on a mental status questionnaire for the elderly person did show gains as a result of the behavioral program.

Social Support Network   Caregiver social networks are often informal and composed of family members, including brothers and sisters, spouses, and adult children. It has been found that caregivers with the lowest levels of depression and the highest satisfaction with their lives are those who have large emotional and social support systems (Gallagher et al., 1989; Schulz, O'Brien, Bookwala, & Fleissner, 1995). Further, these social support systems appear to mitigate some of the difficulties encountered when caring for an elderly relative and provide guidance when decisions about care must be made. Ferris and his colleagues (1987) found that 87.5% of the participants in their study received some type of guidance from family members in decisions to place a relative in a nursing home.

   Given the apparent relationship between social network size and adjustment, some caregiver programs have tried to work on increasing the size of caregivers' networks. Toseland et al. (1990) compared the effectiveness of individual versus group interventions toward this purpose. Although those in group interventions were significantly more likely to increase the size of their social network than individual treatment clients, simply increasing the size of the social network did not necessarily provide satisfaction with the network; participants in the individual condition actually experienced greater satisfaction with their smaller support systems.

The interventions involving telecommunication information and support for caregivers also examined social support. The ComputerLink program, while improving confidence in decision-making, did not reduce social isolation among subjects; nor did it produce gains in decision-making skills (Brennan et al., 1995). However, a program involving peer telephone support and telephone-accessed taped lectures did realize gains in perceived satisfaction with social support (Goodman & Pynoos, 1990).

Despite the fact that many different interventions are centered around increasing social support, caregivers typically fail to identify a need for increased social support, whether it be informal assistance from friends and other relatives, or more formal support, such as respite services or other community resources and services (Smith et al., 1991). In addition, the mere provision of information about community resources is insufficient, since caregivers may have difficulty relinquishing control over caregiving to other people (Smith et al., 1991). Practitioners must be willing to explore with clients their feelings about jeopardizing the care of the elderly person or their relationship with that person, and to reframe the situation such that accepting the use of assistance would offer benefits for the caregiver that would be passed along to the care recipient.

Summary In summary, individual intervention strategies have been found effective in improving caregiver well-being, caregiver-care receiver relationships, and care receiver behaviors. In addition, it appears that the high rate of depression among caregivers (e.g., Bourgeois & Schulz, 1996; Gallagher et al., 1989; McCallion et al., 1994; Zarit & Edwards, 1996), can be screened and treated (Gallagher-Thompson & Steffen, 1994). The findings of Gallagher-Thompson and Steffen (1994) further indicate direction for the type of treatment that should be targeted toward the different stages of caregiving.

Caregiver burden has been less consistently impacted than psychological functioning, a finding that is similar to research results on psychoeducational groups. It could be that the lack of impact on caregiver burden is due to the objective demands of the caregiving situation. As well as governing how much burden caregivers experience, objective demands may worsen over time as the elderly person declines in health (Toseland & Smith, 1990). One recommendation, therefore, has been to implement a case management, multicomponent approach so that some of these objective demands can be alleviated (Toseland

& Smith, 1990).

MULTICOMPONENT INTERVENTIONS

Bourgeois et al. (1996) created the term "multicomponent interventions" to refer to interventions that address several caregiver needs through a variety of services and programs. Any given multicomponent intervention may include a combination of support groups, family meetings, respite care, referrals to community resources, individual psychotherapy, or family therapy. Variables of interest in studies of multicomponent interventions include role strain, nursing home placement, and caregiver well-being (*see* Table 12.4).

Outcomes

Role Strain   Caregivers often experience conflicting demands for their time. The caregiver may be expected to fulfill a number of roles, including that of spouse, parent, employee, son or daughter, or community volunteer. Each role brings with it expectations about what must be done to successfully perform it. Increasing the number of roles that must be performed is likely to lead to a phenomenon referred to as role strain (Ingersoll-Dayton, Chapman, & Neal, 1990; Toseland, Labrecque, Goebel, & Whitney, 1992).

As a measure of role strain, Toseland et al. (1992) studied marital satisfaction in caregiver spouses of elderly veterans and found that over time, marital satisfaction decreased in both the multicomponent treatment group and the referral-only comparison group. However, the multicomponent group, in contrast to the comparison group, reported significantly increased feelings of independence following treatment. Thus, although there was dissatisfaction with the marital relationship, a corresponding increase in independence may have been a positive outcome.

Another area in which role strain may be observed is in the workplace. Ingersoll-Dayton et al. (1990) offered several multicomponent options. Participants at the work site all attended a psychoeducational seminar addressing a variety of issues: normal aging; emotional problems common to the elderly; communication techniques; Medicare and Medicaid information; residential options; caregiver needs; and the availability of community resources. Subjects could then choose to participate in one of three other interventions, which included sessions on care planning, a peer support group, or a buddy system pairing two caregivers as support for each other. The peer support group was chosen as an adjunct significantly more often than the other interventions. The authors found that caregiver employees, regardless of the additional intervention chosen, had higher rates of absenteeism in the 4 weeks following attendance at the psychoeducational seminar than they had in the 4 weeks prior to attending the seminar. Two explanations were provided for this unanticipated finding. It is possible that the relatives for whom they were caring experienced declines during the time of treatment. Alternatively, the employees may have availed themselves of resources and services they had learned about during the intervention and which necessitated their absence from work (Ingersoll-Dayton et al., 1990). Both of these explanations may have to do with the difficulty of balancing the role of caregiving with obligations at the workplace.

Nursing Home Placement One of the goals of intervention may be to reduce the number of nursing home placements for elderly family members. The cost of providing care in a nursing home greatly exceeds that of providing in-home care, although the severity of the care receiver's dementia or difficulty in caring for daily needs may preclude home care (Mittelman et al., 1991; Montgomery & Borgatta, 1989). Several studies in this area examine nursing home placement as an outcome.

Mohide and her colleagues (1990), for example, studied a multicomponent intervention consisting of the following: home visits by nurses; encouragement for the caregiver to attend to personal health; education about dementia and caregiving; bibliotherapy; establishment of caregiving plans; regular and on-demand respite care; and support groups. Nursing home placement was likely to be delayed for those receiving treatment when compared to the control condition (nursing care focused only on the patient's physical needs).

Another study looked at several different components of services (seminars for caregivers, a support group, individualized training in case management, respite services, regular use of an adult day care center, or extended care in a nursing home), offered both separately and in combination, depending on the treatment condition (Montgomery & Borgatta, 1989). Results were reported for both spouse and adult-child caregivers. Spouses were more likely than control group subjects to place their elderly husbands or wives in nursing homes if they had participated in any treatment except for the training in case management. Adult children, on the other hand, had an increased likelihood to place their parents only if they had participated in information seminars and a support group. Regardless of the intervention employed, the elderly persons with the most impaired health and the most difficulty with tasks of daily living were at highest risk for placement. This may have accounted for why spouse caregivers were more likely to have placed their relatives, since they tended to be caring for a severely impaired husband or wife and had to take a lot of responsibility for tasks.

Table 12.4 Multicomponent Interventions

AUTHOR/MODEL	DESIGN/SAMPLE	MEASURES	RESULTS	LIMITATIONS
Haley, Brown, & Levine (1987) *Multiple Psychoeducational/Skills Program* For Alzheimer's disease caregivers ten 90 minute caregivers weekly, Group 1: educational support groups meetings, Group 2: support group plus relaxation & stress management skills training	Experimental, pretest, posttest, and 4 mo follow-up, randomly assigned to 1 to 2 types of support groups. Subjects (spouses & daughters) recruited in 2 stages through a year-long period from agencies. $N = 54$, mean age = 78.3, mostly White female	Standardized and non-standardized measures used: Beck Depression Inventory, Life Satisfaction Index-Z Elderly Caregivers Family Relationship, Health and Daily Living Form, Social Network, Program Satisfaction Questionnaire	Results indicated that although caregivers rated the treatment groups as helpful, group participation did not lead to improvements on objective measure of depression, life satisfaction, social support or coping variables	No SES and other race indicated. Some nonstandardized measures
Haley (1989) *Longitudinal Follow-up Study to Haley, Brown, 1989*	$N = 48$ caregivers who completed all follow-up measures at 29 mos after pretreatment assessment		Findings suggest that treatment group participants decreased level of stress and facilitated some caregivers' successful pursuit of nursing home placement. Marked stability over time indicated on measures of caregiver	

			depression, life satisfaction, social activity, social network, and health	
Ingersoll-Dayton, Chapman, & Neal (1990) *Multiple Intervention Program* at workplace for employees who were caregivers or anticipating caregiving; Phase 1: 7 weekly educational seminars, Phase 2: three 8 week treatment choices of care planning, support group, & buddy system	Quasi-experimental, pretest, posttest at time 1,2, & 3; non-random assignment to 4 treatment options. N = 256 subjects recruited by advertisement at 4 worksites; 14.7% = male, age ranged from 25-73 with mean age = 45 yrs	Non-standardized measures used; self-report questionnaire for 1) helpfulness and impact, 2) stress and strain items, & 3) affect items	Significant increases in knowledge and absenteeism from seminar participation. Support group results indicated somewhat less helpful in reducing stress & helping participants care for themselves. No buddy system choice utilized. Only care planning and support groups were utilized. Due to participation. Overall significant decreases in negative affect were indicated	No information on race or SES provided. Non-standardized measures used. No control group. Lack of follow-up
Kahan, Kemp, Staples, & Brummel-Smith (1985) *Group Support Program* 8 sessions, 2 hrs	Quasi-experimental, pretest, posttest, assigned to treatment group or control group	Family Burden Interview, Zung Self-Rating Depression Scale, Dementia Quiz, Program Rating Sheet	Experimental subjects showed a significant decrease in total family burden, whereas control subjects actually showed	No race or economic status given. Some nonstandardized measures. No follow-up

continued

Table 12.4 *(continued)*

AUTHOR/MODEL	DESIGN/SAMPLE	MEASURES	RESULTS	LIMITATIONS
Cognitive Behavioral approach *Relatives of patients with Alzheimer's disease*	N = 40 subjects recruited from local out-patient clinic		a significant increase. Experimental subjects also showed reduction in their levels of depression. Experimental subjects showed a significantly greater improvement than did control subjects on knowledge of dementia. The acquisition of new knowledge was an important ingredient in reduction of burden & levels of depression	
Mittleman, Ferris, Steinberg et al. (1991). *Multiple Intervention Program*, for Spouse-caregivers of Alzheimer's disease patients to determine *four types of treatment* effectiveness on patient	Quasi-experimental, pretest, posttest, & 8 mo follow-up; random assignment to either treatment group or control group who did receive only routine support. N = 206, subjects	Standardized and non-standardized measures used; newly designed Caregiver Questionnaire, Short Psychiatric Evaluation Scale, Burden Interview, Memory and Behavior	Results were equivocal but those who participated in both the individual/family counseling and support groups were less likely to have nursing home placement for patients	Some measures nonstandardized

institutionalization; four mo structured program that included 2 individual counseling session, 4 family sessions,; followed by required support group, & ad hoc counseling	were excluded if that had received formal counseling or if support group participants; Recruited various social service agencies, 58.3% = female, 41.7% = male, age range = 60 to 70 yrs, 90.3% = White, average income = under $25,000	Problems Checklist, Stokes Social Network Scale, OARS, FACES III Questionnaire	than the control group. Three factors indicated as influence for nursing home placement: Patient's need for assistance with activities of daily living, patient income, and age of patients and caregivers	
Mohide, Pringle, Streiner, Gilbert, Muir, & Tew (1990). *Home management interventions*, 6 mos, 5 major interventions: caregiver-focused health care, education about dementia & caregiving, assistance with problems solving, regularly scheduled in-home respite, & a self-help family caregiver support group	Quasi-experimental, randomization to experimental and control group (community nursing care) N = 60 caregivers living with the demented relative (Canada)	Nonstandardized measures assessed differences in diet, physical activity, & cigarette smoking between intervention & non-intervention groups using biochemical indicators & interviews	After 6 mo intervention period, neither experimental nor control group improved in these areas	Nonstandardized measures used. No mention of physical activity measures. Details of intervention not clear. Attrition at follow-up and different attrition rates between groups

Dementia

continued

Table 12.4 *(continued)*

AUTHOR/MODEL	DESIGN/SAMPLE	MEASURES	RESULTS	LIMITATIONS
Montgomery & Borgatta (1989) Psychoeducational with various combinations of education and respite services. 6 weekly, 2 hr sessions, followed by 6 weekly support group and option of other services	Experimental, pretest, posttest, follow-up at 12 & 20 mos. Random assignment to one of five treatment programs or one control group N = 541 subjects self-referred through service agencies, T.V., radio, or newspaper ads. Eligibility criteria: elder person had to live within the county & family member had to live within 1 hr driving distance. Median age of elderly = 81.6 yrs, 33% male & 67% female, 40% married, 52% widowed, 22% indicated no informal contact w/ persons other than immediate family. For caregivers: 79% were female, 31% spouses of the elderly person, 59% were adult	Standardized and non-standardized measures by caregivers of elderly person's health & Activities of Daily Living Scale, Multidimensional Functional Assessment, OARS Methodology ADL for functional level, a 27 item task inventory used to assess types & extent of tasks performed by the caregivers, level of burden which included objective & subjective burden, and length of living arrangement of elderly person	After 12 mos of service eligibility, caregivers of elderly person remaining in the community reported lower levels of subjective burden. Services appeared to delay nursing home placement among families with adult child caregivers	Some nonstandardized measures; no information on race given; low utilization of services

children, 10% other types of caregivers (grandchildren, friends, & distant relatives). 40% employed full time. Median income = $17,500			
Oktay, & Volland, (1990). *Multiple Post-Hospital Support Program*, patient/caregiver pairs, 1 yr, multi-team approach, ten components: assessment, case management, skilled nursing, counseling, referrals, respite, education, support groups, medical back-up, and on-call help	Quasi-experimental, pretest, posttest with time measures at 3,6,9, and 12 mos; non-random assignment to either treatment or comparison no treatment groups. N = 191 patient/caregiver pairs. Subjects recruited before discharge. Predominately female = 61%, Black = 76%, widowed = 53%, mean age = 76 yrs, mean annual income = $3,880	Standardized and non-standardized measures: *Caregiver stress* by General Health Questionnaire, Symptom checklist for physical health, Negative Impact of Caregiver Scale, caregiver self-reports; *Patient functioning* by Katz Activities of Daily Living Scale. Instrumental Activities of Daily Living Scale, Mental Status Questionnaire, caregiver self-report; *Patient utilization of services* by 3,6,9, and 12 mo interviews and medical records	Results indicated a slight reduction in caregiver stress, with substantial reduction hospital days used by the treatment group. Low attendance at support groups indicated. No evidence of improved patient functioning, but participation in program may have postponed some deaths and nursing home placements	Description did not indicate types of chronic patient illnesses. Due to hospital environment disorganization, results need to be subjected to more rigorous tests. In some cases it was difficult to distinguish findings of caregiver and patient. The amount of previous caregiving experience biased results. Use of some non-standardized measures

continued

Table 12.4 *(continued)*

AUTHOR/MODEL	DESIGN/SAMPLE	MEASURES	RESULTS	LIMITATIONS
Toseland, Labrecque, Goebel, & Whitney (1992). *Multiple Group Program* for spouses of elderly veterans, eight weekly 2 hr sessions that included 4 components: support, education, problem solving, and stress reduction	Experimental, pretest, posttest, single blind, random assignment to treatment or control groups. N = 89, Subjects recruited through staff referral from outpatient clinic and VA medical records. Treatment Groups: mean age = 64.2 yrs 100% wives, 88% White, mean length of caregiving = 5.8 yrs; Control Groups: mean age = 67.7 yrs, 100% wives and White, mean length of caregiving = 8.1 yrs	Global health rating, Physical Symptoms Index, Patient Assessment Tool for Home Care, Burden Scale, Beck Depression Scale, Geriatric Depression Scale, Spielberger State-Trait Anxiety Inventory, Perceived self-efficacy, Help Seeking Coping Index, Index of Coping Responses, Caregivers Knowledge and Use of Community Resources, Informal Support Network, Quality of marital relationship, Identification of pressing problems, Personal Change Scale, Self-appraisal of Change Scale, Program satisfaction	Results indicate that participation in support groups have short-term benefits for spouses of elderly veterans. Treatment group resulted in significant decreases in stress and severity of pressing problems related to caregiving. Subjective burden, and significant increases in use of active coping strategies, knowledge of community resources, perceived independence in the martial relationship, and personal changes in their coping abilities	Some nonstandardized measures used: no follow-up

In a later study, Mittleman et al. (1991) found opposing results to the previous research, but that also could have been because the intervention was so different. In this study, the intervention included counseling, support group participation, and education about Alzheimer's disease and community resources. Results indicated that spouses of Alzheimer's patients were less likely to place their husbands or wives in nursing homes than were those in a comparison group (counselor available upon request, and group support, if desired). Predictors of placement were similar to the earlier study: severe dementia symptoms; a large amount of difficulty with activities of daily living for the elderly person; and high perceived caregiver burden.

Whitlach, Zarit, Goodwin et al. (1995) also found that nursing home placement was associated with higher personal strain and burden. A positive effect from treatment may have further played a role in determining nursing home placements. Caregivers who participated in one of two interventions—support groups, or a combination of individual and family therapy—and reported positive outcomes from treatment were less likely than waiting-list comparison group members or treatment group participants with unsuccessful outcomes to place their elderly relatives in nursing homes.

Some inconsistency exists as to the effects of multicomponent interventions on nursing home placement, although overall results are fairly positive. The inconsistency may have been partly due to the wide range of interventions offered and the subsequent difficulty in making comparisons. It also appears that the level of care necessitated by the elderly person and the amount of burden experienced by the caregiver may determine nursing home placement. These predictors must be targeted by interventions if they are to be successful in reducing nursing home placement.

Another issue afflicting the provision of multicomponent services involves the difficulty of getting caregivers to partake in services offered or to make use of available community resources (Montgomery & Borgatta, 1989; Toseland et al., 1992). Montgomery and Borgatta discuss that the same conditions that have resulted in problems for the caregiver—lack of time and energy due to the burdens of caregiving—are the same factors that preclude the use of services.

Caregiver Well-Being Caregiver well-being refers to outcomes related to psychological functioning, particularly depression, anxiety, stress, and coping. Since depression and anxiety are both quite prevalent in those who care for elderly relatives, reducing or alleviating these conditions is a primary goal of treatment for many caregivers (Mohide et al., 1990; Toseland et al., 1992).

Findings on how multicomponent interventions are able to impact depression are mixed, however. Kahan, Kemp, Staples, & Brummel-Smith (1985) found that a combination of psychoeducation, mutual support, and stress-management training produced significant reductions in depression when compared to a no-treatment control group. The authors believed that increased knowledge about dementia and more realistic expectations of the elderly individual's abilities mitigated the emotional impact of performing duties. At the same time, increased knowledge was not associated with reduced burden, although overall burden was reported to decrease following the multicomponent intervention. Perhaps a decline in the relative's functional status or caregiving duties remained unchanged despite the increase in knowledge.

In another study, Mohide and her colleagues (1990) designed a multicomponent intervention that provided regular nurse home visits, dementia and caregiving education, monthly self-help caregiver support groups, and regular home respite as well as on-demand respite. Despite the intensity of services, depression in caregivers did not decrease. However, depression levels were at least stabilized in comparison to the no-treatment control subjects whose depression tended to worsen. Similar to Mohide et al. (1990), Toseland et al. (1992) found that depression levels remained unchanged in the treatment group, though in this study, comparison group subjects reported improved depression levels.

Anxiety levels also failed to decrease following multicomponent interventions (Mohide et al., 1990; Toseland et al., 1990). In one study, multicomponent intervention group subjects reported moderate anxiety levels, which were stable over time. This was a slight improvement over the nursing-care-only comparison group subjects, who reported increased anxiety by the conclusion of the 6-month study (Mohide et al., 1990). In the other study with anxiety as an outcome, Toseland and colleagues (1992) found no differences in anxiety levels between treatment and comparison conditions at pre- or posttest, though the authors do not mention whether these levels were consistently high, moderate, or low.

The Toseland et al. (1992) study was the only one to evaluate coping as an outcome. They found that active behavioral coping increased in the treatment group, while it remained unchanged in the comparison group. These findings indicate a willingness on the part of the multicomponent intervention group subjects to seek help when needed, whereas the comparison group subjects demonstrated no change in their help-seeking behaviors. It must be noted that increased help-seeking did not translate into improvements on depression or anxiety, although burden was reduced for the spouses of frail elderly veterans following treatment. Positive effects on burden, both objective and subjective, were also noted in Montgomery et al. (1989) following multicomponent intervention.

A final outcome pertinent to caregiver well-being involves caregiver stress levels. Oktay and Volland (1990) compared an intervention involving skilled nursing care, case management, referrals, respite care, group support, education, and counseling to a comparison group that offered home health services and social work services. No differences were reported between treatment and comparison groups in terms of stress.

Summary

While comparisons of multicomponent interventions are made difficult due to the disparate services involved, it appears that such interventions were able to produce gains in certain areas crucial to the experience of caregiving, most notably in the areas of caregiver burden and in delaying nursing home placement. Despite positive gains in these areas, other measures of well-being— anxiety, depression, stress, and coping—did not significantly improve as a result of intervention over various comparison/control conditions. These findings are opposite to the results reported for individual interventions (see above) in which psychological well-being is improved, but not caregiver burden. However, taken together, these results can inform treatment for caregivers. Interventions targeted at skill-building, psychological adjustment, and the amelioration of symptoms such as depression (e.g., Gallagher-Thompson & Steffen, 1994) can improve well-being. At the same time, a range of more tangible services involving the care of the elderly person as offered in multicomponent interventions might be more helpful for reducing burden. In sum, more careful delineation and study of the differential effects of interventions for individuals at different points in their caregiving careers are necessary in order to understand the most cost-effective components that target aspects of caregiver distress (Bourgeois et al., 1996).

LIMITATIONS AND RECOMMENDATIONS FOR RESEARCH

This review has pointed out a number of positive gains produced from interventions with caregivers of the frail elderly. Still, there are a number of limitations that, if addressed, could appreciably strengthen the literature and guide interventions, benefiting both caregivers and the elderly. Limitations involve the lack of attention to different subgroups of caregivers and problems with measurement of outcomes. These issues will be explored in more detail in the sections below.

Although the literature on caregiver interventions has greatly expanded, several authors have noted the predominance of White, middle-class subjects in studies and the lack of attention to caregivers from lower socioeconomic status and ethnic minority groups (Bourgeois et al., 1996; Knight et al., 1993). However, significant numbers of minority caregivers exist. According to a 1997 survey by the National Alliance for Caregiving and the American Association of Retired Persons, of the 22.4 million English-speaking caregiving households nationwide, 82% were White, 11% were African American, 5% were Hispanic, and 2% were Asian. The prevalence of informal caregiving is higher among Asian and African American households (31.7% and 29.4%, respectively) than among Hispanic (26.8%) or White households (24%) [National Alliance of Caregiving and the American Association of Retired Persons, 1997].

Data are needed on the ways non-White ethnic groups view the caregiver role and its associated stressors, as well as how cultural differences should inform practitioners about outreach and the provision of services (Cox & Monk, 1993; Henderson, Gutierrez-Mayka, Garcia, & Boyd, 1993; Segall & Wykle, 1988/1989). In addition, existing evaluation efforts should work toward including sufficient numbers of minority subjects, along with routine analysis of race differences in studies.

As well as attending to race and socioeconomic status, programs should also work toward including more male subjects in caregiving interventions and how women can involve their partners/male relatives in care. The current situation is that almost 70% of spousal caregivers and 80% to 90% of adult child caregivers are female (Miller & Cafasso, 1992). However, a meta-analysis of 14 studies casts doubt on the idea that large variations in caregiving exist between males and females (Miller & Cafasso, 1992). These authors report essentially no significant gender differences in functional impairment of the frail care recipient, total caregiver involvement in care, or in money management tasks. The largest difference involved the greater likelihood of female caregivers to carry out personal care and household tasks and their reports of greater burden than males. Future studies of interventions should not only attempt to involve more males, but gender of caregiver participants should be provided, as well as analysis of gender differences.

Another area to be addressed in studies involves the various life circumstances of caregivers. For example, the concerns of adult child caregivers, which have received some attention by researchers (Smith et al., 1991) may be different than those of spouse caregivers, who have not received the same kind of research attention (Bourgeois et al., 1996). However, McCallion et al. (1994) reviews evidence that spouses are involved with more hours of care, are more isolated, make less use of formal support systems, and suffer more health and physical problems than other informal caregivers, including adult children. These additional stressors may require particular intervention strategies and may produce different responses to treatment.

Another recommendation is to address the length of time in the caregiving role as this might have an effect on treatment outcomes (Knight et al., 1993). For example, the Gallagher-Thompson and Steffen (1994) study suggests that caregiving duration might determine the most appropriate theoretical orientation. In the earlier stages of caregiving, individuals might require work on grief and loss of the elderly person's capacities, while later, certain skills and management of targeted care recipient behaviors may be most important. Indeed, cognitive-behavioral theoretical frameworks have predominated in this literature, with cognitive restructuring, communication skills training, and problem-solving approaches most common. Although emotion-focused approaches may provide benefits for caregivers, particularly at early stages, Bourgeois et al. (1996) have commented on the lack of interventions of this type in the caregiving literature. Future work should concentrate on strengthening theoretical frameworks in studies and matching them to subgroup characteristics of caregivers.

MEASUREMENT ISSUES

Another limitation of the research is the use of nonnstandardized measurement tools. Researchers often have formulated their own program-specific measurement instruments. The use of nonstandardized instruments, however, casts doubt on any findings reported. In addition, the use of many different outcomes, some based on standardized and some based on nonstandardized measures, limits the reader's ability to make comparisons across studies and draw conclusions about the body of knowledge that has developed.

A specific measurement problem involves caregiver burden. There are no standardized measurement instruments to assess burden, despite the frequent use of burden as an outcome in studies. Measurement problems may be one explanation for the lack of effect on burden. Another explanation is that burden may consist of both objective and subjective factors (Biegel, 1995; Montgomery et al., 1985). Given that objective factors, actual time and effort spent caring for another person's needs, may not change due to the declining health of the elderly person, subjective burden, perceptions, feelings, and attitudes about caregiving tasks (Biegel, 1995) may be the only area programs can realistically affect (Biegel, 1995). It also could be that the generally brief nature of caregiver interventions may not be of sufficient intensity to produce an impact on burden (Bourgeois et al., 1996).

Although the assessment of burden is especially troublesome, another issue with measurement is the lack of information on how interventions affect the elderly patient. While a few studies examined nursing home placement, other aspects of the elderly person's functioning could be more routinely addressed, since it is assumed that working with the caregiver not only impacts caregiver distress, but also aids in the quality of care. Given that the elderly population will certainly increase in the near future, caregiving interventions will need to be more responsive to both caregivers and the elderly.

REFERENCES

Barusch, A. S., & Spaid, W. M. (1991). Reducing caregiver burden through short-term training: Evaluation findings from a caregiver support project. *Journal of Gerontological Social Work, 17*, 7–33.

Biegel, D. E. (1995). Caregiver burden. In G. L. Maddox (Ed.), *The Encyclopedia of Aging: A Comprehensive Resource in Gerontology and Geriatrics* (pp. 138–141). New York: Springer.

Bourgeois, M. S., Schulz, R., & Burgio, L. (1996). Interventions for caregivers of patients with Alzheimer's disease: A review and analysis of content, process, and outcomes. *International Journal of Aging and Human Development, 43*, 35–92.

Brennan, P. F., Moore, S. M., & Smyth, K. A. (1995). The effects of a special computer network on caregivers of persons with Alzheimer's disease. *Nursing Research, 44*, 166–172.

Chiverton, C., & Caine, E. D. (1989). Education to assist spouses in coping with alzheimer's disease. *Journal of American Geriatric Society, 37*, 593–598.

Cox, C., & Monk, A. (1993). Hispanic culture and family care of Alzheimer's patients. *Health and Social Work, 18*, 92–100.

Farran, C. J., & Keane-Hagaerty, E. (1994). Interventions for caregivers of persons with dementia: Educational support groups and Alzheimer's association support groups. *Applied Nursing Research, 7*, 112–117.

Ferris, S. H., Steinberg, G., Shulman, E., Kahn, R., & Reisber, B. (1987). Institutionalization of alzheimer's disease patients: Reducing precipitating factors through family counseling. *Home Health Care Services Quarterly, 8*, 23–51.

Gallagher, D., Rose, J., Rivera, P., Lovett, S. & Thompson, L. W. (1989). Prevalence of depression in family caregivers. *The Gerontologist, 29*, 449–456.

Gallagher-Thompson, D., & Steffen, A. M. (1994). Comparative effects of cognitive-behavioral and brief psychodynamic psychotherapies for depressed family caregivers. *Journal of Consulting and Clinical Psychology, 62*, 543–549.

Gallagher-Thompson, D., & DeVries, H. M. (1994). Coping with frustration classes: Development and preliminary outcomes with women who care for relatives with dementia. *The Gerontologist, 34*, 548–552.

Gallagher-Thompson, D. (1995). Caregivers of chronically ill elders. In G. J. Maddox (Ed.), *The encyclopedia of aging: A comprehensive resource in gerontology and geriatrics* (pp. 141–144). New York: Springer.

Gallienne, R. L., Moore, S. M., & Brennan, P. F. (1993). Alzheimer's caregivers. psychosocial support via computer networks. *Journal of Gerontological Nursing, 19*, 15–22.

Glosser, G., & Wexler, D. (1985). Participants' evaluation of educational/support groups for families of patients with Alzheimer's disease and other dementias. *The Gerontological Society of America, 25*, 232–236.

Goldstein, M. Z. (1990). The role of mutual support groups and family therapy for caregivers of demented elderly. *Journal of Geriatric Psychiatry, 23*, 117–128.

Goodman, C. C., & Pynoos, J. (1990). A model telephone information and support program for caregivers of Alzheimer's patients. *The Gerontological Society of America, 30*, 399–404.

Goodman, S. (1991.). Patterns of participation in support groups for dementia caregivers. *Clinical Gerontologist, 10*, 23–34.

Greene, V. L., & Monahan, D. J. (1987). The effect of a professionally guided caregiver support and education group on institutionalization of care receivers. *The Gerontologist, 27*, 716–721.

Haley, W. E., Brown, L. & Levine, E. G. (1987). Experimental evaluation of the effectiveness of group intervention for dementia caregivers. *The Gerontologist, 27*, 376–382.

Haley, W. E., Levine, E. G., Brown, S. L., Berry, J., & Hughes, G. (1987). Psychological, social, and health consequences of caring for a relative with senile dementia. *Journal of American Geriatrics Society, 35*, 405–411.

Haley, W. E. (1989). Group intervention for dementia family caregivers: A longitudinal perspective. *The Gerontologist, 29*, 478–480.

Haas, L., Benedict, J., & Kobos, J. (1996). Psychotherapy by telephone: Risks and benefits for psychologists and consumers. *Professional Psychology Research and Practice, 27*, 154–160.

Henderson, Guttierrez-Mayka, M., Garcia, J., & Boyd, S. (1993). A model for Alzheimer's disease support group development in African American and Hispanic populations. *The Gerontologist, 33*, 409–414.

Ingersoll-Dayton, B., Chapman, N., & Neal, M. (1990). A program for caregivers in the workplace. *The Gerontologist, 30*, 126–130.

Kahan, J., Kemp, B. Staples, F. R. & Brummel-Smith, K. (1985). Decreasing the burden in families caring for a relative with a dementing illness. *Journal Of The American Geriatrics Society, 33*, 664–670.

Kaplan, C. P., & Gallagher-Thompson, D. (1995). Treatment of clinical depression in caregivers of spouses with dementia. *Journal of Cognitive Psychotherapy: An International Quarterly, 9,* 35–44.

Kaye, L. W., & Applegate, J. S. (1993). Family support groups for male caregivers: Benefits of participation. *Journal of Gerontological Social Work, 20,* 167–185.

Knight, B. G., Lutzky, S. M., & Macofsky-Urban, F. (1993). A meta-analytic review of Interventions for caregiver distress: Recommendations for future research. *The Gerontological Society of America, 33,* 240–248.

Lovett, S., & Gallagher, D. (1988). Psychoeducational interventions for family caregivers: Preliminary efficacy data. *Behavior Therapy, 19,* 321–330.

McCallion, P., Toseland, R. W., & Diehl, M. (1994). Social work practice with caregivers of frail older adults. *Research on Social Work Practice, 4,* 64–88.

McCallion, P., & Toseland, R. W. (1995). Supportive group interventions with caregivers of frail older adults. In M. J. Galinsky & J. H. Schopler (Eds.), *Support groups: Current perspectives on theory and practice.* (pp. 11–25). New York: The Haworth Proess, Inc.

Miller, B., & Cafasso, L. (1992). Gender differences in caregiving: Fact or artifact? *The Gerontologist, 32,* 498–507.

Mittelman, M. S., Ferris, S. H., Steinberg, G., Shulman, E., Mackell, J. A., Ambinder, A., Cohen, J. (1991). An intervention that delays institutionalization of alzheimer's disease patients: Treatment of spouse-caregivers. *The Gerontologist, 33,* 730–740.

Mohide, E. A., Pringle, D. M., Streiner, D. L., Gilbert, J. R., Muir, G. & Tew, M. (1990). A randomized trial of family caregiver support in the home management of dementia. *Journal of American Geriatric Society, 38,* 446–454.

Montgomery, R. J. V., & Borgatta, E. F. (1989). The effects of alternative support strategies on family caregiving. *The Gerontologist, 29,* 457–464.

Montgomery, R. J. V., Gonyea, J. G., & Hooyman, N. R. (1985). Caregiving and the experience of subjective and objective burden. *Family Relations,* 19–25.

National Alliance for Caregiving and American Association of Retired Persons (1997). Family caregiving in the U.S.: Findings from a national survey. Washington DC: National Alliance for Caregiving and the American Association of Retired Persons.

Neundorfer, M. M. (1991). Family caregivers of the frail elderly: Impact of caregiving on their health and implications for interventions. *Family Community Health, 14,* 48–58.

Oktay, J. S., & Volland, P. J. (1990). Post-hospital support program for the frail elderly and their caregivers: A quasi-experimental evaluation. *American Journal of Public Health, 80,* 39–46.

Pinkston, E. M., & Linsk, N. L. (1988). Behavioral family intervention with the impaired elderly. *The Gerontologist, 24,* 576–583.

Pinkston, E. M., Linsk, N. L., & Young, R. N. (1988). Home-based behavioral family treatment of the impaired elderly. *Behavior Therapy, 19,* 331–344.

Pratt, C. C., Schmall, V. L., Wright, S., & Cleland, M. (1985). Burden and coping strategies of caregivers to alzheimer's patients. *Family Relations, 34,* 27–33.

Quayhagen, M. P., & Quayhagen, M. (1988). Alzheimer's stress: Coping with the caregiving role. *The Gerontologist, 28,* 391–396.

Quayhagen, M. P., & Quayhagen, M. (1989). Differential effects of family-based strategies on alzheimer's disease. *The Gerontologist, 29*, 150–155.

Robinson, K. M. (1988). A social skills training program for adult caregivers." *Advances in Nursing Science, 10*, 59–72.

Schmidt, G. L., Bonjean, M. J., Widem, A. C., Schefft, B. K., & Steele, D. J. (1988). Brief psychotherapy for caregivers of demented relatives: Comparison of two therapeutic strategies. *Clinical Gerontologist, 7*, 109–125.

Schulz, R., O'Brien, A. T., Bookwala, J., Fleissner, K. (1995). Psychiatric and physical morbidity effects of dementia caregiving: Prevalence, correlates, and causes. *Gerontologist, 35*, 771–791.

Segall, M., & Wykle, M. (1988/1989). The black family's experience with dementia. *Journal of Applied Social Sciences, 13*, 170–191.

Sherrill, J. T., Frank, E., Geary, M., Stack, J. A., & Reynolds, C. F., (1997). Psychoeducational workshops for elderly patients with recurrent major depression and their families. *Psychiatric Services, 48*, 76–81.

Skaff, M. M., & Pearlin, L. I. (1992). Caregiving: Role engulfment and the loss of self. *The Gerontologist, 32*, 656–664.

Skipwith, D. H. (1994). Telephone counseling interventions with caregivers of elders. *Journal of Psychosocial Nursing, 32*, 7–12.

Smith, M. F., Tobin, S. S., & Toseland, R. W. (1992). Therapeutic processes in professional and peer counseling of family caregivers of frail elderly people. *Social Work, 37*, 345–351.

Smith, G. C., Smith, M. F., & Toseland, R, W. (1991). Problems identified by family caregivers in counseling. *The Gerontologist, 31*, 15–22.

Teri, L., & Uomoto, J. M. (1991). Reducing excess disability in dementia patients: Training caregivers to manage patient depression. *Clinical Gerontologist, 10*, 49–63.

Toselan, R. W., Labrecque, M. S., Goebel, S. T., & Whitney, M. H. (1992). An evaluation of a group program for spouses of frail elderly veterans. *The Gerontologist, 32*, 382–390.

Toseland, R. W., Rossiter, C. M., & Labrecque, M. S. (1989). The effectiveness of peer-led and professionally led groups to support family caregivers. *The Gerontological Society of America, 29*, 465–471.

Toseland, R. W., & Rossiter, C. M. (1989). Group interventions to support family caregivers: A review and analysis. *The Gerontologist, 29*, 438–448.

Toseland, R. W., Rossiter, C. M., Peak, T. & Smith, G. C. (1990). Comparative effectiveness of individual and group interventions to support family caregivers. *Social Work*, 209–217.

Toseland, R. W., & Smith, G. C. (1990). Effectiveness of individual counseling by professional and peer helpers for family caregivers of the elderly. *Psychology and Aging, 5*, 256–263.

Townsend, A. L. (1990). Nursing home care and family caregivers' stress and coping. In J. H. Stephens, S. E. Hobfull & D. L. Tennenbaum (Eds.), *Stress and coping in later life families* (pp. 267–285). Washington, DC: Hemisphere Publishing Corporation.

U. S. Senate Special Committee on Aging, and American Association of Retired Persons, Federal Council on the Aging and the Administration on Aging. (1991). *Aging in America: Trends and projections*. Washington, DC, U.S. Department of Health and Human Services.

Whitlatch, C. J., Zarit, S. H., & Von Eye, A. (1991). Efficacy of interventions with caregivers: A reanalysis. *The Gerontologist, 31*, 9–14.

Winogrond, I. R., Fisk, A. A., Kirsling, R. A., & Keyes, B. (1987). The relationship of caregiver burden and morale to Alzheimer's disease patient function in a therapeutic setting. *The Gerontologist, 27*, 336–339.

Wright, L. K., Bennet, G., & Gramling, L. (1998). Telecommunication interventions for caregivers of elders with dementia. *Advances in Nursing Science, 2*, 76–88.

Zarit, S. H., & Edwards, A. B. (1996). Family caregiving: Research and clinical intervention. In R. T. Woods (Ed.), *Handbook of the clinical psychology of aging* (pp. 331–368). Westchester: John Wiley & Sons.

Zarit, S. H., Todd, P. A., & Zarit, J. M. (1986). Subjective burden of husbands and wives as caregivers: A longitudinal study. *The Gerontologist, 26*, 260–266.

Zarit, S. H., Anthony, C. R. & Boutselis, M. (1987). Interventions with care givers of dementia patients: Comparison to two approaches. *Psychology and Aging, 2*, 225–232.

Zarit, S. H., & Zarit, J. M. (1982). Families under stress: Interventions for caregivers of senile dementia patients. *Psychotherapy: Theory, Research and Practice, 19*, 461–471.

MEASURMENT OF FAMILY TREATMENT WITH CAREGIVERS OF THE ELDERLY

Increasingly, practitioners are held accountable for the evaluation of their practice. To assist with evaluation, this section provides the reader with self-report instruments for caregivers of the elderly. Scores from these measurement instruments can be used to guide assessment, clinical practice, and research in this area.

Measures presented in this section involve the following criteria. First, instruments are self-report; that is, they are completed by family members themselves, rather than being interviewer-administered or observational measures. A second criterion for inclusion was that adequate reliability and validity information had to be available for each scale. This area of research tends to be marked by the use of nonstandardized measures. Therefore, commonly used measures, such as the Caregiver's Burden Scale (Zarit, Reever, & Bach-Peterson, 1980; Zarit & Zarit,1982) had to be deleted from this review.

Measures included assess aspects of the caregiving experience such as stress and psychological adjustment. An instrument to assess client satisfaction with services is also presented. Selected psychometric data from the measurement instruments are outlined.

CAREGIVING OUTCOMES

BEHAVIORAL AND MOOD DISTURBANCE SCALE

Authors: Greene, Smith, Gardiner, & Timbury (1982)

Description:

- 34-item self-report completed by caregiving relative of elderly
- Assessing degree of behavior and mood disturbance demonstrated by elderly patient in the home on a 5-point scale ("0" never/ "4" "always")

Reliability:

- Alpha coefficient for total scale = .84 and for subscales ranges from .73 to .90

Validity:

- Factor analysis produced 3 factors:
  1. Apathetic-Withdrawn
  2. Active-Disturbed
  3. Mood Disturbance

Relatives' Stress Scale

Authors: Greene, Smith, Gardiner, & Timbury (1982)

Description:

- 15-item, self-report by caregiver of elderly to assess amount of stress experienced from having to take care of an elderly person
- 5-point scale ("0" not at all/ "4" considerably)

Reliability:

- Alpha coefficient for total scale = .85 and ranging from .72 to .88 for subscales

Validity:

- Scores differentiated between supporters of demented and non-demented dependents
- Significant correlations were found with scores and dependents' cognitive impairment and behavioral disturbance
- Factor analysis indicates 3 factors:
  1. Personal Distress
  2. Life Upset
  3. Negative Feelings toward elderly person

Caregiver Strain Index

Author: Robinson (1983)

Description:

- 13-item, self-report measuring strain associated with caring for the physically ill and impaired elderly

Reliability:

- Internal consistency was .86

Validity:

- Correlates with the ability of the elderly person to perform tasks of daily living

CAREGIVER ADJUSTMENT

BECK DEPRESSION INVENTORY

(*See Chapter One*, Family Treatment with Child Abuse and Neglect)

SYMPTOM CHECKLIST 90—REVISED

(*See Chapter One*, Family Treatment with Child Abuse and Neglect)

BRIEF SYMPTOM INVENTORY

(*See Chapter One*, Family Treatment with Child Abuse and Neglect)

SOCIAL SUPPORT BEHAVIORS SCALE

(*See Chapter Eleven*, Family Treatment with Schizophrenia)

SATISFACTION WITH SERVICES

CLIENT SATISFACTION QUESTIONNAIRE

(*See Chapter One*, Family Treatment with Child Abuse and Neglect)

REFERENCES FOR MEASUREMENT OF FAMILY TREATMENT WITH CAREGIVERS OF THE ELDERLY

Greene, J. G., Smith, R., Gardiner, M., & Timbury, G. C. (1982). Measuring behavioural disturbance of elderly demented patients in the community and its effects on relative: A factor analytic study. *Age and Ageing, 11*, 121–126.

Robinson, B. C. (1983). Validation of a caregiver strain index. *Journal of Gerontology, 38*, 344–348.

Zarit, S., Reever, K., & Bach-Peterson, J. (1980). Relatives of the impaired elderly: Correlates of Feelings of Burden. *The Gerontologist, 20*, 649–655.

Zarit, S. H., & Zarit, J. M. (1982). Families under stress: Interventions for caregivers of senile dementia patients. *Psychotherapy: Theory, research and practice, 19*, 461–471.

INDEX